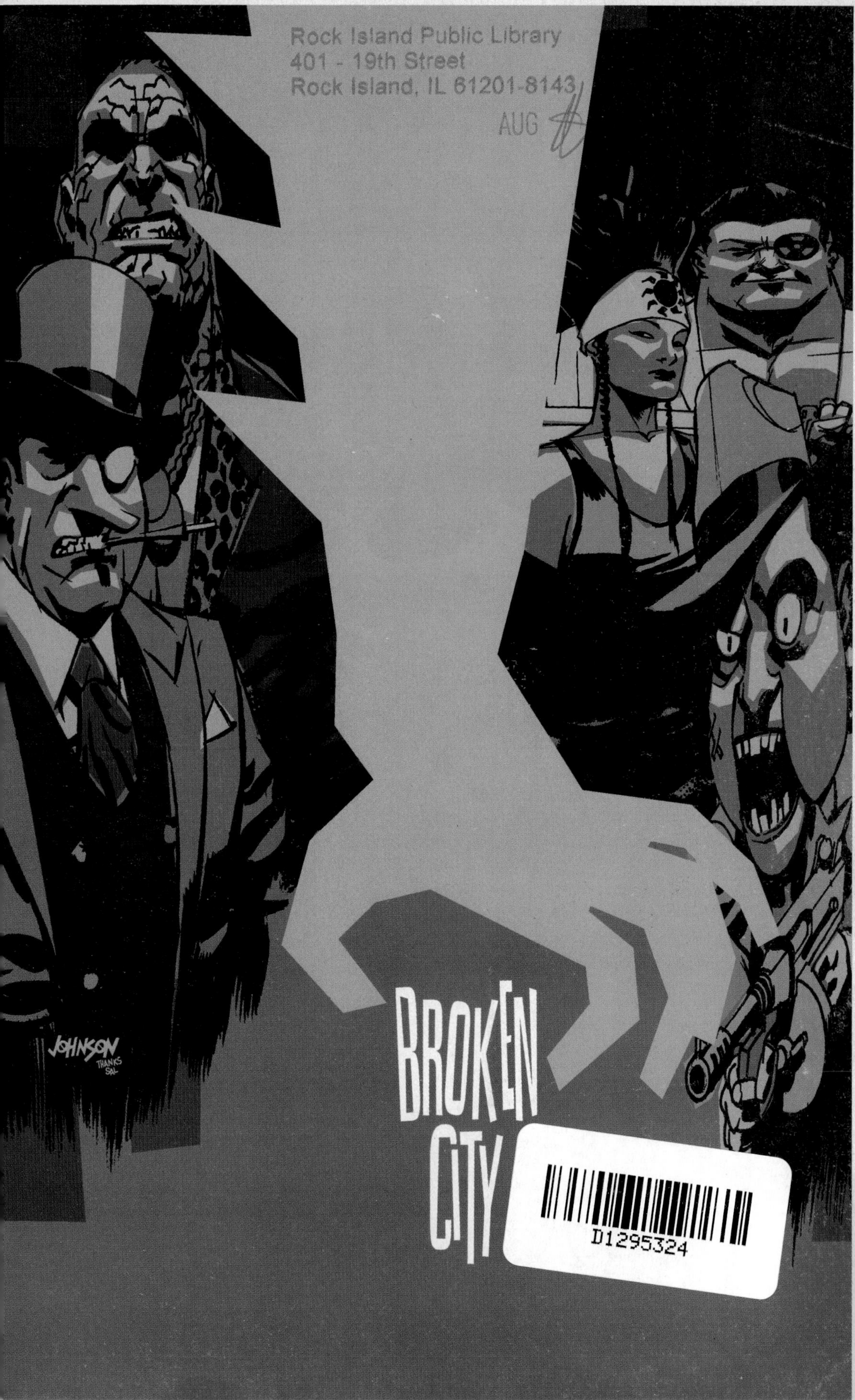
JOHNSON
THANKS SAL
BROKEN CITY

BATMAN: BROKEN CITY
Published by DC Comics. Cover, introduction, and compilation
copyright © 2004 DC Comics. Originally published in single magazine
form as BATMAN 620-625. Copyright © 2003, 2004 DC Comics.
All Rights Reserved. All characters, the distinctive likenesses
thereof and related elements are trademarks of DC Comics.
The stories, characters and incidents featured in this
publication are entirely fictional. DC Comics does not read
or accept unsolicited submissions of ideas, stories or artwork.
DC Comics 1700 Broadway New York, NY 10019.
A Warner Bros. Entertainment Company.
Printed in Canada. First Printing.
Hardcover ISBN: 1-4012-0133-4
Softcover ISBN: 1-4012-0214-4

COVER ILLUSTRATION BY DAVE JOHNSON.

BATMAN
BROKEN CITY

WRITER
BRIAN AZZARELLO

ARTIST
EDUARDO RISSO

LETTERER
CLEM ROBINS

COLORIST
PATRICIA MULVIHILL

ORIGINAL SERIES COVERS
DAVE JOHNSON

BATMAN CREATED BY BOB KANE

Boy, am I lucky!

Starting around 1989, and for several years thereafter, I couldn't wait for the Chicago Comic Con to roll around. It was the one time in the whole year of convention appearances that I knew I would have at least one person in the world that I could torture and treat like dirt. One person that I could take out all of my frustrations on, with careless glee and great abandon. I mean, I had to keep up the façade of "Mr. Nice-Guy" that I had been propagating all those years prior, but somebody had to know the real me. How lucky was I that that someone was this skinny kid who surely couldn't defend himself from an overweight, blowhard, thinks-he's-a-big-shot-in-the-industry-hoo-ha, even if it was just due to the sheer size of me! I could bully him all I wanted! I bullied him mostly because he had the unfortunate circumstance of working for a company that I had previously worked for, but, since it had changed owners from the time I had been there, I decided that I now had the inalienable right to give this kid no end of garbage for his aiding and abetting this new owner. I mean, since I had left the company, how dare they attempt to go on without me?! I became aware of young Brian Azzarello's employment there via a mutual friend, Rafael Nieves, who was co-writing *Tales from the Heart* with Cindy Goff. A great comic book -- if you can get your hands on a copy!

INTRODUCTION
BY BOB SCHRECK

Raf was, and is, a hell of a guy and a hell of a talent, and we often found ourselves chatting it up into the wee hours of some hotel barroom concocting the latest intercompany crossover like *The Banana Splits vs. ElfQuest*! It was during one of these sessions, I believe, that I first met Brian.

Well, after that, we didn't really spend all that much time together, Brian and I, just enough for me to download my hate and bile from the last 12 months and then be on my merry way. In all honesty, Brian always knew that I was just funnin' with him and I knew from Raf that he could take a good razzing with the best of them. What I didn't know was that this poor recipient of my horrid attempts to embarrass and humiliate him for having the audacity to work for my former employer would, along with his assembled team, go on to break all the boundaries with the creation of their award-winning Vertigo series, 100 BULLETS. What I also didn't know was that he would eventually become one of the most talented and award-winning writers of our time, bringing new dimensions to the crime fiction genre of comic book storytelling and adding to that prestigious canon of the likes of Frank Miller, Howard Chaykin, and David Lapham.

My luck graced me again as, years later, I watched BATMAN soar to the top of the charts for an entire year, thanks to the fantastic work of Jeph Loeb, Jim Lee, Scott Williams, and Alex Sinclair, only to be followed up by these magnificent six issues you now hold in your hands. And my luck continued as Brian and his team made the monthly streets of Gotham ooze an inky black of words and pictures that reminded us of a time when Miller and Mazzucchelli were doing their much-celebrated *Batman: Year One*. Brian certainly brought his "A" game by delivering to us a moment that adds so much to the history and mythos of this lasting character that I still shake my head in disbelief that it hadn't been thought of before. He also brought us an edge to the character that is rarely seen in the monthly pages, for a time considered a place for tamer stuff.

As Brian tells it, we actually owe it all to Eduardo Risso, whose love for Batman and respect for Frank Miller and the many other fine talents who had left their mark on the character over the years was the impetus to get the entire project rolling in the first place. What started as a hardcover soon became six issues that will certainly leave a high watermark for those in the future to aspire to. You can tell just by looking that nothing Eduardo did on this series was left to chance. While he followed his keen artistic instincts, he challenged every brush stroke and made sure that nothing was there that didn't absolutely inform the story. He wasn't left in the lurch, either. His collaborator-in-color, Trish Mulvilhill, once again delivered her finest effort by accentuating Eduardo's every intention with her excellent eye for mood and creating a visual tension through color.

Every present has its giftwrap, and this is one package that always sported the most amazing covers, bar none. Dave Johnson, like the rest of his 100 BULLETS team, knocks it out of the park with each and every new, amazing cover he delivers, and boy did he deliver on this run! Truly, some of his finest work ever. And then there's Clem Robins, the letterer's letterer. Clem and I go back a ways as well, and I have come to know and trust him beyond words. He's the best.

I am the luckiest guy I know, as Vertigo editor Will Dennis and his able assistant editors, Casey Seijas and Zachary Rau, had the day-to-day chore of wrangling their 100 BULLETS team into the BATMAN corral and making sure we didn't skip a deadline, all the while doing it with great style. My many thanks to Will, Casey, and Zack for all the skills they brought to the editorial table and for letting me co-pilot and enjoy the view for a change.

And, finally, my sincere thanks to Brian, Eduardo, Trish, Clem, and Dave, and my sincere wishes for their fast return to Gotham as I continue to stand in awe of the magic they bring to each and every page they set their hearts to.

I am truly lucky. Really! Most important, because I've had the honor and pleasure of knowing Brian for over 15 years... and he hasn't killed me yet!

Thank you, one and all. Bravo!

— Bob Schreck
February 8, 2004

ANYBODY WHO LIVES HERE KNOWS GOTHAM IS REALLY BUILT OF TINDERSTICKS AND GUNPOWDER, WITH OILY KEROSENE CRUDELY BURPING OUT OF ITS SEWERS.

THAT'S WHY WHEN IT RAINS, IT'S NOT SO MUCH WATER...

...AS IT IS A RELIEF.

WRITTEN BY **BRIAN AZZARELLO**

ILLUSTRATED BY **EDUARDO RISSO**

COLORED BY PATRICIA MULVIHILL • LETTERED BY CLEM ROBINS

COVER BY DAVE JOHNSON • ASSISTANT EDITOR ZACHARY RAU

EDITED BY WILL DENNIS & BOB SCHRECK

BATMAN CREATED BY BOB KANE

ALL THE CHISELED GRANITE AND JUTTING SPOKES OF STEEL GIVE THE IMPRESSION THAT THIS CITY HAS AN IRON JAW...

...BUT IT ONLY FOOLS OUT-OF-TOWNERS.

BROKEN CITY
PART ONE

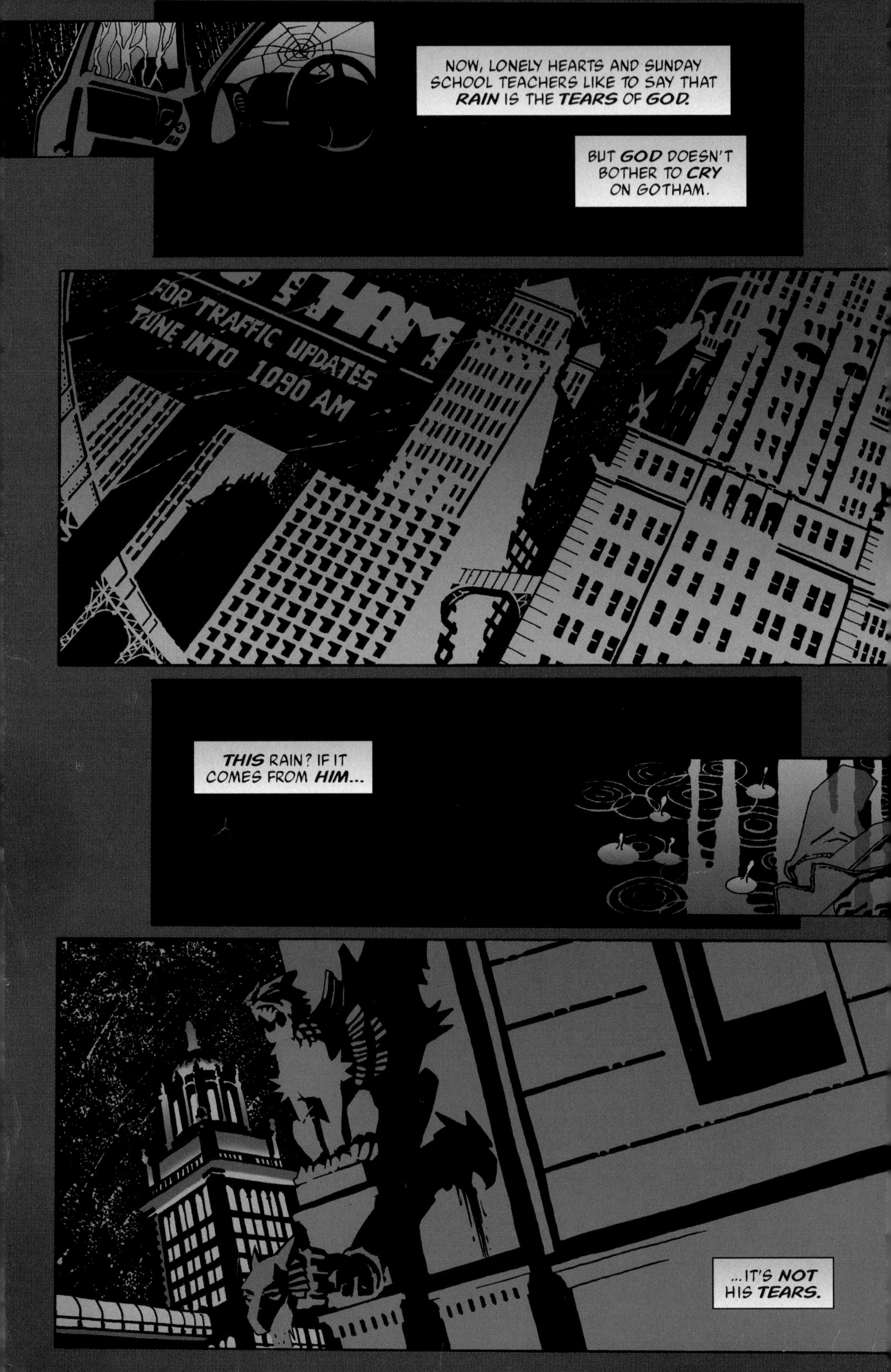
NOW, LONELY HEARTS AND SUNDAY SCHOOL TEACHERS LIKE TO SAY THAT **RAIN** IS THE **TEARS** OF **GOD.**
BUT **GOD** DOESN'T BOTHER TO **CRY** ON GOTHAM.
FOR TRAFFIC UPDATES TUNE INTO 1090 AM
THIS RAIN? IF IT COMES FROM **HIM...**
...IT'S **NOT** HIS **TEARS.**

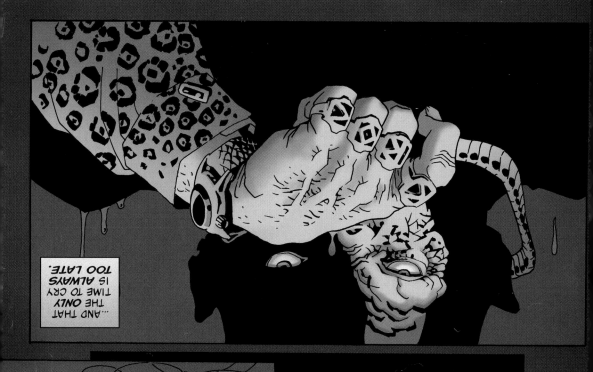

...AND THAT
THE ONLY
TIME TO CRY
IS ALWAYS
TOO LATE.

NO PLACE IN
HEAVEN FOR ME OR
GOTHAM CITY...

BEFORE I LEARNED
THERE IS NO
PITY IN GOD...

I DID--ONCE--A
LIFE AGO--BEFORE
I WAS WHAT I AM.

THOUGH I CAN'T
IMAGINE MY LIFE
WITHOUT IT, I
WOULDN'T CRY FOR
GOTHAM EITHER.

I HAVE TO
CONFESS, I THINK
THERE'S A LITTLE
OF ME IN GOD--A
SENSE OF HUMOR,
NOBODY GETS.

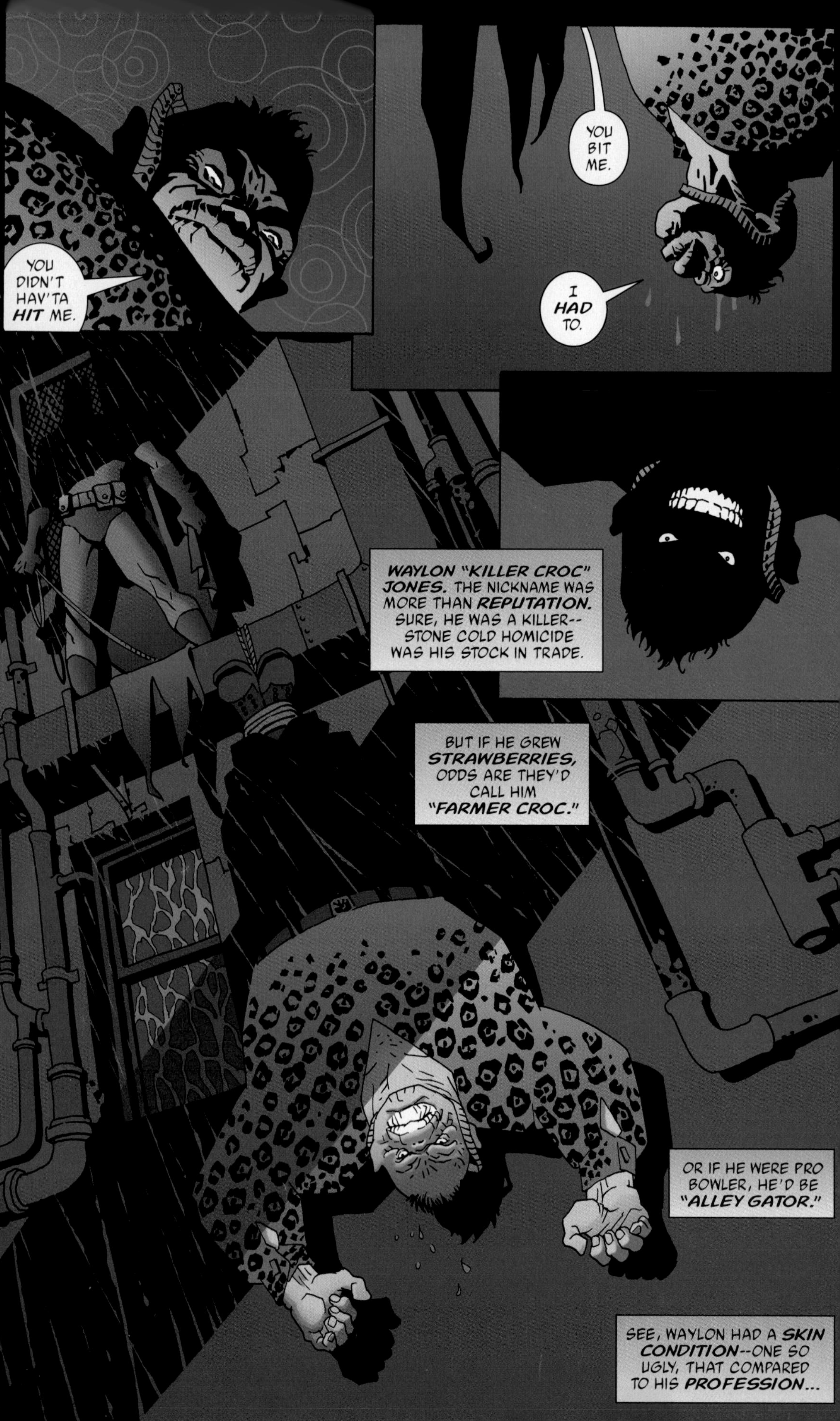
YOU DIDN'T HAV'TA **HIT** ME.
YOU BIT ME.
I **HAD** TO.
WAYLON "KILLER CROC" JONES. THE NICKNAME WAS MORE THAN **REPUTATION.** SURE, HE WAS A KILLER-- STONE COLD HOMICIDE WAS HIS STOCK IN TRADE.
BUT IF HE GREW **STRAWBERRIES,** ODDS ARE THEY'D CALL HIM **"FARMER CROC."**
OR IF HE WERE PRO BOWLER, HE'D BE **"ALLEY GATOR."**
SEE, WAYLON HAD A **SKIN CONDITION**--ONE SO UGLY, THAT COMPARED TO HIS **PROFESSION...**

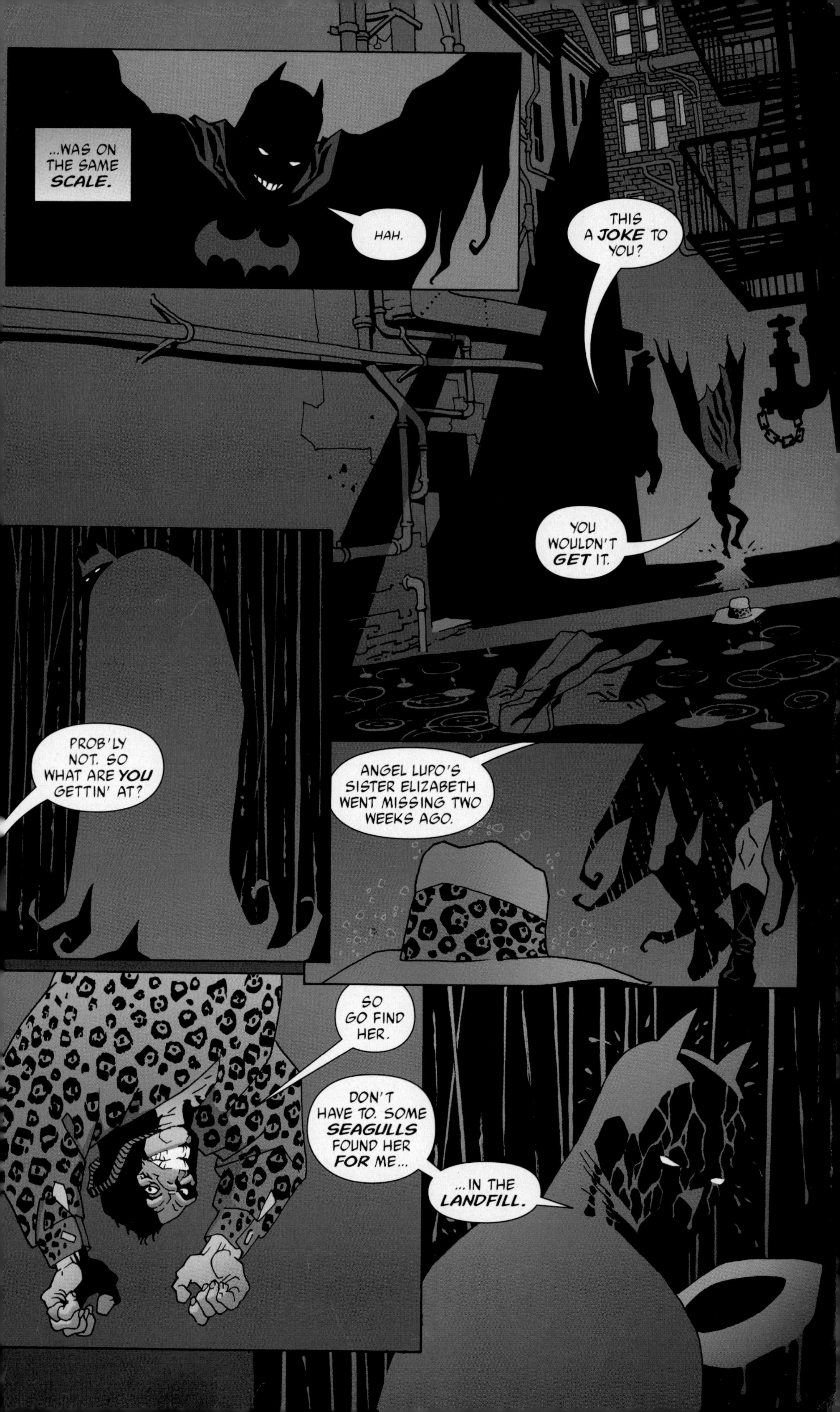
...WAS ON THE SAME ***SCALE.***
HAH.
THIS A ***JOKE*** TO YOU?
YOU WOULDN'T ***GET*** IT.
PROB'LY NOT. SO WHAT ARE ***YOU*** GETTIN' AT?
ANGEL LUPO'S SISTER ELIZABETH WENT MISSING TWO WEEKS AGO.
SO GO FIND HER.
DON'T HAVE TO. SOME ***SEAGULLS*** FOUND HER ***FOR*** ME...
...IN THE ***LANDFILL.***

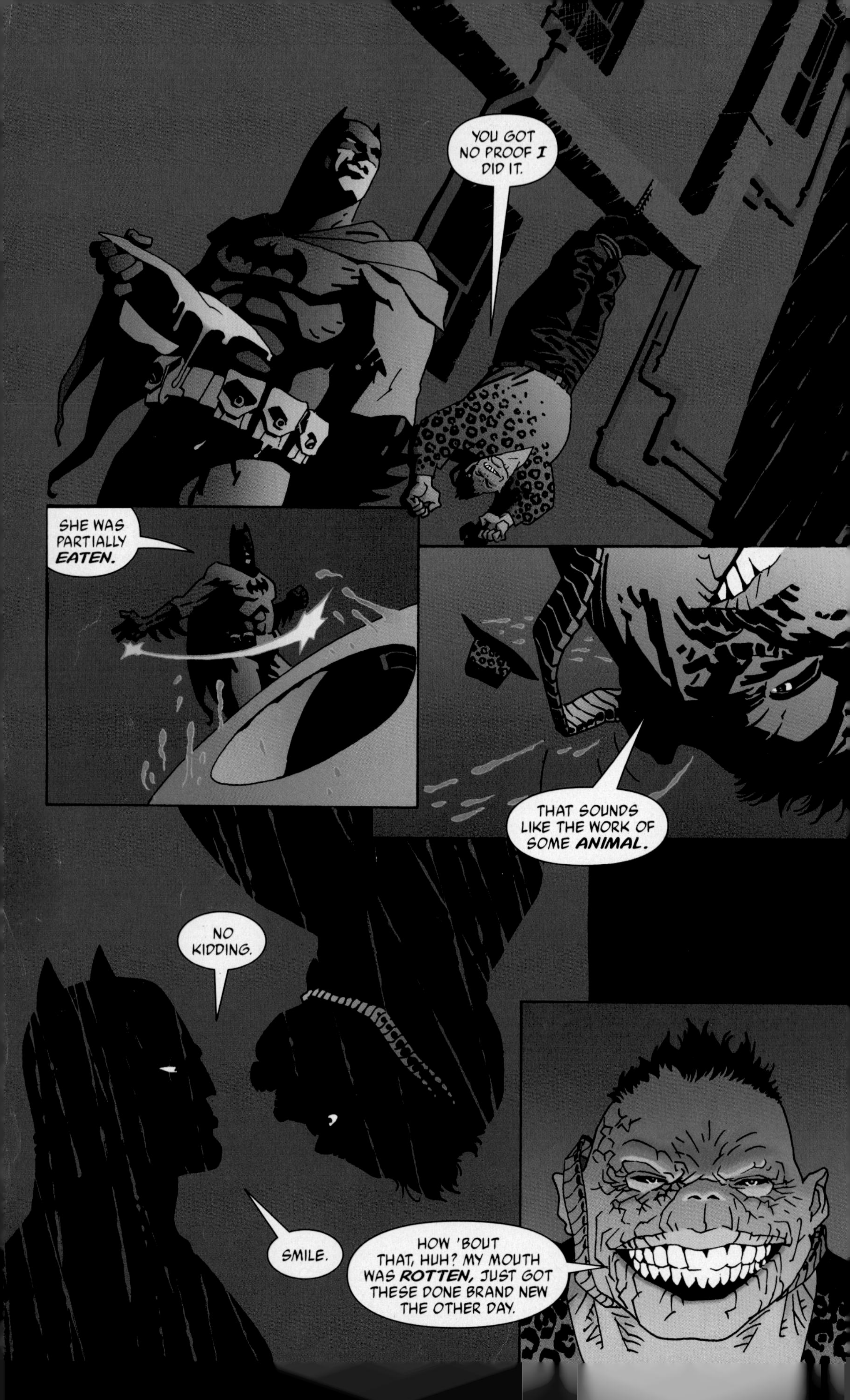
YOU GOT NO PROOF *I* DID IT.
SHE WAS PARTIALLY ***EATEN.***
THAT SOUNDS LIKE THE WORK OF SOME ***ANIMAL.***
NO KIDDING.
SMILE.
HOW 'BOUT THAT, HUH? MY MOUTH WAS ***ROTTEN,*** JUST GOT THESE DONE BRAND NEW THE OTHER DAY.

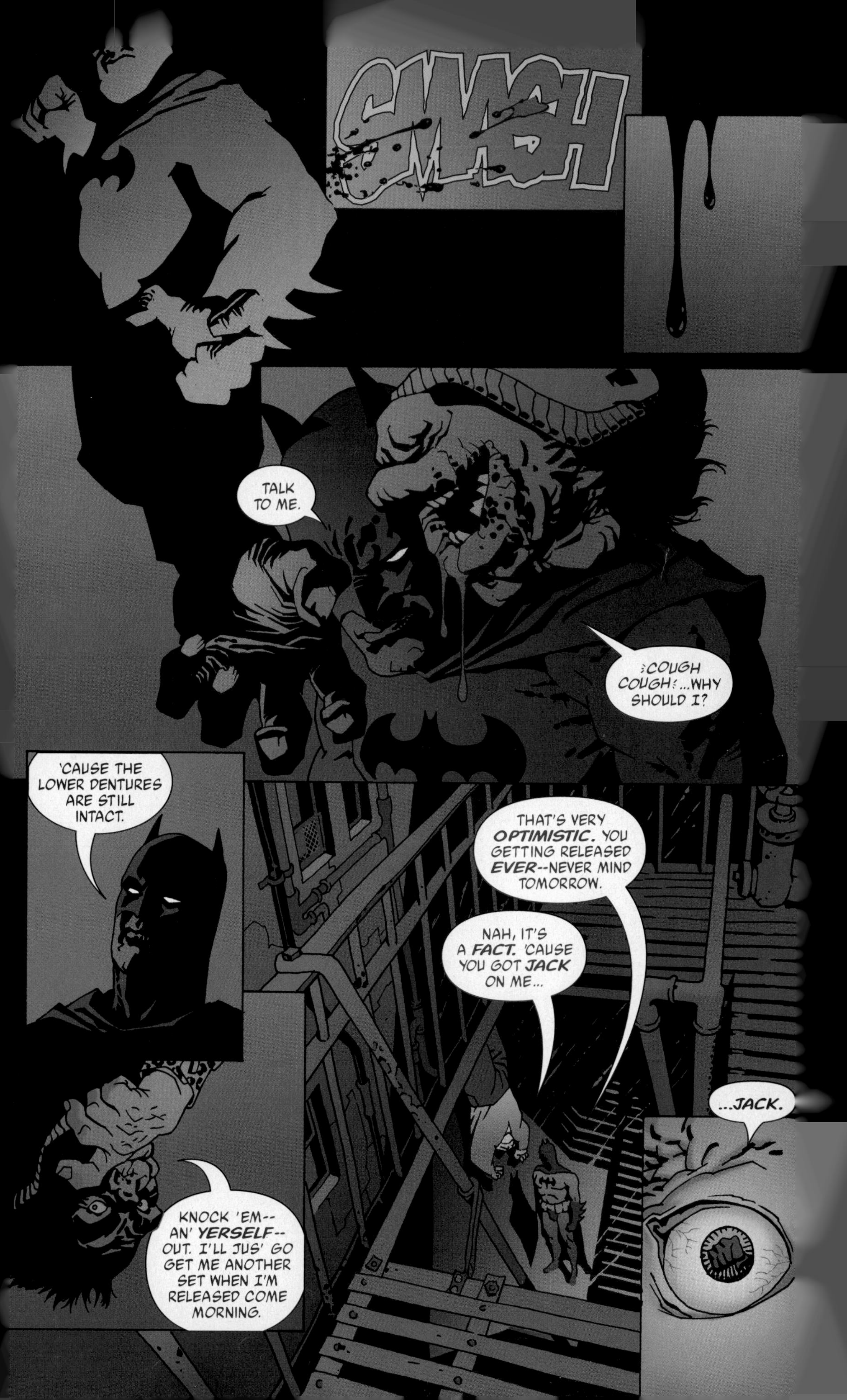
SMASH
TALK TO ME.
:COUGH COUGH: ...WHY SHOULD I?
'CAUSE THE LOWER DENTURES ARE STILL INTACT.
KNOCK 'EM-- AN' **YERSELF**-- OUT. I'LL JUS' GO GET ME ANOTHER SET WHEN I'M RELEASED COME MORNING.
THAT'S VERY **OPTIMISTIC.** YOU GETTING RELEASED **EVER**--NEVER MIND TOMORROW.
NAH, IT'S A **FACT.** 'CAUSE YOU GOT **JACK** ON ME...
...**JACK.**

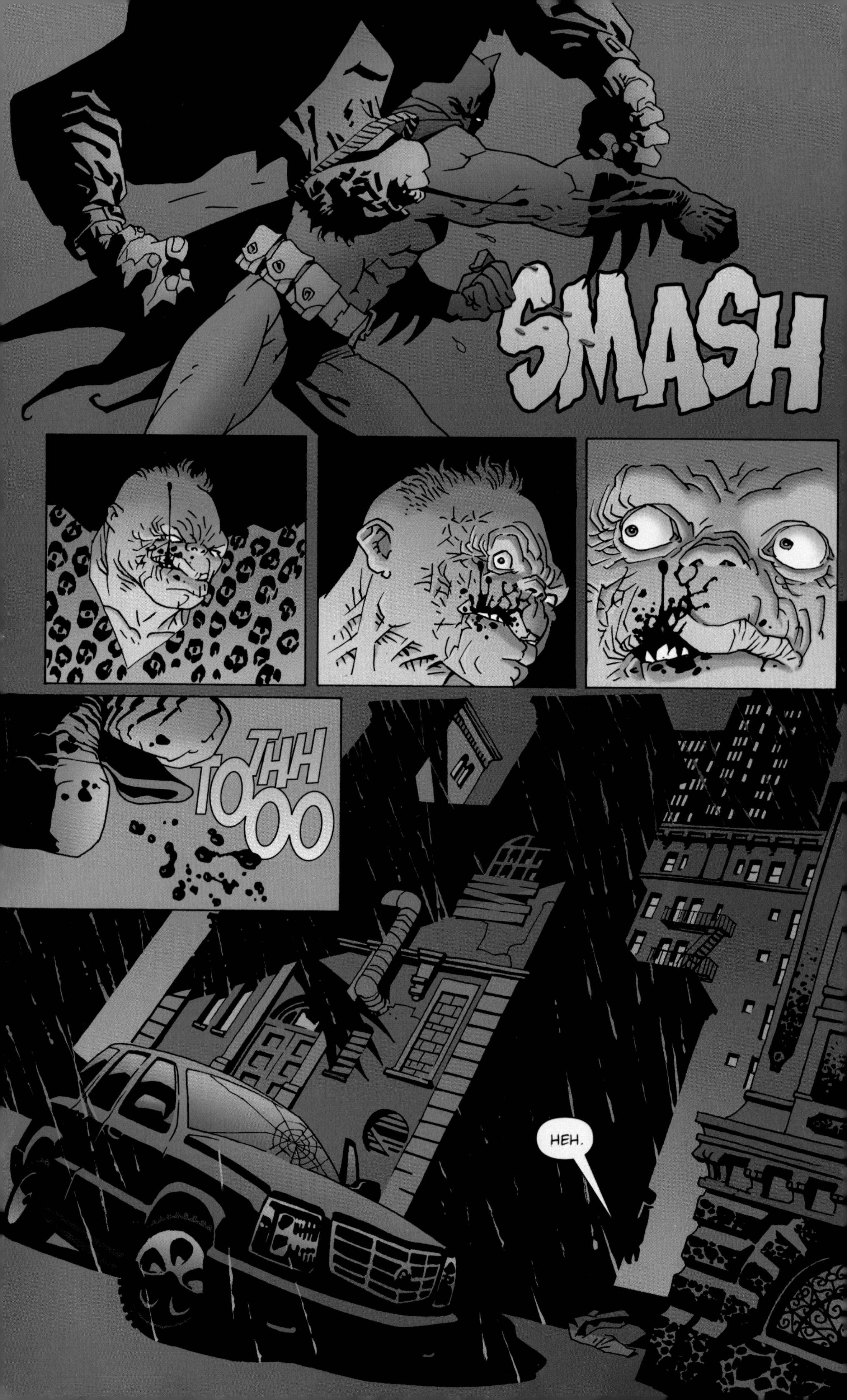
SMASH
THH
TOOOO
HEH.

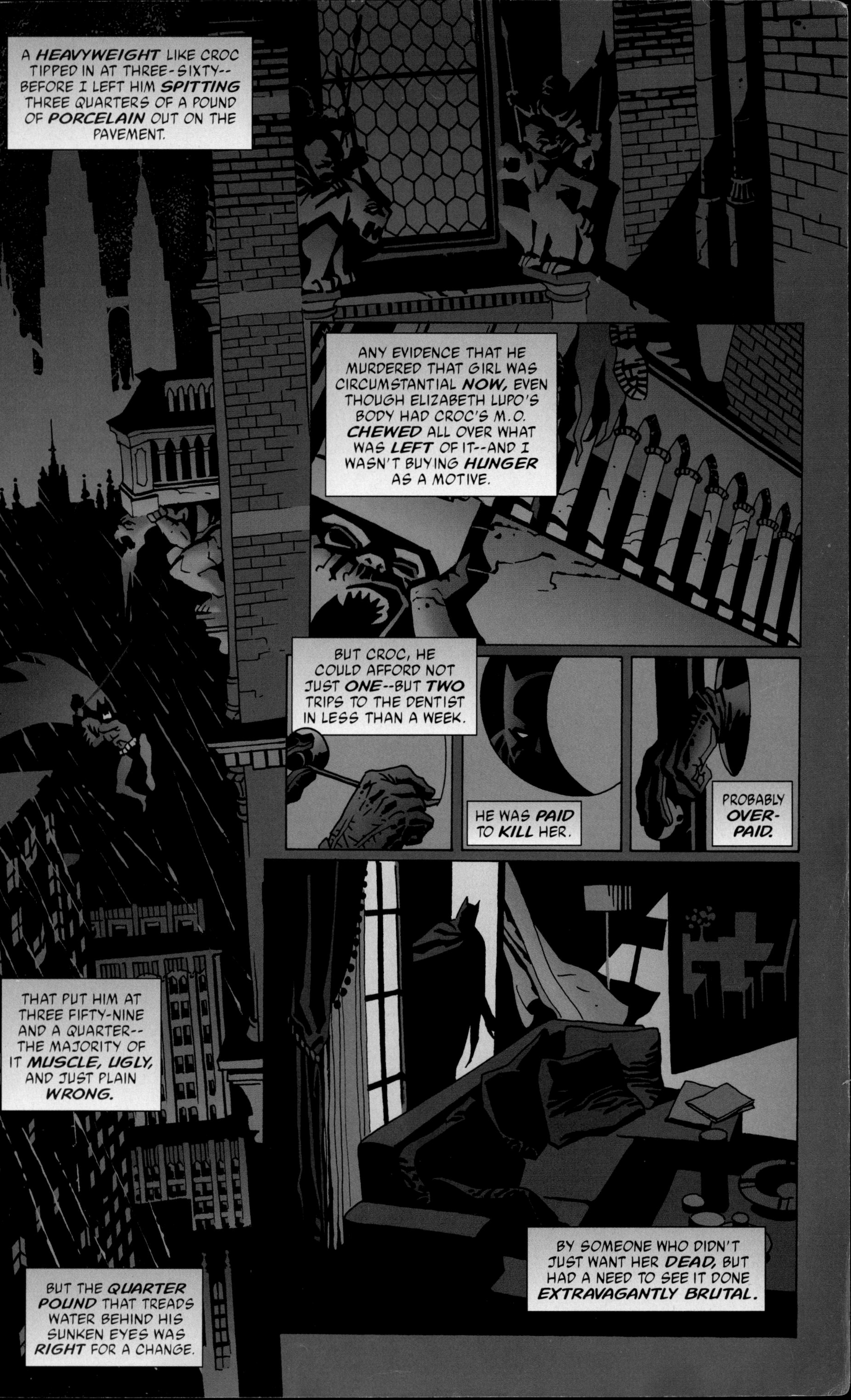
A HEAVYWEIGHT LIKE CROC TIPPED IN AT THREE-SIXTY--BEFORE I LEFT HIM SPITTING THREE QUARTERS OF A POUND OF PORCELAIN OUT ON THE PAVEMENT.
THAT PUT HIM AT THREE FIFTY-NINE AND A QUARTER--THE MAJORITY OF IT MUSCLE, UGLY, AND JUST PLAIN WRONG.
BUT THE QUARTER POUND THAT TREADS WATER BEHIND HIS SUNKEN EYES WAS RIGHT FOR A CHANGE.
ANY EVIDENCE THAT HE MURDERED THAT GIRL WAS CIRCUMSTANTIAL NOW, EVEN THOUGH ELIZABETH LUPO'S BODY HAD CROC'S M.O. CHEWED ALL OVER WHAT WAS LEFT OF IT--AND I WASN'T BUYING HUNGER AS A MOTIVE.
BUT CROC, HE COULD AFFORD NOT JUST ONE--BUT TWO TRIPS TO THE DENTIST IN LESS THAN A WEEK.
HE WAS PAID TO KILL HER.
PROBABLY OVER-PAID.
BY SOMEONE WHO DIDN'T JUST WANT HER DEAD, BUT HAD A NEED TO SEE IT DONE EXTRAVAGANTLY BRUTAL.

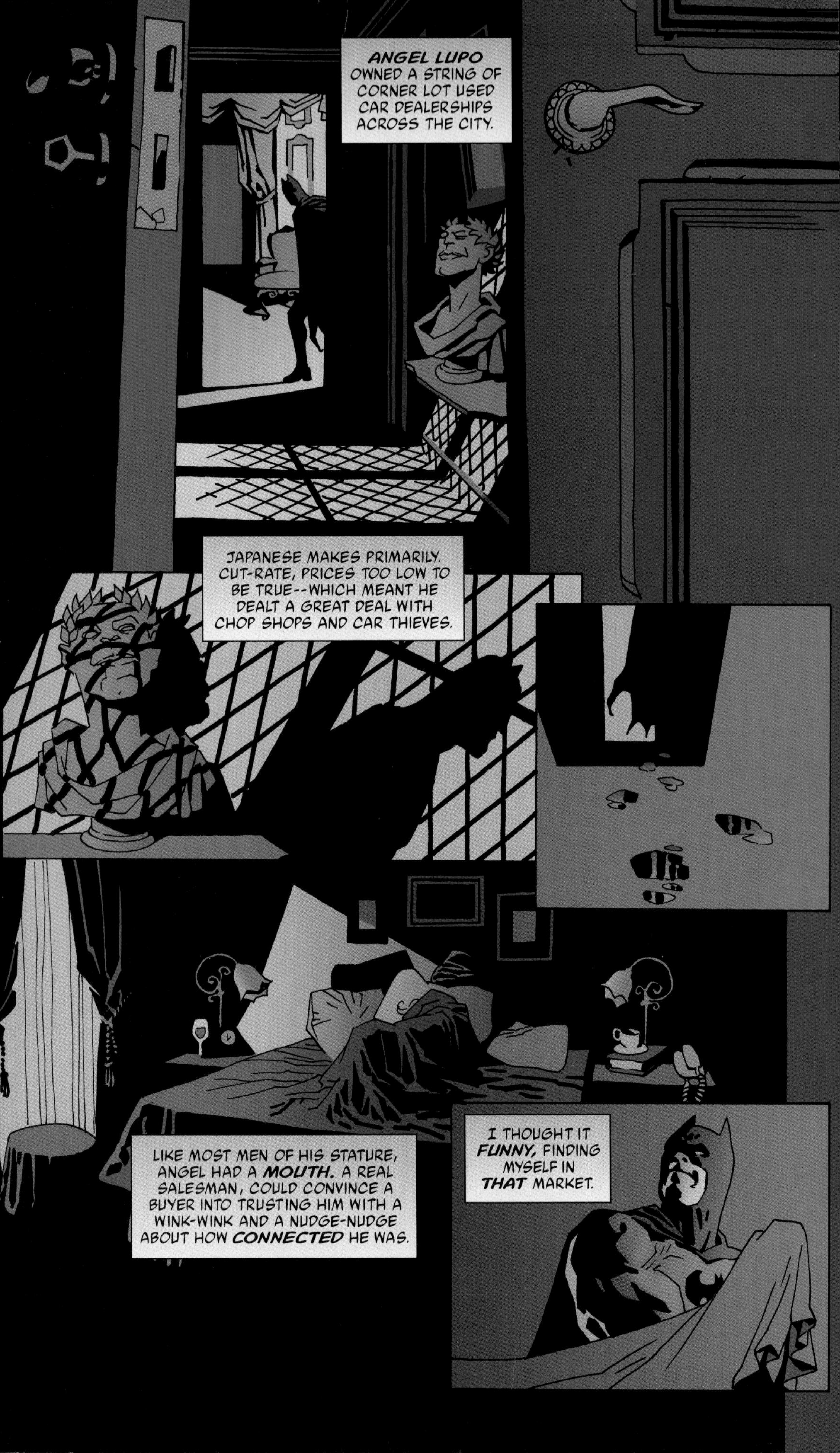

ANGEL LUPO OWNED A STRING OF CORNER LOT USED CAR DEALERSHIPS ACROSS THE CITY.
JAPANESE MAKES PRIMARILY. CUT-RATE, PRICES TOO LOW TO BE TRUE--WHICH MEANT HE DEALT A GREAT DEAL WITH CHOP SHOPS AND CAR THIEVES.
LIKE MOST MEN OF HIS STATURE, ANGEL HAD A ***MOUTH.*** A REAL SALESMAN, COULD CONVINCE A BUYER INTO TRUSTING HIM WITH A WINK-WINK AND A NUDGE-NUDGE ABOUT HOW ***CONNECTED*** HE WAS.
I THOUGHT IT ***FUNNY,*** FINDING MYSELF IN ***THAT*** MARKET.

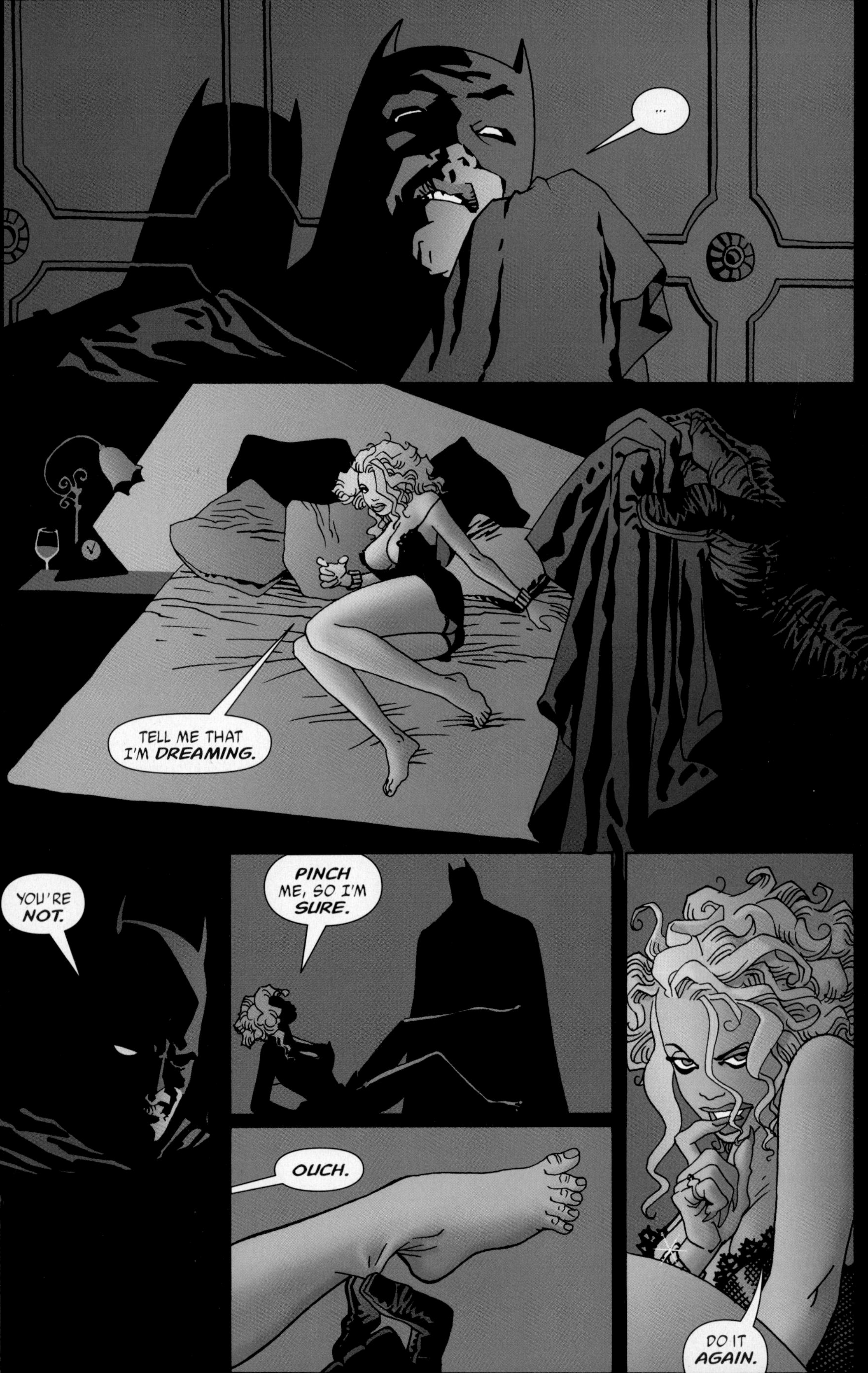
...
TELL ME THAT I'M *DREAMING.*
YOU'RE *NOT.*
PINCH ME, SO I'M *SURE.*
OUCH.
DO IT *AGAIN.*

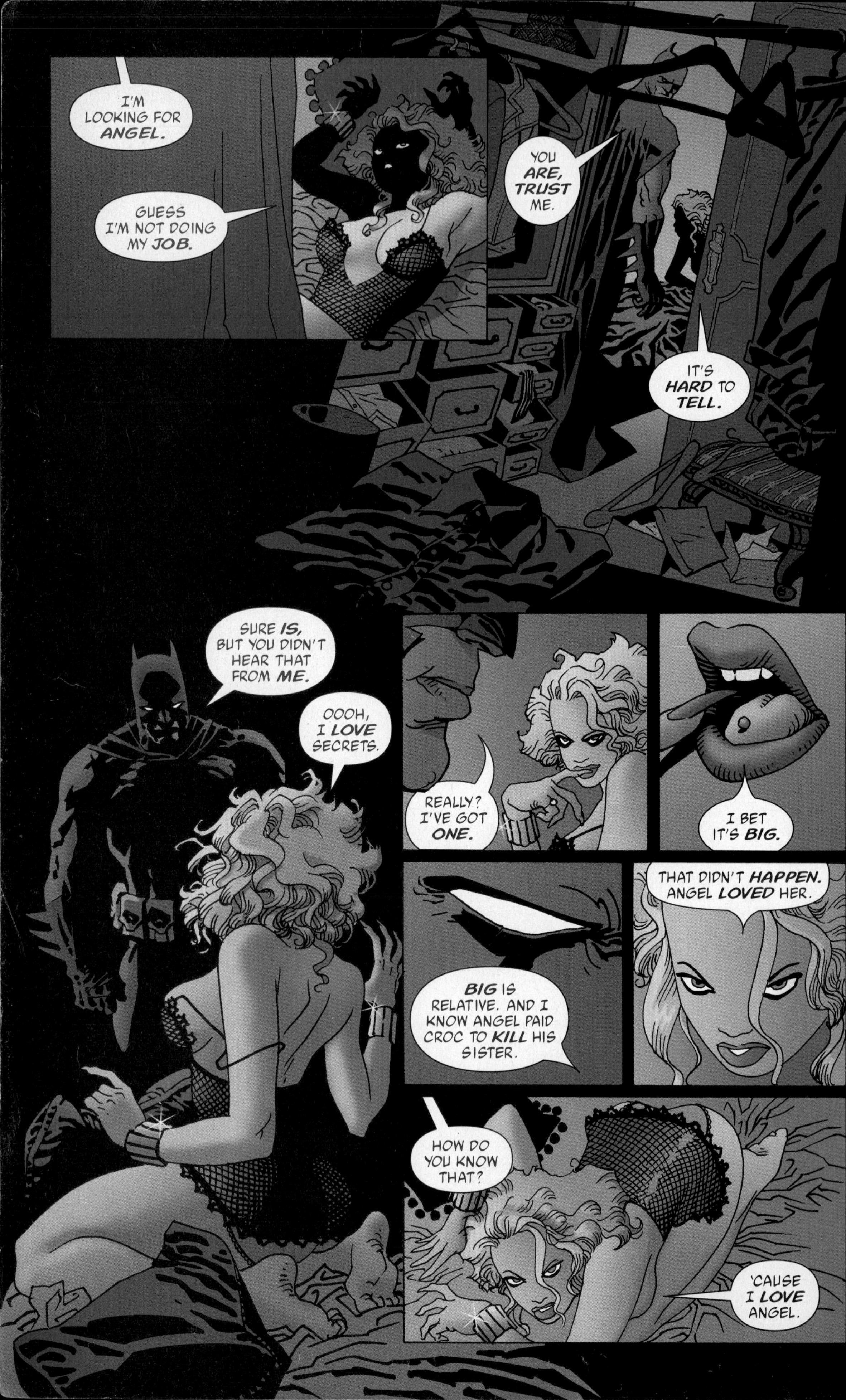
I'M LOOKING FOR ANGEL.
GUESS I'M NOT DOING MY JOB.
YOU ARE, TRUST ME.
IT'S HARD TO TELL.
SURE IS, BUT YOU DIDN'T HEAR THAT FROM ME.
OOOH, I LOVE SECRETS.
REALLY? I'VE GOT ONE.
I BET IT'S BIG.
BIG IS RELATIVE. AND I KNOW ANGEL PAID CROC TO KILL HIS SISTER.
THAT DIDN'T HAPPEN. ANGEL LOVED HER.
HOW DO YOU KNOW THAT?
'CAUSE I LOVE ANGEL.

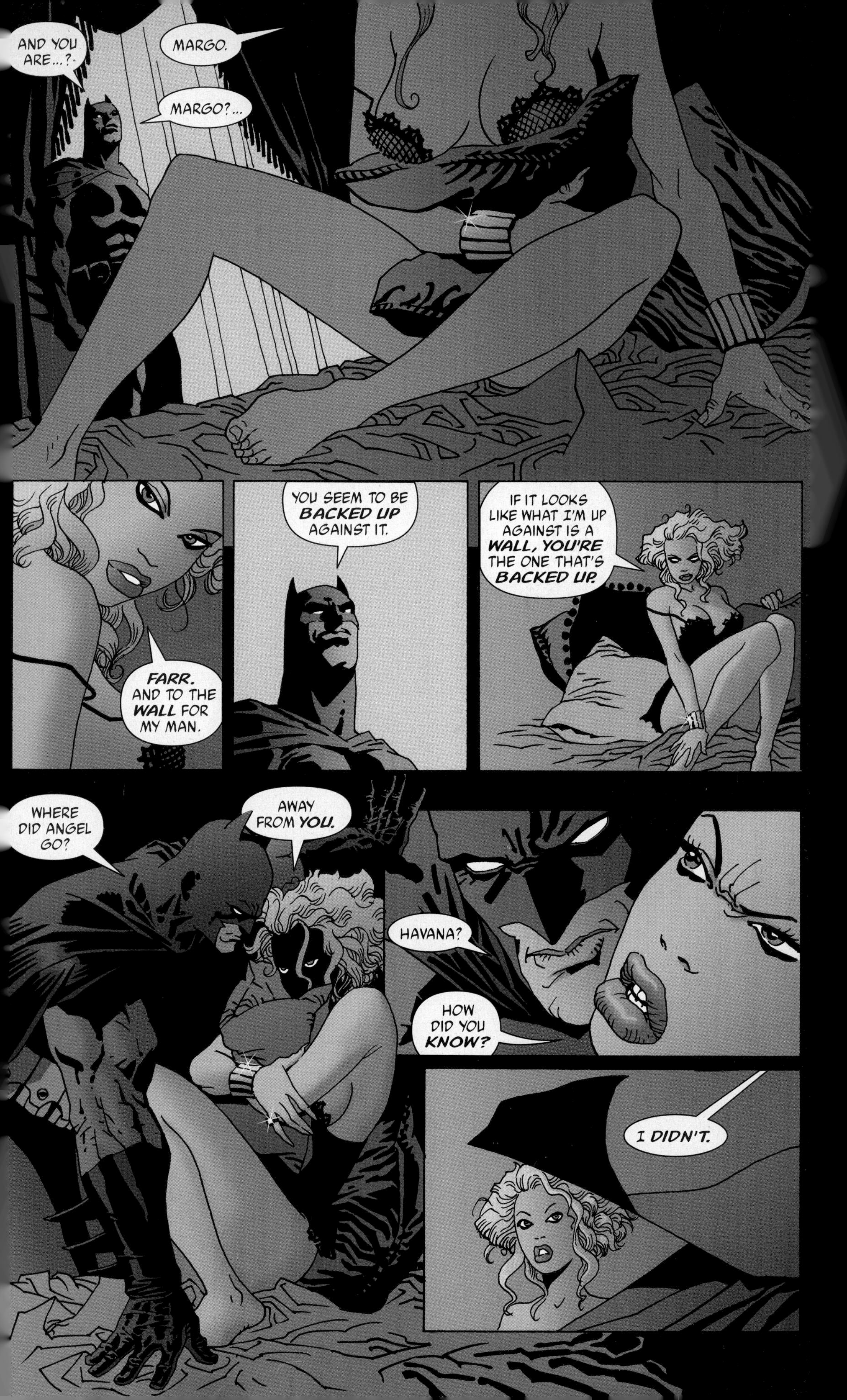
AND YOU ARE...?
MARGO.
MARGO?...
FARR. AND TO THE WALL FOR MY MAN.
YOU SEEM TO BE BACKED UP AGAINST IT.
IF IT LOOKS LIKE WHAT I'M UP AGAINST IS A WALL, YOU'RE THE ONE THAT'S BACKED UP.
WHERE DID ANGEL GO?
AWAY FROM YOU.
HAVANA?
HOW DID YOU KNOW?
I DIDN'T.

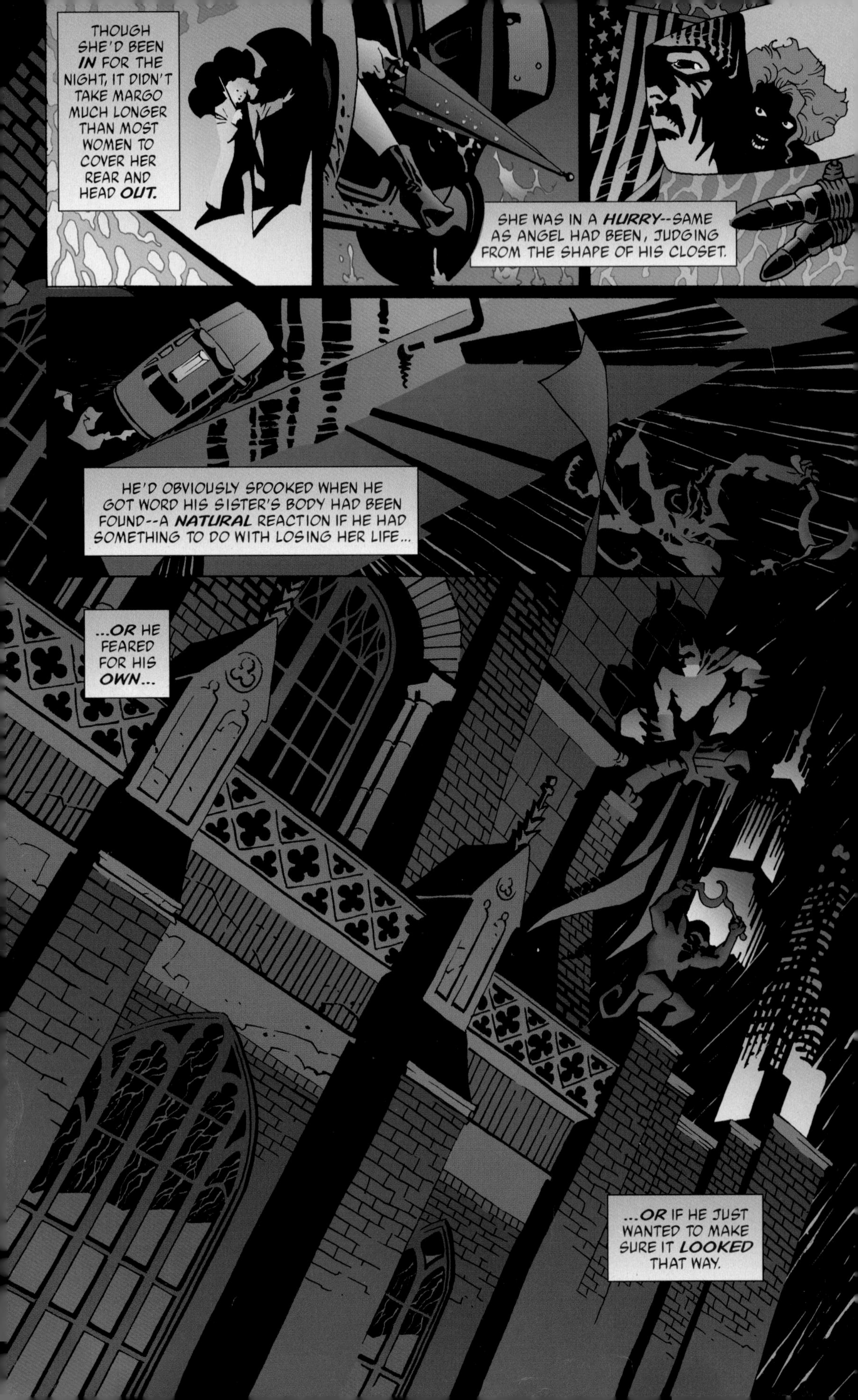
THOUGH SHE'D BEEN IN FOR THE NIGHT, IT DIDN'T TAKE MARGO MUCH LONGER THAN MOST WOMEN TO COVER HER REAR AND HEAD OUT.
SHE WAS IN A HURRY--SAME AS ANGEL HAD BEEN, JUDGING FROM THE SHAPE OF HIS CLOSET.
HE'D OBVIOUSLY SPOOKED WHEN HE GOT WORD HIS SISTER'S BODY HAD BEEN FOUND--A NATURAL REACTION IF HE HAD SOMETHING TO DO WITH LOSING HER LIFE...
...OR HE FEARED FOR HIS OWN...
...OR IF HE JUST WANTED TO MAKE SURE IT LOOKED THAT WAY.

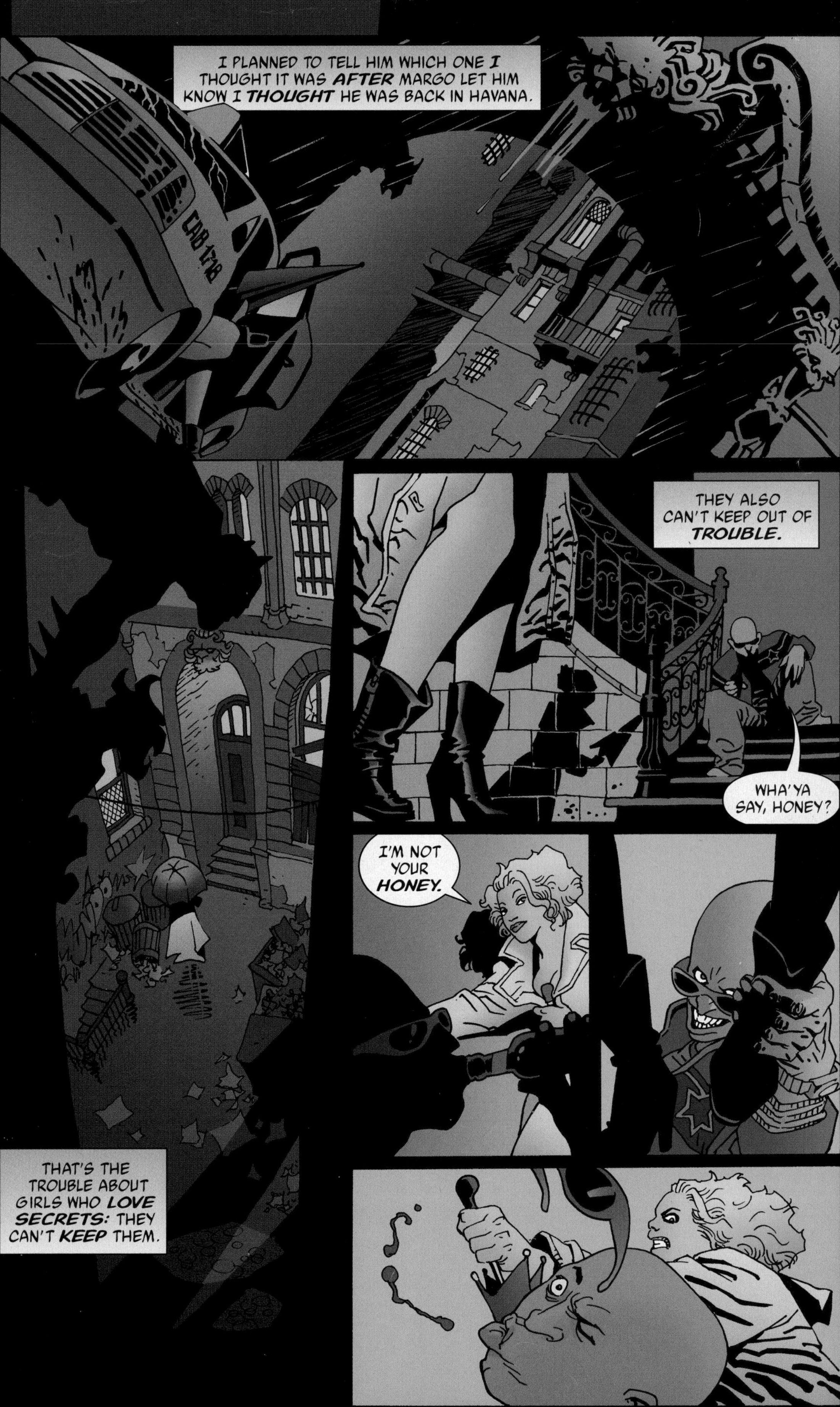
I PLANNED TO TELL HIM WHICH ONE *I* THOUGHT IT WAS ***AFTER*** MARGO LET HIM KNOW *I* ***THOUGHT*** HE WAS BACK IN HAVANA.
CAB 1718
THEY ALSO CAN'T KEEP OUT OF ***TROUBLE.***
WHA'YA SAY, HONEY?
I'M NOT YOUR ***HONEY.***
THAT'S THE TROUBLE ABOUT GIRLS WHO ***LOVE SECRETS:*** THEY CAN'T ***KEEP*** THEM.

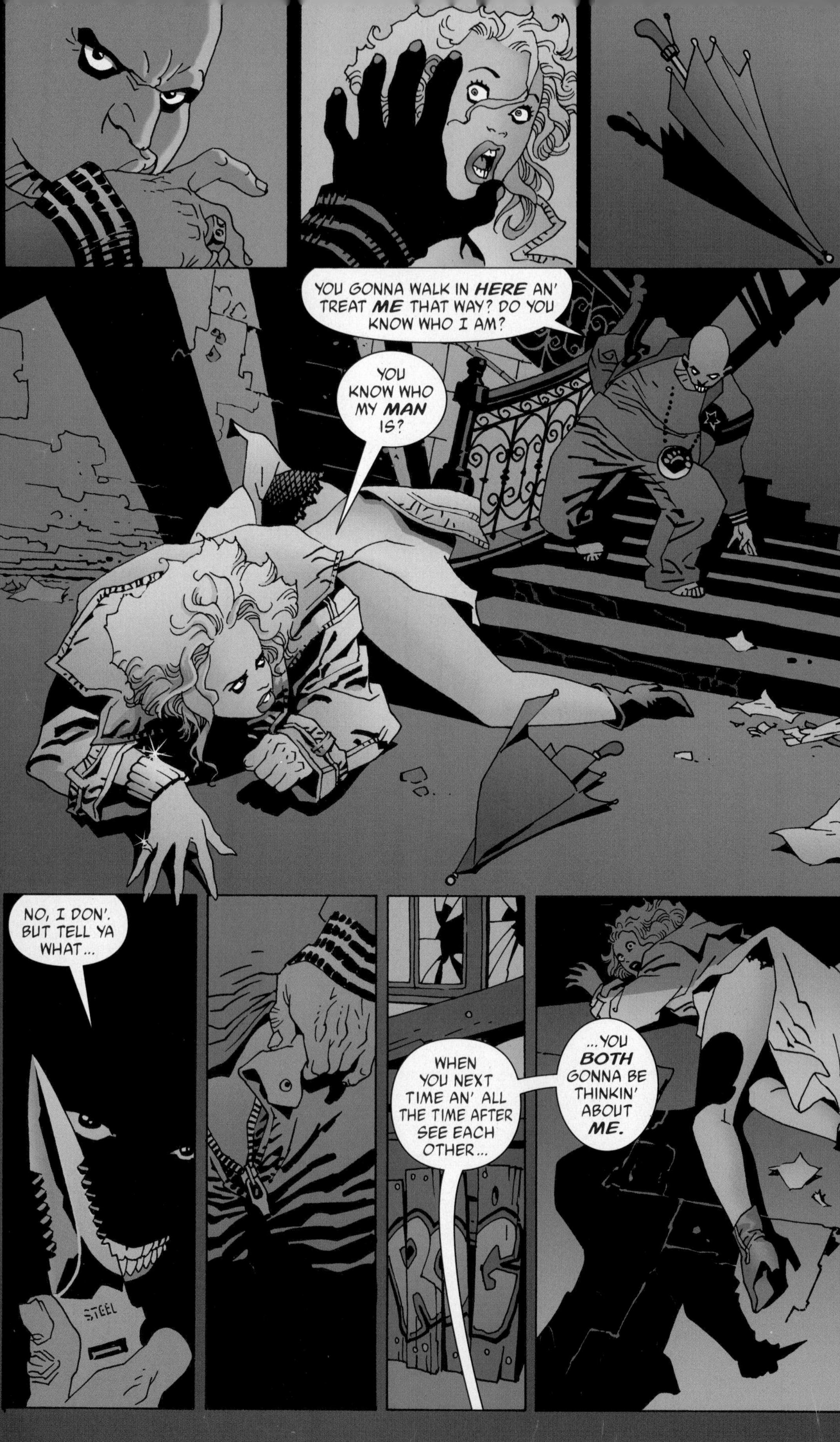
YOU GONNA WALK IN HERE AN' TREAT ME THAT WAY? DO YOU KNOW WHO I AM?
YOU KNOW WHO MY MAN IS?
NO, I DON'. BUT TELL YA WHAT...
WHEN YOU NEXT TIME AN' ALL THE TIME AFTER SEE EACH OTHER...
...YOU BOTH GONNA BE THINKIN' ABOUT ME.
STEEL

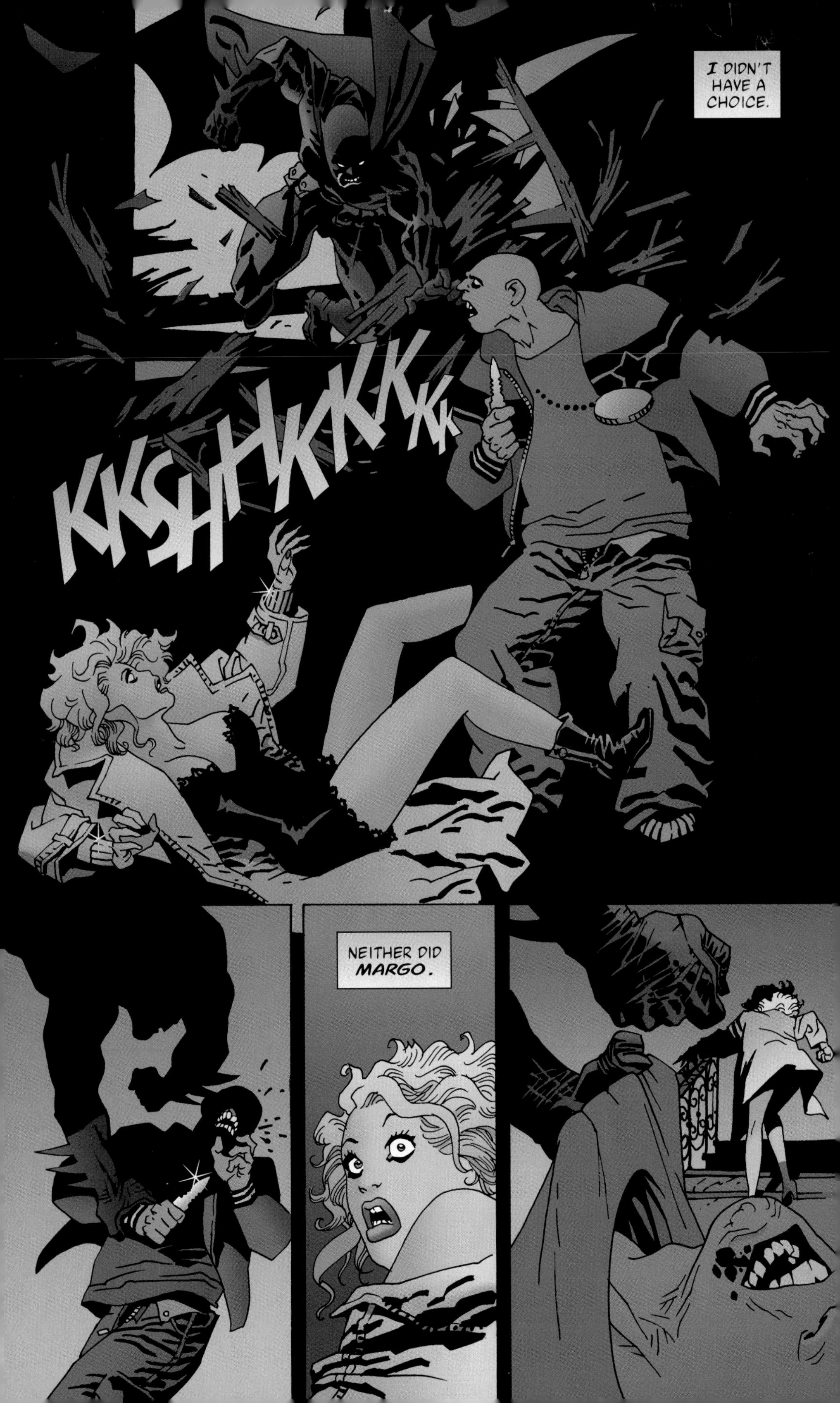
I DIDN'T HAVE A CHOICE.
KKSHHKKKKKK
NEITHER DID MARGO.

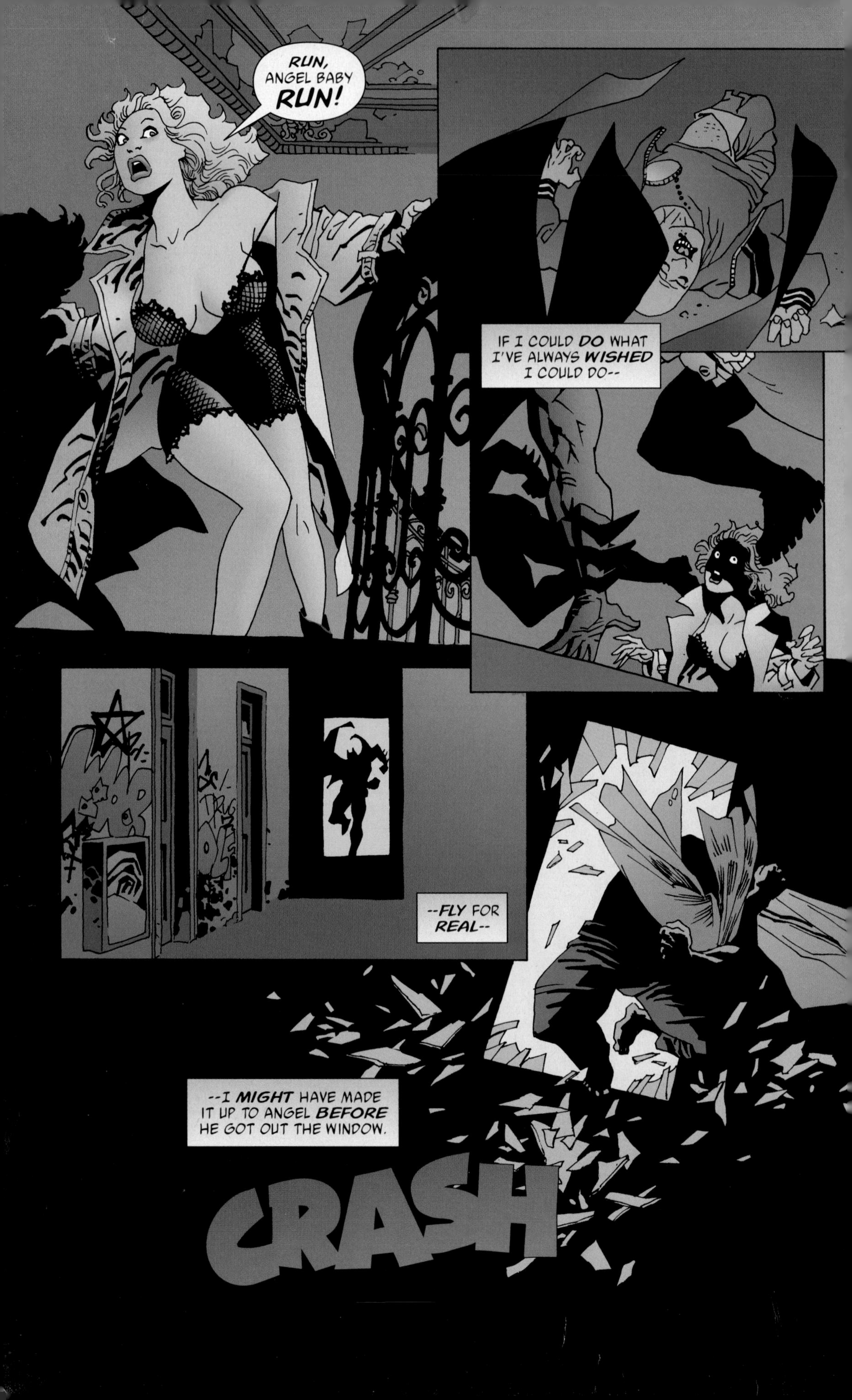
RUN, ANGEL BABY RUN!
IF I COULD DO WHAT I'VE ALWAYS WISHED I COULD DO--
--FLY FOR REAL--
--I MIGHT HAVE MADE IT UP TO ANGEL BEFORE HE GOT OUT THE WINDOW.
CRASH

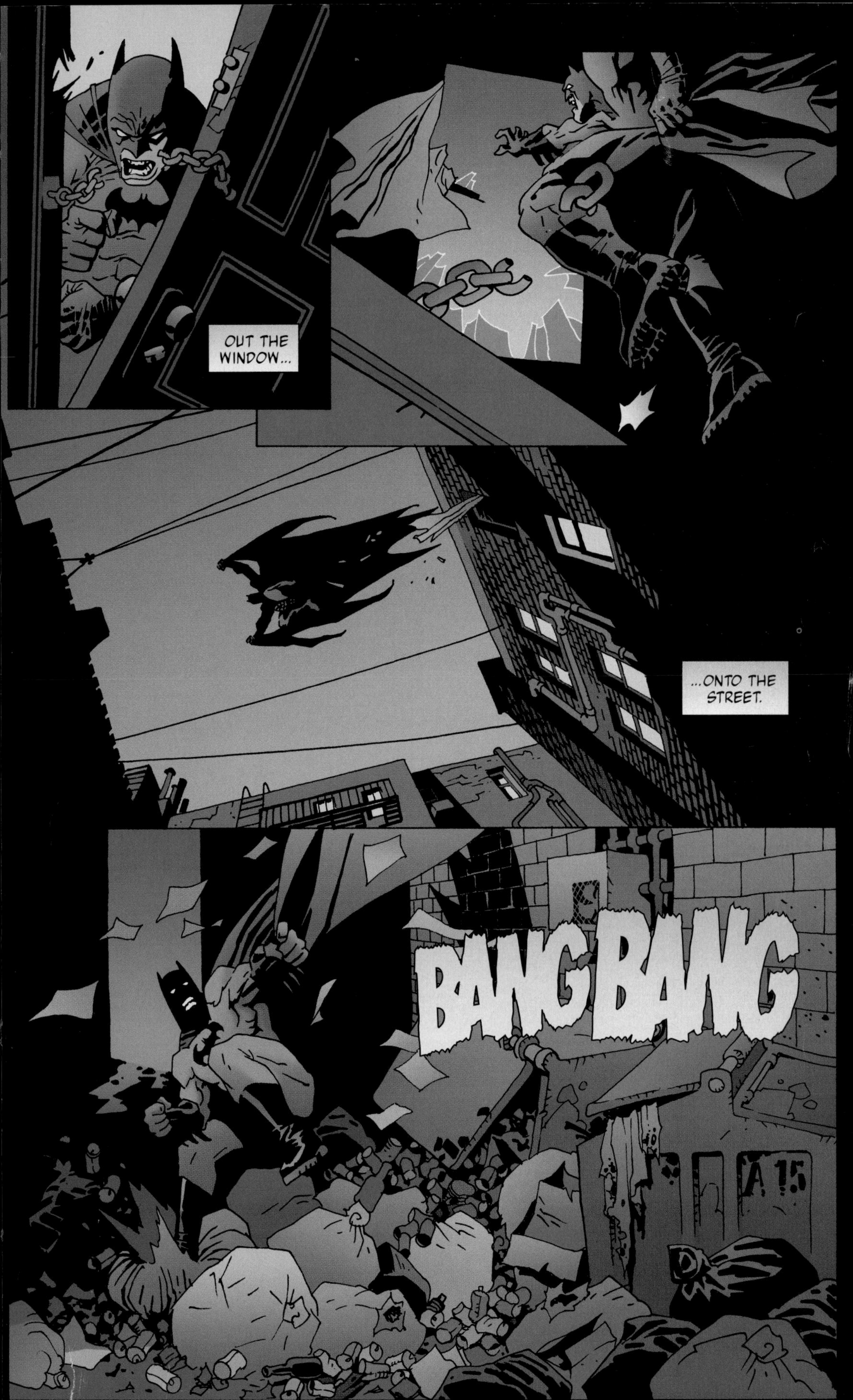
OUT THE WINDOW...
...ONTO THE STREET.
BANG BANG
A 15

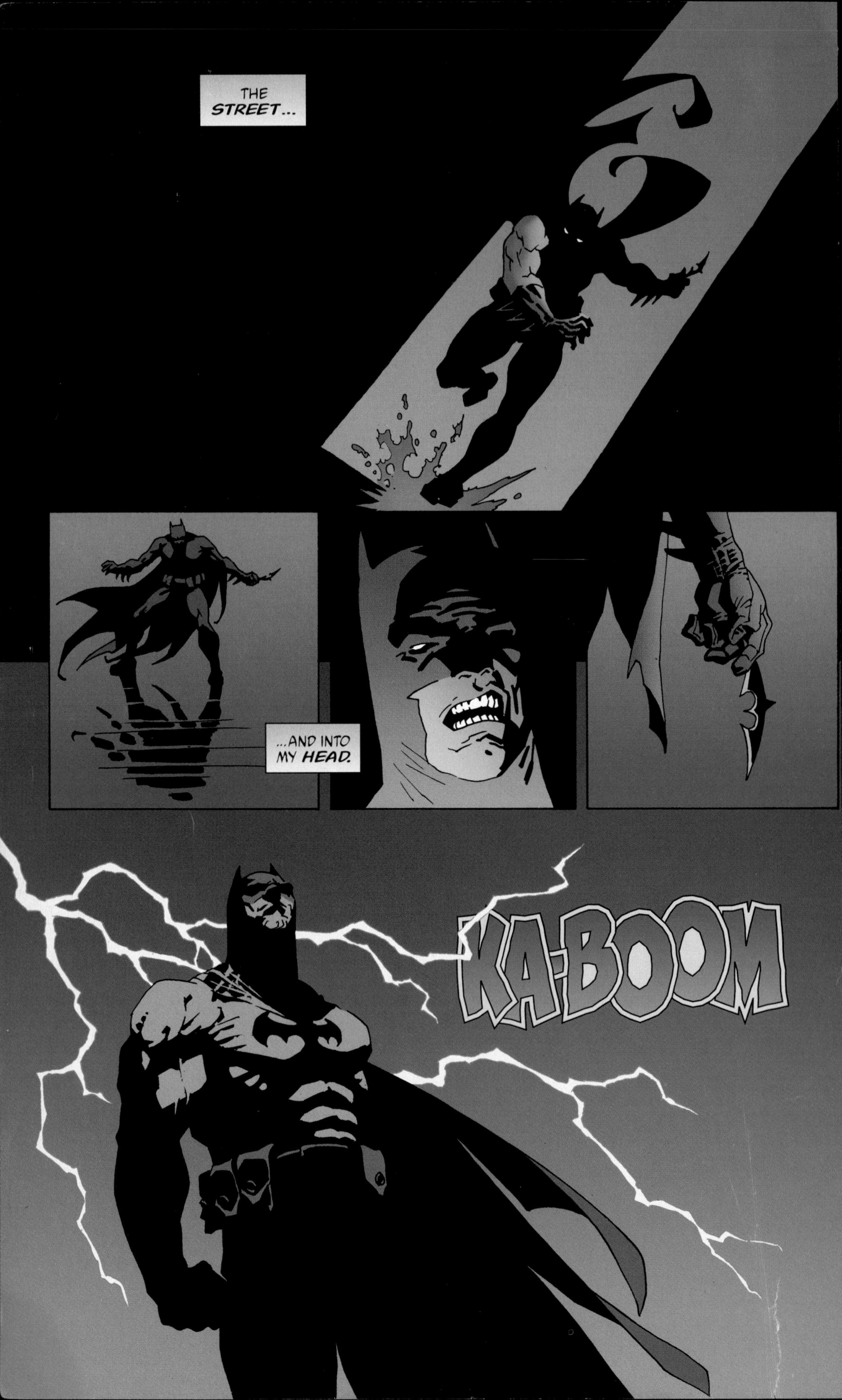
THE STREET...
...AND INTO MY HEAD.
KA-BOOM

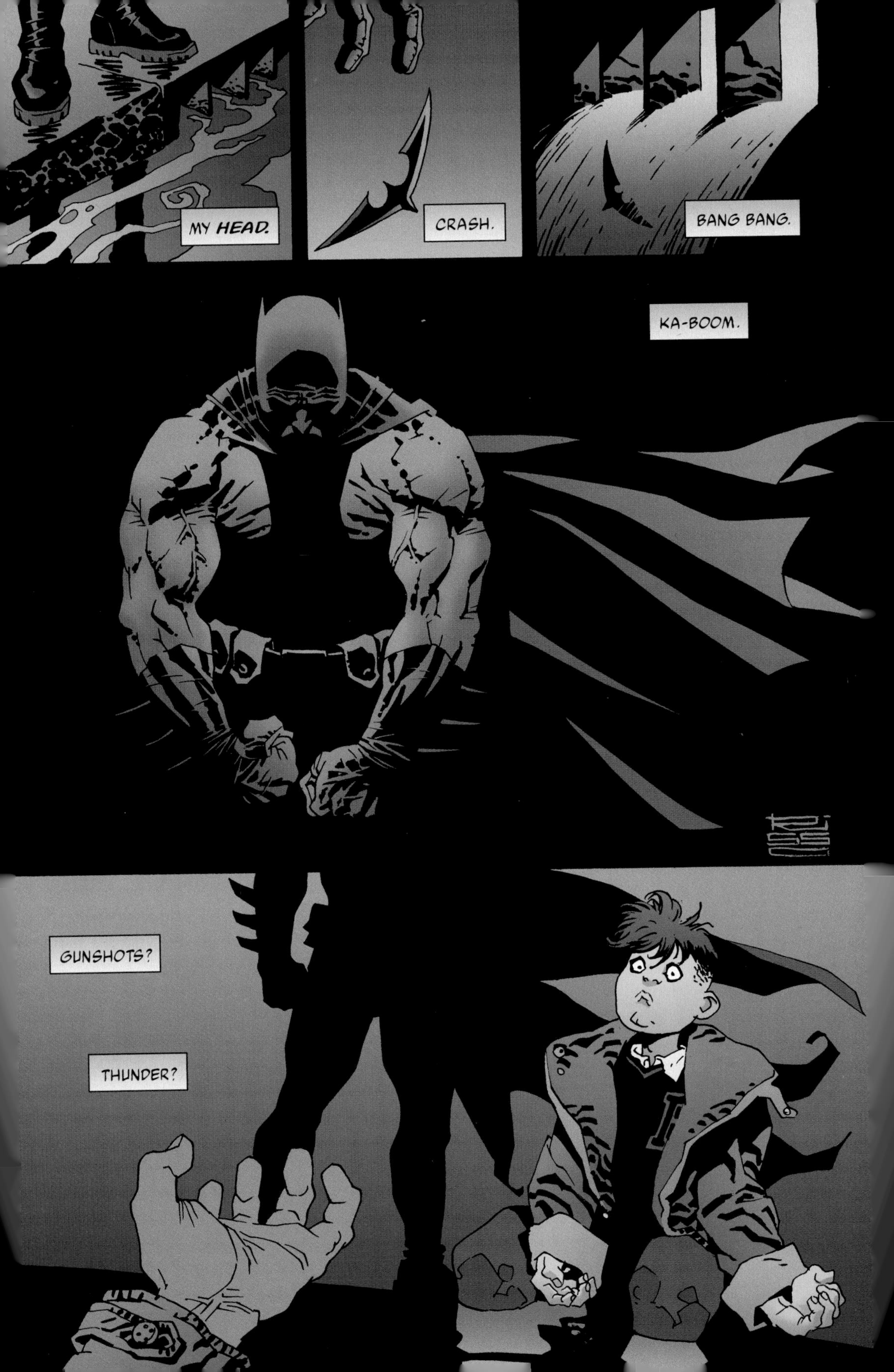
MY HEAD.
CRASH.
BANG BANG.
KA-BOOM.
GUNSHOTS?
THUNDER?

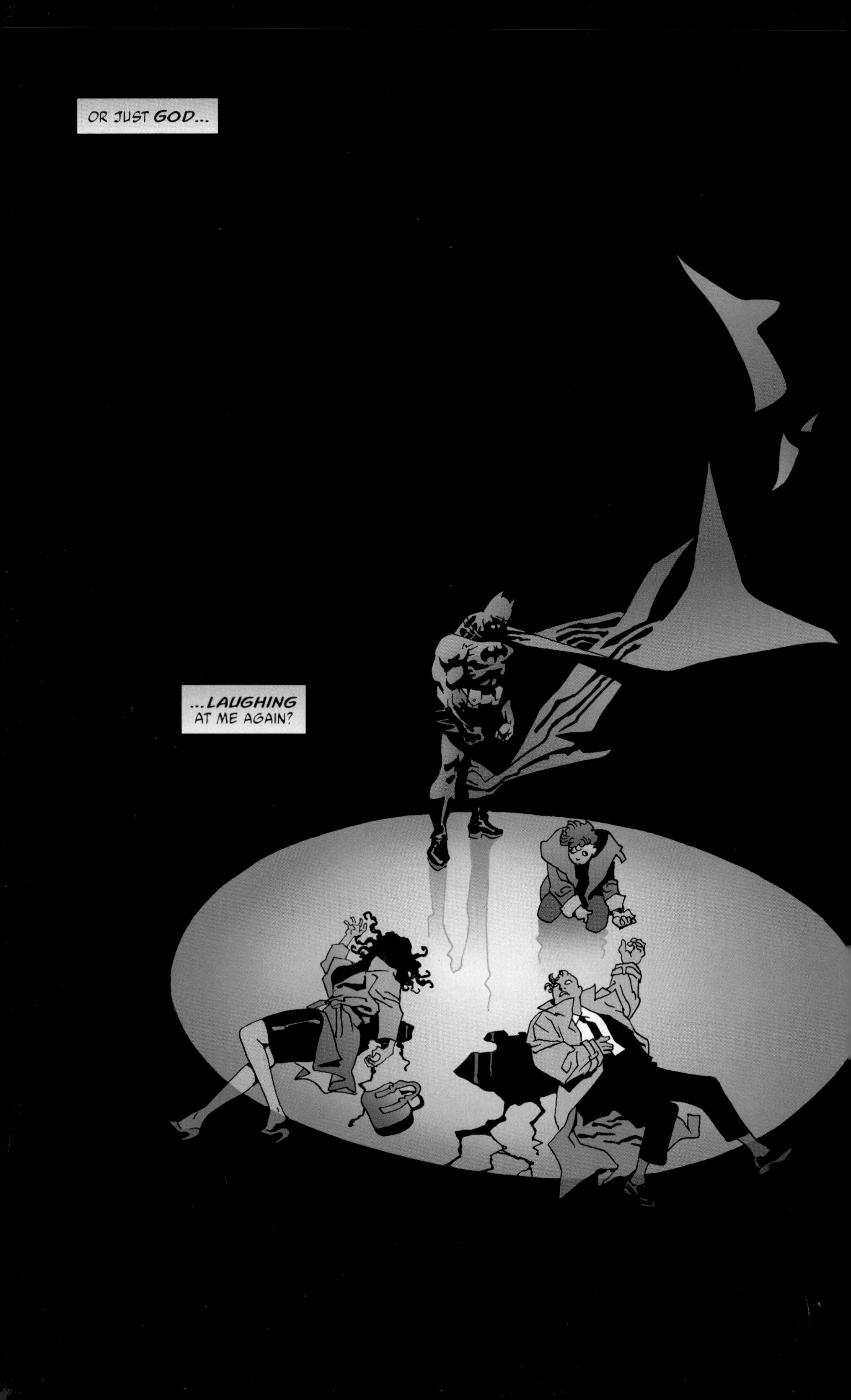
OR JUST **GOD**...
...**LAUGHING** AT ME AGAIN?

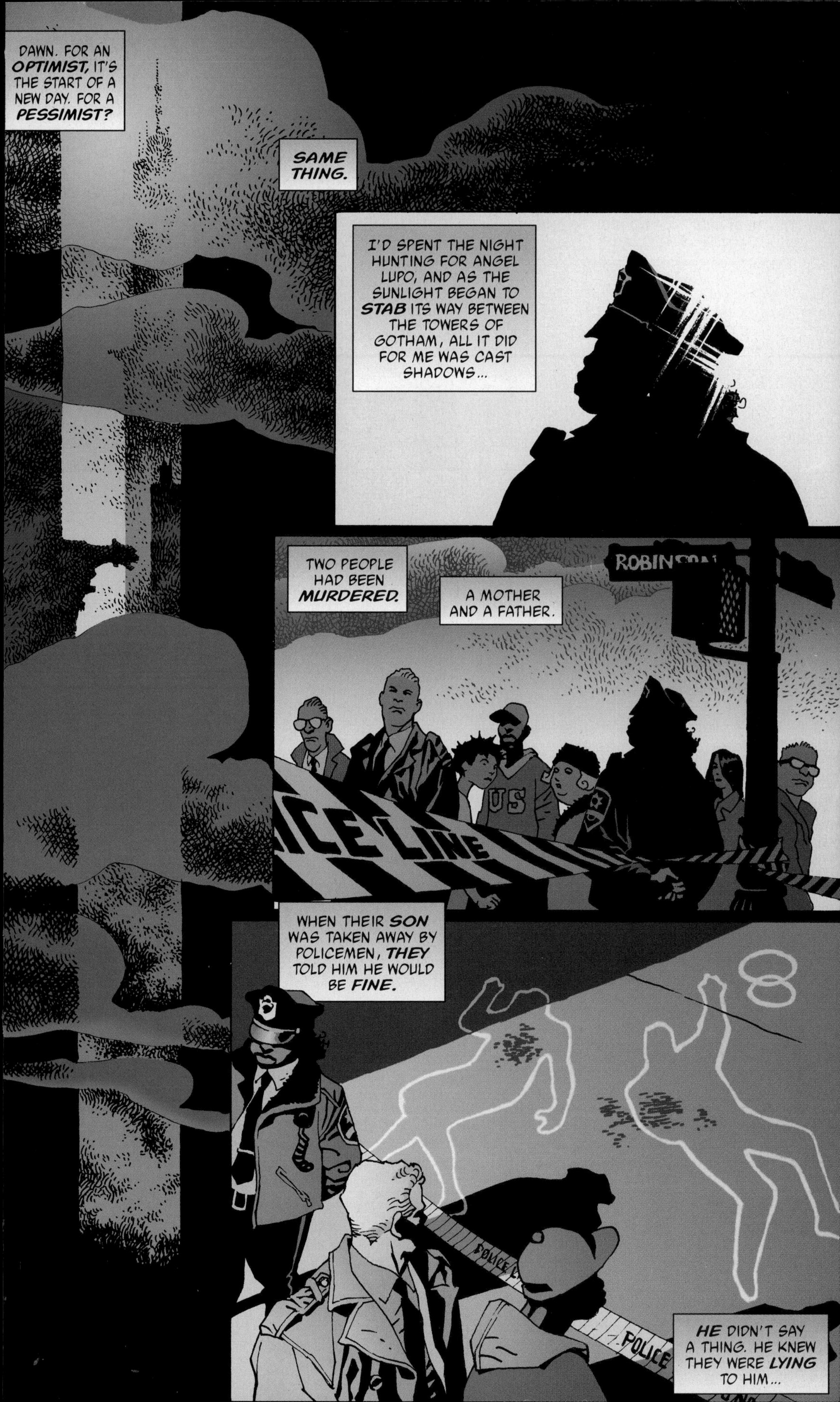
DAWN. FOR AN OPTIMIST, IT'S THE START OF A NEW DAY. FOR A PESSIMIST?
SAME THING.
I'D SPENT THE NIGHT HUNTING FOR ANGEL LUPO, AND AS THE SUNLIGHT BEGAN TO STAB ITS WAY BETWEEN THE TOWERS OF GOTHAM, ALL IT DID FOR ME WAS CAST SHADOWS...
TWO PEOPLE HAD BEEN MURDERED.
A MOTHER AND A FATHER.
WHEN THEIR SON WAS TAKEN AWAY BY POLICEMEN, THEY TOLD HIM HE WOULD BE FINE.
HE DIDN'T SAY A THING. HE KNEW THEY WERE LYING TO HIM...

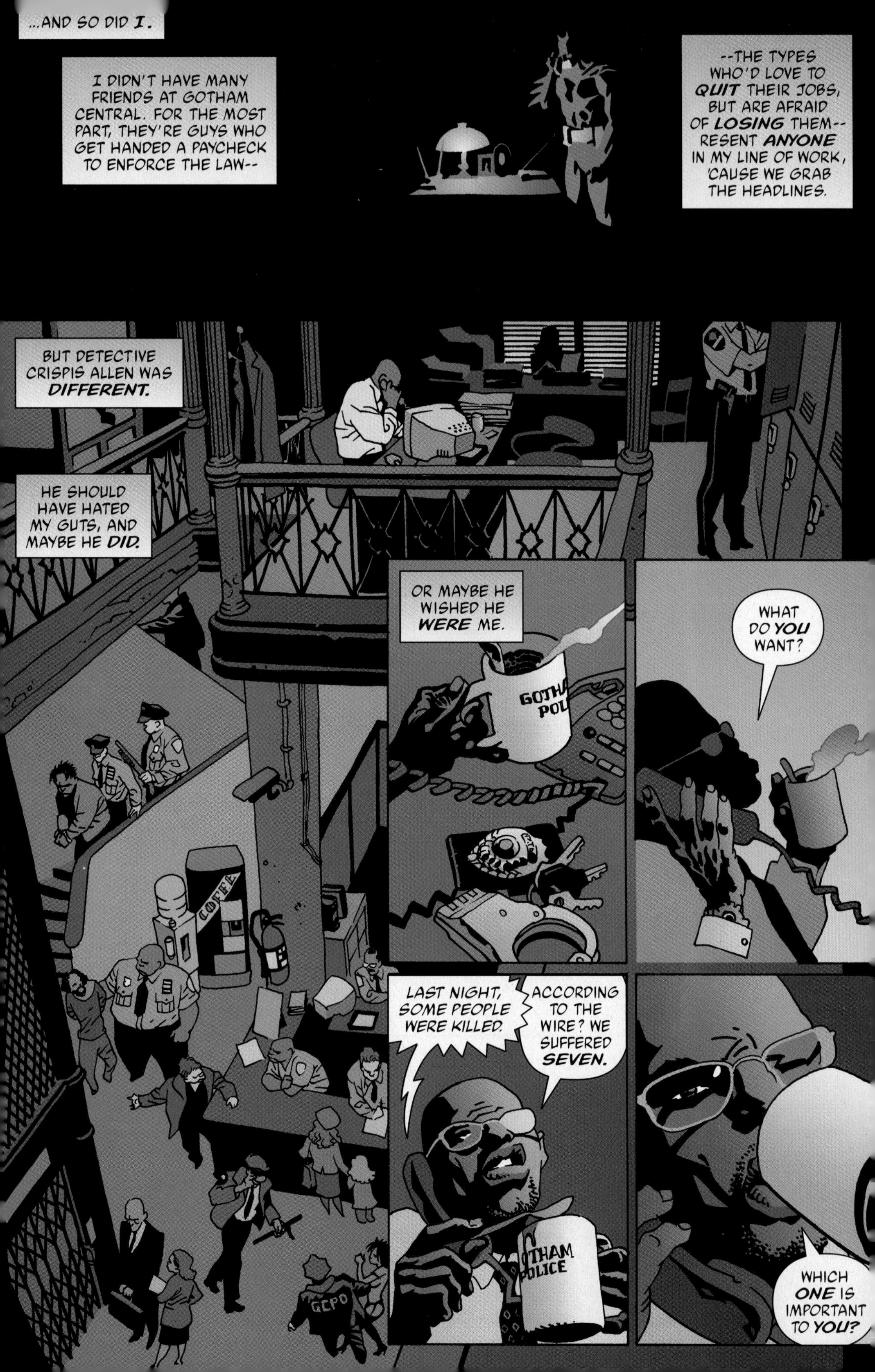
...AND SO DID I.
I DIDN'T HAVE MANY FRIENDS AT GOTHAM CENTRAL. FOR THE MOST PART, THEY'RE GUYS WHO GET HANDED A PAYCHECK TO ENFORCE THE LAW--
--THE TYPES WHO'D LOVE TO QUIT THEIR JOBS, BUT ARE AFRAID OF LOSING THEM--RESENT ANYONE IN MY LINE OF WORK, 'CAUSE WE GRAB THE HEADLINES.
BUT DETECTIVE CRISPIS ALLEN WAS DIFFERENT.
HE SHOULD HAVE HATED MY GUTS, AND MAYBE HE DID.
OR MAYBE HE WISHED HE WERE ME.
GOTHA POL
WHAT DO YOU WANT?
COFFE
LAST NIGHT, SOME PEOPLE WERE KILLED.
ACCORDING TO THE WIRE? WE SUFFERED SEVEN.
GOTHAM POLICE
GCPD
WHICH ONE IS IMPORTANT TO YOU?

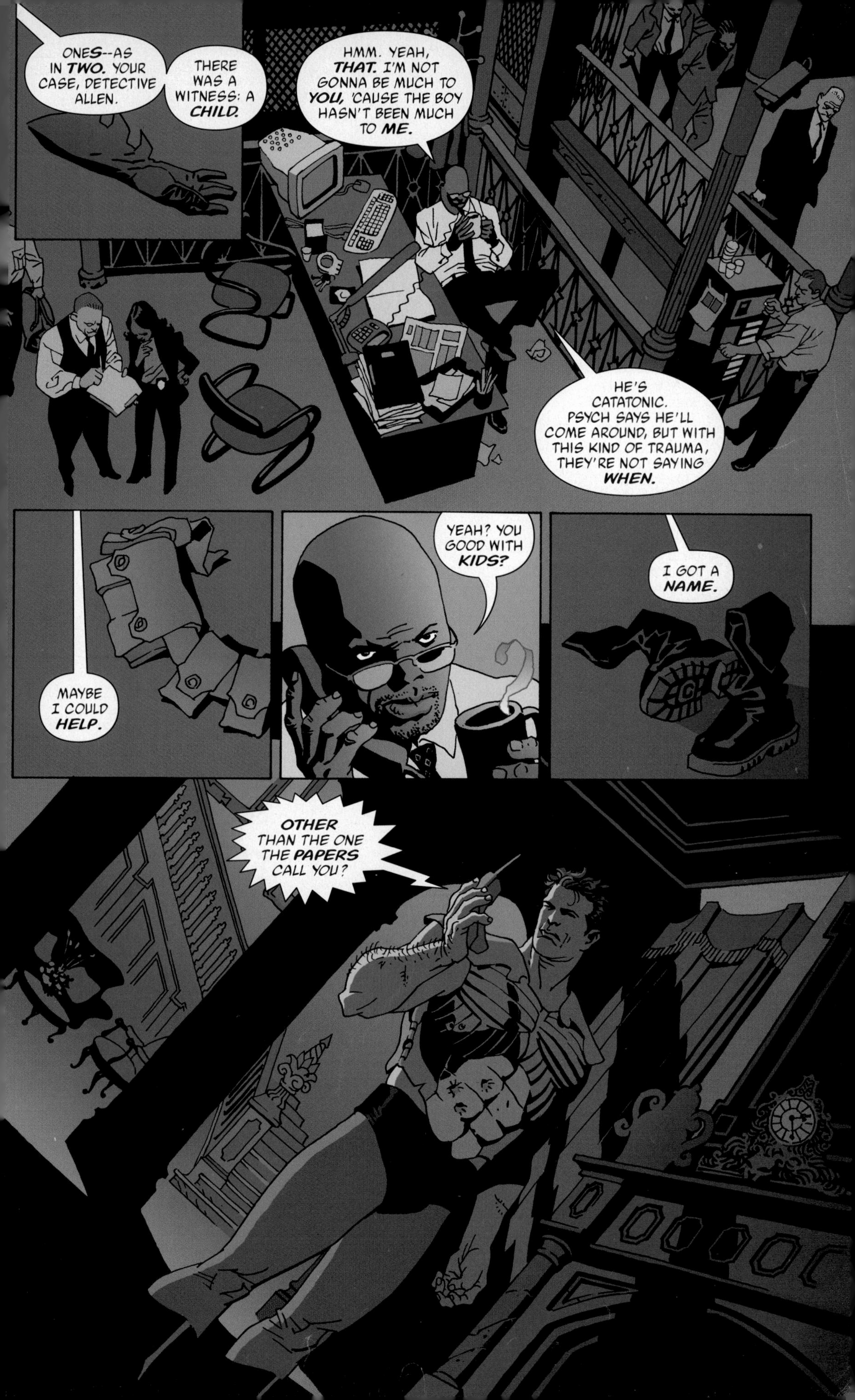
ONES--AS IN **TWO.** YOUR CASE, DETECTIVE ALLEN.
THERE WAS A WITNESS: A **CHILD.**
HMM. YEAH, **THAT.** I'M NOT GONNA BE MUCH TO **YOU,** 'CAUSE THE BOY HASN'T BEEN MUCH TO **ME.**
HE'S CATATONIC. PSYCH SAYS HE'LL COME AROUND, BUT WITH THIS KIND OF TRAUMA, THEY'RE NOT SAYING **WHEN.**
MAYBE I COULD **HELP.**
YEAH? YOU GOOD WITH **KIDS?**
I GOT A **NAME.**
OTHER THAN THE ONE THE **PAPERS** CALL YOU?

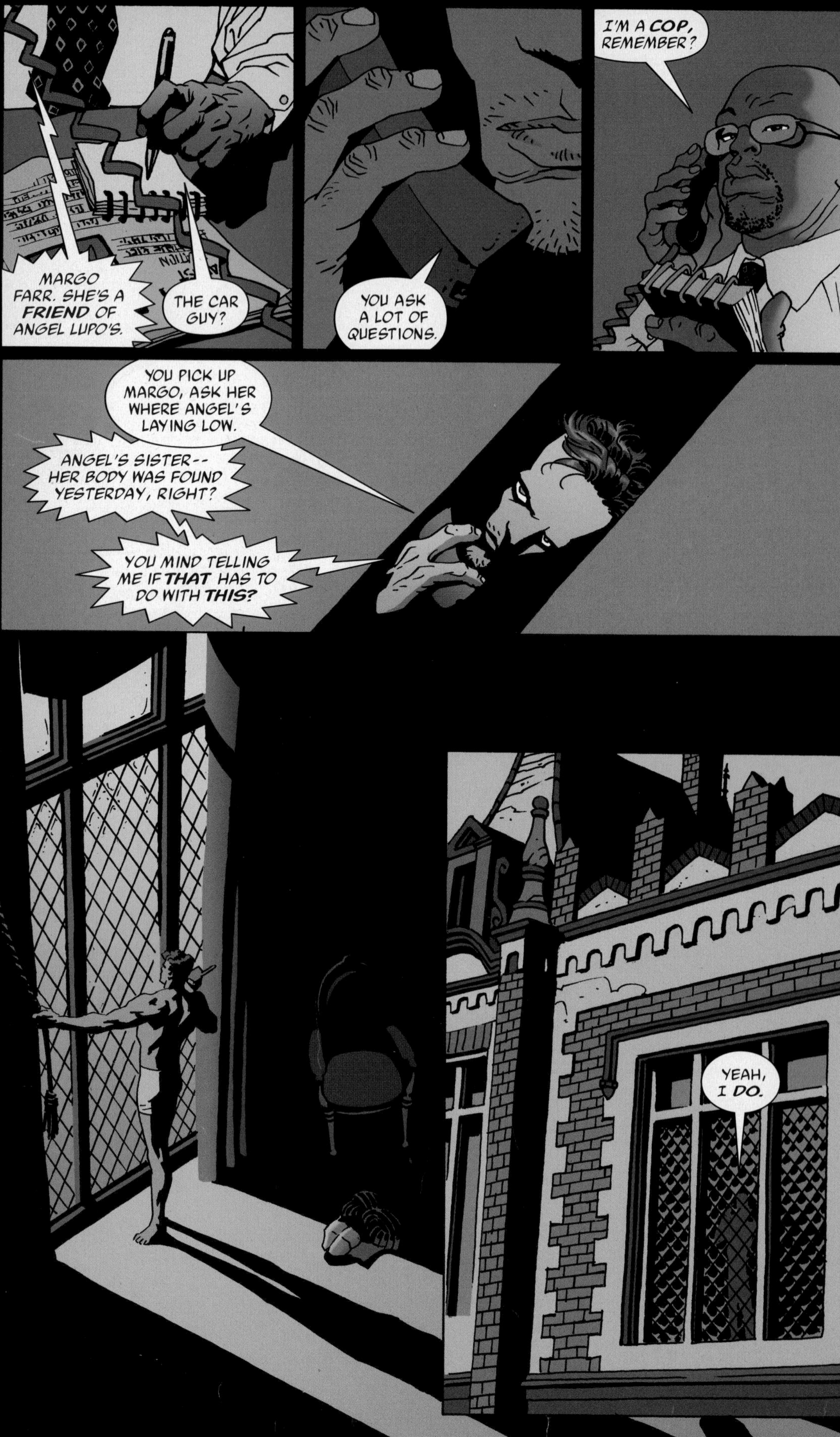
MARGO FARR. SHE'S A **FRIEND** OF ANGEL LUPO'S.
THE CAR GUY?
YOU ASK A LOT OF QUESTIONS.
I'M A **COP**, REMEMBER?
YOU PICK UP MARGO, ASK HER WHERE ANGEL'S LAYING LOW.
ANGEL'S SISTER-- HER BODY WAS FOUND YESTERDAY, RIGHT?
YOU MIND TELLING ME IF **THAT** HAS TO DO WITH **THIS?**
YEAH, I **DO.**

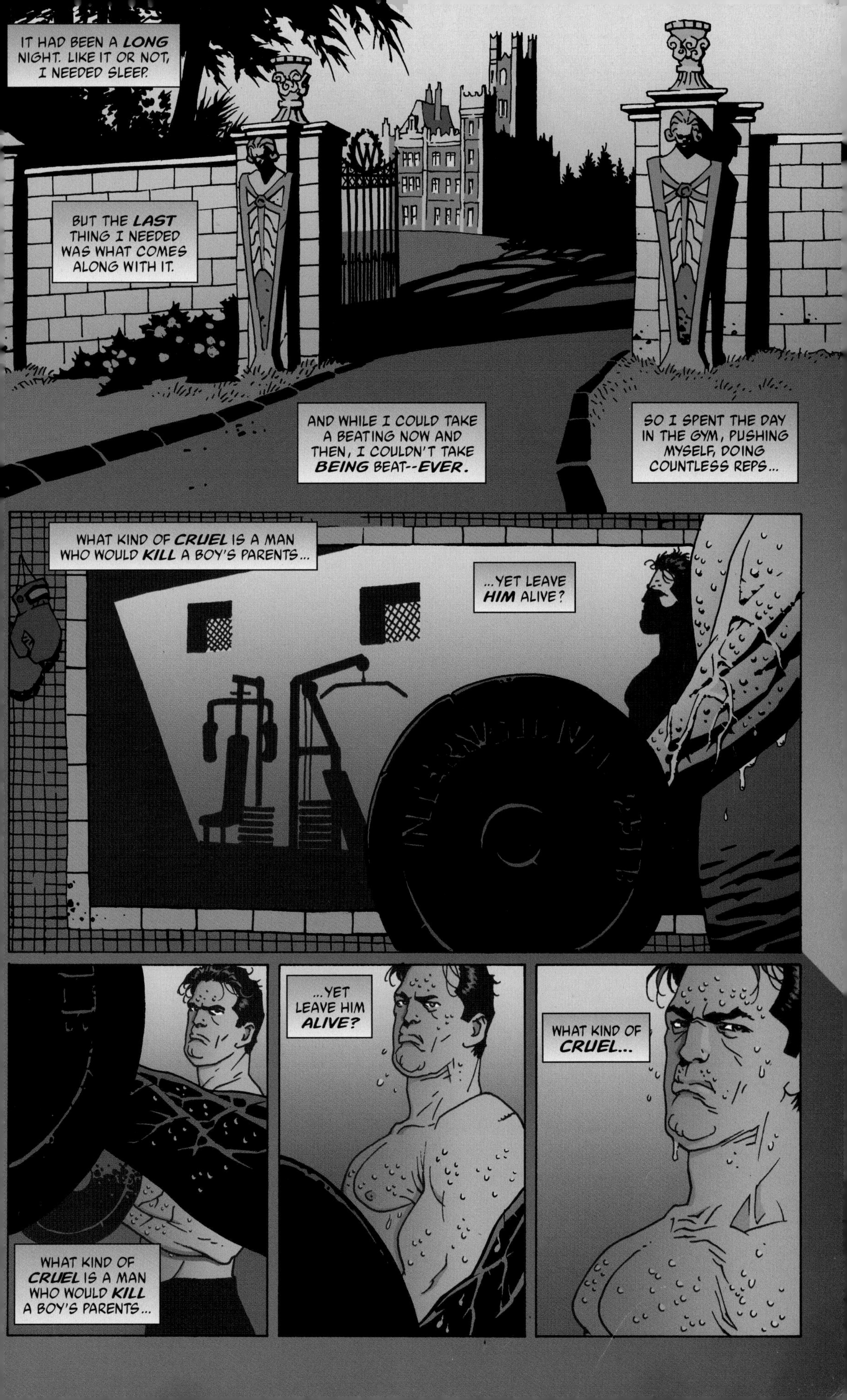
IT HAD BEEN A LONG NIGHT. LIKE IT OR NOT, I NEEDED SLEEP.
BUT THE LAST THING I NEEDED WAS WHAT COMES ALONG WITH IT.
AND WHILE I COULD TAKE A BEATING NOW AND THEN, I COULDN'T TAKE BEING BEAT--EVER.
SO I SPENT THE DAY IN THE GYM, PUSHING MYSELF, DOING COUNTLESS REPS...
WHAT KIND OF CRUEL IS A MAN WHO WOULD KILL A BOY'S PARENTS...
...YET LEAVE HIM ALIVE?
WHAT KIND OF CRUEL IS A MAN WHO WOULD KILL A BOY'S PARENTS...
...YET LEAVE HIM ALIVE?
WHAT KIND OF CRUEL...

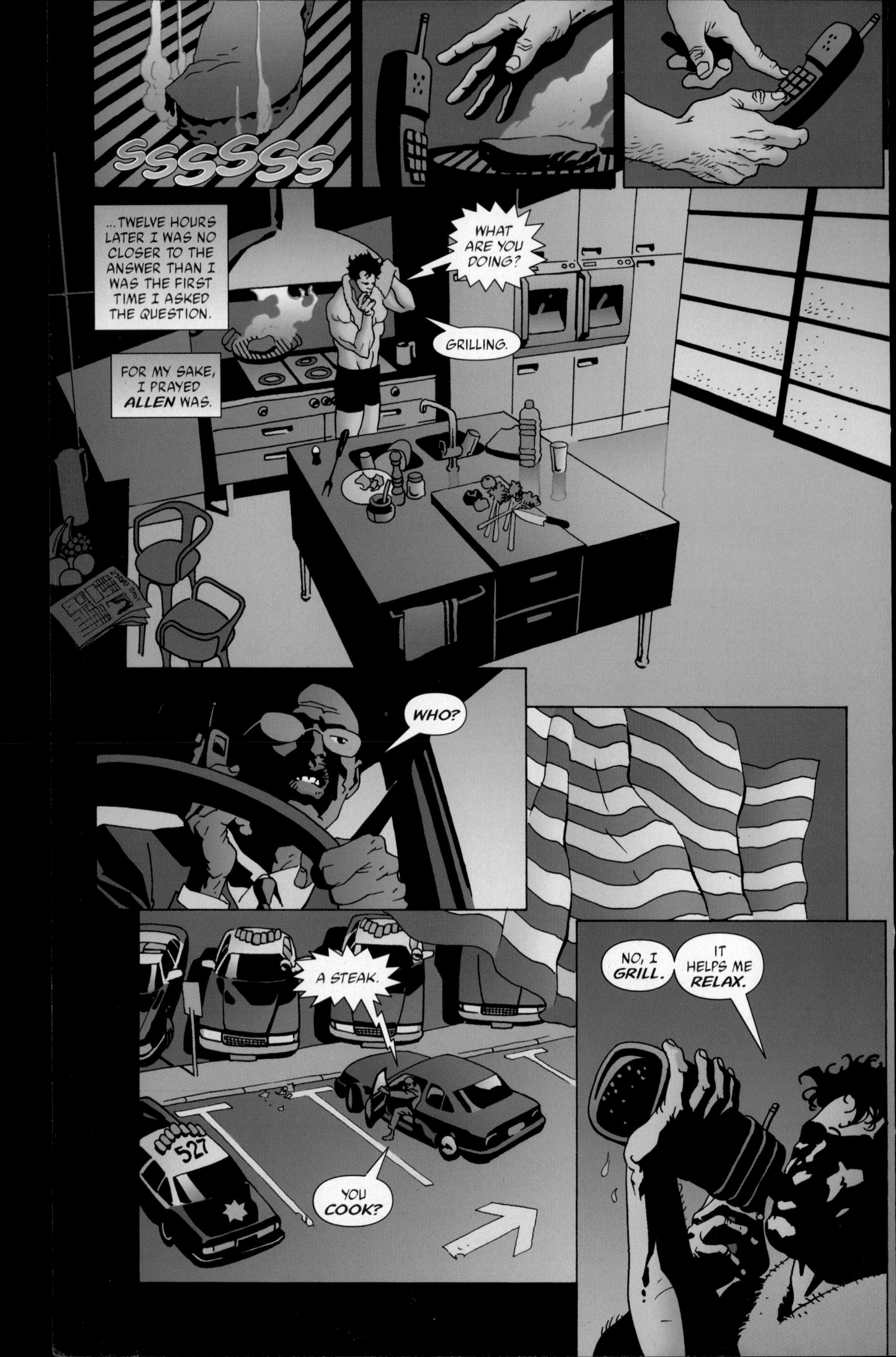
SSSSSS
...TWELVE HOURS LATER I WAS NO CLOSER TO THE ANSWER THAN I WAS THE FIRST TIME I ASKED THE QUESTION.
WHAT ARE YOU DOING?
GRILLING.
FOR MY SAKE, I PRAYED **ALLEN** WAS.
WHO?
A STEAK.
YOU **COOK?**
NO, I **GRILL.**
IT HELPS ME **RELAX.**

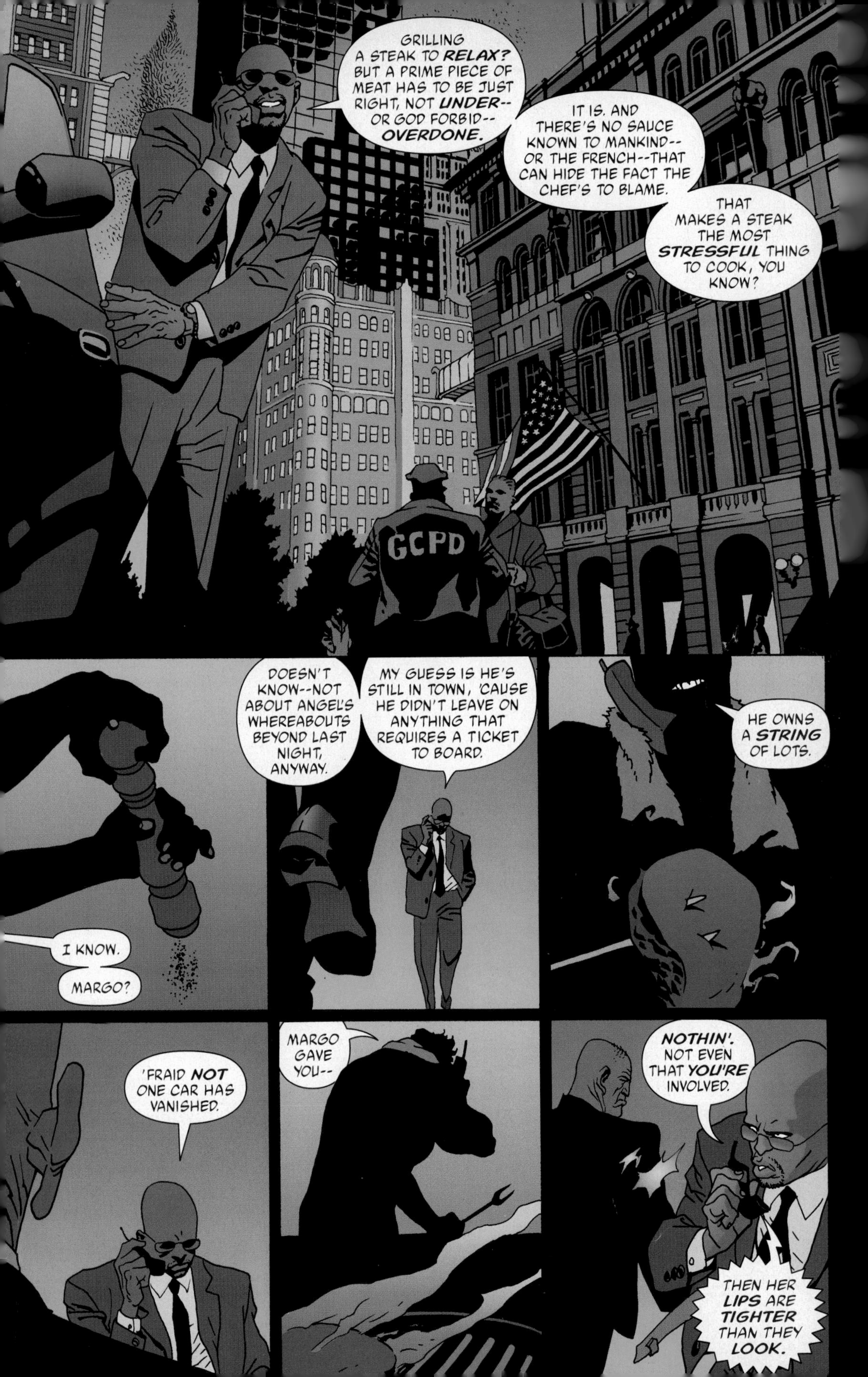
GRILLING A STEAK TO **RELAX?** BUT A PRIME PIECE OF MEAT HAS TO BE JUST RIGHT, NOT **UNDER**-- OR GOD FORBID-- **OVERDONE.**
IT IS. AND THERE'S NO SAUCE KNOWN TO MANKIND-- OR THE FRENCH--THAT CAN HIDE THE FACT THE CHEF'S TO BLAME.
THAT MAKES A STEAK THE MOST **STRESSFUL** THING TO COOK, YOU KNOW?
GCPD
DOESN'T KNOW--NOT ABOUT ANGEL'S WHEREABOUTS BEYOND LAST NIGHT, ANYWAY.
MY GUESS IS HE'S STILL IN TOWN, 'CAUSE HE DIDN'T LEAVE ON ANYTHING THAT REQUIRES A TICKET TO BOARD.
HE OWNS A **STRING** OF LOTS.
I KNOW.
MARGO?
'FRAID **NOT** ONE CAR HAS VANISHED.
MARGO GAVE YOU--
NOTHIN'. NOT EVEN THAT **YOU'RE** INVOLVED.
THEN HER **LIPS** ARE **TIGHTER** THAN THEY **LOOK.**

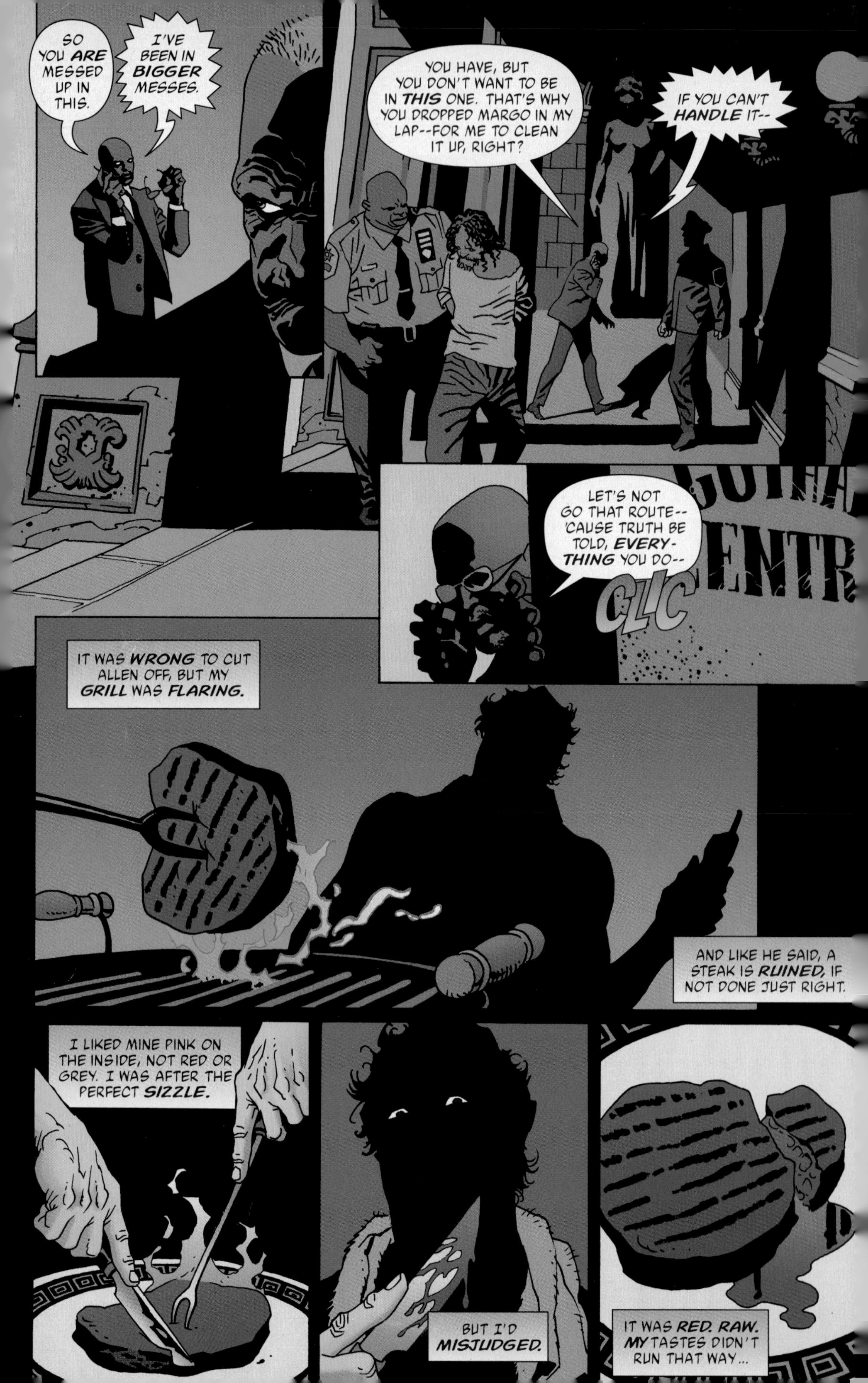
SO YOU **ARE** MESSED UP IN THIS.
I'VE BEEN IN **BIGGER** MESSES.
YOU HAVE, BUT YOU DON'T WANT TO BE IN **THIS** ONE. THAT'S WHY YOU DROPPED MARGO IN MY LAP--FOR ME TO CLEAN IT UP, RIGHT?
IF YOU CAN'T **HANDLE** IT--
LET'S NOT GO THAT ROUTE-- 'CAUSE TRUTH BE TOLD, **EVERY-THING** YOU DO--
CLIC
ENTR
IT WAS **WRONG** TO CUT ALLEN OFF, BUT MY **GRILL** WAS **FLARING.**
AND LIKE HE SAID, A STEAK IS **RUINED,** IF NOT DONE JUST RIGHT.
I LIKED MINE PINK ON THE INSIDE, NOT RED OR GREY. I WAS AFTER THE PERFECT **SIZZLE.**
BUT I'D **MISJUDGED.**
IT WAS **RED. RAW. MY** TASTES DIDN'T RUN THAT WAY...

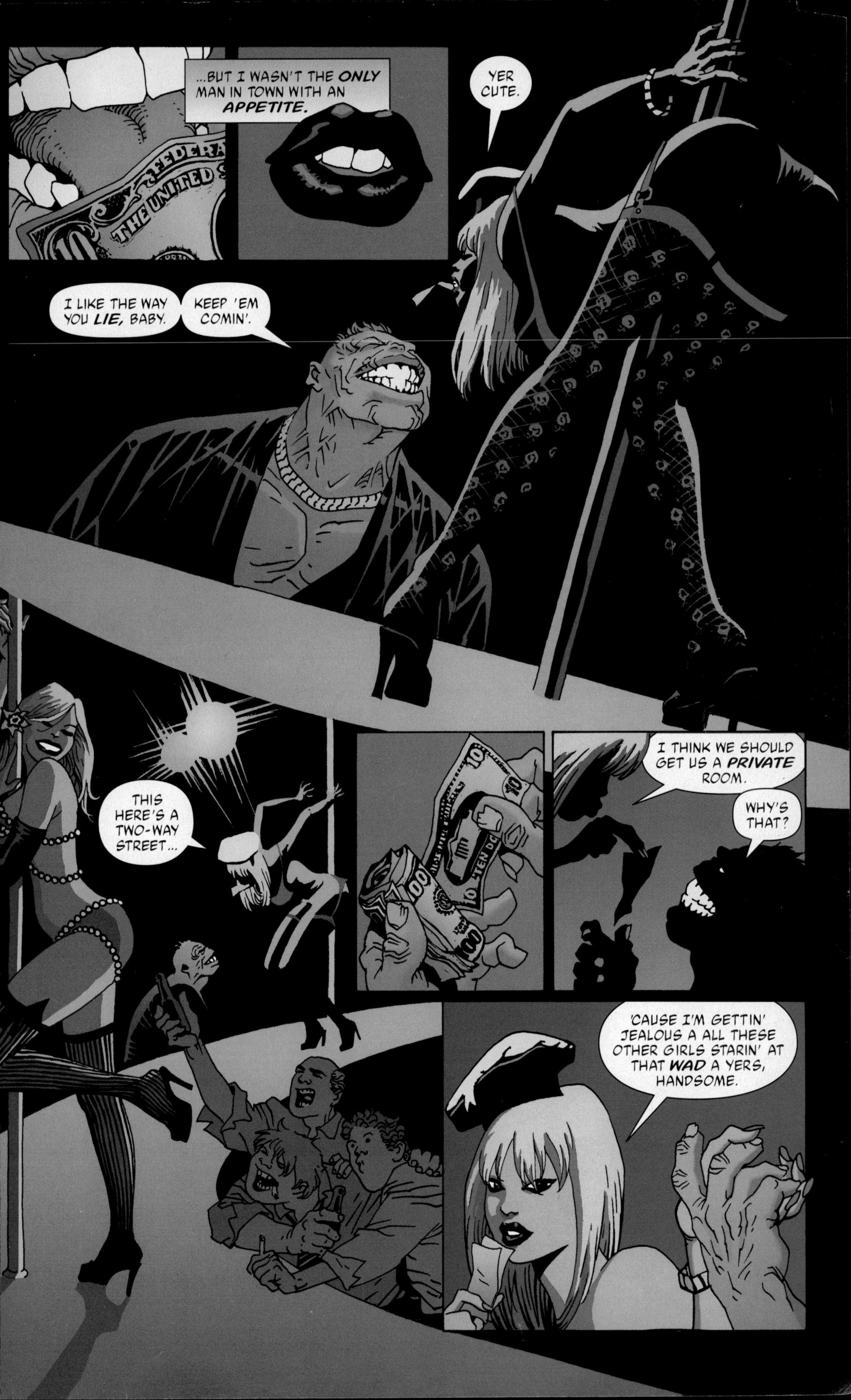

...BUT I WASN'T THE **ONLY** MAN IN TOWN WITH AN **APPETITE.**
YER CUTE.
I LIKE THE WAY YOU **LIE,** BABY.
KEEP 'EM COMIN'.
THIS HERE'S A TWO-WAY STREET...
I THINK WE SHOULD GET US A **PRIVATE** ROOM.
WHY'S THAT?
'CAUSE I'M GETTIN' JEALOUS A ALL THESE OTHER GIRLS STARIN' AT THAT **WAD** A YERS, HANDSOME.

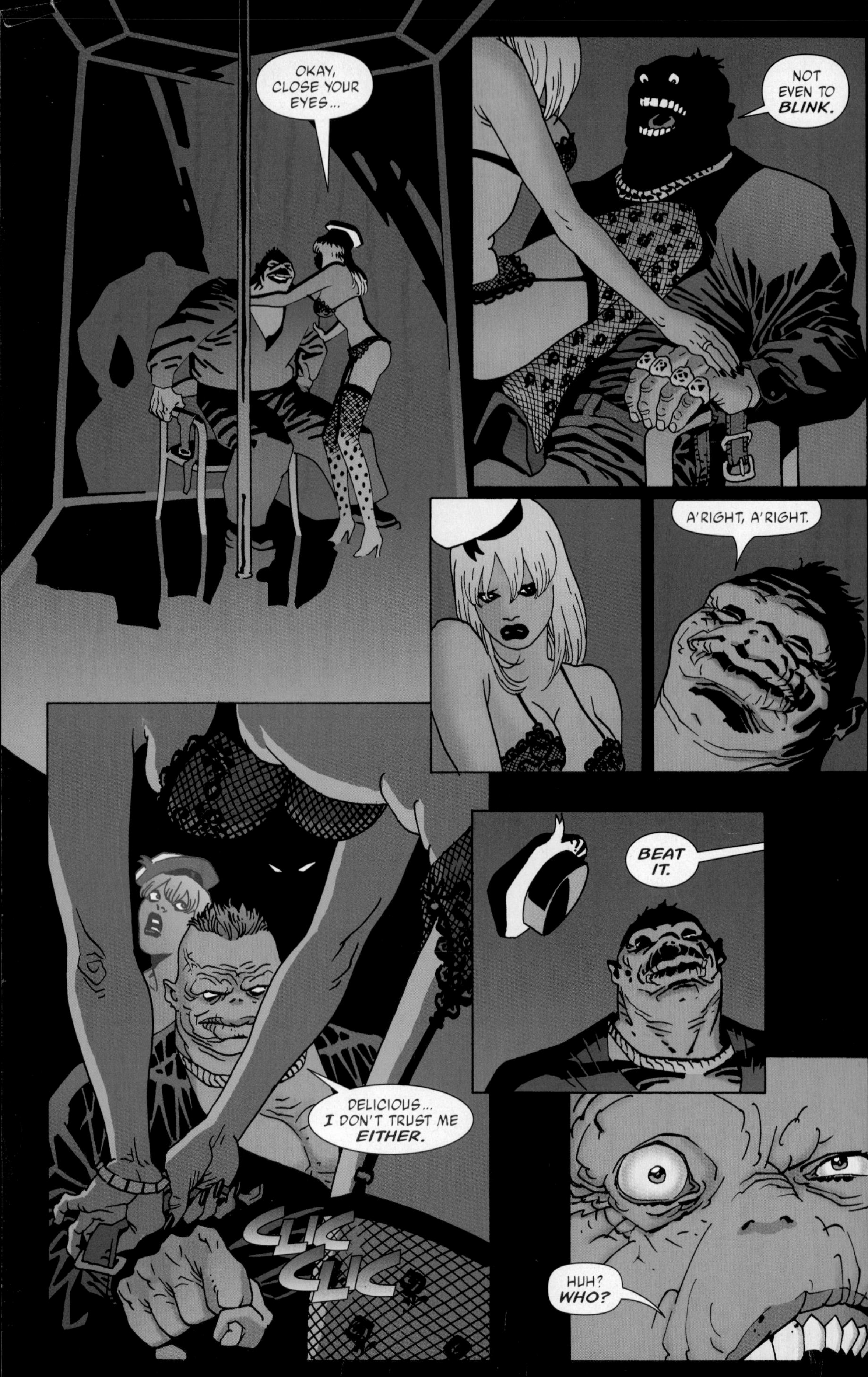
OKAY, CLOSE YOUR EYES...
NOT EVEN TO BLINK.
A'RIGHT, A'RIGHT.
BEAT IT.
DELICIOUS... I DON'T TRUST ME EITHER.
CLIC CLIC
HUH? WHO?

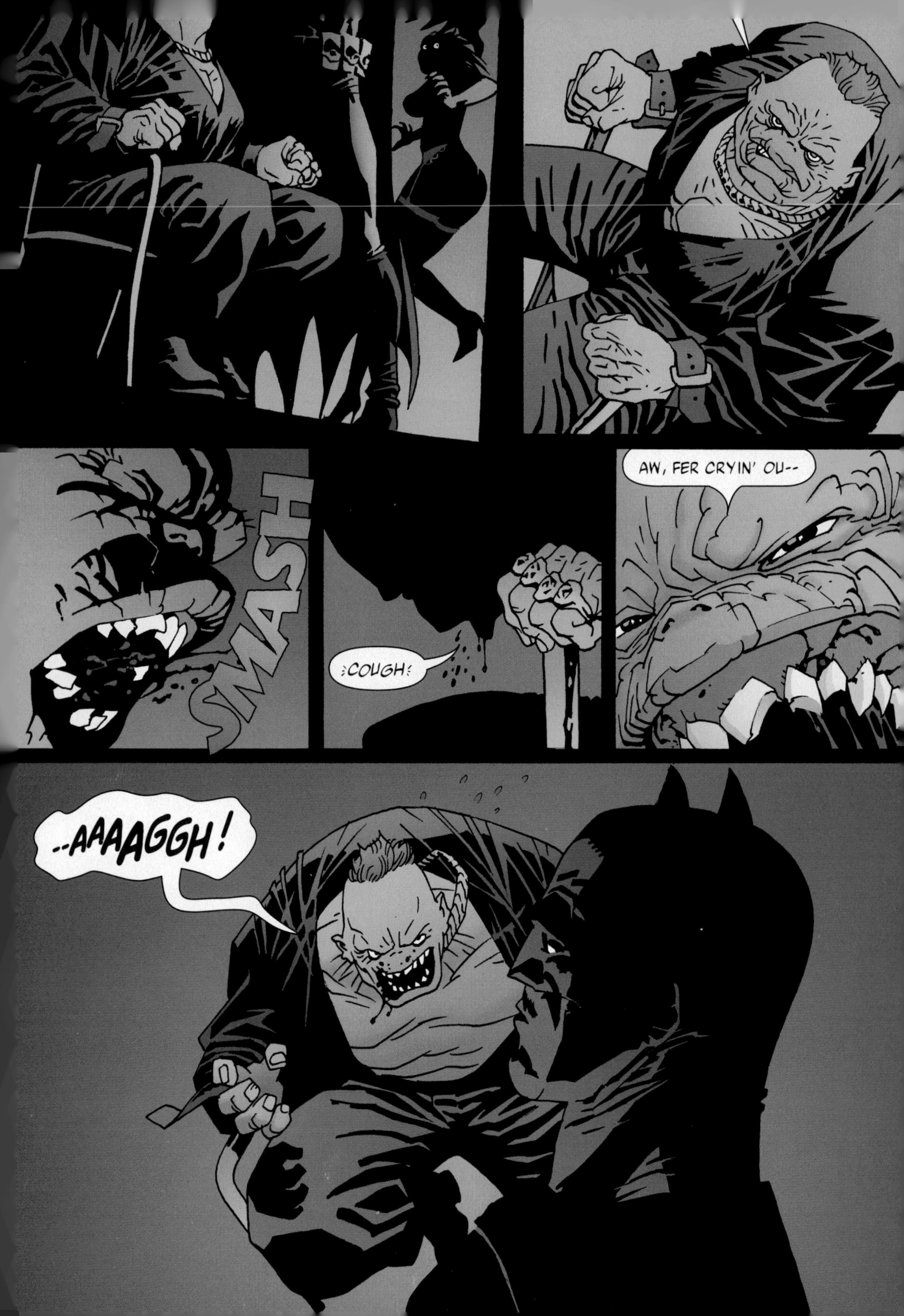
SMASH
COUGH
AW, FER CRYIN' OU--
--AAAAGGH!

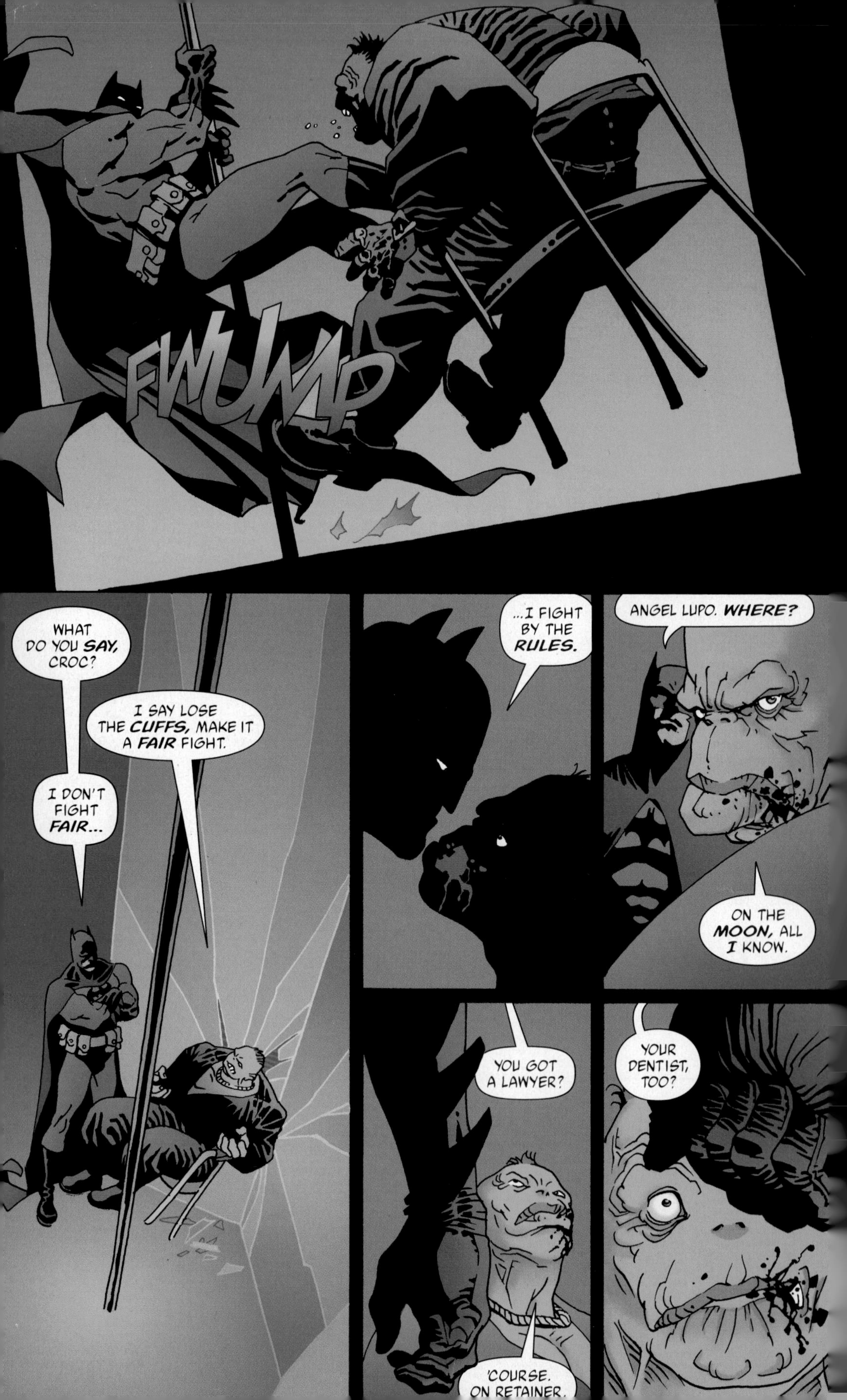
FWUMP
WHAT DO YOU **SAY**, CROC?
I SAY LOSE THE **CUFFS**, MAKE IT A **FAIR** FIGHT.
I DON'T FIGHT **FAIR**...
...I FIGHT BY THE **RULES**.
ANGEL LUPO. **WHERE?**
ON THE **MOON**, ALL **I** KNOW.
YOU GOT A LAWYER?
'COURSE. ON RETAINER.
YOUR DENTIST, TOO?

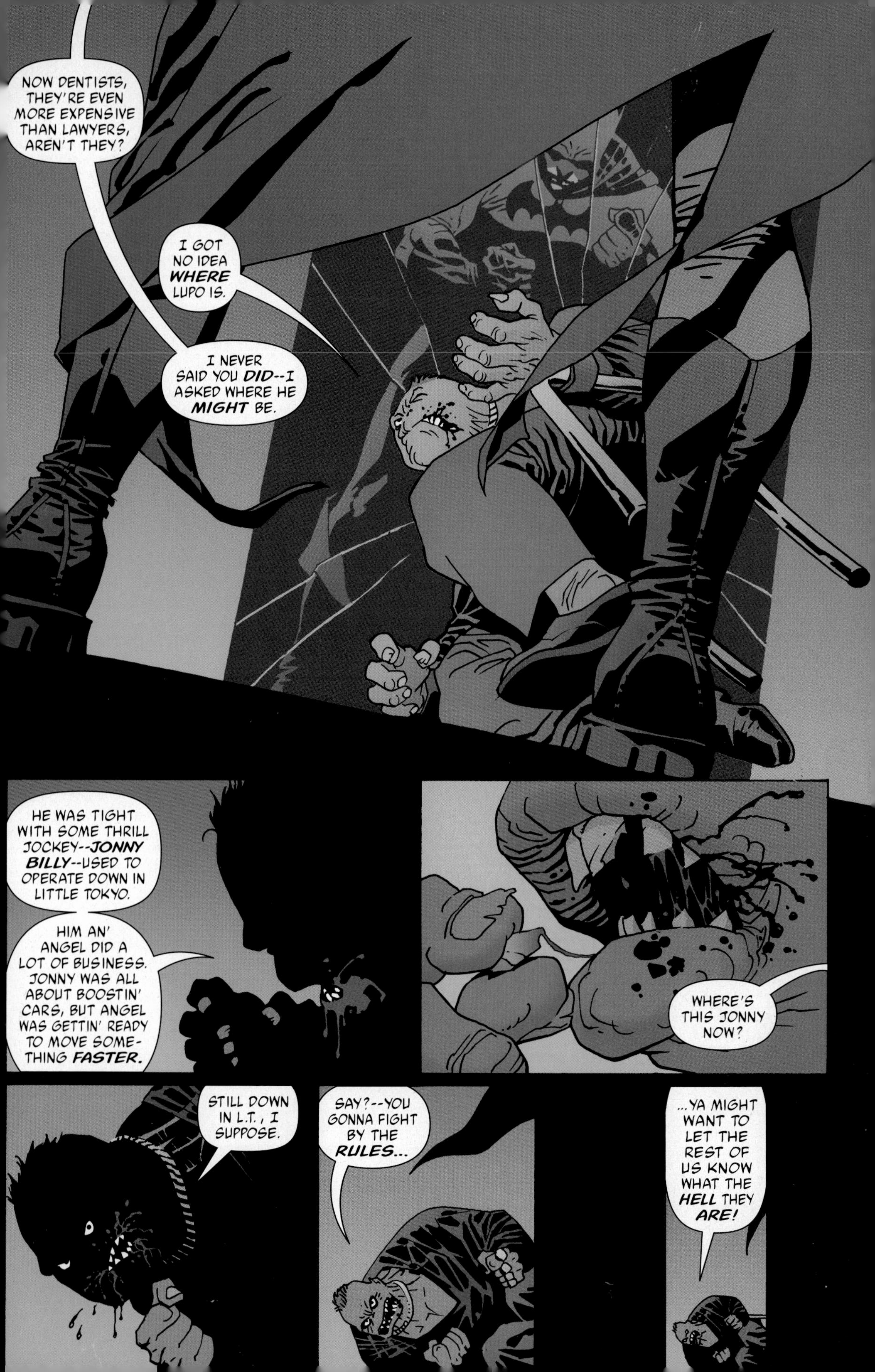
NOW DENTISTS, THEY'RE EVEN MORE EXPENSIVE THAN LAWYERS, AREN'T THEY?
I GOT NO IDEA **WHERE** LUPO IS.
I NEVER SAID YOU **DID**--I ASKED WHERE HE **MIGHT** BE.
HE WAS TIGHT WITH SOME THRILL JOCKEY--**JONNY BILLY**--USED TO OPERATE DOWN IN LITTLE TOKYO.
HIM AN' ANGEL DID A LOT OF BUSINESS. JONNY WAS ALL ABOUT BOOSTIN' CARS, BUT ANGEL WAS GETTIN' READY TO MOVE SOMETHING **FASTER.**
WHERE'S THIS JONNY NOW?
STILL DOWN IN L.T., I SUPPOSE.
SAY?--YOU GONNA FIGHT BY THE **RULES...**
...YA MIGHT WANT TO LET THE REST OF US KNOW WHAT THE **HELL** THEY **ARE!**

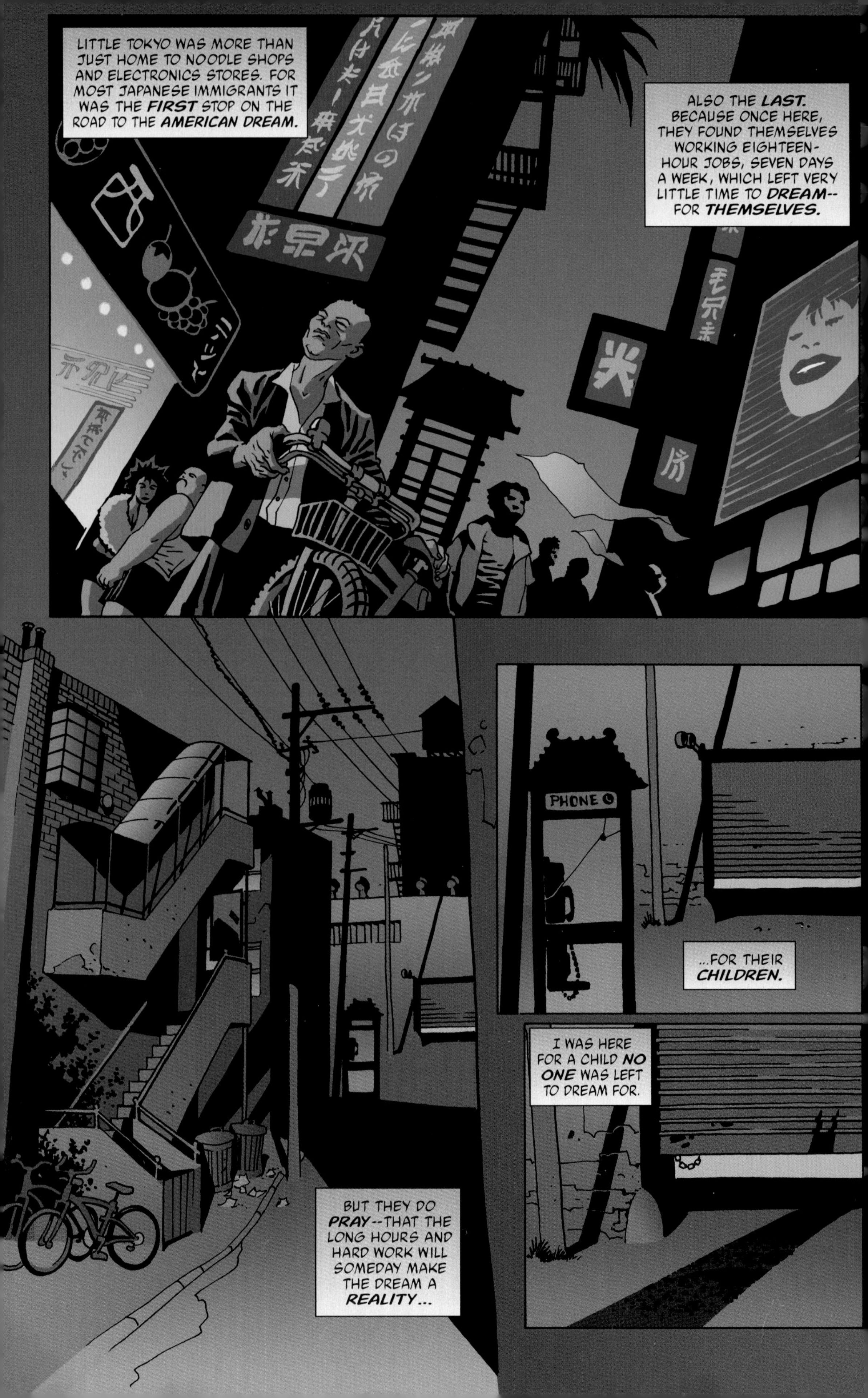
LITTLE TOKYO WAS MORE THAN JUST HOME TO NOODLE SHOPS AND ELECTRONICS STORES. FOR MOST JAPANESE IMMIGRANTS IT WAS THE **FIRST** STOP ON THE ROAD TO THE **AMERICAN DREAM.**
ALSO THE **LAST.** BECAUSE ONCE HERE, THEY FOUND THEMSELVES WORKING EIGHTEEN-HOUR JOBS, SEVEN DAYS A WEEK, WHICH LEFT VERY LITTLE TIME TO **DREAM**-- FOR **THEMSELVES.**
BUT THEY DO **PRAY**--THAT THE LONG HOURS AND HARD WORK WILL SOMEDAY MAKE THE DREAM A **REALITY...**
PHONE
...FOR THEIR **CHILDREN.**
I WAS HERE FOR A CHILD **NO ONE** WAS LEFT TO DREAM FOR.

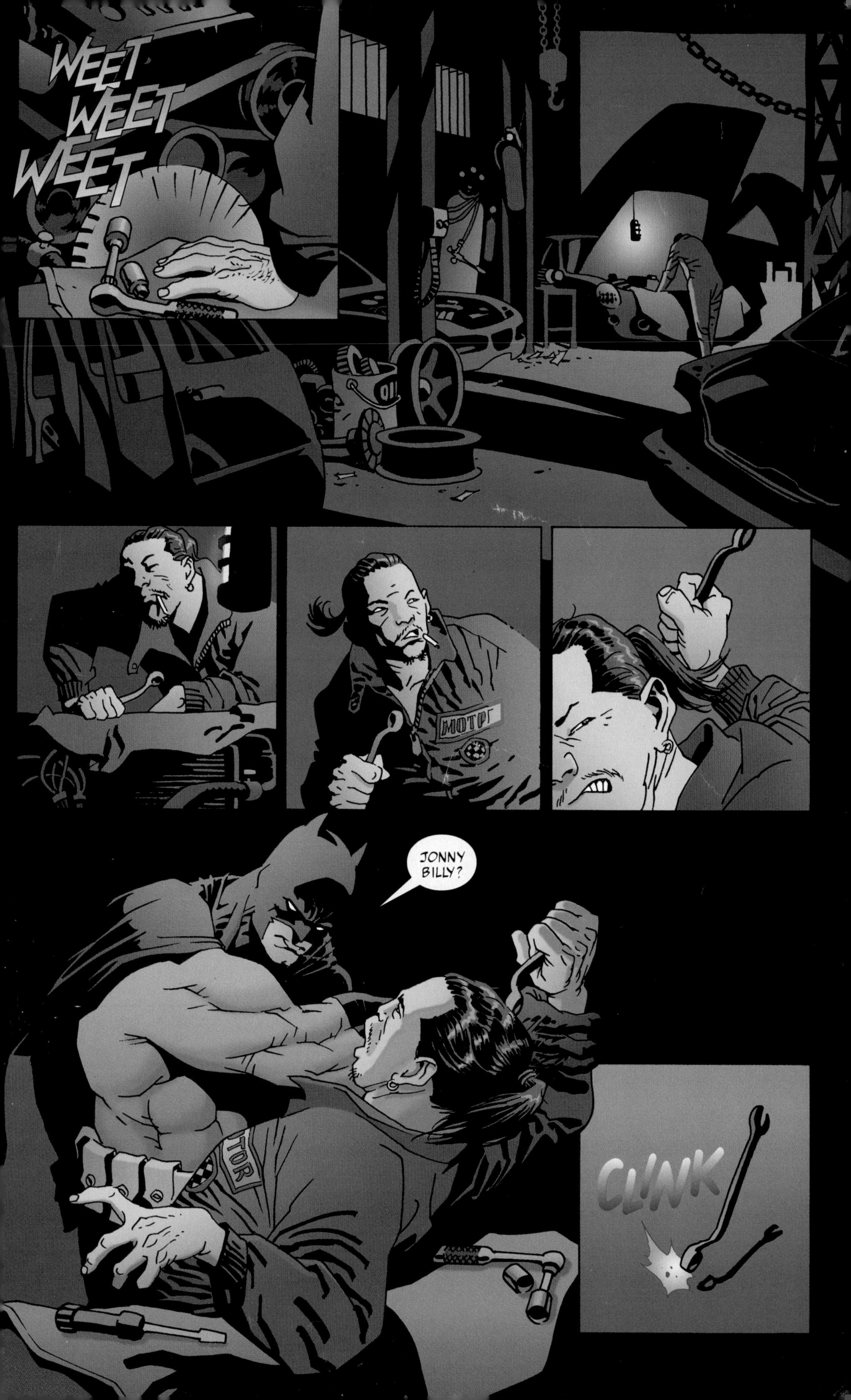
WEET
WEET
WEET
JONNY BILLY?
CLINK

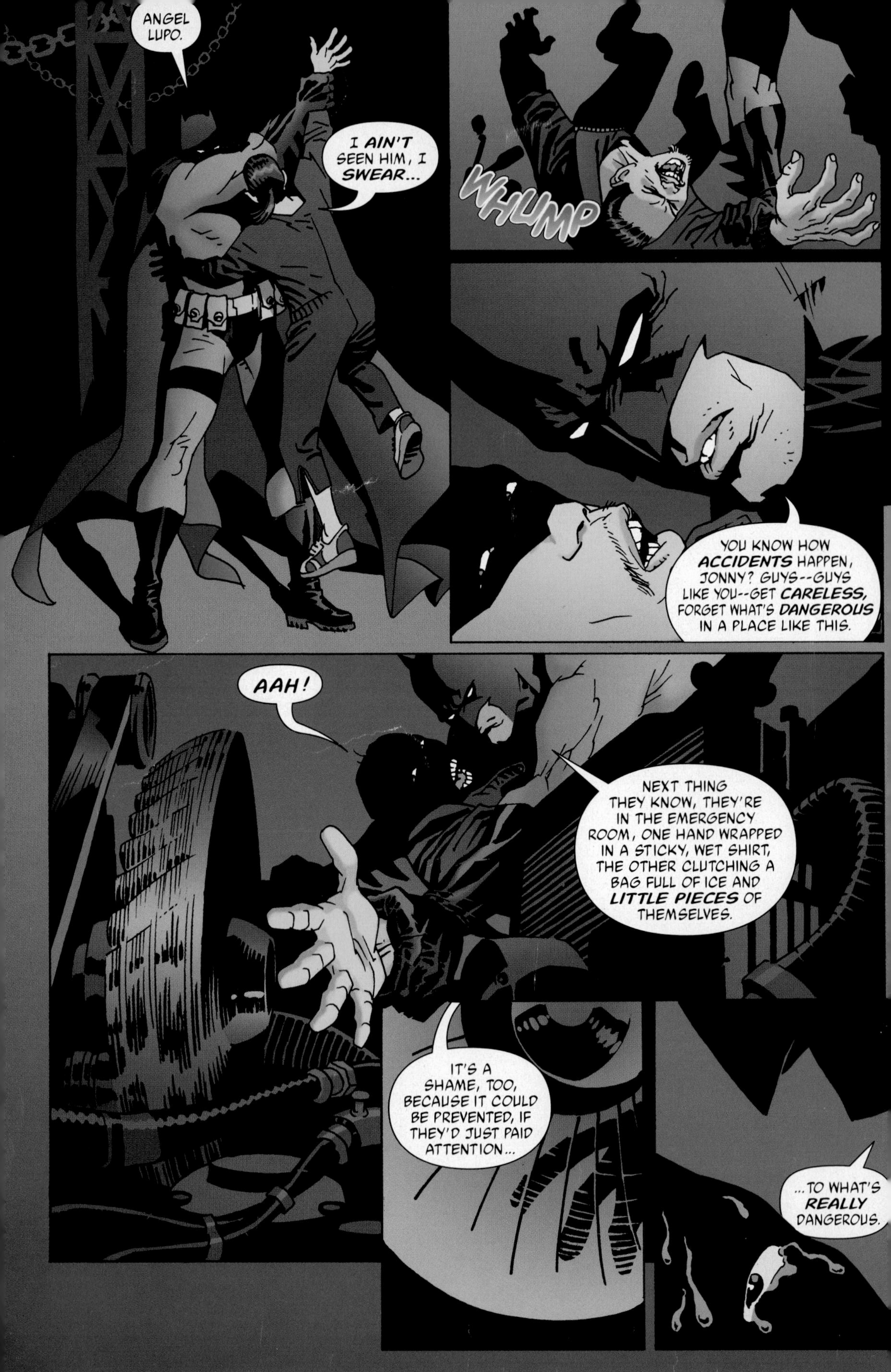
ANGEL LUPO.
I AIN'T SEEN HIM, I SWEAR...
WHUMP
YOU KNOW HOW ACCIDENTS HAPPEN, JONNY? GUYS--GUYS LIKE YOU--GET CARELESS, FORGET WHAT'S DANGEROUS IN A PLACE LIKE THIS.
AAH!
NEXT THING THEY KNOW, THEY'RE IN THE EMERGENCY ROOM, ONE HAND WRAPPED IN A STICKY, WET SHIRT, THE OTHER CLUTCHING A BAG FULL OF ICE AND LITTLE PIECES OF THEMSELVES.
IT'S A SHAME, TOO, BECAUSE IT COULD BE PREVENTED, IF THEY'D JUST PAID ATTENTION...
...TO WHAT'S REALLY DANGEROUS.

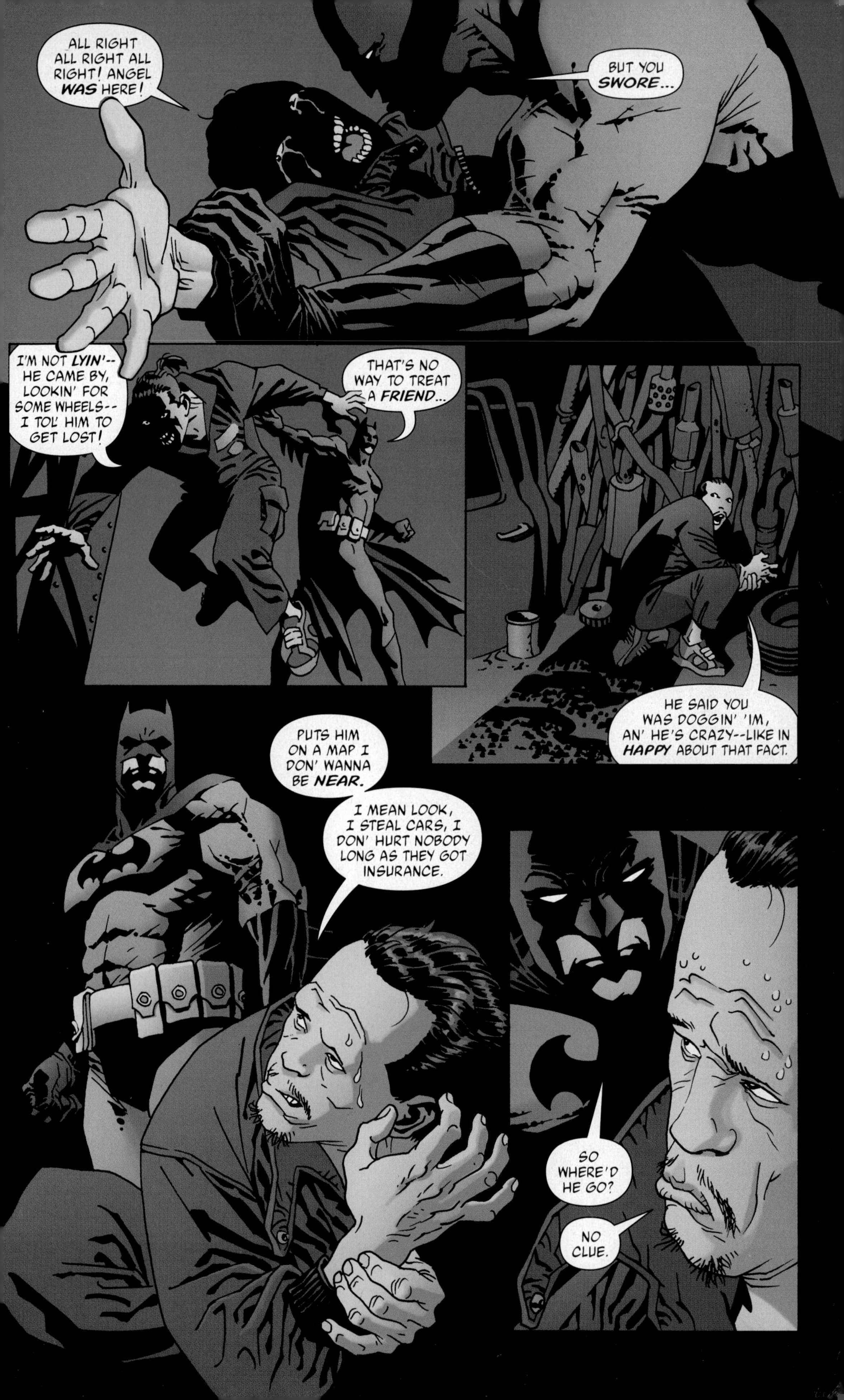
ALL RIGHT ALL RIGHT ALL RIGHT! ANGEL WAS HERE!
BUT YOU SWORE...
I'M NOT LYIN'-- HE CAME BY, LOOKIN' FOR SOME WHEELS-- I TOL' HIM TO GET LOST!
THAT'S NO WAY TO TREAT A FRIEND...
HE SAID YOU WAS DOGGIN' 'IM, AN' HE'S CRAZY--LIKE IN HAPPY ABOUT THAT FACT.
PUTS HIM ON A MAP I DON' WANNA BE NEAR.
I MEAN LOOK, I STEAL CARS, I DON' HURT NOBODY LONG AS THEY GOT INSURANCE.
SO WHERE'D HE GO?
NO CLUE.

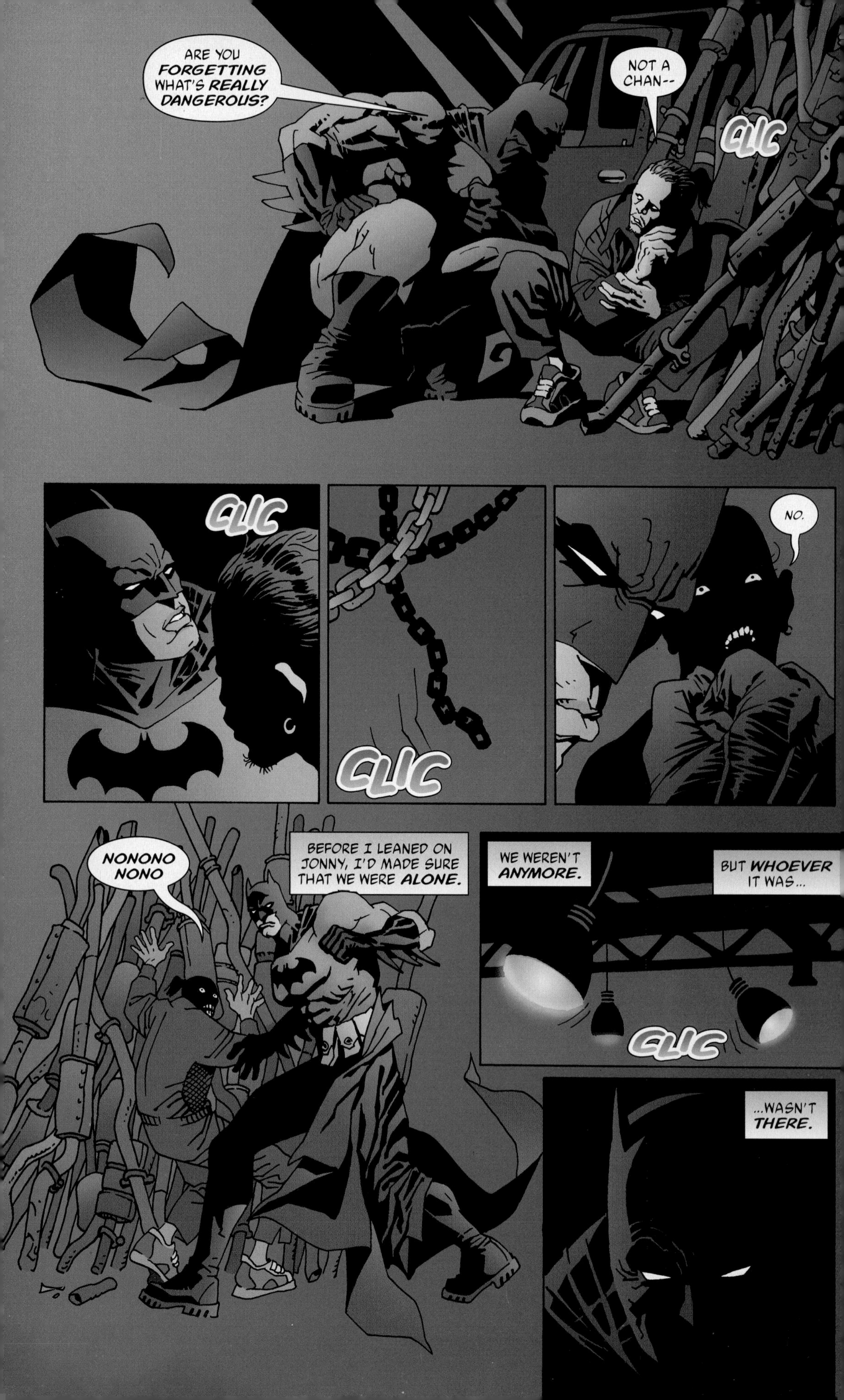

ARE YOU **FORGETTING** WHAT'S **REALLY DANGEROUS?**
NOT A CHAN--
CLIC
CLIC
CLIC
NO.
NONONO NONO
BEFORE I LEANED ON JONNY, I'D MADE SURE THAT WE WERE **ALONE**.
WE WEREN'T **ANYMORE**.
BUT **WHOEVER** IT WAS...
CLIC
...WASN'T **THERE**.

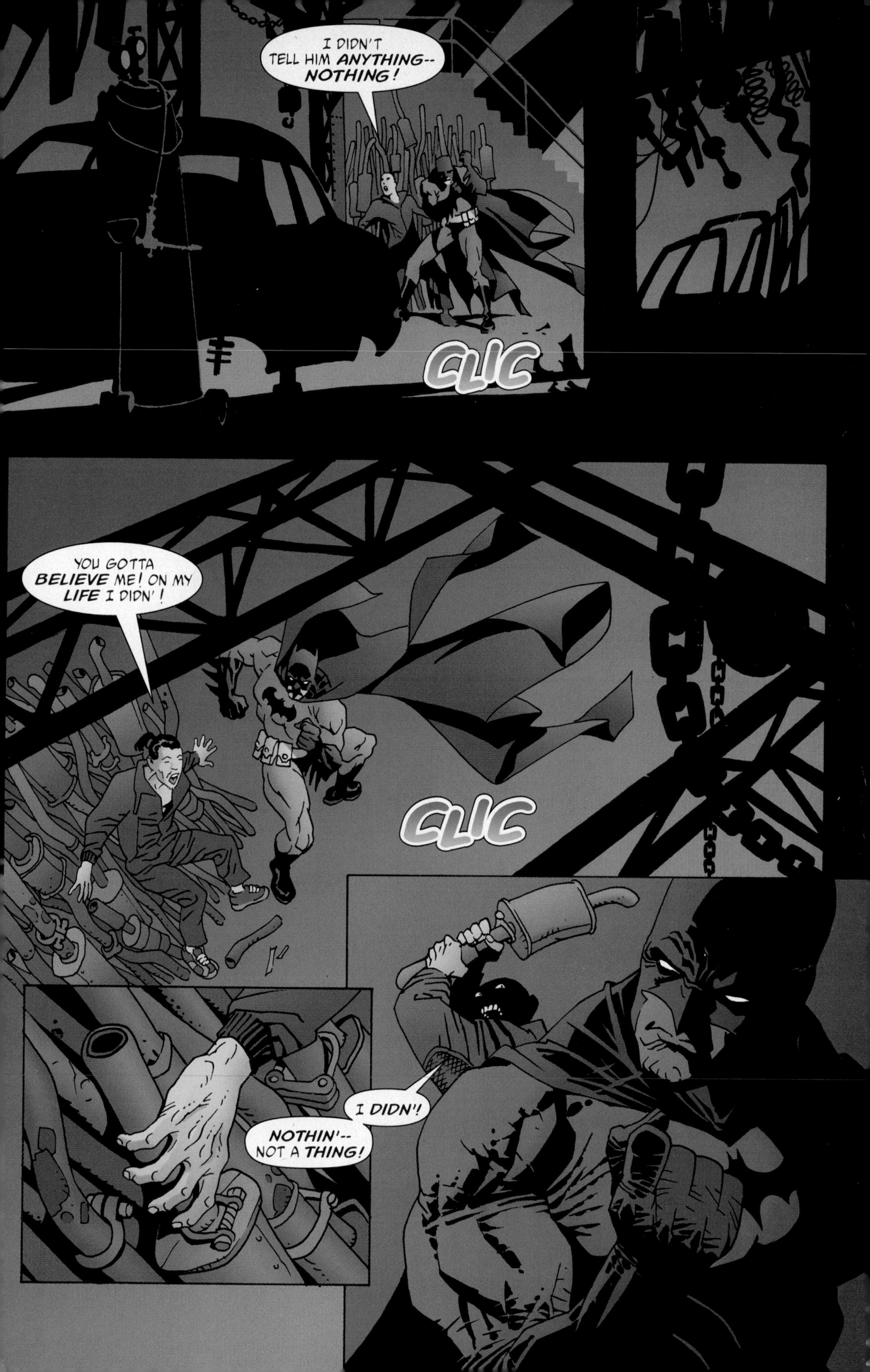
I DIDN'T TELL HIM ANYTHING-- NOTHING!
CLIC
YOU GOTTA BELIEVE ME! ON MY LIFE I DIDN'!
CLIC
I DIDN'!
NOTHIN'-- NOT A THING!

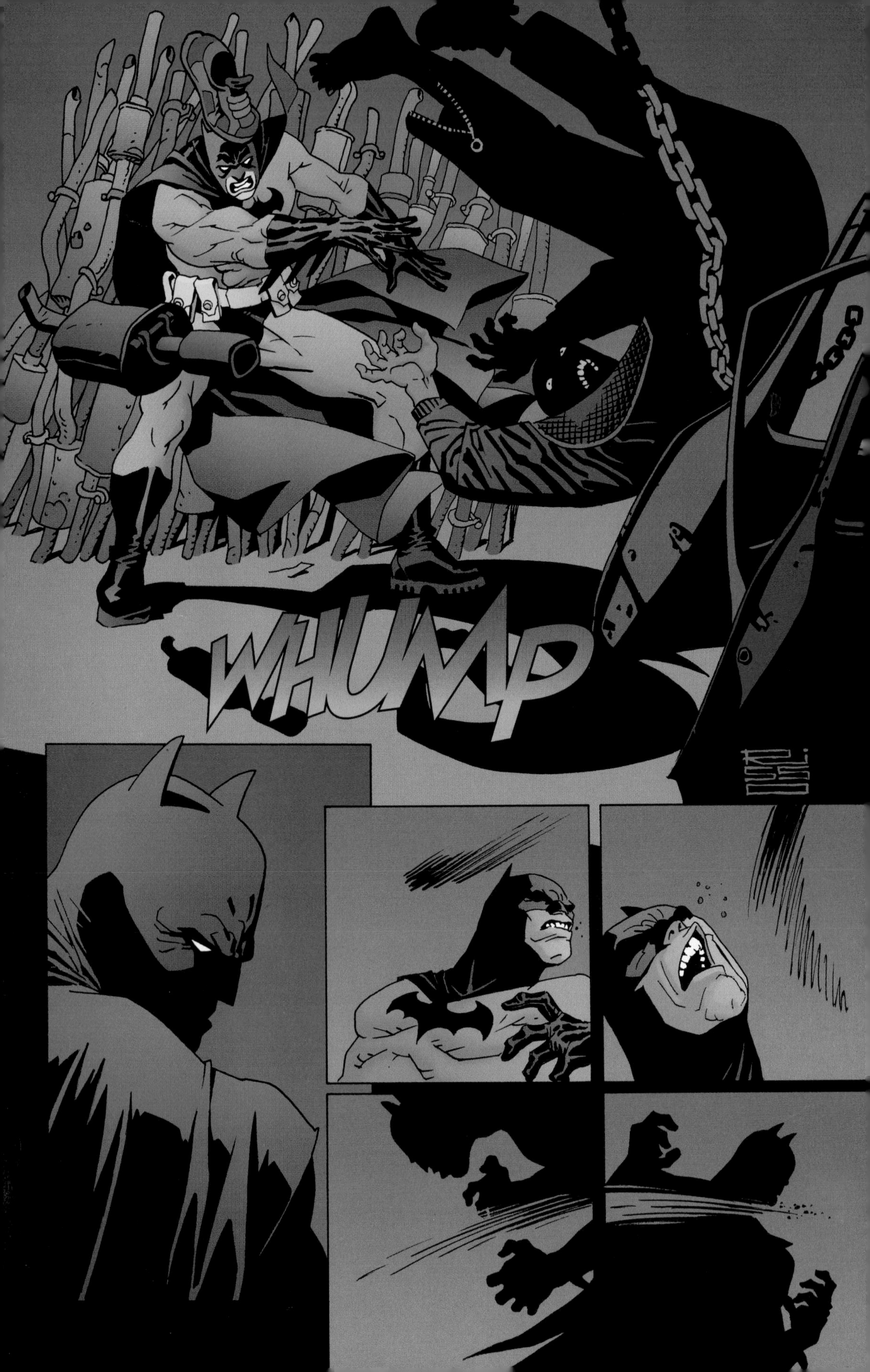
WHUMP

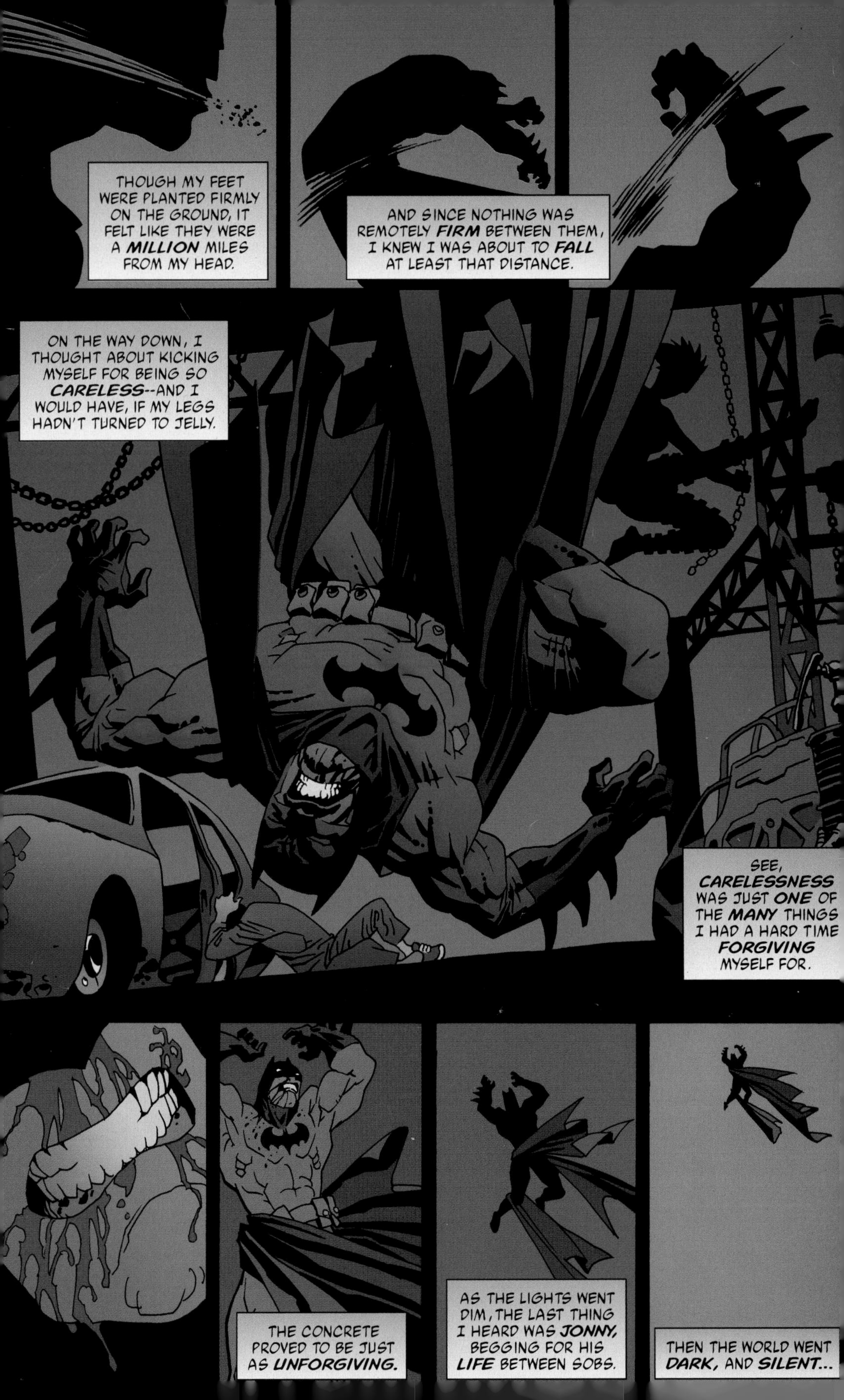
THOUGH MY FEET WERE PLANTED FIRMLY ON THE GROUND, IT FELT LIKE THEY WERE A **MILLION** MILES FROM MY HEAD.
AND SINCE NOTHING WAS REMOTELY **FIRM** BETWEEN THEM, I KNEW I WAS ABOUT TO **FALL** AT LEAST THAT DISTANCE.
ON THE WAY DOWN, I THOUGHT ABOUT KICKING MYSELF FOR BEING SO **CARELESS**--AND I WOULD HAVE, IF MY LEGS HADN'T TURNED TO JELLY.
SEE, **CARELESSNESS** WAS JUST **ONE** OF THE **MANY** THINGS I HAD A HARD TIME **FORGIVING** MYSELF FOR.
THE CONCRETE PROVED TO BE JUST AS **UNFORGIVING.**
AS THE LIGHTS WENT DIM, THE LAST THING I HEARD WAS **JONNY,** BEGGING FOR HIS **LIFE** BETWEEN SOBS.
THEN THE WORLD WENT **DARK,** AND **SILENT...**

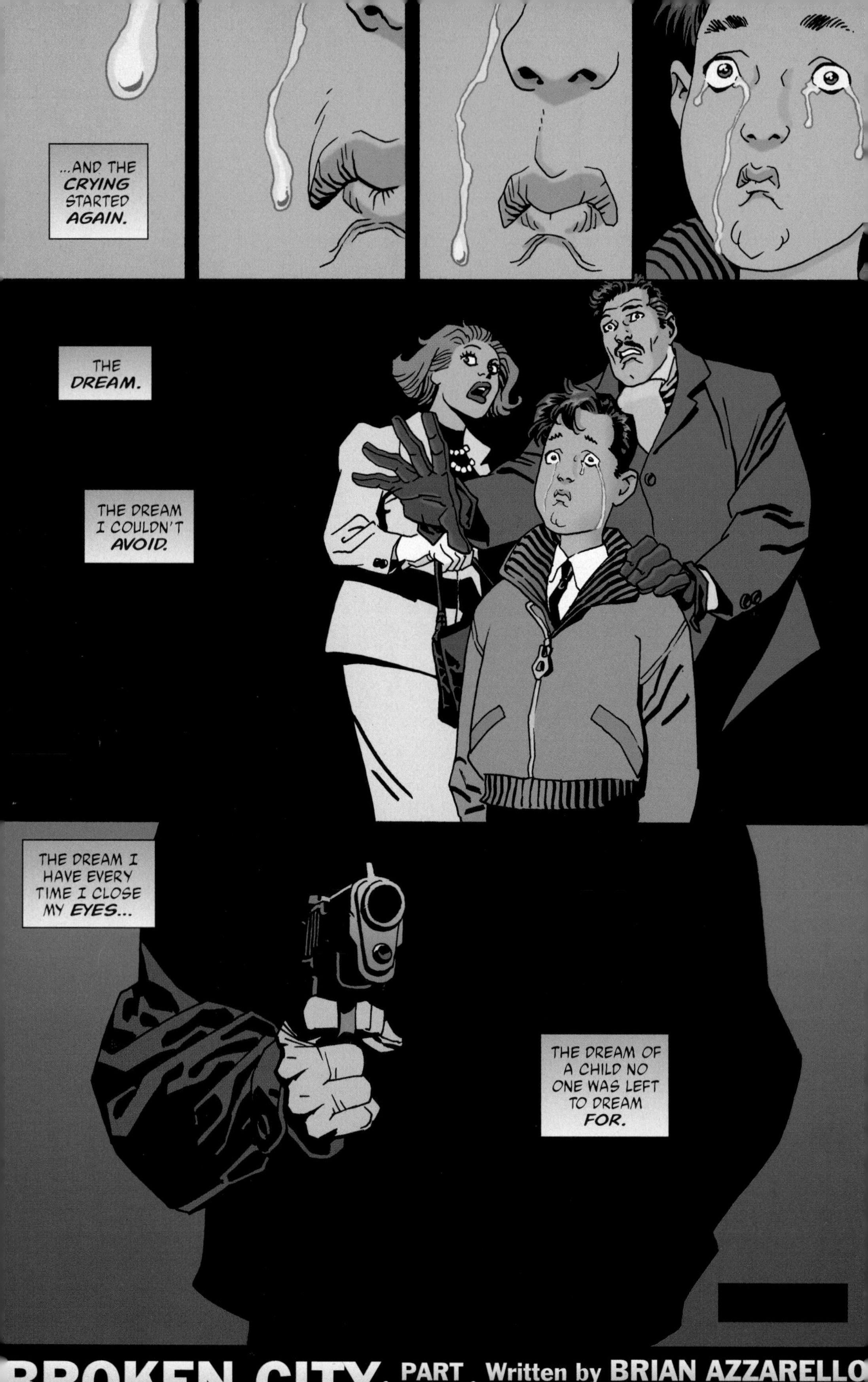
...AND THE CRYING STARTED AGAIN.
THE DREAM.
THE DREAM I COULDN'T AVOID.
THE DREAM I HAVE EVERY TIME I CLOSE MY EYES...
THE DREAM OF A CHILD NO ONE WAS LEFT TO DREAM FOR.

BROKEN CITY · PART TWO · Written by BRIAN AZZARELLO Illustrated by EDUARDO RISSO

Colored by Patricia Mulvihill · Lettered by Clem Robins · Cover by Dave Johnson
Ass't Ed Zachary Rau · Edited by Will Dennis and Bob Schreck · Batman created by Bob Kane

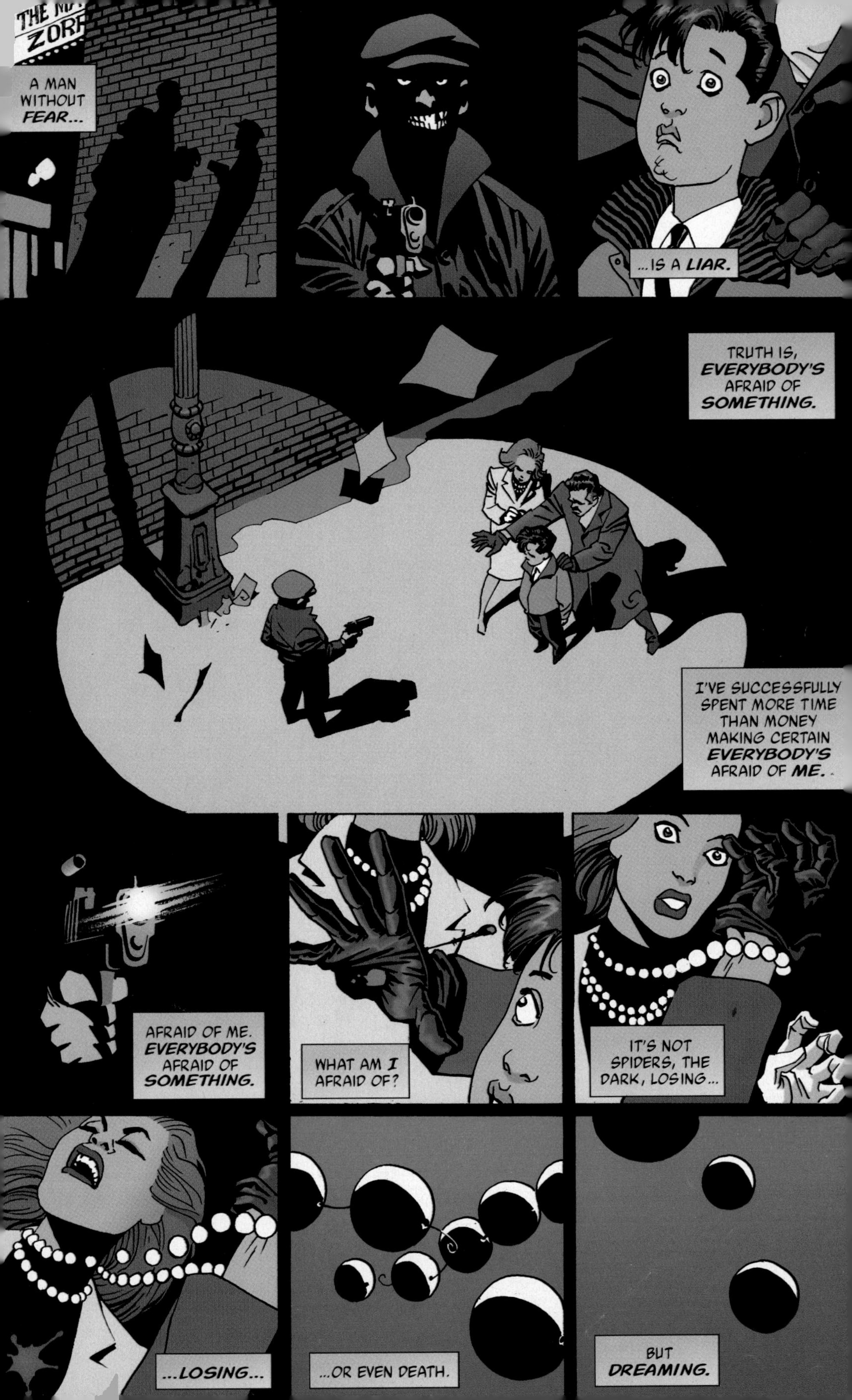
A MAN WITHOUT FEAR...
...IS A LIAR.
TRUTH IS, EVERYBODY'S AFRAID OF SOMETHING.
I'VE SUCCESSFULLY SPENT MORE TIME THAN MONEY MAKING CERTAIN EVERYBODY'S AFRAID OF ME.
AFRAID OF ME. EVERYBODY'S AFRAID OF SOMETHING.
WHAT AM I AFRAID OF?
IT'S NOT SPIDERS, THE DARK, LOSING...
...LOSING...
...OR EVEN DEATH.
BUT DREAMING.

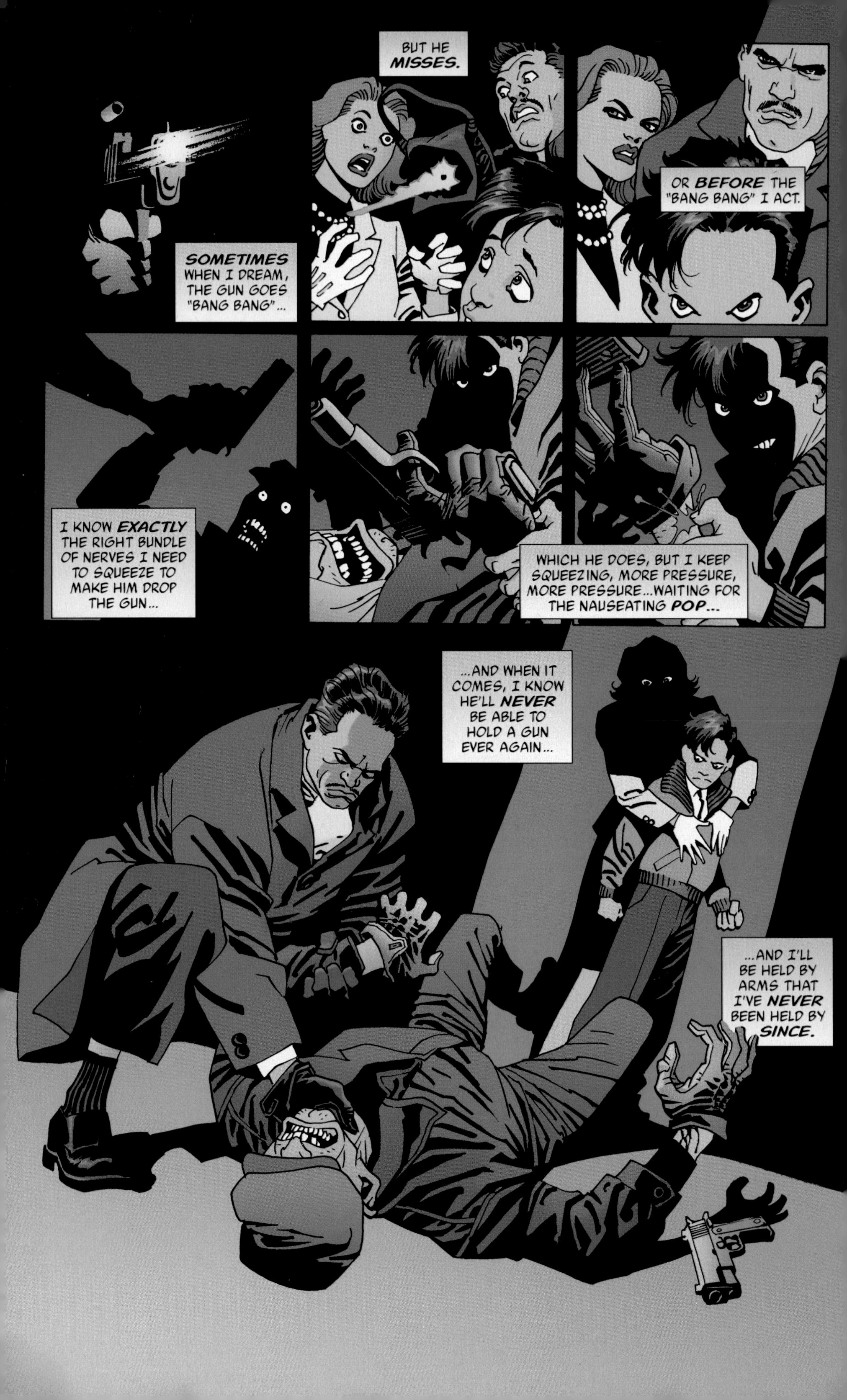
SOMETIMES WHEN I DREAM, THE GUN GOES "BANG BANG"...
BUT HE MISSES.
OR BEFORE THE "BANG BANG" I ACT.
I KNOW EXACTLY THE RIGHT BUNDLE OF NERVES I NEED TO SQUEEZE TO MAKE HIM DROP THE GUN...
WHICH HE DOES, BUT I KEEP SQUEEZING, MORE PRESSURE, MORE PRESSURE...WAITING FOR THE NAUSEATING POP...
...AND WHEN IT COMES, I KNOW HE'LL NEVER BE ABLE TO HOLD A GUN EVER AGAIN...
...AND I'LL BE HELD BY ARMS THAT I'VE NEVER BEEN HELD BY SINCE.

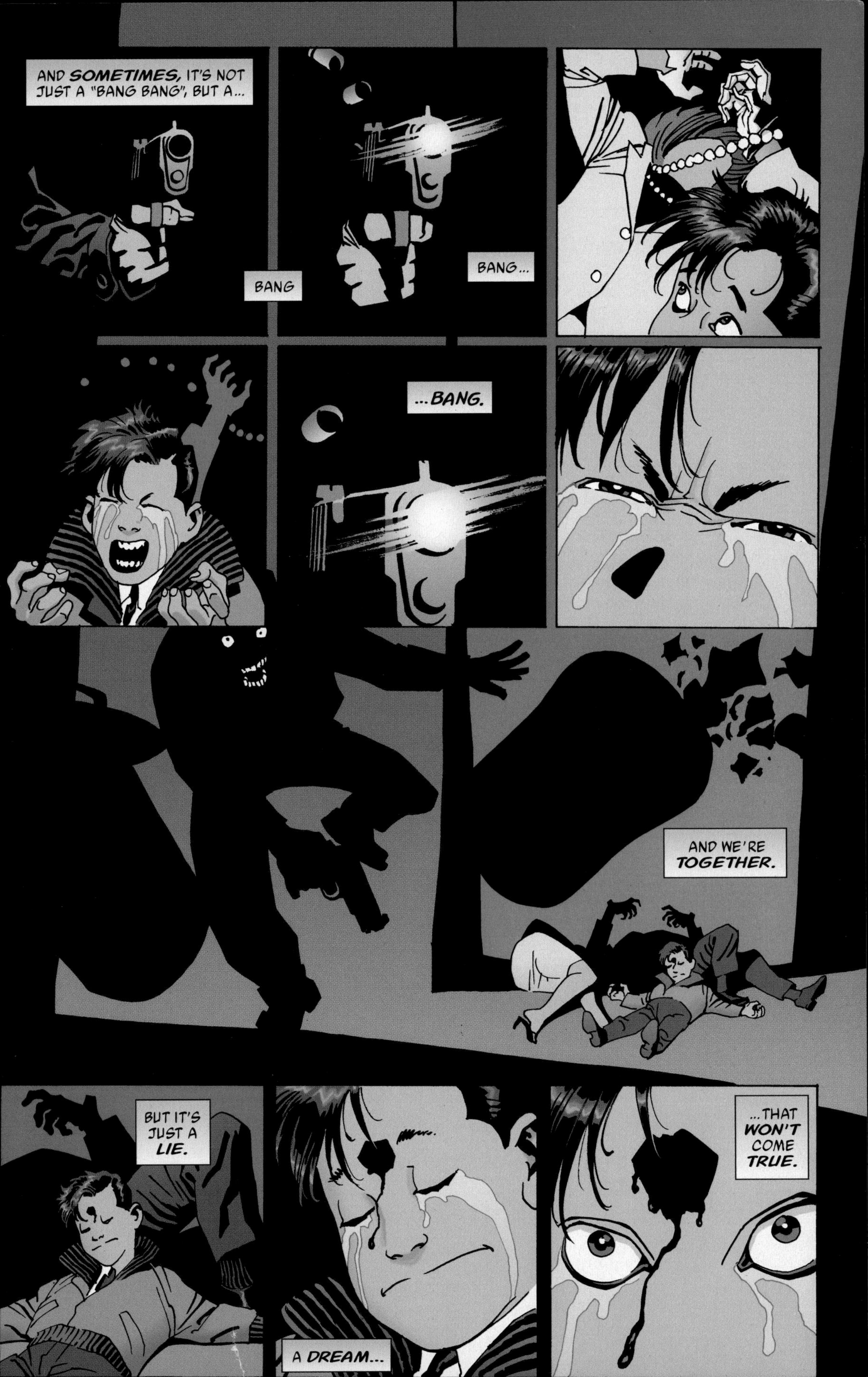
AND **SOMETIMES,** IT'S NOT JUST A "BANG BANG", BUT A...
BANG
BANG...
...**BANG.**
AND WE'RE **TOGETHER.**
BUT IT'S JUST A **LIE.**
A **DREAM...**
...THAT **WON'T** COME **TRUE.**

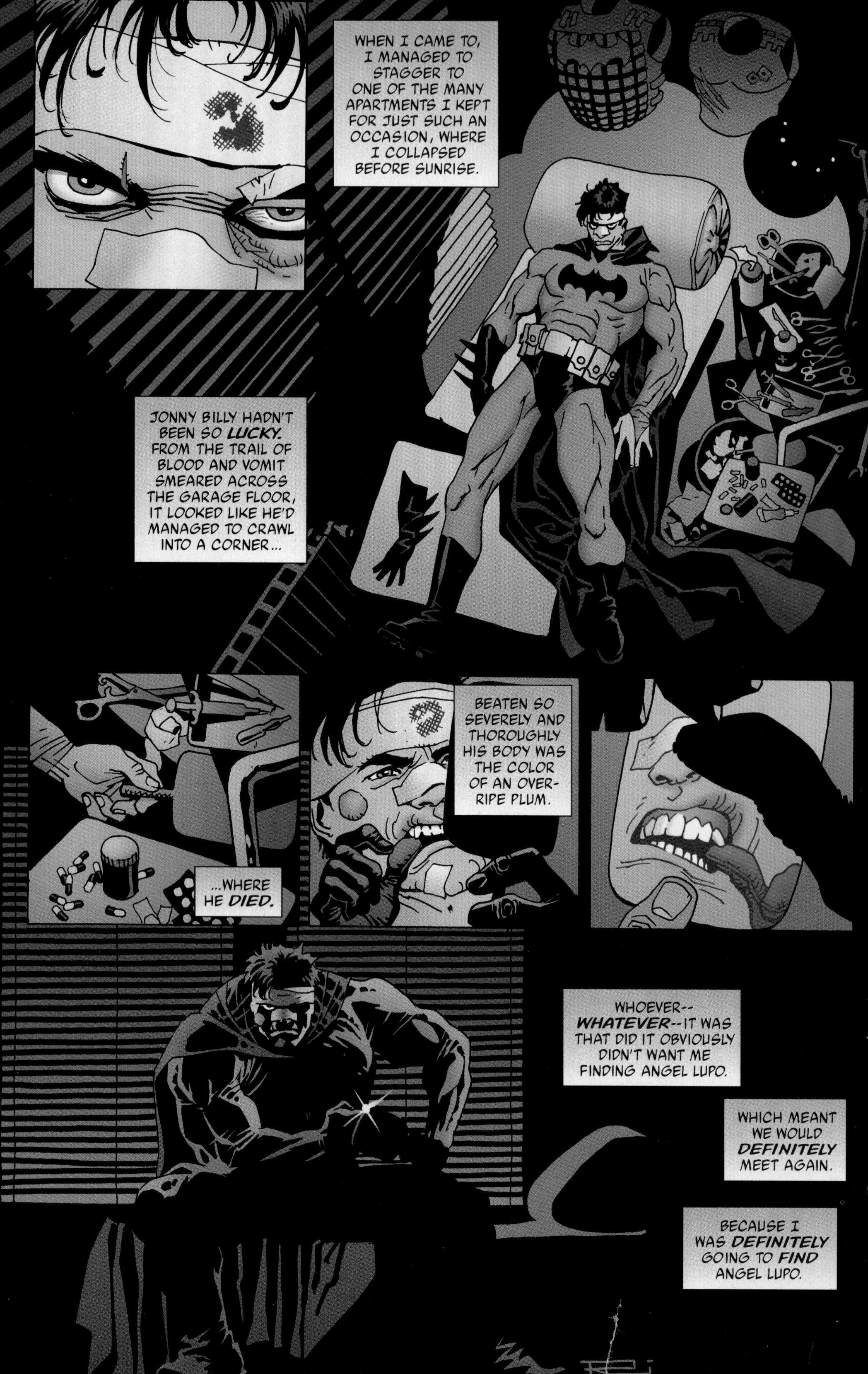
WHEN I CAME TO, I MANAGED TO STAGGER TO ONE OF THE MANY APARTMENTS I KEPT FOR JUST SUCH AN OCCASION, WHERE I COLLAPSED BEFORE SUNRISE.
JONNY BILLY HADN'T BEEN SO **LUCKY.** FROM THE TRAIL OF BLOOD AND VOMIT SMEARED ACROSS THE GARAGE FLOOR, IT LOOKED LIKE HE'D MANAGED TO CRAWL INTO A CORNER...
...WHERE HE **DIED.**
BEATEN SO SEVERELY AND THOROUGHLY HIS BODY WAS THE COLOR OF AN OVER-RIPE PLUM.
WHOEVER-- **WHATEVER**--IT WAS THAT DID IT OBVIOUSLY DIDN'T WANT ME FINDING ANGEL LUPO.
WHICH MEANT WE WOULD **DEFINITELY** MEET AGAIN.
BECAUSE I WAS **DEFINITELY** GOING TO **FIND** ANGEL LUPO.

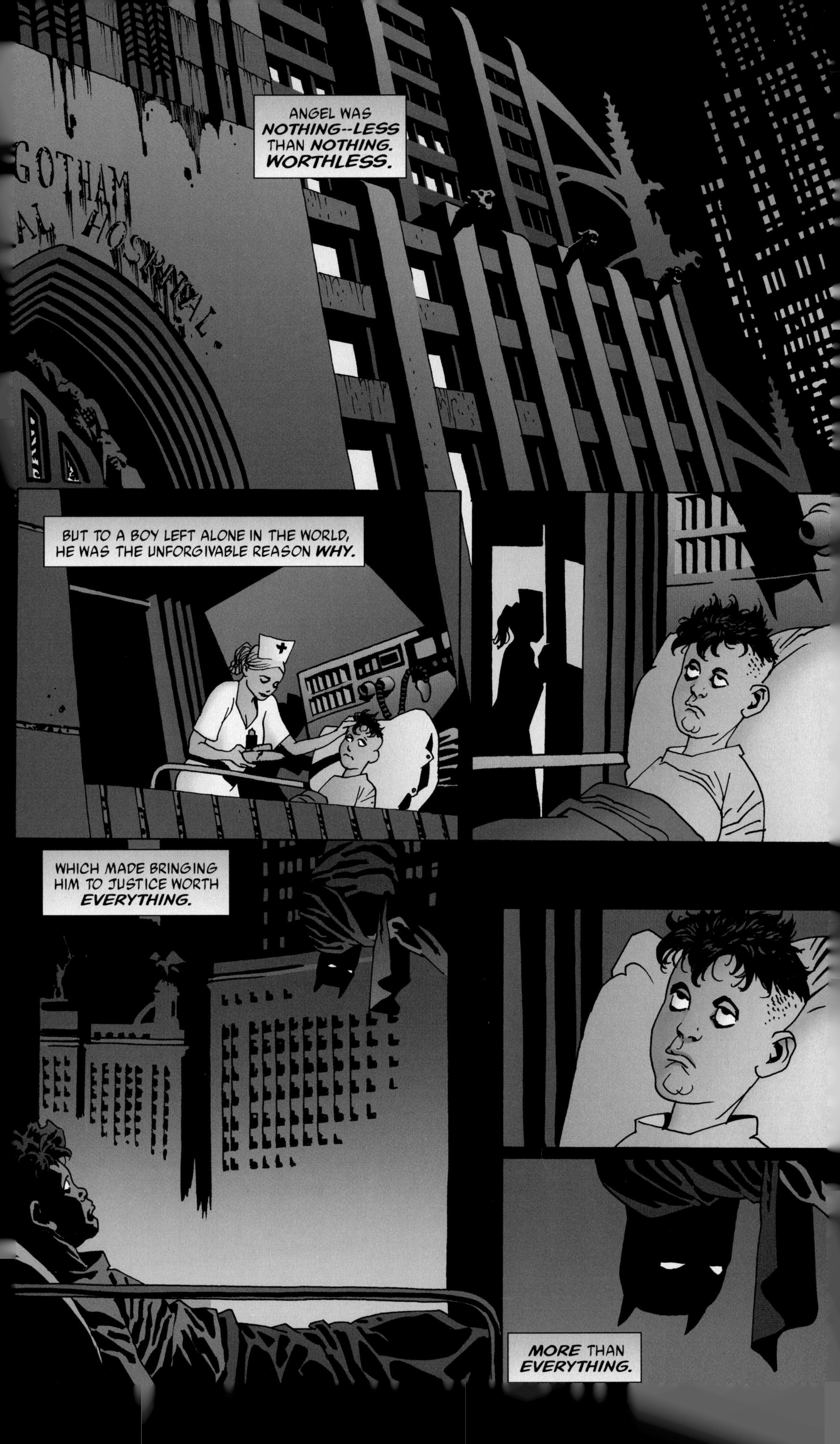
GOTHAM
AL HOSPITAL
ANGEL WAS NOTHING--LESS THAN NOTHING. WORTHLESS.
BUT TO A BOY LEFT ALONE IN THE WORLD, HE WAS THE UNFORGIVABLE REASON WHY.
WHICH MADE BRINGING HIM TO JUSTICE WORTH EVERYTHING.
MORE THAN EVERYTHING.

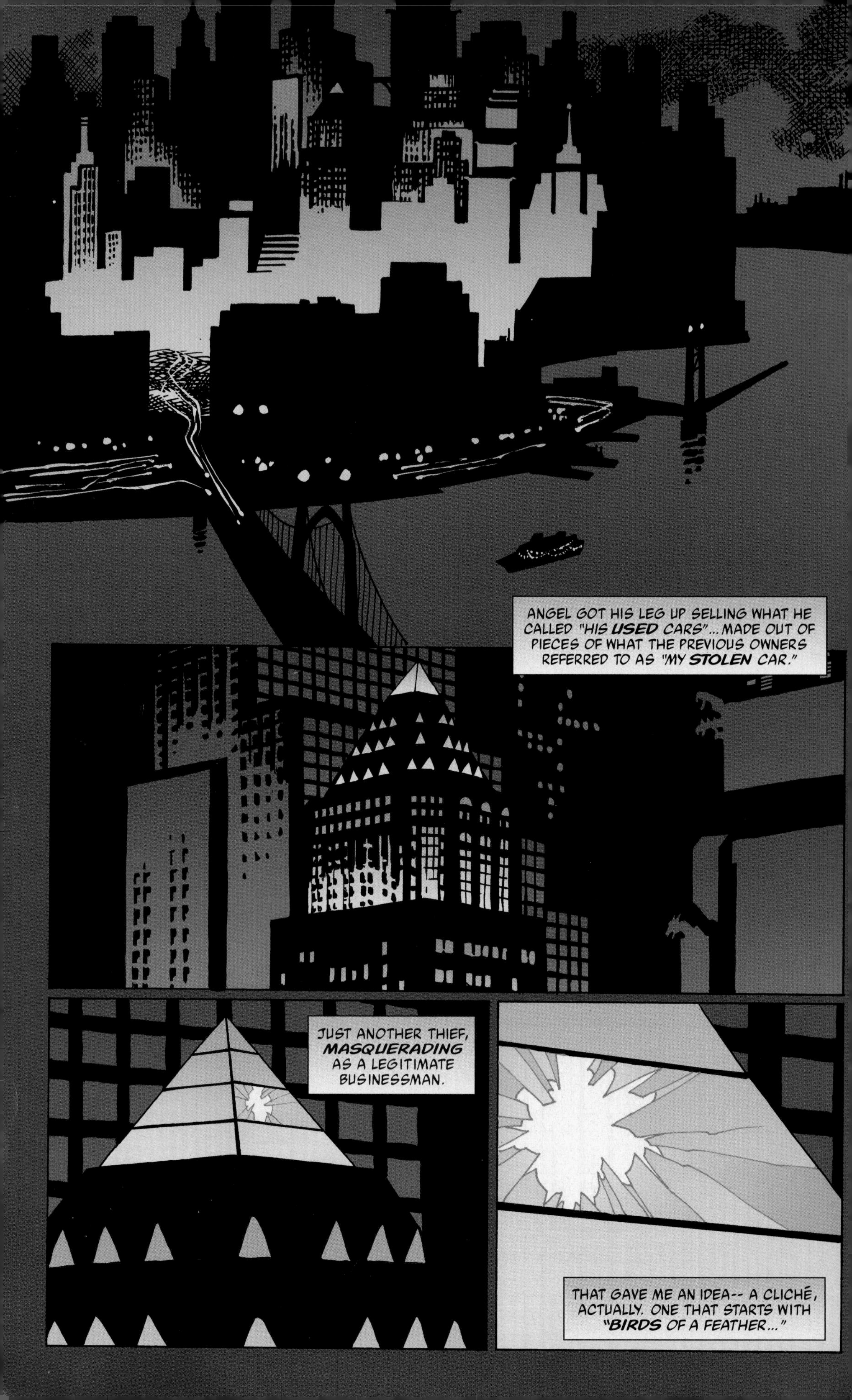
ANGEL GOT HIS LEG UP SELLING WHAT HE CALLED "HIS *USED* CARS"... MADE OUT OF PIECES OF WHAT THE PREVIOUS OWNERS REFERRED TO AS "MY *STOLEN* CAR."
JUST ANOTHER THIEF, *MASQUERADING* AS A LEGITIMATE BUSINESSMAN.
THAT GAVE ME AN IDEA-- A CLICHÉ, ACTUALLY. ONE THAT STARTS WITH "*BIRDS* OF A FEATHER..."

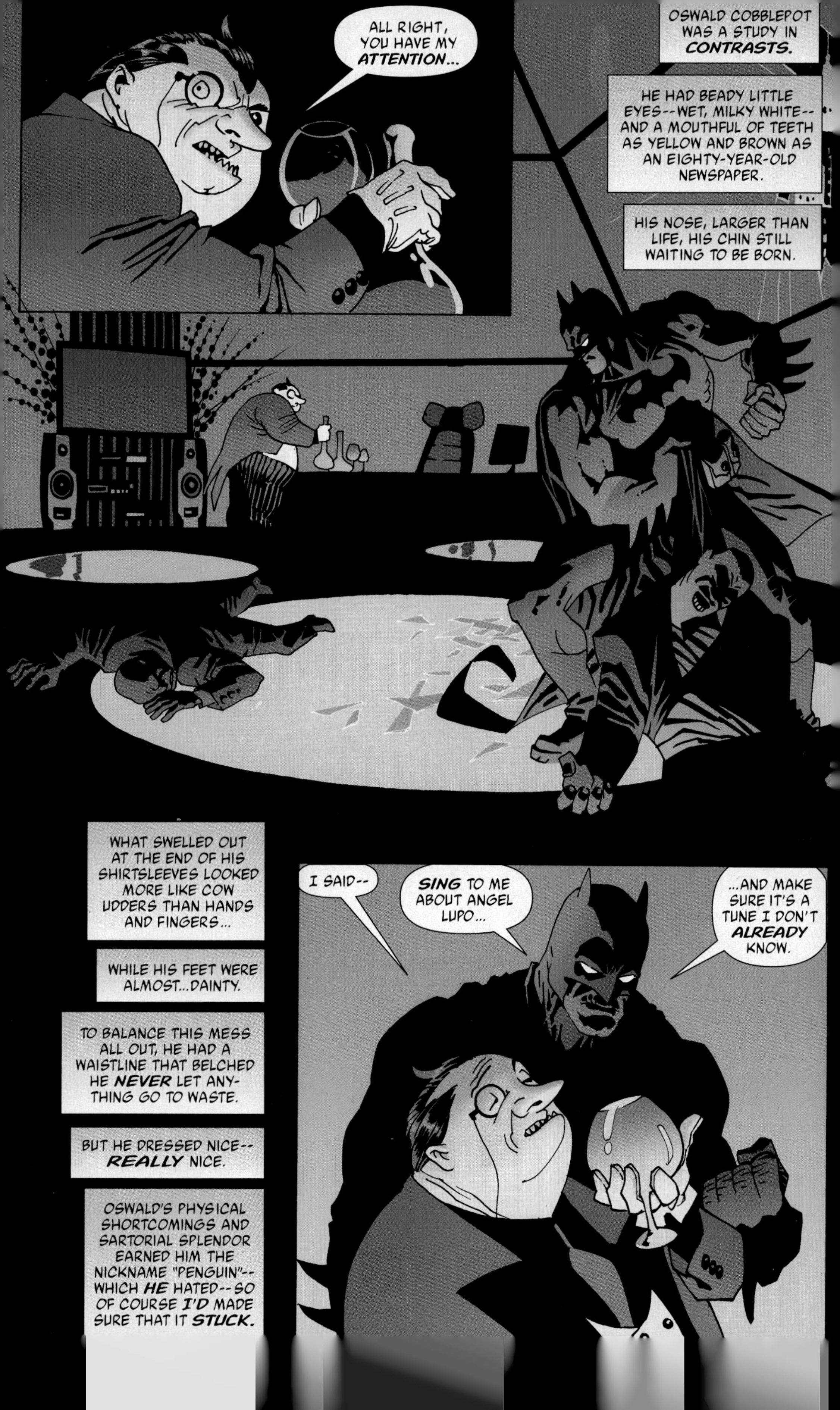
OSWALD COBBLEPOT WAS A STUDY IN **CONTRASTS.**
ALL RIGHT, YOU HAVE MY **ATTENTION...**
HE HAD BEADY LITTLE EYES--WET, MILKY WHITE--AND A MOUTHFUL OF TEETH AS YELLOW AND BROWN AS AN EIGHTY-YEAR-OLD NEWSPAPER.
HIS NOSE, LARGER THAN LIFE, HIS CHIN STILL WAITING TO BE BORN.
WHAT SWELLED OUT AT THE END OF HIS SHIRTSLEEVES LOOKED MORE LIKE COW UDDERS THAN HANDS AND FINGERS...
WHILE HIS FEET WERE ALMOST...DAINTY.
TO BALANCE THIS MESS ALL OUT, HE HAD A WAISTLINE THAT BELCHED HE **NEVER** LET ANY-THING GO TO WASTE.
BUT HE DRESSED NICE--**REALLY** NICE.
OSWALD'S PHYSICAL SHORTCOMINGS AND SARTORIAL SPLENDOR EARNED HIM THE NICKNAME "PENGUIN"--WHICH **HE** HATED--SO OF COURSE **I'D** MADE SURE THAT IT **STUCK.**
I SAID--
SING TO ME ABOUT ANGEL LUPO...
...AND MAKE SURE IT'S A TUNE I DON'T **ALREADY** KNOW.

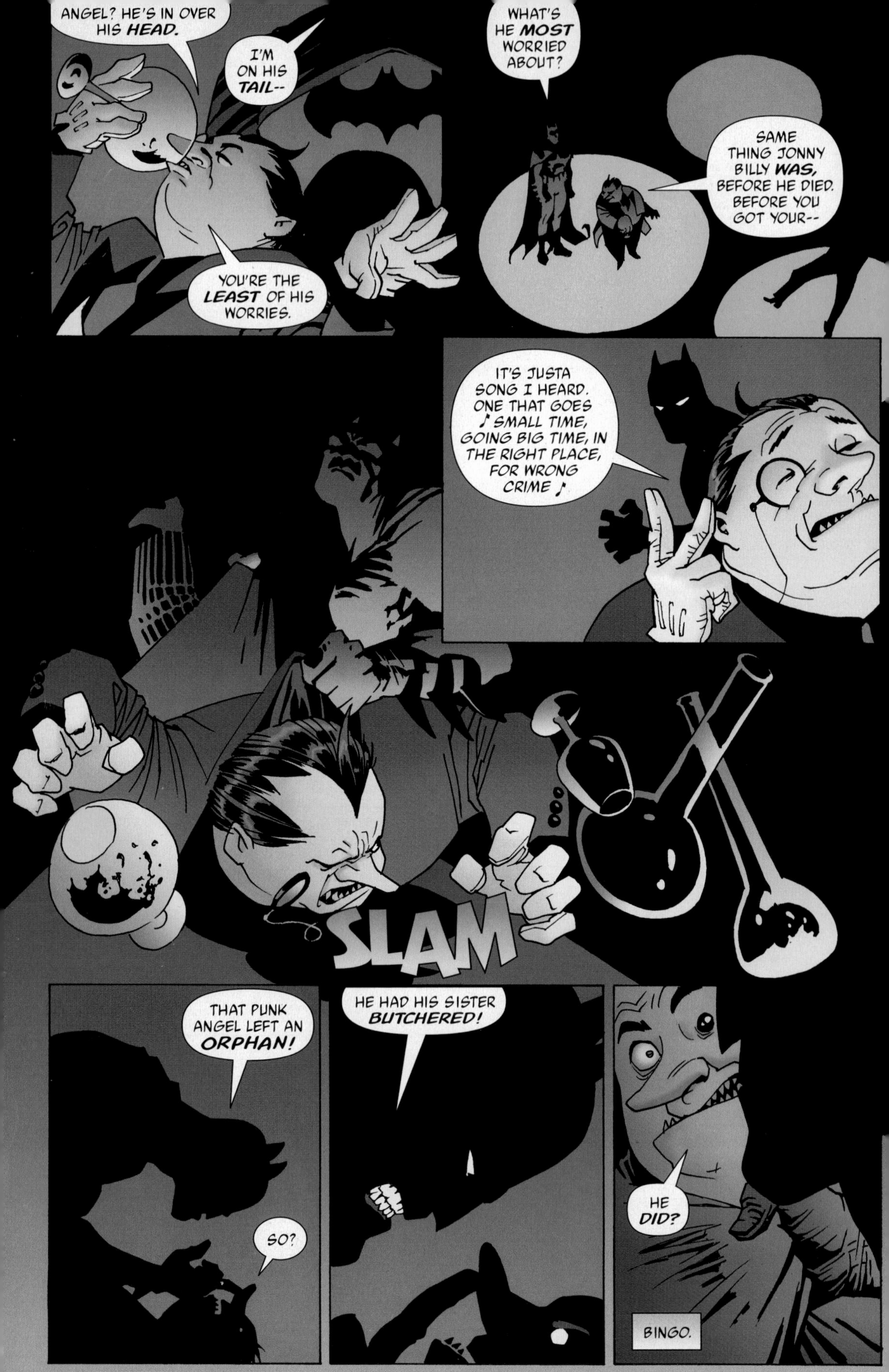
ANGEL? HE'S IN OVER HIS **HEAD.**
I'M ON HIS **TAIL**--
YOU'RE THE **LEAST** OF HIS WORRIES.
WHAT'S HE **MOST** WORRIED ABOUT?
SAME THING JONNY BILLY **WAS,** BEFORE HE DIED. BEFORE YOU GOT YOUR--
IT'S JUSTA SONG I HEARD. ONE THAT GOES ♪ SMALL TIME, GOING BIG TIME, IN THE RIGHT PLACE, FOR WRONG CRIME ♪
SLAM
THAT PUNK ANGEL LEFT AN **ORPHAN!**
SO?
HE HAD HIS SISTER **BUTCHERED!**
HE **DID?**
BINGO.

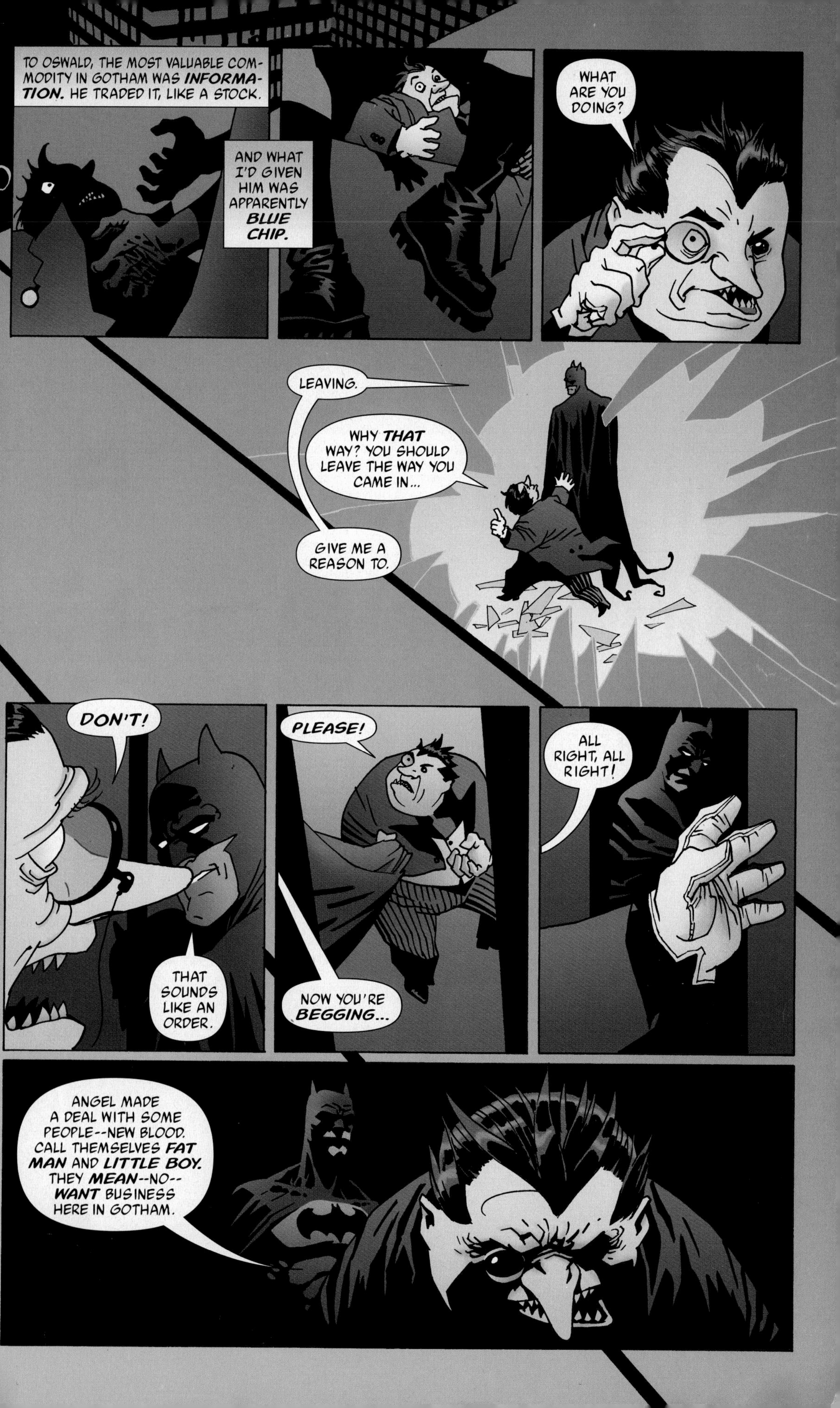
TO OSWALD, THE MOST VALUABLE COMMODITY IN GOTHAM WAS ***INFORMATION.*** HE TRADED IT, LIKE A STOCK.
AND WHAT I'D GIVEN HIM WAS APPARENTLY ***BLUE CHIP.***
WHAT ARE YOU DOING?
LEAVING.
WHY ***THAT*** WAY? YOU SHOULD LEAVE THE WAY YOU CAME IN...
GIVE ME A REASON TO.
DON'T!
THAT SOUNDS LIKE AN ORDER.
PLEASE!
NOW YOU'RE ***BEGGING...***
ALL RIGHT, ALL RIGHT!
ANGEL MADE A DEAL WITH SOME PEOPLE--NEW BLOOD. CALL THEMSELVES ***FAT MAN*** AND ***LITTLE BOY.*** THEY ***MEAN***--NO--***WANT*** BUSINESS HERE IN GOTHAM.

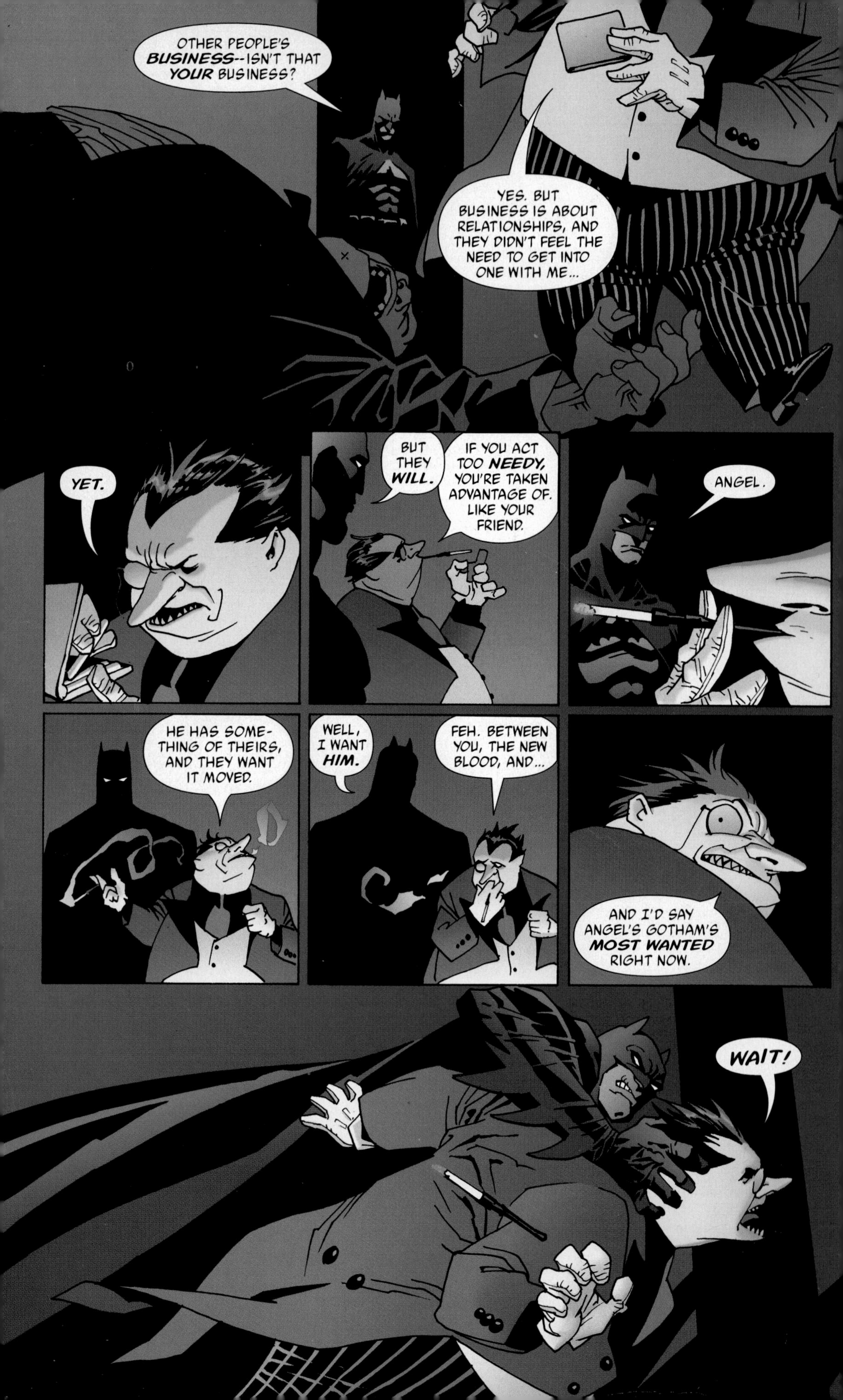
OTHER PEOPLE'S **BUSINESS**--ISN'T THAT **YOUR** BUSINESS?
YES. BUT BUSINESS IS ABOUT RELATIONSHIPS, AND THEY DIDN'T FEEL THE NEED TO GET INTO ONE WITH ME...
YET.
BUT THEY **WILL.**
IF YOU ACT TOO **NEEDY,** YOU'RE TAKEN ADVANTAGE OF. LIKE YOUR FRIEND.
ANGEL.
HE HAS SOME-THING OF THEIRS, AND THEY WANT IT MOVED.
WELL, I WANT **HIM.**
FEH. BETWEEN YOU, THE NEW BLOOD, AND...
AND I'D SAY ANGEL'S GOTHAM'S **MOST WANTED** RIGHT NOW.
WAIT!

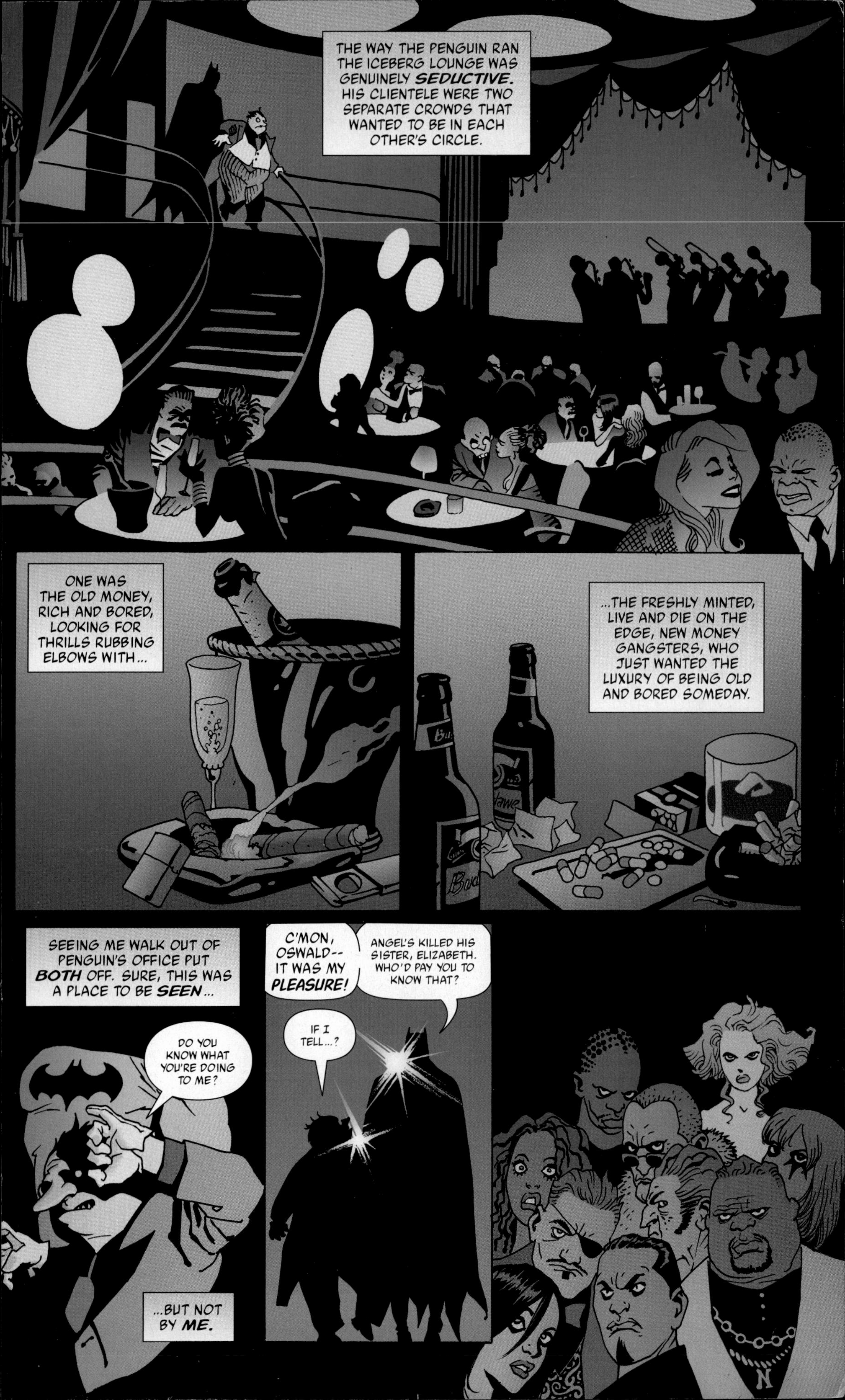
THE WAY THE PENGUIN RAN THE ICEBERG LOUNGE WAS GENUINELY **SEDUCTIVE.** HIS CLIENTELE WERE TWO SEPARATE CROWDS THAT WANTED TO BE IN EACH OTHER'S CIRCLE.
ONE WAS THE OLD MONEY, RICH AND BORED, LOOKING FOR THRILLS RUBBING ELBOWS WITH...
...THE FRESHLY MINTED, LIVE AND DIE ON THE EDGE, NEW MONEY GANGSTERS, WHO JUST WANTED THE LUXURY OF BEING OLD AND BORED SOMEDAY.
SEEING ME WALK OUT OF PENGUIN'S OFFICE PUT **BOTH** OFF. SURE, THIS WAS A PLACE TO BE **SEEN**...
DO YOU KNOW WHAT YOU'RE DOING TO ME?
...BUT NOT BY **ME.**
C'MON, OSWALD-- IT WAS MY **PLEASURE!**
ANGEL'S KILLED HIS SISTER, ELIZABETH. WHO'D PAY YOU TO KNOW THAT?
IF I TELL...?

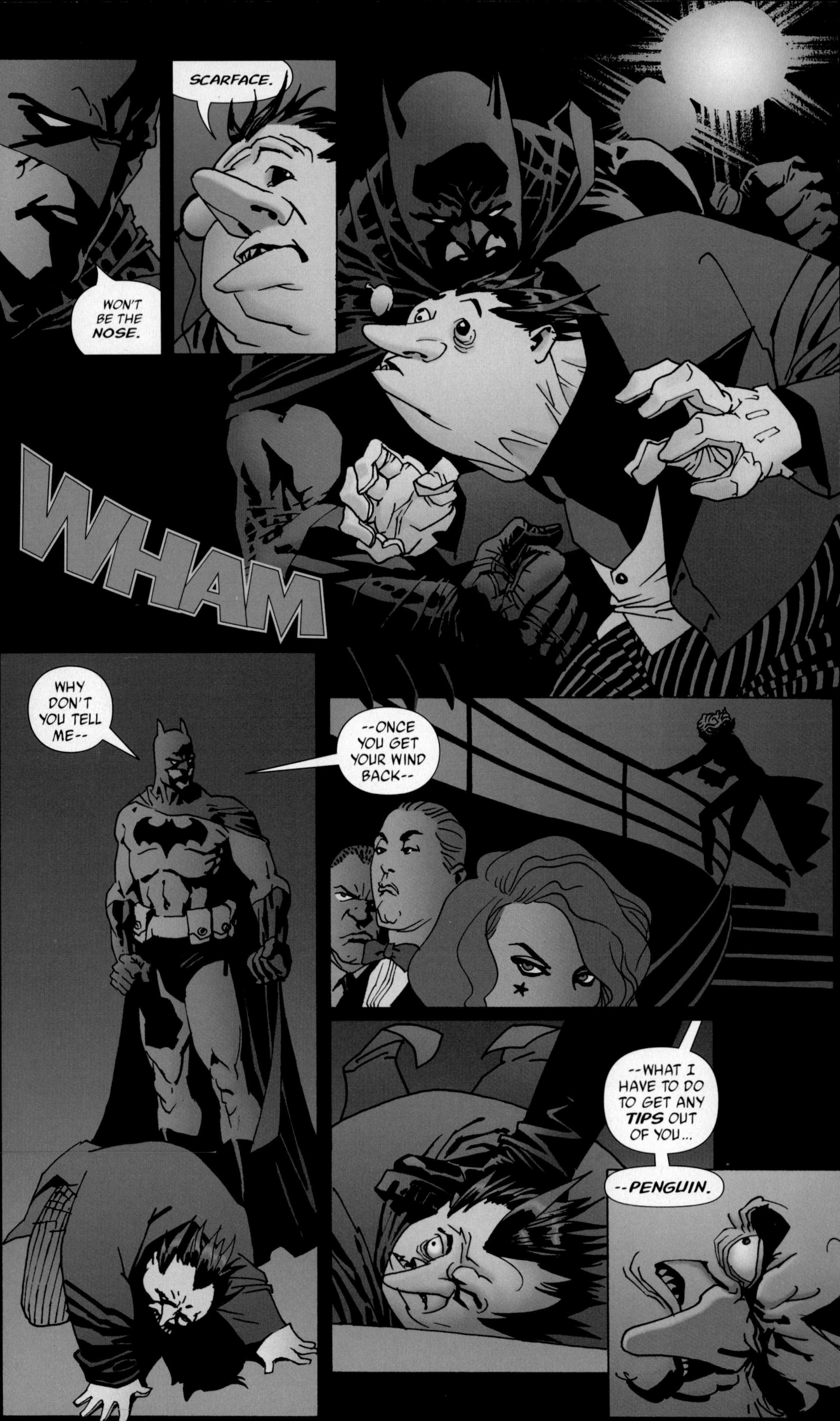
SCARFACE.
WON'T BE THE NOSE.
WHAM
WHY DON'T YOU TELL ME--
--ONCE YOU GET YOUR WIND BACK--
--WHAT I HAVE TO DO TO GET ANY TIPS OUT OF YOU...
--PENGUIN.

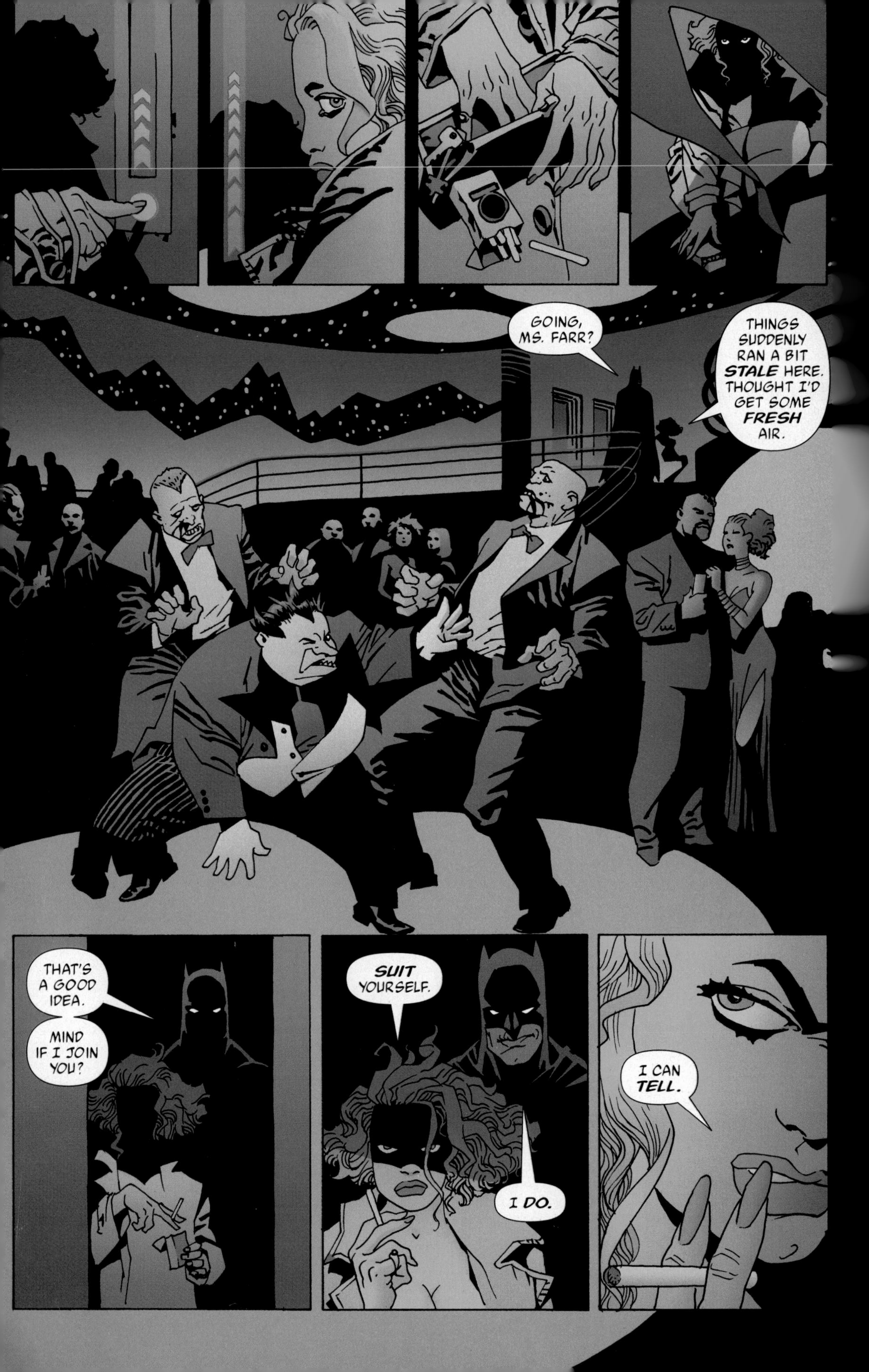
GOING, MS. FARR?
THINGS SUDDENLY RAN A BIT STALE HERE. THOUGHT I'D GET SOME FRESH AIR.
THAT'S A GOOD IDEA.
MIND IF I JOIN YOU?
SUIT YOURSELF.
I DO.
I CAN TELL.

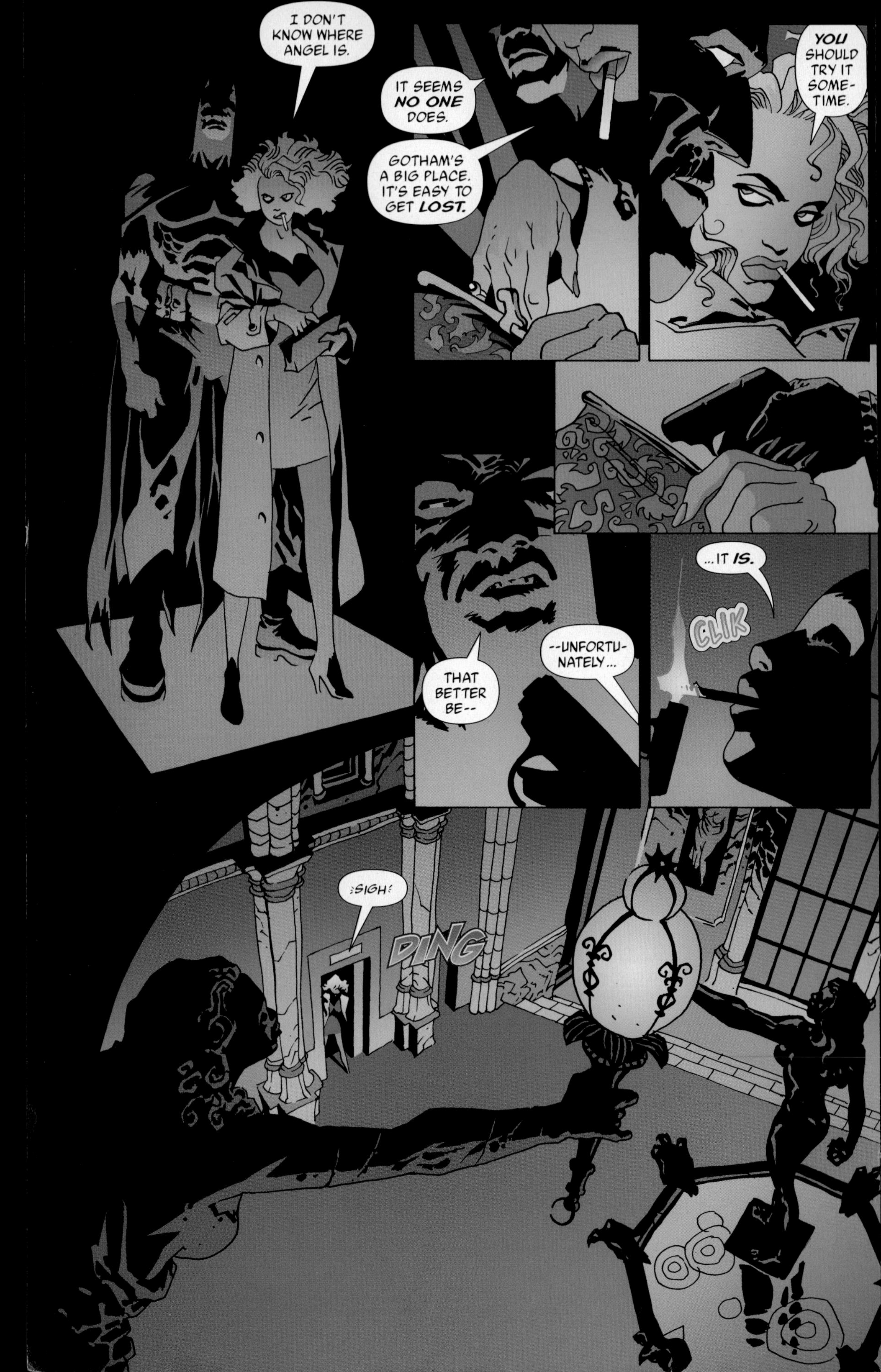
I DON'T KNOW WHERE ANGEL IS.
IT SEEMS **NO ONE** DOES.
GOTHAM'S A BIG PLACE. IT'S EASY TO GET **LOST.**
YOU SHOULD TRY IT SOME-TIME.
THAT BETTER BE--
--UNFORTU-NATELY...
CLIK
...IT **IS.**
DING
:SIGH:

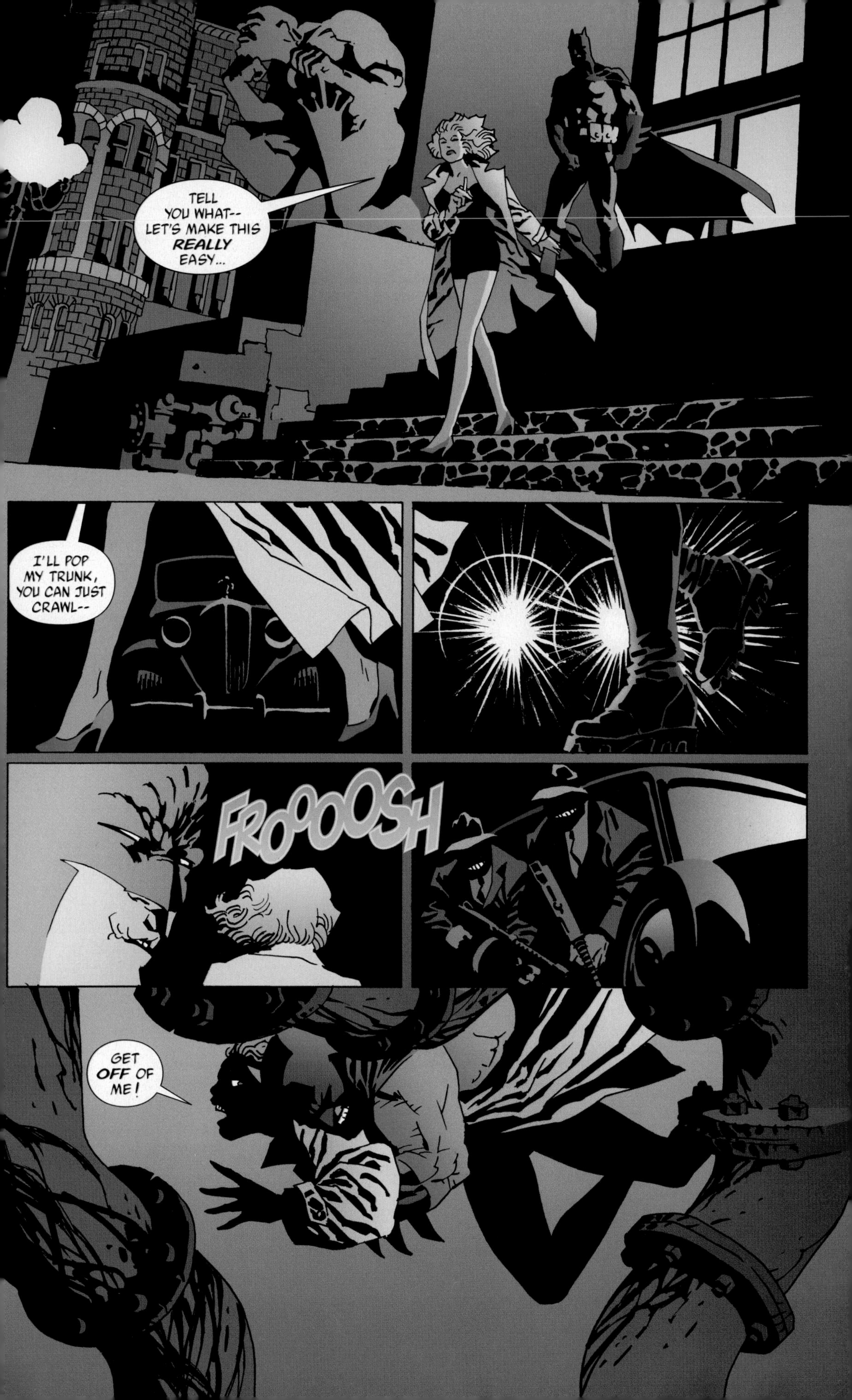
TELL YOU WHAT-- LET'S MAKE THIS **REALLY** EASY...
I'LL POP MY TRUNK, YOU CAN JUST CRAWL--
FROOOOSH
GET **OFF** OF ME!

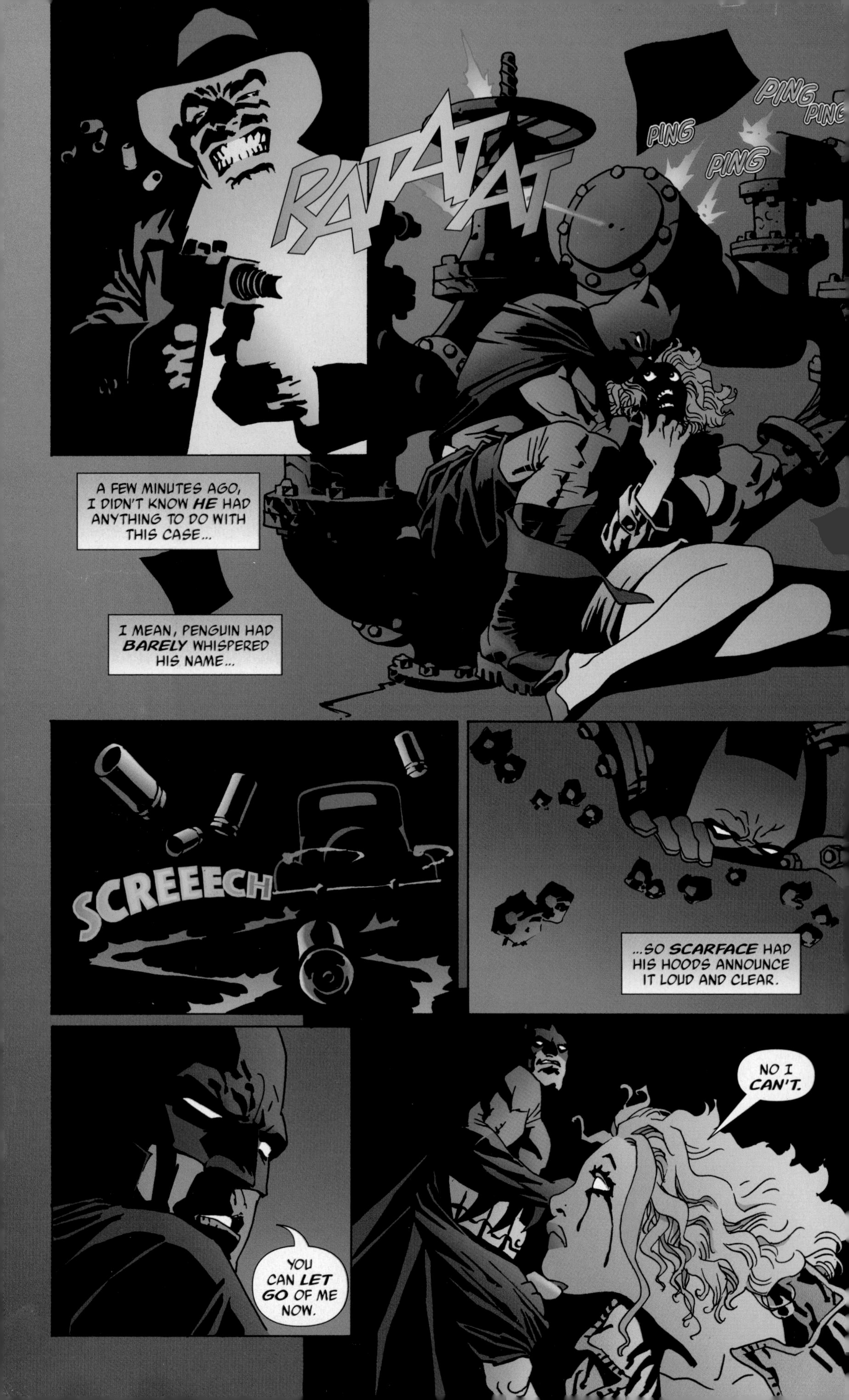

RATATAT
PING
PING
PING
PING
A FEW MINUTES AGO, I DIDN'T KNOW **HE** HAD ANYTHING TO DO WITH THIS CASE...
I MEAN, PENGUIN HAD **BARELY** WHISPERED HIS NAME...
SCREEECH
...SO **SCARFACE** HAD HIS HOODS ANNOUNCE IT LOUD AND CLEAR.
YOU CAN **LET GO** OF ME NOW.
NO I **CAN'T.**

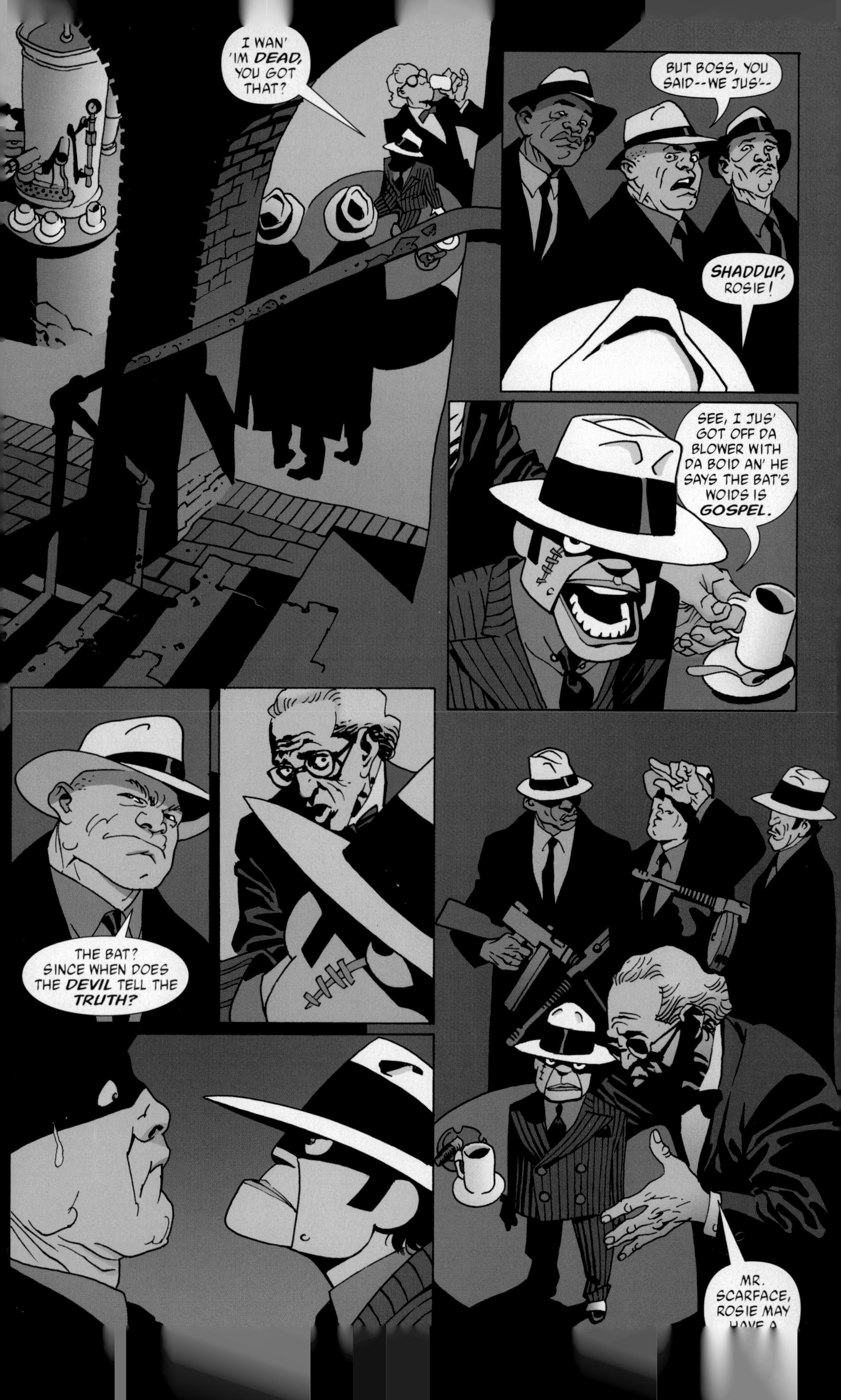
I WAN' 'IM **DEAD**, YOU GOT THAT?
BUT BOSS, YOU SAID--WE JUS'--
SHADDUP, ROSIE!
SEE, I JUS' GOT OFF DA BLOWER WITH DA BOID AN' HE SAYS THE BAT'S WOIDS IS **GOSPEL**.
THE BAT? SINCE WHEN DOES THE **DEVIL** TELL THE **TRUTH?**
MR. SCARFACE, ROSIE MAY HAVE A

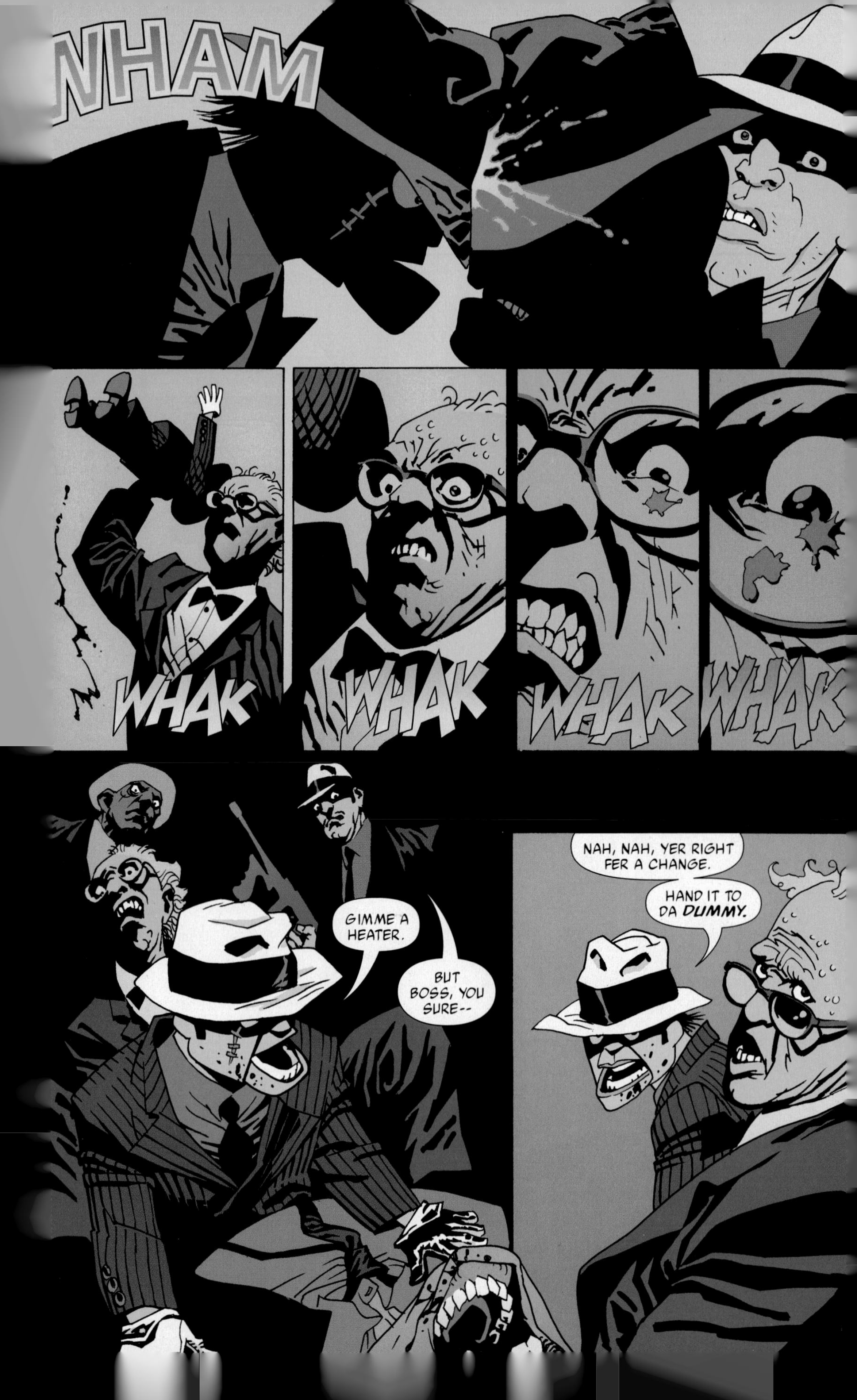
NHAM
WHAK
WHAK
WHAK
WHAK
GIMME A HEATER.
BUT BOSS, YOU SURE--
NAH, NAH, YER RIGHT FER A CHANGE.
HAND IT TO DA *DUMMY*.

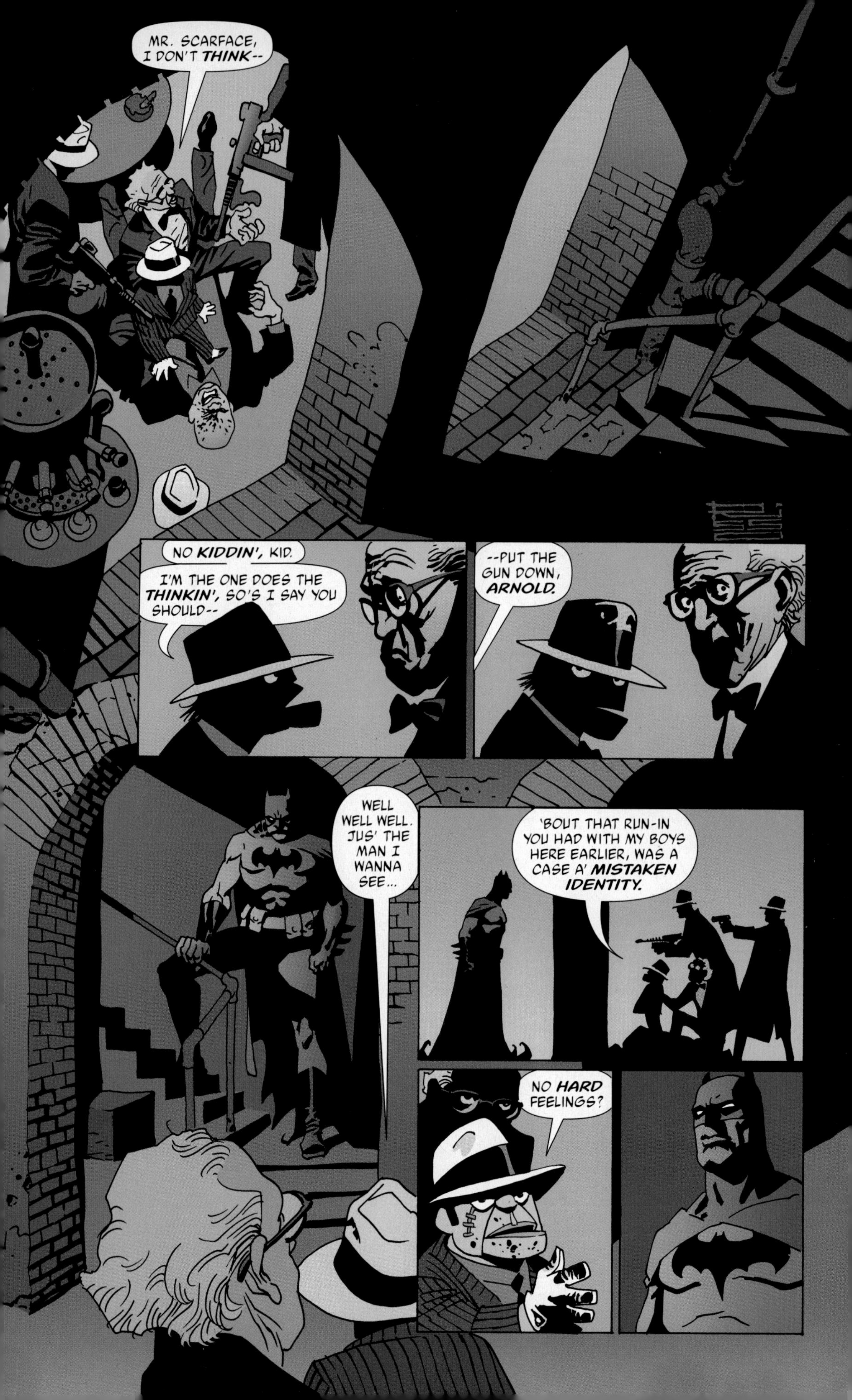
MR. SCARFACE, I DON'T THINK--
NO KIDDIN', KID.
I'M THE ONE DOES THE THINKIN', SO'S I SAY YOU SHOULD--
--PUT THE GUN DOWN, ARNOLD.
WELL WELL WELL. JUS' THE MAN I WANNA SEE...
'BOUT THAT RUN-IN YOU HAD WITH MY BOYS HERE EARLIER, WAS A CASE A' MISTAKEN IDENTITY.
NO HARD FEELINGS?

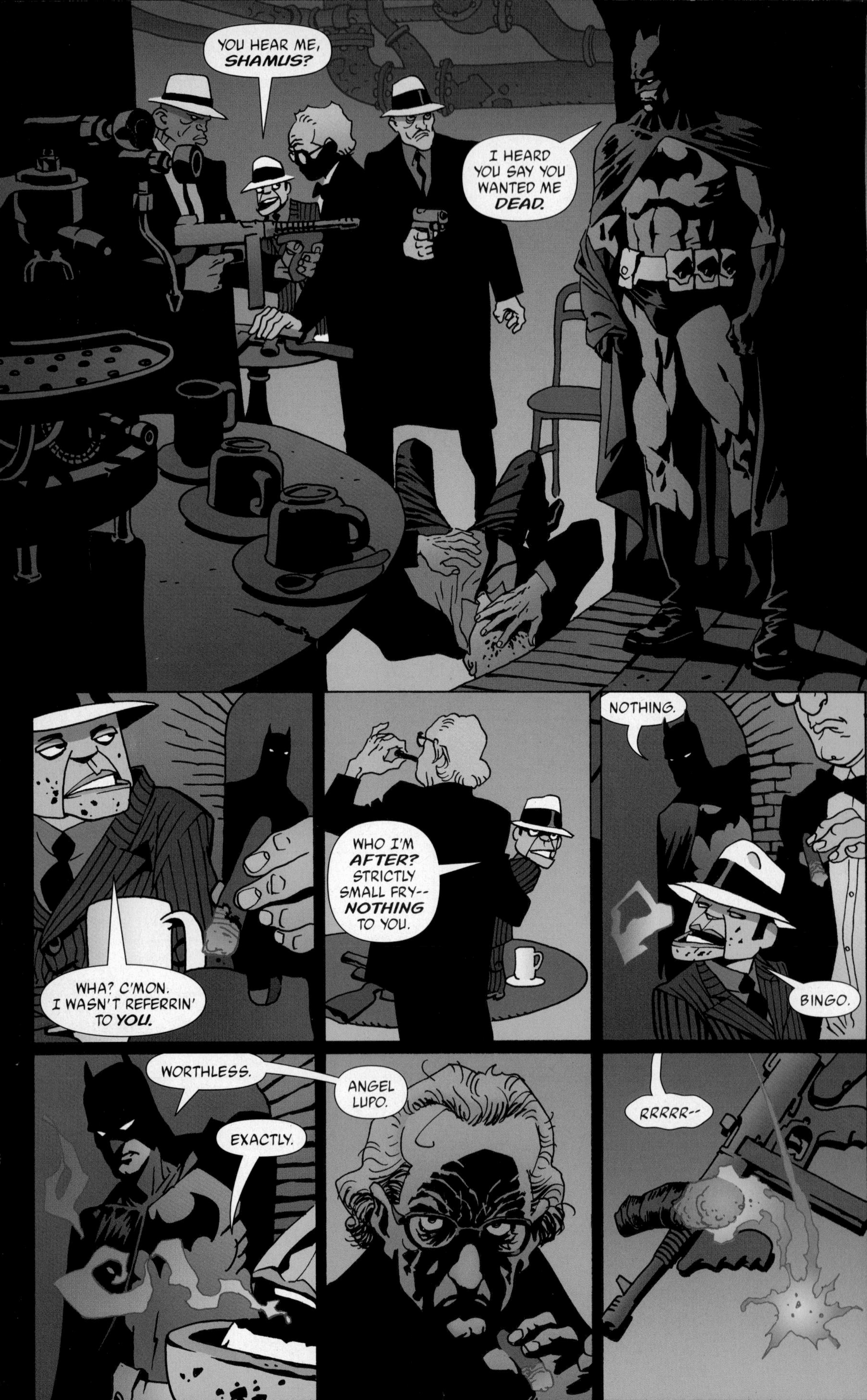
YOU HEAR ME, **SHAMUS?**
I HEARD YOU SAY YOU WANTED ME **DEAD.**
WHA? C'MON. I WASN'T REFERRIN' TO **YOU.**
WHO I'M **AFTER?** STRICTLY SMALL FRY-- **NOTHING** TO YOU.
NOTHING.
BINGO.
WORTHLESS.
ANGEL LUPO.
EXACTLY.
RRRRR--

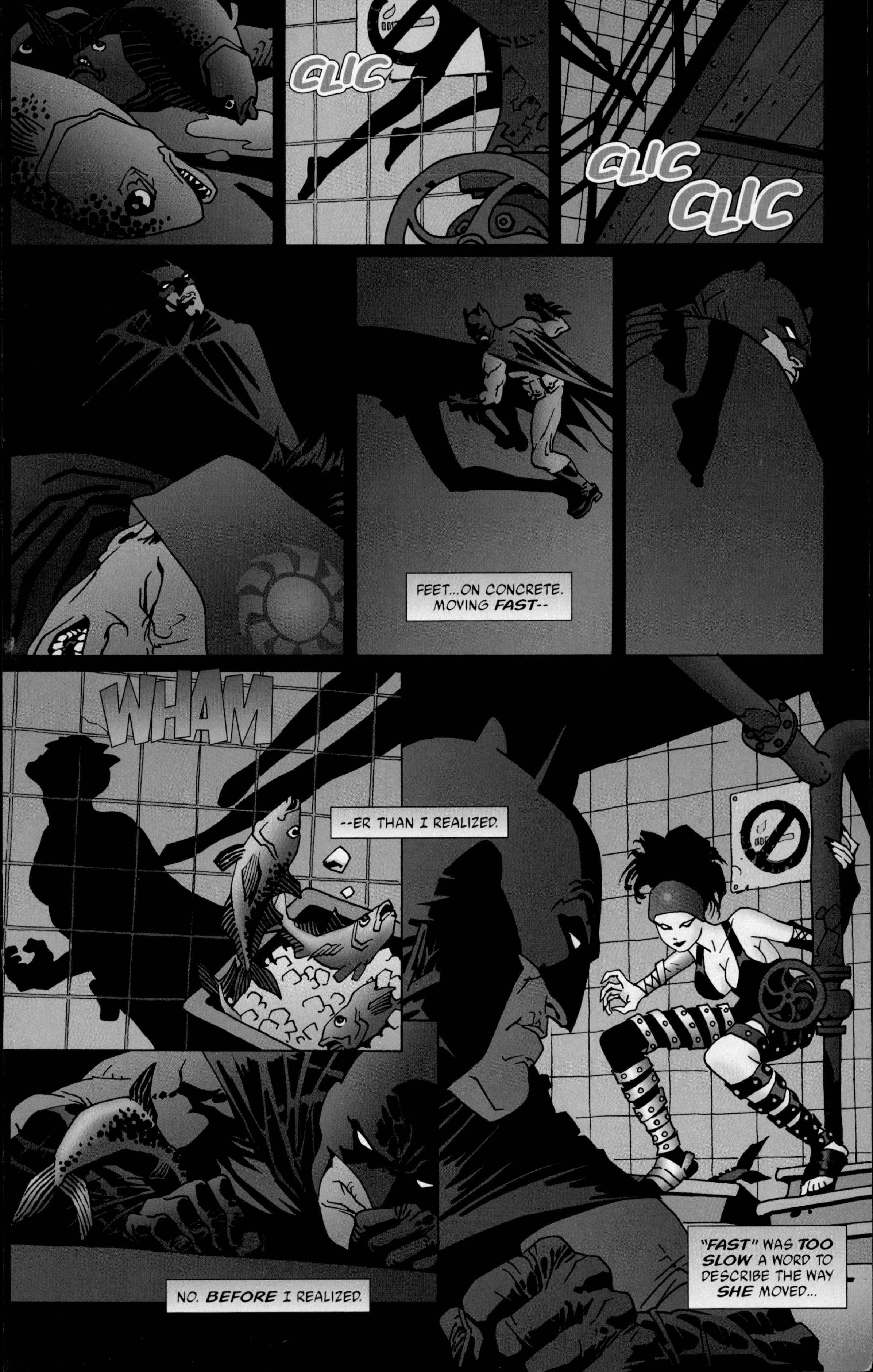
CLIC
CLIC
CLIC
FEET...ON CONCRETE. MOVING FAST--
WHAM
--ER THAN I REALIZED.
NO. BEFORE I REALIZED.
"FAST" WAS TOO SLOW A WORD TO DESCRIBE THE WAY SHE MOVED...

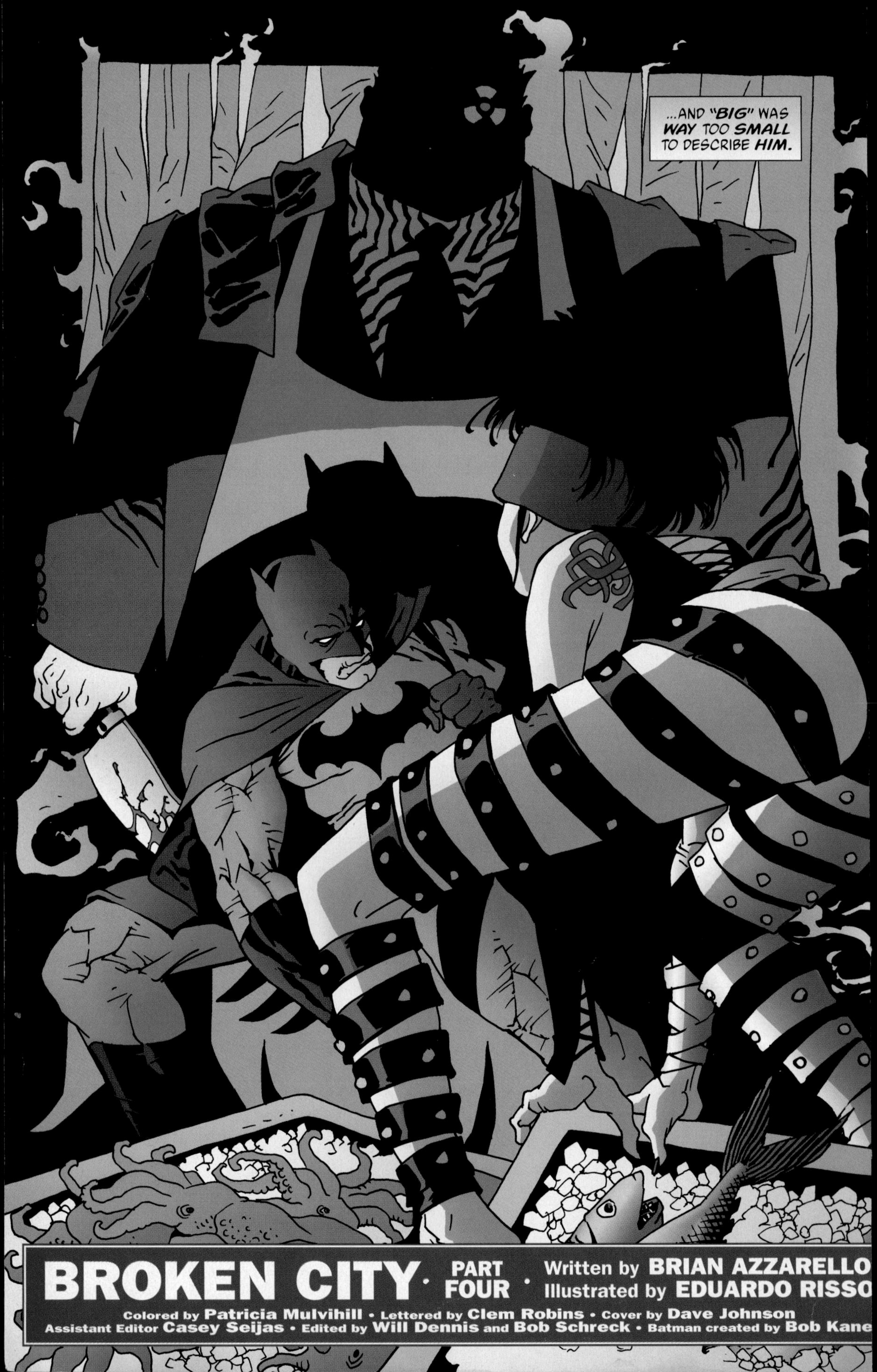
...AND "BIG" WAS WAY TOO SMALL TO DESCRIBE HIM.
BROKEN CITY · PART FOUR · Written by BRIAN AZZARELLO Illustrated by EDUARDO RISSO
Colored by Patricia Mulvihill · Lettered by Clem Robins · Cover by Dave Johnson
Assistant Editor Casey Seijas · Edited by Will Dennis and Bob Schreck · Batman created by Bob Kane

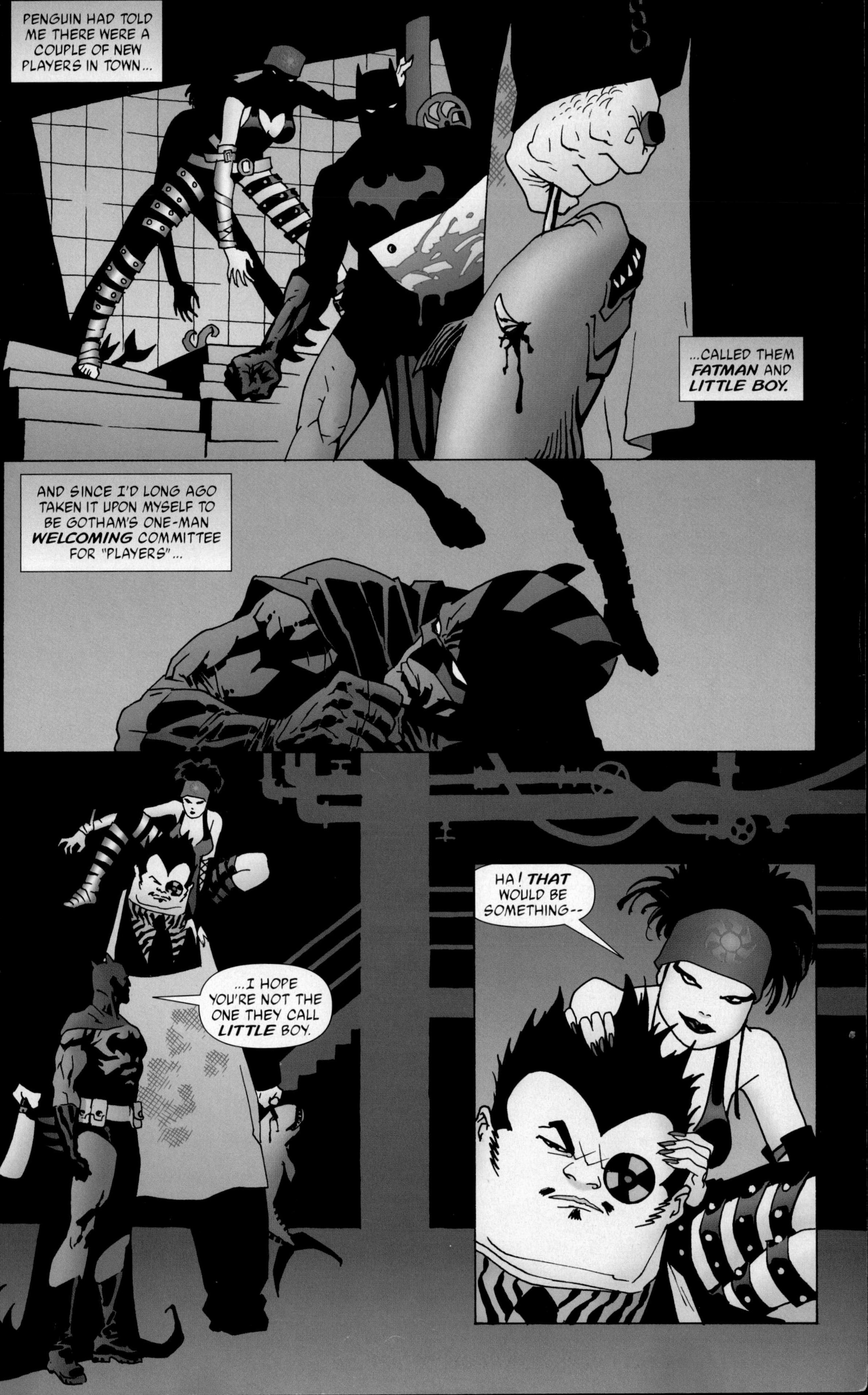
PENGUIN HAD TOLD ME THERE WERE A COUPLE OF NEW PLAYERS IN TOWN...
...CALLED THEM ***FATMAN*** AND ***LITTLE BOY.***
AND SINCE I'D LONG AGO TAKEN IT UPON MYSELF TO BE GOTHAM'S ONE-MAN ***WELCOMING*** COMMITTEE FOR "PLAYERS"...
...I HOPE YOU'RE NOT THE ONE THEY CALL ***LITTLE*** BOY.
HA! ***THAT*** WOULD BE SOMETHING--

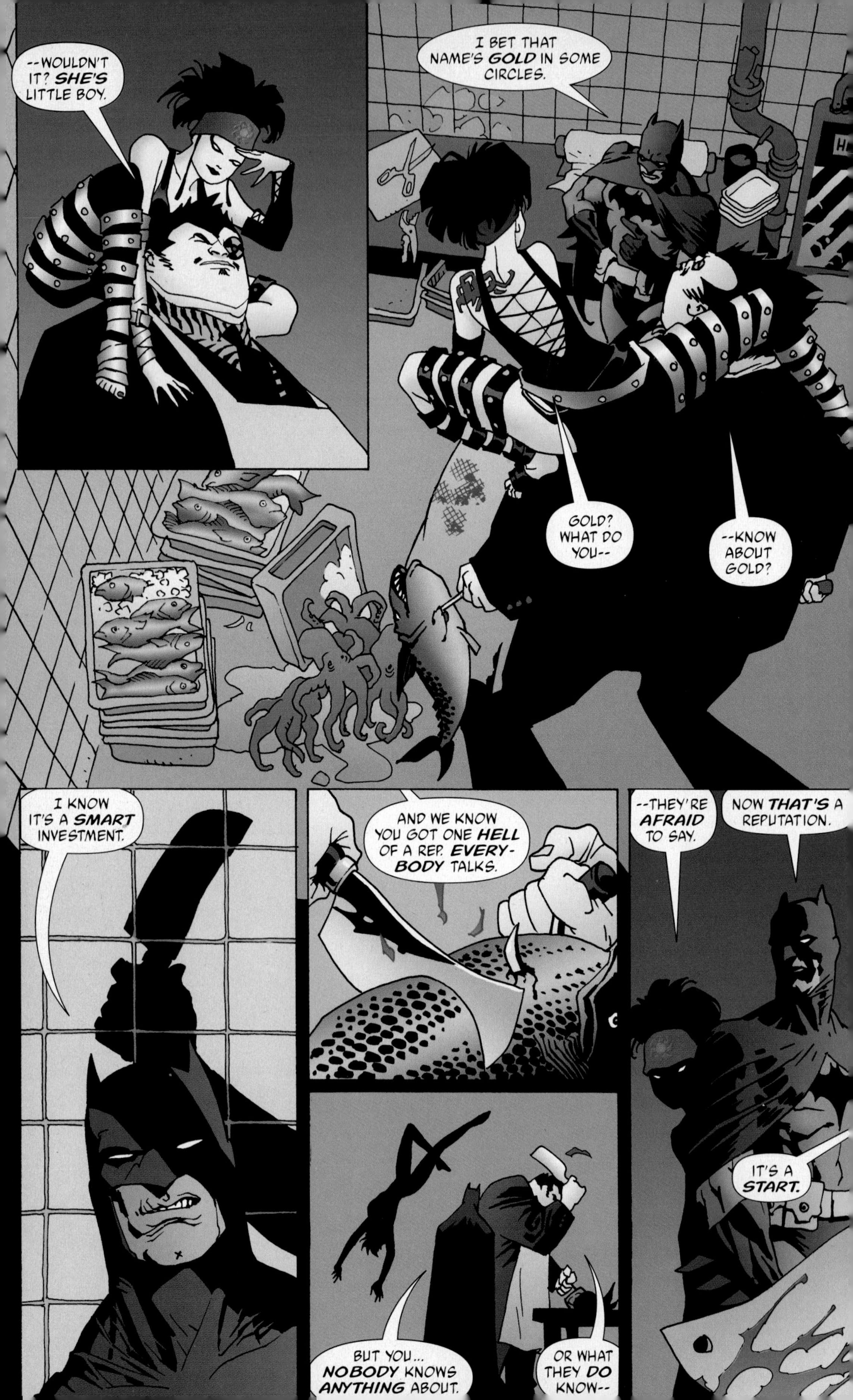
--WOULDN'T IT? **SHE'S** LITTLE BOY.
I BET THAT NAME'S **GOLD** IN SOME CIRCLES.
GOLD? WHAT DO YOU--
--KNOW ABOUT GOLD?
I KNOW IT'S A **SMART** INVESTMENT.
AND WE KNOW YOU GOT ONE **HELL** OF A REP. **EVERY-BODY** TALKS.
BUT YOU... **NOBODY** KNOWS **ANYTHING** ABOUT.
OR WHAT THEY **DO** KNOW--
--THEY'RE **AFRAID** TO SAY.
NOW **THAT'S** A REPUTATION.
IT'S A **START.**

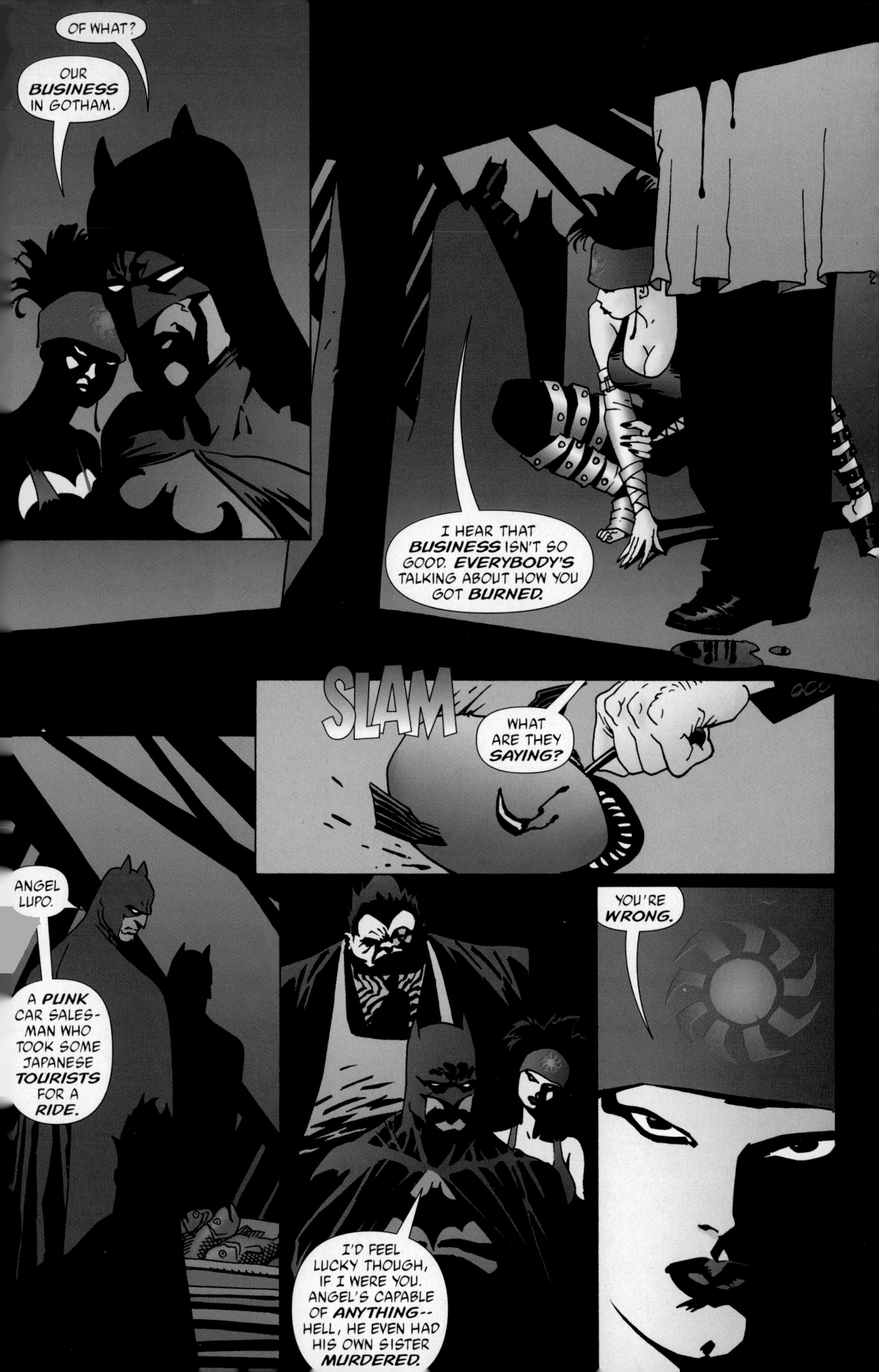
OF WHAT?
OUR BUSINESS IN GOTHAM.
I HEAR THAT BUSINESS ISN'T SO GOOD. EVERYBODY'S TALKING ABOUT HOW YOU GOT BURNED.
SLAM
WHAT ARE THEY SAYING?
ANGEL LUPO.
A PUNK CAR SALES-MAN WHO TOOK SOME JAPANESE TOURISTS FOR A RIDE.
I'D FEEL LUCKY THOUGH, IF I WERE YOU. ANGEL'S CAPABLE OF ANYTHING-- HELL, HE EVEN HAD HIS OWN SISTER MURDERED.
YOU'RE WRONG.

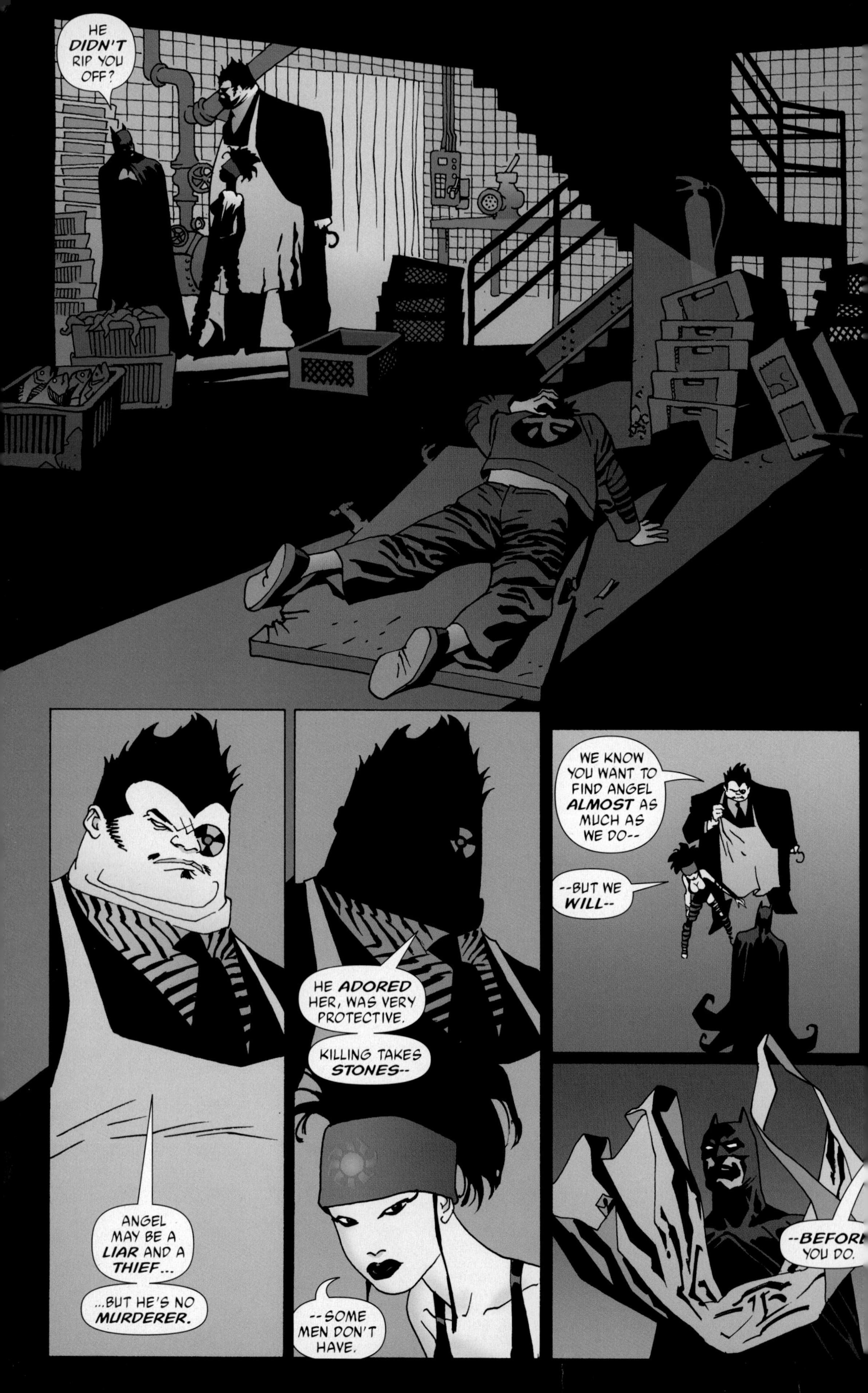
HE **DIDN'T** RIP YOU OFF?
ANGEL MAY BE A **LIAR** AND A **THIEF**...
...BUT HE'S NO **MURDERER.**
HE **ADORED** HER, WAS VERY PROTECTIVE.
KILLING TAKES **STONES**--
--SOME MEN DON'T HAVE.
WE KNOW YOU WANT TO FIND ANGEL **ALMOST** AS MUCH AS WE DO--
--BUT WE **WILL**--
--**BEFOR**
YOU DO.

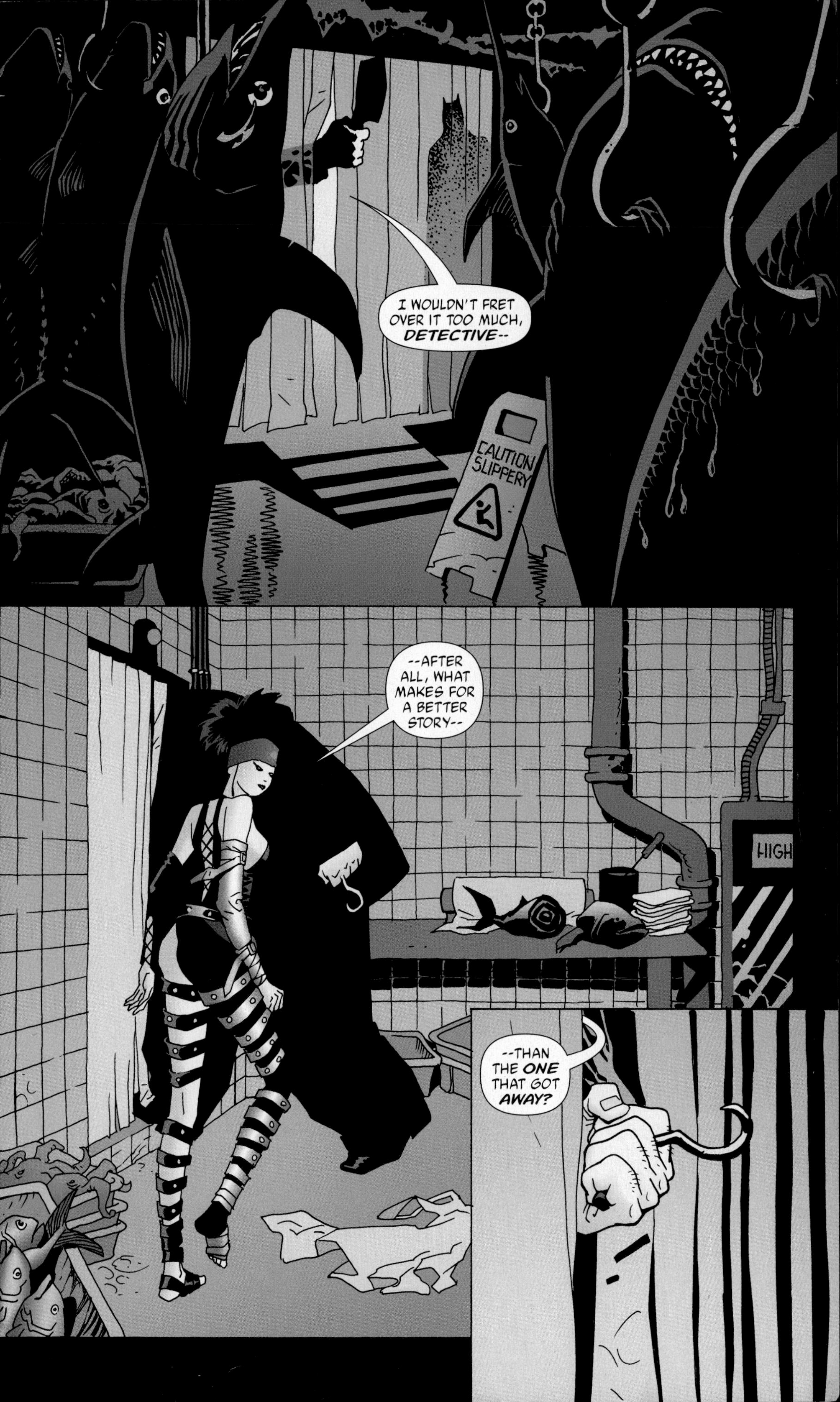
I WOULDN'T FRET OVER IT TOO MUCH, **DETECTIVE**--
CAUTION SLIPPERY
--AFTER ALL, WHAT MAKES FOR A BETTER STORY--
HIGH
--THAN THE **ONE** THAT GOT **AWAY?**

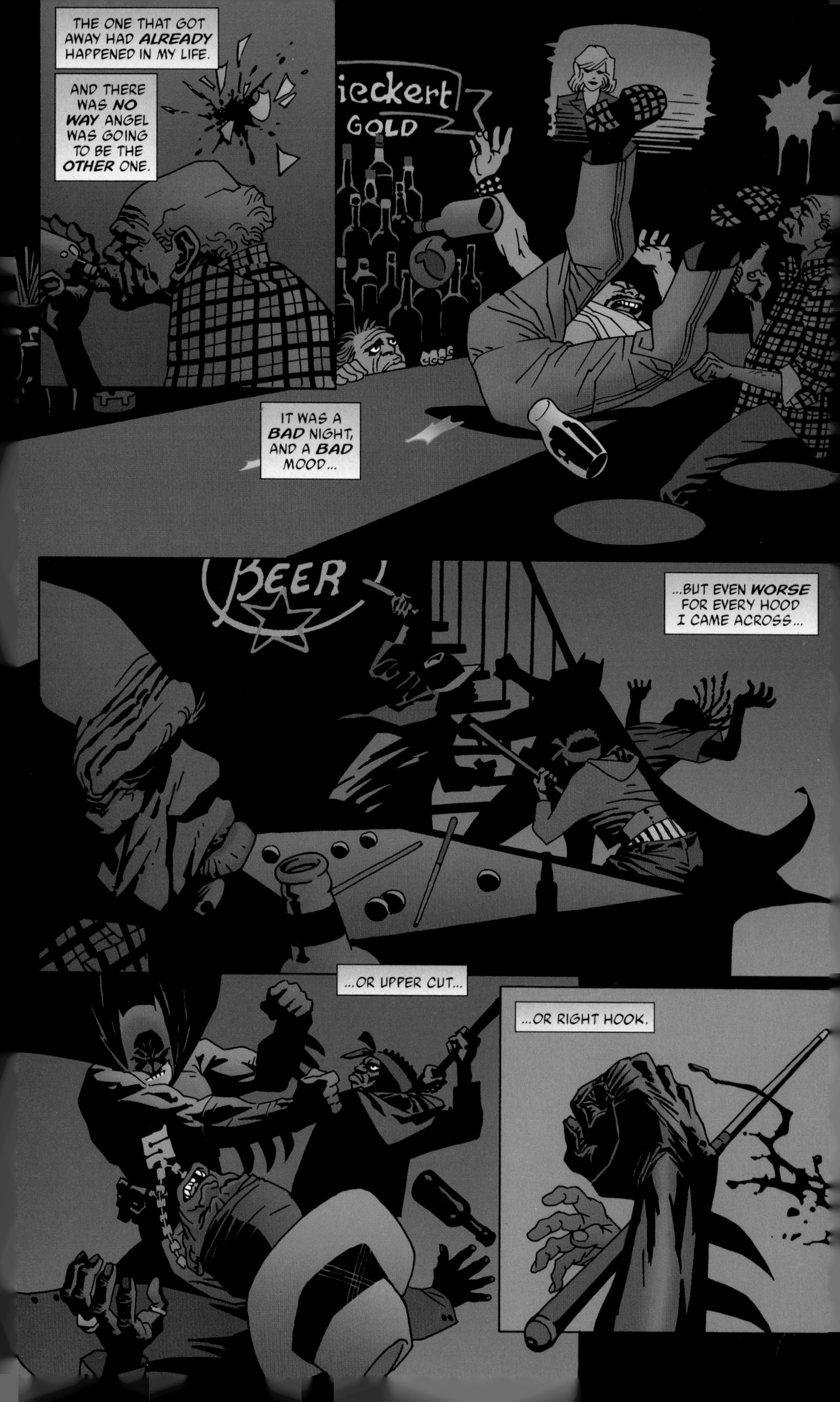
THE ONE THAT GOT AWAY HAD **ALREADY** HAPPENED IN MY LIFE.
AND THERE WAS **NO WAY** ANGEL WAS GOING TO BE THE **OTHER** ONE.
ieckert GOLD
IT WAS A **BAD** NIGHT, AND A **BAD** MOOD...
BEER
...BUT EVEN **WORSE** FOR EVERY HOOD I CAME ACROSS...
...OR UPPER CUT...
...OR RIGHT HOOK.

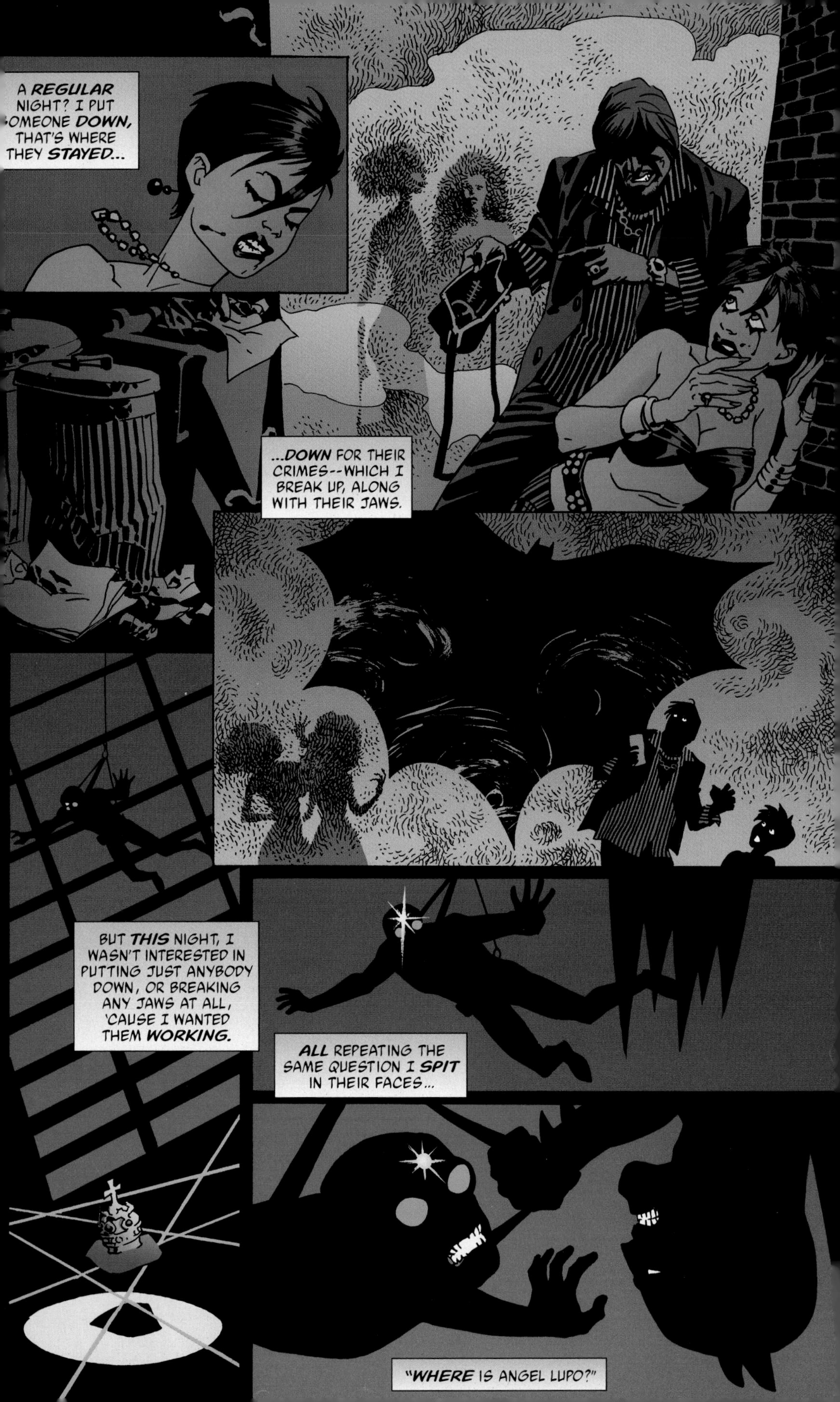
A **REGULAR** NIGHT? I PUT SOMEONE **DOWN,** THAT'S WHERE THEY **STAYED...**
...DOWN FOR THEIR CRIMES--WHICH I BREAK UP, ALONG WITH THEIR JAWS.
BUT **THIS** NIGHT, I WASN'T INTERESTED IN PUTTING JUST ANYBODY DOWN, OR BREAKING ANY JAWS AT ALL, 'CAUSE I WANTED THEM **WORKING.**
ALL REPEATING THE SAME QUESTION I **SPIT** IN THEIR FACES...
"**WHERE** IS ANGEL LUPO?"

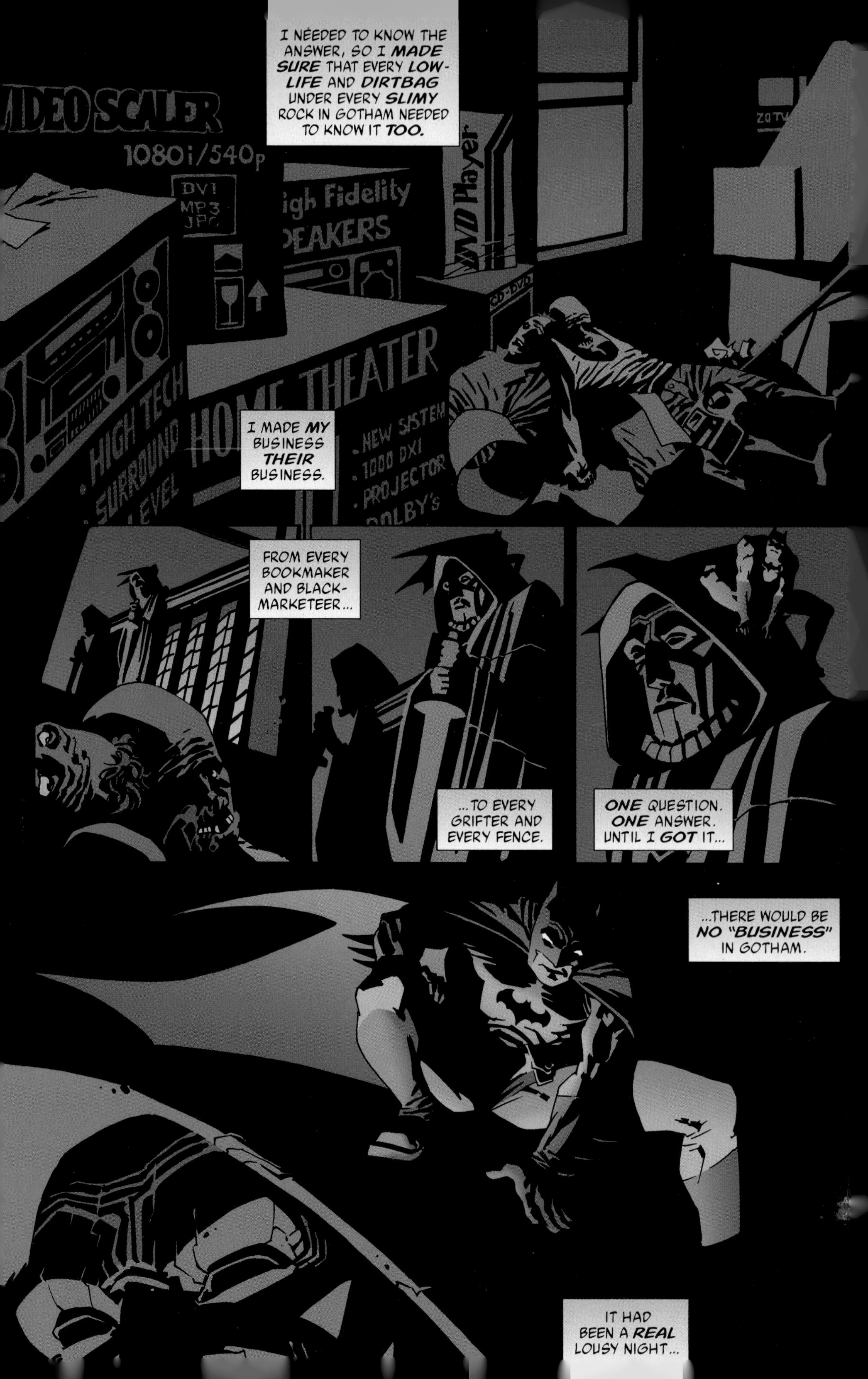
I NEEDED TO KNOW THE ANSWER, SO I **MADE SURE** THAT EVERY **LOW-LIFE** AND **DIRTBAG** UNDER EVERY **SLIMY** ROCK IN GOTHAM NEEDED TO KNOW IT **TOO.**
VIDEO SCALER
1080i/540p
DVI
MP3
JPG
High Fidelity
PEAKERS
DVD Player
CD-DVD
HIGH TECH
SURROUND
LEVEL
HOME THEATER
NEW SYSTEM
1000 DXI
PROJECTOR
DOLBY's
I MADE **MY** BUSINESS **THEIR** BUSINESS.
FROM EVERY BOOKMAKER AND BLACK-MARKETEER...
...TO EVERY GRIFTER AND EVERY FENCE.
ONE QUESTION. **ONE** ANSWER. UNTIL **I GOT** IT...
...THERE WOULD BE **NO "BUSINESS"** IN GOTHAM.
IT HAD BEEN A **REAL** LOUSY NIGHT...

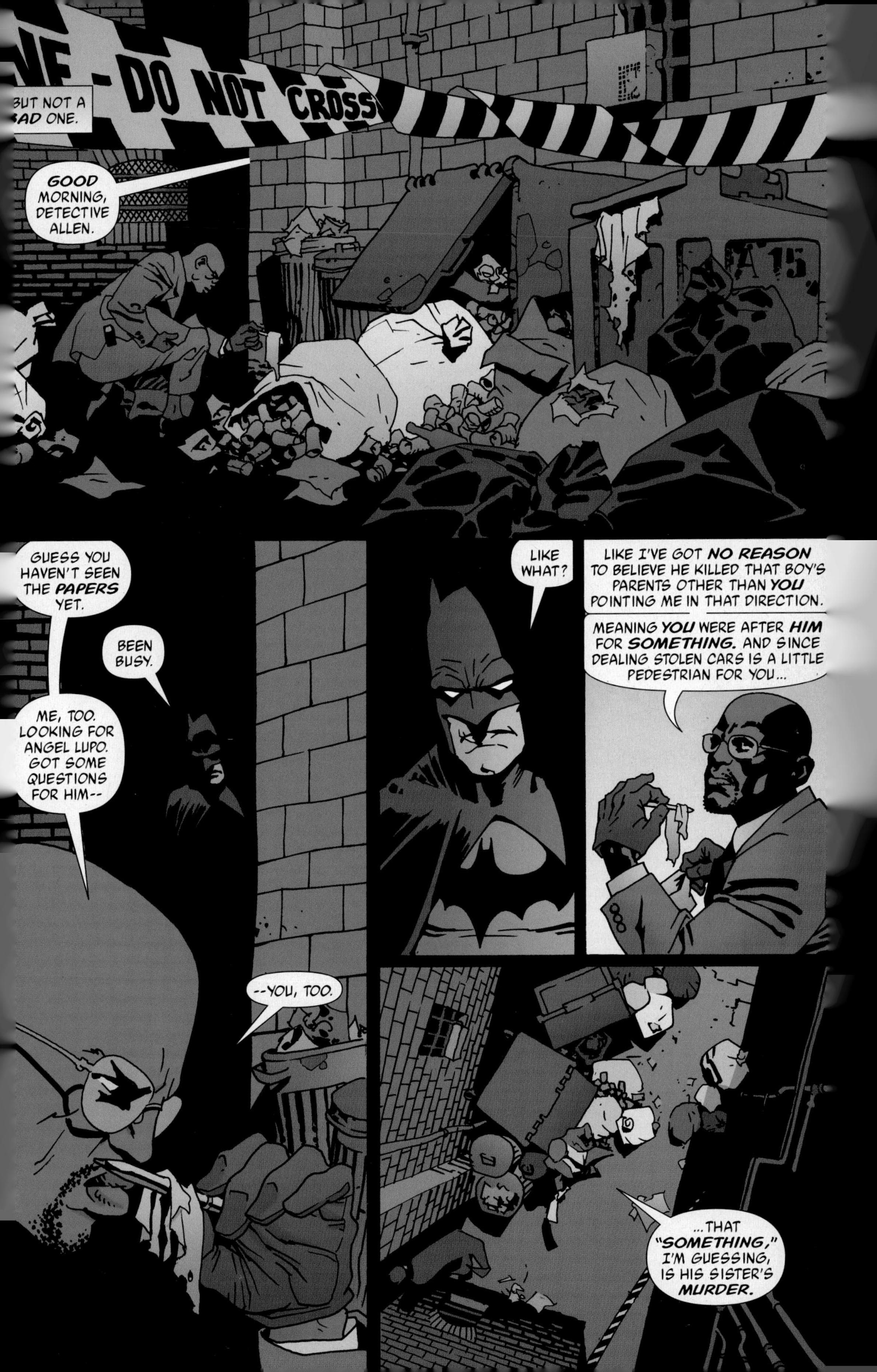
DO NOT CROSS
UT NOT A AD ONE.
GOOD MORNING, DETECTIVE ALLEN.
GUESS YOU HAVEN'T SEEN THE PAPERS YET.
BEEN BUSY.
ME, TOO. LOOKING FOR ANGEL LUPO. GOT SOME QUESTIONS FOR HIM--
--YOU, TOO.
LIKE WHAT?
LIKE I'VE GOT NO REASON TO BELIEVE HE KILLED THAT BOY'S PARENTS OTHER THAN YOU POINTING ME IN THAT DIRECTION.
MEANING YOU WERE AFTER HIM FOR SOMETHING. AND SINCE DEALING STOLEN CARS IS A LITTLE PEDESTRIAN FOR YOU...
...THAT "SOMETHING," I'M GUESSING, IS HIS SISTER'S MURDER.

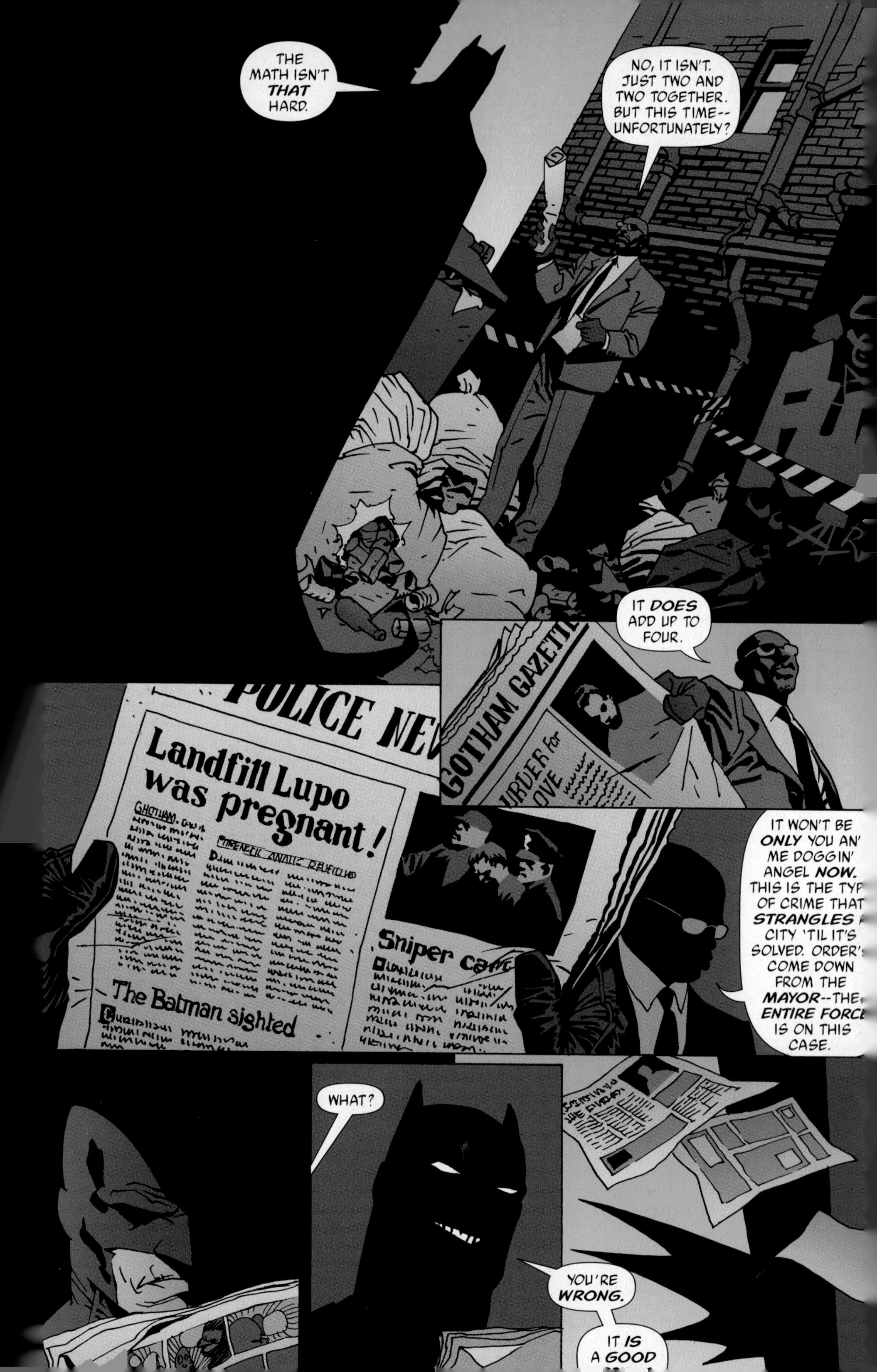

THE MATH ISN'T **THAT** HARD.
NO, IT ISN'T. JUST TWO AND TWO TOGETHER. BUT THIS TIME-- UNFORTUNATELY?
IT **DOES** ADD UP TO FOUR.
GOTHAM GAZETTE
POLICE NEWS
Landfill Lupo was pregnant!
Sniper cam
The Batman sighted
IT WON'T BE **ONLY** YOU AN' ME DOGGIN' ANGEL **NOW.** THIS IS THE TYPE OF CRIME THAT **STRANGLES** A CITY 'TIL IT'S SOLVED. ORDER'S COME DOWN FROM THE **MAYOR**--THE **ENTIRE FORCE** IS ON THIS CASE.
WHAT?
YOU'RE **WRONG.**
IT **IS** A **GOOD**

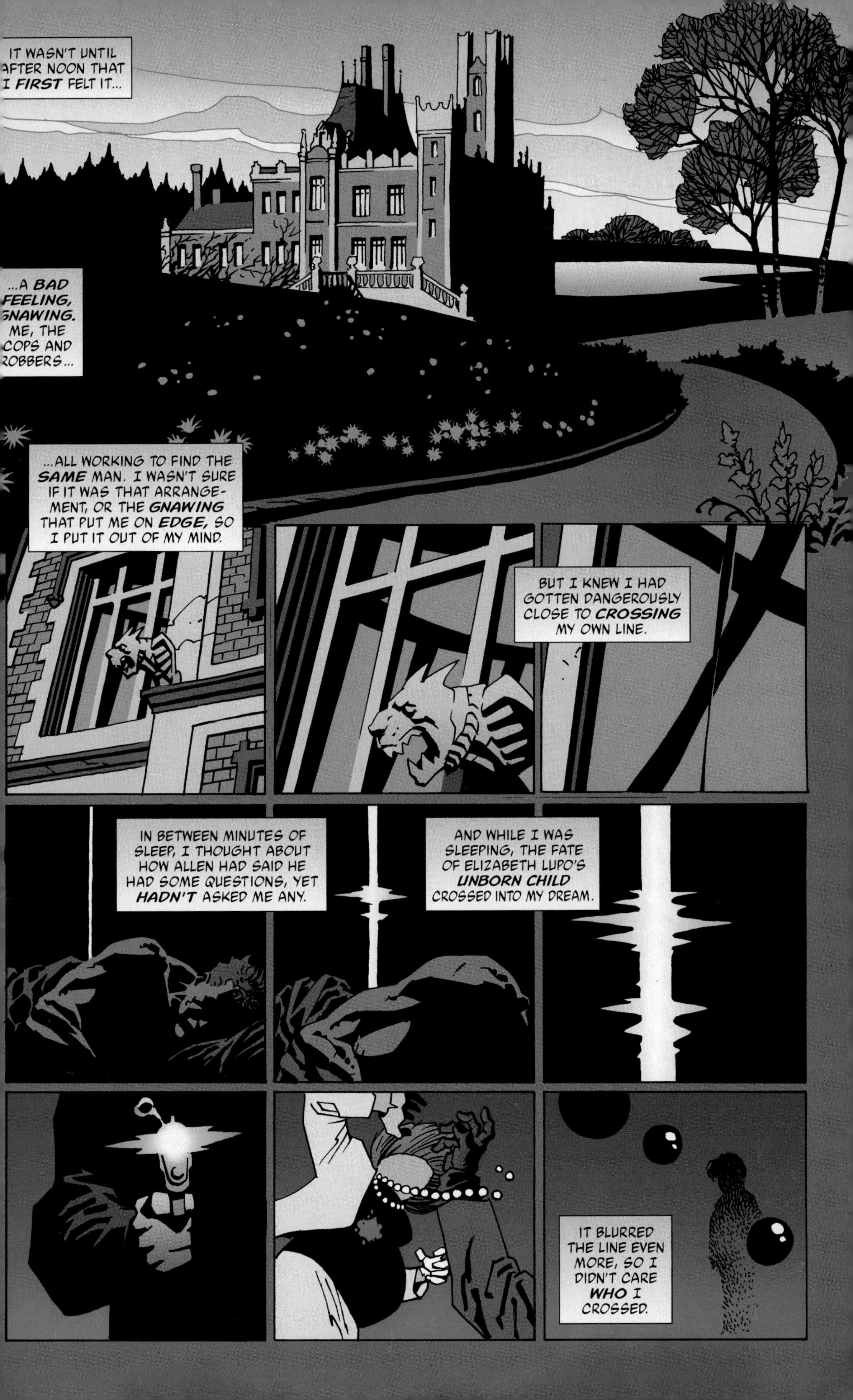
IT WASN'T UNTIL AFTER NOON THAT I **FIRST** FELT IT...
...A **BAD FEELING, GNAWING.** ME, THE COPS AND ROBBERS...
...ALL WORKING TO FIND THE **SAME** MAN. I WASN'T SURE IF IT WAS THAT ARRANGE-MENT, OR THE **GNAWING** THAT PUT ME ON **EDGE,** SO I PUT IT OUT OF MY MIND.
BUT I KNEW I HAD GOTTEN DANGEROUSLY CLOSE TO **CROSSING** MY OWN LINE.
IN BETWEEN MINUTES OF SLEEP, I THOUGHT ABOUT HOW ALLEN HAD SAID HE HAD SOME QUESTIONS, YET **HADN'T** ASKED ME ANY.
AND WHILE I WAS SLEEPING, THE FATE OF ELIZABETH LUPO'S **UNBORN CHILD** CROSSED INTO MY DREAM.
IT BLURRED THE LINE EVEN MORE, SO I DIDN'T CARE **WHO** I CROSSED.

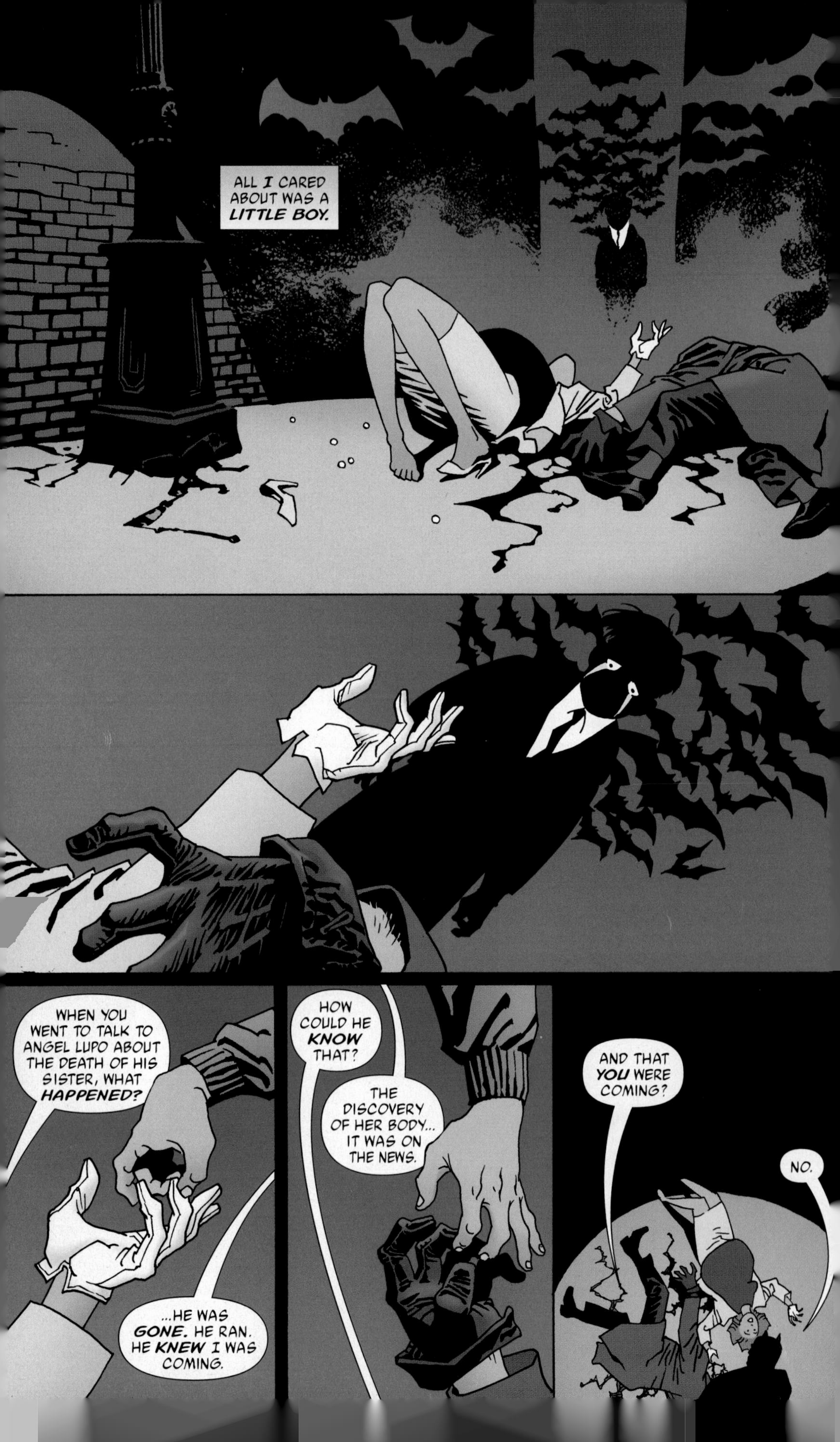
ALL I CARED ABOUT WAS A LITTLE BOY.
WHEN YOU WENT TO TALK TO ANGEL LUPO ABOUT THE DEATH OF HIS SISTER, WHAT HAPPENED?
...HE WAS GONE. HE RAN. HE KNEW I WAS COMING.
HOW COULD HE KNOW THAT?
THE DISCOVERY OF HER BODY... IT WAS ON THE NEWS.
AND THAT YOU WERE COMING?
NO.

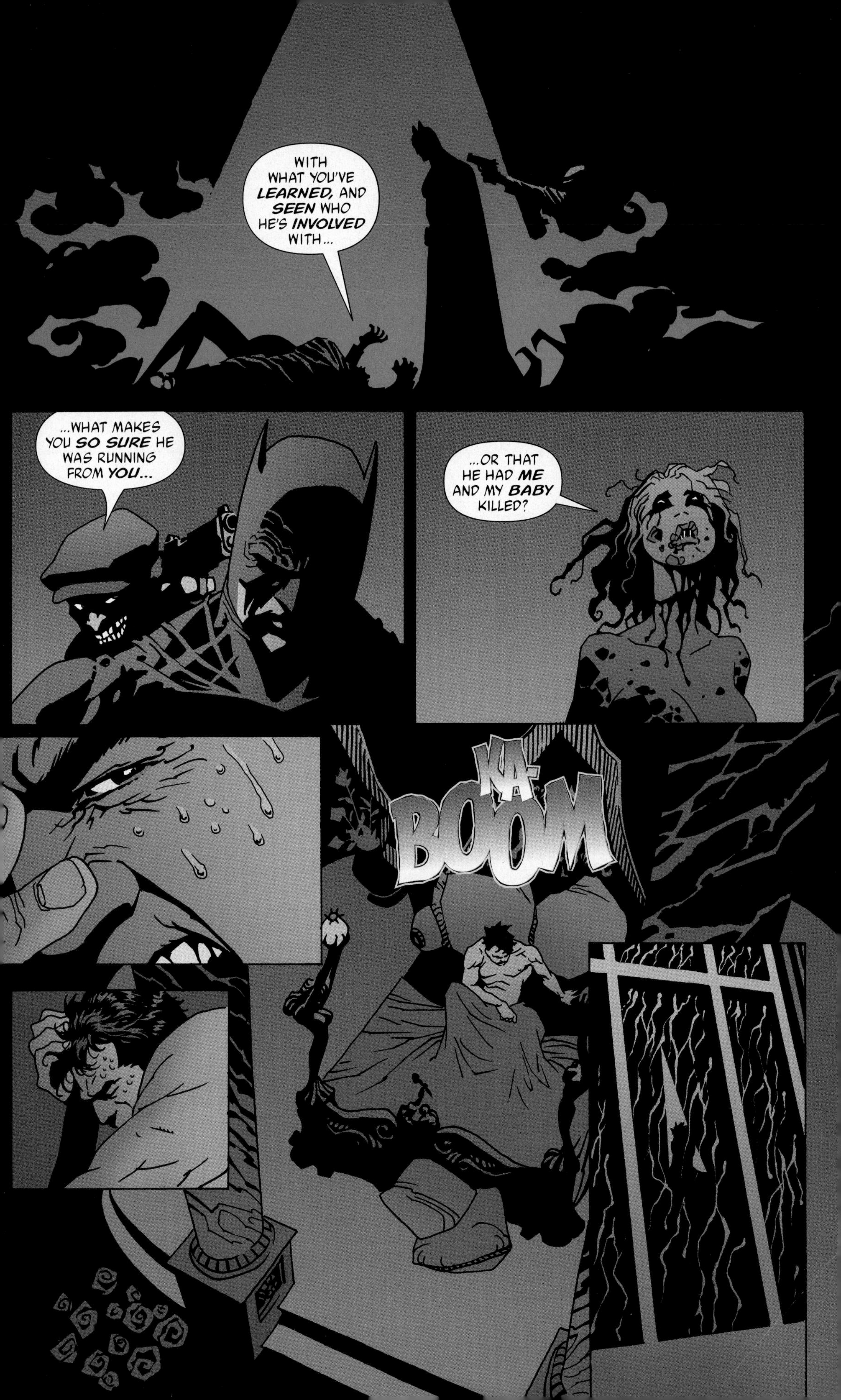
WITH WHAT YOU'VE ***LEARNED,*** AND ***SEEN*** WHO HE'S ***INVOLVED*** WITH...
...WHAT MAKES YOU ***SO SURE*** HE WAS RUNNING FROM ***YOU...***
...OR THAT HE HAD ***ME*** AND MY ***BABY*** KILLED?
KA-BOOM

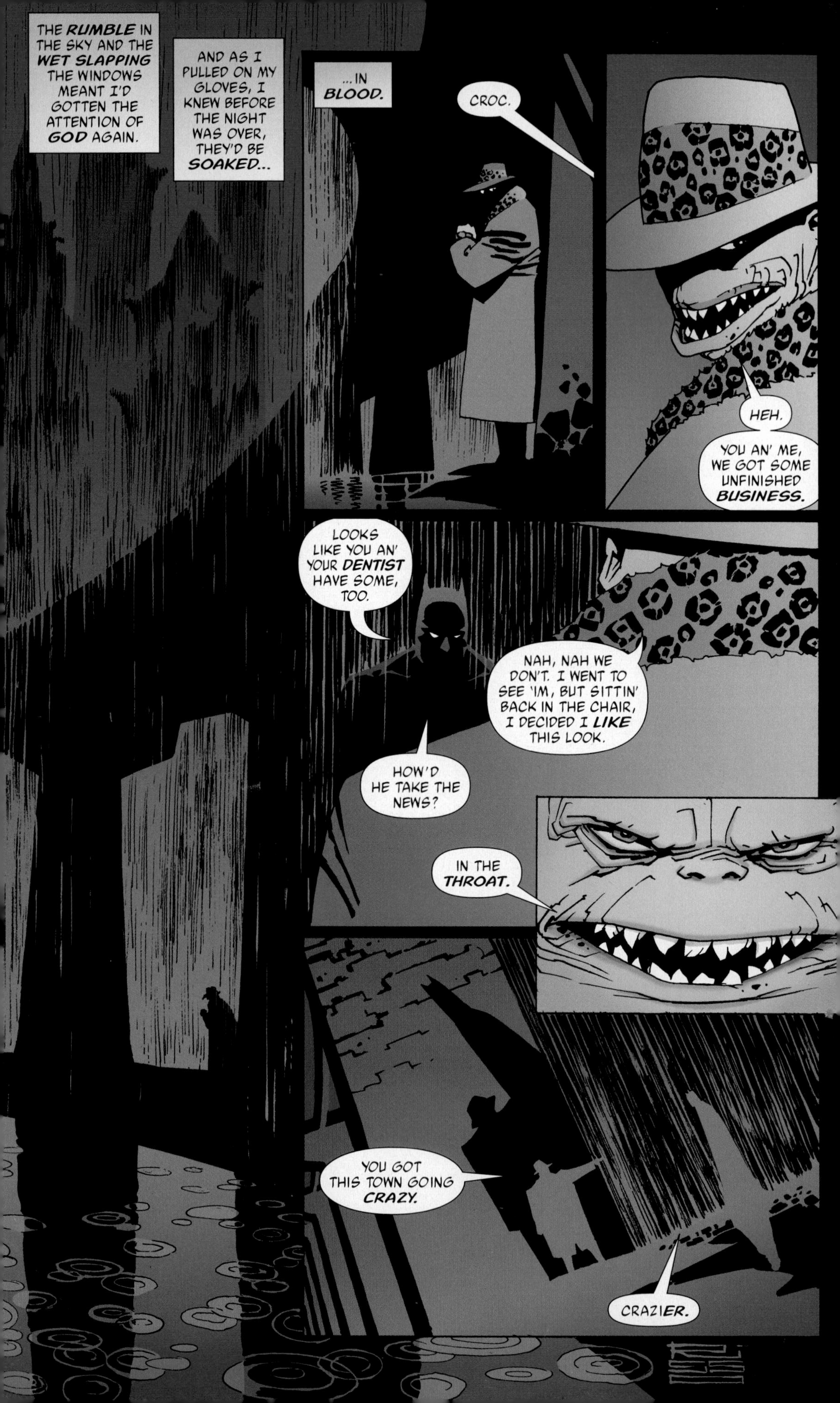
THE **RUMBLE** IN THE SKY AND THE **WET SLAPPING** THE WINDOWS MEANT I'D GOTTEN THE ATTENTION OF **GOD** AGAIN.
AND AS I PULLED ON MY GLOVES, I KNEW BEFORE THE NIGHT WAS OVER, THEY'D BE **SOAKED...**
...IN **BLOOD.**
CROC.
HEH.
YOU AN' ME, WE GOT SOME UNFINISHED **BUSINESS.**
LOOKS LIKE YOU AN' YOUR **DENTIST** HAVE SOME, TOO.
NAH, NAH WE DON'T. I WENT TO SEE 'IM, BUT SITTIN' BACK IN THE CHAIR, I DECIDED I **LIKE** THIS LOOK.
HOW'D HE TAKE THE NEWS?
IN THE **THROAT.**
YOU GOT THIS TOWN GOING **CRAZY.**
CRAZIER.

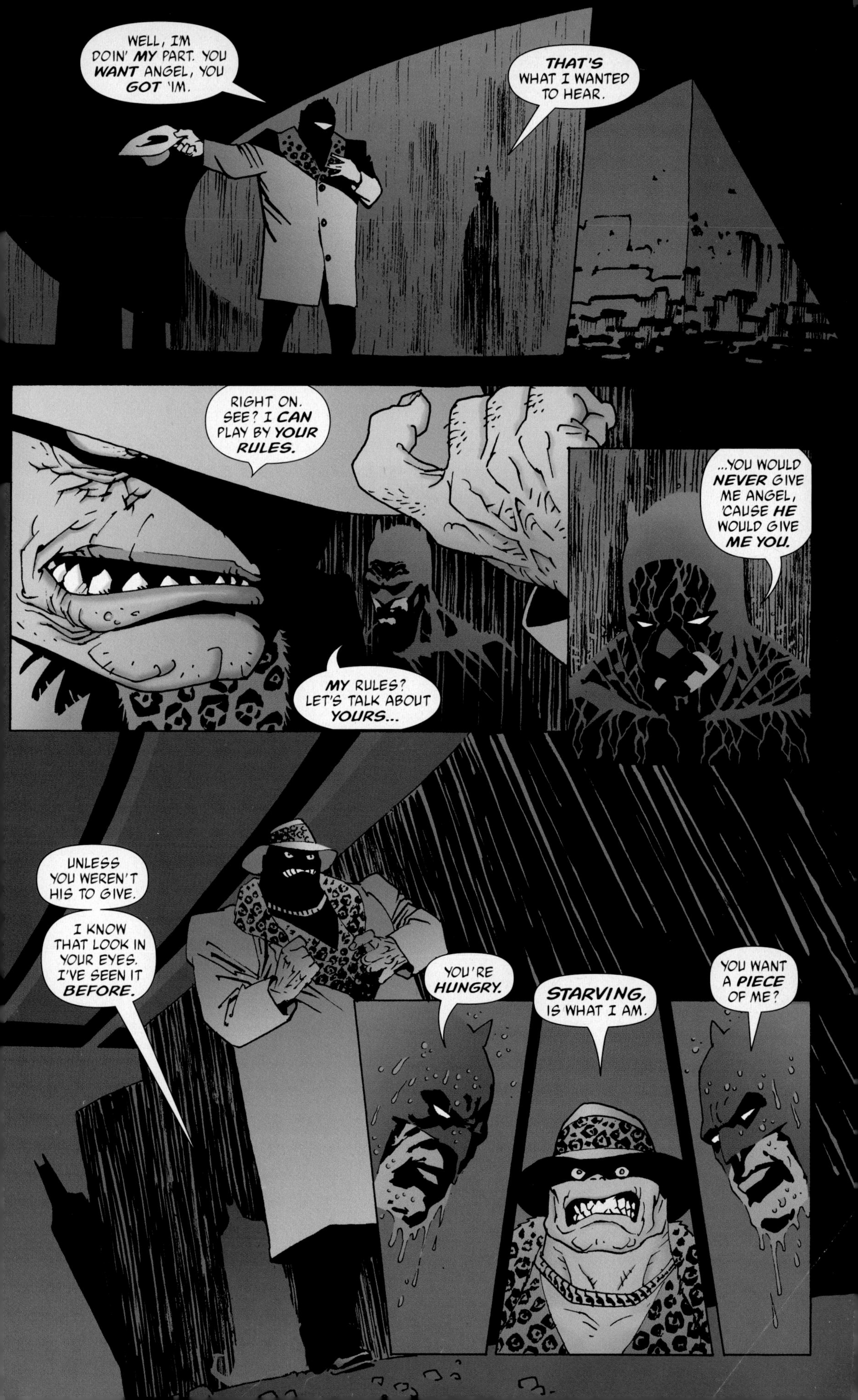
WELL, I'M DOIN' **MY** PART. YOU **WANT** ANGEL, YOU **GOT** 'IM.
THAT'S WHAT I WANTED TO HEAR.
RIGHT ON. SEE? I **CAN** PLAY BY **YOUR RULES.**
MY RULES? LET'S TALK ABOUT **YOURS...**
...YOU WOULD **NEVER** GIVE ME ANGEL, 'CAUSE **HE** WOULD GIVE **ME YOU.**
UNLESS YOU WEREN'T HIS TO GIVE.
I KNOW THAT LOOK IN YOUR EYES. I'VE SEEN IT **BEFORE.**
YOU'RE **HUNGRY.**
STARVING, IS WHAT I AM.
YOU WANT A **PIECE** OF ME?

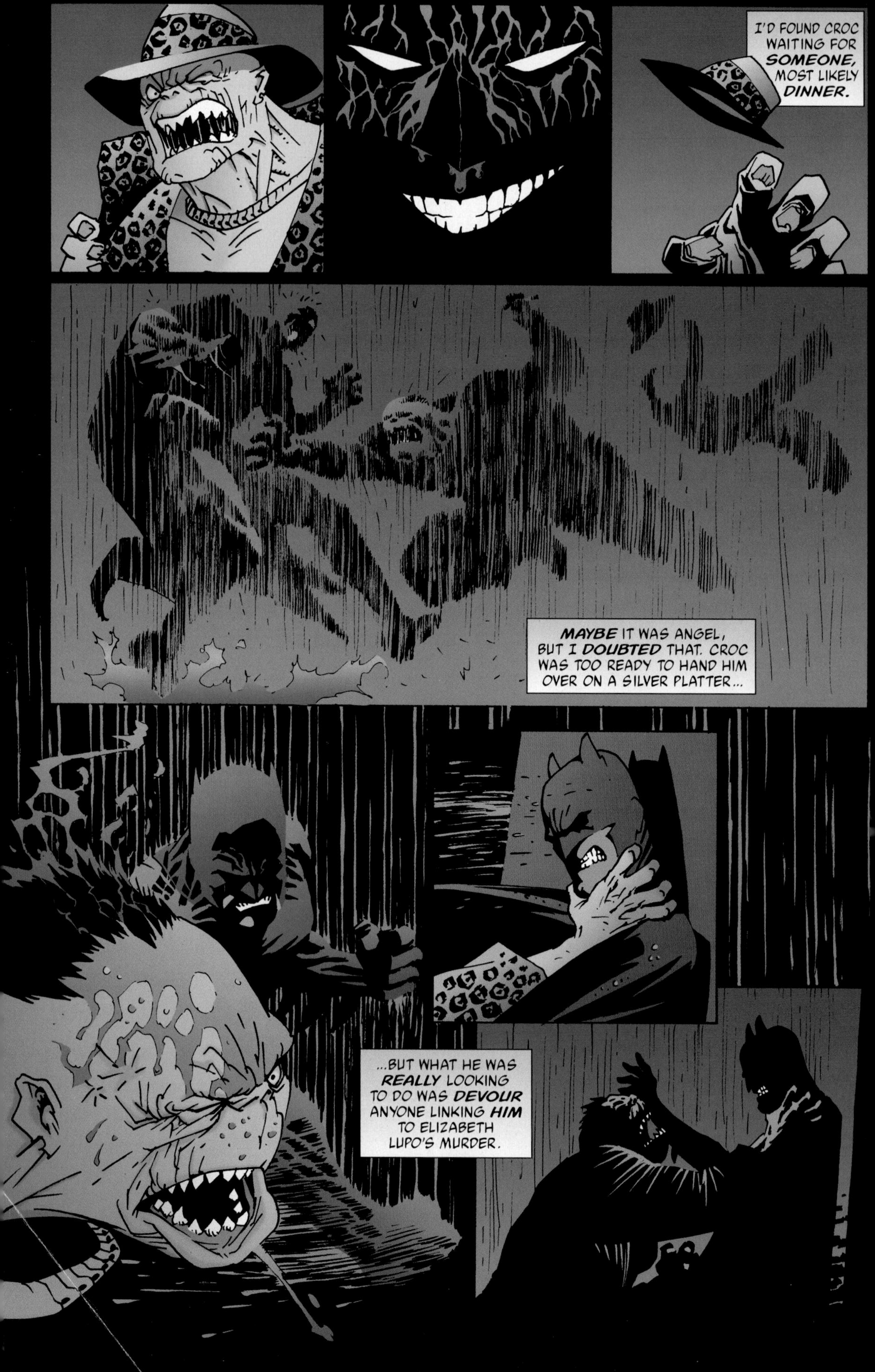
I'D FOUND CROC WAITING FOR **SOMEONE,** MOST LIKELY **DINNER.**
MAYBE IT WAS ANGEL, BUT I ***DOUBTED*** THAT. CROC WAS TOO READY TO HAND HIM OVER ON A SILVER PLATTER...
...BUT WHAT HE WAS ***REALLY*** LOOKING TO DO WAS ***DEVOUR*** ANYONE LINKING ***HIM*** TO ELIZABETH LUPO'S MURDER.

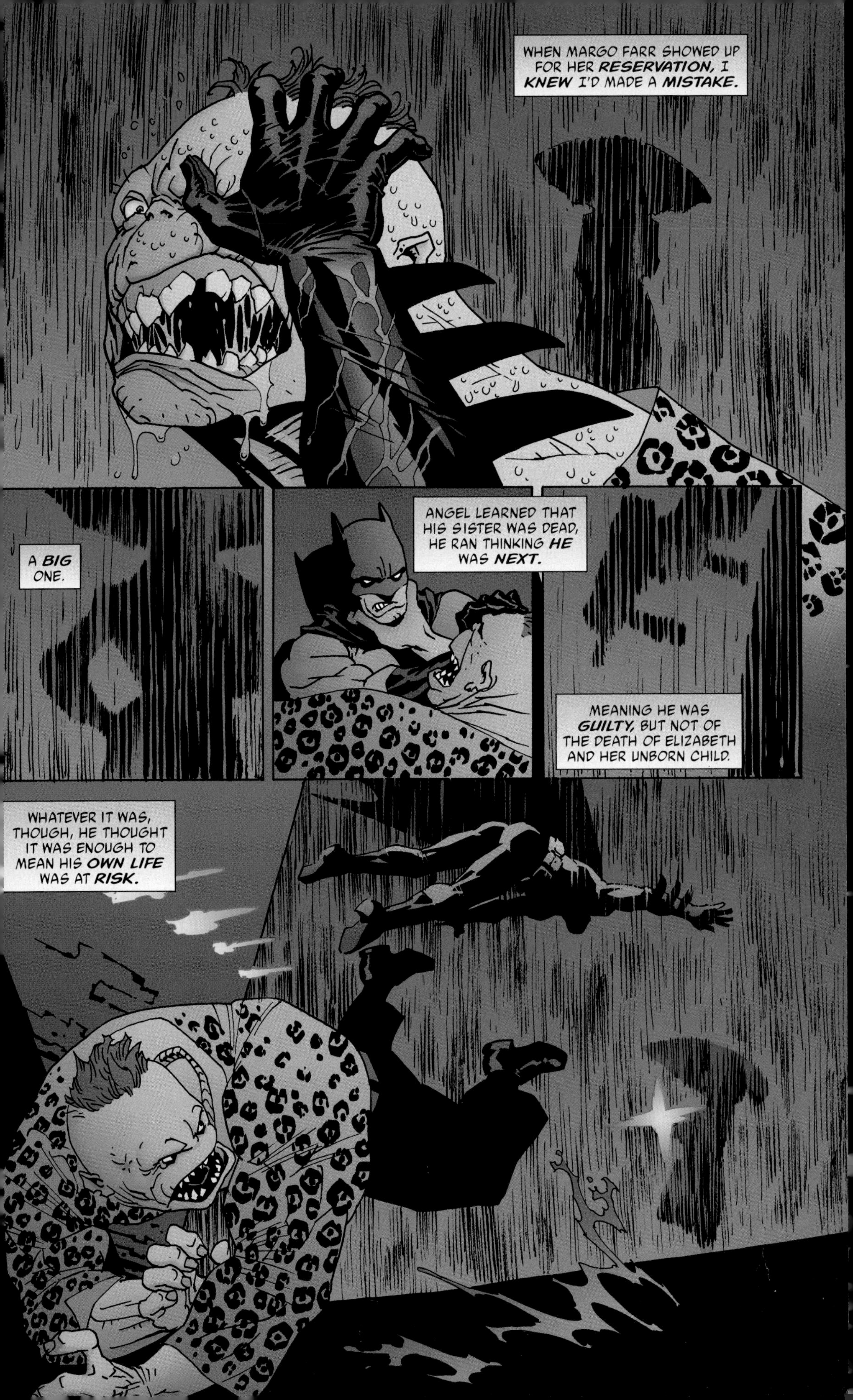
WHEN MARGO FARR SHOWED UP FOR HER **RESERVATION**, I **KNEW** I'D MADE A **MISTAKE**.
A **BIG** ONE.
ANGEL LEARNED THAT HIS SISTER WAS DEAD, HE RAN THINKING **HE** WAS **NEXT**.
MEANING HE WAS **GUILTY**, BUT NOT OF THE DEATH OF ELIZABETH AND HER UNBORN CHILD.
WHATEVER IT WAS, THOUGH, HE THOUGHT IT WAS ENOUGH TO MEAN HIS **OWN LIFE** WAS AT **RISK**.

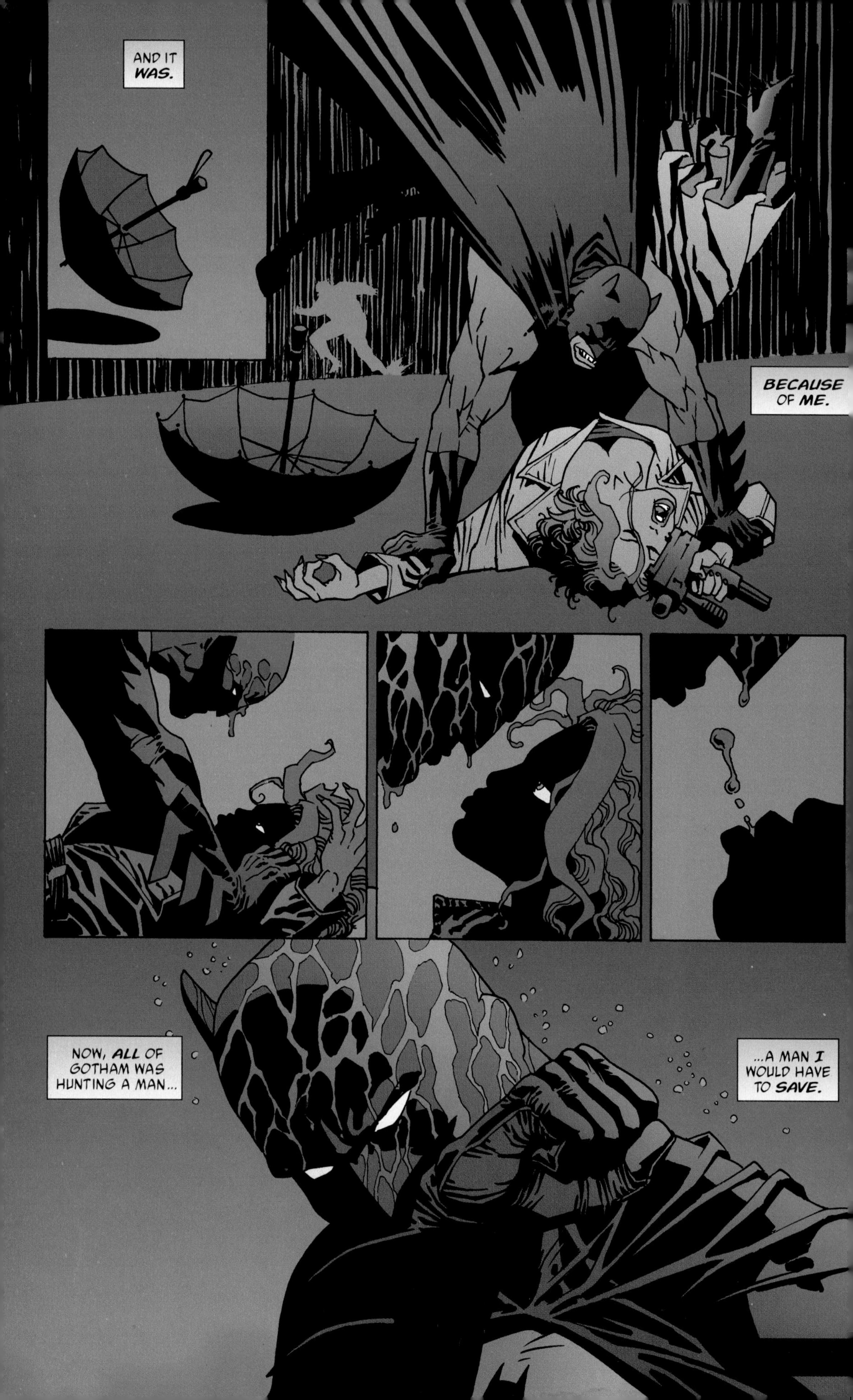
AND IT **WAS.**
BECAUSE* OF *ME.
NOW, ***ALL*** OF GOTHAM WAS HUNTING A MAN...
...A MAN ***I*** WOULD HAVE TO ***SAVE.***

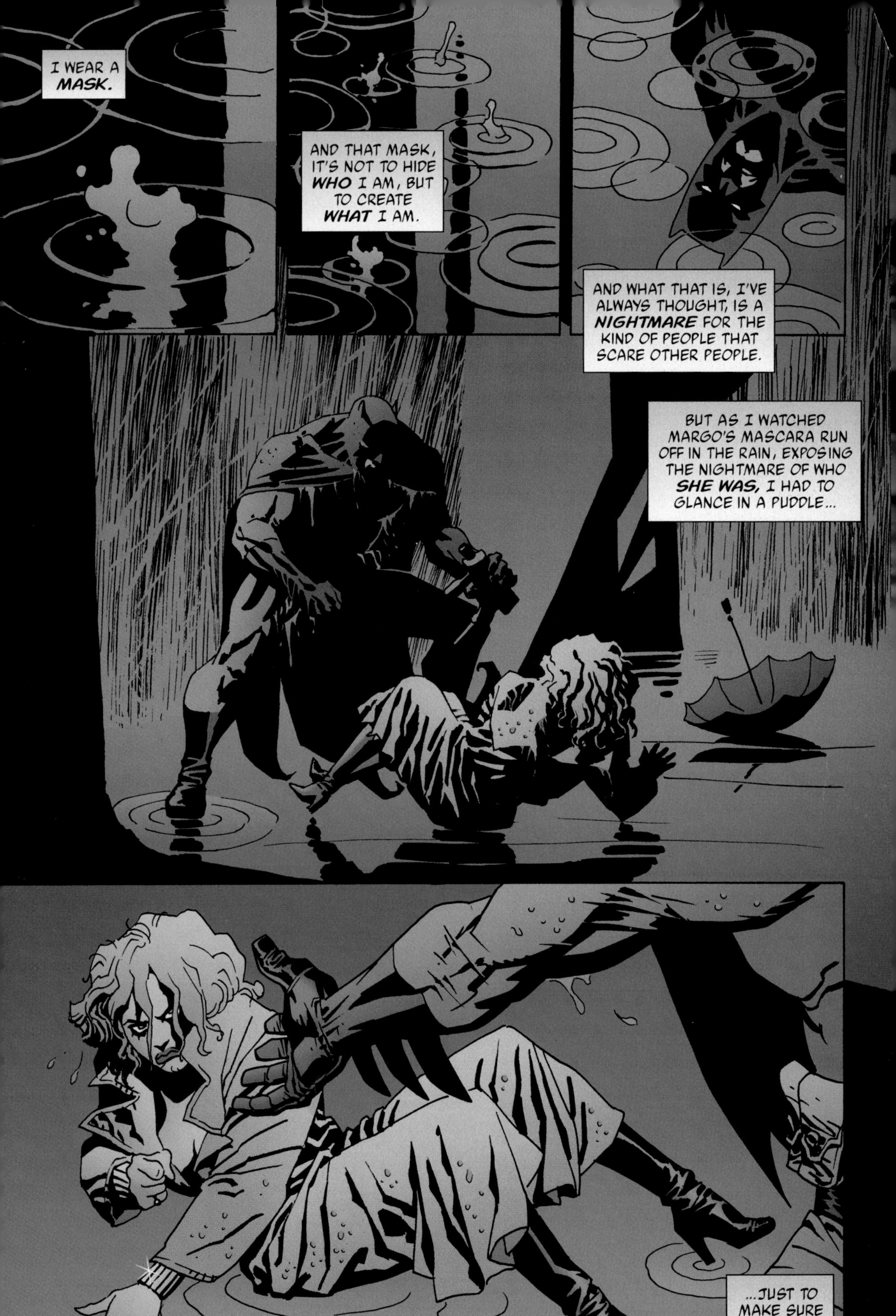
I WEAR A **MASK.**
AND THAT MASK, IT'S NOT TO HIDE **WHO** I AM, BUT TO CREATE **WHAT** I AM.
AND WHAT THAT IS, I'VE ALWAYS THOUGHT, IS A **NIGHTMARE** FOR THE KIND OF PEOPLE THAT SCARE OTHER PEOPLE.
BUT AS I WATCHED MARGO'S MASCARA RUN OFF IN THE RAIN, EXPOSING THE NIGHTMARE OF WHO **SHE WAS,** I HAD TO GLANCE IN A PUDDLE...
...JUST TO MAKE SURE WHAT **I AM** WAS STILL THERE.

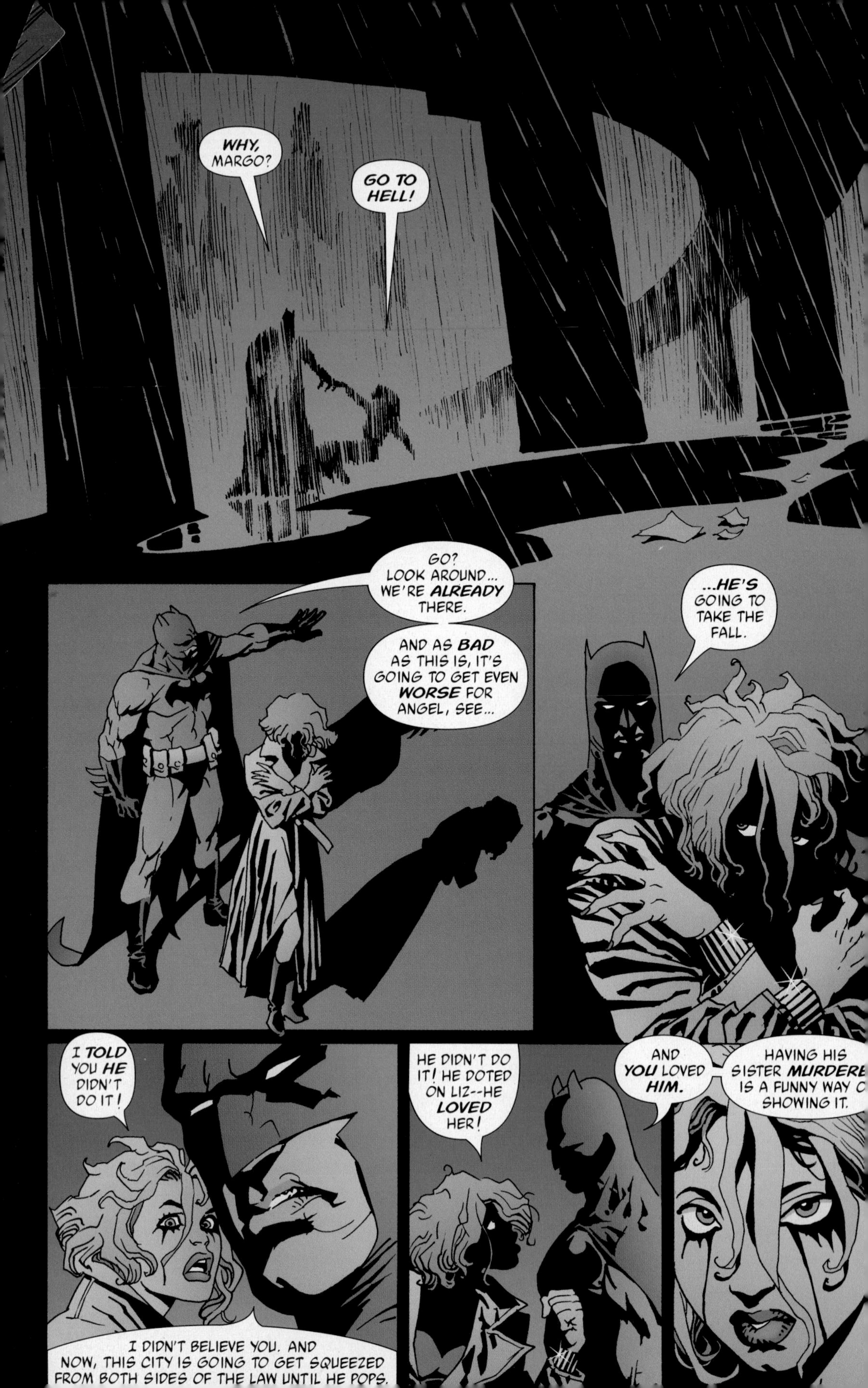
WHY, MARGO?
GO TO HELL!
GO? LOOK AROUND... WE'RE ALREADY THERE.
AND AS BAD AS THIS IS, IT'S GOING TO GET EVEN WORSE FOR ANGEL, SEE...
...HE'S GOING TO TAKE THE FALL.
I TOLD YOU HE DIDN'T DO IT!
I DIDN'T BELIEVE YOU. AND NOW, THIS CITY IS GOING TO GET SQUEEZED FROM BOTH SIDES OF THE LAW UNTIL HE POPS.
HE DIDN'T DO IT! HE DOTED ON LIZ--HE LOVED HER!
AND YOU LOVED HIM.
HAVING HIS SISTER MURDERE IS A FUNNY WAY C SHOWING IT.

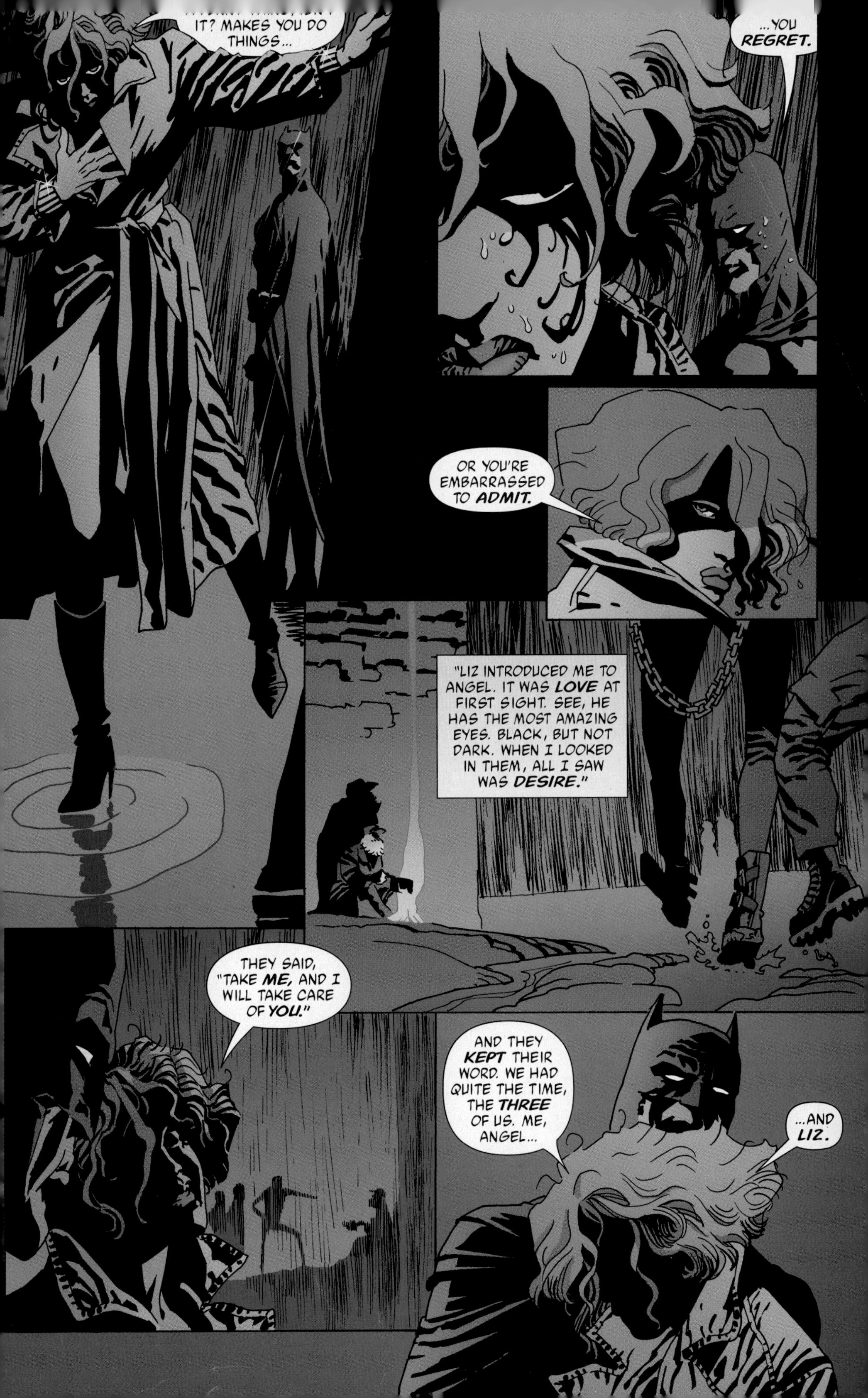

IT? MAKES YOU DO THINGS...
...YOU *REGRET.*
OR YOU'RE EMBARRASSED TO *ADMIT.*
"LIZ INTRODUCED ME TO ANGEL. IT WAS *LOVE* AT FIRST SIGHT. SEE, HE HAS THE MOST AMAZING EYES. BLACK, BUT NOT DARK. WHEN I LOOKED IN THEM, ALL I SAW WAS *DESIRE.*"
THEY SAID, "TAKE *ME,* AND I WILL TAKE CARE OF *YOU.*"
AND THEY *KEPT* THEIR WORD. WE HAD QUITE THE TIME, THE *THREE* OF US. ME, ANGEL...
...AND *LIZ.*

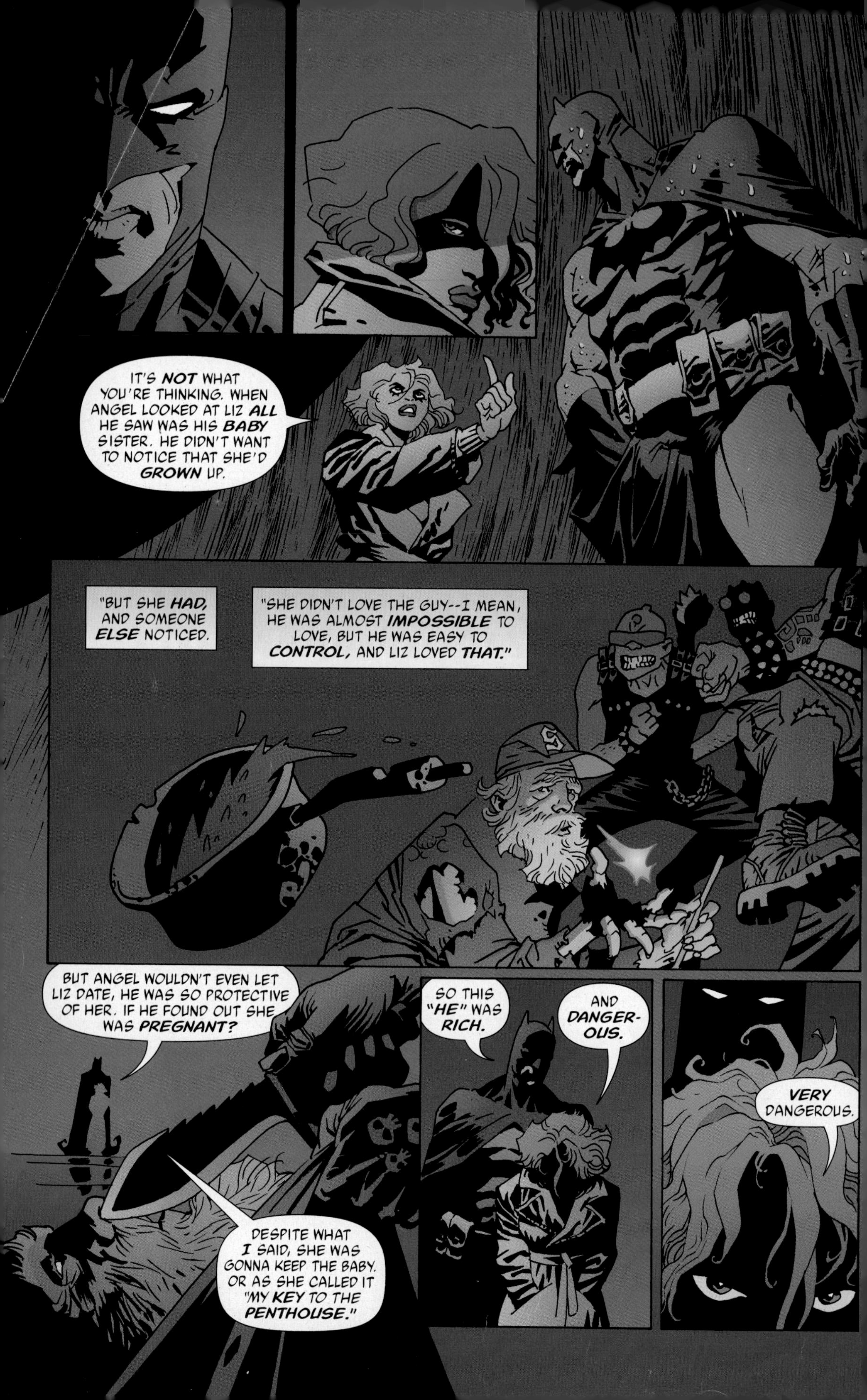

IT'S **NOT** WHAT YOU'RE THINKING. WHEN ANGEL LOOKED AT LIZ **ALL** HE SAW WAS HIS **BABY** SISTER. HE DIDN'T WANT TO NOTICE THAT SHE'D **GROWN** UP.
"BUT SHE **HAD,** AND SOMEONE **ELSE** NOTICED.
"SHE DIDN'T LOVE THE GUY--I MEAN, HE WAS ALMOST **IMPOSSIBLE** TO LOVE, BUT HE WAS EASY TO **CONTROL,** AND LIZ LOVED **THAT.**"
BUT ANGEL WOULDN'T EVEN LET LIZ DATE, HE WAS SO PROTECTIVE OF HER. IF HE FOUND OUT SHE WAS **PREGNANT?**
DESPITE WHAT **I** SAID, SHE WAS GONNA KEEP THE BABY. OR AS SHE CALLED IT "MY **KEY** TO THE **PENTHOUSE.**"
SO THIS "**HE**" WAS **RICH.**
AND **DANGER-OUS.**
VERY DANGEROUS.

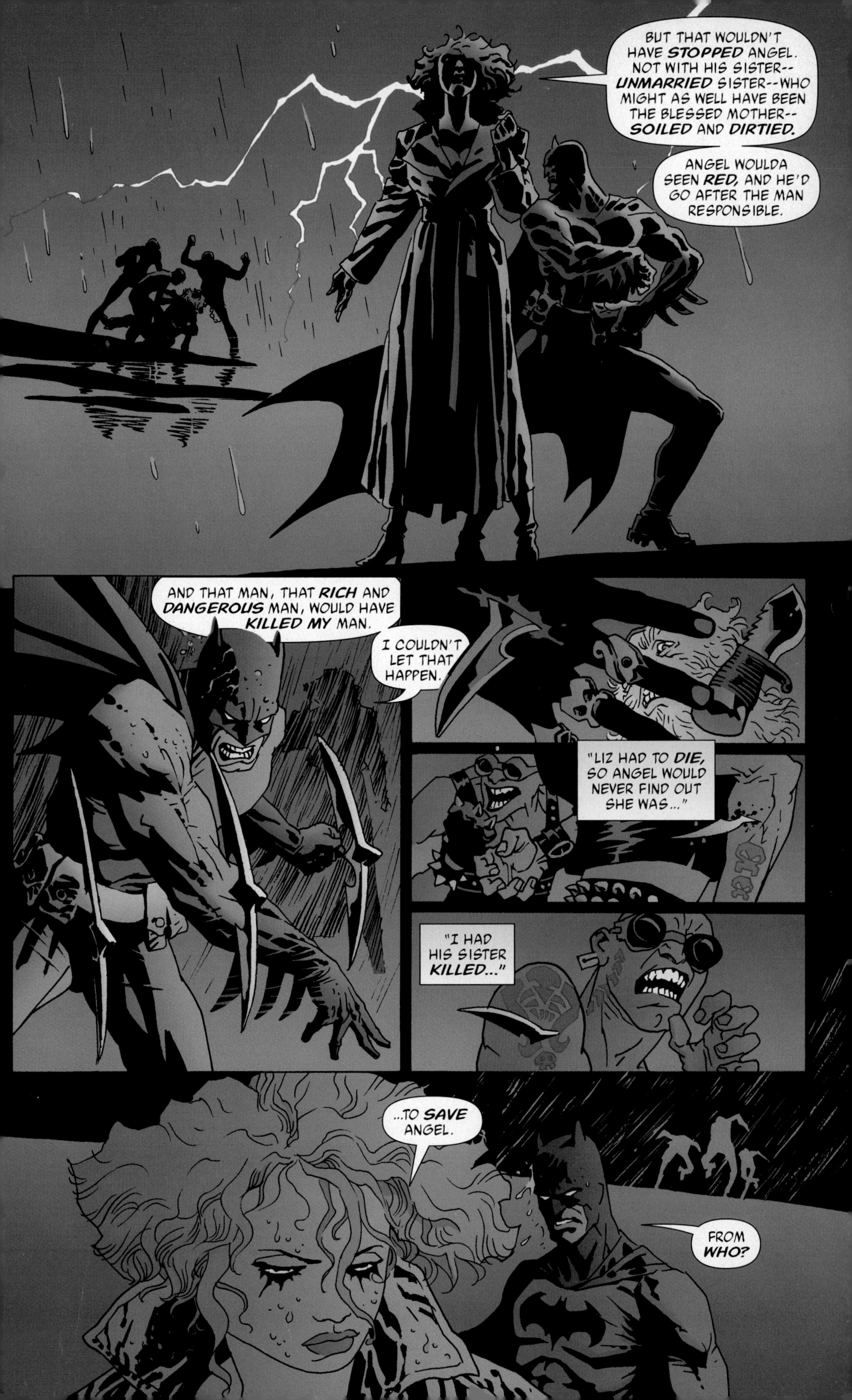
BUT THAT WOULDN'T HAVE **STOPPED** ANGEL. NOT WITH HIS SISTER-- **UNMARRIED** SISTER--WHO MIGHT AS WELL HAVE BEEN THE BLESSED MOTHER-- **SOILED** AND **DIRTIED.**
ANGEL WOULDA SEEN **RED,** AND HE'D GO AFTER THE MAN RESPONSIBLE.
AND THAT MAN, THAT **RICH** AND **DANGEROUS** MAN, WOULD HAVE **KILLED MY** MAN.
I COULDN'T LET THAT HAPPEN.
"LIZ HAD TO **DIE,** SO ANGEL WOULD NEVER FIND OUT SHE WAS..."
"I HAD HIS SISTER **KILLED...**"
...TO **SAVE** ANGEL.
FROM **WHO?**

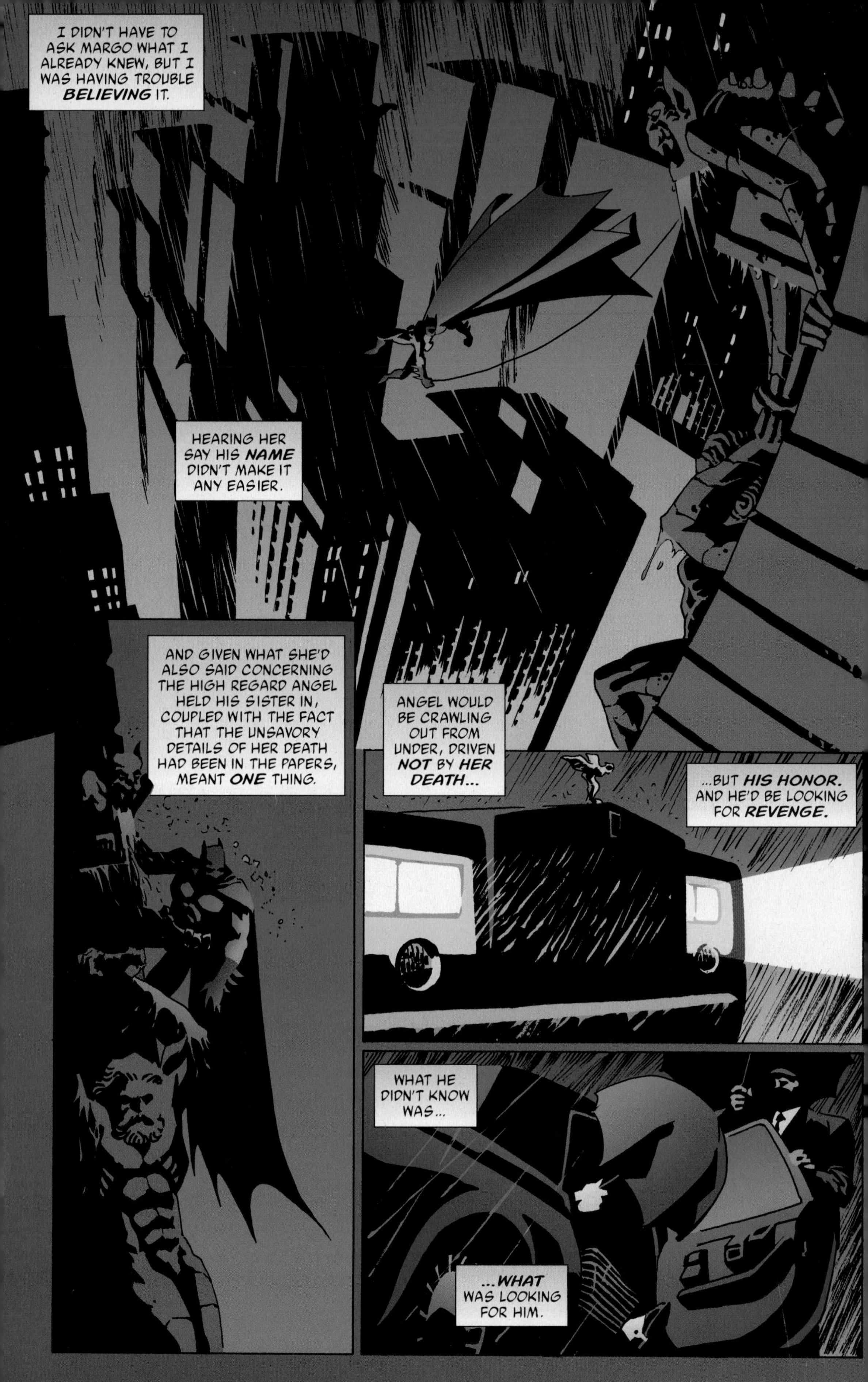
I DIDN'T HAVE TO ASK MARGO WHAT I ALREADY KNEW, BUT I WAS HAVING TROUBLE **BELIEVING** IT.
HEARING HER SAY HIS **NAME** DIDN'T MAKE IT ANY EASIER.
AND GIVEN WHAT SHE'D ALSO SAID CONCERNING THE HIGH REGARD ANGEL HELD HIS SISTER IN, COUPLED WITH THE FACT THAT THE UNSAVORY DETAILS OF HER DEATH HAD BEEN IN THE PAPERS, MEANT **ONE** THING.
ANGEL WOULD BE CRAWLING OUT FROM UNDER, DRIVEN **NOT** BY **HER DEATH...**
...BUT **HIS HONOR.** AND HE'D BE LOOKING FOR **REVENGE.**
WHAT HE DIDN'T KNOW WAS...
...WHAT WAS LOOKING FOR HIM.

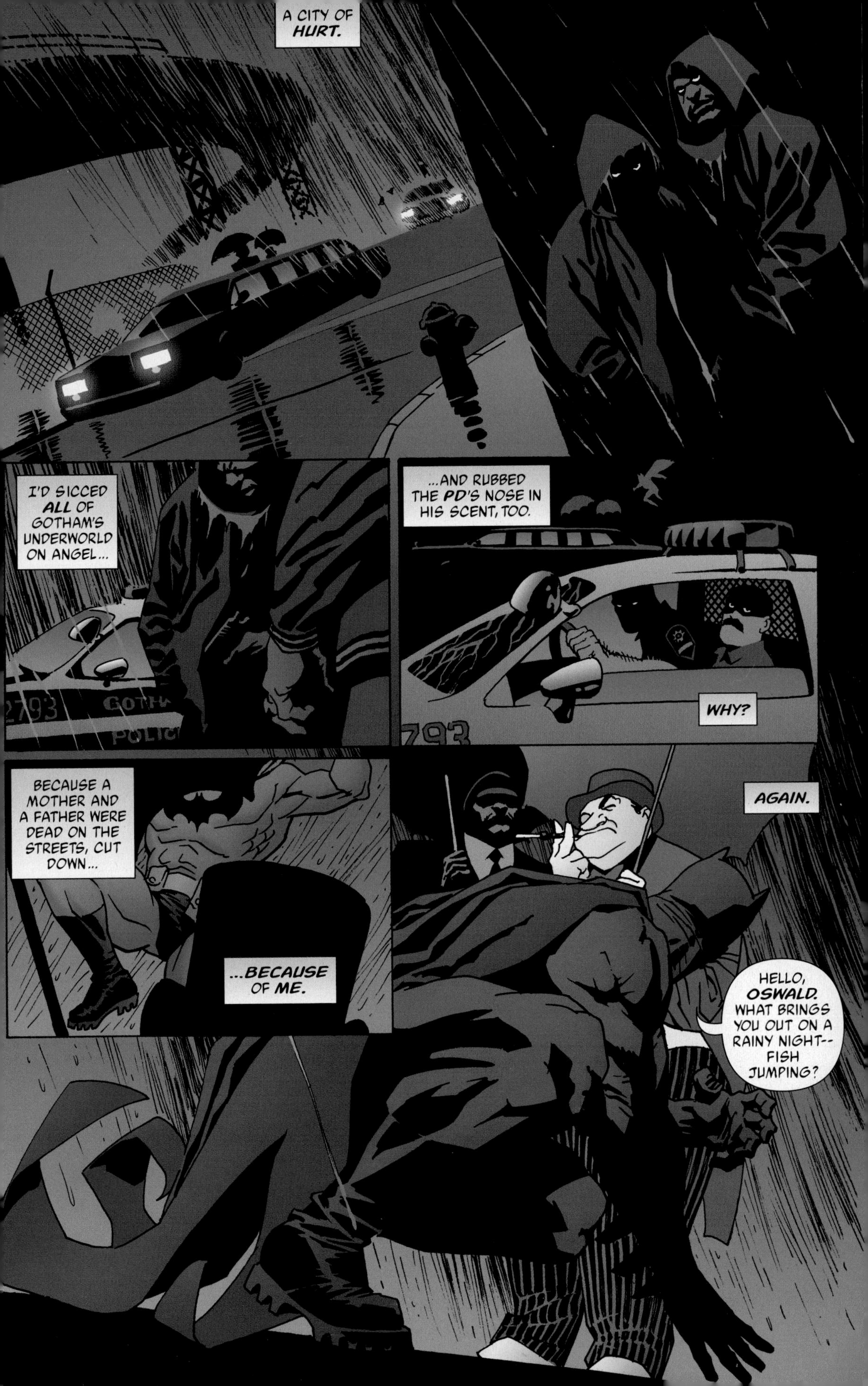
A CITY OF HURT.
I'D SICCED ALL OF GOTHAM'S UNDERWORLD ON ANGEL...
...AND RUBBED THE PD'S NOSE IN HIS SCENT, TOO.
WHY?
BECAUSE A MOTHER AND A FATHER WERE DEAD ON THE STREETS, CUT DOWN...
...BECAUSE OF ME.
AGAIN.
HELLO, OSWALD. WHAT BRINGS YOU OUT ON A RAINY NIGHT--FISH JUMPING?

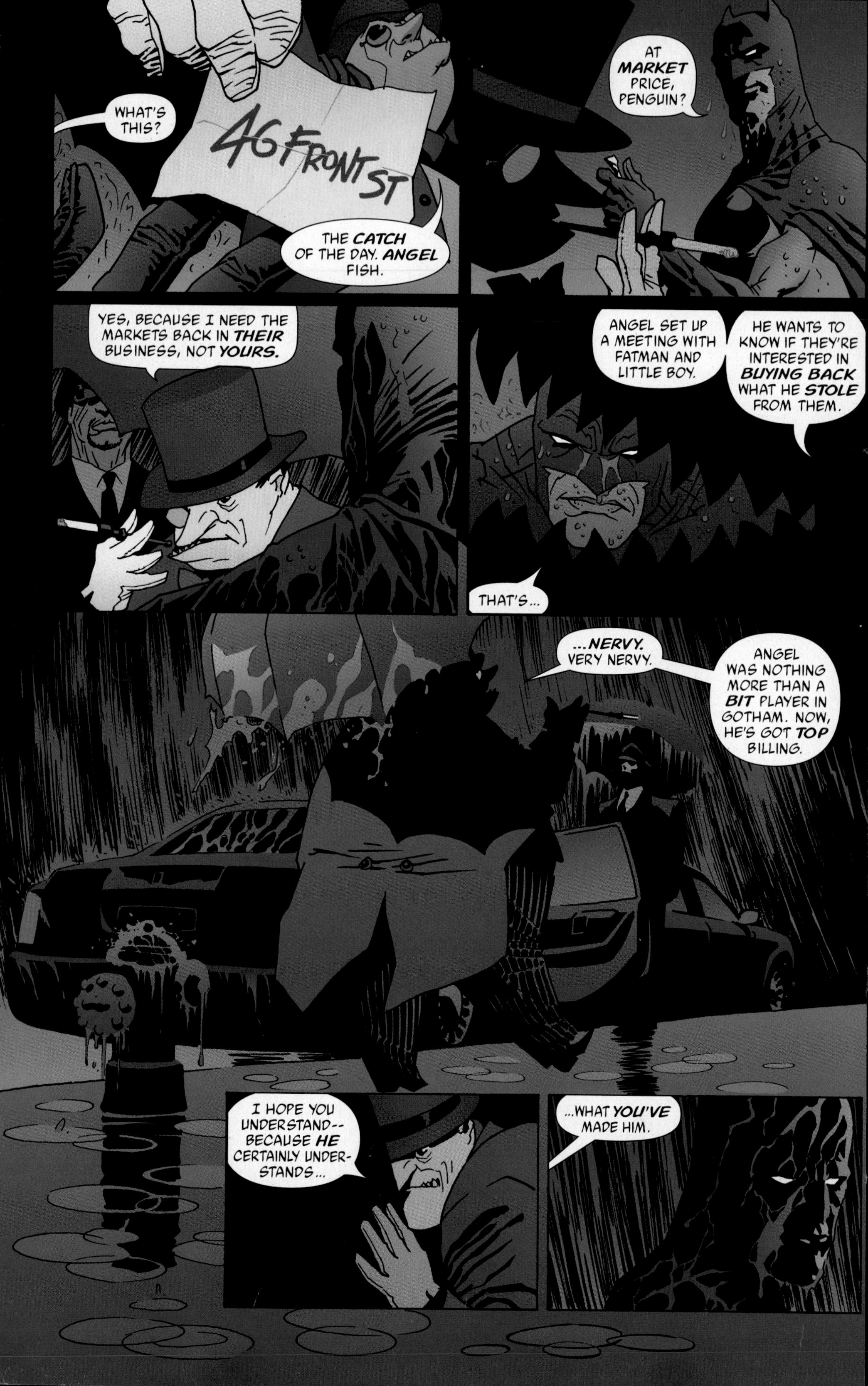
WHAT'S THIS?
46 FRONT ST
THE **CATCH** OF THE DAY. **ANGEL** FISH.
AT **MARKET** PRICE, PENGUIN?
YES, BECAUSE I NEED THE MARKETS BACK IN **THEIR** BUSINESS, NOT **YOURS.**
ANGEL SET UP A MEETING WITH FATMAN AND LITTLE BOY.
HE WANTS TO KNOW IF THEY'RE INTERESTED IN **BUYING BACK** WHAT HE **STOLE** FROM THEM.
THAT'S...
...NERVY. VERY NERVY.
ANGEL WAS NOTHING MORE THAN A **BIT** PLAYER IN GOTHAM. NOW, HE'S GOT **TOP** BILLING.
I HOPE YOU UNDERSTAND-- BECAUSE **HE** CERTAINLY UNDERSTANDS...
...WHAT **YOU'VE** MADE HIM.

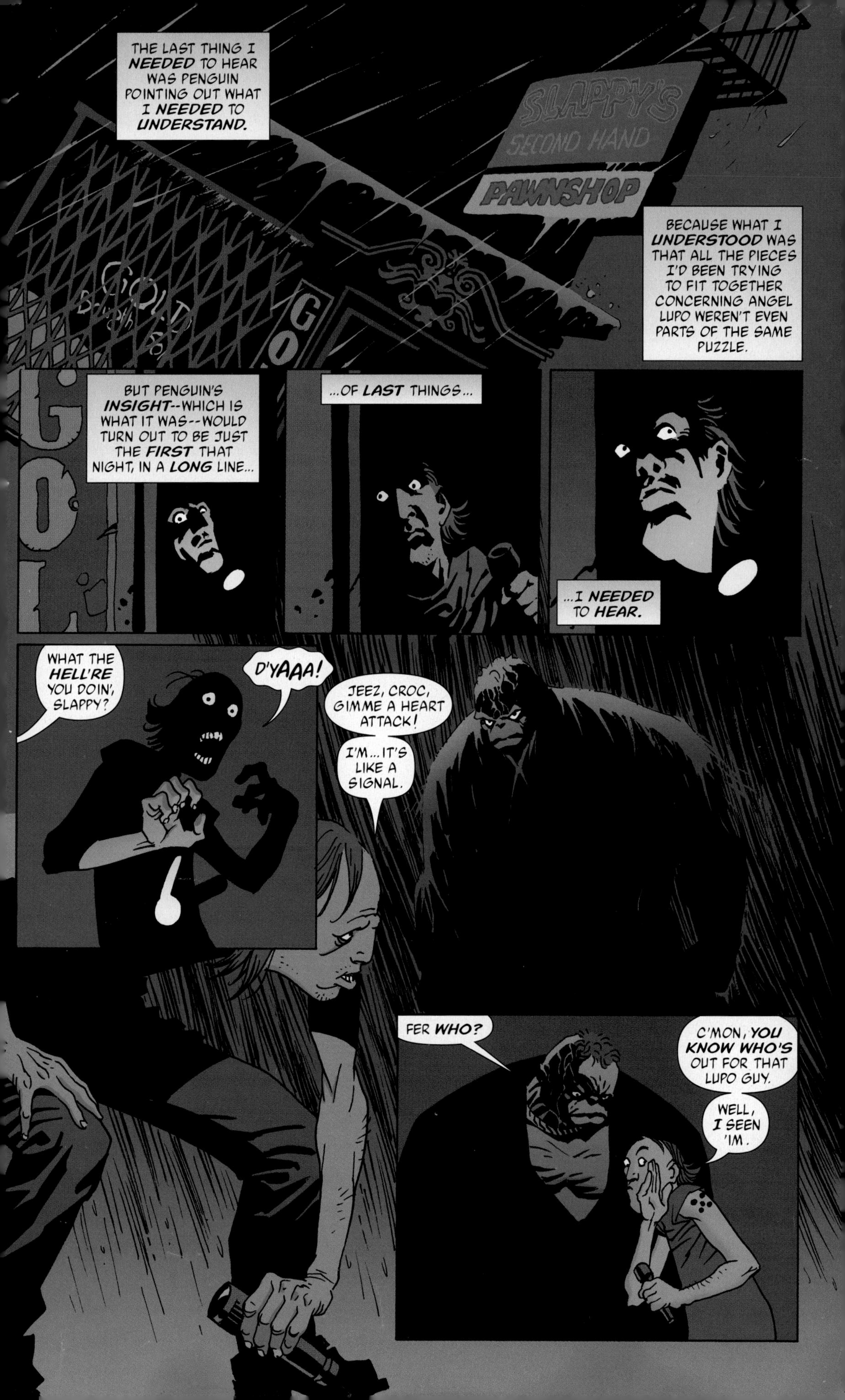
THE LAST THING I NEEDED TO HEAR WAS PENGUIN POINTING OUT WHAT I NEEDED TO UNDERSTAND.
SLAPPY'S SECOND HAND
PAWNSHOP
BECAUSE WHAT I UNDERSTOOD WAS THAT ALL THE PIECES I'D BEEN TRYING TO FIT TOGETHER CONCERNING ANGEL LUPO WEREN'T EVEN PARTS OF THE SAME PUZZLE.
BUT PENGUIN'S INSIGHT--WHICH IS WHAT IT WAS--WOULD TURN OUT TO BE JUST THE FIRST THAT NIGHT, IN A LONG LINE...
...OF LAST THINGS...
...I NEEDED TO HEAR.
WHAT THE HELL'RE YOU DOIN', SLAPPY?
D'YAAA!
JEEZ, CROC, GIMME A HEART ATTACK!
I'M... IT'S LIKE A SIGNAL.
FER WHO?
C'MON, YOU KNOW WHO'S OUT FOR THAT LUPO GUY.
WELL, I SEEN 'IM.

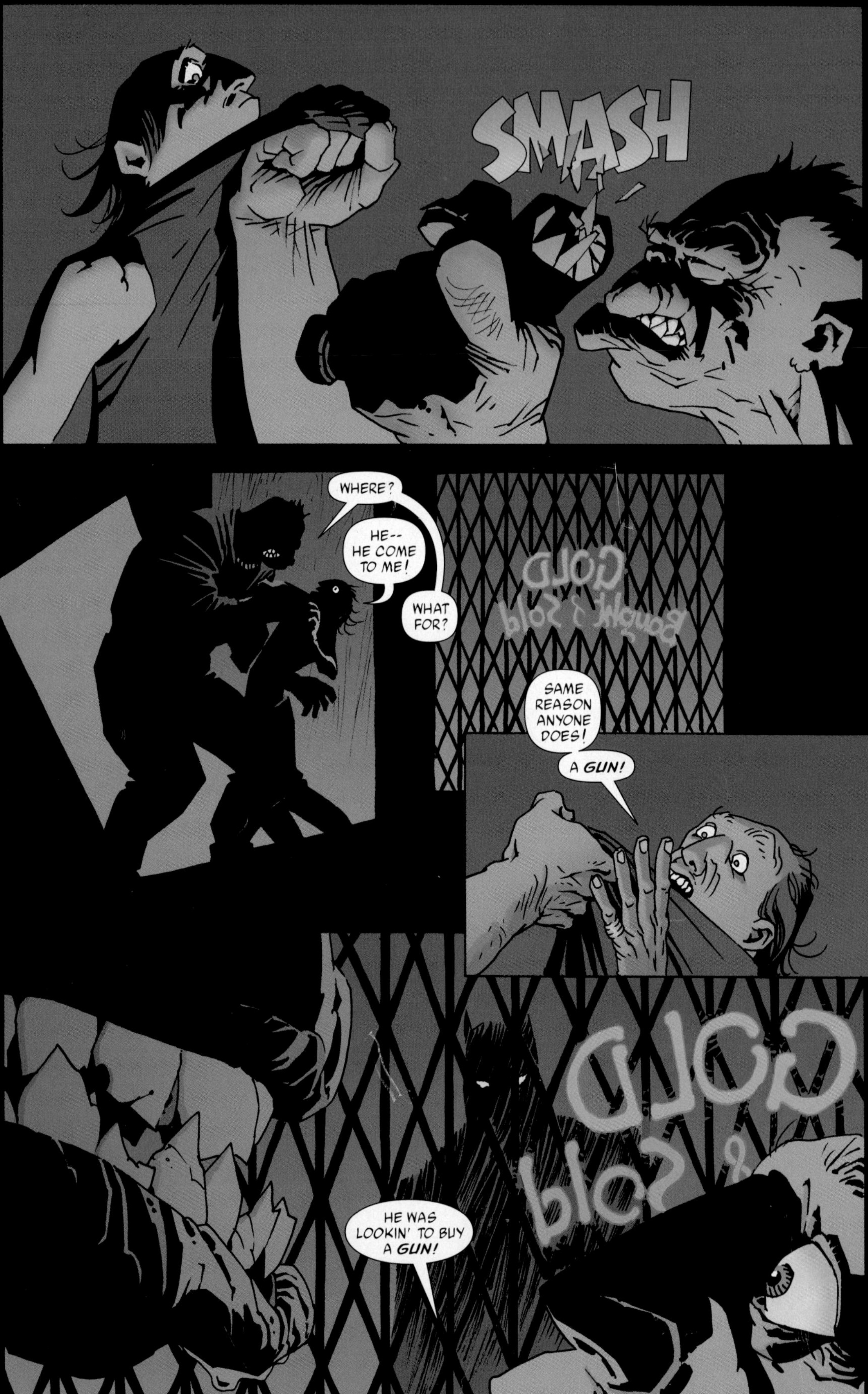
SMASH
WHERE?
HE--
HE COME
TO ME!
WHAT
FOR?
SAME
REASON
ANYONE
DOES!
A GUN!
HE WAS
LOOKIN' TO BUY
A GUN!

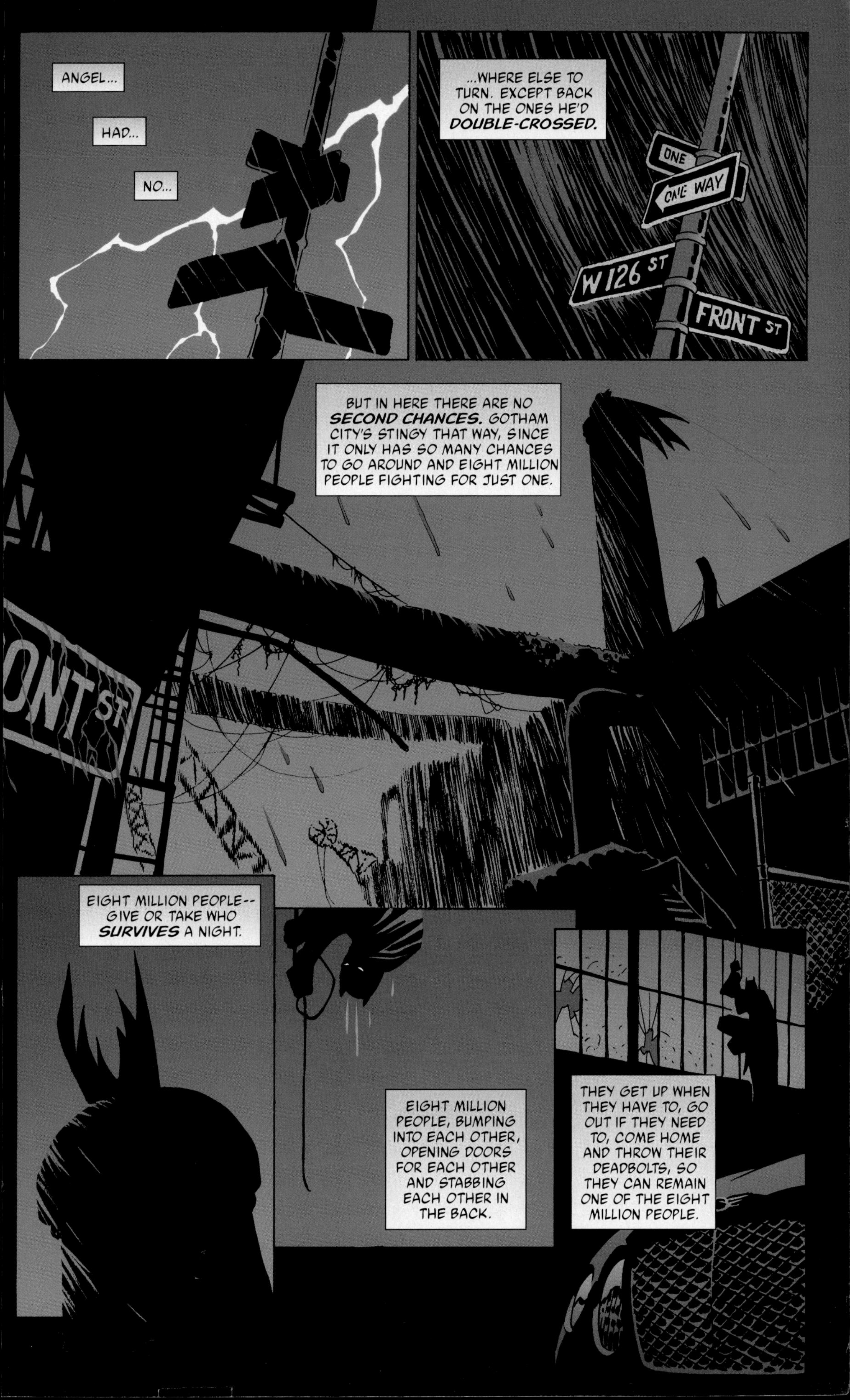
ANGEL...
HAD...
NO...
...WHERE ELSE TO TURN. EXCEPT BACK ON THE ONES HE'D DOUBLE-CROSSED.
ONE
ONE WAY
W 126 ST
FRONT ST
BUT IN HERE THERE ARE NO SECOND CHANCES. GOTHAM CITY'S STINGY THAT WAY, SINCE IT ONLY HAS SO MANY CHANCES TO GO AROUND AND EIGHT MILLION PEOPLE FIGHTING FOR JUST ONE.
EIGHT MILLION PEOPLE-- GIVE OR TAKE WHO SURVIVES A NIGHT.
EIGHT MILLION PEOPLE, BUMPING INTO EACH OTHER, OPENING DOORS FOR EACH OTHER AND STABBING EACH OTHER IN THE BACK.
THEY GET UP WHEN THEY HAVE TO, GO OUT IF THEY NEED TO, COME HOME AND THROW THEIR DEADBOLTS, SO THEY CAN REMAIN ONE OF THE EIGHT MILLION PEOPLE.

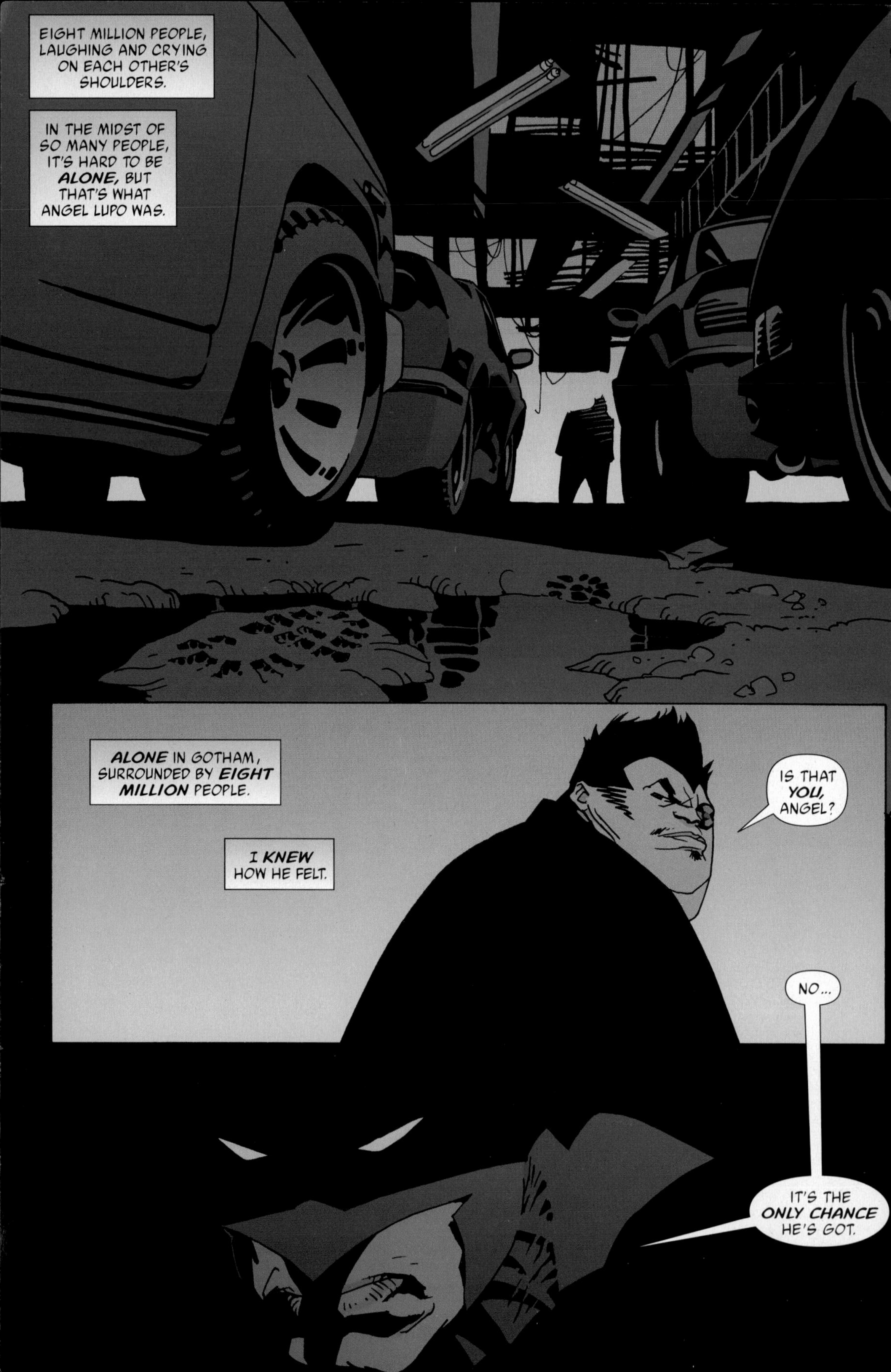
EIGHT MILLION PEOPLE, LAUGHING AND CRYING ON EACH OTHER'S SHOULDERS.
IN THE MIDST OF SO MANY PEOPLE, IT'S HARD TO BE ***ALONE,*** BUT THAT'S WHAT ANGEL LUPO WAS.
ALONE IN GOTHAM, SURROUNDED BY ***EIGHT MILLION*** PEOPLE.
IS THAT ***YOU,*** ANGEL?
I KNEW HOW HE FELT.
NO...
IT'S THE ***ONLY CHANCE*** HE'S GOT.

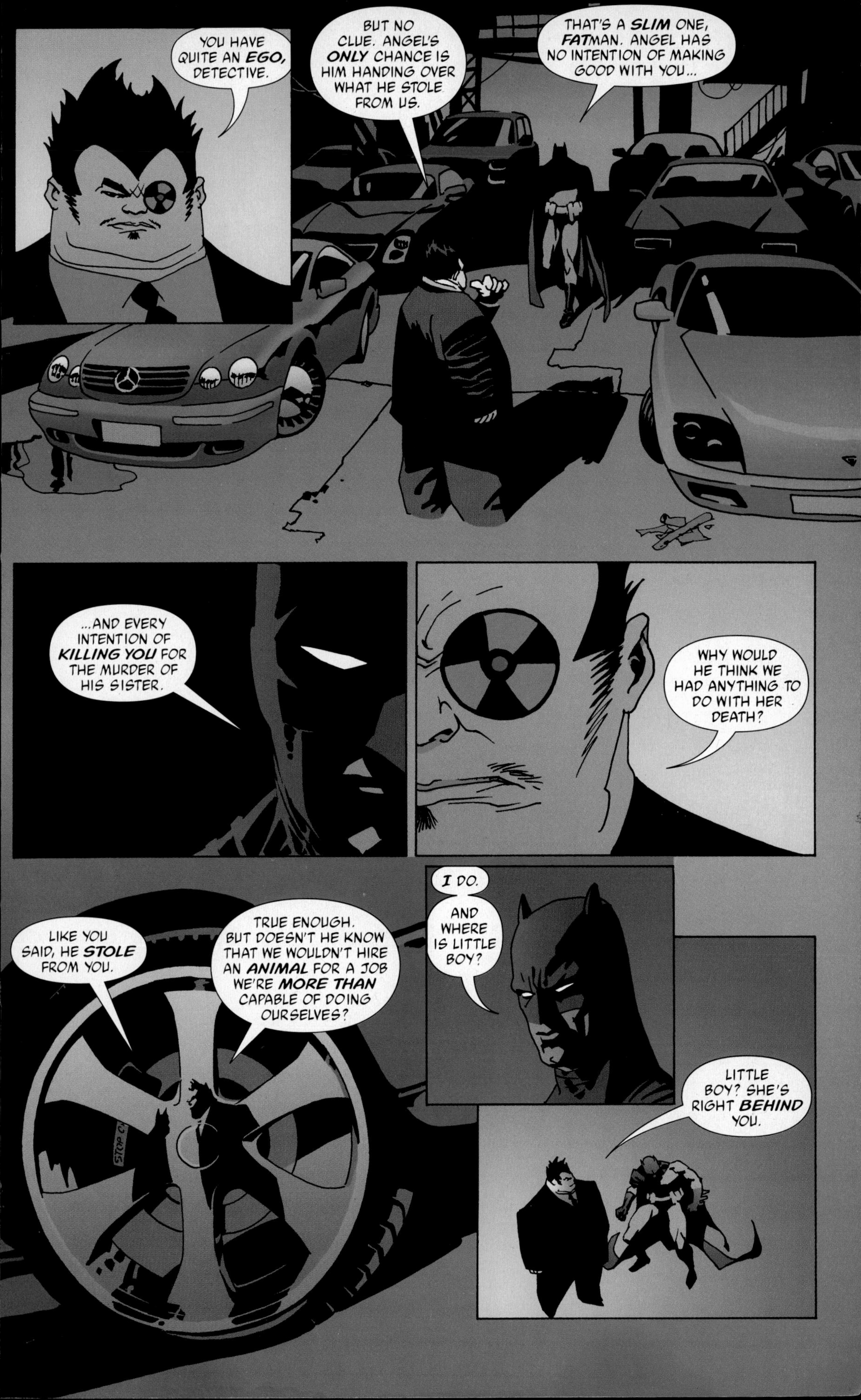
YOU HAVE QUITE AN **EGO,** DETECTIVE.
BUT NO CLUE. ANGEL'S **ONLY** CHANCE IS HIM HANDING OVER WHAT HE STOLE FROM US.
THAT'S A **SLIM** ONE, **FAT**MAN. ANGEL HAS NO INTENTION OF MAKING GOOD WITH YOU...
...AND EVERY INTENTION OF **KILLING YOU** FOR THE MURDER OF HIS SISTER.
WHY WOULD HE THINK WE HAD ANYTHING TO DO WITH HER DEATH?
LIKE YOU SAID, HE **STOLE** FROM YOU.
TRUE ENOUGH. BUT DOESN'T HE KNOW THAT WE WOULDN'T HIRE AN **ANIMAL** FOR A JOB WE'RE **MORE THAN** CAPABLE OF DOING OURSELVES?
I DO.
AND WHERE IS LITTLE BOY?
LITTLE BOY? SHE'S RIGHT **BEHIND** YOU.

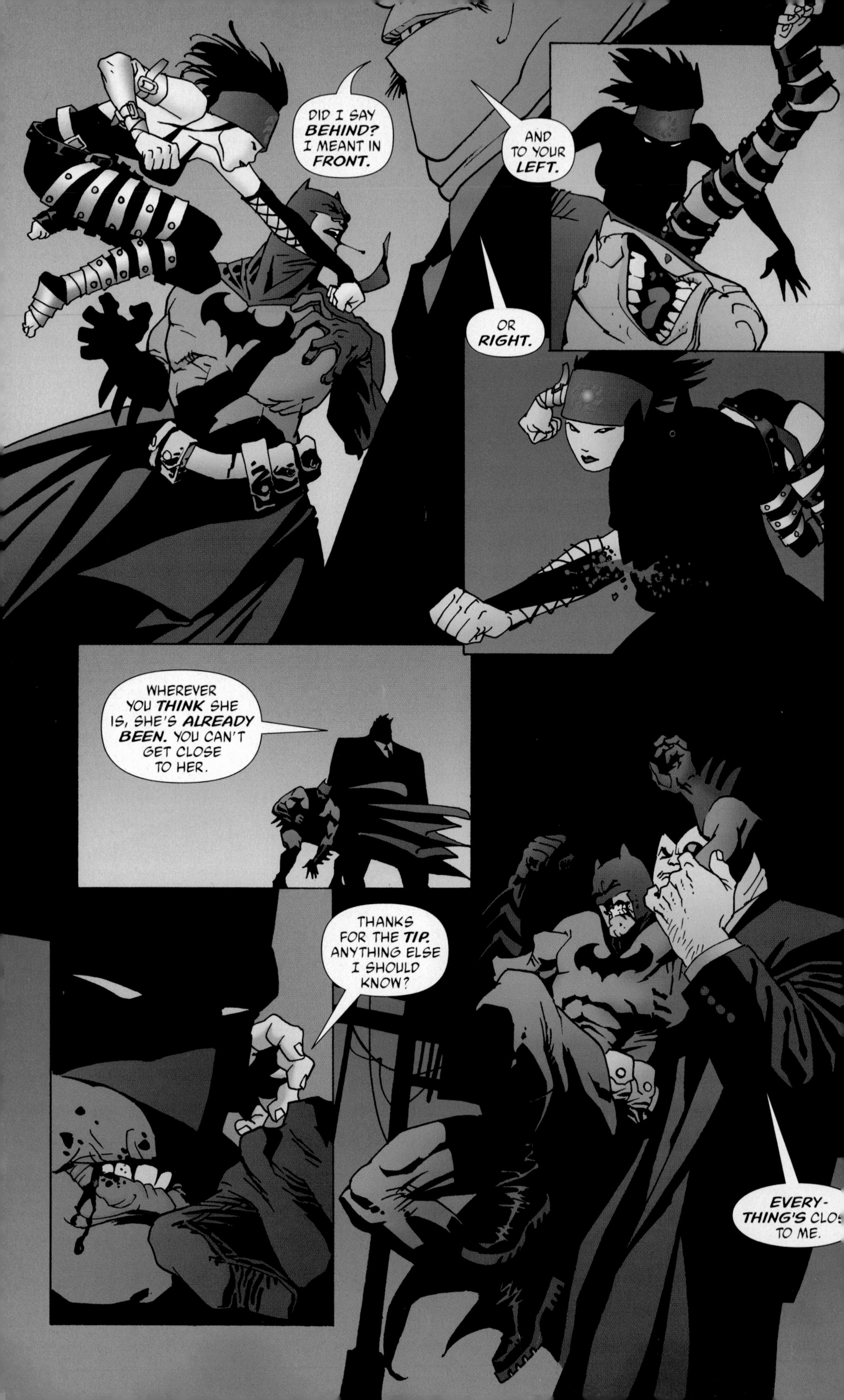

DID I SAY **BEHIND?** I MEANT IN **FRONT.**
AND TO YOUR **LEFT.**
OR **RIGHT.**
WHEREVER YOU **THINK** SHE IS, SHE'S **ALREADY BEEN.** YOU CAN'T GET CLOSE TO HER.
THANKS FOR THE **TIP.** ANYTHING ELSE I SHOULD KNOW?
EVERY-THING'S CLOS TO ME.

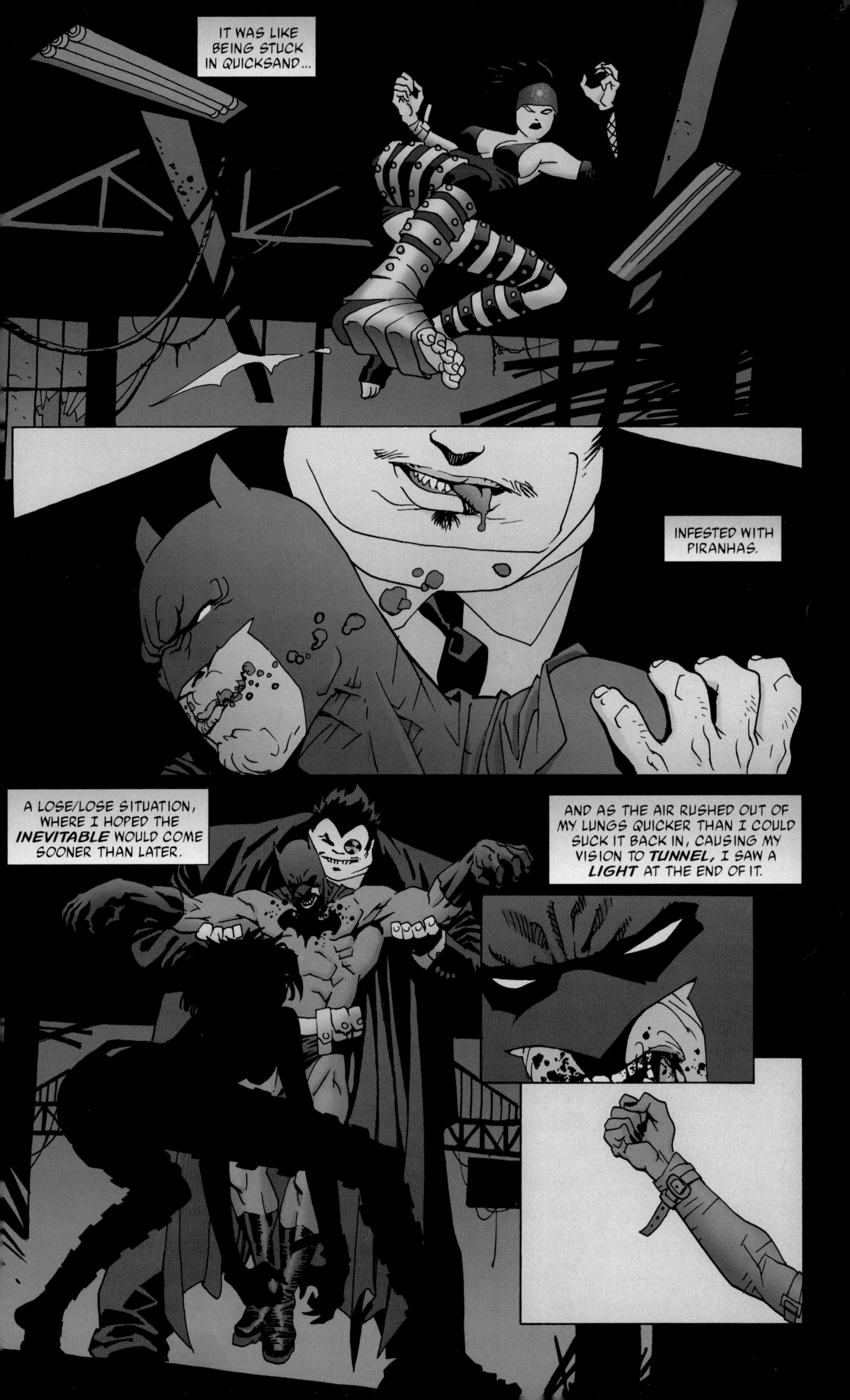
IT WAS LIKE BEING STUCK IN QUICKSAND...
INFESTED WITH PIRANHAS.
A LOSE/LOSE SITUATION, WHERE I HOPED THE ***INEVITABLE*** WOULD COME SOONER THAN LATER.
AND AS THE AIR RUSHED OUT OF MY LUNGS QUICKER THAN I COULD SUCK IT BACK IN, CAUSING MY VISION TO ***TUNNEL,*** I SAW A ***LIGHT*** AT THE END OF IT.

LITTLE BOY WASN'T *FAST*...
SHE WAS *AHEAD* OF ME. AND AS THOSE PIRANHAS BIT...
AND BIT...
AND BIT...
I DIDN'T PAY ATTENTION TO ANY *MOUTH*...
...BECAUSE I WAS LOOKING FOR A *TAIL*.

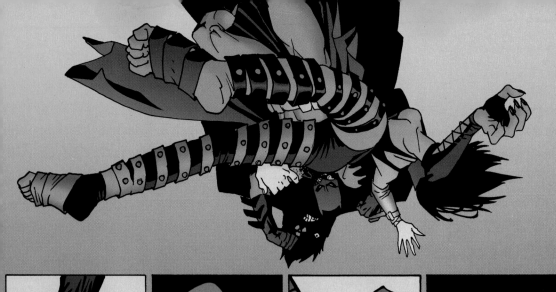

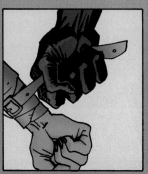

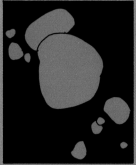

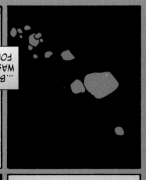

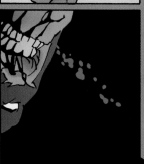

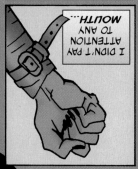

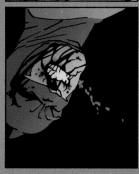

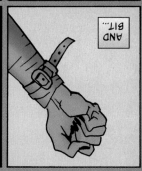

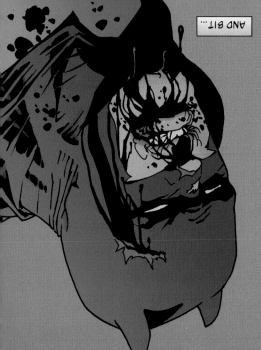

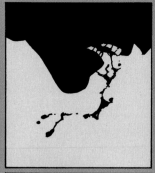

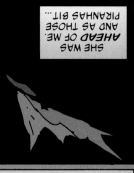

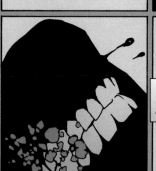

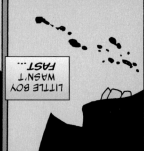

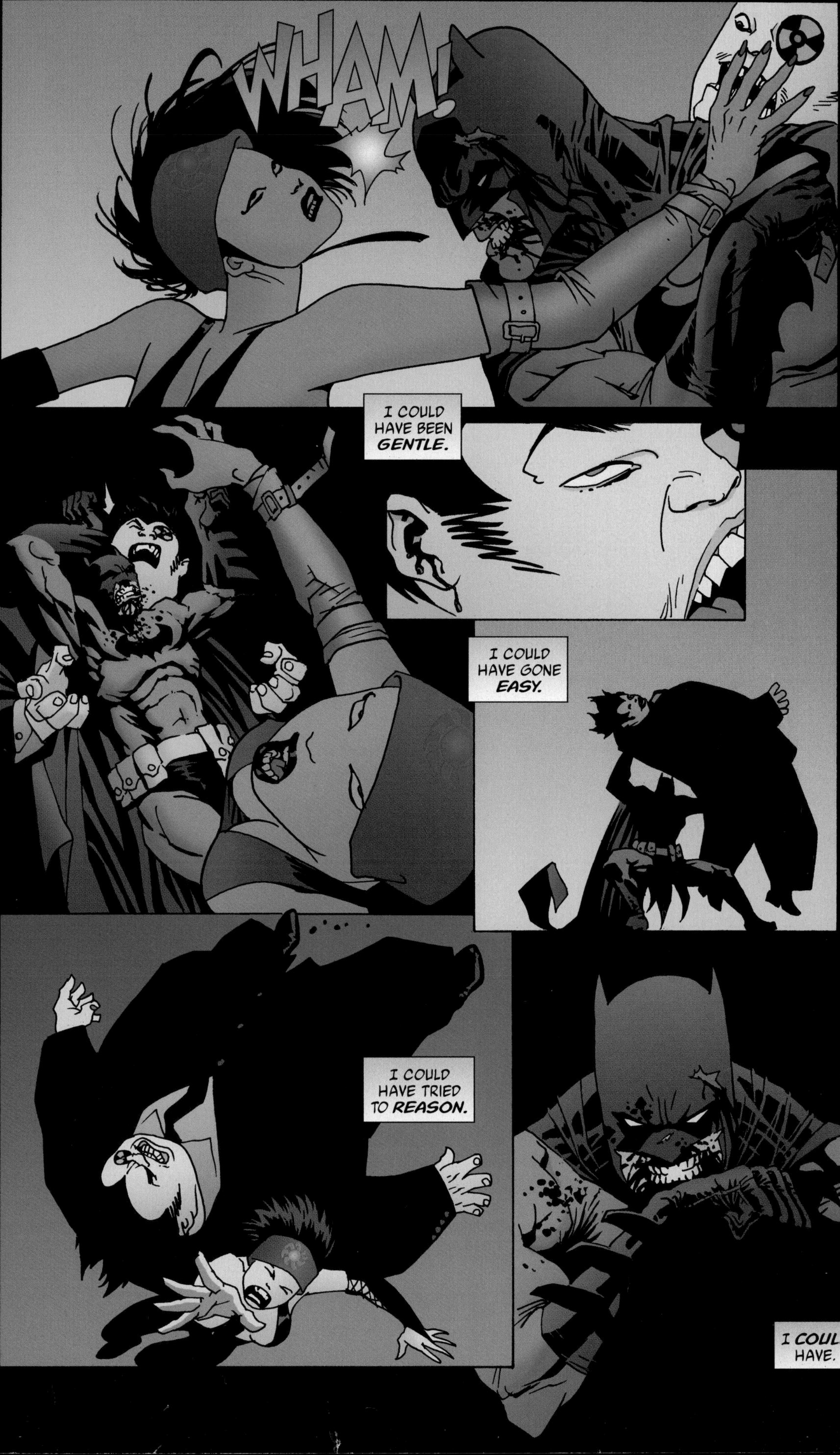
WHAM!
I COULD HAVE BEEN GENTLE.
I COULD HAVE GONE EASY.
I COULD HAVE TRIED TO REASON.
I COULD HAVE.

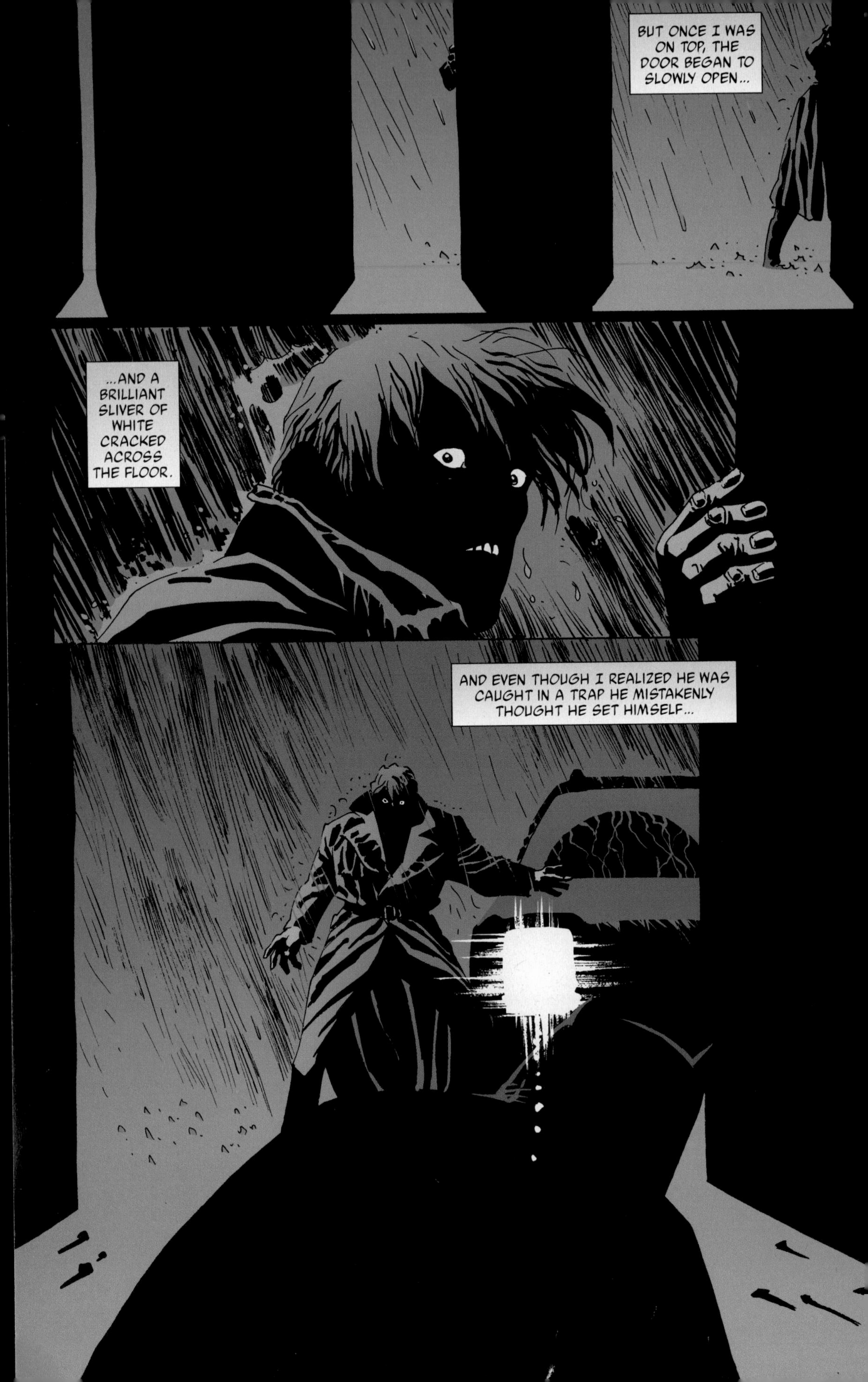
BUT ONCE I WAS ON TOP, THE DOOR BEGAN TO SLOWLY OPEN...
...AND A BRILLIANT SLIVER OF WHITE CRACKED ACROSS THE FLOOR.
AND EVEN THOUGH I REALIZED HE WAS CAUGHT IN A TRAP HE MISTAKENLY THOUGHT HE SET HIMSELF...

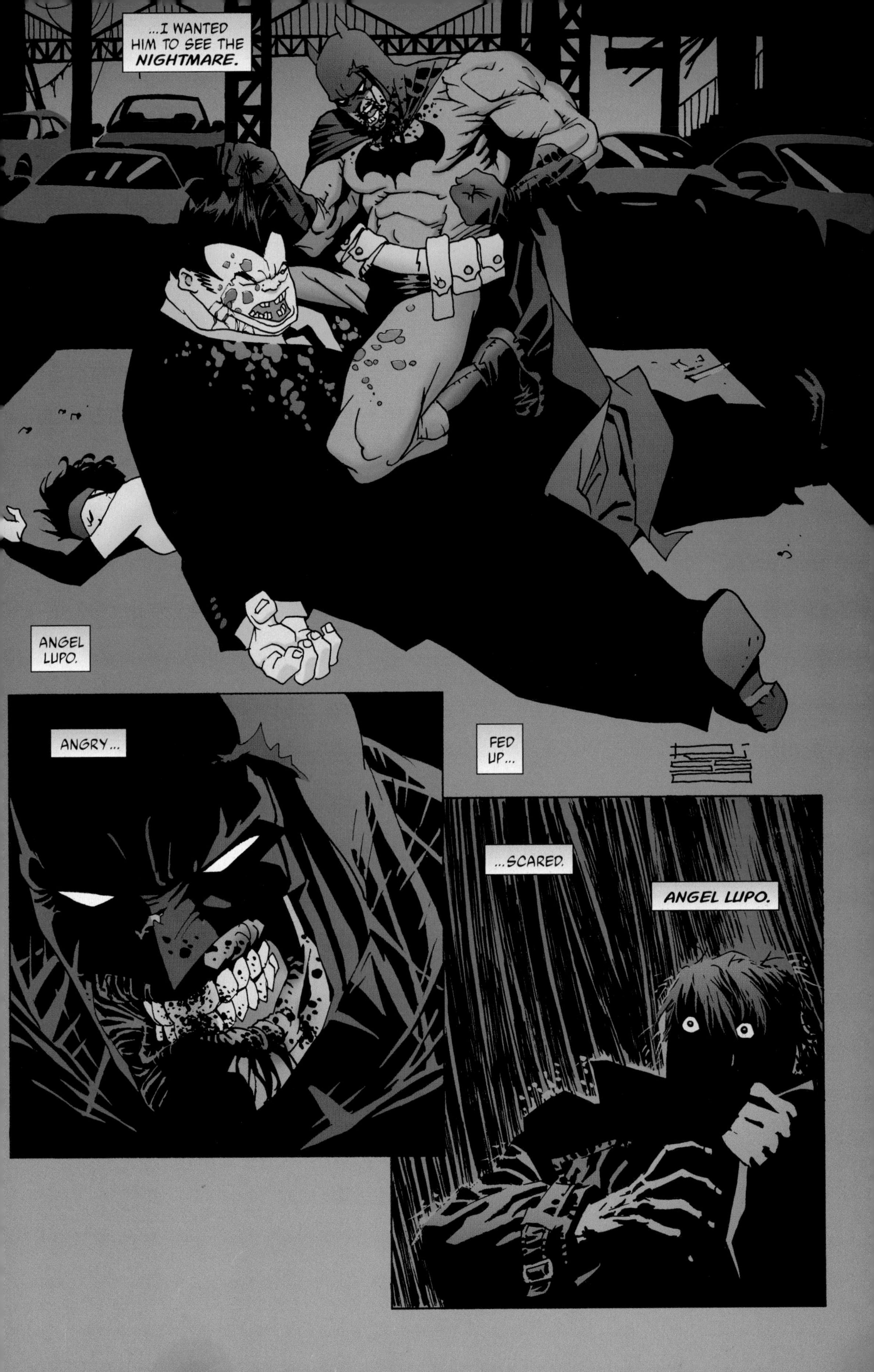
...I WANTED HIM TO SEE THE NIGHTMARE.
ANGEL LUPO.
ANGRY...
FED UP...
...SCARED.
ANGEL LUPO.

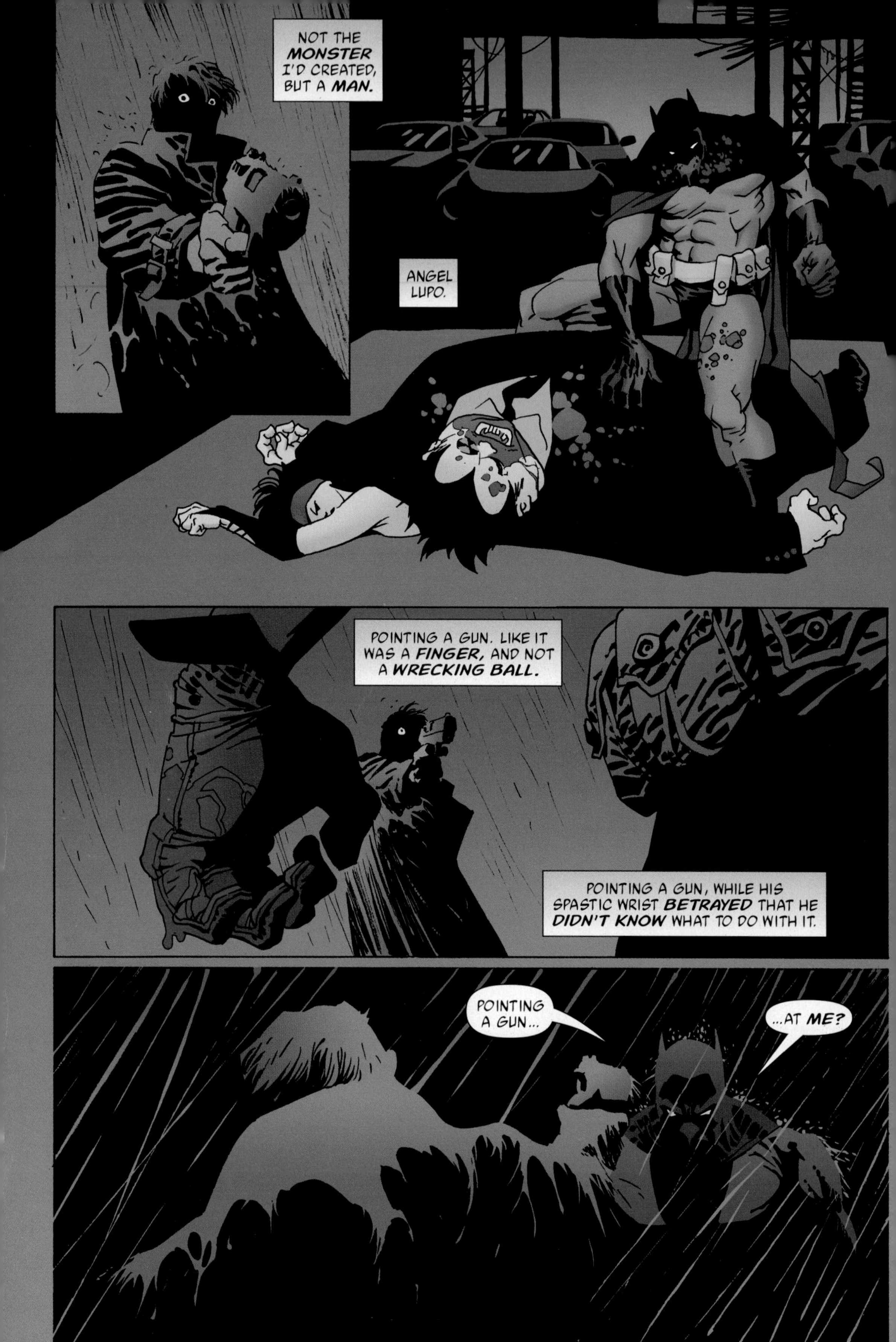
NOT THE **MONSTER** I'D CREATED, BUT A **MAN.**
ANGEL LUPO.
POINTING A GUN. LIKE IT WAS A **FINGER,** AND NOT A **WRECKING BALL.**
POINTING A GUN, WHILE HIS SPASTIC WRIST **BETRAYED** THAT HE **DIDN'T KNOW** WHAT TO DO WITH IT.
POINTING A GUN...
...AT **ME?**

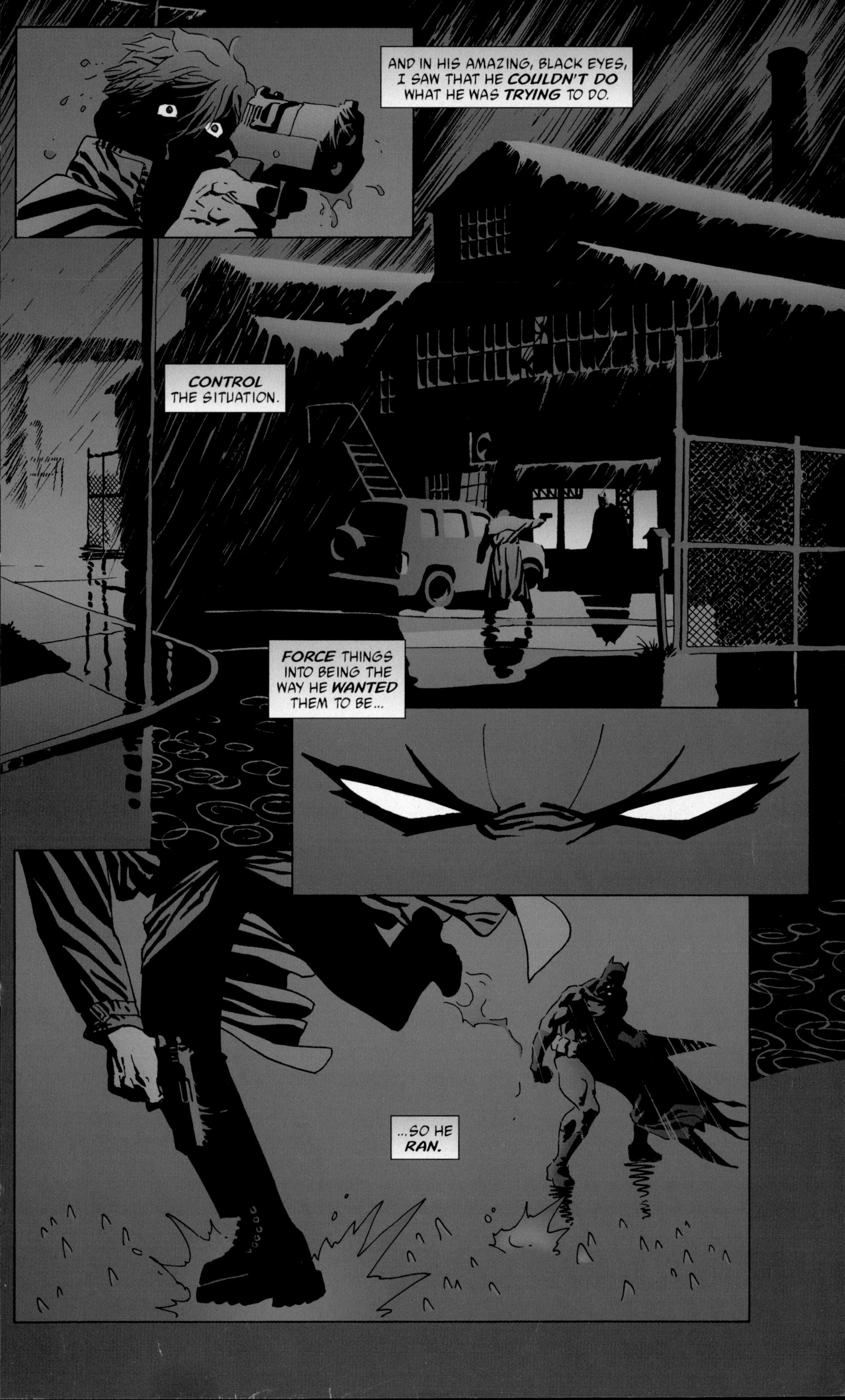
AND IN HIS AMAZING, BLACK EYES, I SAW THAT HE COULDN'T DO WHAT HE WAS TRYING TO DO.
CONTROL THE SITUATION.
FORCE THINGS INTO BEING THE WAY HE WANTED THEM TO BE...
...SO HE RAN.

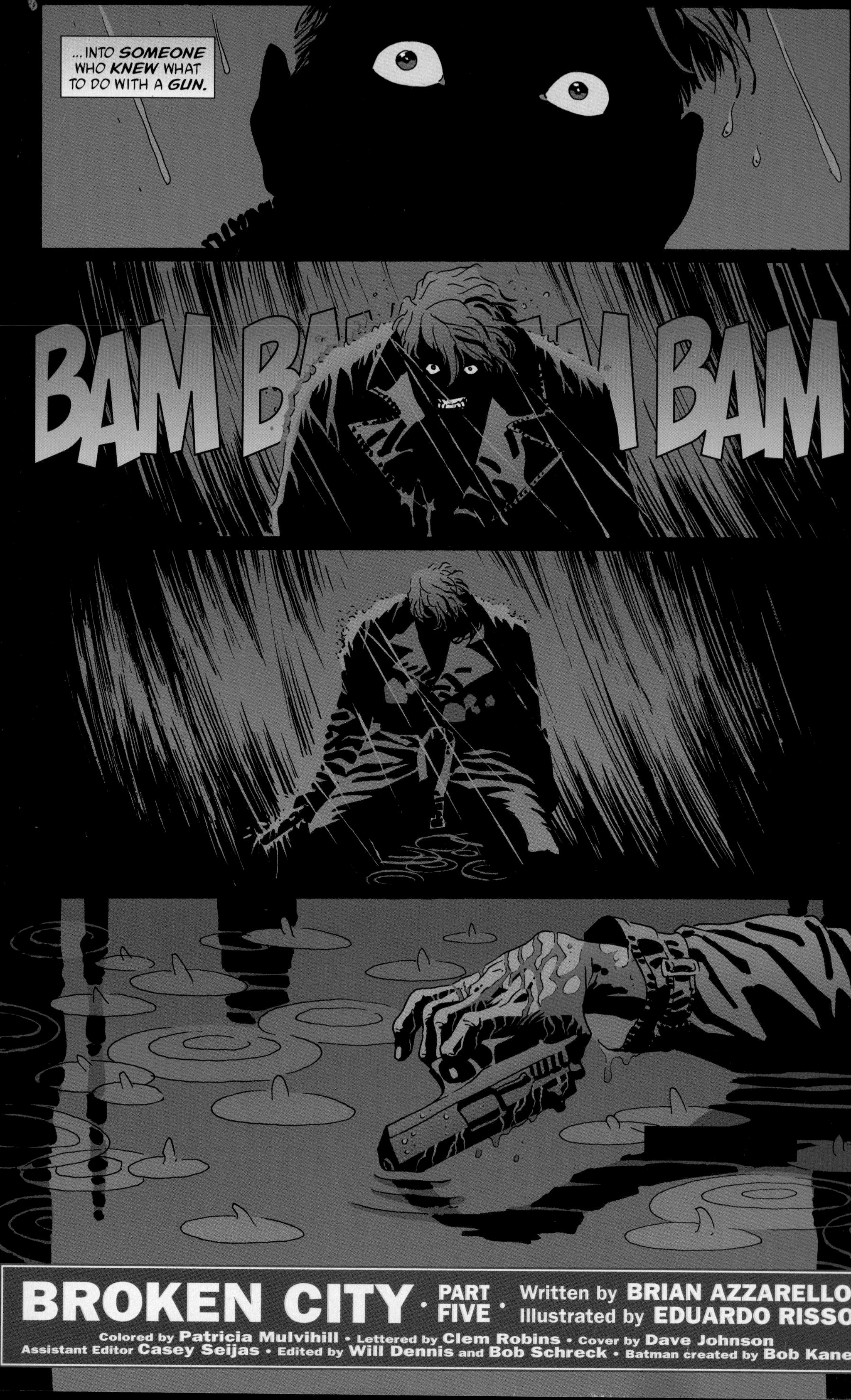
...INTO SOMEONE WHO KNEW WHAT TO DO WITH A GUN.
BAM BA
M BAM
BROKEN CITY · PART FIVE · Written by BRIAN AZZARELLO Illustrated by EDUARDO RISSO
Colored by Patricia Mulvihill • Lettered by Clem Robins • Cover by Dave Johnson
Assistant Editor Casey Seijas • Edited by Will Dennis and Bob Schreck • Batman created by Bob Kane

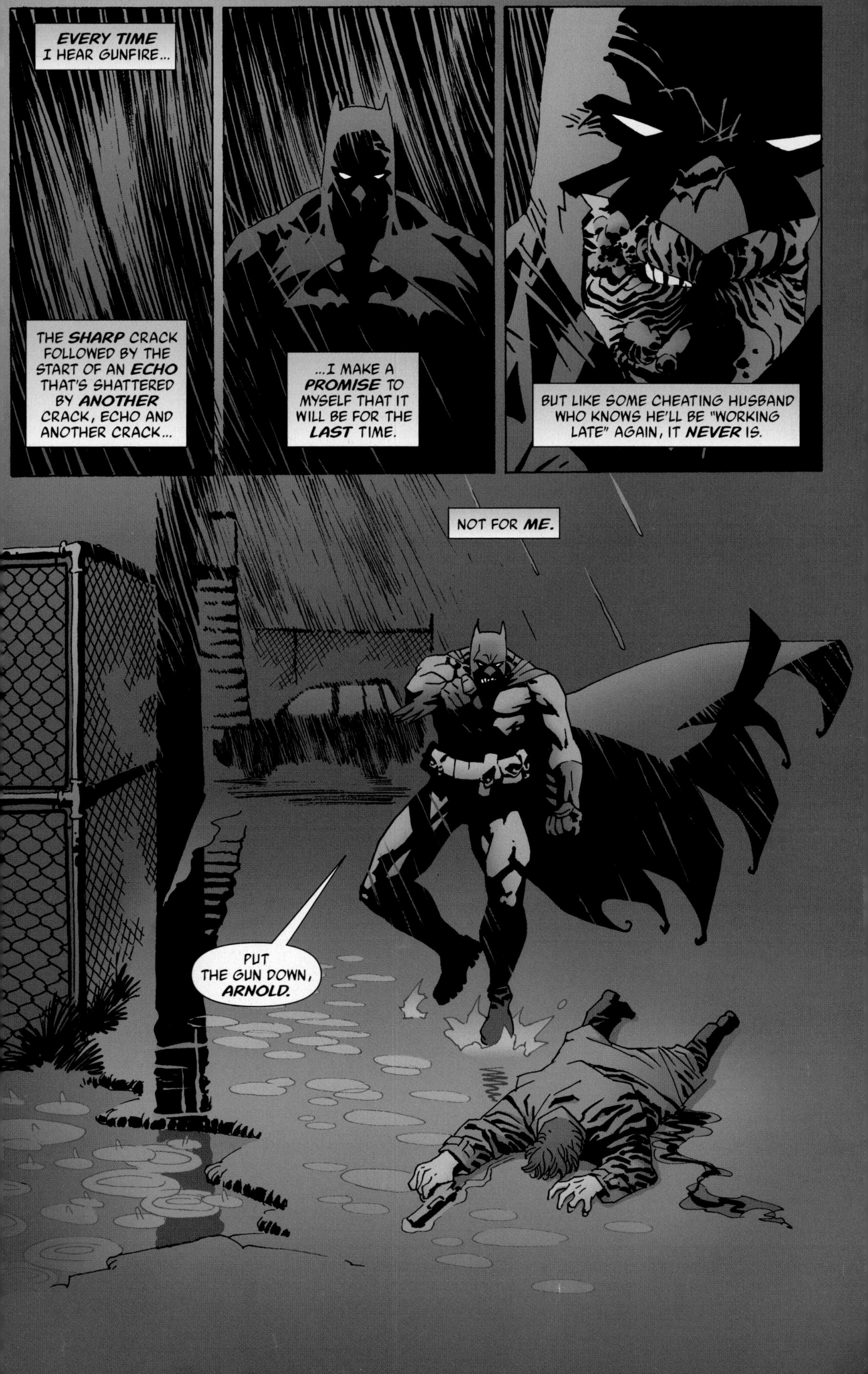
EVERY TIME I HEAR GUNFIRE...
THE SHARP CRACK FOLLOWED BY THE START OF AN ECHO THAT'S SHATTERED BY ANOTHER CRACK, ECHO AND ANOTHER CRACK...
...I MAKE A PROMISE TO MYSELF THAT IT WILL BE FOR THE LAST TIME.
BUT LIKE SOME CHEATING HUSBAND WHO KNOWS HE'LL BE "WORKING LATE" AGAIN, IT NEVER IS.
NOT FOR ME.
PUT THE GUN DOWN, ARNOLD.

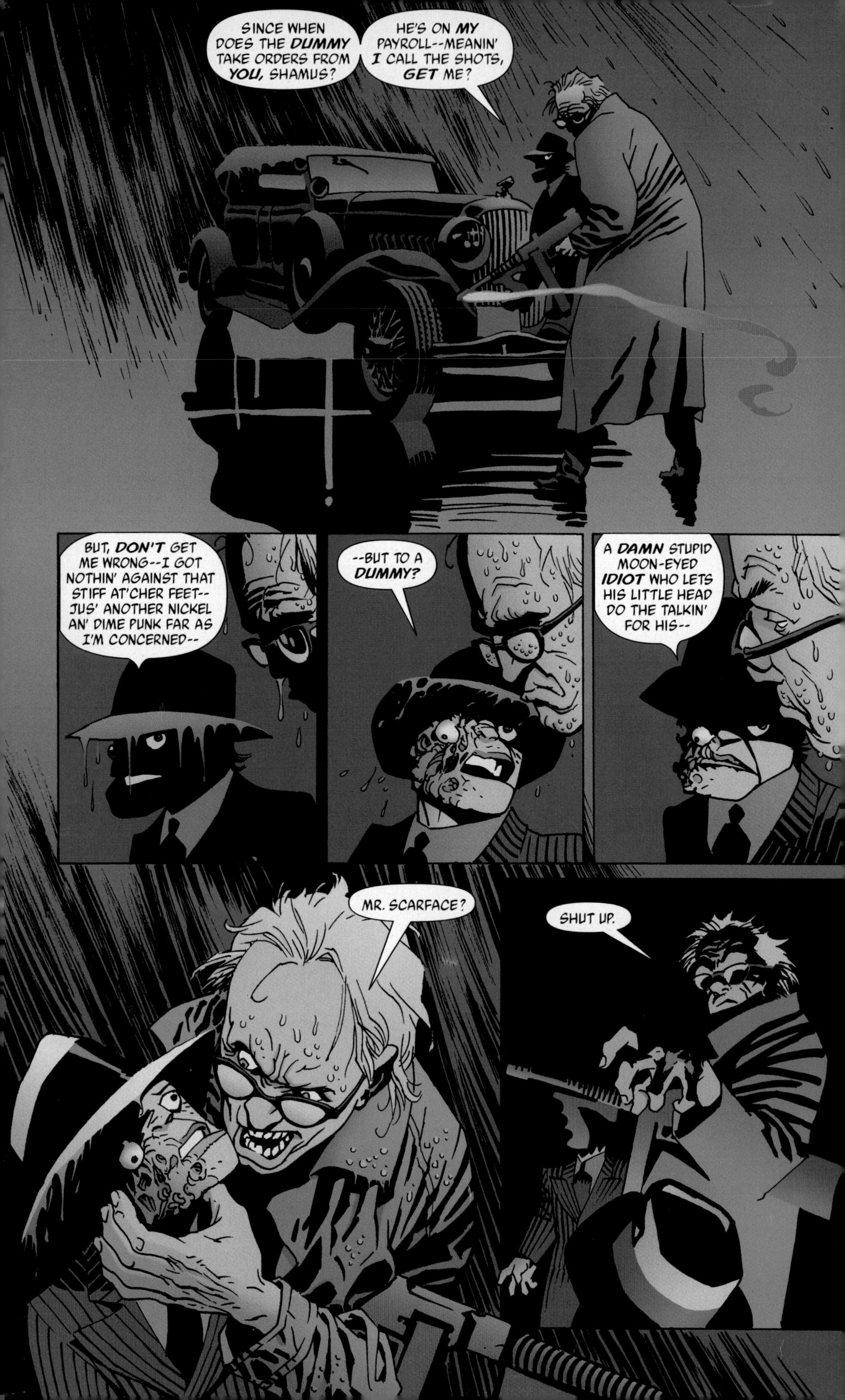
SINCE WHEN DOES THE **DUMMY** TAKE ORDERS FROM **YOU,** SHAMUS?
HE'S ON **MY** PAYROLL--MEANIN' **I** CALL THE SHOTS, **GET** ME?
BUT, **DON'T** GET ME WRONG--I GOT NOTHIN' AGAINST THAT STIFF AT'CHER FEET--JUS' ANOTHER NICKEL AN' DIME PUNK FAR AS I'M CONCERNED--
--BUT TO A **DUMMY?**
A **DAMN** STUPID MOON-EYED **IDIOT** WHO LETS HIS LITTLE HEAD DO THE TALKIN' FOR HIS--
MR. SCARFACE?
SHUT UP.

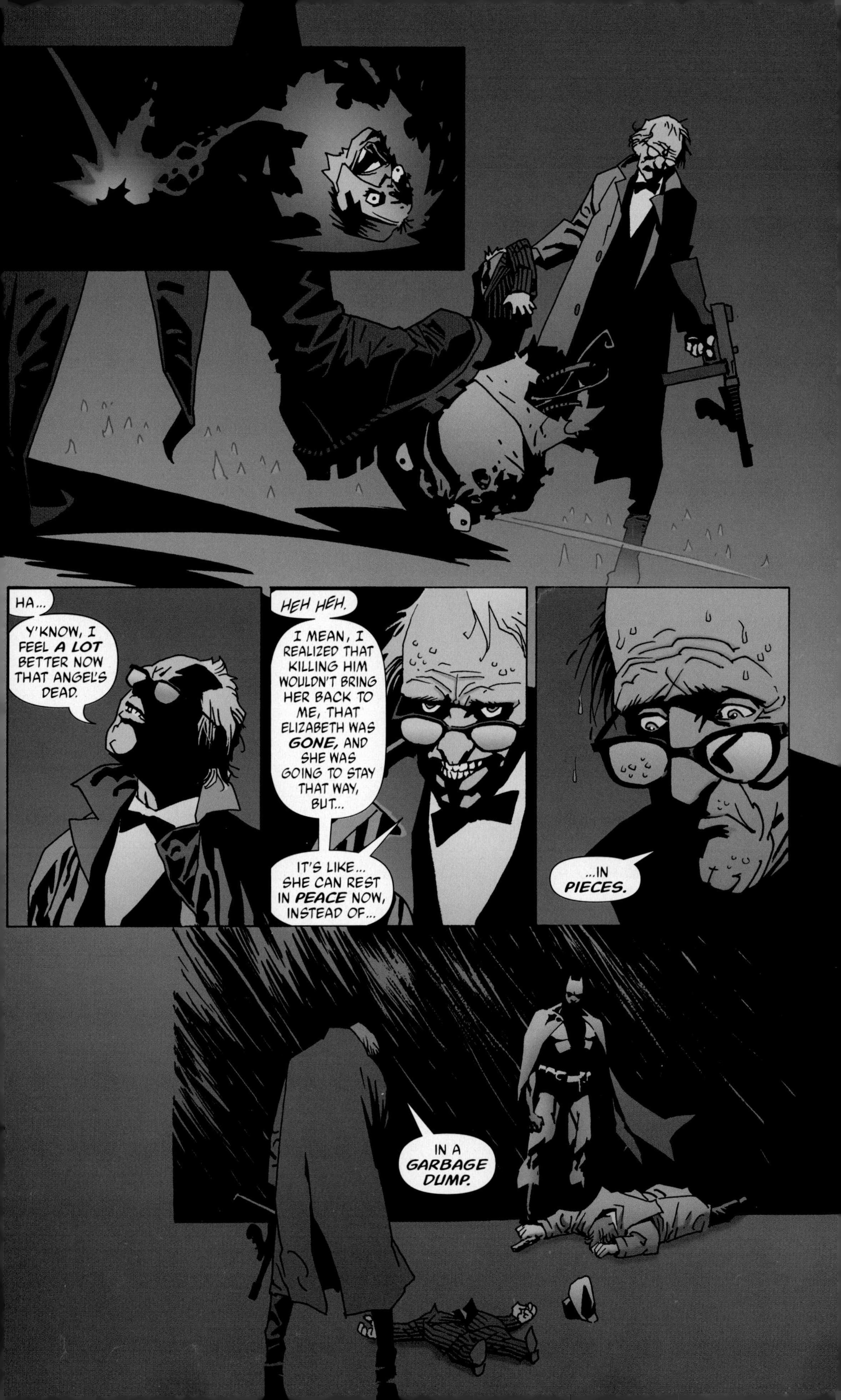
HA...
Y'KNOW, I FEEL A LOT BETTER NOW THAT ANGEL'S DEAD.
HEH HEH.
I MEAN, I REALIZED THAT KILLING HIM WOULDN'T BRING HER BACK TO ME, THAT ELIZABETH WAS GONE, AND SHE WAS GOING TO STAY THAT WAY, BUT...
IT'S LIKE... SHE CAN REST IN PEACE NOW, INSTEAD OF...
...IN PIECES.
IN A GARBAGE DUMP.

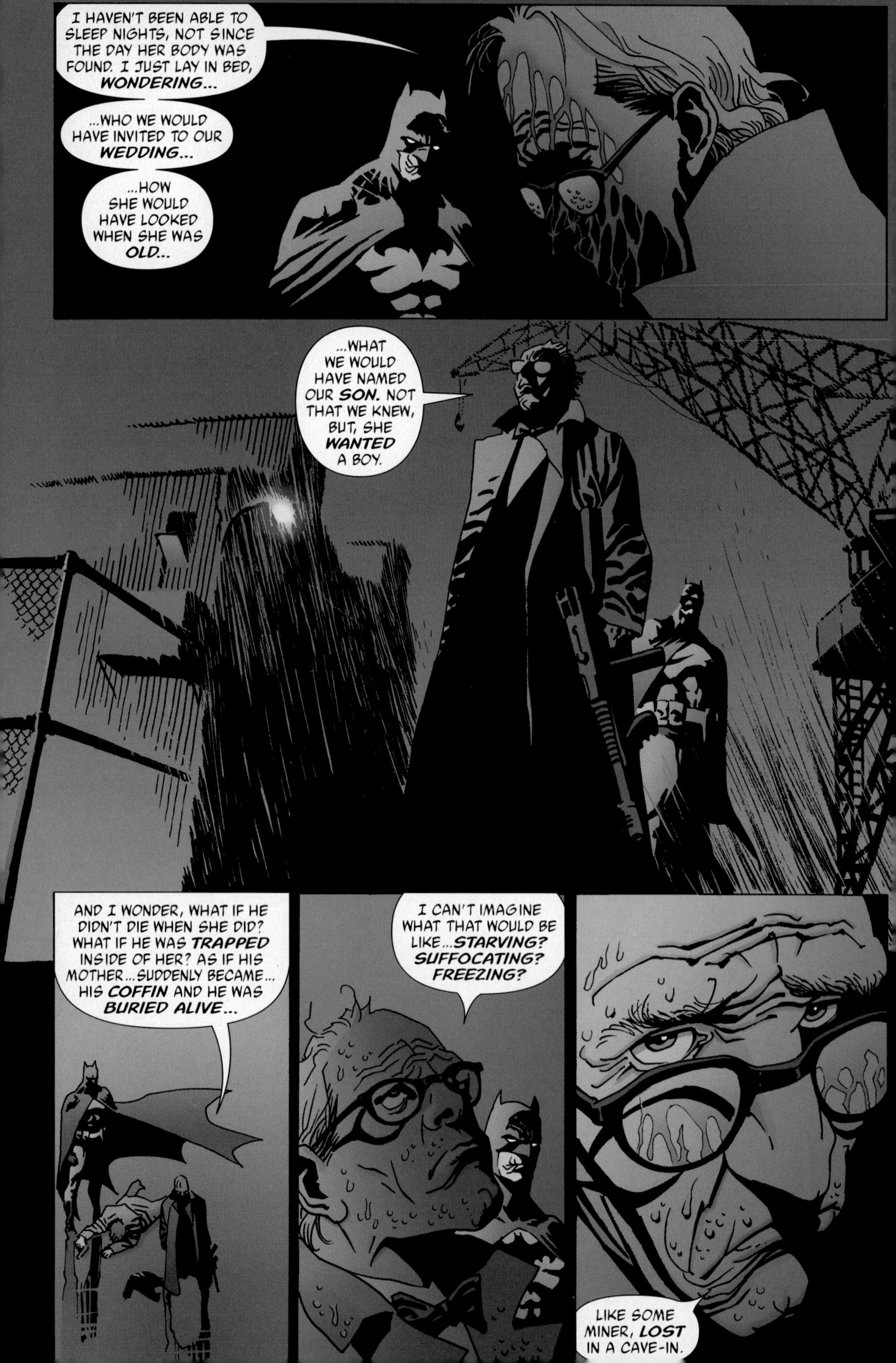
I HAVEN'T BEEN ABLE TO SLEEP NIGHTS, NOT SINCE THE DAY HER BODY WAS FOUND. I JUST LAY IN BED, **WONDERING...**
...WHO WE WOULD HAVE INVITED TO OUR **WEDDING...**
...HOW SHE WOULD HAVE LOOKED WHEN SHE WAS **OLD...**
...WHAT WE WOULD HAVE NAMED OUR **SON.** NOT THAT WE KNEW, BUT, SHE **WANTED** A BOY.
AND I WONDER, WHAT IF HE DIDN'T DIE WHEN SHE DID? WHAT IF HE WAS **TRAPPED** INSIDE OF HER? AS IF HIS MOTHER...SUDDENLY BECAME... HIS **COFFIN** AND HE WAS **BURIED ALIVE...**
I CAN'T IMAGINE WHAT THAT WOULD BE LIKE...**STARVING? SUFFOCATING? FREEZING?**
LIKE SOME MINER, **LOST** IN A CAVE-IN.

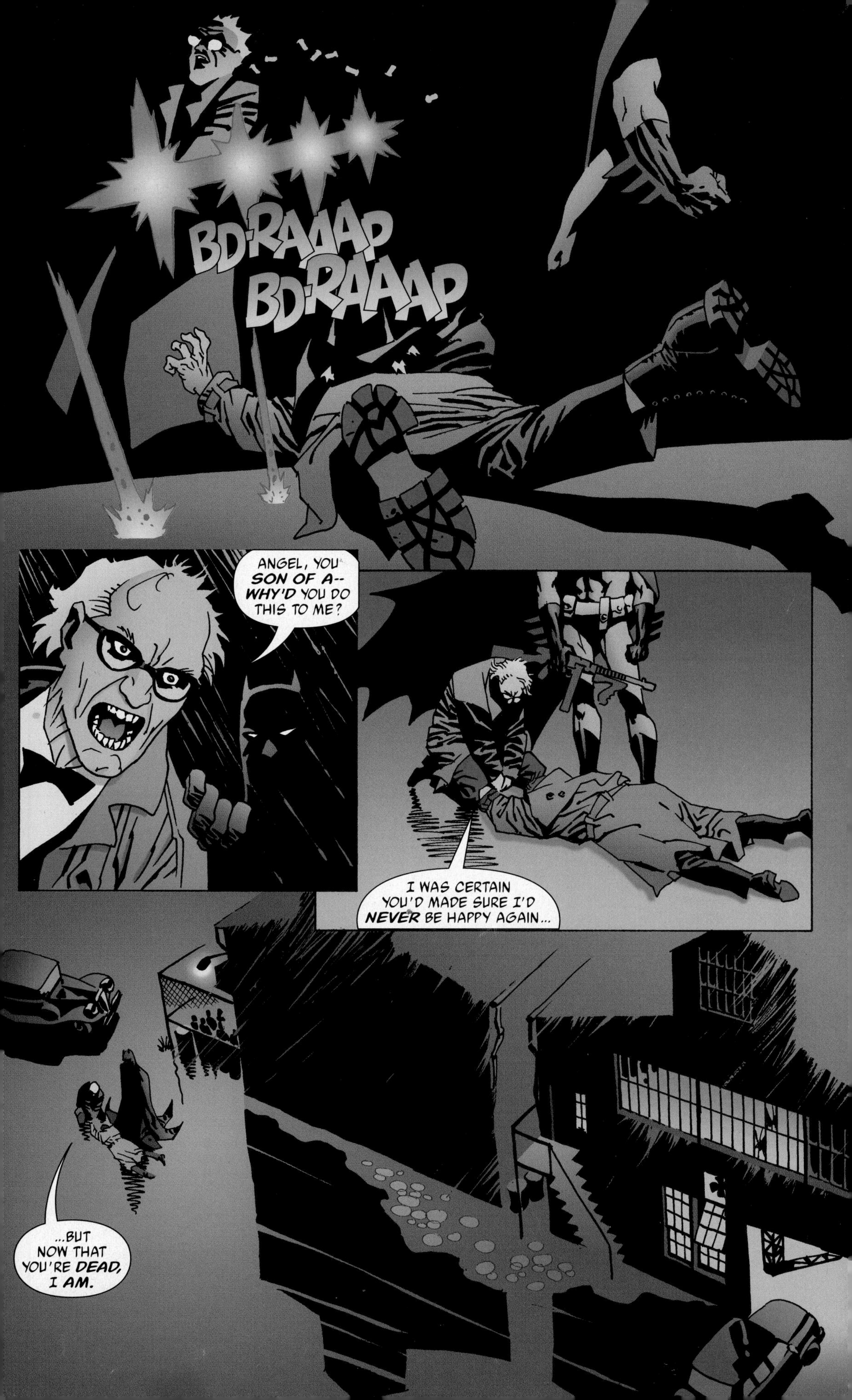
BD-RAAAP
BD-RAAAP
ANGEL, YOU **SON OF A--** **WHY'D** YOU DO THIS TO ME?
I WAS CERTAIN YOU'D MADE SURE I'D **NEVER** BE HAPPY AGAIN...
...BUT NOW THAT YOU'RE **DEAD,** **I AM.**

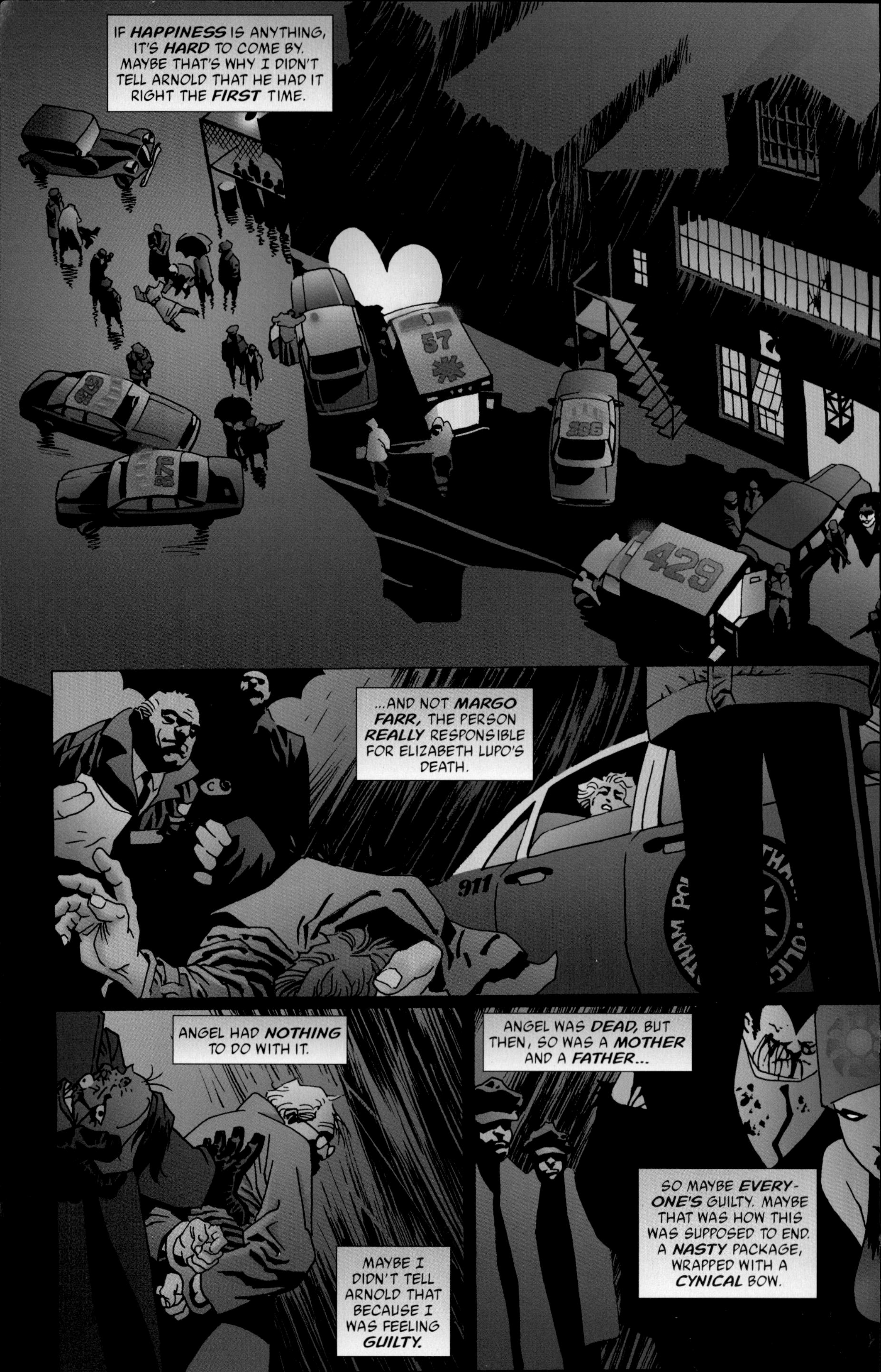
IF HAPPINESS IS ANYTHING, IT'S HARD TO COME BY. MAYBE THAT'S WHY I DIDN'T TELL ARNOLD THAT HE HAD IT RIGHT THE FIRST TIME.
57
206
429
...AND NOT MARGO FARR, THE PERSON REALLY RESPONSIBLE FOR ELIZABETH LUPO'S DEATH.
911
ANGEL HAD NOTHING TO DO WITH IT.
MAYBE I DIDN'T TELL ARNOLD THAT BECAUSE I WAS FEELING GUILTY.
ANGEL WAS DEAD, BUT THEN, SO WAS A MOTHER AND A FATHER...
SO MAYBE EVERY-ONE'S GUILTY. MAYBE THAT WAS HOW THIS WAS SUPPOSED TO END. A NASTY PACKAGE, WRAPPED WITH A CYNICAL BOW.

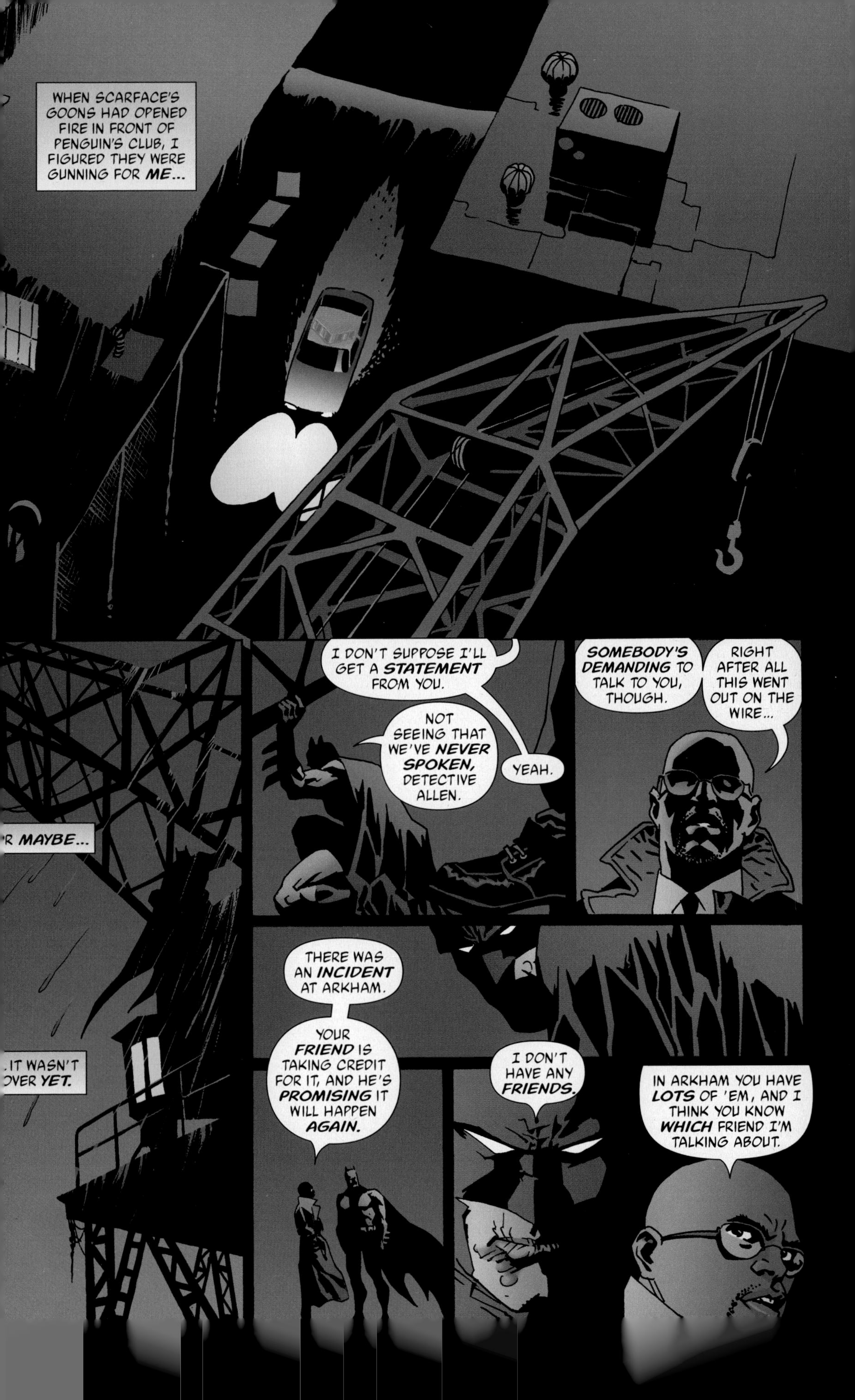
WHEN SCARFACE'S GOONS HAD OPENED FIRE IN FRONT OF PENGUIN'S CLUB, I FIGURED THEY WERE GUNNING FOR **ME**...
R **MAYBE**...
I DON'T SUPPOSE I'LL GET A **STATEMENT** FROM YOU.
NOT SEEING THAT WE'VE **NEVER SPOKEN,** DETECTIVE ALLEN.
YEAH.
SOMEBODY'S DEMANDING TO TALK TO YOU, THOUGH.
RIGHT AFTER ALL THIS WENT OUT ON THE WIRE...
.IT WASN'T
OVER **YET.**
THERE WAS AN **INCIDENT** AT ARKHAM.
YOUR **FRIEND** IS TAKING CREDIT FOR IT, AND HE'S **PROMISING** IT WILL HAPPEN **AGAIN.**
I DON'T HAVE ANY **FRIENDS.**
IN ARKHAM YOU HAVE **LOTS** OF 'EM, AND I THINK YOU KNOW **WHICH** FRIEND I'M TALKING ABOUT.

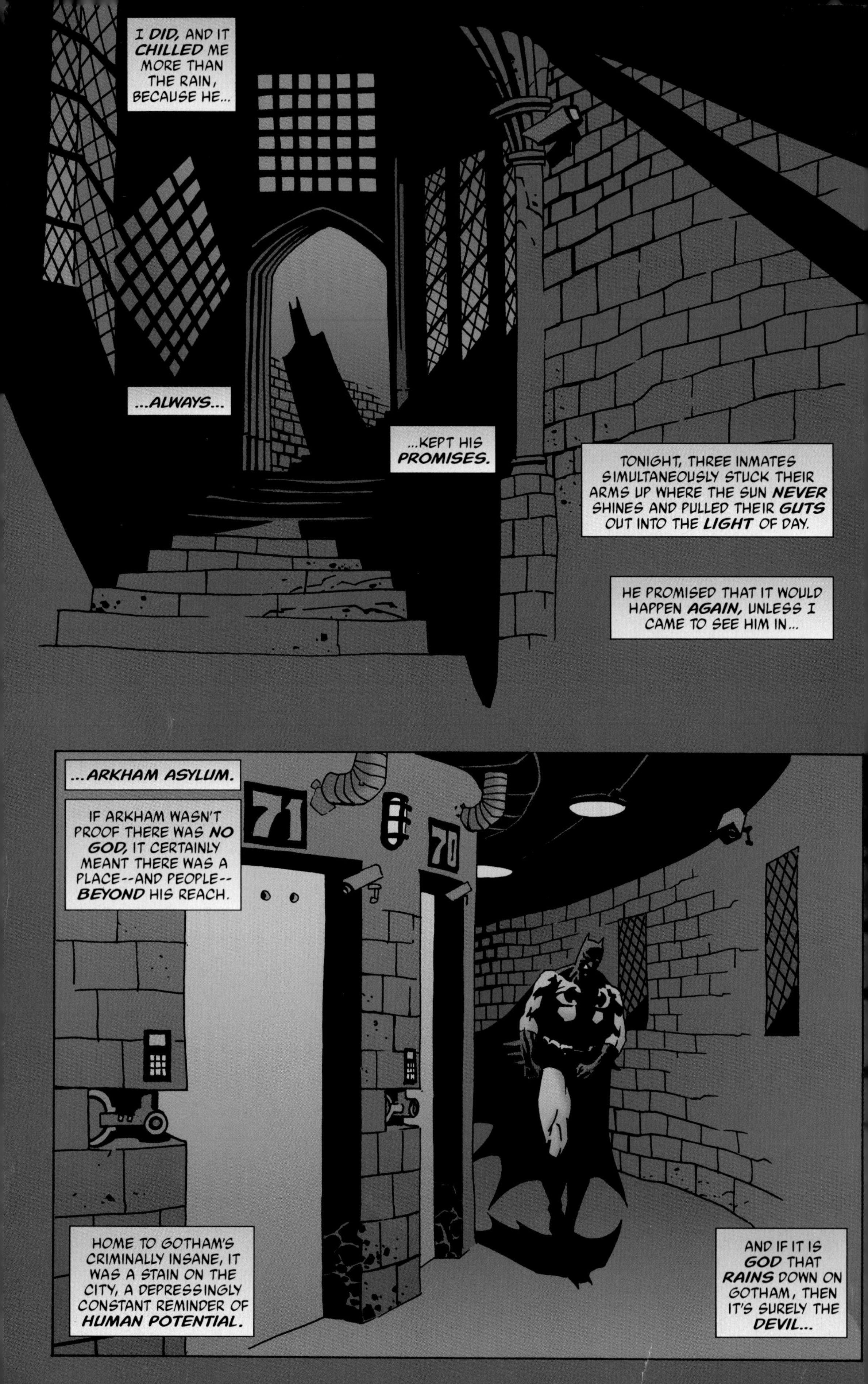
I DID, AND IT CHILLED ME MORE THAN THE RAIN, BECAUSE HE...
...ALWAYS...
...KEPT HIS PROMISES.
TONIGHT, THREE INMATES SIMULTANEOUSLY STUCK THEIR ARMS UP WHERE THE SUN NEVER SHINES AND PULLED THEIR GUTS OUT INTO THE LIGHT OF DAY.
HE PROMISED THAT IT WOULD HAPPEN AGAIN, UNLESS I CAME TO SEE HIM IN...
...ARKHAM ASYLUM.
IF ARKHAM WASN'T PROOF THERE WAS NO GOD, IT CERTAINLY MEANT THERE WAS A PLACE--AND PEOPLE--BEYOND HIS REACH.
71
70
HOME TO GOTHAM'S CRIMINALLY INSANE, IT WAS A STAIN ON THE CITY, A DEPRESSINGLY CONSTANT REMINDER OF HUMAN POTENTIAL.
AND IF IT IS GOD THAT RAINS DOWN ON GOTHAM, THEN IT'S SURELY THE DEVIL...

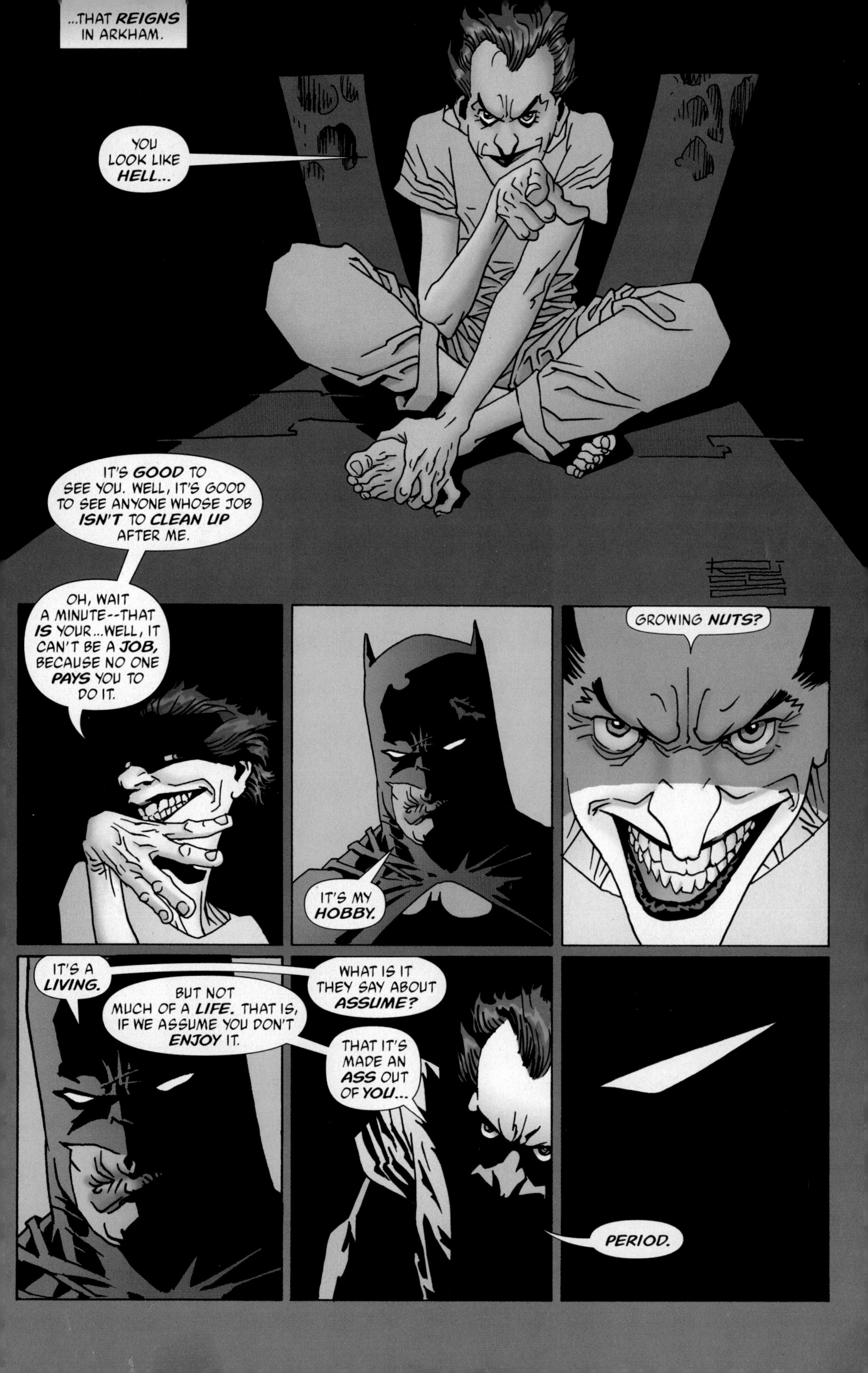
...THAT REIGNS IN ARKHAM.
YOU LOOK LIKE HELL...
IT'S GOOD TO SEE YOU. WELL, IT'S GOOD TO SEE ANYONE WHOSE JOB ISN'T TO CLEAN UP AFTER ME.
OH, WAIT A MINUTE--THAT IS YOUR...WELL, IT CAN'T BE A JOB, BECAUSE NO ONE PAYS YOU TO DO IT.
IT'S MY HOBBY.
GROWING NUTS?
IT'S A LIVING.
BUT NOT MUCH OF A LIFE. THAT IS, IF WE ASSUME YOU DON'T ENJOY IT.
WHAT IS IT THEY SAY ABOUT ASSUME?
THAT IT'S MADE AN ASS OUT OF YOU...
PERIOD.

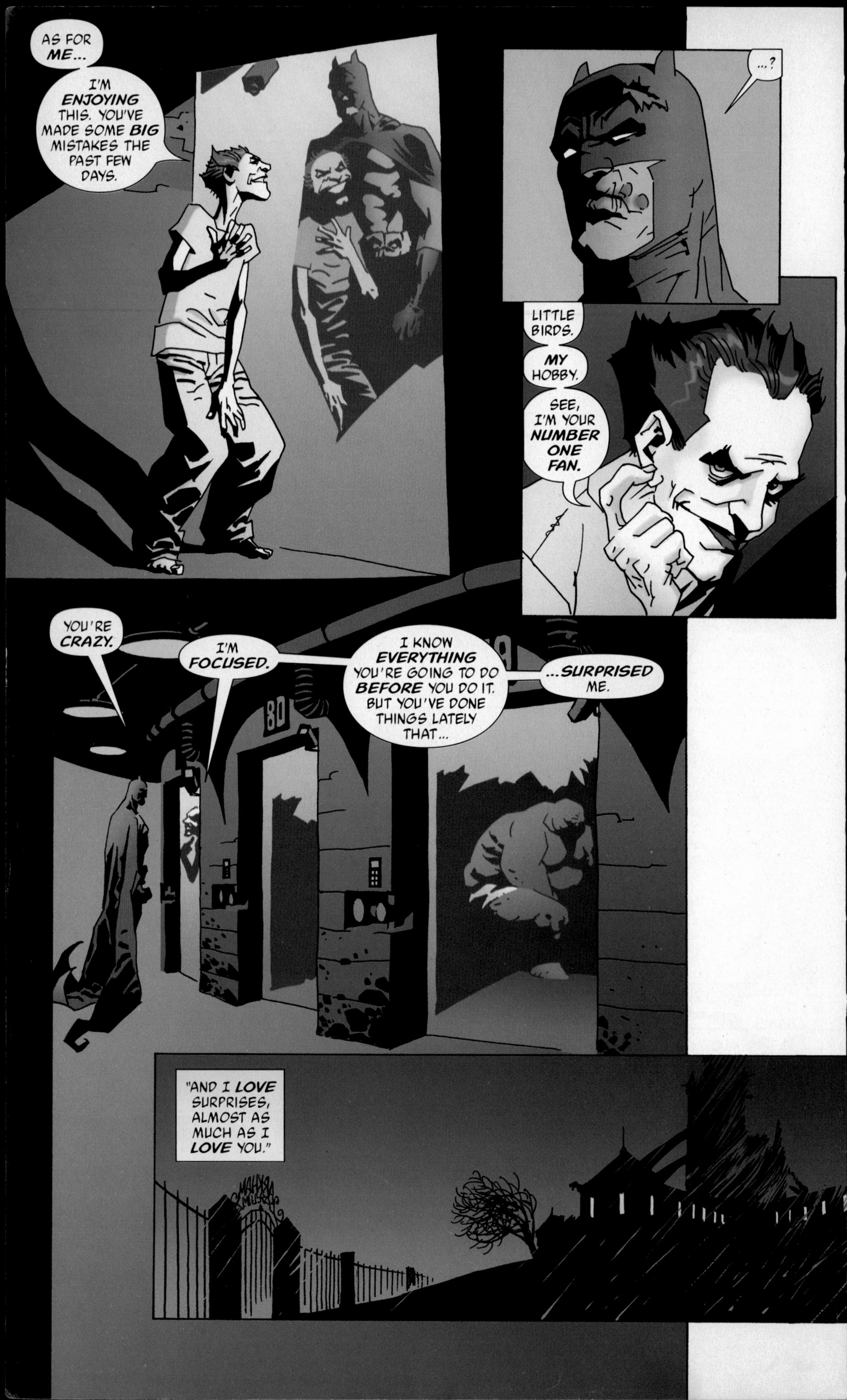

AS FOR **ME**...
I'M **ENJOYING** THIS. YOU'VE MADE SOME **BIG** MISTAKES THE PAST FEW DAYS.
...?
LITTLE BIRDS.
MY HOBBY.
SEE, I'M YOUR **NUMBER ONE FAN.**
YOU'RE **CRAZY.**
I'M **FOCUSED.**
I KNOW **EVERYTHING** YOU'RE GOING TO DO **BEFORE** YOU DO IT. BUT YOU'VE DONE THINGS LATELY THAT...
...**SURPRISED** ME.
"AND I **LOVE** SURPRISES, ALMOST AS MUCH AS I **LOVE** YOU."

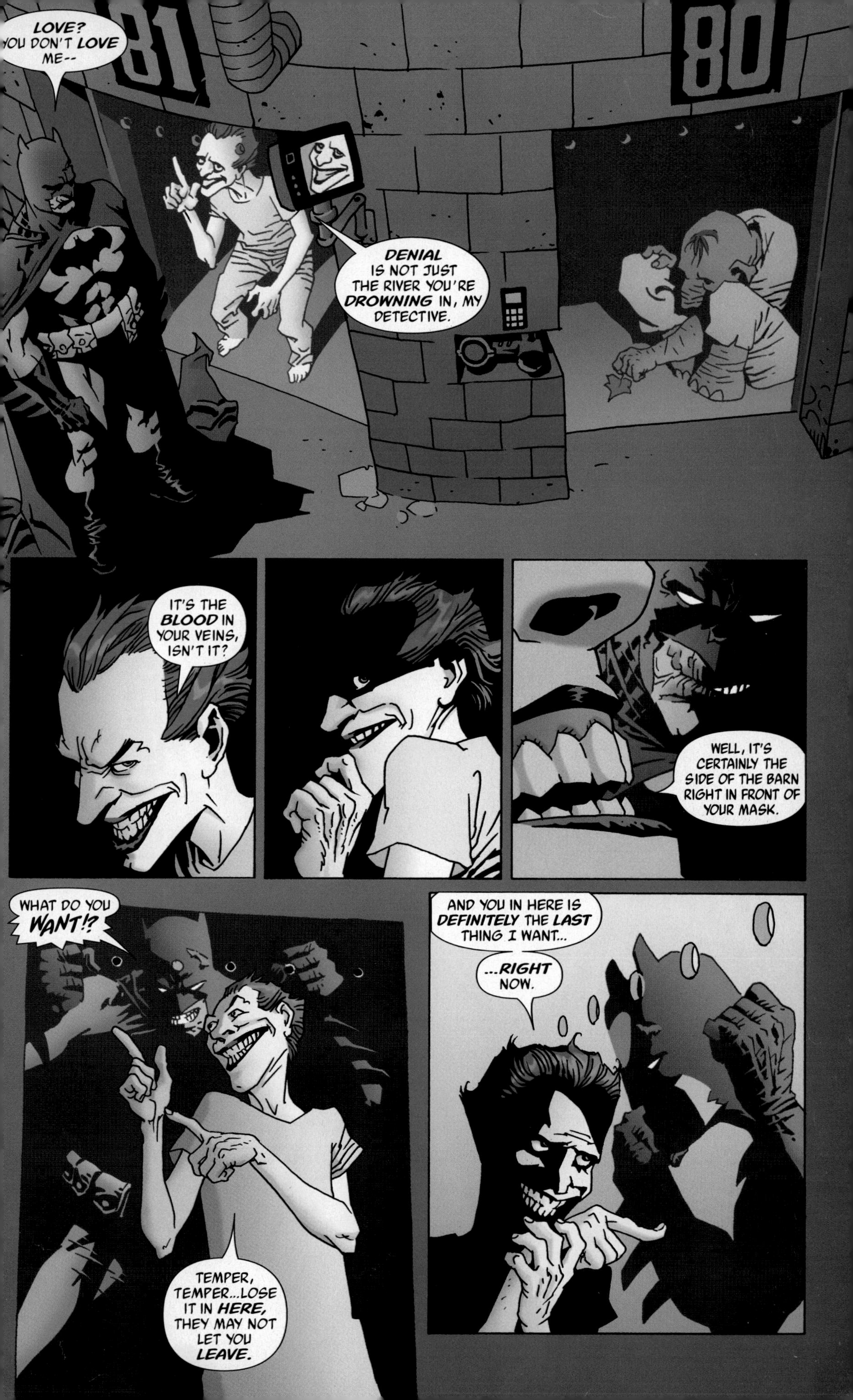

LOVE? YOU DON'T LOVE ME--
81
80
DENIAL IS NOT JUST THE RIVER YOU'RE DROWNING IN, MY DETECTIVE.
IT'S THE BLOOD IN YOUR VEINS, ISN'T IT?
WELL, IT'S CERTAINLY THE SIDE OF THE BARN RIGHT IN FRONT OF YOUR MASK.
WHAT DO YOU WANT!?
TEMPER, TEMPER...LOSE IT IN HERE, THEY MAY NOT LET YOU LEAVE.
AND YOU IN HERE IS DEFINITELY THE LAST THING I WANT...
...RIGHT NOW.

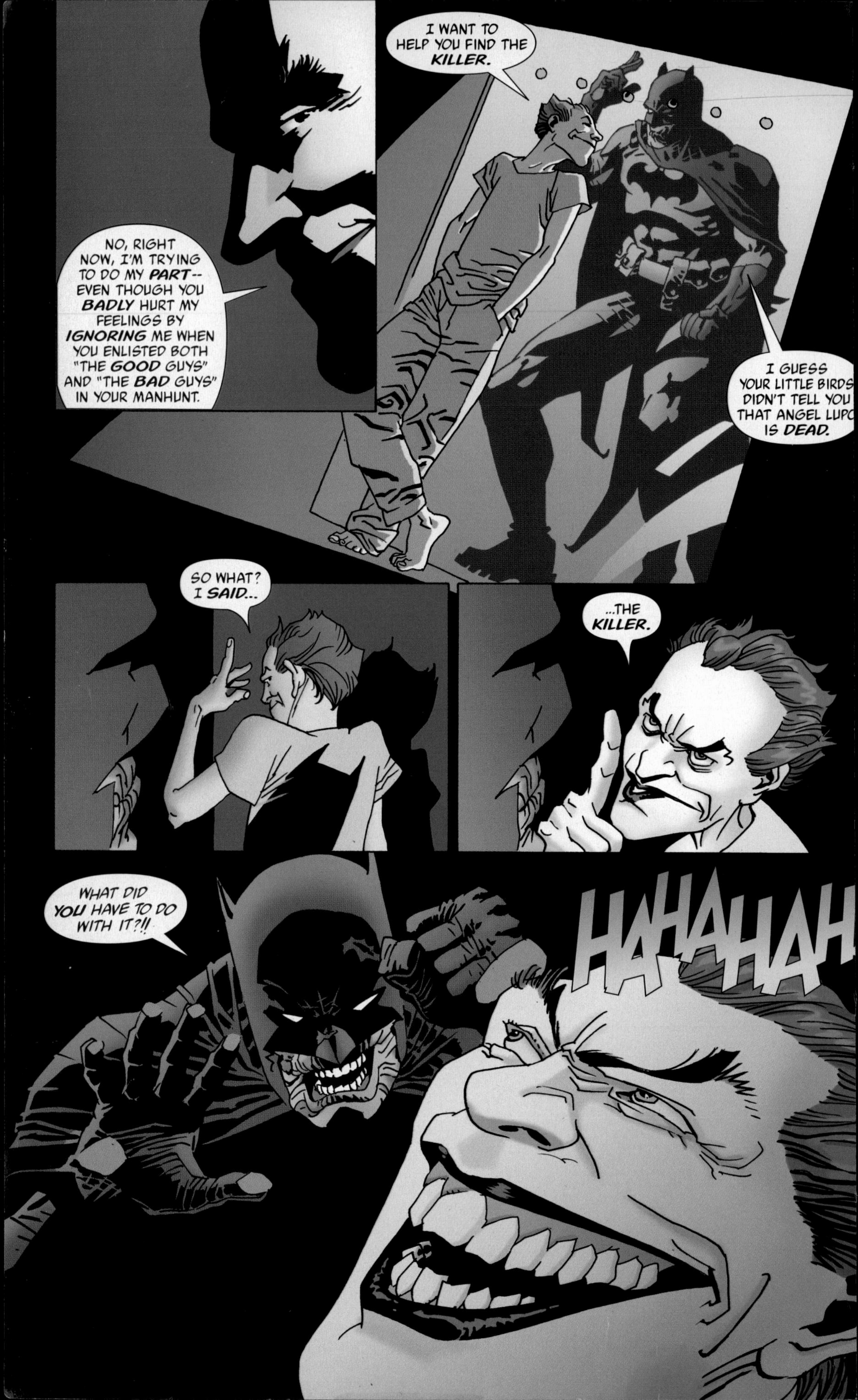
I WANT TO HELP YOU FIND THE **KILLER.**
NO, RIGHT NOW, I'M TRYING TO DO MY **PART**-- EVEN THOUGH YOU **BADLY** HURT MY FEELINGS BY **IGNORING** ME WHEN YOU ENLISTED BOTH "THE **GOOD** GUYS" AND "THE **BAD** GUYS" IN YOUR MANHUNT.
I GUESS YOUR LITTLE BIRDS DIDN'T TELL YOU THAT ANGEL LUPO IS **DEAD.**
SO WHAT? I **SAID...**
...THE **KILLER.**
WHAT DID **YOU** HAVE TO DO WITH IT?!!
HAHAHAH

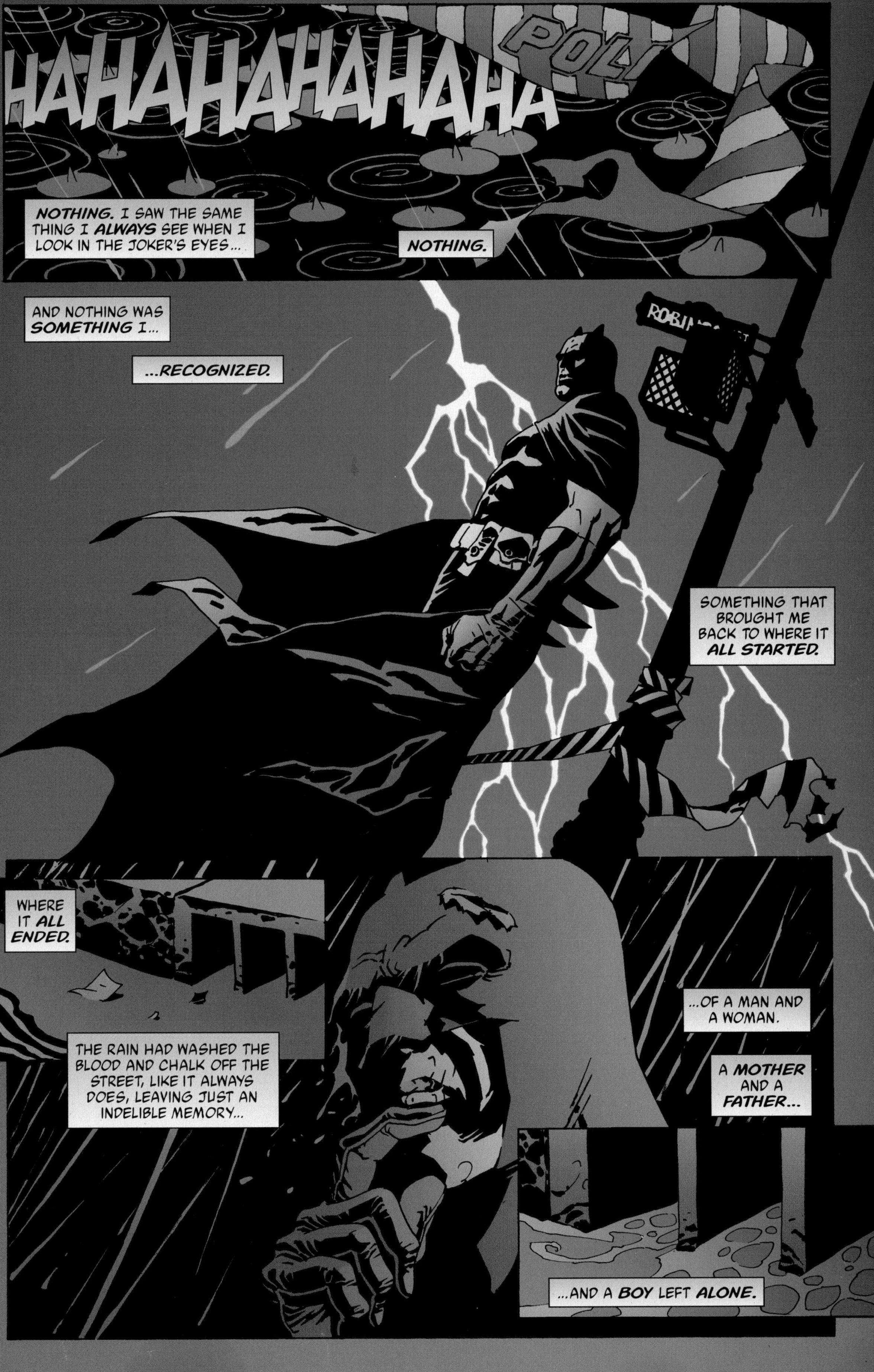
HAHAHAHAHAHAHA
POLI
NOTHING. I SAW THE SAME THING I ALWAYS SEE WHEN I LOOK IN THE JOKER'S EYES...
NOTHING.
AND NOTHING WAS SOMETHING I...
...RECOGNIZED.
SOMETHING THAT BROUGHT ME BACK TO WHERE IT ALL STARTED.
WHERE IT ALL ENDED.
THE RAIN HAD WASHED THE BLOOD AND CHALK OFF THE STREET, LIKE IT ALWAYS DOES, LEAVING JUST AN INDELIBLE MEMORY...
...OF A MAN AND A WOMAN.
A MOTHER AND A FATHER...
...AND A BOY LEFT ALONE.

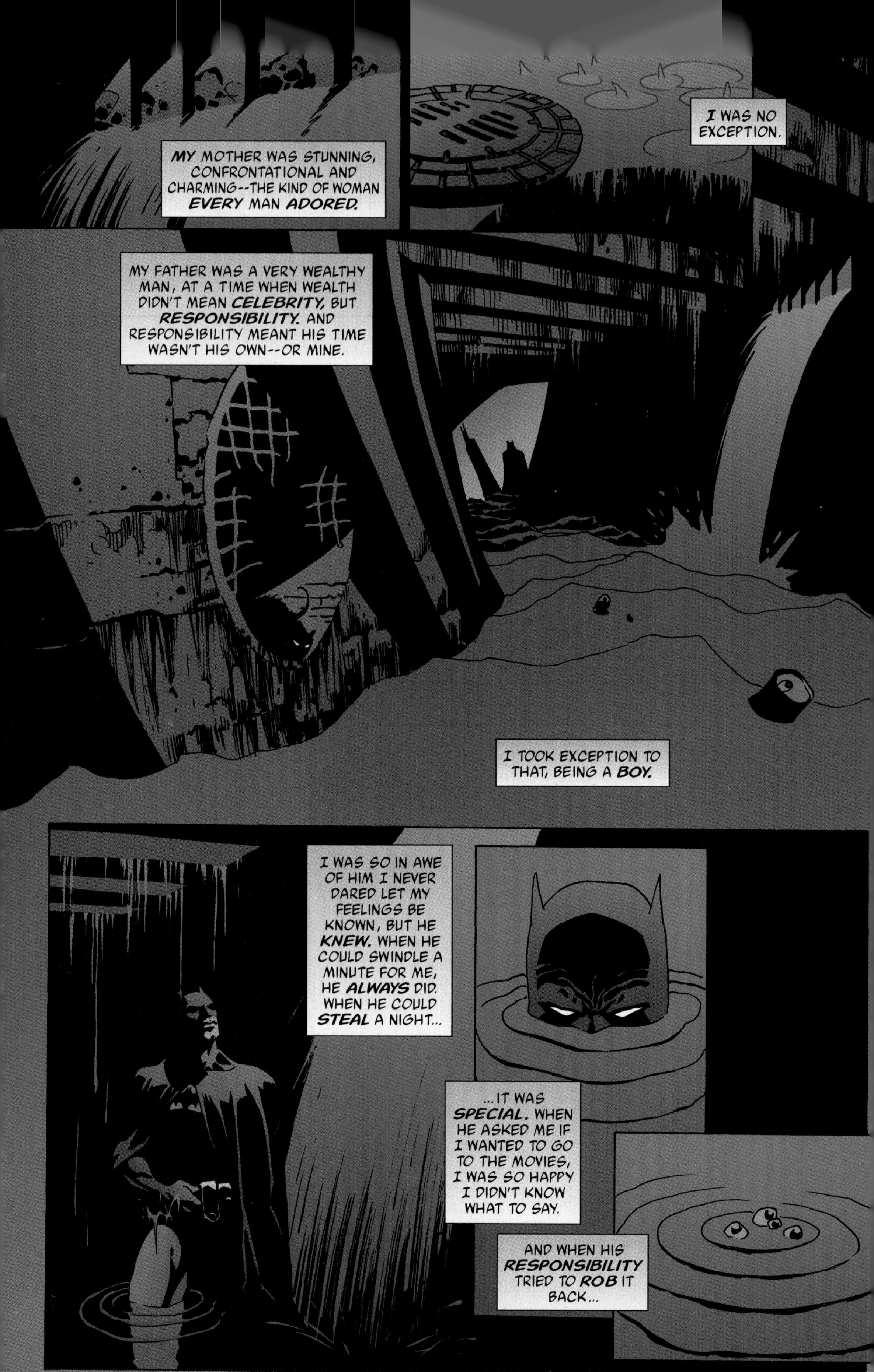
MY MOTHER WAS STUNNING, CONFRONTATIONAL AND CHARMING--THE KIND OF WOMAN EVERY MAN ADORED.
I WAS NO EXCEPTION.
MY FATHER WAS A VERY WEALTHY MAN, AT A TIME WHEN WEALTH DIDN'T MEAN CELEBRITY, BUT RESPONSIBILITY. AND RESPONSIBILITY MEANT HIS TIME WASN'T HIS OWN--OR MINE.
I TOOK EXCEPTION TO THAT, BEING A BOY.
I WAS SO IN AWE OF HIM I NEVER DARED LET MY FEELINGS BE KNOWN, BUT HE KNEW. WHEN HE COULD SWINDLE A MINUTE FOR ME, HE ALWAYS DID. WHEN HE COULD STEAL A NIGHT...
...IT WAS SPECIAL. WHEN HE ASKED ME IF I WANTED TO GO TO THE MOVIES, I WAS SO HAPPY I DIDN'T KNOW WHAT TO SAY.
AND WHEN HIS RESPONSIBILITY TRIED TO ROB IT BACK...

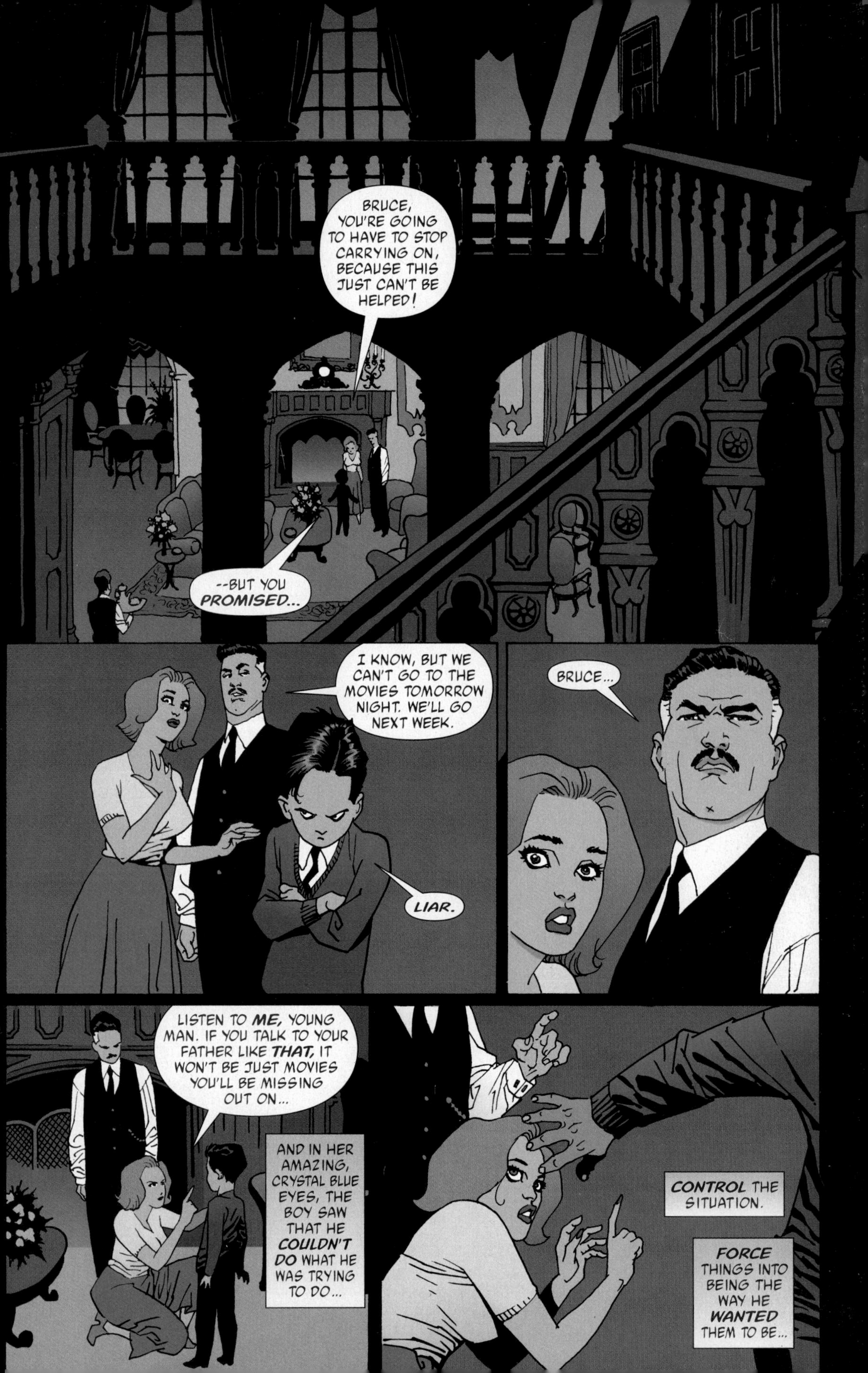
BRUCE, YOU'RE GOING TO HAVE TO STOP CARRYING ON, BECAUSE THIS JUST CAN'T BE HELPED!
--BUT YOU **PROMISED...**
I KNOW, BUT WE CAN'T GO TO THE MOVIES TOMORROW NIGHT. WE'LL GO NEXT WEEK.
LIAR.
BRUCE...
LISTEN TO **ME,** YOUNG MAN. IF YOU TALK TO YOUR FATHER LIKE **THAT,** IT WON'T BE JUST MOVIES YOU'LL BE MISSING OUT ON...
AND IN HER AMAZING, CRYSTAL BLUE EYES, THE BOY SAW THAT HE **COULDN'T DO** WHAT HE WAS TRYING TO DO...
CONTROL THE SITUATION.
FORCE THINGS INTO BEING THE WAY HE **WANTED** THEM TO BE...

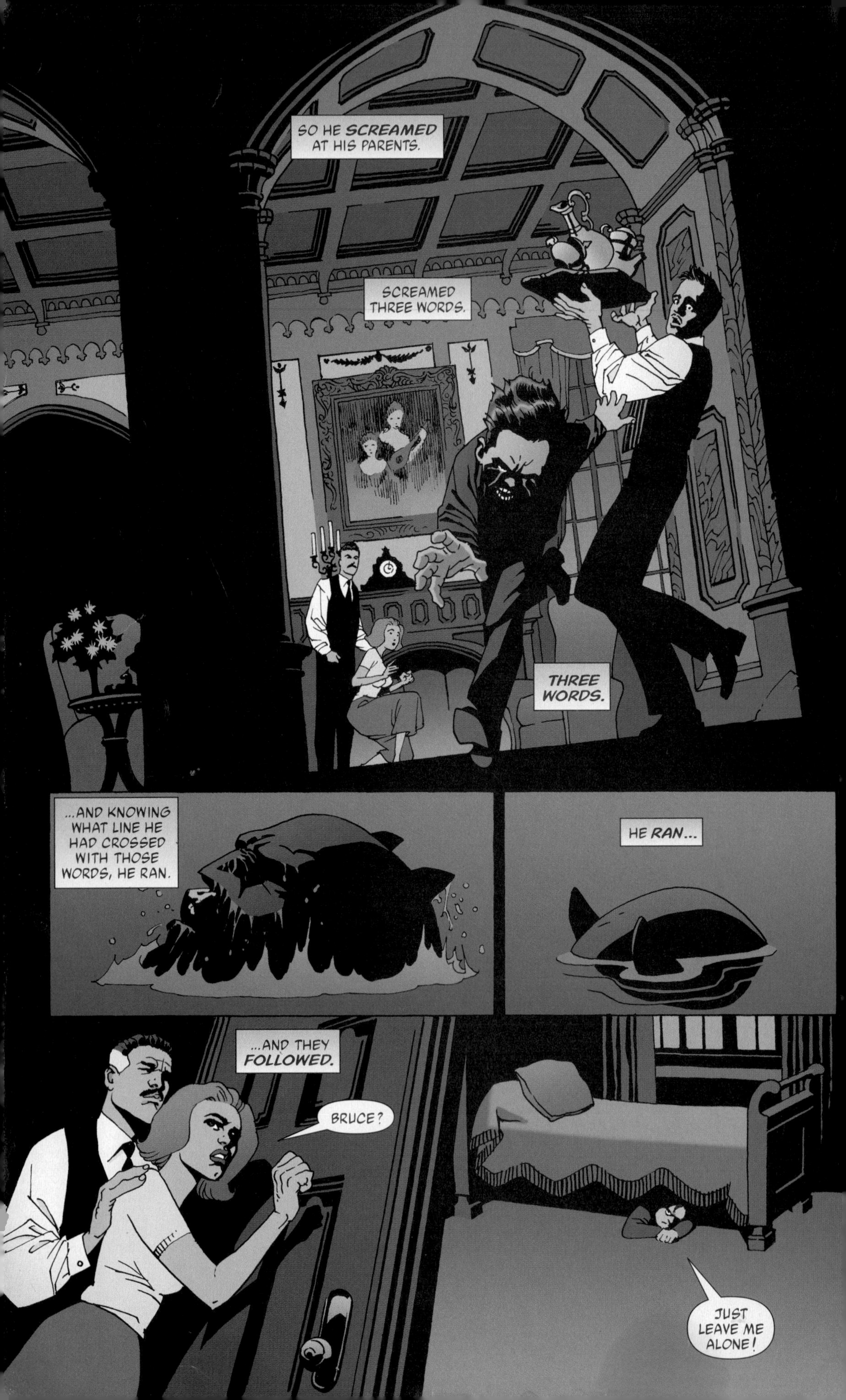
SO HE SCREAMED AT HIS PARENTS.
SCREAMED THREE WORDS.
THREE WORDS.
...AND KNOWING WHAT LINE HE HAD CROSSED WITH THOSE WORDS, HE RAN.
HE RAN...
...AND THEY FOLLOWED.
BRUCE?
JUST LEAVE ME ALONE!

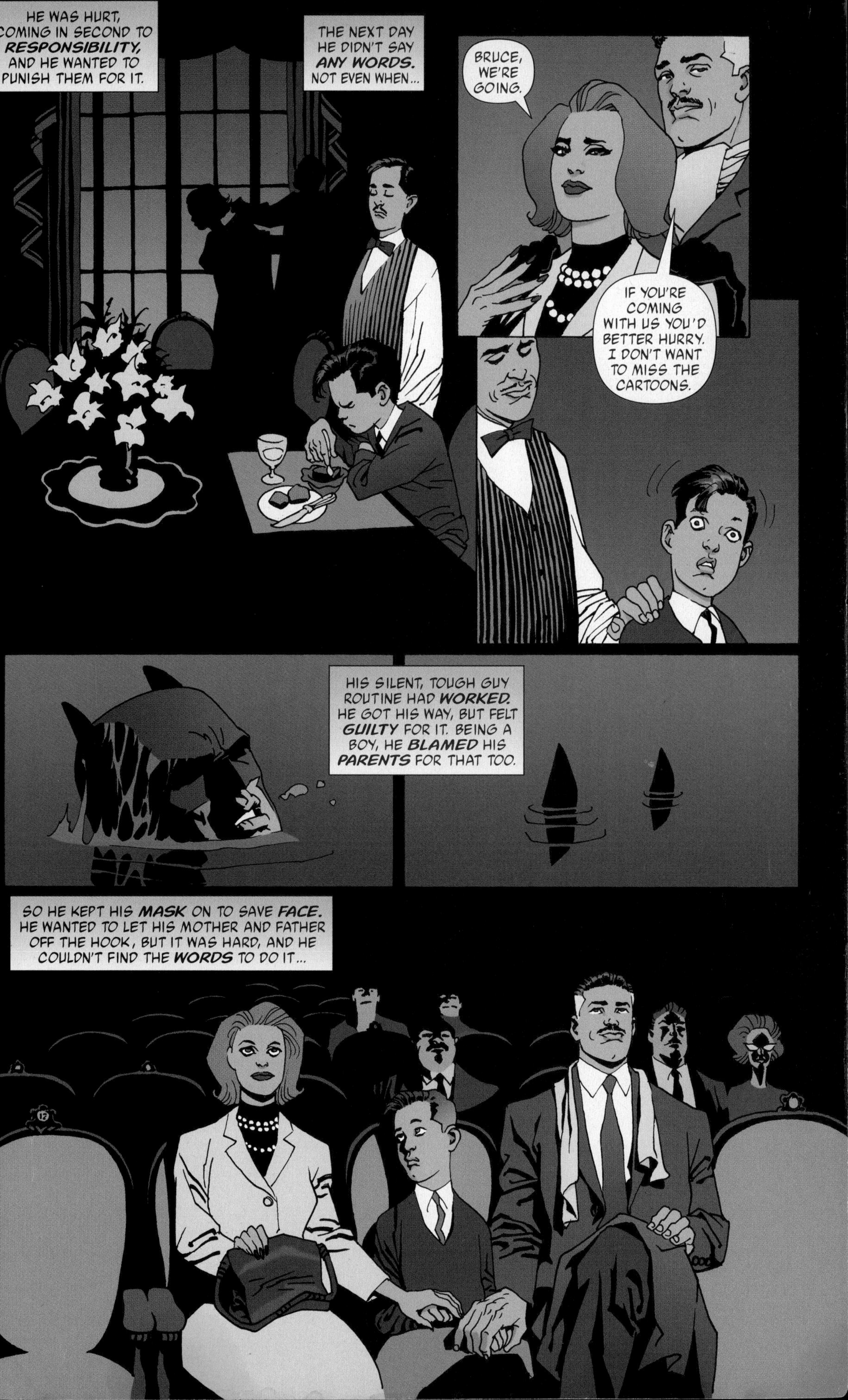
HE WAS HURT, COMING IN SECOND TO RESPONSIBILITY, AND HE WANTED TO PUNISH THEM FOR IT.
THE NEXT DAY HE DIDN'T SAY ANY WORDS. NOT EVEN WHEN...
BRUCE, WE'RE GOING.
IF YOU'RE COMING WITH US YOU'D BETTER HURRY. I DON'T WANT TO MISS THE CARTOONS.
HIS SILENT, TOUGH GUY ROUTINE HAD WORKED. HE GOT HIS WAY, BUT FELT GUILTY FOR IT. BEING A BOY, HE BLAMED HIS PARENTS FOR THAT TOO.
SO HE KEPT HIS MASK ON TO SAVE FACE. HE WANTED TO LET HIS MOTHER AND FATHER OFF THE HOOK, BUT IT WAS HARD, AND HE COULDN'T FIND THE WORDS TO DO IT...

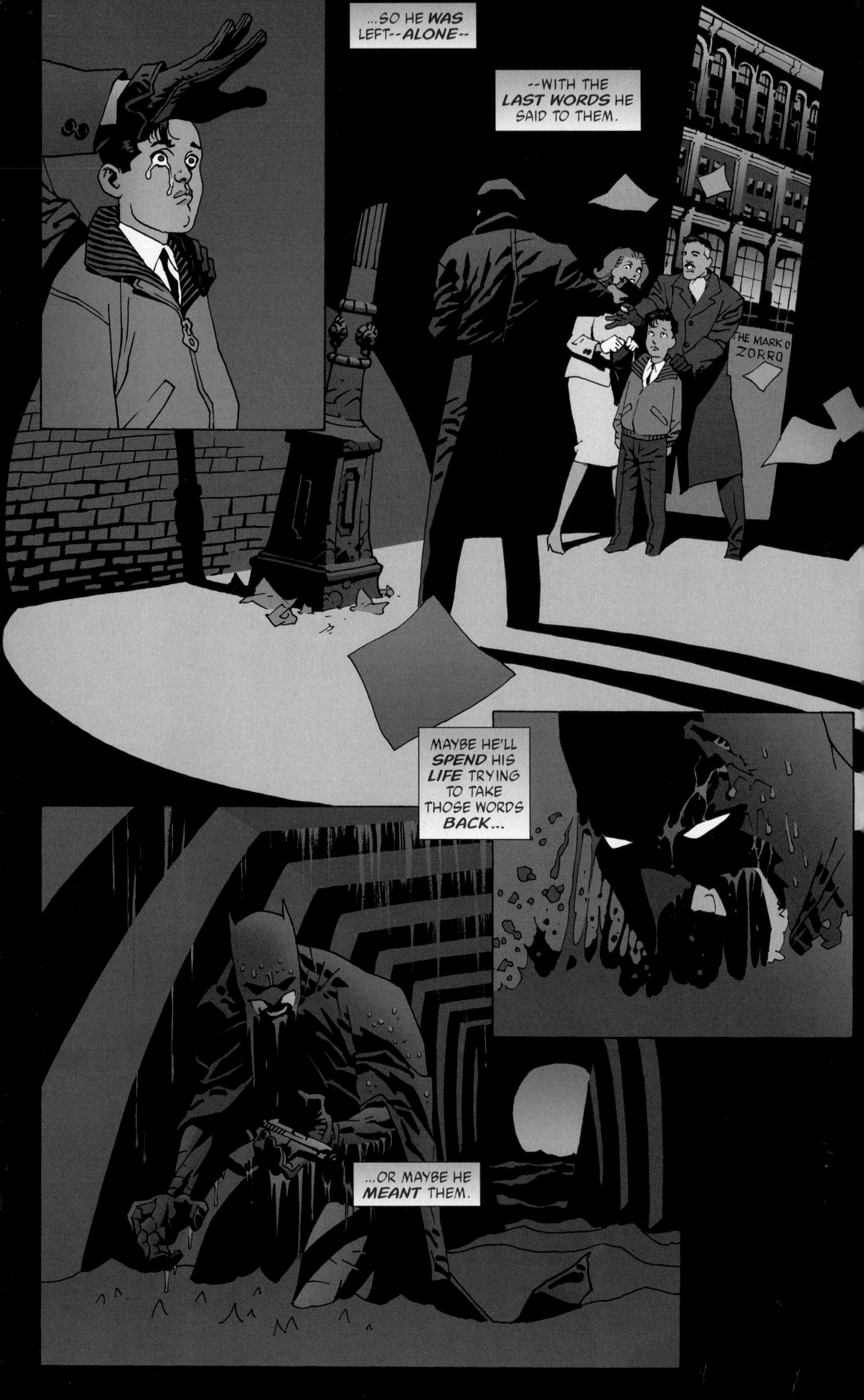
...SO HE **WAS** LEFT--**ALONE**--
--WITH THE **LAST WORDS** HE SAID TO THEM.
THE MARK O
ZORRO
MAYBE HE'LL **SPEND** HIS **LIFE** TRYING TO TAKE THOSE WORDS **BACK**...
...OR MAYBE HE **MEANT** THEM.

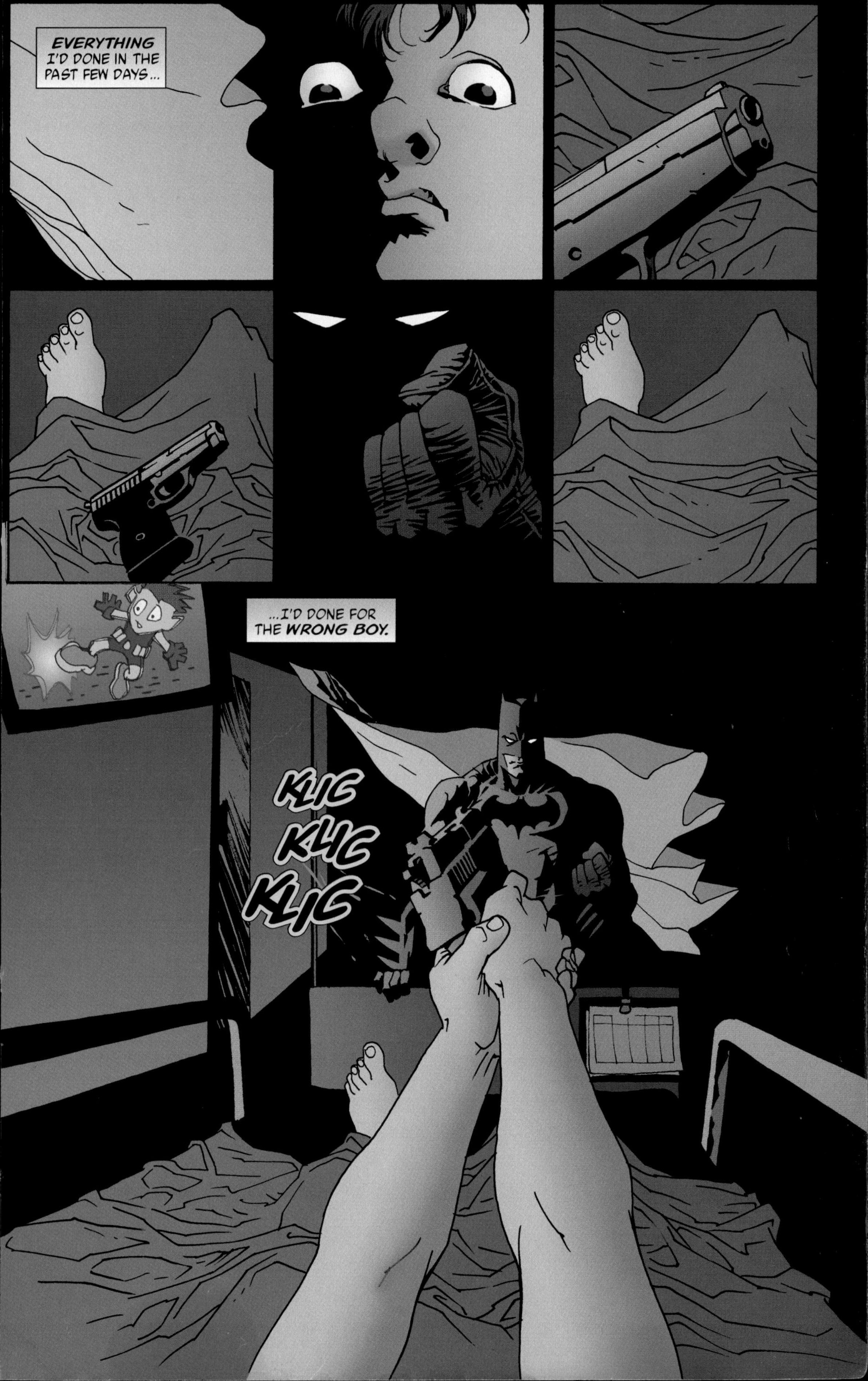
EVERYTHING I'D DONE IN THE PAST FEW DAYS...
...I'D DONE FOR THE WRONG BOY.
KLIC
KLIC
KLIC

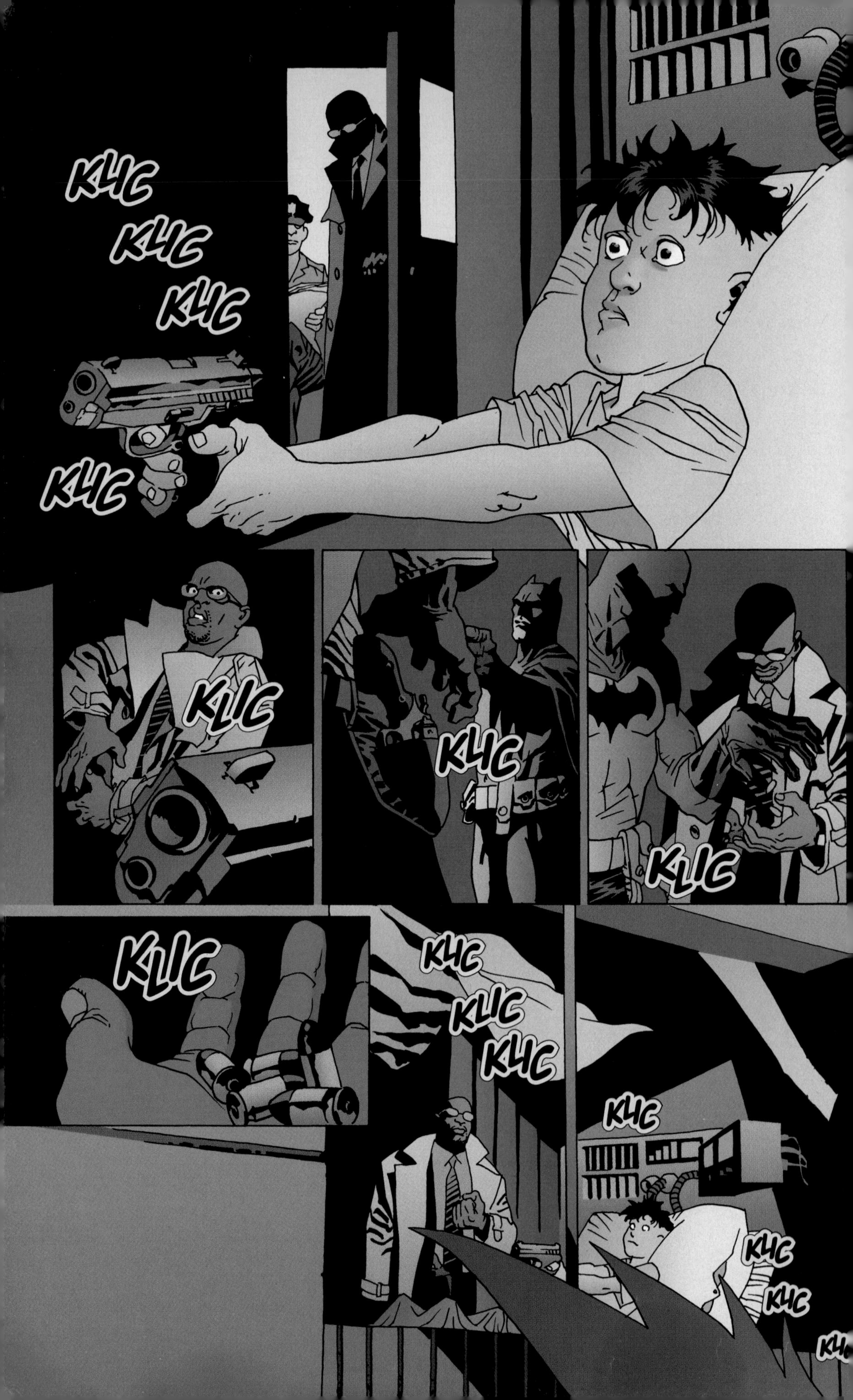
KLIC
KLIC
KLIC
KLIC
KLIC
KLIC
KLIC
KLIC
KLIC
KLIC
KLIC
KLIC
KLIC
KLIC

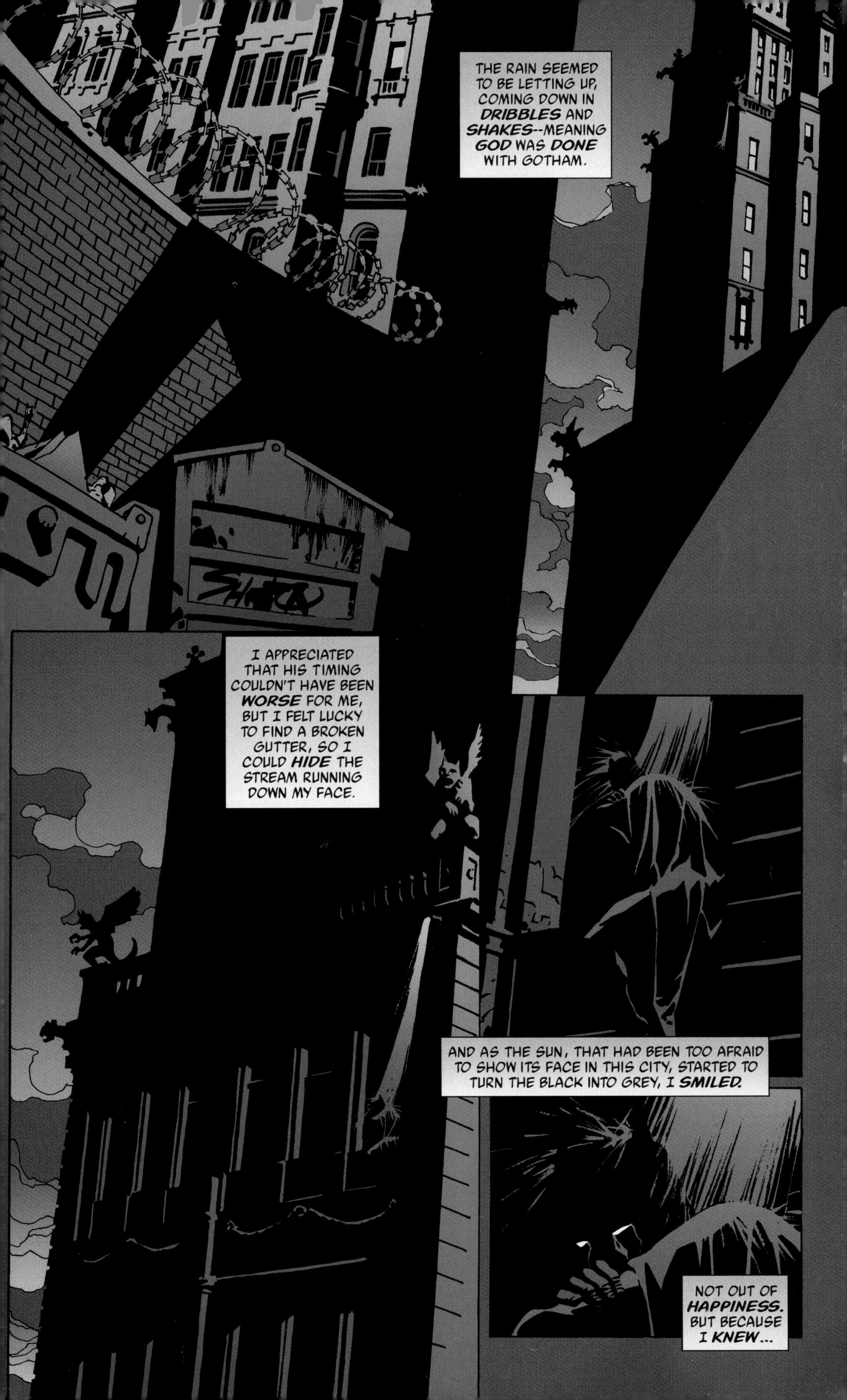
THE RAIN SEEMED TO BE LETTING UP, COMING DOWN IN **DRIBBLES** AND **SHAKES**--MEANING **GOD** WAS **DONE** WITH GOTHAM.
I APPRECIATED THAT HIS TIMING COULDN'T HAVE BEEN **WORSE** FOR ME, BUT I FELT LUCKY TO FIND A BROKEN GUTTER, SO I COULD **HIDE** THE STREAM RUNNING DOWN MY FACE.
AND AS THE SUN, THAT HAD BEEN TOO AFRAID TO SHOW ITS FACE IN THIS CITY, STARTED TO TURN THE BLACK INTO GREY, I **SMILED.**
NOT OUT OF **HAPPINESS.** BUT BECAUSE I **KNEW...**

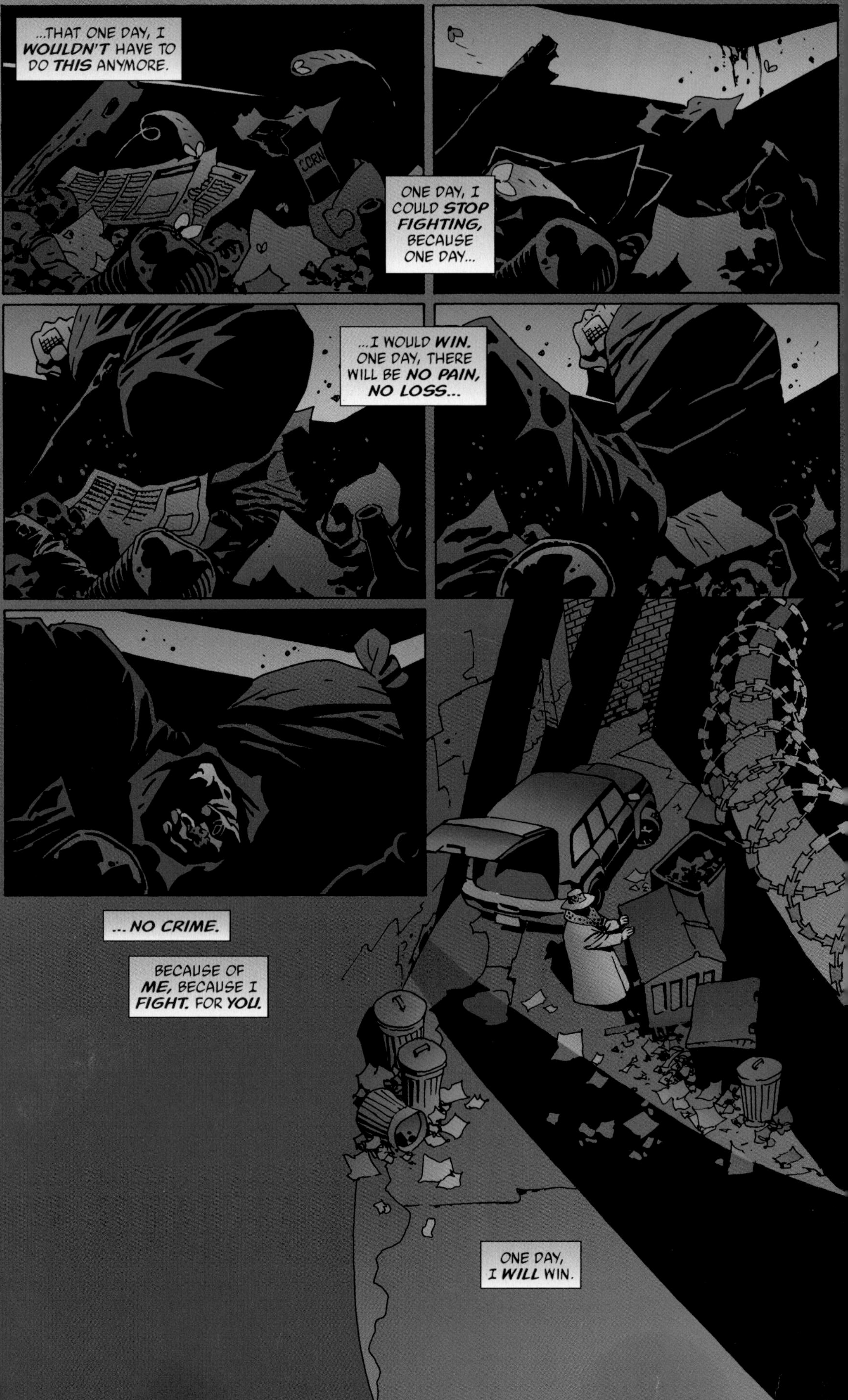
...THAT ONE DAY, I WOULDN'T HAVE TO DO THIS ANYMORE.
ONE DAY, I COULD STOP FIGHTING, BECAUSE ONE DAY...
...I WOULD WIN. ONE DAY, THERE WILL BE NO PAIN, NO LOSS...
...NO CRIME.
BECAUSE OF ME, BECAUSE I FIGHT. FOR YOU.
ONE DAY, I WILL WIN.

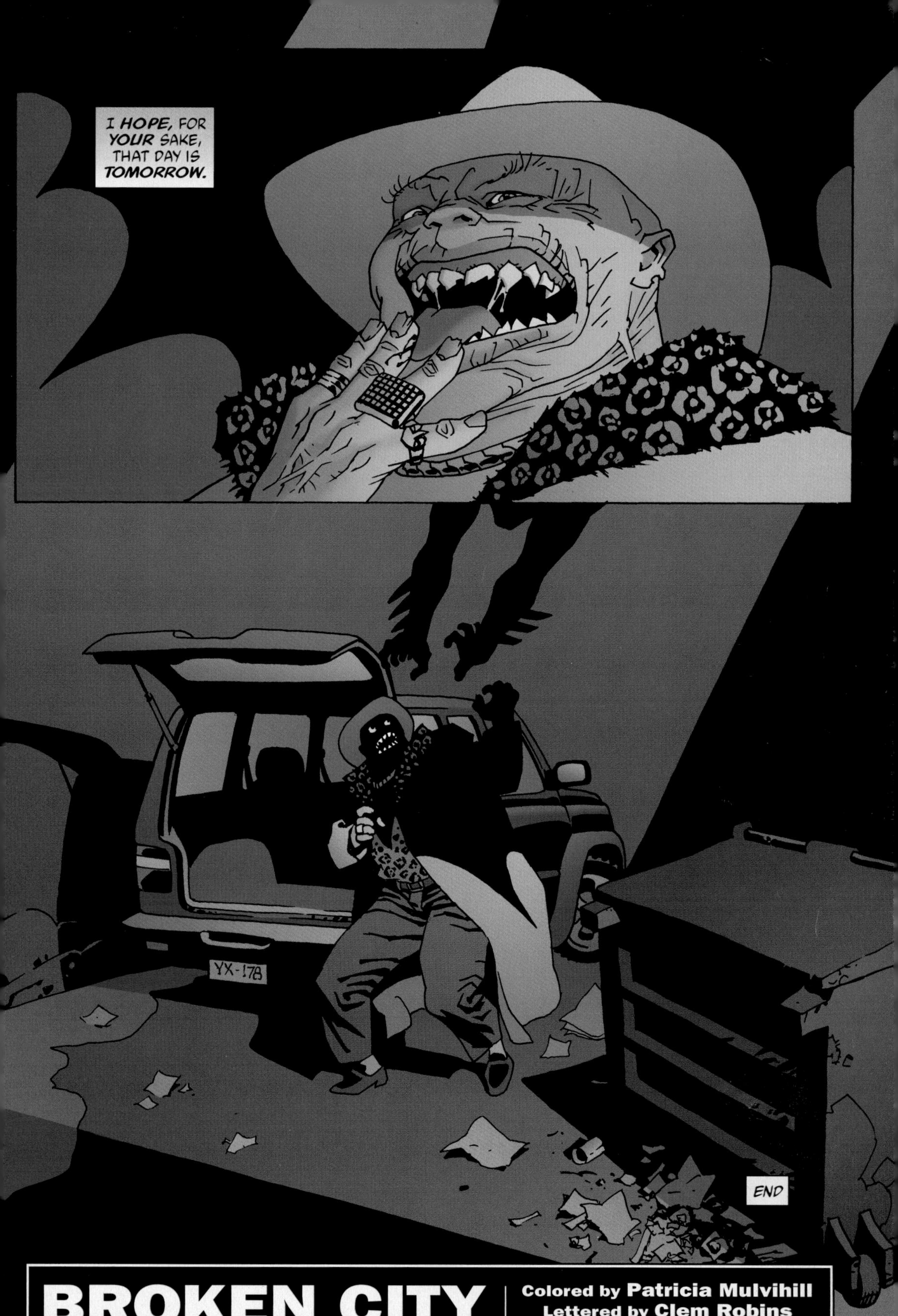
I HOPE, FOR YOUR SAKE, THAT DAY IS TOMORROW.
YX-178
END

BROKEN CITY
CONCLUSION

Written by BRIAN AZZARELLO
Illustrated by EDUARDO RISSO

Colored by Patricia Mulvihill
Lettered by Clem Robins
Cover by Dave Johnson
Assistant Editor Casey Seijas
Edited by Will Dennis
and Bob Schreck
Batman created by Bob Kane

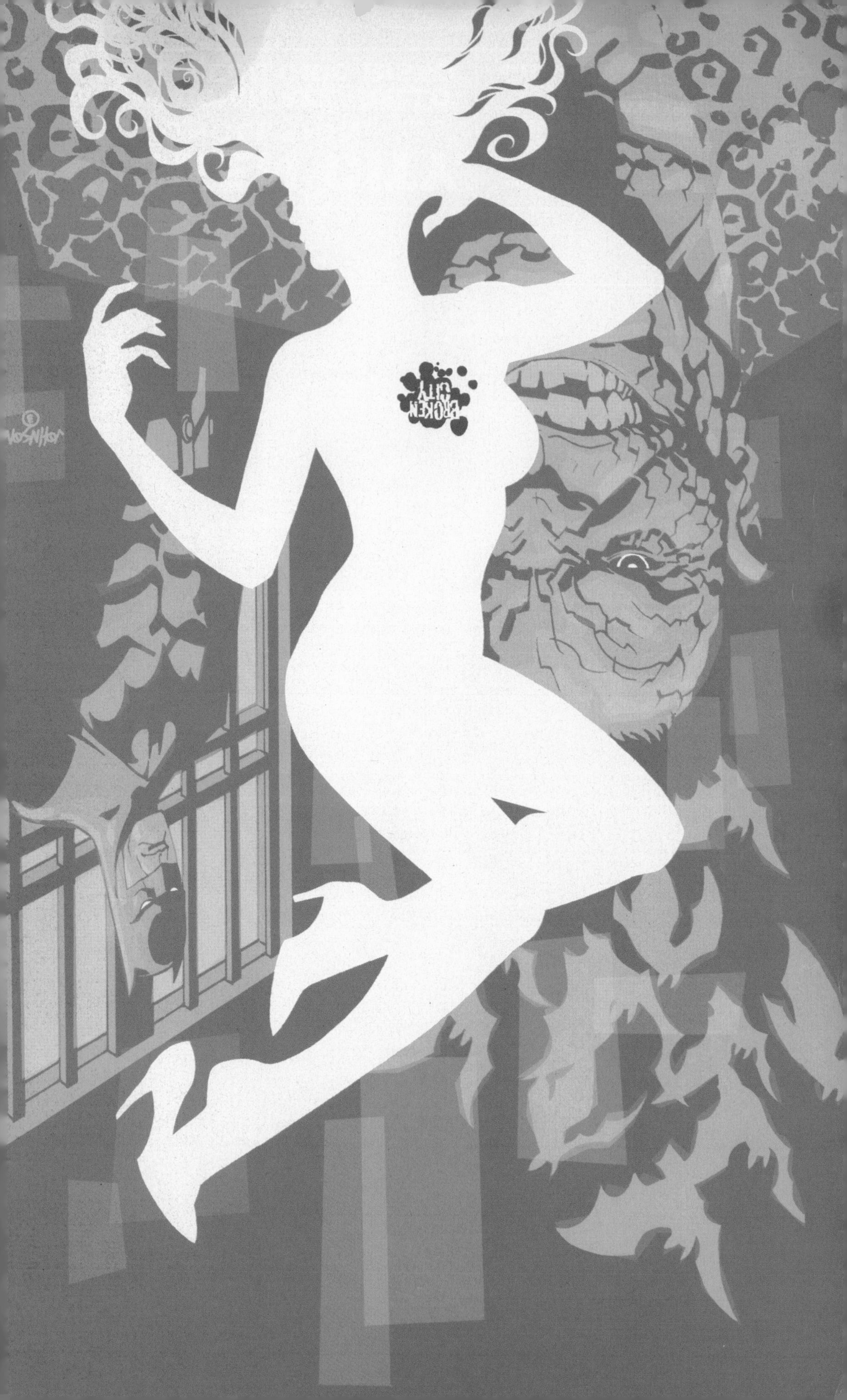
BROKEN CITY
JOHNSON

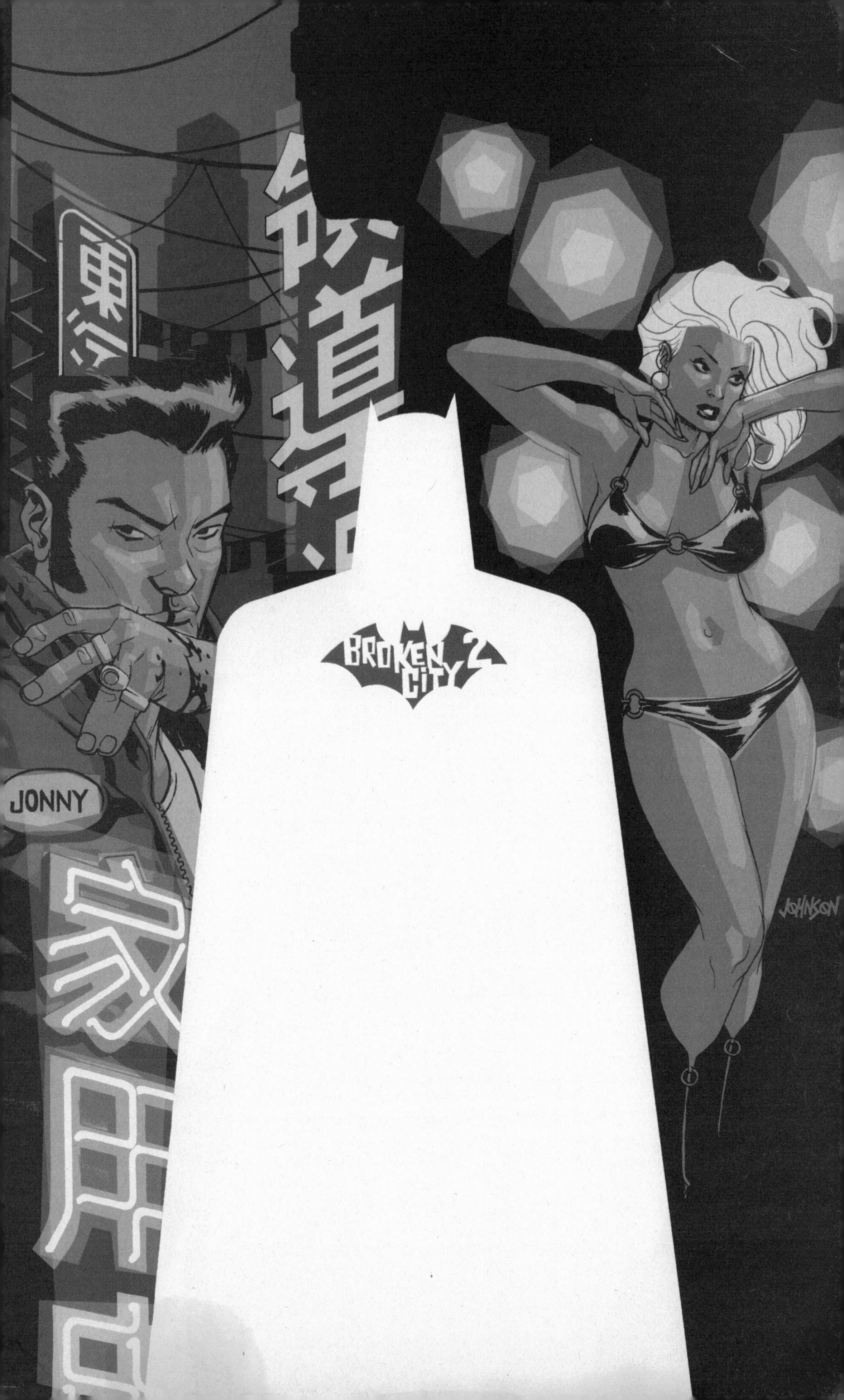
BROKEN CITY 2
JONNY
JOHNSON

Broken City 3
JOHNSON ©

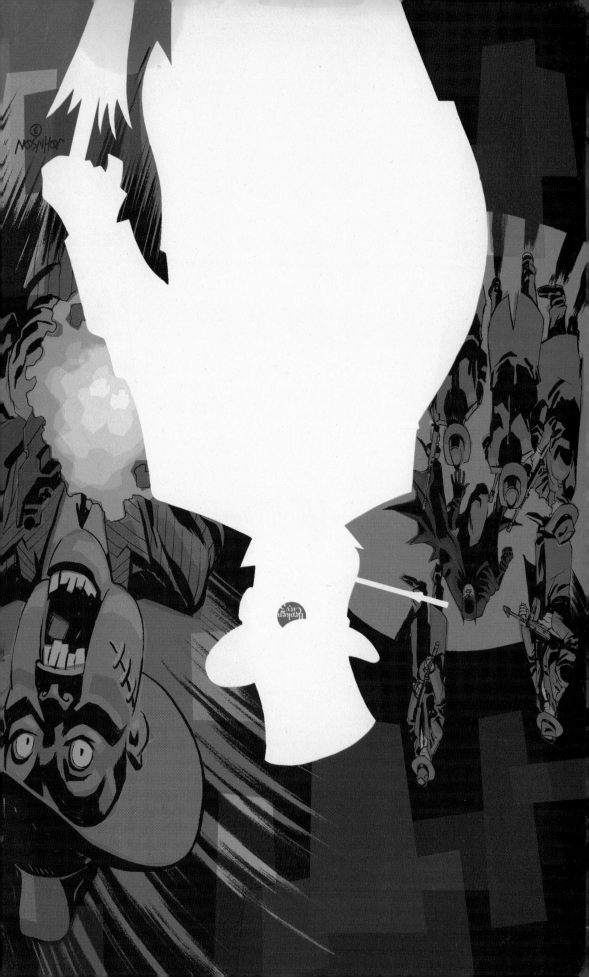

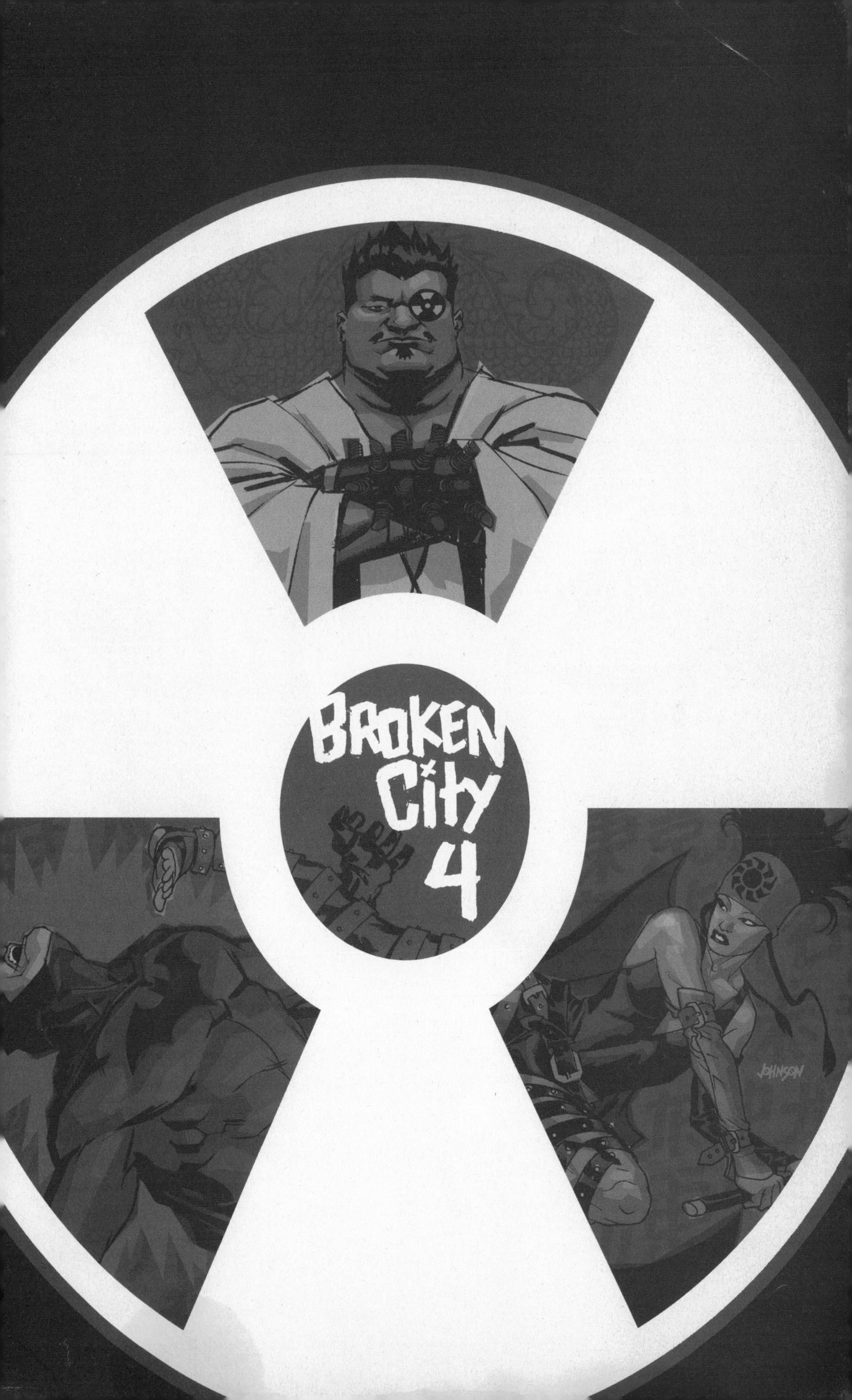
BROKEN
CITY
4
JOHNSON

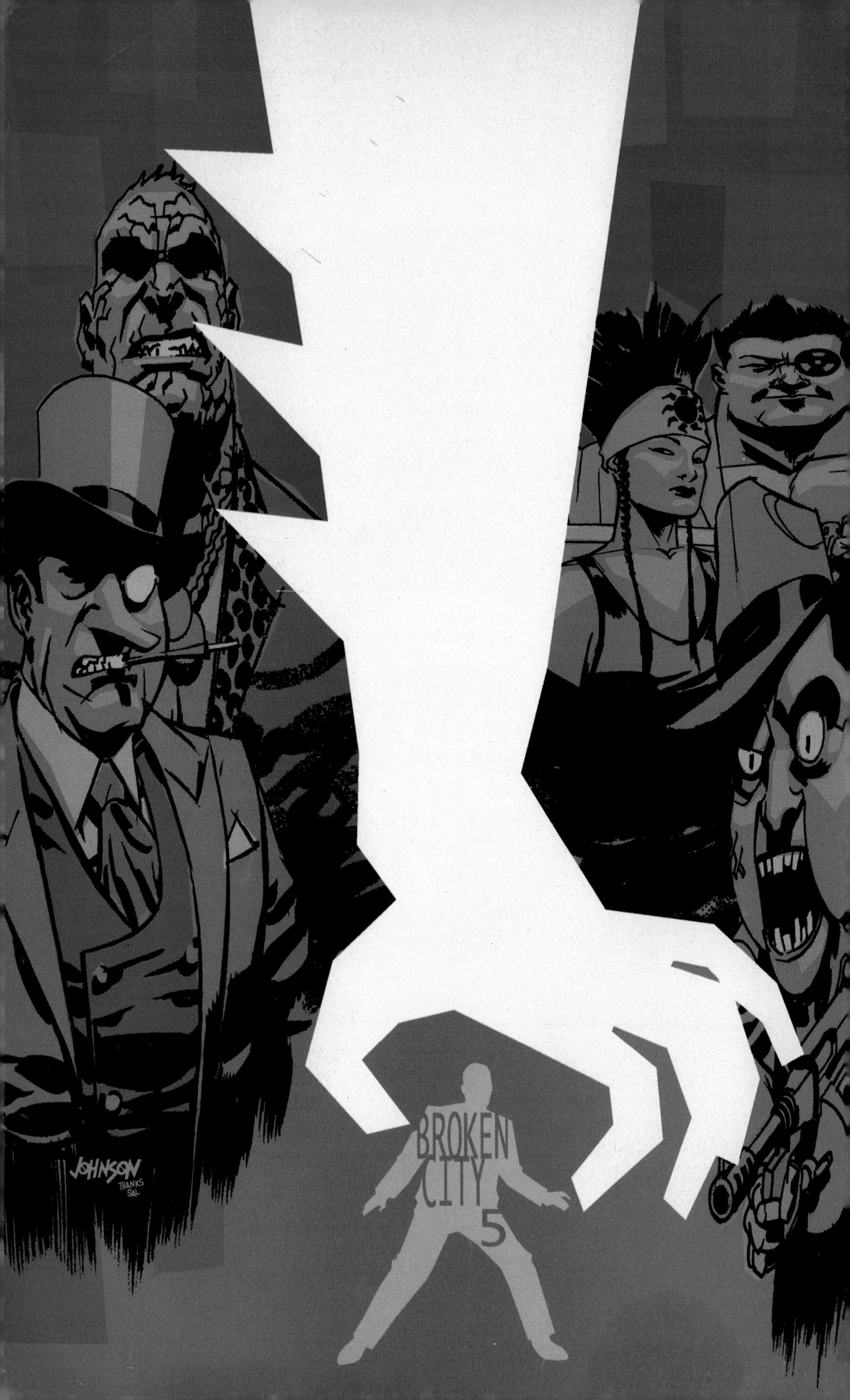
BROKEN
CITY
5
JOHNSON
THANKS
SAL

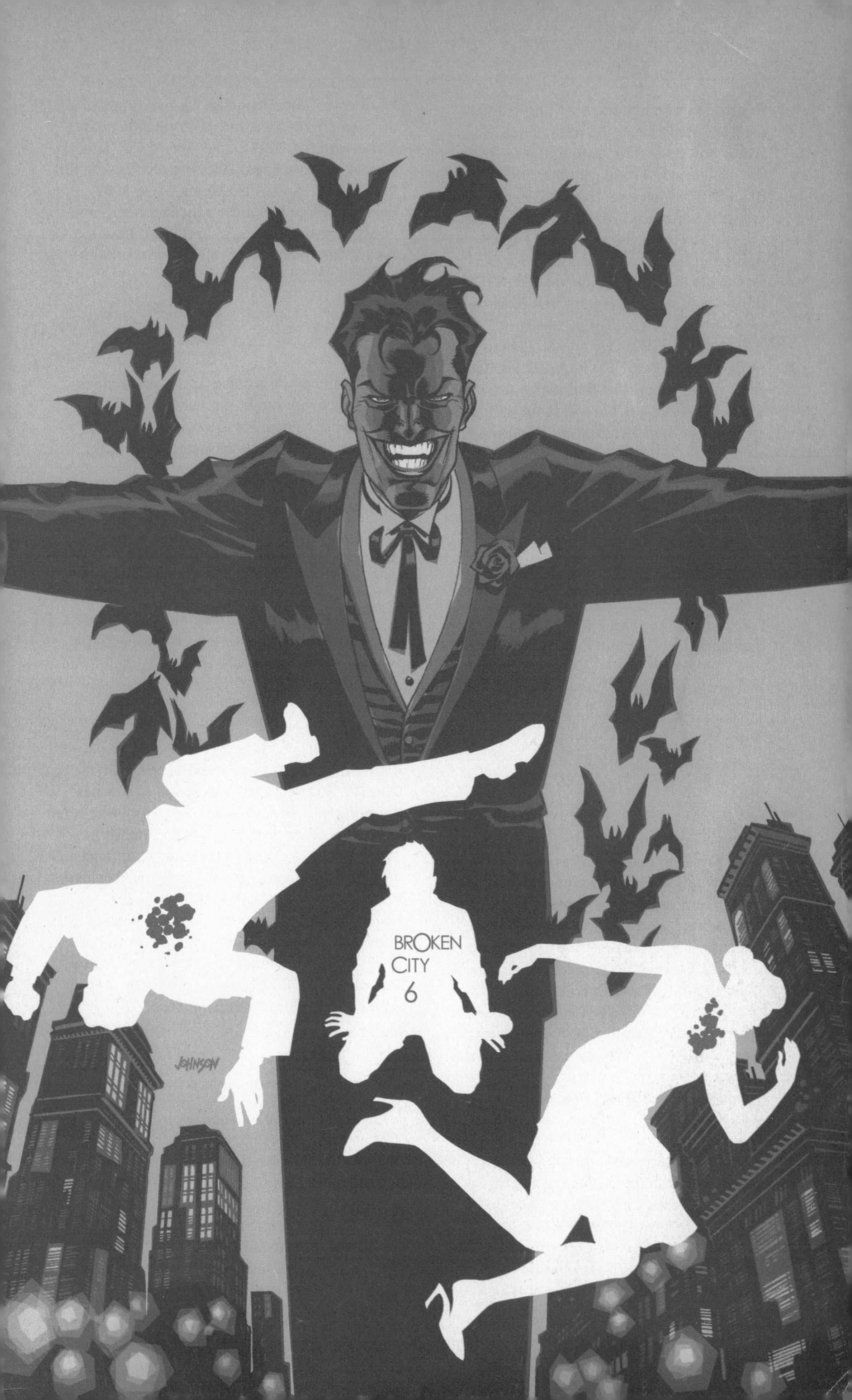
BROKEN
CITY
6
JOHNSON

Brian Azzarello

Brian Azzarello has been writing comics professionally since the mid-1990's. He is the writer and co-creator with Eduardo Risso of the acclaimed Vertigo monthly series 100 BULLETS, which won the 2002 Harvey and Eisner Awards for best continuing series.

Azzarello's other writing credits for DC Comics include BATMAN and JONNY DOUBLE (both with Risso), SUPERMAN (with artist Jim Lee) GANGLAND, BATMAN/DEATHBLOW and an Eisner-nominated run on HELLBLAZER. He has also written *Cage* and *Banner* for Marvel Comics. In 2004, Brian will team with artist Jim Lee for a year's worth of Superman stories in addition to writing LEX LUTHOR: MAN OF STEEL, a miniseries.

Brian has been cited as one of *Wizard* magazine's top ten writers and has been profiled and/or reviewed in *Entertainment Weekly*, *GEAR*, *The Chicago Tribune*, and countless other publications. He lives in Chicago with his wife, artist Jill Thompson, and still does not have a website.

Eduardo Risso

Eduardo Risso was born in 1959 in Leones, Argentina and began his career in 1981 doing illustrations for the newspaper *La Nacion* and various magazines. In 1987, Risso collaborated with writer Ricardo Barreiro on his first comic book, *Parque Chas*, and published in the anthology *Fierro*. He followed this with other Barreiro collaborations including *Cain* and *Los Misterios de la Luna Roja*. In 1989, Risso's first French work, *Fulu*, was published in *Vécu magazine* and after that by *Glénat*, in all, five books, all written by frequent collaborator Carlos Trillo, were published. By 1997, Risso's work was discovered in America and he was hired to illustrate Dark Horse Comics' adaptation of *Aliens: Resurrection*. A year later, he collaborated for the first time with Brian Azzarello on the JONNY DOUBLE miniseries. The duo worked so well together that they created 100 BULLETS, which continues to be published as a monthy comic and a series of collected editions. Risso also continues to work with Trillo, including four volumes of *Je Suis un Vampire* and *Lectures Macabres*.

Risso won the 2001 Eisner Award for "best serialized story," two 2002 Harvey Awards for "best artist" and "best series," two 2002 Eisner Awards for "best penciller/inker" and "best continuing series" and the Yellow Kid Award for "best artist," all for his work on 100 BULLETS.

Clem Robins

Clem Robins has worked as a letterer since 1977, for every major publisher and far too many minor ones. He is the winner of the prestigious Susan Lucci Award, for never having won any lettering awards. His illustrations have appeared in various magazines over the years, and his TV courtroom sketches have been featured on CNN. He teaches figure drawing and artistic anatomy at the Art Academy of Cincinnati, and his instructional book *The Art of Figure Drawing* has recently gone into its second printing. He lives in Norwood, Ohio with his very long-suffering wife Lisa.

Patricia Mulvihill

Patricia Mulvihill lives in a much-too-small New York City apartment, where she drinks large quantities of industrial-strength tea. She spends a great deal of time learning about the hidden mysteries of her computer and devising excuses to travel. She is shamelessly, ruthlessly devoted to 100 BULLETS. Her extensive credits include virtually every major character and title from DC Comics over the last decade including a noteworthy run on WONDER WOMAN. Don't ask her what her favorite color is...please.

Dave Johnson

Winner of the 2002 Eisner Award for Best Cover Artist, Dave continues to provide a fresh graphic voice to comics. His work with Brian Azzarello and Eduardo Risso began with the celebrated 100 BULLETS and continues the association with BROKEN CITY. Additionally, Dave is known for SUPERMAN: RED SON and currently works at Warner Bros. Animation.

The Seafarers THE MEN-OF-WAR

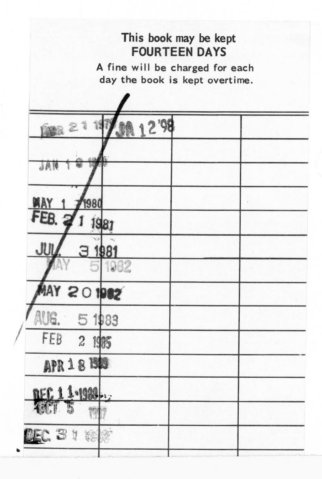

This book may be kept
FOURTEEN DAYS
A fine will be charged for each
day the book is kept overtime.

APR 2 1 1978 JA 12 '98		
JAN 1 8 1980		
MAY 1 7 1980		
FEB. 2 1 1981		
JUL. 3 1981		
MAY 5 1982		
MAY 2 0 1982		
AUG. 5 1983		
FEB 2 1985		
APR 1 8 1989		
DEC 1 1 1989		
OCT 5 1997		
DEC 3 1 1997		

TIME
LIFE
BOOKS ®

Other Publications:

THE ENCYCLOPEDIA OF COLLECTIBLES
THE GREAT CITIES
WORLD WAR II
HOME REPAIR AND IMPROVEMENT
THE WORLD'S WILD PLACES
THE TIME-LIFE LIBRARY OF BOATING
HUMAN BEHAVIOR
THE ART OF SEWING
THE OLD WEST
THE EMERGENCE OF MAN
THE AMERICAN WILDERNESS
THE TIME-LIFE ENCYCLOPEDIA OF GARDENING
LIFE LIBRARY OF PHOTOGRAPHY
THIS FABULOUS CENTURY
FOODS OF THE WORLD
TIME-LIFE LIBRARY OF AMERICA
TIME-LIFE LIBRARY OF ART
GREAT AGES OF MAN
LIFE SCIENCE LIBRARY
THE LIFE HISTORY OF THE UNITED STATES
TIME READING PROGRAM
LIFE NATURE LIBRARY
LIFE WORLD LIBRARY
FAMILY LIBRARY:
HOW THINGS WORK IN YOUR HOME
THE TIME-LIFE BOOK OF THE FAMILY CAR
THE TIME-LIFE FAMILY LEGAL GUIDE
THE TIME-LIFE BOOK OF FAMILY FINANCE

The Cover: Her hull abristle with cannon, a Dutch man-of-war fires a salute into the blue-white haze, announcing her entry into harbor while suggesting the hull-splintering might she could unleash in a less tranquil circumstance. The painting is by the great Dutch marine artist Willem van de Velde the Younger.

The Title Page: This gleaming bronze cannon, which bears the emblem of the Admiralty of Rotterdam, was in the arsenal of a 17th Century Dutch fighting ship. Weighing nearly two tons, the cannon could hurl a 12-pound shot one mile.

The Seafarers

THE MEN-OF-WAR

by David Howarth
AND THE EDITORS OF TIME-LIFE BOOKS

TIME-LIFE BOOKS, ALEXANDRIA, VIRGINIA

The Seafarers

Editorial Staff for The Men-of-War:
Editor: George G. Daniels
Picture Editor: Jane Coughran
Designer: Herbert H. Quarmby
Text Editors: Anne Horan. Sterling Seagrave
Staff Writers: William C. Banks. Carol Dana.
Stuart Gannes. Gus Hedberg
Chief Researcher: Martha T. Goolrick
Researchers: Mary G. Burns. Philip Brandt George.
W. Mark Hamilton. Katie Hooper McGregor. Blaine
McCornick Reilly. Peggy L. Sawyer. Kathleen Shortall
Art Assistant: Michelle René Clay
Editorial Assistant: Adrienne George

Editorial Production
Production Editor: Douglas B. Graham
Operations Manager: Gennaro C. Esposito
Assistant Production Editor: Feliciano Madrid
Quality Control: Robert L. Young (director). James J. Cox
(assistant). Michael G. Wight (associate)
Art Coordinator: Anne B. Landry
Copy Staff: Susan B. Galloway (chief). Sheirazada Hann.
Elise D. Ritter. Florence Keith. Celia Beattie
Picture Department: Marguerite Johnson

Correspondents: Elisabeth Kraemer (Bonn); Margot
Hapgood. Dorothy Bacon (London); Susan Jonas. Lucy T.
Voulgaris (New York); Maria Vincenza Aloisi. Josephine
du Brusle (Paris); Ann Natanson (Rome).
Valuable assistance was also provided by: Janny
Hovinga (Amsterdam); Ole Schierbeck (Copenhagen);
Penny Newman (London); Bill Lyon (Madrid); Carolyn T.
Chubet. Miriam Hsia (New York); Alison Raphael
(Rio de Janeiro); Mary Johnson (Stockholm); Traudl
Lessing (Vienna).

The editors are indebted to Barbara Hicks. Karin Hills.
Barbara Levitt and Philip C. F. Smith for their help in the
preparation of this book.

The Author:
David Howarth, who has written a number
of books on seafaring, brings to his work a
practical knowledge of ships and the sea.
During World War II he rose from seaman to
lieutenant commander in the Royal Navy
and spent four years in the Shetland Islands
organizing fishing boats with crews of Norwegian volunteers to land agents and arms
in occupied Norway. After the War he designed and built boats, before turning to
writing full time. His books include Sovereign of the Seas, Trafalgar and Panama.

The Consultants:
John Horace Parry, Gardiner Professor of
Oceanic History and Affairs at Harvard
University, received his Ph.D. from Cam-
bridge University. Among his numerous
historical studies are The Discovery of the
Sea and The Spanish Seaborne Empire.

Geoffrey Vaughan Scammell is director of
studies in history at Cambridge University's Pembroke College and the author of numerous articles on maritime history.

Philip Bosscher is a lecturer at the Royal
Netherlands Naval Academy and a lieutenant commander in the Netherlands Royal
Navy. The author of several books and articles on Dutch naval history, he studied at
the Universities of Bologna, Leiden and
Freiburg, Germany.

William Avery Baker is a naval architect
and curator of the Hart Nautical Museum at
the Massachusetts Institute of Technology.
He has designed reproductions of a number
of 17th and 18th Century ships and written
books on maritime history and ship design.

David Lyon is an expert in historical ships'
plans and a board member of the Nautical
Archeological Trust. He has participated in
the underwater survey of the 16th Century
British warship Mary Rose and is the author
of Navies of the Revolution.

Library of Congress Cataloging in Publication Data
Howarth. David Armine (date)
   The men-of-war.
   (The seafarers ; v.5)
   Bibliography: p.
   Includes index.
   1. Navies—History—17th century. 2. Naval art and
science—History—17th century. 3. Anglo-Dutch War.
1652-1654. 4. Anglo-Dutch War. 1664-1667. I. Time-Life
Books. II. Title. III. Series
V47.H68   359'.009'032   78-18476
ISBN 0-8094-2668-4
ISBN 0-8094-2667-6 lib. bdg.

Contents

Essay Rivals to inherit the earth   6

Chapter 1 **A marriage of cannon and sail**   14

Essay The "Wasa" reborn from the deep   40

Chapter 2 **Titanic trials for the new navies**   46

Essay In celebration of the waters around them   68

Chapter 3 **A Spanish interlude between the wars**   76

Chapter 4 **The nemesis of the dockyard thieves**   96

Essay The fire ship: a triumph of the incendiary's art   116

Chapter 5 **"To fly is the fashion of cowards"**   124

Chapter 6 **Twin catastrophes: God's fire, Holland's revenge**   146

Essay The greater victory that might have been   162

BIBLIOGRAPHY   170

ACKNOWLEDGMENTS   171

PICTURE CREDITS   172

INDEX   173

Rivals to inherit the earth

"Whosoever commands the sea commands trade; whosoever commands the trade of the world commands the riches of the world, and consequently the world itself." Thus did Sir Walter Raleigh in the early 1600s set down a doctrine that would alter the course of Western civilization—and for centuries serve as a virtual declaration of war on the high seas.

For almost a hundred years after the heroic burst of exploration at the end of the 15th and beginning of the 16th Centuries, Spain and Portugal ruled the world's oceans, harvesting without challenge the riches of their newly discovered lands. In 1580 Spain conquered Portugal and became sole lord of the seas. But by the turn of the 17th Century, two new maritime powers had emerged to drive the old order into decline, as this series of paintings by the Dutch marine artist Hendrick Corneliszoon Vroom shows.

In England there was an upsurge in trade and exploration in the 1500s as the fetters of the Dark Ages fell away. This explosion of commerce led to the development of bigger, more seaworthy ships, and a growing corps of professional seamen to sail them. Inevitably there were clashes with Spain, and out of them grew ever more heavily armed English warships designed to contest Spain's—or anyone else's—claim to sovereignty on the seas. Indeed, the English, in the Narrow Seas around their island, claimed that right for themselves.

At about the same time, the industrious and ambitious Dutch across the North Sea from England were sending forth fleets of armed merchantmen to wrest African and Far Eastern markets from the Spanish Crown. And gradually, the Dutch, too, developed their own sailing warships to attack the Spanish and protect their own convoys.

Soon these two young and aggressive imperial powers would be at each other's throats. Their weapons would be the new warships—the men-of-war—that they were now forming into great national Navies. For neither the English nor the Dutch were content to see the other inherit Spain's former monopoly on seaborne trade. Echoing an opinion held by most of his countrymen shortly before the eruption in 1652 of the first two Anglo-Dutch naval wars, one English captain declared, "The trade of the world is too little for us two, therefore one must down."

Drifting in on the tide, a flotilla of five blazing English ships—deliberately set on fire—descends on the Spanish Armada as it lies off Calais in 1588. These fire ships were so terrifying that the Spaniards at this stage of the engagement did not trade broadsides with English men-of-war, as Hendrick Vroom shows in this painting, but fled without even firing a shot.

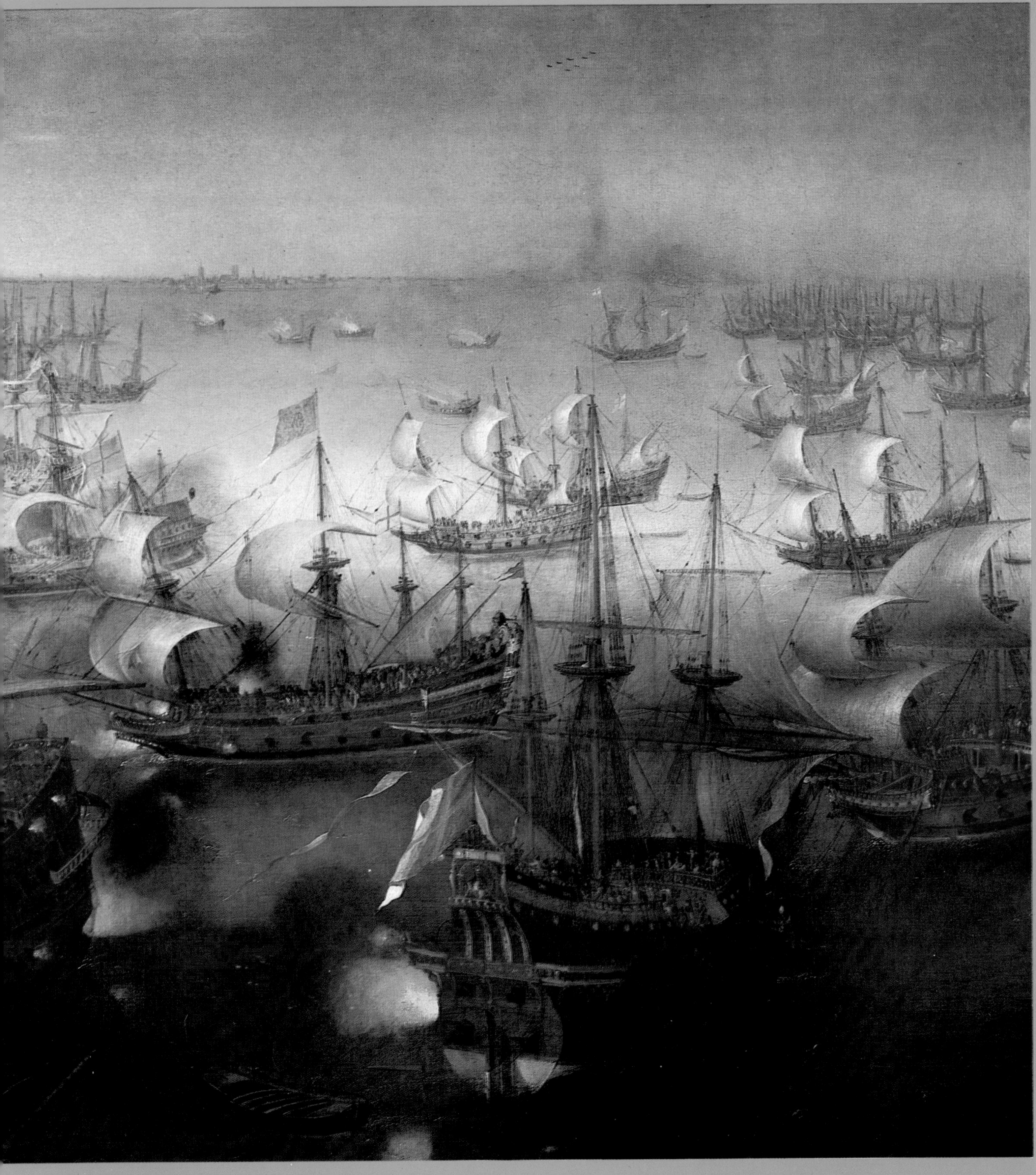

Driving downwind under full sail, an early Dutch man-of-war, the Maen, crushes the Spanish galley Padilla beneath her bows off the Flemish coast in 1602. Desperate to break the growing Dutch control of north European waters, Spain sent a small fleet of the swift Mediterranean galleys to confront the Dutch, but the tender, lightly armed craft proved to be helpless against their sturdy, cannon-carrying opponents.

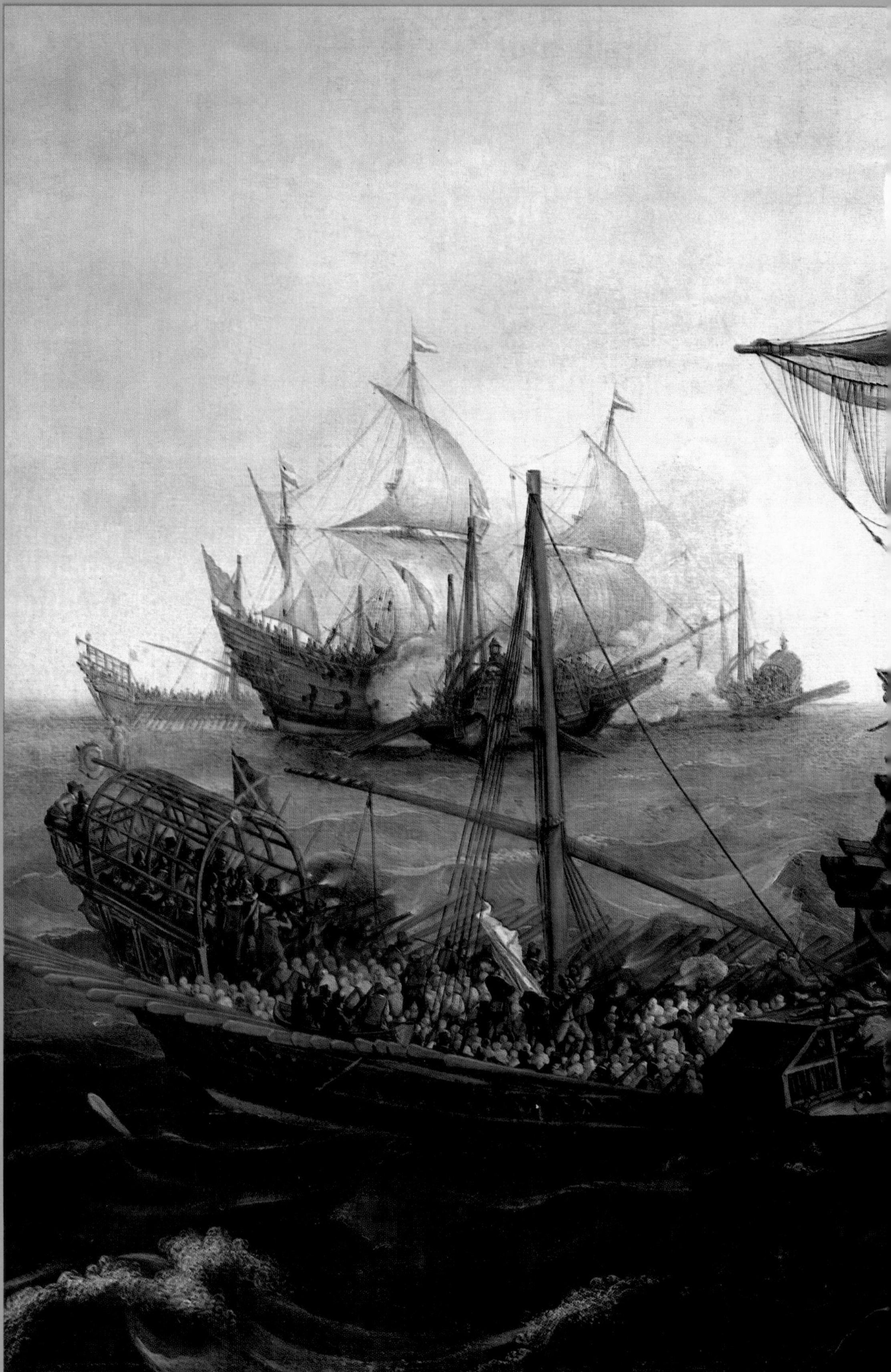

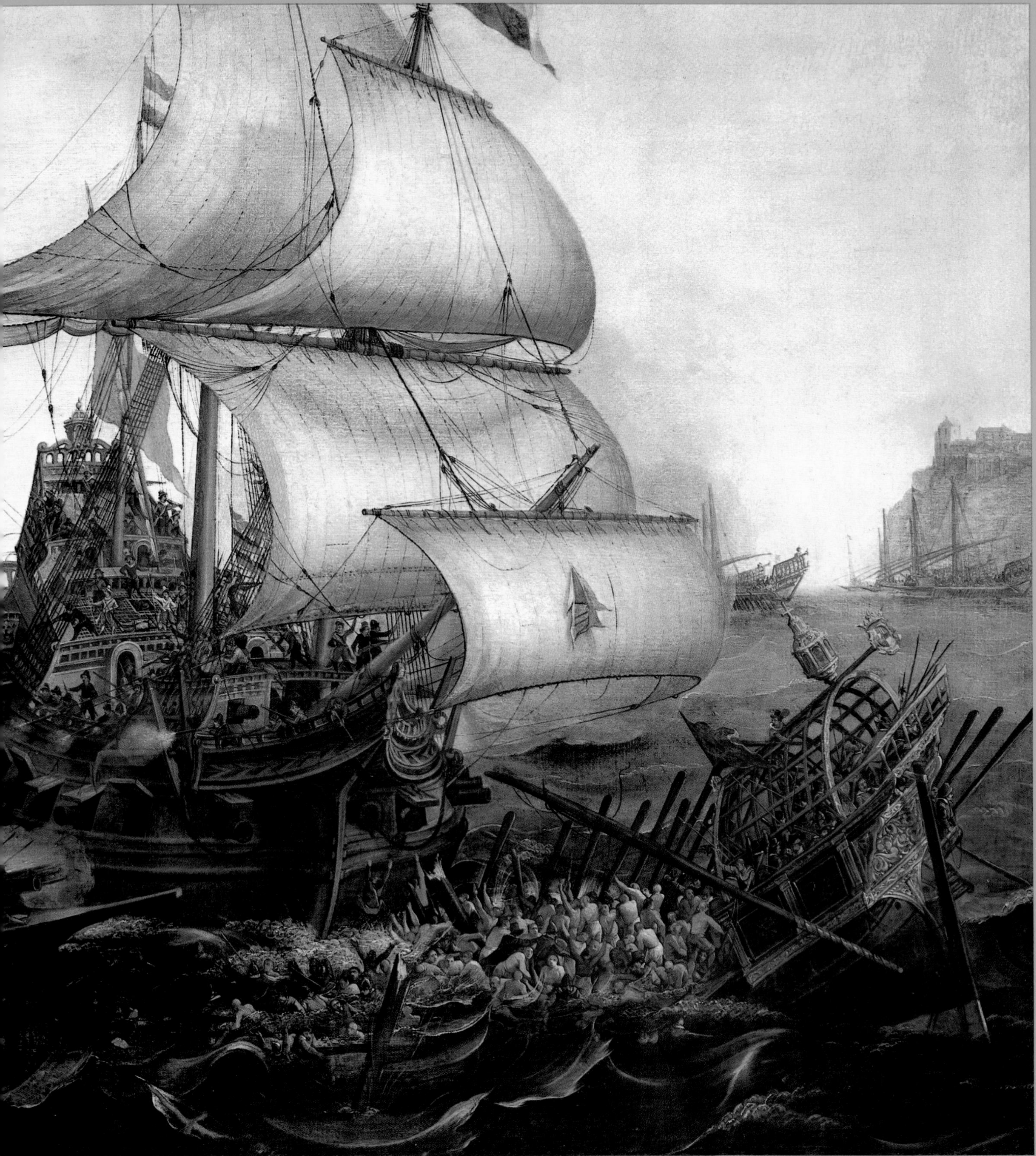

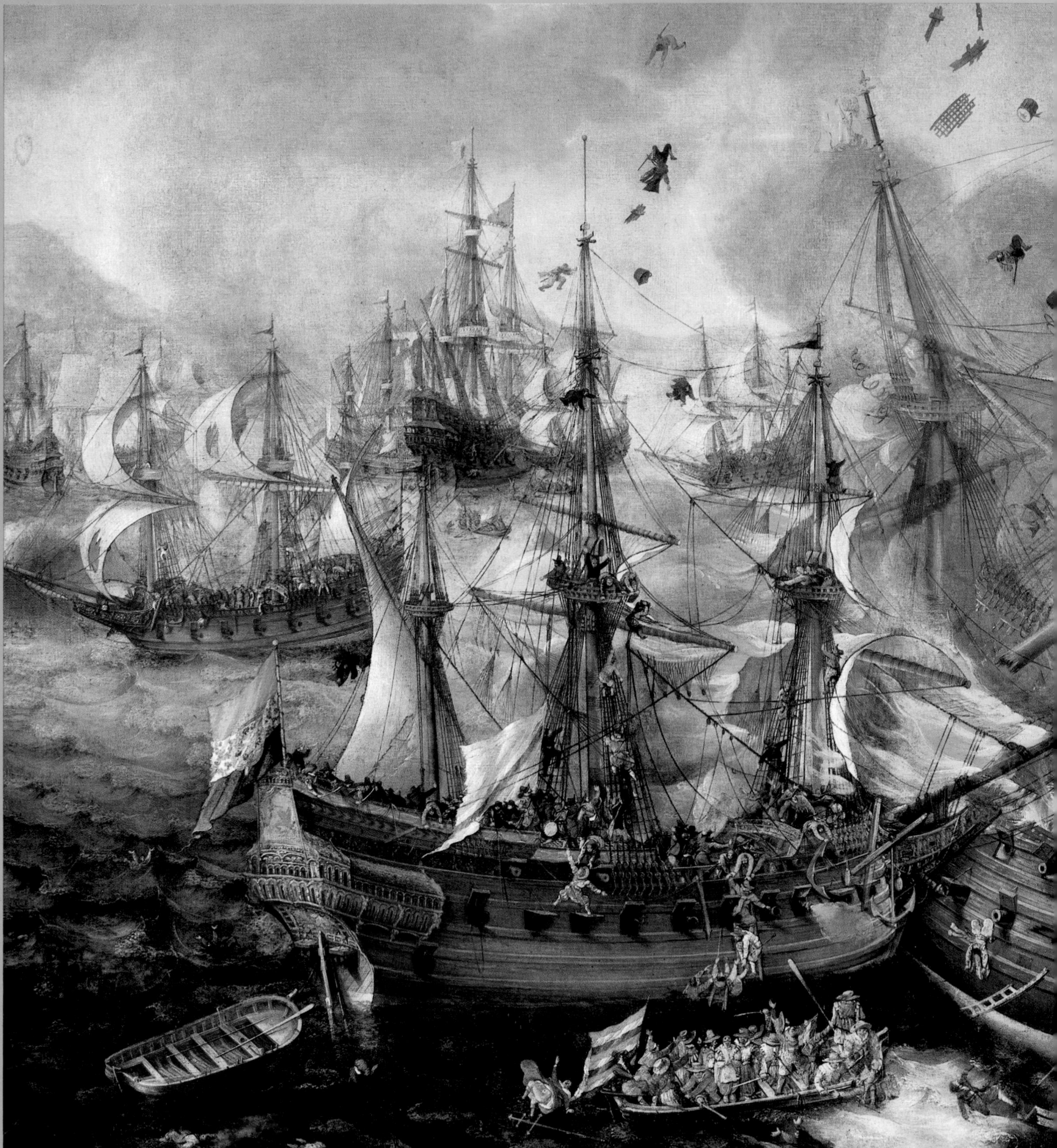

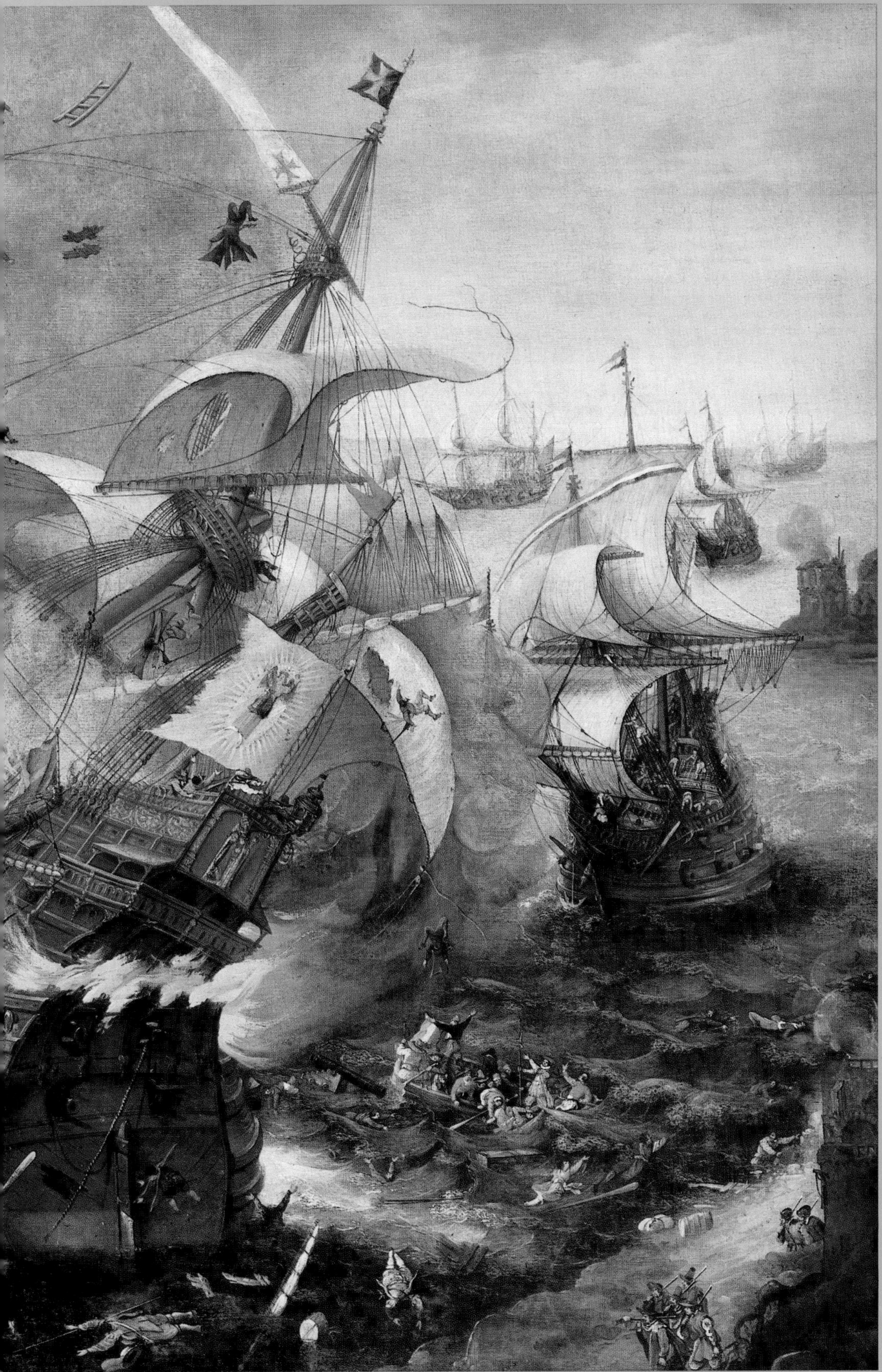

As a Dutch warship rams amidships, the magazine of a much larger Spanish flagship explodes, hurling men and debris hundreds of feet into the air during a battle near Gibraltar in 1607. With this bold attack in Spanish home waters, Dutch Admiral Jacob van Heemskerck sought to discourage Spain from launching armadas into northern waters. Van Heemskerck himself was killed in the battle but his fleet won the day, sinking or disabling 14 of the Spanish ships.

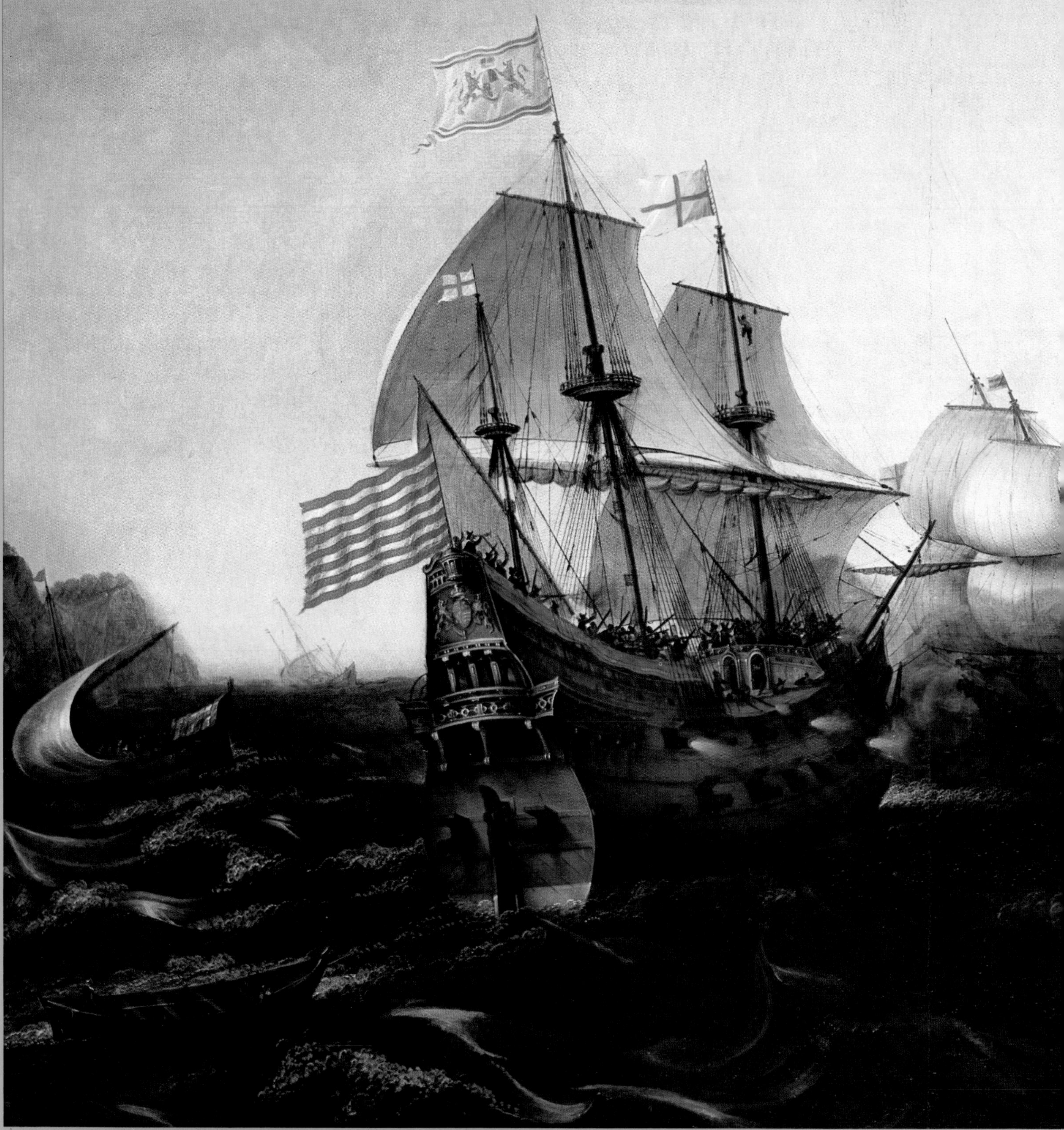

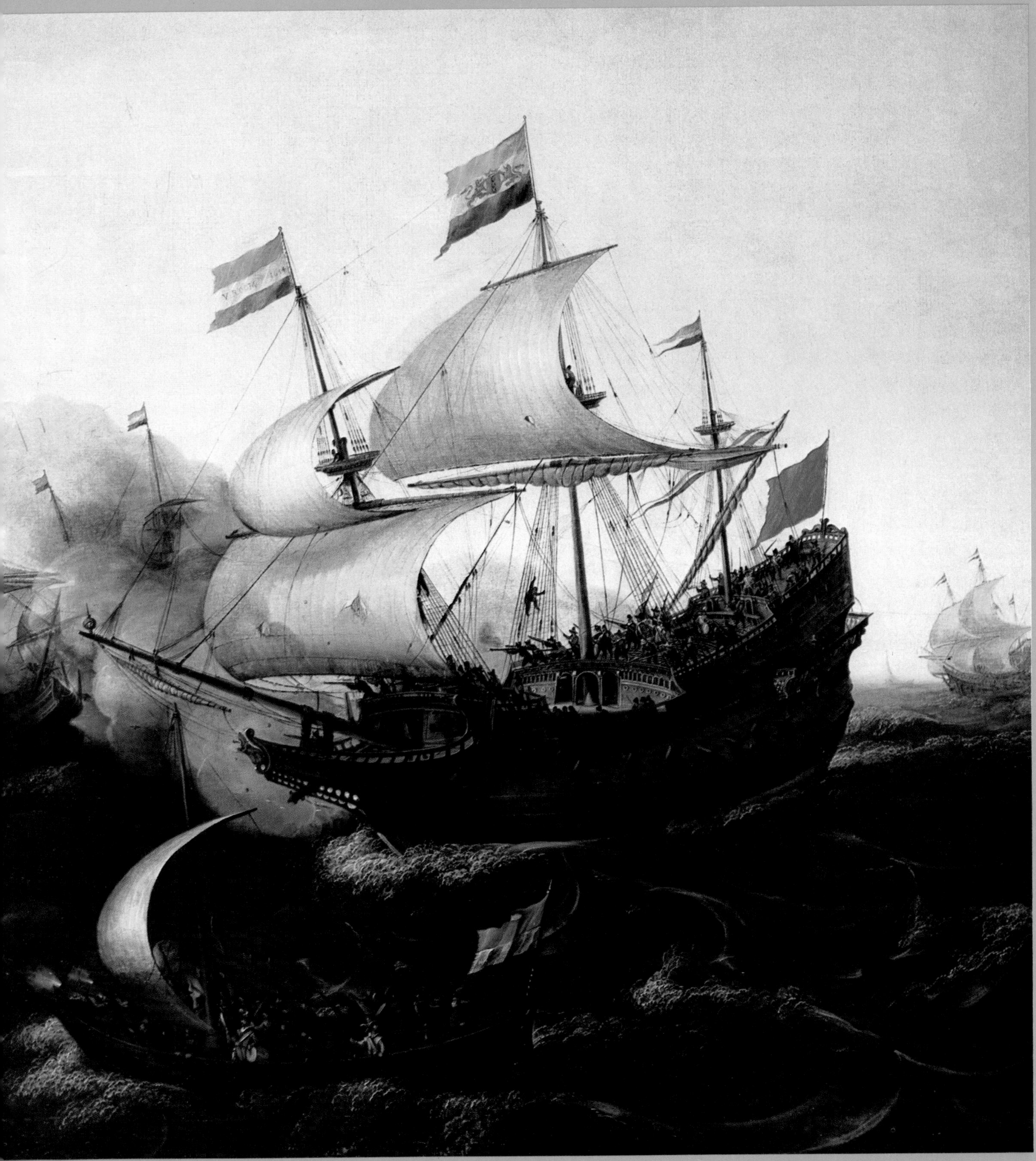

With the striped flag of a vice admiral flying from her sternpost, the English man-of-war Vanguard lets go a broadside at a Dutchman during a skirmish in the English Channel in the early 1600s. Claiming sovereignty over the Channel, England insisted that all of the foreign ships dip their flags in salute when passing; the Dutch skipper refused and unfurled his red flag of battle. As Spanish strength faded, the two emergent powers found themselves increasingly at odds, until war became inevitable.

Chapter 1

A marriage of cannon and sail

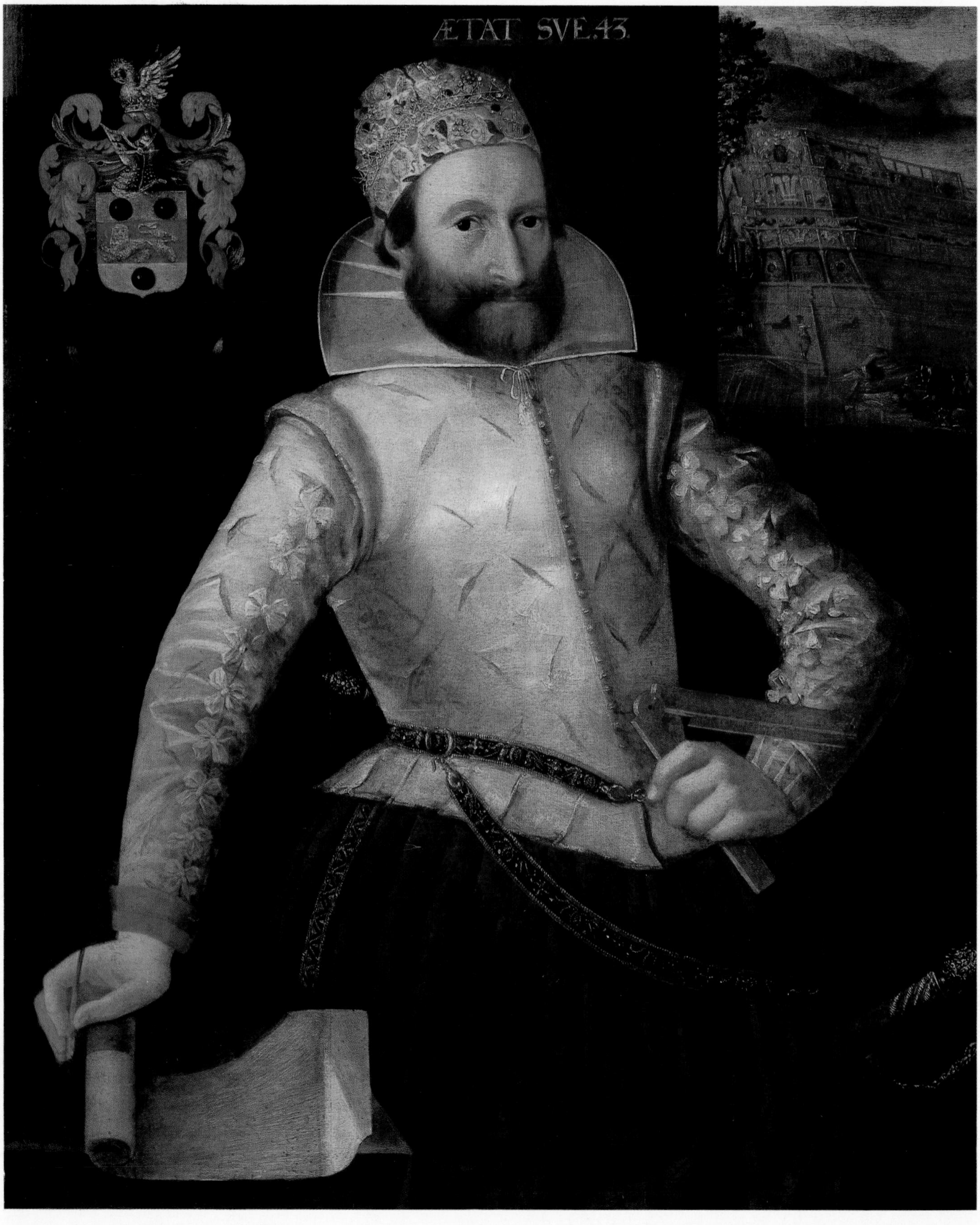
ÆTAT SVE.43

n the year 1607, an English shipwright named Phineas Pett wrote in his journal: "I began a curious model, the most part whereof I wrought with my own hands; which being most fairly garnished with carving and painting, and placed in a frame arched, covered and curtained with crimson taffety, was, the 10th day of November, by me presented to the Lord High Admiral at his lodging at Whitehall."

The Lord High Admiral was Howard of Effingham, who had commanded Queen Elizabeth I's fleet against the Spanish Armada 19 years before, and the curious model was of a new warship. In basic design she resembled the most up-to-date of the Elizabethan ships now in His Majesty's service—low-built, four-masted and square-rigged, with long rows of cannon firing through gunports in her sides. But there was a vast difference in scale. At a projected 1,200 tons, she was almost half again as big as any warship in existence. And the extra size provided sufficient height for greatly improved armament. Most Elizabethan ships had two rows of cannon, one on the main deck and a second firing through ports on the deck below. But the new ship was tall enough for an additional covered gun deck, making three fearsome ranks of artillery in all. She thus would carry 64 heavy guns, 50 per cent more than the older ships, and a correspondingly bigger crew of some 500 men.

The Lord High Admiral was much attracted by the design, and he quickly passed the model on to King James I who, according to Pett, was "exceedingly delighted." The King commissioned Pett to build the great ship in the royal dockyards at Woolwich on the Thames.

This was a considerable coup for Pett, and it brought an immediate howl of protest from rival shipwrights—with some reason. Though Pett came from a family that had produced at least a dozen master builders in the past half century, most of whom (to the confusion of later historians) were christened either Phineas or Peter, this particular Phineas was noted mainly for his vanity and peppery disposition. At 37, he had built only two ships before, and both of them were small. One was not much more than a toy—a miniature replica of the *Ark Royal,* which had served as the English flagship in the fight against the Spanish Armada—for Prince Henry, King James's eldest son, to sail in the safety of the Thames above London Bridge. The other was a merchant ship that Pett had built on speculation, and he had been accused by the King's Commission of purloining timber from the royal dockyards to construct it. The charge had never been proved, and it was a common enough practice of the time, in any event. But this allegation, combined with his difficult personality and seeming lack of talent, left Pett more or less permanently on the outs with his peers.

None of Pett's rivals could believe he was competent to complete such a ship as he proposed. It seemed to them that he had hit on this grandiose design merely to bring himself to the notice of the King and to secure a profitable commission. From the start, his rivals spied on his work at Woolwich, and as it progressed they sent biting reports to the King.

"First, the mould is altogether unperfect," wrote seven of them in a formal deposition, adding that "she hath too much floor" (meaning too many timbers lying transverse to her keel) and that "her breadth lieth too

Splendidly attired in a white doublet and embroidered cap, shipwright Phineas Pett gives every evidence of the wealth and position that accrued to him in 1610 as designer and builder of a great warship for England's King James I. The Prince Royal, seen here on the ways outside Pett's window, was the first vessel to carry three decks of cannon —an arsenal that made her, as was said at the time, "a ship to fight for a kingdom."

high, and so she will draw too much water, and thereby be dangerous and unfit for our shoal seas.'' Caviling over her lavish decorations— which were to include a set of roaring lions' heads above 14 of her gunports—they charged Pett with constructing a showpiece instead of a proper warship. Moreover, work so far completed was "very ill done." The timber was "cross-grained and overgrown"; the frame was "unfit for any use but a dung boat"—and the projected price of £20,000, enough for six smaller ships, was four times as much as it should have been.

At last the din grew so loud that the King himself decided to go down to Woolwich to hold an inquiry. The result was a remarkable scene in the shipyard, on a May morning in 1609. Thousands of people turned up to watch. The great keel of the new ship, 115 feet in length, lay on the chocks in the building dock: the stem and stern and some of the frame had been erected, and the lower part of the planking was in place. The workmen's canteen was hung with draperies to make it fit for the royal presence. While everyone waited for the King, Pett's critics, so the embattled shipwright said, "pryed up and down the yard, belching out nothing but disgraces, despiteful speeches, and base opprobrious terms." They predicted that he would be hanged.

At the inquiry, no fewer than 50 witnesses were called to testify. Pett spent much of the day in the tiresome position required of a defendant— on his knees in front of the King. James listened carefully to all the complaints, and listened, too, to Pett's rather lame explanation that the attacks on him were entirely due to malice and jealousy. The King climbed all over the partly built ship to judge matters for himself.

In the end, to the surprise of almost everyone present, King James decided in Pett's favor. In a Solomonic stroke, he appointed two of the most severe critics to advise Pett, but Pett was allowed to finish the job. The ship was completed and launched in 1610. She was named the *Prince Royal*, and in spite of everything said against her, she was a complete vindication of her builder.

The "floor" the critics had found too timbered helped support the added weight of heavy guns. The draft they had found too deep steadied her under the impact of the guns' recoil—as she was to prove in a long and distinguished combat career. Even the lavish décor fulfilled a purpose; showiness in the years to come would be one way in which the 17th Century naval powers might advertise their authority on the high seas.

Indeed, it could be said that the *Prince Royal* was a ship whose day had come. She arrived on the scene just at a time when naval strength, rarely before more than an adjunct to prowess on land, suddenly became a vital end in itself. The first years of the 17th Century found England engaged in a fierce competition for supremacy with its chief commercial and maritime rival: the lusty young Dutch Republic across the North Sea. Dutch merchantmen plied the world's seas and oceans in such numbers that a Dutch official in the early 1600s boasted, "The Hollanders have well nigh beaten all nations, by traffic, out of the seas, and have become the only carrier of goods throughout the world." This was an exaggeration, and one that annoyed the English exceedingly, for their own vessels were sailing to all points of the compass on missions of exploration, colonization and, above all, trade. Nevertheless, there was

Taking in sail to reduce speed, the Prince Royal enters Flushing harbor in Holland on a state visit in 1613. The first of a long line of three-tiered English men-of-war, the Prince Royal proved successful in battle, but initially the new design won only grudging acceptance. One English admiral complained that the extra gun deck created "so great a smoke within board that people must use their arms like blind men, not knowing how to go about their work, or having a sight of the ship whom they encounter."

some truth in the Dutch claim to maritime supremacy, and the English made up their minds to end it.

Inevitably, these rival ambitions led to a clash of arms. And when it came, the war was of titanic proportions. The battlefield was the sea, and the weapons were something that had never existed before: great sailing navies composed of state-owned men-of-war like the *Prince Royal*, vessels specifically designed for fighting, mounting cannon of great destructive power and manned by professional mariners who went into combat with an agreed and rehearsed set of tactics. All this was new to fighting at sea: the men-of-war, the armament, the combatant crewmen, the tactics, the standing national navies. What was new, too, was the vast shoreside establishment known as the Admiralty, which evolved to buttress the contending fleets with dockyards, arsenals and victualers, and a hierarchy that issued commands and dealt with violations of the rules.

The battles between the English and the Dutch, taking place in two brief but intense wars—the first from 1652 to 1654, the second from 1665 to 1667—were the most evenly matched in the whole of naval history. In sheer numbers they involved as many as 250 men-of-war, 12,000 guns and 60,000 sailors all hammering furiously away at each other. The fleets ranged up and down the English Channel, and back and forth across the North Sea between the coasts of the Netherlands and England. They charged into battle, wrote a chronicler of the struggle, "with trumpets sounding, and drums beating in every ship, the seamen waving in defiance their hats, and the officers their plumed beavers." Sometimes the Dutch had the best of it, and sometimes the English; ofttimes they fought until both sides were too exhausted to fight any more. Once, the fighting went on for four incredible days, and then was halted only because of a merciful turn to foul weather. After each battle, both fleets limped back to their ports to repair the damage and to replace the dead and wounded; they were ready a few weeks later to put to sea for yet another thunderous fight.

In the end, the Anglo-Dutch wars produced no clear-cut winner. The belligerents were forced to conclude that the world was big enough for both to conduct trade profitably — and that there were enemies abroad far more dangerous than those presently appearing over their respective guns. What did come out of the wars was the prototype of the modern navy and a set of tactics that lasted, with changes of varying degree, right up to the age of the submarine and aircraft.

There were a number of reasons why sophisticated warfare at sea was slow to develop, particularly in northern Europe. For one thing, the world of the Middle Ages was severely circumscribed; the great explorers had yet to discover the Americas and open up the treasure stores of the East Indies. Medieval commerce was conducted largely overland or by river and coastal routes; thus the opportunities for collisions of interest at sea were few.

European seamanship, all through those centuries, was stifled as well by chivalry. In medieval times, every court and castle was a center of the cult of chivalry, and every aristocrat was bred in its mystique. As its name implies, chivalry (from the French *cheval*, for horse) was totally centered on horsemanship. For the knight, fighting and hunting on horseback were among the greatest achievements in life. But horsemanship was always an opposite of seamanship. There was—and is—nothing more incongruous than a horseman in a boat, except perhaps a sailor on a horse. Knights believed that the only proper form of combat was on a horse, and in armor. But at sea, they could not mount their horses; they could not use their favorite weapons, the lance and the sword. And presumably they could not wear their armor—or if they did, they must have been oppressed by the thought that if the ship sank, or if they fell or were forced overboard, they would go to the bottom like a stone. One can observe that all through the Middle Ages, knights hated going to sea, and when they had to do it, to reach a battlefield, they got ashore again as quickly as possible. Thus the major warlike use of ships was in transporting armies, while the technique of fighting at sea was largely ignored.

Many medieval kings possessed a few ships of their own, but not nearly enough to carry their armies, with their horses and equipment. When they wanted to send an army overseas, they chartered or commandeered their subjects' merchant ships, with their regular masters and

As bowmen and pikemen let fly at close quarters, English and French knights in full armor fight hand to hand on the decks of medieval ships at the Battle of Sluys off the French coast in 1340. More than 400 ships took part in this epic battle, won by the English at the start of the Hundred Years' War, but it could hardly be called a naval victory because the vessels themselves were unarmed, designed only to carry troops to board the enemy.

crews. At such times the ships were temporarily altered with fortifications—just in case they might encounter an enemy en route. Hence the forecastle and the aftercastle. These had to be very lightly built, or the ships would have been top-heavy. If the ships did happen to meet an enemy, the castles gave some protection against arrows and could be used as platforms from which to hurl down missiles. They were often built with little Gothic windows and battlements, and even with dummy brickwork painted on, like toy reproductions of the castles on shore. At best, they were unseaman-like structures, and were the despair of the vessels' regular captains. But the captains had no say in the matter. When knights came aboard they took charge, and captains were expected to do as they were told.

In any event, battles at sea were relatively rare. With a single square sail, these medieval ships could proceed at only a few knots per hour, and they could be sailed only with the wind abaft the beam. Thus when the wind was fair—to cross the English Channel for example—it was safe to assume that vessels on the other side would be stuck in harbor. Meeting a hostile fleet at sea, all through those centuries, was highly unusual.

When it happened, and if both sides were equally willing to fight, they ran alongside each other and threw grappling irons on board. In addition to a hail of missiles, the combatants would throw a combustible liquid called Greek fire, which they had copied from the Saracens during the Crusades. The primary ingredient was naphtha, and it could set an enemy ship ablaze. But it was a tricky business; fire was always a danger-

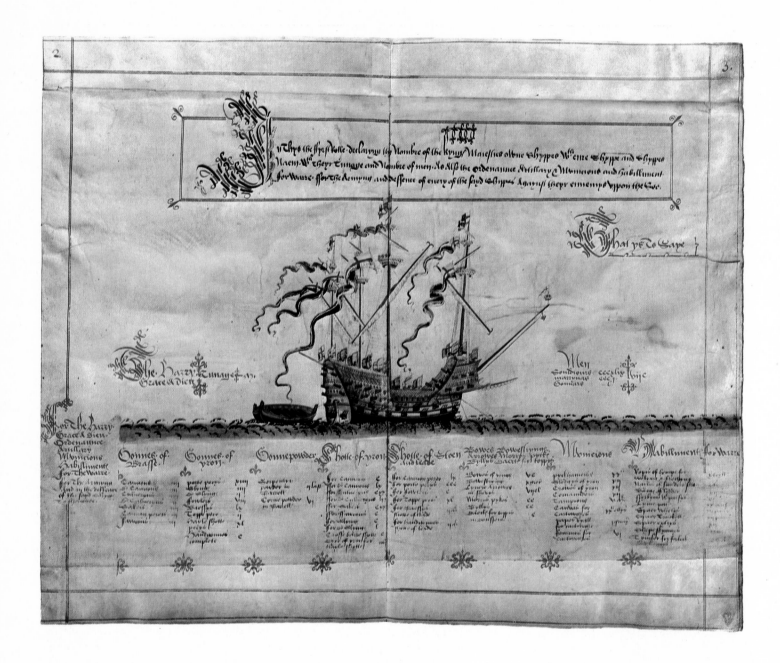

ous weapon at sea because it could easily spread and destroy both ships.

In 1350 England's King Edward III met a hostile Spanish fleet in the English Channel and experimented with the Mediterranean tactic of ramming the leading Spaniard, in galley fashion. He slammed into the Spaniard so enthusiastically that the mast of his ship came crashing down, carrying with it all the men who were perched aloft to fling down arrows, rocks and bars of iron. The jolt also split some of the planking of the hull, and Edward's knights had to turn their hands to the menial job of bailing. The Spaniard suffered a considerable amount of damage but managed to stay afloat.

Some time later Edward's son, the Black Prince, who was commanding another ship, tried the same tactic with even more shattering results. His own ship sank. But before it went down, he and the members of his

With silk banners streaming from her four masts and cannon bristling along her sides, Henry VIII's Great Harry rides majestically at anchor in this illumination from a 16th Century illustrated list of naval vessels. The most powerful ship of her day, she represented a transition in design, combining the high fore-and-aft "castles" of the Middle Ages with the tiers of guns that heralded the coming age of artillery duels. The writing describes the ship's armament, from her 122 guns to her store of 1,200 bowstrings and 750 sheaves of arrows.

crew succeeded in boarding a Spanish vessel and throwing her crew overboard to their deaths. That was the general custom, and Chaucer, in his poem "Shipman," had a verse for it:

If e'er he fought, and gained the upper hand,
He cast men overboard to swim to land.

The only medieval weapons invented specially for use in ships seem more like a practical joke than a serious tool of warfare. They were called triboli, and they were bits of iron with three spikes, so designed that whichever way they fell they stood on two spikes with one spike pointing upward. The idea was to throw liquid soap on the enemy's deck, then handfuls of triboli; the enemy, if the scenario went as planned, would slip on the soap and sit down on the triboli.

Such weapons were ingenious, perhaps, but limited. What was needed before naval warfare could evolve was a means of sinking an enemy ship from a distance—in other words, cannon. Small cannon were installed on northern European ships as early as 1406, when a ship called the *Christopher of the Tower* included three guns of wrought iron built up from eight-foot bars and welded into crude tubes. They probably fired no more than a half-pound shot—too small to damage a ship—and were useful mainly to repel boarders. In 1488 during the interminable wars of the period, England's King Henry VII built a four-masted ship called the *Regent*, recorded as having carried more guns than any other vessel in history. There were 225 of them, all mounted on the upper decks and castles. But they were also very small. They could not hurt an enemy ship at a distance—and indeed the *Regent* was lost when she grappled a French ship in the old-fashioned way and both caught fire.

To fight at a distance required bigger guns with longer range. But to mount such heavy guns on the forecastles and aftercastles, where the other weapons went, would have upset the ship's stability. More than 100 years elapsed before anyone figured out how to put such weight aboard without capsizing the ship—much less how to deal with the problem of the guns' recoil.

The credit for the epoch-making solution is traditionally given to Henry VIII. In 1512 he sent to a Flanders foundry for some cast-bronze, smoothbore, muzzle-loading guns. To test them, he blasted a row of English village houses (after first thoughtfully clearing the dwellings of their occupants). Satisfied with the devastation, Henry ordered his shipwrights to find a way of mounting the same kind of guns on ships.

One James Baker, an English shipwright, is supposed to have had the brain storm that satisfied the King's command. And the answer, when he found it, was altogether simple: to mount the guns low on the cargo deck and fire them broadside through portholes cut in the ship's hull.

The most celebrated ship to carry the new invention was a 1,000-ton monster known as the *Great Harry*, after the King who built her. Launched in 1514, she was covered from stem to stern in the fashion of the day with multicolored flags, pennants and other painted symbols of medieval chivalry, and on state occasions her sails were of gold damask. But ranged along the hull was Baker's inspiration: a tier of openings through which poked the snouts of the cannon. The ports were cut

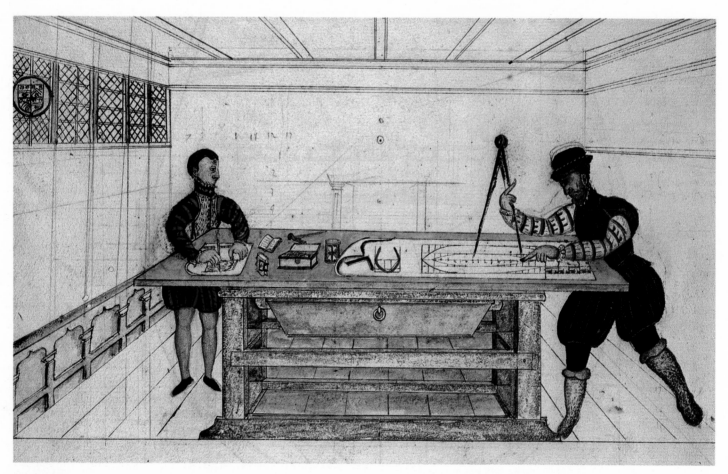

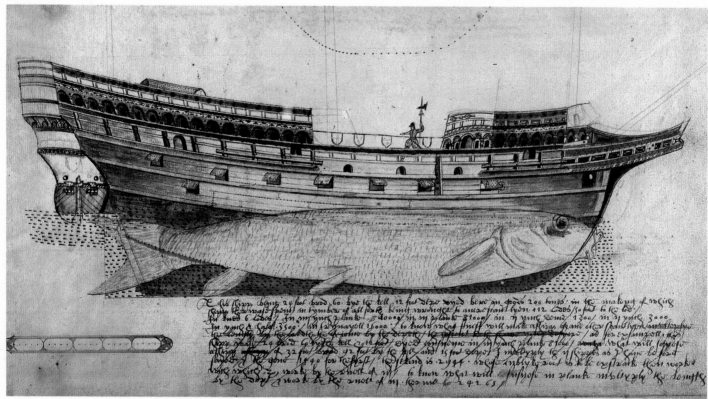

*Wielding a formidable compass, an
Elizabethan shipbuilder measures off the
arcs in his design while an apprentice
transcribes the number of degrees, in this
1560s painting by Matthew Baker, himself
a renowned shipwright of the day. Baker
was the first to be accorded the official title
of Master Shipwright and the first
ever known to set down on paper complete
and detailed plans for his ships.*

*To allow a smooth, swift flow of water
along the hull, the Elizabethans designed
their ships with what they called
a "cod's head and mackerel tail," a
configuration with the maximum breadth
just forward of midships, and a sharp
taper aft—a point graphically illustrated
in this painting by Matthew Baker.
Beneath his rendering, Baker has written
detailed calculations for the timber
requirements of this vessel in order "to
know what stueff will make a shipp."*

round, in imitation of the porthole, through which merchant ships had just begun to lade their cargoes, and were hinged across the top. Like the new lading porthole, the gunports could be closed when the ship was under sail, and opened to thrust out the guns as needed. The guns themselves—including 21 in gleaming bronze—ranged in caliber from a modest two and a half inches to a mighty eight-inch weapon that threw an iron ball of perhaps 50 pounds. The smallest could hit a target at 280 yards; the biggest could reach out more than 1,600 yards.

Delighted with his acquisition, Henry ordered a number of such ships expressly for defending the realm, and by 1547 he could boast a fleet of 53 vessels in addition to the *Great Harry*.

Alas, as with most new inventions, gunports advanced by trial and error, bringing some classic disasters. In the summer of 1545, Henry ordered his warships to sea when a fleet of hostile Frenchmen was reported to be off Portsmouth. The commander of the *Great Harry* prudently closed his gunports; the knight in charge of the *Mary Rose* had left his open. As soon as the *Mary Rose* felt the wind and heeled, she flooded through her open lower gunports, which lay only 16 inches above the water line and, in full view of the King and his court and the wife of the unfortunate knight, sank to the bottom, drowning most of her crew.

The lesson was obvious: gunports must be placed higher. Other strides were made as well. Fore-and-aft castles were done away with, and reliance placed first and foremost on gunnery. Men would grapple and board only as a final act to capture a ship that was already crippled.

Sir John Hawkins, as treasurer of Queen Elizabeth's ships, was the man who made the bold decision to eliminate the castles. He was a practical seaman, a veteran of slaving and some privateering voyages to Africa, South America and the Caribbean, and he knew from experience how the towering old castles ruined the sailing qualities of a ship. He came up with an entirely new kind of fighting ship—a race-built ship.

The phrase did not mean that the ship was fast, though she was. The word race derived from the French *ras*, meaning shaven or flat, and it describes what Hawkins did to the castles: he razed them. Hawkins' ship, called the *Revenge*, had fine lines with little superstructure, and lay rakishly low in the water. She was not particularly large, and beside the high old ships she looked even smaller than she was. If she had ever been boarded and forced to fight at close quarters, she would have been at a hopeless disadvantage against the older kind. But she was meant to avoid that situation. Without the windage of the old top-hamper, she was faster and more maneuverable, better to windward and quicker on the helm; the word the Elizabethans used was nimbler. She could outsail the older ships, and keep her range and beat them with her deadly guns.

This kind of ship not only brought a new technique of fighting on the sea, it also gave seamen a new and better status. Hitherto in wartime, the captain and crew had manned the ships but the soldiers did whatever fighting there was to be done. But the race-built ship was a sailor's weapon. As the Elizabethans also said, she was not "pestered" with soldiers. The sailors manned the guns, the captain was in command and success depended on skill in seamanship.

The first great test came in fighting the Spanish Armada in 1588. All

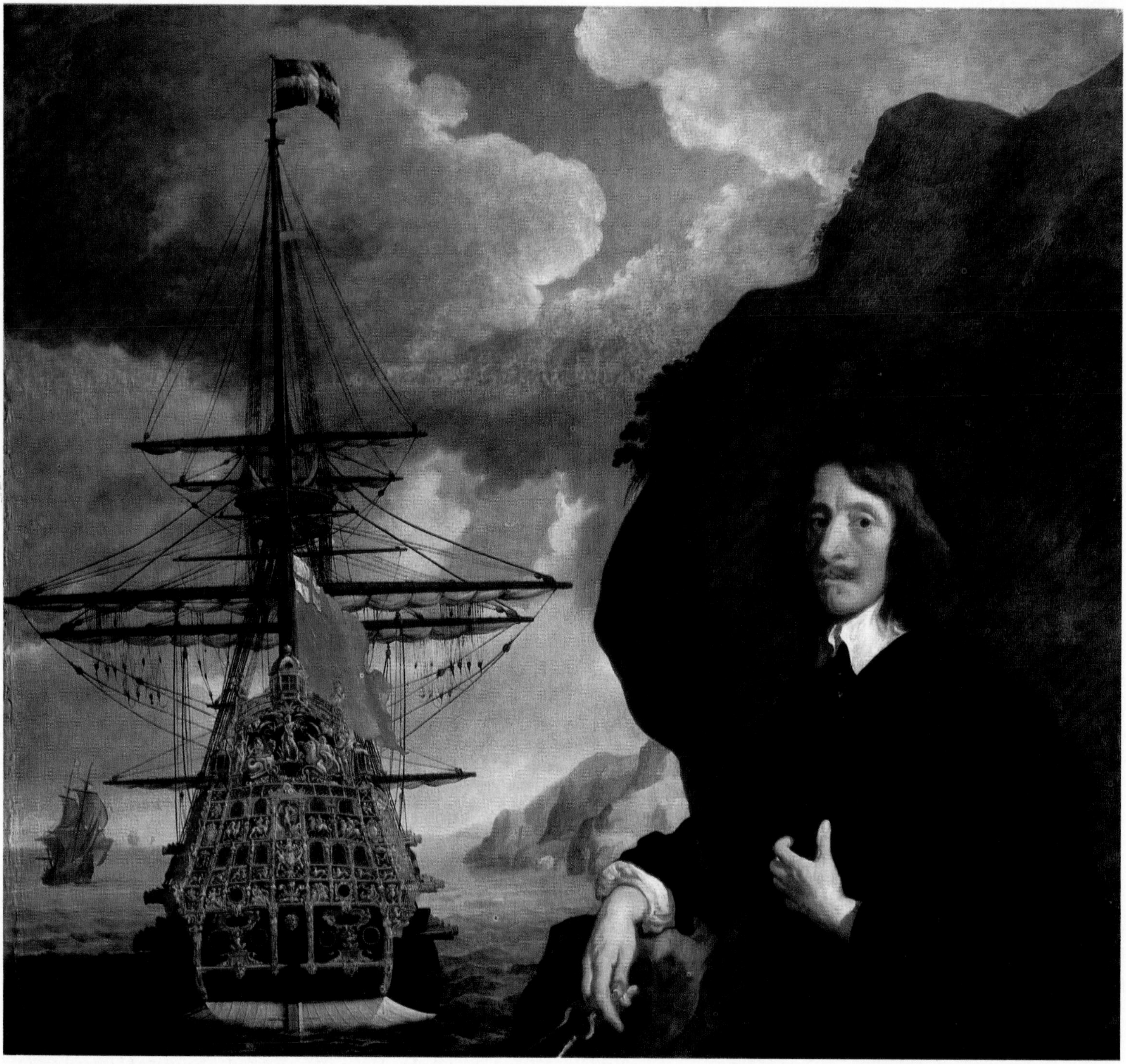

Dividers in hand, master shipbuilder Peter Pett is shown with his masterpiece, the Sovereign of the Seas, in this contemporary portrait. Built for King Charles I in 1637, she was lavishly carved and decorated, but she was still a formidable warship all the same: her 1,500-ton size and 104 guns were scarcely exceeded during the next 200 years.

the Spanish ships were of the old design, high castled, manned by sailors who were under soldiers' orders, still intent on grappling and boarding if it came to a fight. The majority of the English fleet were chartered merchantmen built for trading and were much the same; they did very little good except to make an imposing array. It was the race-built ships that gave the lead, and as the Spanish fleet sailed slowly and majestically up the English Channel, its sailors were horrified to see that several English ships could sail rings round them. "The worst of them," a Spanish captain wrote bitterly, "without their main course or topsails, can beat the best sailers we have." And in the end, it was the race-built ships that charged in and defeated the Spaniards by better sailing and maneuverability, never allowing them a chance to come alongside and board.

Those Elizabethan ships—the *Ark Royal* and the *Revenge* were perhaps the most famous of them—had all the essentials of a naval weapon. But still, they suffered from a lack of organization within the fleet. When the English charged the Spaniards on July 28, 1588, off Calais, each captain chose his own opponent, and nobody in the gigantic melee could see what was happening or make any ordered plan.

The *Prince Royal,* which Phineas Pett launched in 1610, represented a further improvement on the race-built ships, not because she was so far advanced in overall design, but because she was vastly bigger and more powerful. For a whole generation the *Prince Royal* remained the biggest warship in the world; England was generally at peace in those years, and she was used as a showpiece and a transport for royalty. Because of her imposing size, she was a symbol of the majesty of the realm and was used by King James I on the highest state occasions as a royal yacht.

In 1635 it was King Charles I's turn to feel the royal urge to possess a ship that was bigger and grander yet. So he sent for Phineas Pett. By then, Pett's son Peter was in charge of the dockyard at Woolwich, and between them they produced the family's masterpiece: the *Sovereign of the Seas*.

The *Sovereign of the Seas* must be reckoned one of the most astonishing ships in history. In appearance as in name she symbolized the ancient claim to the sovereignty that England was now beginning to take seriously. From stem to stern she was carved, painted and gilded with decorations that made the *Prince Royal*'s lion-headed designs plain by comparison. The decorations were an expression of 17th Century Baroque in all its extravagance, a mélange of symbols representing almost every age, civilization and faith known to Western Europe.

Her bow had statues of the Anglo-Saxon King Edgar, triumphantly trampling seven prostrate Celtic kings beneath his feet, while a Roman cupid rode among them on a tamed lion. The stern was carved in relief to represent the Greek heroes Hercules and Jason the Argonaut. The sides and bulkheads were adorned with caryatids, unicorns and dragons, combined with signs of the zodiac. The full length of the middle gun deck sported a carved frieze showing 17th Century guns and muskets, intermixed with medieval swords, battle-axes, suits of armor, trumpets, drums, flags and banners. Finally, filling a dual function of décor and utilitarianism, the *Sovereign of the Seas* had at her stern a giant lantern so big it was said 12 men could stand upright inside it; in 1661 Samuel

A contest of Cavaliers vs. Roundheads

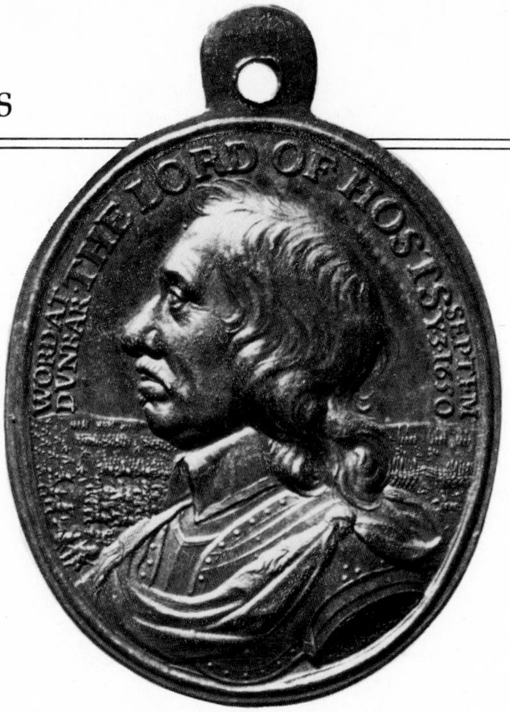
WORD AT DUNBAR
THE LORD OF HOSTS

Appearing gaunt and stern, Oliver Cromwell surveys his revolutionary troops in this medallion that was struck to commemorate the defeat of Royalist forces at Dunbar on September 3, 1650. Parliament overruled Cromwell's protests against the use of his portrait on the medallion but accepted his idea for the Biblical legend — "The Lord of Hosts" — Cromwell's motto in that battle.

Charles I is beheaded outside his Banqueting House in Whitehall on January 30, 1649, and the executioner holds aloft his grisly prize. The King's body was embalmed and buried in St. George's Chapel at Windsor next to Henry VIII.

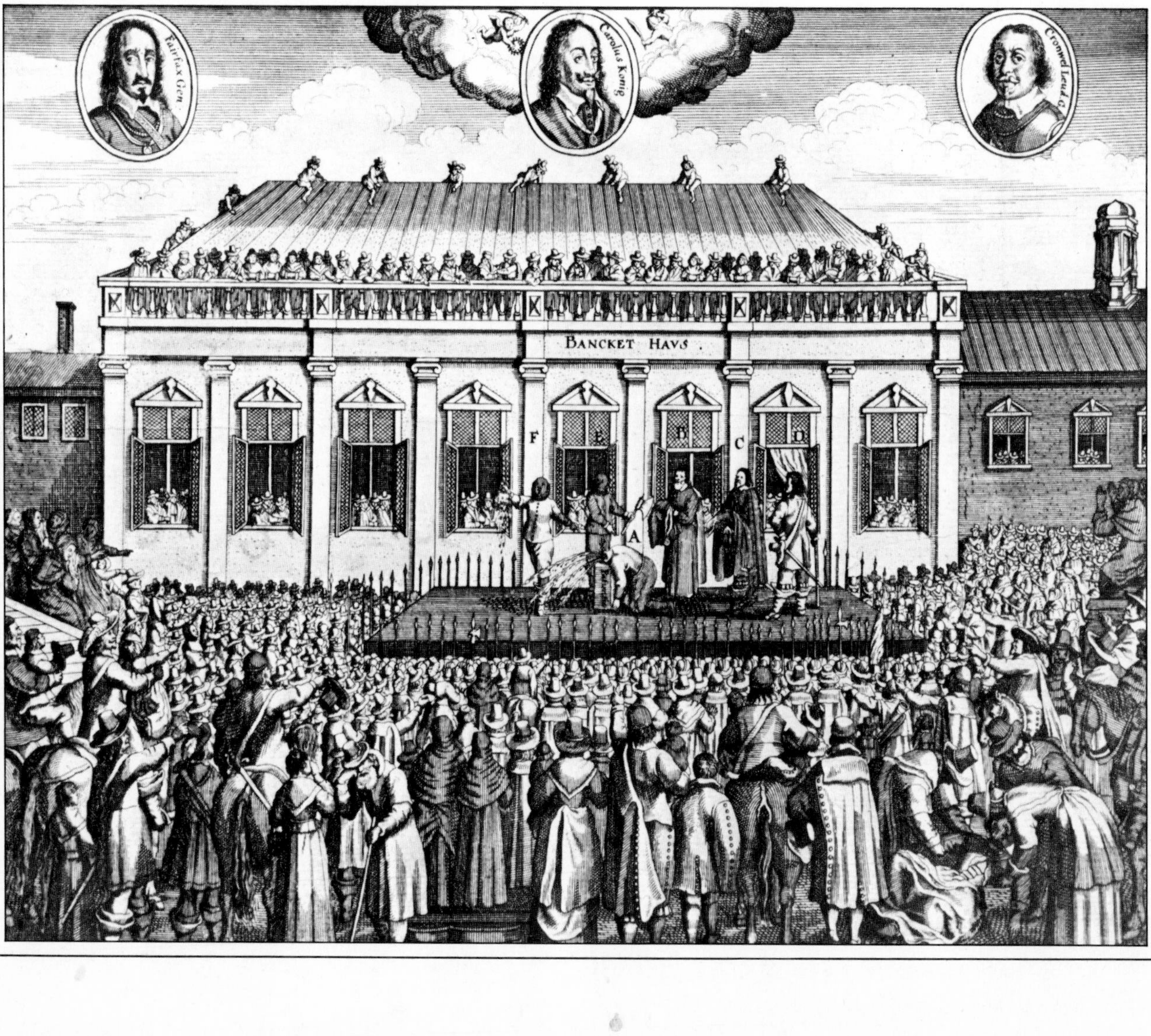
Fairfax Gen
Carolus Konig
BANCKET HAVS

"And now God being displeased with England, sent an evil spirit of Division betwixt the King and Parliament; which Division being industriously fomented by Incendiaries, soon brake forth into the flame of open Hostility." So wrote a contemporary historian in explanation of the political strife that tore England asunder in the years 1642 through 1651. Yet a man of the times might well think it the work of the devil himself, so deep and so violent were the issues among Englishmen.

It was a period when Puritanism clashed with the Church of England; when unorthodox theological beliefs spawned radical political views; when the age-old divine right of kings was challenged by a sentiment for constitutional government.

The unfortunate monarch who became the focal point of all this foment was Charles I, who acceded to the throne in 1625. A different ruler might have cooled the fevers of unrest, but Charles frustrated friends, alienated supporters and inexorably turned an increasingly Puritan-dominated Parliament against him.

Charles reacted by dissolving one Parliament after another, and for 11 years he ruled England alone. Only in 1640, when pressed for money to fight the Presbyterian Scots, upon whom he had attempted to impose the Church of England, did he reconvoke Parliament. Yet within two years he unsuccessfully tried to seize and confine the opposition members of Parliament. It was the last straw. England erupted in civil war. Pitched battles pitted the Royalist Cavaliers against the Parliamentary Roundheads (so called from their closely cropped, wigless heads). In the end, Charles was defeated, tried for treason for waging war on his subjects and, in January 1649, beheaded.

By now, the shining beacon of libertarian hope was Oliver Cromwell, a sometime member of Parliament and one of the most able officers of the Parliamentary forces. After Charles's execution, Cromwell was sent to Ireland, where he crushed dissident factions. In 1650 and 1651 he routed two last Royalist attempts to restore the monarchy with young Charles II as king, and thus emerged as the leader of the new Commonwealth. Among the first of his actions was to approve the Navigation Act of 1651, which was designed to strengthen England's mercantile power. Although this led to the first of the naval wars with the Dutch, it also laid the cornerstone for the future ascendancy of the British Navy.

Cromwell, proclaimed Lord Protector of the Commonwealth in 1653, ran what in effect was a military dictatorship, one conceived and prosecuted by the Puritan ethic—harsh, moralistic, punitive—yet one without which a strong constitutional form of government in Britain might not have emerged. But it was a government of one man's personality. When Oliver Cromwell died of a fever at the age of 59 in 1658, the torch passed to his son Richard, who within a year proved to be unequal to the task. Restoration of the monarchy in the person of Charles I's exiled son, Charles II, was the inevitable consequence.

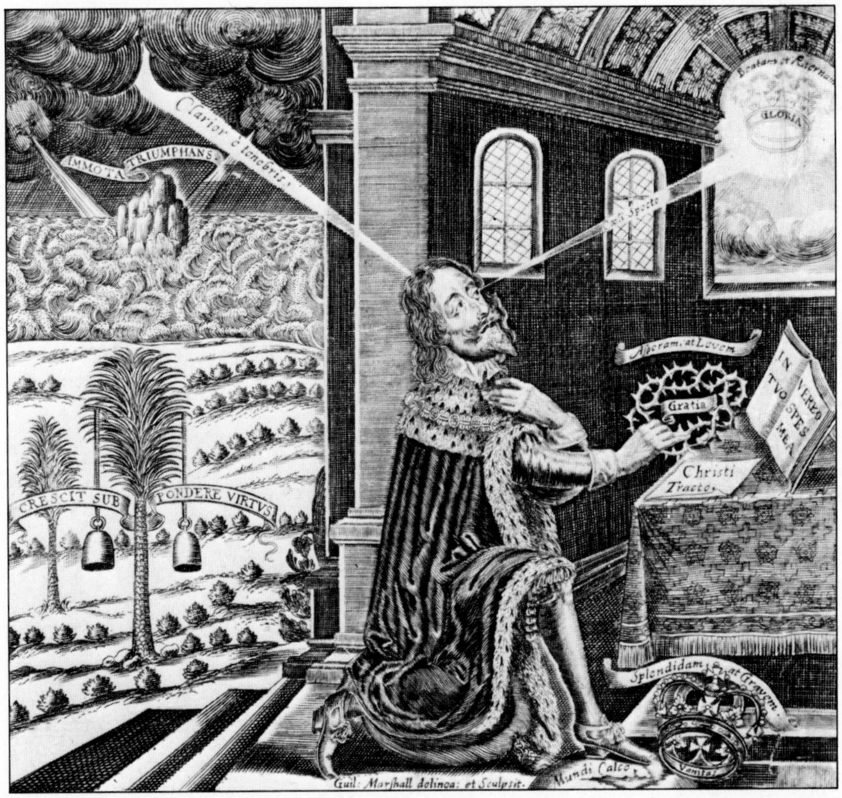
IMMOTA TRIUMPHANS
Clarior e tenebris
GLORIA
Gratia
IN VERBO TVO SPES MEA
Christi Tracto
CRESCIT SUB PONDERE VIRTUS
Mundi Calco
Guil: Marshall delineo: et Sculpsit.

Surrounded by ethereal visions, celestial rays and pious Latin mottoes, King Charles I raises his eyes toward heaven in an engraving from Eikon Basilike. This book, published on the day of his burial, contained prayers and meditations on the King's life, and fostered the Royalists' faithful vision of Charles as a martyr.

Sanctuary for the fugitive heir

Charles II was 19 when his father, Charles I, was executed. Royalists immediately proclaimed him king, but all his hopes for regaining the throne were dashed when Oliver Cromwell defeated his supporters at the Battle of Worcester in 1651.

As Cromwell's forces swept through the land, Charles became a fugitive, seeking to escape into exile. For six weeks he and various loyal followers edged toward the sea—one day concealing themselves in the branches of a huge oak tree, another time in a barn—until finally the King set sail from Shoreham to take sanctuary in France, the Netherlands and later Germany.

Charles remained in exile for more than eight years, while Royalists at home secretly plotted for his restoration. With Oliver Cromwell's death in 1658, there arose a strident call for a resumption of the monarchy. Charles II returned to England in 1660 and was crowned the following year.

He proved a dissipated, sensual and cynically self-centered man and his reign was characterized by intrigues and misgovernment. Yet during the 25 years of his rule, the Royal Navy, for all its misadventures against the Dutch, grew to such formidable proportions that England's claim to sovereignty of the seas became a reality.

Disguised as a lady's manservant on the leading horse, Charles II makes his escape from Cromwell's forces following the Royalist defeat at Worcester in 1651. The lady riding behind His Majesty is Jane Lane, sister of a Royalist colonel. She loyally followed Charles into exile and after the Restoration was granted a pension of £1,000 a year by the King.

Pepys, the famed diarist, naval administrator and gentleman about London, was to test its capacity by shutting five ladies into it with himself and moving about to kiss them all.

The Sovereign's cost was an enormous £40,000, twice the price that the shipwrights of King James's day had thought outrageous in the Prince Royal. Again, the Petts had made a great leap forward in size: the Sovereign came to 1,500 tons and her overall length was 232 feet. The vast quantities of oak needed to build her were more than the forests of nearby Kent and Sussex could supply; timber had to be shipped 400 miles from Northumberland.

When she was finished she mounted 104 bronze guns—two thirds again as many as the Prince Royal had carried. Among them were 20 cannon firing 60-pound shot, eight demicannon of 30-pound shot, 32 culverins of 18-pound shot and 44 demiculverins of 9-pound shot—a mix of ordnance that would enable her to fire more than a ton of screaming metal in one murderous broadside. To crew this giant in battle required 800 men.

Like the Prince Royal before her, the new nautical wonder raised a storm of criticism while she was being built—this time not so much from other shipwrights, but from the highly respected Elder Brethren of Trinity House. Trinity House was then—and still is, some 341 years later—the institution responsible for the lighthouses, beacons and buoys on the coasts of England. Its Elder Brethren were an executive council composed of eminent mariners and navigators, and they expected their opinions to be heard on any nautical matter.

Alarmed at the Sovereign's draft of more than 20 feet, they wrote to the King's principal secretary. "The art or wit of man," they stated firmly, "can not build a ship well conditioned and fit for service with three tier of ordnance." (On that point the Brethren had miscalculated; with her top deck, the Sovereign actually had four ranks of cannon.) And what anchors could hold this behemoth when she was forced to lie exposed in an open roadstead? "Anchors and cables must hold proportion," the Brethren continued, "and being made, they will not be manageable, the strength of man can not wield nor work them. But could they do it, the ship would be little bettered in point of safety, for we are doubtful whether cables and anchors can hold a ship of this bulk in a great storm."

Naval experts have often been absurdly conservative, and have often been proved by events to be hopelessly wrong. The King took no notice of the Elder Brethren's outburst. The Sovereign was duly launched and she had an exceptionally long life, reaching the age of nearly 60.

Curiously, for a ship of such formidable might, she was seldom to go into battle in her early years. No reason for this was given in naval annals. Perhaps she was too costly to be risked; perhaps it was thought her large size would make her too conspicuous in the battle line; possibly it was difficult to find men enough to crew her. Eventually, in the 1690s, other ships began to approach her size. And then she came into her own as a man-of-war, and fought magnificently in the Battle of Barfleur against the French in May 1692, when she was 55 years old. When at last she succumbed in 1696, it was not as a battle casualty but as the victim of a careless accident; she burned because a cook left a lighted candle in his cabin. With her size and armament, she would not have been out of place at Trafalgar a century later. In fact, Horatio Nelson's *Victory* and the other great 100-gunners of that day could trace their ancestry to her.

Charles I made a second important contribution to the foundation of the Navy. He instituted the first nationwide tax to build a fleet. This tax was known as ship money and had its origin in medieval times when kings levied taxes on the coastal towns in lieu of their providing ships. Charles extended the duty to all towns and counties throughout the country, and raised it to unprecedented heights. While inland taxpayers understood that England's future lay in the seas and supported the principle of the tax, they found the extent of it onerous. They opposed the tax on the grounds it had not been voted by Parliament, and it was one of the things that led to Charles's downfall.

Over the course of half a dozen years, Charles built around 50 vessels known as the "Ship Money Fleet." But the King ignored two other interlocked and vital concerns. One was that to man a navy, men would have to be paid regularly. Another was that a new religious strain was gaining ground—Puritanism, with its literal interpretation of Biblical injunctions and its dour austerity. While the seamen went payless, a part of the ship money went toward such sinful extravagances as ungodly graven images on the *Sovereign of the Seas.* Adding fuel to the flames of hard feeling, Charles made the fatal mistake of dismissing his Parliament: a body that by this time, although consisting basically of squires and gentry, had large numbers of rich merchants whose increasingly valuable cargo vessels needed more and more protection out on the high seas—and a body of men too powerful to trifle with.

In August 1642 Parliament's rising fury at its stubborn and arrogant King erupted into civil war, and for the next seven years England was a nation torn asunder, divided not only in its loyalties to Charles but also on broad moral and religious grounds *(pages 26-28).* The man who rose to command the forces of Parliament as the war progressed was Oliver Cromwell, born into the north of England's landed gentry, brilliant in battle, rigidly Puritan in his beliefs, terrifying in his hatreds. And it was he who ordered Charles's execution in the bitter winter of 1649 after the Royalist forces had finally been crushed.

The English Navy's role in all this was that of enthusiastic Parliamentary ally. Disaffected from a King who could not or would not pay them, the Navy's officers and men supported Parliament, giving it command of the seas and coasts around England, and enabled the government to conduct foreign trade, collect customs and prevent the Royalists from importing munitions. King Charles's nephew Prince Rupert tried with a handful of ships to wage the Royalist fight at sea but was swiftly driven from European waters to sanctuary in the Caribbean. More than that, in the end it was the Navy that Oliver Cromwell counted on to secure his victory and forestall any counterrevolution.

When all was lost for the Royalists, the King's son and heir, young Charles II, fled to the Netherlands, where he was well received by his Dutch uncle, William II, the stadtholder, or chief magistrate of the land. Now the new political powers in England had an additional reason for viewing Dutch ships as a menace on the seas. The young Charles was lurking over there, waiting for the chance to claim his crown—and a goodly part of the Dutch fleet was presumed to be at Charles's disposal.

It seemed vital to Cromwell and his colleagues, as they took over the reins of the new government, that they look to England's fleet. Cromwell procured a huge annual grant of £400,000 for the Navy. The wages of seamen were raised from less than 15 shillings a month to an unprecedented 20 shillings a month, and for the first time something of an effort was made to pay the men regularly. But with the purse strings in the hands of the upper classes, the welfare of the lower classes, even in Cromwell's day, was not a matter of overriding concern. Payment of wages fell far in arrears and remained a continual source of irritation.

The vast bulk of the naval appropriations went into a massive ship-building program that brought the fleet 207 new warships in 11 years. Among them was a vessel named to memorialize the battle that secured Cromwell's victory—the *Naseby*. Though not so huge as the *Sovereign of the Seas*, the *Naseby* was both larger (at 1,655 tons) and more heavily gunned (at 80 guns) than the first of the line, the old *Prince Royal*, and incorporated a number of important innovations in hull and rigging design (*pages 32-33*). She and the scores of vessels that were coming off the ways were to be the standard capital ships of the fleet upon which England would depend in the coming wars against the Dutch.

Across the North Sea, the United Provinces of the Netherlands could only view the English Naval build-up with alarm. While the Dutch had received Charles II in exile, they had no intention of putting any warships at his disposal, and were in no way anxious to involve themselves in a civil war between Royalists and Parliamentarians. As it was, their relations with the English were tender enough over the far larger and more dangerous issue of worldwide trade and maritime sovereignty.

The roots of the Anglo-Dutch conflict at sea went back centuries, to the very nature of the two lands and their people. The Netherlands was poorly endowed with natural resources. Low and marshy, constantly at the mercy of the encroaching sea, the area could support only a small farming population. But it was blessed with one enormous strategic advantage: it lay athwart a network of rivers that seemed to come from everywhere, making the Netherlands a gateway to the interior of Europe on the one hand and to the oceans of the world on the other.

Seizing this advantage as the worldwide trade of Europe grew and expanded, the Dutch learned how to make the bounty of others a boon for themselves. They became what the journalist Daniel Defoe, writing in later years, called "the Factors and Brokers of Europe. They buy to sell again, take in to send out and the greatest part of their vast Commerce consists in being supply'd from All Parts of the World, that they may supply All the World again." In Amsterdam, Leiden, Haarlem, Gouda and perhaps half a dozen other cities with populations of 20,000 to 40,000—the densest cluster of cities anywhere in Europe—the Dutch salted fish hauled from English waters, built ships of timber hewn in the Baltic, bleached linen spun in Germany, processed salt mined in France, and refined spices fetched from the East Indies.

Thus the Dutch had prospered through the ages, though they had been governed by a series of foreign rulers—Burgundians, Austrian Haps-

Metamorphosis of the man-of-war

The first ship that could truly be called a man-of-war was the *Henri Grâce à Dieu*, the flagship of Henry VIII, who frenchified her name in the courtly fashion of the day. His subjects anglicized it to *Great Harry*, and great she was. Launched in 1514, she carried 186 cannon along her decks, and while most of them were small breech-loaders for close-quarter fighting, they were together more powerful than any other floating arsenal in history. In 1540 the *Great Harry* was refitted with two tiers of muzzle-loading, long-range bronze and iron cannon—some weighing two tons and capable of hurling a 66-pound shot 500 yards.

Yet she was a ship in transition. Of her 700-man complement, 400 were infantrymen who were expected to fight from her decks and the lofty upper works, called castles.

Bedecked with flags and sporting sails dyed yellow to simulate a cloud of regal gold, the Henri Grâce à Dieu, pride of Henry VIII, was the first to carry significant numbers of cannon while retaining the old-fashioned castles, the sheer hooks on her yardarms, and a grappling hook on her bowsprit, all used in close combat. Her keel length was some 150 feet, only about twice the measure of her huge beam.

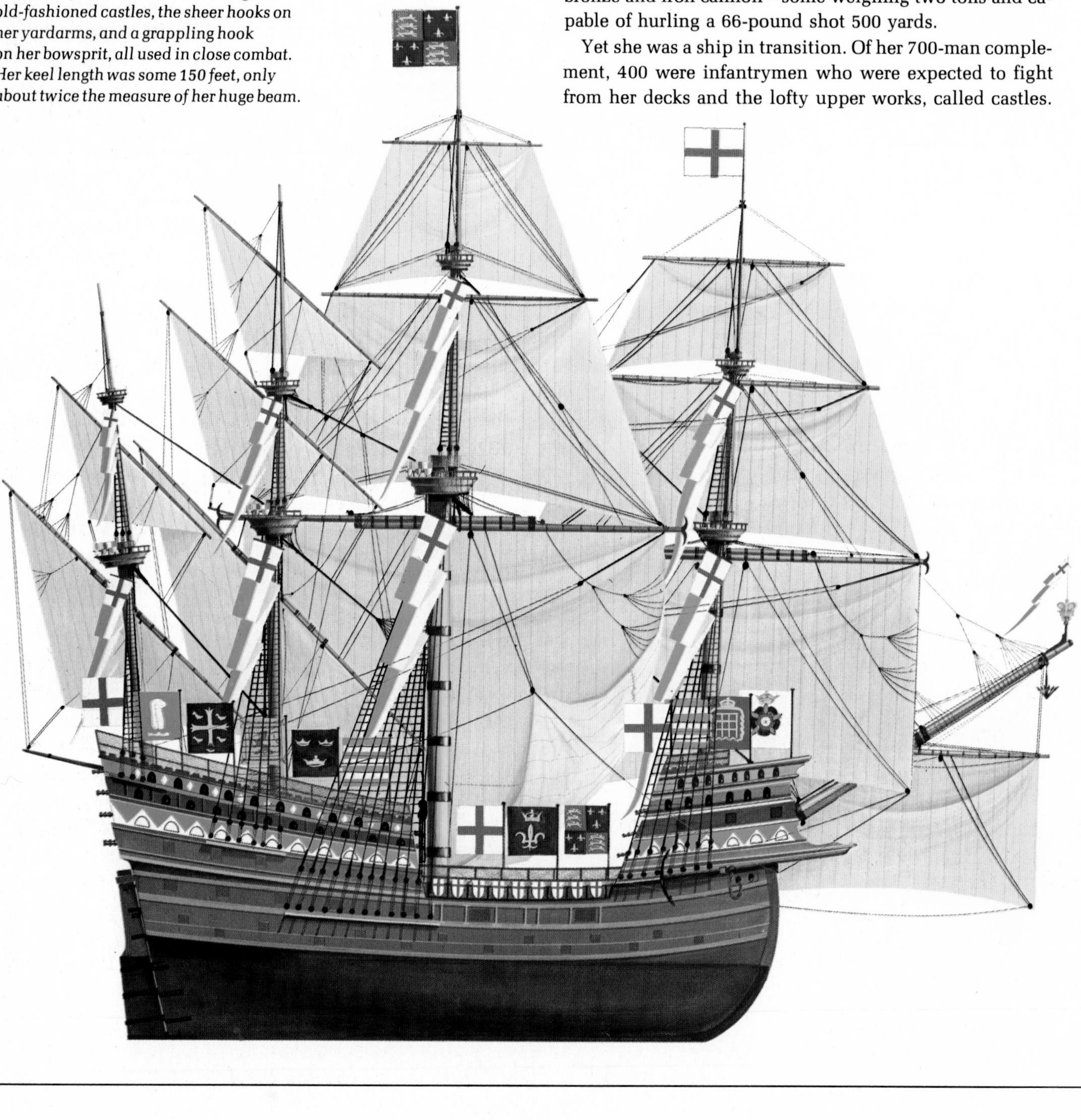

The broad-beamed hull required five lateen sails on two mizzenmasts to aid in steering. Even then she was awkward and top-heavy, unseaworthy in all but the lightest weather. Over the next century the English warship improved in both handling and firepower. With the launching of the *Naseby* in 1655, the man-of-war achieved a form that survived for 200 years. The flagship of Oliver Cromwell, the *Naseby* carried 80 cannon ranging from 12-pounders to 42-pounders. Gone were the clumsy castles and the soldiers; the *Naseby* had a crew of 600 highly trained seamen, who could fight hand to hand but specialized in long-range cannon duels. In contrast to her Tudor ancestor, the *Naseby's* greatest beam was at her water line. This made her a better sailer in heavy weather and a more stable gun platform.

Low and lean, the 80-gun Naseby of Oliver Cromwell was a prototype of every man-of-war until the coming of steam. With a keel of 131 feet and a length-to-beam ratio of better than 3 to 1, she was swift (up to 12 knots), maneuverable and sturdy. She was beautiful as well, decorated with gilded carvings from her ornate quarter galleries to the figurehead that depicted the Great Protector on horseback.

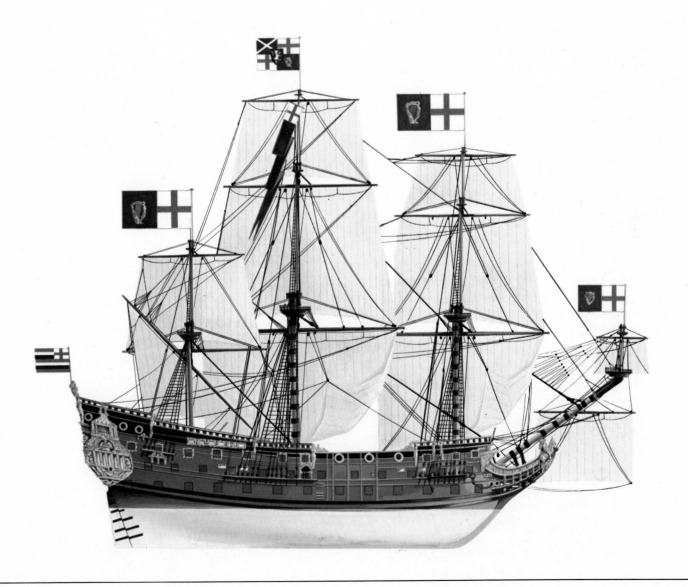

burgs and finally the Spanish. With the truce of 1609, the seven northern provinces of the Netherlands won independence from Spain after 41 years of warfare. From then on, the Dutch genius for commerce knew no bounds. Dutch traders sailed west across the Atlantic to found the colony of New Amsterdam on the coast of North America; they journeyed south into the Caribbean to claim half a dozen islands and a corner of South America in what is now Brazil; they traveled east around Africa to contest the Portuguese for the spice trade of the Malay Archipelago.

In all this, the near neighbors of the Dutch across the North Sea were equally aggressive. The English were also finding profit in the oceans. By 1607 venturesome Englishmen had spanned the Atlantic to found a New World colony they named Jamestown after their king; soon there were English enclaves all along the North American coast, and in the Caribbean. In the East in 1602 English traders had established a base, or "factory," at Bantam in the Spice Islands, where the Dutch were also establishing themselves. They pushed on from there to Surat in India.

As might be expected, it was the competition for spices that first brought the English and the Dutch into conflict—though the two regarded each other amiably enough at first. Under an agreement reached in 1619 by the Amsterdam-based merchants of the Dutch East India Company and their English counterparts in London, the Dutch granted the English permission to install a factor on Amboina, near the Banda Islands, an obscure archipelago that lies south of the Moluccas, 260 miles south of the equator and 400 miles off the desolate northern coast of Australia. But agreements reached in London and Amsterdam did not always suit human tempers in the steamy tropics halfway round the world, where the combination of isolation, strange and ghastly diseases and alien customs bred special animosities.

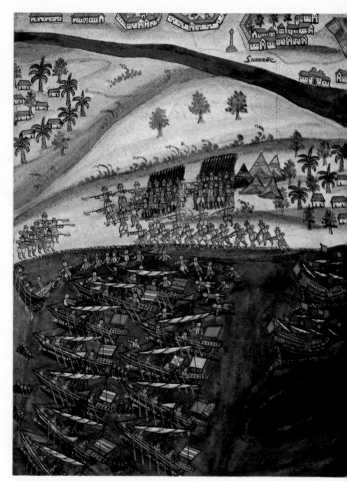

The remoteness of such trading posts as 17th Century Amboina is almost beyond imagining now. The distance under sail was something like 15,000 nautical miles, down through the Atlantic almost to Brazil, east across the Cape of Good Hope, past Madagascar and the southern end of India and Ceylon, along the whole length of Sumatra and Java. But in the 17th Century, time was a truer measurement than mileage. With luck, the outward voyage could take eight months. To send a message home took longer, usually a year and sometimes two, because it had to wait for a ship that was homeward bound.

Inevitably, events in Amboina were always out of step with events in England and the Netherlands, and men out there were guided not by governments or home-based trading company policy, but by their emotions—which mainly, in such isolation, were fear, jealousy and greed. One English factor wrote insultingly of the tubby Dutchmen with whom he shared the Indies market: "Theis buterboxes are groanne soe insolent that yf they be suffred but a whit longer, they will make claims to the whole Indies, so that no man shall trade but themselves or by thear leave; but I hope to see ther pride take a falle." The Dutch were equally nettled by the English factors. "We sit here," complained a Dutch trader in a letter home to Amsterdam, "tied to them as to a troublesome wife."

In 1623 the grievances ceased to be in the least humorous. The Dutch governor of Amboina believed that the English factor was plotting to attack his fortress and murder him, using Japanese mercenaries. The Dutchman commanded about 1,000 troops and sailors, while the number of Englishmen on the island totaled no more than 20. Nevertheless, the Dutch governor rounded up the Englishmen, put them to torture and executed 10 of them. The surviving 10 were set free and fled in terror to describe this "foule and bloody act."

When news of the executions reached London a year later, it roused Englishmen to fury. Handbills appeared on coffeehouse doors and on roadside trees giving every gruesome detail of the "Massacre of Amboina." Politicians thundered for a war of revenge. War against the Netherlands was the very last thing the English East India Company wanted. It pointed out calmly enough that the dastardly deed was the fault of one Dutchman and not of the Dutch as a nation. The Dutch government apologized and offered financial recompense. But irrational anger smouldered on in England for years.

Meanwhile, there were other causes of friction between the Dutch and the English. For some 400 years, ever since the reign of King John from 1199 to 1216, English monarchs had fancied the title Sovereign of the Seas. (Thus the name of Charles I's great warship.) Since they seldom ventured far from home when the term first came into use, the "seas" to the English meant the ones lapping their own shores—the North Sea, the English Channel and the narrow body of water connecting those two, the Strait of Dover. Over the centuries the English had come to require ships of other nations to recognize the claim by saluting as they passed through the Strait, furling their topsails or hauling down their flags.

The claim was harmless enough in medieval days, when traffic through the Strait was relatively scant. In the quickening pace of the 17th Century, however, it took on new meaning, especially to the Dutch, whose ocean-plying vessels could not reach Amsterdam, their commercial entrepôt on the North Sea, without passing through the Strait of Dover. Now, as they came through with their rich cargoes of spices, silver, silks, jewels and foodstuffs, the Dutch ships were called upon to make that salute to a growing fleet of English warships such as the *Prince Royal* with her glowering gunports.

Facing this gauntlet and an increasingly hostile climate, the Dutch from the early 1600s on started building a war fleet of their own to convoy merchantmen as they came up the English Channel or down the North Sea. The Dutch leaders were content, for the time being, to placate the English by offering the ritual salute, but it was only good sense to give the cargo fleets an armed escort—just in case.

The men-of-war the Dutch built drew on the most advanced technology of the day, some of it borrowed from the English after their victory over the Armada, some of it developed independently. They were race-built and square-rigged and were quite fast. But they were less stable than the English ships in heavy seas, which from time to time put them at a disadvantage in the actions to come. The fact that they were smaller than the English warships may have had something to do with their problem. The largest Dutch ship, the *Brederode*, carried 54 guns, compared with the *Prince Royal*'s 64 and the *Naseby*'s 80; most of the Dutch ships mounted between 20 and 30 guns.

At 17th Century Surat, on the west coast of India, Portuguese galleys are routed by Dutchmen who have arrived in the five square-rigged warships anchored at right. The Portuguese soon drove out the Dutch interlopers. However, in 1612 the Portuguese were ousted once more, this time by the English, and the English and the Dutch thereafter struck a shaky alliance to trade jointly at Surat.

The Dutch never explained their reasoning, but some historians have suggested that the Dutch built smaller warships because their shipyards were in shallow harbors, or because they had to be able to navigate the shallow waters off their own coast. Yet their merchant ships were as big as any. Some naval tacticians all through history have preferred a small, maneuverable ship to a big one, and perhaps the Dutch had that kind of temperament. Besides, they had no king to insist on ships that showed his prestige and they were building not so much for fleet actions as for convoy escort. In any case, they had many reasons for building small.

The act that finally and irrevocably pushed the two rivals into war was an intolerable extension of the English claim to sovereignty of the seas. In 1651 the English Council of State passed a Navigation Act, by which all trade into English ports was reserved for ships that were English built and owned, and manned by largely English crews. Moreover, the English fleet was authorized to engage foreign ships that refused to strike their flags upon meeting English men-of-war. The Dutch assumed that the act was deliberately aimed against them and they were undoubtedly right. Certainly it reinforced the ancient claim of sovereignty, and gave English warships a legal excuse to shoot first and ask questions later.

At this point the Dutch commenced to prepare in earnest for war. On March 3, 1652, Dutch leaders at The Hague ordered the fitting-out of 150 additional ships of war to join the 76 already patrolling the Channel and North Sea. From this it was obvious to the English that the Dutch intended to make their position clear by force. They were not mollified when the Dutch embassy in London blandly assured Parliament that the Netherlands "had no intention of doing the slightest harm to any of their allies, or to neutral states—far less to England—but merely to preserve their own free navigation." For their part, the English, with a fleet of 85 warships and many more on the way, appeared equally ready for a test of strength, and they seem to have racked their brains for grievances. All the old commercial jealousies were dug up and paraded in the pamphlet press. An inflamed populace demanded an end to Dutch fishing in waters anywhere near England and railed against Dutch Baltic trade. Observing the uproar, one chronicler noted, "The Dutch have too much trade, and the English are resolved to take it from them."

The generation-old Massacre of Amboina was revived and fanned to new fury. The English press railed against the "unjust, cruel, and barbarous proceedings" of the Dutch on Amboina. Sir George Downing, the English Minister in The Hague, later noted that the Dutch were for "*mare liberum* in the British Seas, but *mare clausum* on the coast of Africa and in the East Indies"—in favor of open seas where the English roamed, but closed seas where their own interests were involved. A Swedish diplomat may have been right when he wrote home from London: "Both these nations, and especially this one here, are insufferably arrogant; it is possible that God will yet humble their pride."

When war began, it began out of an almost ludicrous chance encounter. On a spring morning off Devon, in 1652, Captain Anthony Young put to sea in a small man-of-war named the *President*, with two other equally small ships. As he cleared land he saw a squadron of a dozen ships

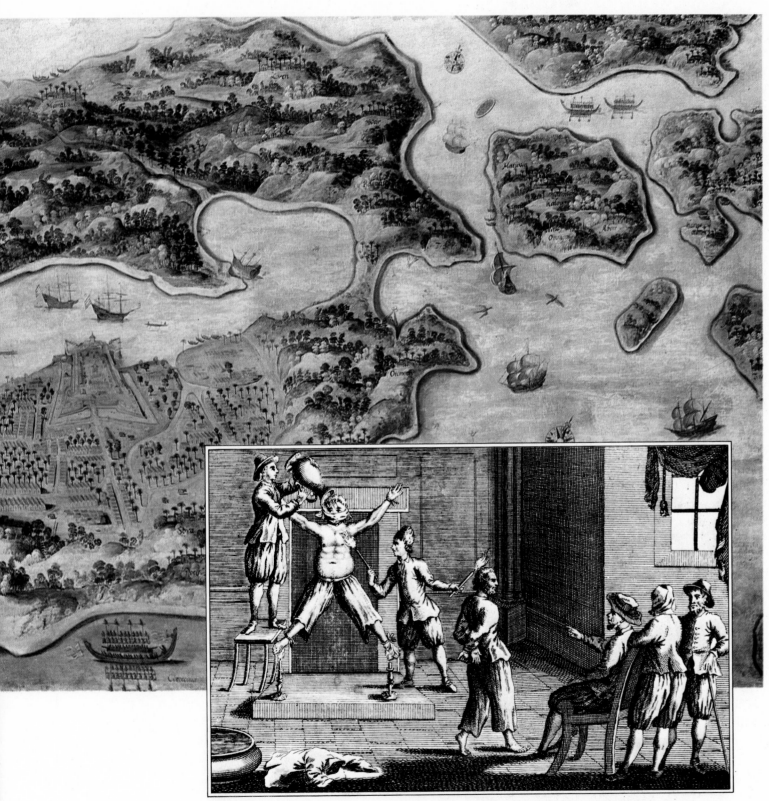

Amboina, a prime port for cloves and nutmegs in the East Indies, appears prosperous and peaceful in this early-17th Century painting. Yet in 1623 violence erupted when the Dutch tortured and executed several English merchants accused of plotting against the Dutch governor. The incident, shown in the grisly English engraving inset above, enraged England. "This no English patience can bear," wrote one pamphleteer; "the blood of the innocent cries out against it: the honor of the nation suffereth in it."

beating up channel from the Atlantic. He thought they were English and
went to have a look, but found they were Dutch merchantmen homeward
bound, escorted by three warships wearing the flags of an admiral, a vice
admiral and a rear admiral. So he called on them, as the English often
had in the past, to salute by lowering their flags.

The admiral did so, but that was not enough for Young: he wanted all
three flags down. The vice admiral, coming astern, refused, and shouted
through a speaking trumpet to Young, no doubt with appropriate oaths,
that if the Englishman wanted it lowered he could come and lower it
himself. Young took him at his word and sent his shipmaster in a boat.
Naturally, the Dutchmen refused to let him board and sent him back
again. After more demands and more refusals, Young angrily fired a
broadside and the Dutchman with equal anger fired one back. The Dutch
rear admiral and Young's other ships started shooting too—and then the
vice admiral changed his mind and hauled down the offending flag.

*In the sunny courtyard of the Amsterdam
bourse, black-frocked merchants
and speculators gather to discuss the latest
quotations for everything from Swedish
copper to Bordeaux wine. For most
of the 17th Century, Amsterdam was the
hub of northern European capitalism,
providing a dependable currency exchange
and the world's first stock market, where
investors could speculate on the progress of
the Dutch overseas trading companies
by purchasing "actions"—the
precursors of modern stock certificates.*

One man had been killed in the *President*, and she had some damage, so a new argument began, shouted across the intervening water. Young demanded that the vice admiral's ship come into harbor with him to pay for the damage. At that, the admiral joined in to say that he had not interfered while they were arguing only about the flag, but he would not let one of his ships be taken to port. Young gave it up. He was quite pleased with himself and felt that honor had been satisfied. "I do believe I gave him his bellyful of it," he wrote in his report.

Nothing more might have happened, but farther up the Channel, in the Strait of Dover, large fleets of both countries happened to be in sight of each other. The English were under their commander in chief, General-at-Sea Robert Blake. He flew his flag in the 48-gun *James*. Opposite him was Lieutenant Admiral Maarten Harpertszoon Tromp in the *Brederode*. Each was minding his own business but eying the other suspiciously.

There was a strong northeasterly wind, and the English fleet of 21 ships was divided; nine ships under Rear Admiral Nehemiah Bourne were in the Downs—the roadstead off the east of Kent that is sheltered by the Goodwin Sands—and the remainder were some distance to the west in Rye Bay. The Dutch fleet, with almost twice as many ships, had come across the Channel from the coast of France and was anchored between the two parts of the English fleet, in the lee of the land, off Dover.

Tromp had politely sent two ships into the Downs to explain to the nervous English that he had been losing anchors and cables off France in the blustery weather, and had only come across for shelter. The English only half believed him. To have a large Dutch fleet anchored off one of England's principal ports made everyone nervous. Thus far, as he lay at anchor, Tromp had met no English ships to salute in the ritual fashion. But it was not only the ships of England that expected the salute. Tromp may not have known, but the castle at Dover expected it too. While he lay anchored there, the garrison of the castle fired some shots to remind him, but he failed to respond properly. On the contrary, he made a bit of noise himself by having his musketeers fire volleys of shots. Both parts of the English fleet weighed anchor and began to converge on Dover to see what was happening. The Dutch saw them coming, and they also weighed and discreetly stood off toward the coast of France again.

So far so good. But two hours later, before the English fleet had joined off Dover, the Dutch abruptly reversed course and began to come back. What had happened? None of the English knew. In fact, a single Dutch ship had come up from westward, bringing a captain who had been present at the farcical action off Devon. His name was Captain Joris Van der Saanen, and he went on board the *Brederode* by boat and told Tromp that the merchant convoy, with goods worth a great deal, was anchored in the lee of the English coast and that the English were about to seize it.

This was untrue. But Van der Saanen's report, along with his highly colored account of the run-in with Young, triggered a violent change in Tromp's intentions, or so it seemed. The Dutch fleet came about. Blake and the English were astonished to see the 42 Dutch warships bearing down on them, led by Tromp in the *Brederode*, and more astonished still to see a flag being hoisted below the *Brederode*'s ensign—the blood-red flag that every seaman knew was the signal for battle.

The "Wasa" reborn from the deep

Baring his great fangs, a carved lion from the recovered Swedish Wasa snarls ferociously, his tongue still red with original paint and his features still flecked with gilding after 333 years underwater. Mounted high on the sterncastle, this lion and its twin formed a part of the royal coat of arms, as can be seen in the rendering below, which gives an overall view of the fantastic wealth of decoration on the great vessel. Ranging from classical gods to grotesque human heads, these wooden carvings formed a dazzling display along the stern galleries.

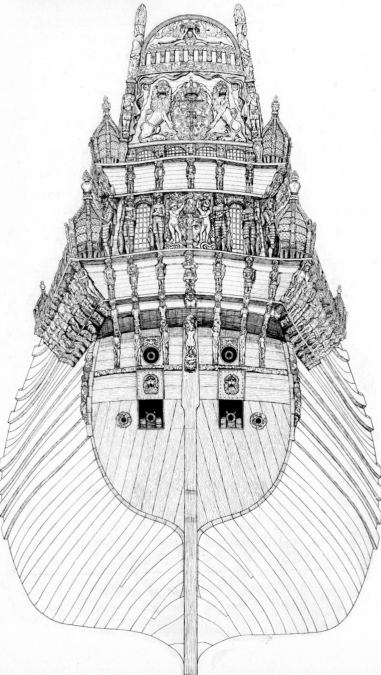

Shortly after Sunday vespers on August 10, 1628, the crew of the Swedish warship *Wasa* set her foresail, mizzen lateen sail and two topsails to snare the light breezes that would ease her out of Stockholm harbor on her maiden voyage. But as she sailed on a reach across the harbor, a squall suddenly howled out of the southwest. The great ship reeled, recovered and then heeled hard over again. This time the sea poured in through her lower gunports—still open while she was making the harbor passage—and in minutes Sweden's mightiest vessel filled and sank in 110 feet of water.

In 17th Century Sweden the foundering of the *Wasa* was an embarrassment of epic proportions. But in the 20th Century her spectacular recovery has given the world a first-hand look at a man-of-war from 300 years past.

The Swedish government started its salvage operation in 1958, and in three and a half years spent two million dollars to bring the great ship to the surface. Over time she had lost her beaked prow, her sterncastle and most of her masts, but the icy water and accumulating layers of harbor silt had preserved the ship so remarkably well that after only minor structural repairs she was able to float on her own.

Constructed by a Dutch shipwright hired by the Swedish Crown, the *Wasa* embodied the latest in warship design as it was evolving between the two premier maritime powers of Europe: the Netherlands and England. Race-built and square-rigged, she carried 64 cannon in several tiers along her 204-foot hull. Her three masts soared as high as 165 feet above her keel, and she carried 10 sails—13,000 square feet of canvas in all. Had she survived to reach the sea, she probably could have made 11 knots in a good breeze.

Most of her 133-man shakedown crew were rescued when she sank. Only 18 skeletons were found on board. But the men left behind thousands of items that provide a vivid record of sailors' life: clothes, eating utensils, even a butter-box filled with rancid butter.

But the most fascinating aspect of the *Wasa* lies in the glory of her decorations. It was the habit of 17th Century monarchs to proclaim their power and wealth with lavish vessels. King Gustavus II outdid the world with the *Wasa*. Her stern and sides were one gilded mass of more than 1,000 carvings, like the one at left. "Building small ships, the King declared, "is only a waste of young trees."

In firing position abutting open gunports, empty gun carriages add a ghostly aura to the Wasa's lower gun deck, whose woodwork glistens under the constant spray of a chemical preservative. These carriages once cradled 48 great bronze 24-pounders, almost all of which were salvaged shortly after the ship sank.

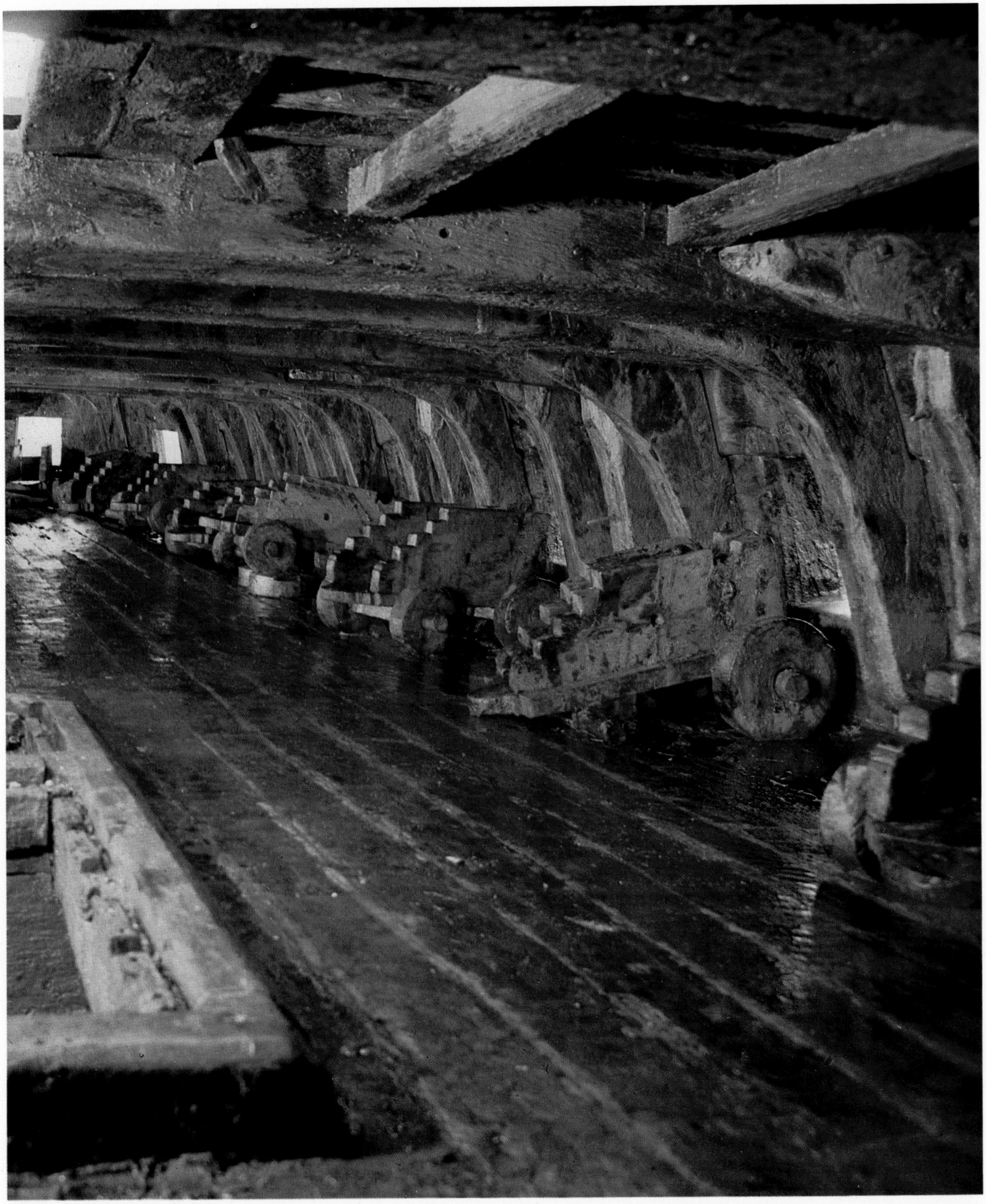

TAFFRAIL DECORATION

WASA SHEAF   GROTESQUE HEAD   SHIELD WITH BIRD'S HEAD

CHERUB WITH LUTE

Far more than mere decoration for decoration's sake, the magnificent carvings that adorned the Wasa conveyed with symbols many popular and inspirational themes of their day. Lions, griffins and crowns symbolized the majesty and power of the King, while Roman emperors attested to his noble and ancient lineage. Angelic figures and Biblical scenes reminded seamen of the righteousness of their sovereign's cause, and of course mermaids and sea-gods were fashioned to glorify the traditional lore of the sea.

ROMAN WARRIOR

LION MASK

MERMAID

A treasure-trove of 17th Century artifacts, abandoned in haste as the Wasa went down, was uncovered when archeologists sifted through the 700 tons of silt that had settled inside the hull during the centuries. Neatly stowed in the seaman's chest at far right were leather work gloves, a broad-brimmed hat, a comb and a thimble. The earthenware pot at center right was probably heated directly on an open fire in fair weather.

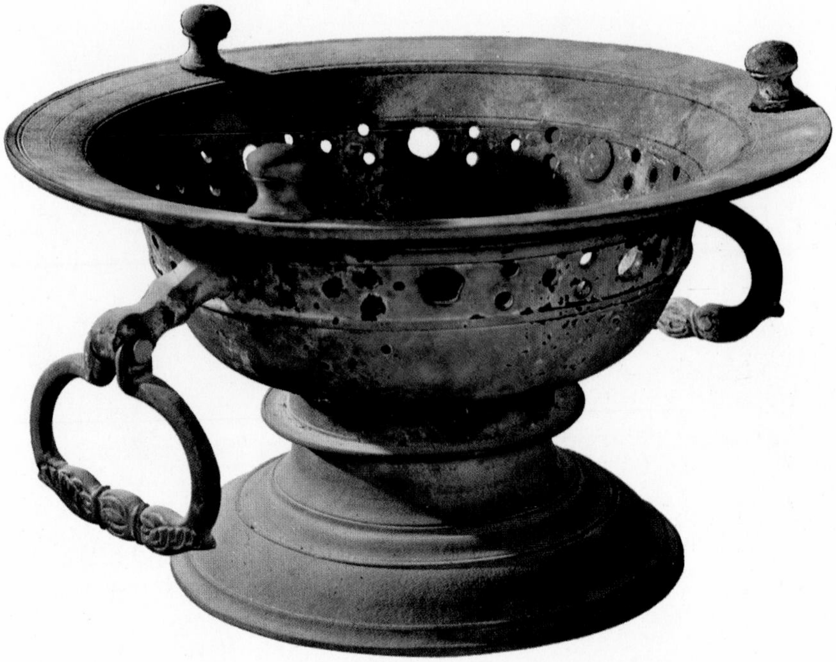

PEWTER BRAZIER

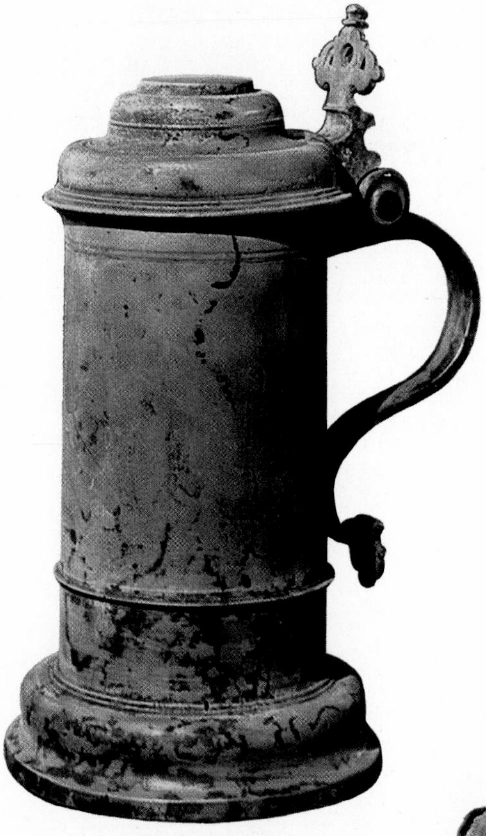

PEWTER TANKARD

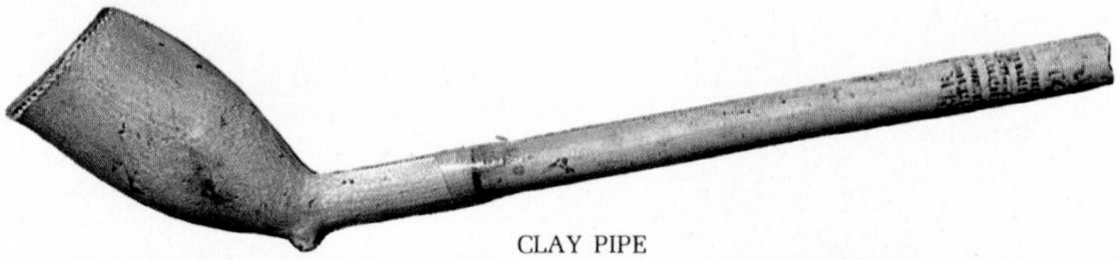

CLAY PIPE

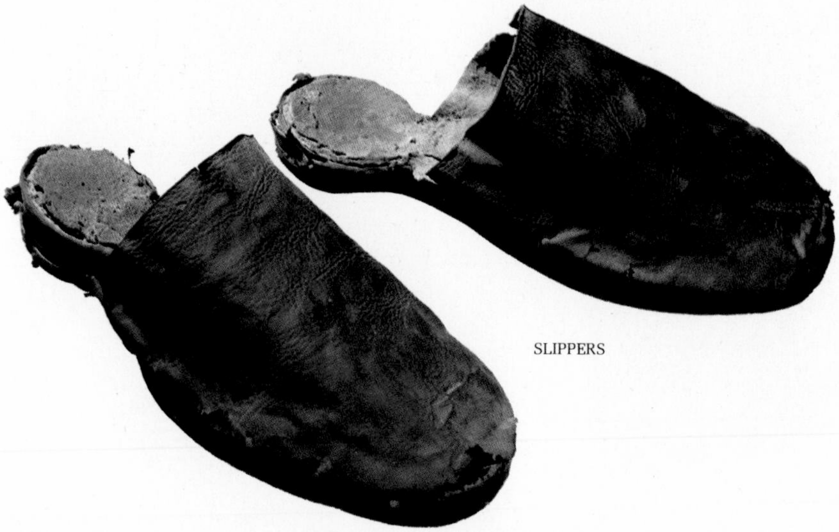

SLIPPERS

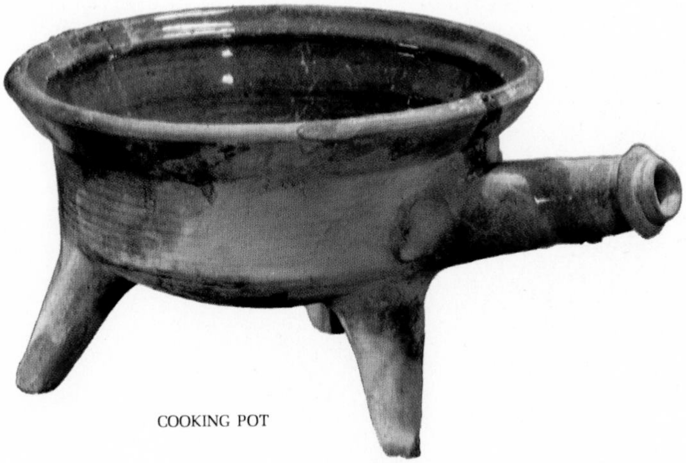

COOKING POT

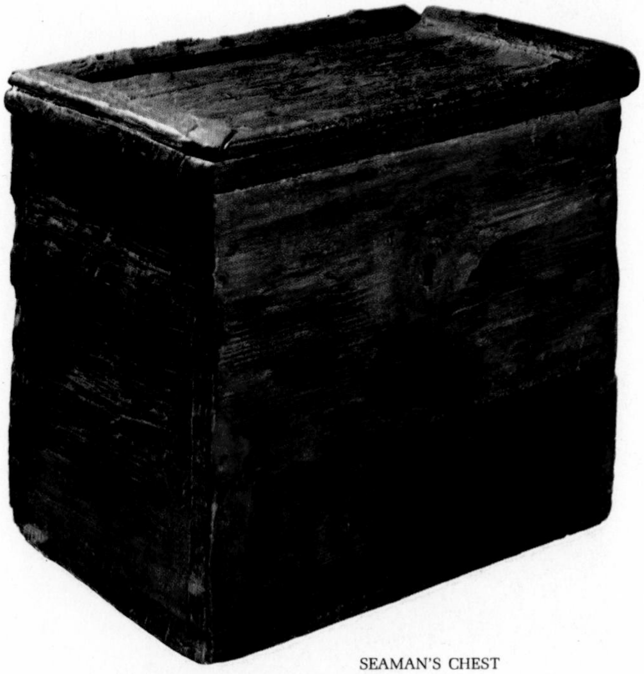

SEAMAN'S CHEST

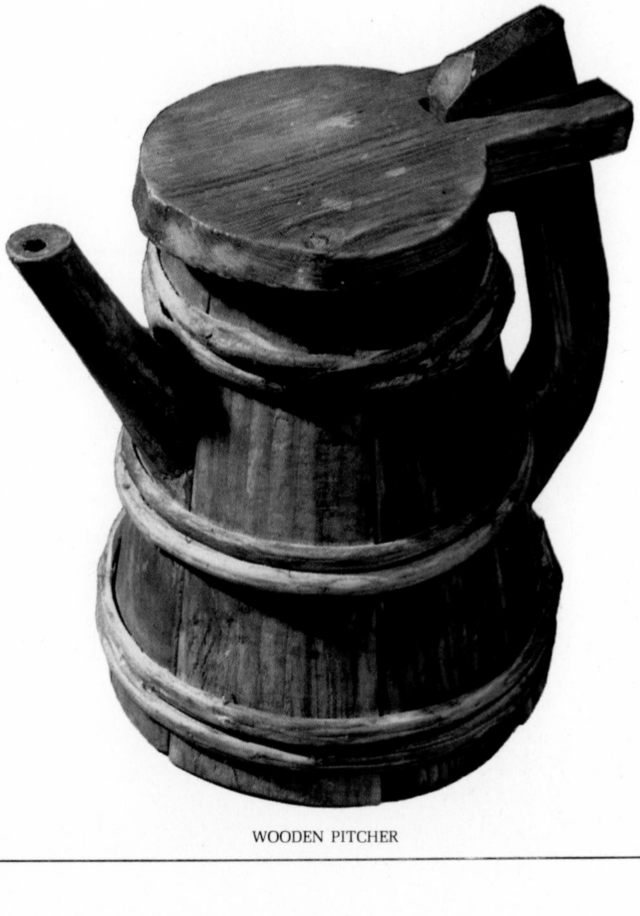

WOODEN PITCHER

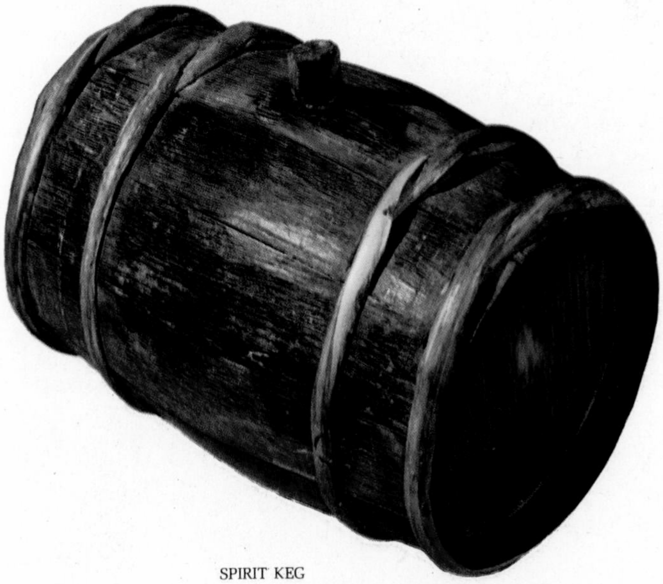

SPIRIT KEG

Chapter 2

Titanic trials for the new navies

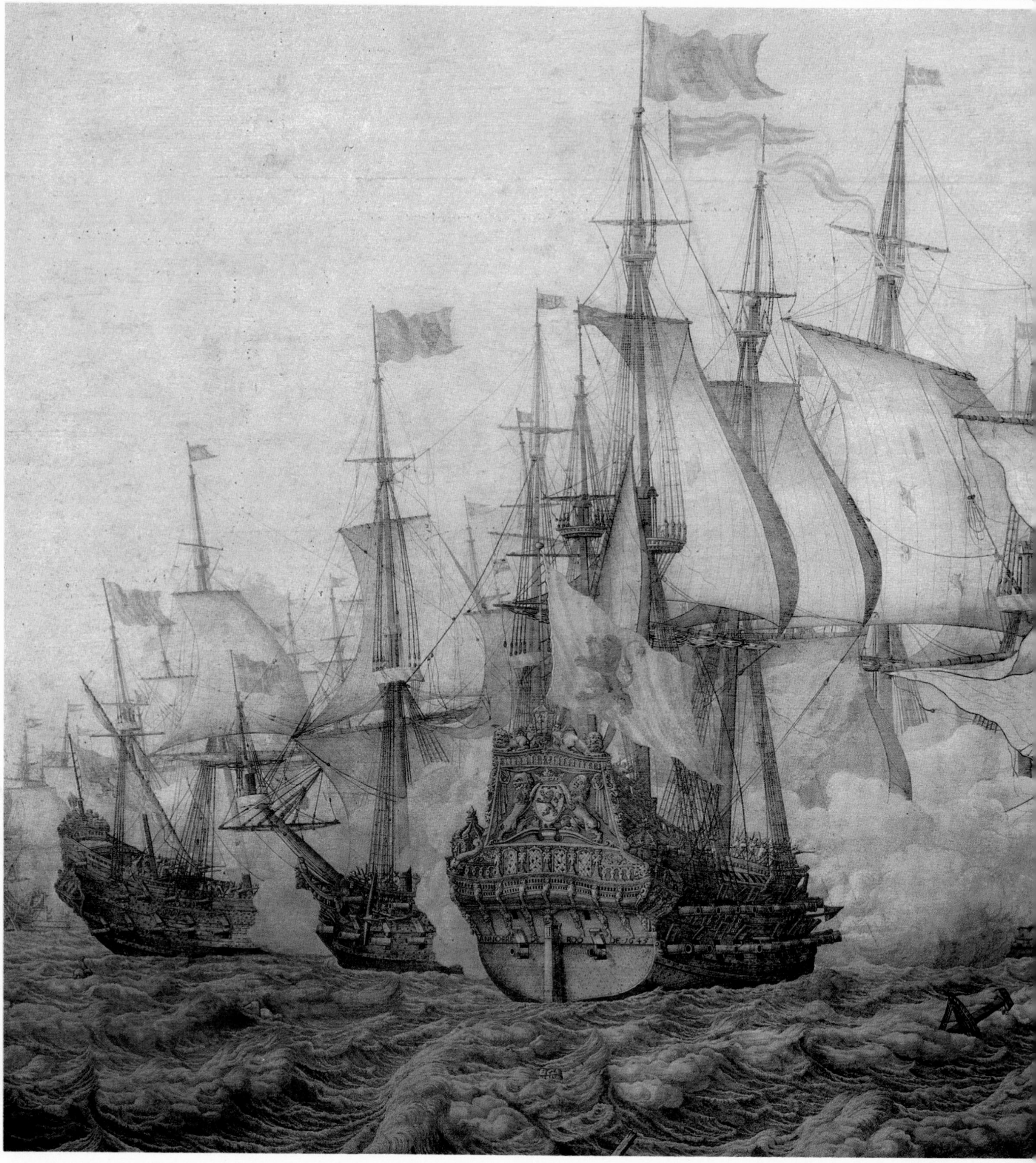

With thunderous broadsides the English and Dutch fleets hammer away at each other in the 1653 Battle of Gabbard Shoal—a debacle for the Dutch.

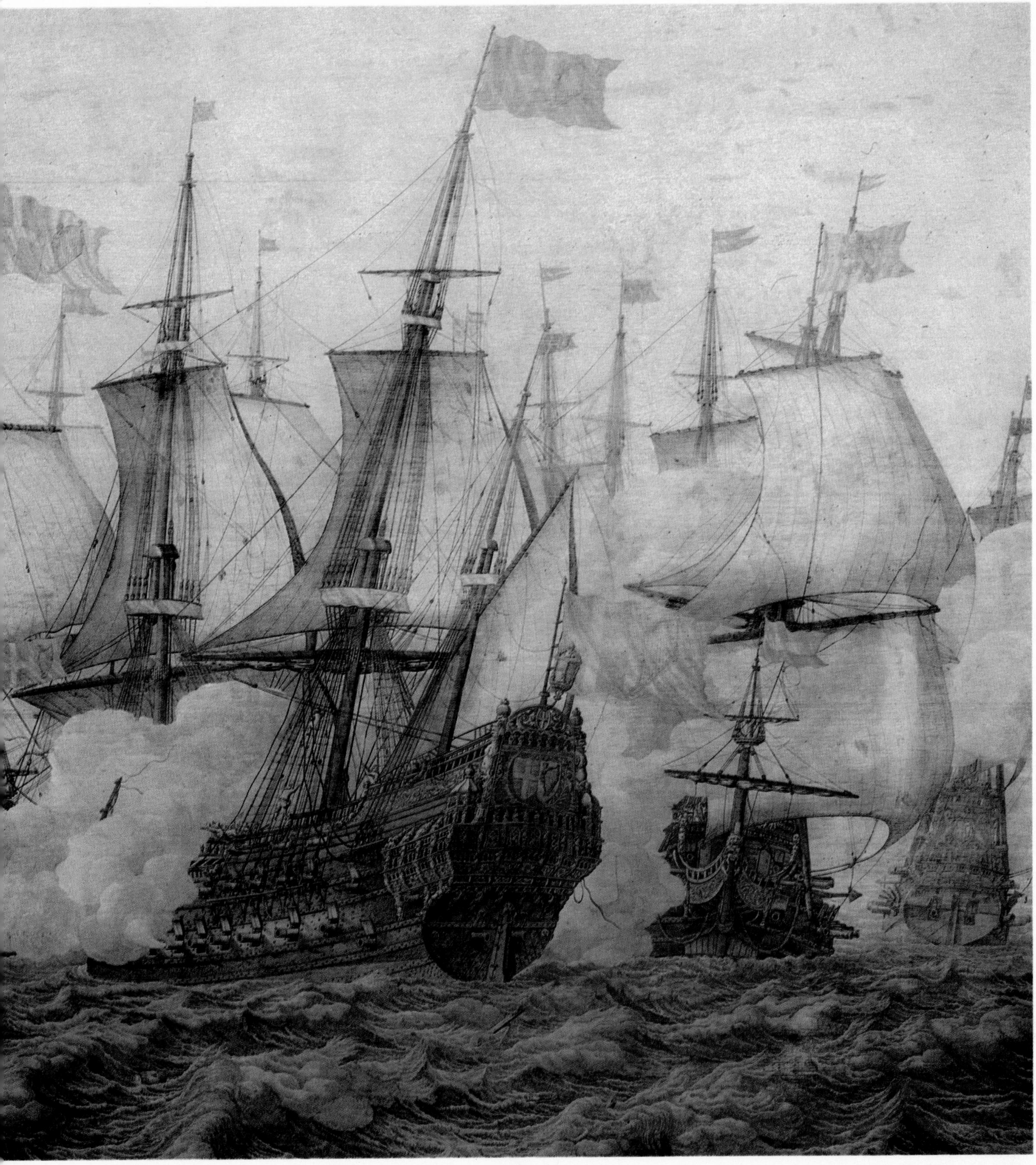

The two commanders approaching each other in that moment of climax off Dover on a spring day in 1652 could hardly have been less alike. Maarten Harpertszoon Tromp was a "tarpaulin"—a lifelong seaman—who had worked his way to the top. Robert Blake was a wealthy country squire, merchant and soldier who had spent relatively little time at sea until Oliver Cromwell appointed him to command at the age of 50. The only things Tromp and Blake had in common were stubborn bravery, tactical genius and the seasoning that comes with age; both were in their mid-fifties, which in those days was getting old for an active man.

Yet in a period of merely 15 months, from May 1652 through August 1653, these two disparate men would be the major protagonists in the opening round of one of the greatest struggles in maritime history. The Dutch and English fleets under their leadership would fight no fewer than seven major sea battles, and in the course of these contests they would define the true meaning of war at sea.

Tromp was the son of an officer on an early Dutch man-of-war; his mother washed sailors' shirts to supplement the family income. At the age of nine, Tromp went to sea with his father and was present in a major battle with the Spaniards off Gibraltar. Three years later they sailed together on a merchant ship to Africa, where they were attacked by English pirates and Tromp's father was slain. According to legend the 12-year-old boy rallied the Dutch crew with the cry: "Won't you avenge my father's death?" But the pirates seized him and forced him to serve as a cabin boy for two years. Set free, he supported his mother and three sisters by working in a Rotterdam shipyard, went to sea again at 19, and three years later was captured once more—this time by Barbary corsairs off Tunis. He was kept as a slave till he was 24, and by then had so impressed the bey of Tunis with his skill in gunnery and navigation that he was again set free. By 1624, at age 26, he was the captain of a Dutch man-of-war, and at age 31 he became flag captain of the budding fleet. Within eight years he had risen to the rank of lieutenant admiral of Holland and was, in effect, commander in chief of the fleet.

Always conscious of his humble origin, Tromp was firm but kind to his crews, who called him *Bestevaer*–Granddad. His men, said a contemporary, "thought it a great honor to fight under him, and even if they lost an arm or a leg in action, they boasted that they had lost their limb in the ship and in the service of Admiral Tromp." At 44 he had the curious distinction of being knighted by King Charles I of England for escorting Queen Henrietta Maria and the crown jewels to Holland, where she sold them to raise money for arms to equip the English Royalist forces in the Civil War against Parliament. "I falling on my knee," Tromp recalled later, "the King struck me on my left shoulder; and that being done, I kissed the King's hand, and he helped me up and wished me luck. I answered the King, 'My life is for Your Majesty.' "

Tromp may or may not have meant it. But his vow was never tested, for the Dutch took no part in the English Civil War, which ended with Charles's defeat and beheading. Still, that chivalrous promise marked Tromp as totally different from the cold and curt commander of the Parliamentary fleet facing the Dutch off the Downs that day in May 1652.

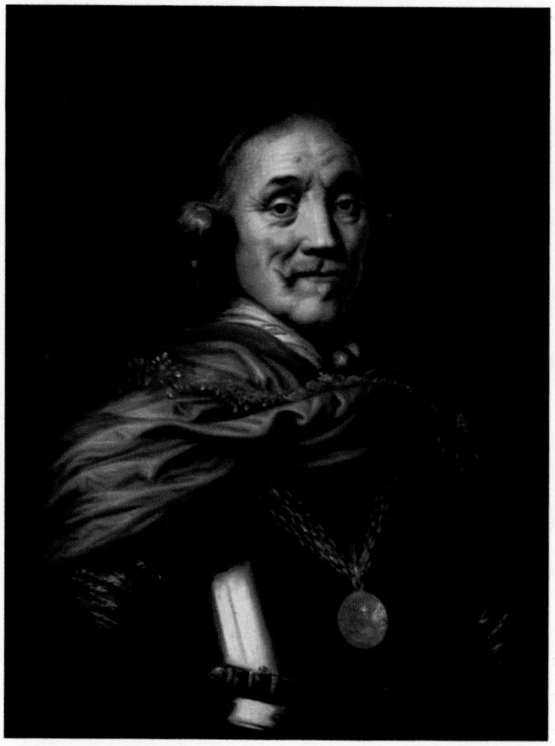

Maarten Tromp, the salty old admiral who led the Dutch fleet in five battles during the two-year war, was respected among his crews as a "tarpaulin"—an officer who had come up through the ranks. A persistent legend has it that after his victory at Dungeness he flew a broom from his mainmast as a symbol of his intention to sweep the English Channel clear of enemy ships, a tale dismissed by historians.

Robert Blake was born in the west of England, the scion of well-to-do merchants and shipowners who traded with the farthest colonies. He studied at Oxford, took over the family business at 27 when his father died, and for the next 15 years or so applied himself assiduously to mercantile affairs. Stern, shrewd, scholarly and stiffly Puritan, he was naturally attracted to Cromwell's cause in the Civil War against King Charles. And as a lieutenant colonel in a Parliamentary foot regiment, he soon proved himself the scourge of Royalist forces. Though Blake called it a "strange surprise extremely beyond my merits," it was understandable when in 1649 Cromwell chose to appoint his totally loyal and dedicated officer as one of three generals-at-sea to command England's warships. What Blake did not know about warfare at sea he would soon learn—of that Cromwell could be sure.

Dour and humorless, a fierce disciplinarian, Blake was the last man on earth any seaman would call Granddad. But he quickly cleared the seas around England of Royalist warships and proved himself an entirely worthy adversary of the brilliant Dutch admiral, Maarten Tromp.

People watching the converging fleets from the cliffs of Dover on May 29, 1652, seem to have had no doubt about what was going to happen. At 10 that morning they had seen Blake and his small fleet of 12 men-of-war claw their way slowly up from Rye Bay against a foul northeasterly head wind, and they had watched the Dutch fleet of 42 men-of-war weigh anchor at the sight of Blake and stand close-hauled away toward Calais. Then abruptly the Dutch fleet had turned in a cluster of sails and run back before the wind straight for Blake. So certain was it that a battle was in the offing that 40 English volunteers put off in a boat from Dover to join the fun. They boarded Blake's flagship, the *James*, and Blake, in a rare moment of joviality, gave each of them a beer mug of old Malaga wine and drank one himself.

Both commanders afterward said that the other had started the fracas. In his report, Tromp stated that Blake "got to windward of us, firing shots through our hull and sails, with the obvious intention of sinking us. Whereupon we turned and gave them a broadside." For his part, Blake described how the Dutch "bore directly with us, Tromp the headmost; whereupon we lay by and put ourselves into a fighting posture, judging they had a resolution to engage. Being come within musket-shot I gave order to fire at his flag, which was done thrice. After the third shot he let fly a broadside at us."

With all the claims and counterclaims of provocation, it was never resolved who had in fact fired the first broadside. But at once the two great men-of-war—the *James* of 48 guns and the *Brederode* with 54 guns—loosed broadside after broadside at each other, locked in close combat, with each fleet coming up astern of the two flagships and joining in the battle. One Dutch captain later confessed that "how the fight began he knoweth not, being a great distance off; but seeing his admiral fight, he fought likewise according to his orders."

Though fewer in number, Blake's ships were mostly larger and more heavily gunned than the Dutch. Spectators on the cliff tops watched as the two fleets coalesced into a totally unorganized mass: 42 Dutch, 12

Robert Blake, commander of the English fleet in 1652 during the First Dutch War, was a brilliant infantry officer in Cromwell's army until he was called upon to defend the new Commonwealth at sea. He showed a rare concern for the needs of his crews, once complaining to Cromwell that "though supply come timely, yet if beer come not with it, we shall be undone that way."

English, all steering different courses, all blazing away point-blank.

Down in the claustrophobic gloom of the gun decks, there was a hell of noise: the concussion of guns, the crash of broken wood and the whiz of lethal splinters, shouts and cries and screams—and occasionally cheers. It was a hellish sight as well: the swirling smoke, the flash of powder, the corpses and bits of corpses that were shoved out of gunports into the sea, the wounded carried below, the blood that flowed from side to side across the holystoned decks as the ships heeled with the impact of broadsides, the small boys who ran through it all, each carrying powder to his gun. Even more agonizing were the cockpits below the water line, lit only by candle lanterns, where the surgeons hacked and sawed off the mangled limbs of stoic men.

On the upper decks, masts and spars came crashing down and buried men in tangles of canvas and rigging. Hailstorms of musketry and sheets of razor-edged junk swept the decks. Captains and helmsmen steered instinctively to avoid collisions, but the battle was fought in clouds of gun smoke sometimes so thick that nobody could see the length of the ship. And here and there in the acrid fog, men-of-war crashed together, and then the decks suddenly swarmed with men attacking each other hand to hand with cutlasses and pikes.

For four desperate hours the battle continued, with neither side getting much the better of it. Then, in the gathering dusk, Major John Bourne and his division of nine ships from the Downs, taking advantage of the northeasterly wind, came down upon Tromp's straggling rear division. With these reinforcements the odds against the English were dramatically lowered. Tromp's fleet found itself waging battle to both the front and the rear.

At nightfall the battle stopped. Nobody thought of fighting in the dark, when there was no way at all to distinguish friend from foe. The Dutch drew away toward France, showing stern lights to keep together. They left two small ships behind, the 37-gun *St. Maria* and the 30-gun *St. Laurens*—both dismasted and riddled through the hull. The ships were taken by the English and their crews captured. The *St. Laurens* was towed back to England as a war prize. The *St. Maria* was abandoned in a sinking condition. But in the morning her hull was still afloat and a Dutch crew retrieved her and towed her home.

Although 63 ships had been engaged and many were floating wrecks, not a single one had been sunk. The Dutch tended to aim their fire at spars, sails and rigging, hoping to immobilize an enemy ship, after which it could be captured or destroyed by fire ships (*pages 116-123*). The English, on the other hand, concentrated their firepower on the hull, seeking to demolish armament and kill crew. Yet even then, in those days of solid, nonexplosive shot, the wooden hull itself rarely sank unless a powder magazine was touched off. Shot holes were nearly always above the water line because the surface of the ocean deflected virtually every shot; a ball that did penetrate the water soon lost all its momentum. The worst that could happen was a hit between wind and water—directly at the water line—where the ship could flood before her carpenters could make repairs. But able carpenters could plug almost any hole in an amazingly short time.

Blake's flagship, the *James*, was in the hottest of the fight that day, with 70 shot holes in the hull and an uncountable number in the rigging. More than 40 of her crew were killed or seriously wounded (nobody counted the minor wounds), and her mizzenmast went by the boards. But after a night's repairs she was under sail again and ready to join the battle once more.

The English claimed a victory because the Dutch had retired, and because they had taken the *St. Laurens* as a prize. But it was more nearly a standoff. Nevertheless, the loss of a man-of-war irked the Dutch, and a few days later Tromp wrote Blake a letter of charming impertinence: "Sir,—On the 29th of last month we met each other at sea. My intention was to greet you; but, seeing that I was attacked, I was forced as a man of honor to defend myself. It has however today been reported to me that one of our ships has been brought into your road in Downs. It is the only one of ours missing, and I beg you for friendship's sake to be pleased to restore this ship."

Although Blake had apparently visited Rotterdam during his youthful voyages and he and Tromp had many times encountered each other's ships at sea under more amicable conditions, there is no evidence that Tromp's reference to friendship was anything but sarcasm.

Blake replied with anger. "Sir," he wrote, "It is not without great astonishment that I have read yours of 2nd June wherein, though representing yourself as a person of honour, you introduce many gross misstatements; and this, after having fought with the fleet of the Parliament of the English Republic, instead of employing the customary respect, which the occasion demanded. I presume Parliament will keenly resent this great insult and the spilling of the blood of their unoffending subjects, and that you will moreover find, in the undersigned, one ever ready to carry out their commands."

If Blake had returned the *St. Laurens*, the crew that had captured her would have been even more outraged than Parliament, for the Naval tradition of awarding prize money was by that time well established. A 1649 act of Parliament gave officers and men one-half the value of any warship captured, the other half going to a fund for sick and wounded sailors, widows and orphans. But payments had a way of getting bogged down in the bureaucracy of the Prize Courts; ofttimes the money was not paid for years, and sometimes it was forgotten altogether— which encouraged crews to take matters into their own hands when and if they could.

After the battle, Cromwell hastened to Dover to inspect damage to the fleet, confer with Blake and interrogate captives. Under questioning, Captain Bastiaen Tuynemans of the captured *St. Laurens* agreed that Tromp, not Blake, had fired the first broadside—although he had been too far in the rear to know. His confession stemmed from bitterness at being left behind by his comrades. "He cries out," Major John Bourne reported, "against Tromp and the rest for their cowardly carriage in leaving them to our mercy."

Cromwell returned to London to fulminate against the Dutch and prepare the country for full-scale naval war. At this point the English

Navy counted 85 combat ships and another 40 in various stages of construction. An order went out from the Council of State to impress seamen between 15 and 50 to man the vessels. Supplies of victuals, shot and gunpowder, 600 barrels of it, were sent to Dover.

To make control of the fleet more effective, Blake and Cromwell decided to divide the ships into three squadrons—red, white and blue. Blake himself would command the red, or vanguard, and he would rotate command of the other two squadrons among senior officers, one of whom was William Penn, whose son and namesake would soon win fame as founder of the New World colony of Pennsylvania. The senior Penn was already known as an outstanding officer in the Parliamentary army. In the past, however, there had been questions about his loyalty; in fact, Cromwell had had him apprehended and taken into custody for a month in 1648 on suspicion of his having corresponded with the de-

A Dutch corner on cartography

Tlandt ontrent Doueren zeijende doer de hoofden
Douers
S.Margaret
Grauesent
Tilbury
Holhauen
Bornham
Brikelsey
Walton
Root Clif
A
N
G L I Æ
P A R
S.
De Zee Custen tusschen Douere en Orfordts nesse, daer de Teemse de Vermaerde Riuire vā Lonen gelegens is, met alle sanden ons diepte, naer haren wesen en ghedaente.
Door Lucas Iansz. Wage.
Rochester
Sandwich
Norborow
John
Margat
Whitstaple
Roculuer
Santosyts
Walton
Orwelhouen
Goen fliet
Spiets
Knock
Ter voor landt
O C E A N V S
S E P
T R O N A L I S
N O O R D T
Z E E

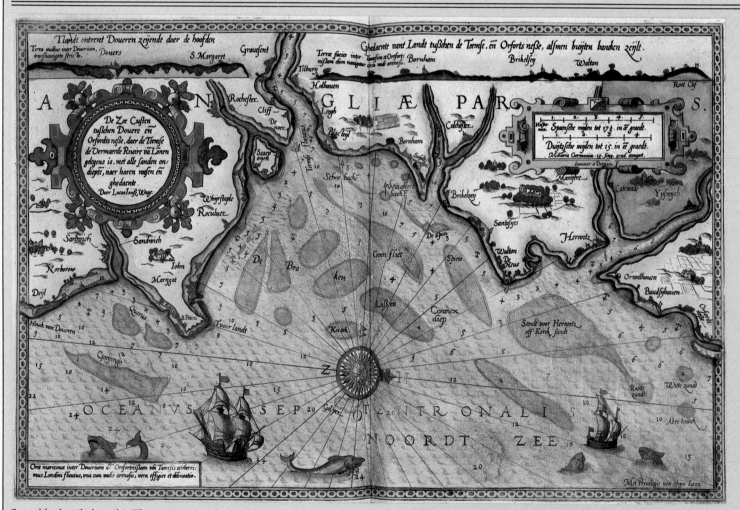

Superbly detailed, as this Thames estuary chart shows, the maps of cartographer Lucas Waghenaer were standard seamen's aids in the 17th Century.

posed Charles I. But Penn had been exonerated, and his military talents were so great that he was now appointed Blake's vice admiral.

Though the Dutch and English were not to declare a formal war for another three months, a state of war clearly existed between the two nations. The English decided to strike at Dutch commerce. Blake was ordered to attack the Dutch herring fleet, which for generations had been fishing off the coasts of England and Scotland. He was also instructed, while in the North Sea, to intercept a homeward-bound Dutch convoy of Indiamen that was expected to avoid the English Channel by sailing round the north of Scotland. Blake chose as his flagship the old *Prince Royal,* the vessel now known as the *Resolution.* And on July 6, with a fleet of 61 men-of-war, he headed north for Scotland, where the Dutch convoy would have to pass. He would have been interested to learn that Tromp was hard on his heels.

If the English were the great innovators in naval design throughout the 16th and 17th Centuries, the Dutch were the experts in nautical chartmaking. So superior were Dutch charts of the period, in fact, that the English used Dutch maps to sail their own estuaries and coasts—and to fight their wars with the Dutch.

A people heavily dependent upon trade and fishing, the Dutch were in the forefront of the emerging science of navigation. As early as 1500 they had issued a series of written port-to-port sailing instructions for northern European waters. In the mid-16th Century these instructions were compiled in a printed volume supplemented by woodcut charts of the coastlines. And by 1584 a Dutch cartographer named Lucas Waghenaer had taken the great step of producing a complete sea atlas for northern and western European waters that featured highly detailed copperplate-engraved maps.

Waghenaer's atlas, known as *The Mariner's Mirror,* contained no fewer than 44 charts that gave shoals, soundings, banks and landmarks, standardized symbols to represent anchorages, buoys and various hazards, and silhouettes showing the view of the shore from the sea. The atlas also included the latest sailing instructions for each chart, plus tables on tides and declination of the sun.

The English were so impressed that Charles Howard, the English Lord Admiral, called the atlas an aid "very necessary to our seamen" and immediately ordered a translation. Appearing in 1588, it became the standard for English coastal navigators.

It was not until almost a century later, well after the two Dutch wars, that the English attempted their own sea atlas. In 1671, one John Seller published *The English Pilot,* advertised as "being furnished with new and exact draughts, charts and descriptions." But many of Seller's charts were actually poor copies of Dutch charts—or worse yet, were made directly from out-of-date Dutch and French engraving plates bought up by Seller.

It took another decade for Charles II to authorize the first complete survey of England's coast. The result, in 1691, was Captain Greenvile Collins' *Great Britain's Coasting Pilot,* the first authoritative English sea atlas and the basis of English maritime cartography.

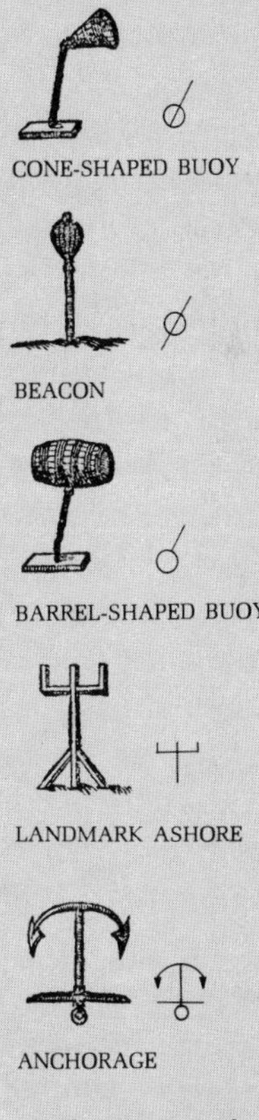
CONE-SHAPED BUOY
BEACON
BARREL-SHAPED BUOY
LANDMARK ASHORE
ANCHORAGE

Waghenaer was the first chartmaker to use standardized symbols to convey offshore navigational information. Circles intersected by lines indicated buoys and beacons, pitchfork-like crosstrees represented navigational landmarks, and anchors showed safe anchorages.

The Dutch had been no less quick to repair and bolster their war fleet. On July 11 Tromp seized a small English merchantman and learned from her skipper that a large English fleet under Blake had been heading north. Guessing his adversary's intent, Tromp brought together 83 men-of-war and nine fire ships, and immediately set out in pursuit. But from the outset of the chase the Fates conspired against him. Beating into adverse winds, he was soon forced to turn back; he headed south, in hopes of destroying the English division that had been left to guard the Channel. But then the fickle winds changed and he ran before them after Blake, as originally planned, through heavy seas that created perverse housekeeping problems for the Dutch fleet.

For some reason—possibly because they had departed in such great haste—the Dutch had loaded a considerable amount of their food on storeships, which were proceeding independently in the wake of the fleet. And now, in the stormy seas, the warships found it next to impossible to rendezvous with the supply squadron. Tromp worriedly wrote to the States-General: "If we miss the victuals and provisions, with 11,000 or more men on board, who daily consume at least 50 or 60 barrels of beer and as many of water, and above 60,000 pounds of hard bread in a week, and other provisions in proportion; in such a case there would be nothing to do but disembark the men in Norway or elsewhere (as England and Scotland are hostile), and to see the crews desert and the whole fleet ruined, which God forbid."

As it turned out, Tromp never was able to rendezvous with the supply ships, and while the shortage of supplies did not force him to call off the mission, as he had feared, it did have a deleterious effect on the morale and efficiency of his men.

Blake, meanwhile, was wreaking havoc on the Dutch herring fleet. Each year, hundreds upon hundreds of Dutch busses, 20- to 30-ton boats, fished their way southward from the Shetland Islands to herring shoals near the Scottish and English coasts. Blake found it a simple matter to overwhelm the few Dutch men-of-war on guard duty and capture the busses. "Divers Dutch are slain and wounded," Blake reported. More than 900 of the fishermen were taken captive; their catches were seized, and the men were then set free with a stern warning never to venture northward again.

As Blake headed south and Tromp hurried north, the two fleets passed each other on the dark and dismal night of August 3. There is no record that the English were aware of the Dutch, and only scant evidence that one or two Dutch lookouts spied the lights of the English. In any event, word of the sighting was not relayed to Tromp until late in the afternoon of the next day. But soon Tromp's fleet was hit by a violent storm. "As night fell," he wrote later, "an extraordinary gale came up and increased so that it was impossible to tack without the sails being rent or blown into ribbons, or quite carried away. Being in this extreme peril, and all thinking we must perish, each one did his best for ship and life: some tacked, others ran before the wind." A Dutch chronicler of the day wrote: "Ships seemed buried by the sea in horrible abysses, rose out of them only to be tossed up to the clouds; here masts were beaten down, there the deck was overflowed with the prevailing waves. The tempest was so

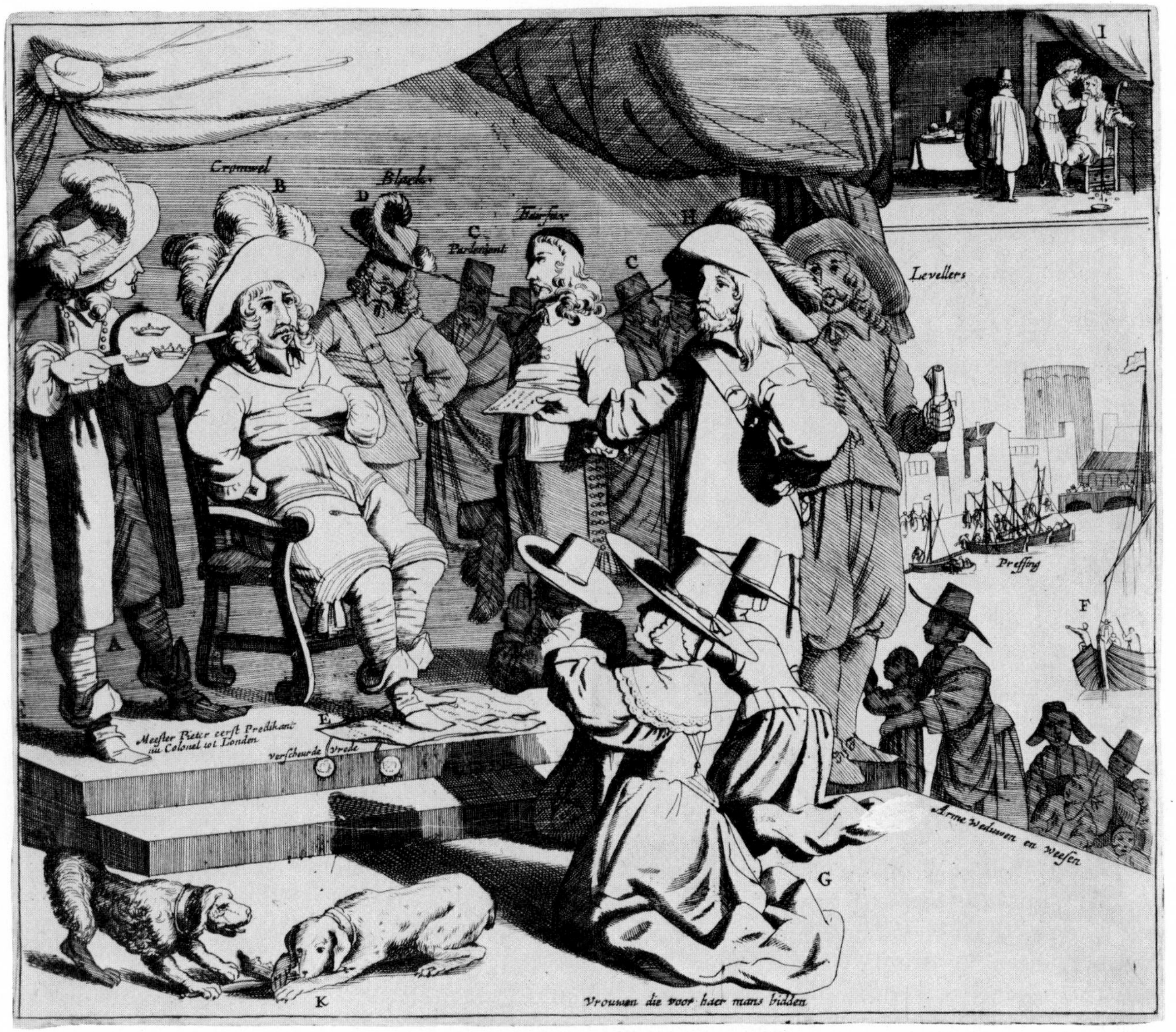

Cromwel
B
Blacke
D
C
Parlement
Fairfax
H
C
Levellers
I
A
Meester Pieter eerst Predikant
nu Colonel tot London
E
Verscheurde Vrede
F
Arme Weduwen en Weesen
G
K
Vrouwen die voor haer mans bidden

A bitter Dutch cartoon of Cromwell's England shows the Lord Protector surrounded by his "Council of Blood," while a Puritan divine applies a bellows to his ear, pumping his head full of dreams of power. At his feet the wives of the unfortunates who are being pressed into war duty on the ships in the background plead piteously for their husbands' release and, at left, two mongrels gnaw at the crown and scepter of the deposed House of Stuart. The inset at top right shows Cromwell being purged of his bad blood.

much mistress of the ships, they could be governed no longer. On every side appeared the forerunners of a dismal wreck."

When at last the storm abated, Tromp found to his dismay that "of the 92 ships of war there were only 34 remaining." He felt himself "extraordinarily punished by the mighty hand of God" and saw no alternative save "for the best to make for home with the ships at present with us." Blake had thus got away scot free with his devastating fisheries raid. Tromp's only consolation was that as the storm died, the Dutch Indiamen that he had been sent to protect appeared and fell in with his fleet. There were eight of them and they had come through the 50-mile-wide Fair Isle channel at the height of the gale, hidden from the English frigates by the storm.

Yet for Tromp it was a melancholy return to the Netherlands on August 20, shepherding less than half of the great fleet he had taken to sea. During the next few weeks, many of the missing vessels limped home alone or in small groups until all but a few could be accounted for. Nevertheless, it was regarded as a disaster of the greatest magnitude, and a scapegoat had to be named. Tromp was called to account by the States-General, the ruling body of the Netherlands, and was forced to resign his command.

With Tromp's disgrace, Vice Admiral Witte de With was given command of the fleet. De With was a long-experienced sailor and had served with some distinction in a number of sea fights during the war of independence against Spain. But he had been passed over for fleet command in favor of Tromp. This had done nothing to improve de With's disposition, which was caustic, jealous, boorish and cruel—exacting discipline that was considered extreme even in an age when the lash and keelhauling were commonplace. If ordinary seamen loved Tromp, they detested de With—and would soon show it in the most embarrassing manner.

By October 7 a Dutch fleet of 62 men-of-war was ready once more, and de With boasted that he would lead them into battle and only the devil would lead them out again. For his flagship de With chose Tromp's old vessel, the powerful *Brederode*, but as he was being rowed over to where she was lying at anchor the unthinkable happened. The *Brederode*'s crew actually refused to let the new commander come on board—and even threatened to fire a broadside into his longboat if he persisted in trying. Livid with rage, de With had himself rowed to his former ship, the smaller *Prins Willem*—where, to his incalculable fury, he found the entire crew, from the captain down, uproariously drunk, possibly in celebration of having got rid of him.

Catastrophe then mounted on catastrophe. On October 8 de With tried to take advantage of an easterly wind and charge into the Downs to catch the English fleet while it was anchored on a lee shore. At the last moment the wind shifted to the west, balking de With and allowing Blake to get his fleet under way. Worse, many of de With's captains refused to fight.

Once he was home, de With furiously accused his captains of cowardice. "They seem in every way to try to show the white feather," he fumed, "indeed brandish it so that we are put to shame before the world. Never in all my life have I seen such cowardice among sea captains as these have shown."

A commission composed of seven members, one from each of the provinces, was convened to examine the debacle. But the inquiry dissolved in a flood of accusation and counteraccusation. De With found himself alone, friendless. He emerged as the scapegoat and was dismissed from his command.

The war had now been going on for almost six months, and thus far the English obviously had the best of it. The retreat from Dover, the capture of the herring fleet, Tromp's disgrace and now the rout of de With had shaken the Dutch profoundly. What is more, the war was beginning to pinch where Cromwell had intended—in Dutch pocketbooks. Merchantmen loaded with goods lay in harbor awaiting safe convoy to the open seas. Clearly something had to be done, and clearly Maarten Tromp, not Witte de With, was the man to do it.

In accepting reappointment, Tromp could not resist a swipe at those

Dutch Admiral Witte de With, who briefly replaced Tromp during the war, was so pugnacious that he was known as "The Bellicose." On one occasion he actually flew into a tantrum when his superior officers, in the face of overwhelming numbers, shied away from an opportunity to engage the enemy.

who had forced his earlier resignation. "Fighting the enemy, and venturing my life gives me not the least trouble," he wrote in a letter to the States-General. "But all my trouble arises from this, that after having contributed all that is in me to the service of the country, I may be molested on my return home with subtle questions, by ill-disposed and hostile persons—it being unheard of that a commander in chief of a whole force should have to answer why he did not rather do this, and why he rather did that."

On December 1 Tromp put to sea with a fleet of 78 men-of-war, which was soon augmented by 29 more vessels from Zeeland. It was an immense fleet, but Tromp could have used even more ships, for his mission was to sweep a clear path through the Strait of Dover to the Channel and the open Atlantic for a vast convoy of no fewer than 300 merchantmen following in his wake. On December 9 the English spotted him standing down past the Goodwin Sands on a stiff southwesterly breeze. After a hasty council of war, Blake sailed out to challenge Tromp's 107 vessels with a fleet of 42 men-of-war. It was a decision historians later called "rash to the verge of madness."

Once Blake became aware of the immensity of Tromp's war fleet, it was too late to turn back, for the wind veered suddenly into the northwest and blew hard. This obliged the Dutch fleet to claw in close to the English coastline for shelter, and Blake only avoided being carried out among the Dutch men-of-war by hugging the shore even more closely.

Both fleets anchored that night in the lee of the Downs and set sail at the same time next morning. The wind was still fresh from the northwest, and as the coastline curved out toward Dungeness, Blake's fleet was forced inexorably into Tromp's path. The *Garland* and the *Bonaventure*, both major ships of 44 and 36 guns, were soon surrounded, battered and boarded, and their captains were slain. Flying his flag in the 44-gun *Triumph* for this battle, Blake himself was nearly killed; his ship was horribly pounded and lost her foremast. Half-a-dozen other ships were reduced to riddled hulks by the overwhelming numbers of Dutch warships. Three English ships were sunk, in addition to the two that were captured. The remnants of the English fleet slunk back to Dover when darkness halted the battle, and the triumphant Tromp sent word back to the huge merchant convoy that it was safe for them to pass.

Now it was the turn of the English to be sick at heart and to look for fault. In their soul-searching they found their way to several historic decisions on the conduct of the new navies that were evolving. Blake wrote to the Council of State complaining, as had the Dutchman de With, that in his fleet "there was much baseness of spirit, not among the merchantmen only, but many of the State's ships." To buttress his command and make the iron discipline of Cromwell's regime more visible in the fleet, one of Blake's old comrades-in-arms, General Richard Deane, was transferred from his post in Scotland to serve directly with Blake. A second veteran field commander, General George Monck, was also detached to join them.

The Council of State also convened a board of inquiry, as Blake requested, to investigate the conduct of captains under fire. Nobody was surprised that the masters of armed merchantmen, which were still

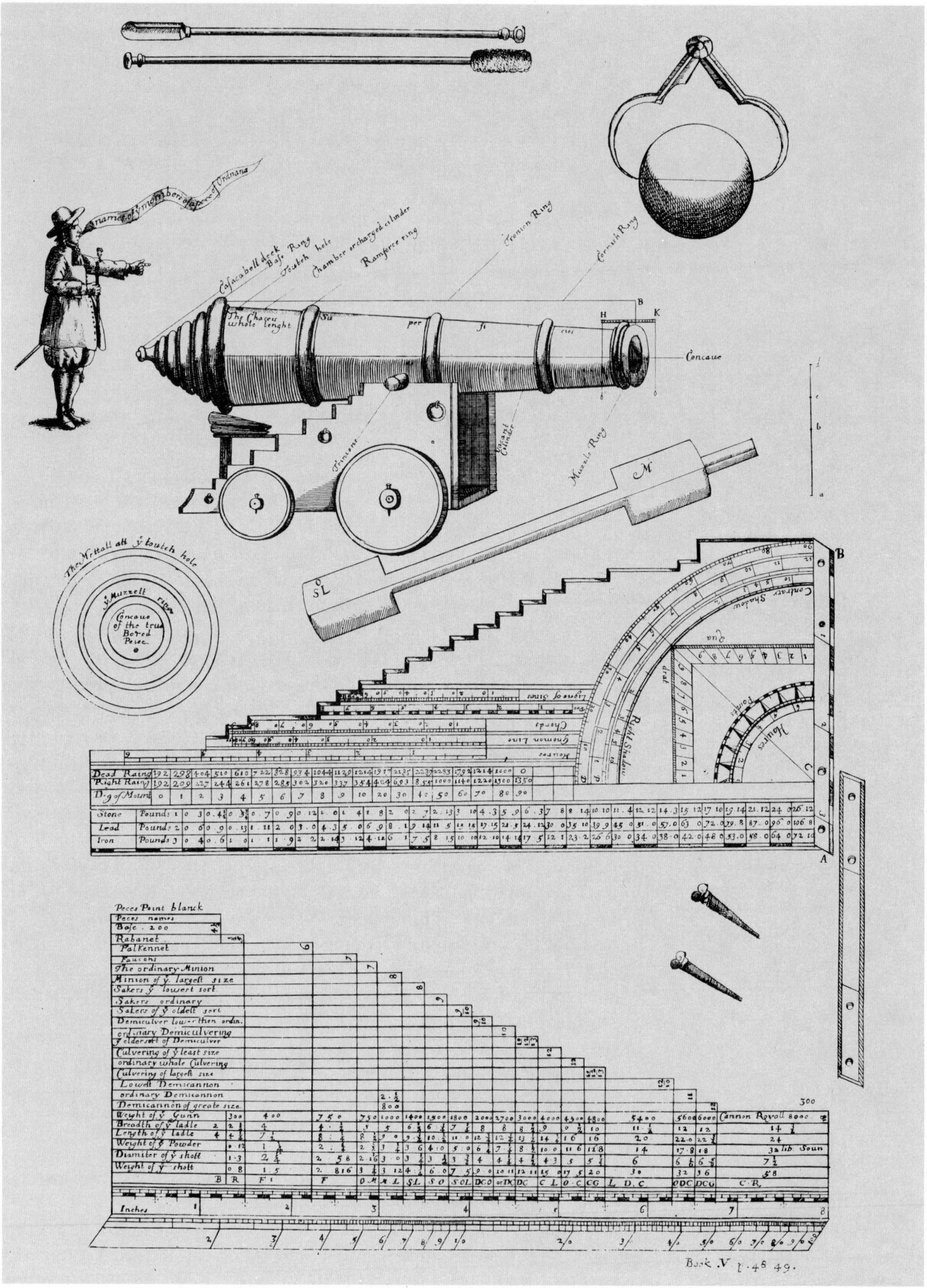
Concave
Trunion Ring
Chords
Inches
Peces Point blanck
Stone
Lead
Iron
Dead Raing
Right Raing
Weight of ỹ Gunn
Breadth of ỹ ladle
Length of ỹ ladle
Weight of ỹ Powder
Diamiter of ỹ shott
Weight of ỹ shott
Cannon Royall 8000
Book V p. 48 49.

A page from a 17th Century English Naval manual shows a large cannon mounted on a sea truck and labeled, as the gunner points out, with "the names of the members of a pece of ordnance." A powder ladle and swabbing sponge are at top alongside a set of calipers used to check shot caliber. The concentric circles at center left give the dimension of the cannon barrel. At bottom are the screws, plate, and front and back panels of an instrument that could be used variously as a gunner's quadrant, calculator, navigational device and bore measure.

hired by the Navy to round out the fleet, might hang back from the heat of battle; many of them were owners or part owners of their vessels and did not trust their government—with excellent reason—to compensate them for loss or damage. The board of inquiry agreed that henceforth merchant captains should not command their own ships during battle but must serve under Naval officers.

It was a different matter with captains of warships owned by the state. Their conduct was as much an essential part of naval tactics as any later development, for the first navies began not only without technique but without tradition. It was Cromwell's army officers, men like Blake, who founded the Naval tradition that in later centuries was the backbone of England's national pride.

The immediate result of Blake's protest was that six captains who had skulked off at Dungeness were dismissed and briefly shut up in the Tower of London. Blake, with his Puritan sense of justice and rectitude, did not hesitate to include his own brother Benjamin on the list. The English also used the occasion to devise a permanent set of rules for their naval establishment.

The Articles of War of 1653, inspired by Blake, became the first rule book in a series of Naval Discipline Acts that governed the English Navy ever after. At first glance it was a fearsome document. It had 39 articles, 25 of which prescribed the death penalty, 13 without option. Although the act applied to all ranks, it was aimed first and foremost at captains, setting down exactly what the state expected of them. Thus Article XII read: "Every captain and officer shall in his own person, and according to his place, hearten and encourage the seamen and common men to fight courageously, and not to behave themselves faintly, nor yield to the enemy, or cry for quarter, upon pain of death or such other punishment as the offence shall deserve." And Article XIV provided the same penalty for "all that shall in time of any fight or engagement withdraw or keep back or not come into the fight and engage, and do his utmost to take, fire, kill, and endamage the enemy."

This first disciplinary act had a profound effect on Navy men, both high and low—and for an interesting reason. Though its wording was harsh, it established a code of conduct that was far more precise than the amorphous old "laws and customs of the sea," which could mean anything a martinet wished them to mean. Men now knew exactly what was expected of them. And because the act was tempered with mercy in practice, seamen and officers alike entered into their duties with more willingness.

The defeat at Dungeness fired Blake with a fierce desire for revenge, and the opportunity soon came. In February 1653, two months after Dungeness, Tromp again was obliged to escort a great fleet of 150 merchantmen through the Channel inbound toward Holland. He had rendezvoused with the merchantmen and was convoying his charges up the Channel when he met the English near Portland. The merchantmen bore off toward France, while Tromp interposed his fleet between them and the enemy. This time the two fleets were about equal in number, with 75 warships for Tromp and 70 for Blake. But the English once more had the advantage of bigger ships and—no doubt because of the disciplinary act of the previous January—much better behaved captains and crews.

For three days, Blake forced Tromp to fight a long, bloody, running defensive battle up the Channel. The casualties on both sides were terrible. Ship after ship put into port on both coasts, pounded near to kindling and laden with dead and maimed men. A newssheet gave a grisly description of the first captured Dutch prizes: "All the men-of-war who are taken are much dyed with blood, their masts and tackles being moiled with brains, hair, pieces of skulls; dreadful sights though glorious, as being a signal token of the Lord's goodness to this Nation."

By the beginning of the third day, the Dutch had lost five men-of-war sunk or burned, and four captured; about every ship was damaged to some degree. But the English were suffering as well: one ship had been sunk and heavy damage was everywhere evident. Blake's flagship, the *Triumph*, lost her flag captain, the admiral's secretary and 100 of her 350 crewmen—and Blake himself had been wounded in the thigh by a flying bar of iron. He refused to go below and continued to direct the battle.

Late in the afternoon of the third day, Blake collected his squadrons and paused while he contemplated yet another attack. On board the Dutch flagship, the veteran *Brederode*, Tromp was in a dilemma: "If we had fought half an hour longer," he explained later, "we should have exhausted all the ammunition we had still left and inevitably have fallen into the enemy's hands." But Tromp gamely lowered his topsails in the traditional signal to Blake that he accepted the challenge. That gallant act saved the day. Blake, his own fleet spent, veered off—"to our great good fortune," Tromp observed. From what Blake's pilots had told him, the Dutch had worked themselves into a trap, which would give him time to rest his fleet and attack in the morning.

The running fight had carried Tromp and his fleet below Cape Gris-Nez in France, so far that he would not, according to the English pilots, be able to work his way back around the cape against the heavy northwesterly wind then blowing.

But the pilots were mistaken. For in the night, through an impressive feat of seamanship, Tromp led his fleet with lights extinguished and shortened sail into the wind around Cape Gris-Nez and home. The battered *Brederode* barely made it. In the winds, Tromp later recalled, the tottering masts of the flagship began "to creak and to go by the board." He struck all sail and rigged jury masts for the last leg home.

The English were not overly pleased with their victory. Though Blake had managed to capture a number of the fleeing Dutch merchantmen, the bulk of the convoy had escaped to home ports during the battle. And Tromp, for all the damage to his fleet, had also made it to safety with most of his ships. The fight, as always, had been something of a free-for-all, and thus inconclusive.

Though Blake had adopted a three-squadron division of the fleet, he and his commanders could exercise only the most rudimentary tactical control once the battle started. The squadron commander led the way into the fight, with the rest of his ships crowding in behind as best they could. Each captain chose his opponent and fought him as he pleased. At the end, they retired when and if they saw the flagship break off the fight. What was desperately needed was a set of orderly, coordinated battle tactics as well as a system of signaling that would work in combat.

No one had attempted such a thing with sailing ships before. Nor had there ever been such awesome numbers of cannon-firing warships engaged in battle. Moreover, until recently there had been no corps of professional officers who were ready, willing and able to carry out a series of tactical orders.

On April 8, 1653, Blake, Monck and Deane signed two historic documents in the evolution of the man-of-war and the fighting navy. One was entitled *Instructions for the Better Ordering of the Fleet in Sailing*. The *Sailing Instructions* admonished captains not to compete for favored windward positions when sailing or tacking but to maintain formation and defer to those of superior rank; in no case was a captain to go upwind of his squadron chief. The *Sailing Instructions* laid out, as well, a complete set of communications, utilizing signal guns, flags, various sail positions or lights in the night, to convey changes of course, decisions to heave to, anchor, hold a conference and so forth. In case his ship sprang a leak or met with some other disability, for example, a captain was "to make a sign thereof by firing two guns distinctly one from another, and hauling up his low sails."

The second document was entitled *Instructions for the Better Ordering of the Fleet in Fighting*, and it was a quantum jump forward in naval tactics. In it are the first orders for forming a line of battle—each ship following the one before in precise formation—which became the standard fleet tactic until the time of Horatio Nelson. There were 14 of these *Fighting Instructions*, and No. 3 stated firmly: "As soon as they shall see the General engage, then each squadron shall take the best advantage they can to engage the enemy next unto them, and in order hereunto all the ships of every squadron shall endeavour to keep in line with their chief." The *Fighting Instructions* went on to describe various maneuvers for maintaining the line, what to do if the squadron chief was disabled or an enemy ship was captured, and the like. As in the *Sailing Instructions*, various combinations of flags and signal guns would be used to transmit orders to the various ships in the squadrons. It was a far cry from the simple blood-red battle ensign of yore.

In itself, the line of battle was a simple, obvious way of using a fighting fleet. Almost all guns on a man-of-war were mounted on the sides; ahead and astern there were only a few small weapons, called bow chasers and stern chasers. So firepower was concentrated on the beam, and the bow and stern were vulnerable. In an uncoordinated melee the full power of a ship could rarely be brought to bear without danger of hitting a friendly vessel. But in a line ahead, as the battle line came to be called, each ship enjoyed a clear field of fire for broadsides. And except for the first and last in line, all bows and sterns were protected as well.

William Penn, who was Blake's vice admiral and at this time commander of the fleet's blue squadron, was given credit for the idea. But there is some evidence that he drew it from conversations with Tromp before the war. Tromp had first conceived the notion early in his career but had been hampered by lack of a signaling system and of competent

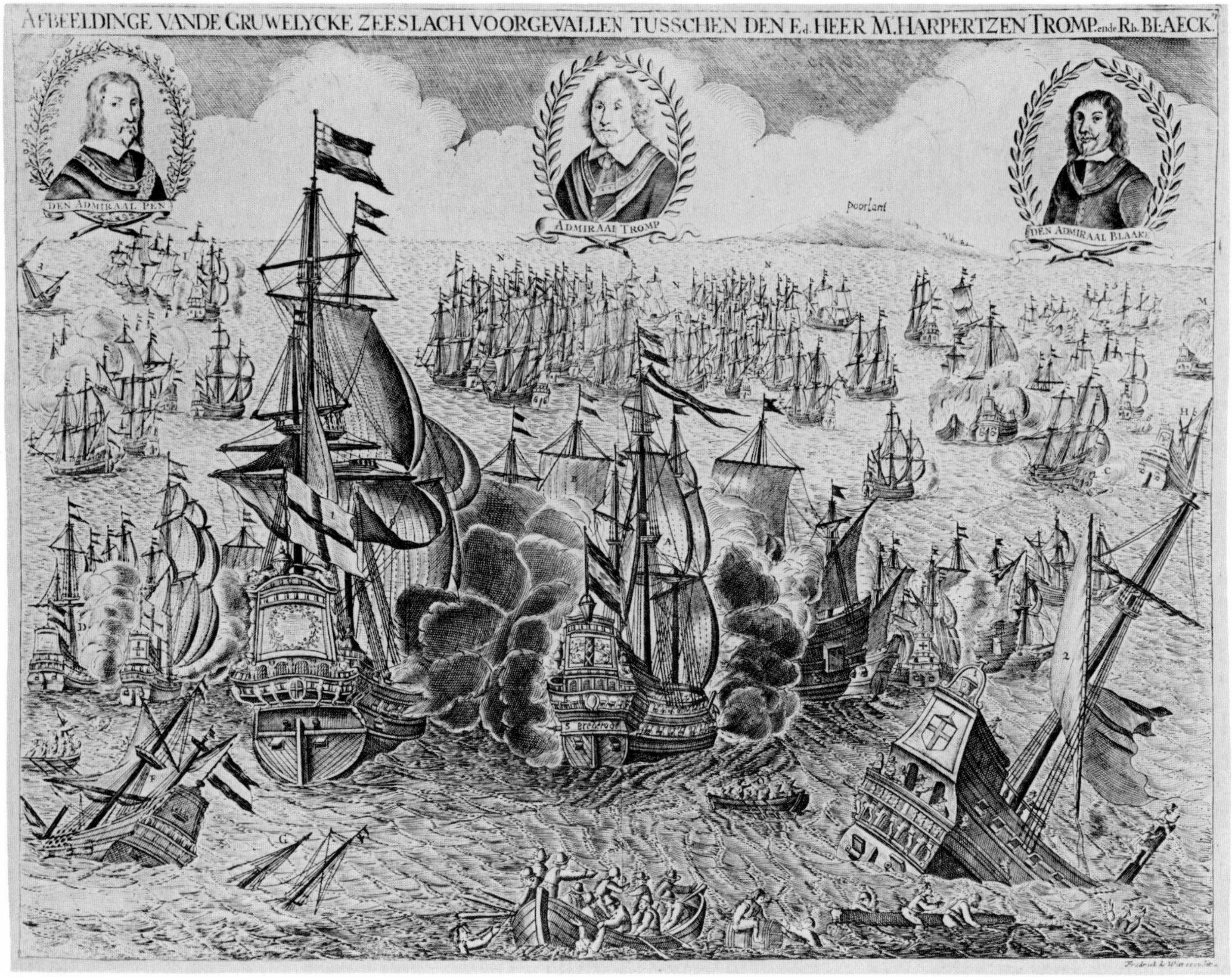
AFBEELDINGE VANDE GRUWELYCKE ZEESLACH VOORGEVALLEN TUSSCHEN DEN Ed. HEER M.HARPERTZEN TROMP ende Rb. BLAECK
DEN ADMIRAAL PEN
ADMIRAAL TROMP
DEN ADMIRAAL BLAAKE
poorlant

Shepherding a convoy of Dutch merchantmen up the English Channel on February 28, 1653, Maarten Tromp in the Brederode (center) fights off an onslaught of English warships under the command of Robert Blake and William Penn, not far off the English headland of Portland Bill. Tromp's fleet sustained serious losses but held the English at bay.

officers to carry it out. The English had now greatly refined Tromp's original idea: they had devised the beginnings of a signaling system, and they were building up a core of professional fighting mariners to apply the new tactics.

The first time the English tried their new battle plan, the results proved inconclusive, not because they lost the fight—in fact, they won—but because they were unable to put the tactics to a real test. The action also cost them the life of one of their foremost naval leaders. Blake was not involved; the leg wound he had suffered during the three-day battle off Portland had turned out to be more serious than was at first believed, and command had passed to Monck and Deane. On June 12 they were at sea in the *Resolution*, Phineas Pett's sturdy old *Prince Royal*, when they sighted the Dutch off the Gabbard Shoal in the North Sea.

It is intriguing that the English and Dutch Navies, without really knowing how many vessels the other side would assemble for battle, almost always chanced to meet with equal numbers. On this day the English had 100 ships, and the Dutch had 98. The English made an attempt to form a line of battle, but the winds were so light and perverse that they were only partially successful. Then, as they bore slowly down on the Dutch in a straggling line, the first enemy broadside that was fired at close range brought tragedy.

As this barrage swept down on the *Resolution*, a whirling, scythelike length of chain hit Deane full on and chopped him into pieces. Monck was standing by Deane's side and was drenched in the sudden shower of blood. He could do nothing but tear off his cloak, lay it over the grisly remains and, choking back his horror, return his attention to the battle.

In the feeble winds the ships drifted aimlessly, and soon the battle was an old-fashioned melee. But gradually the new English attention to discipline began to wear down the Dutch. "Our fleet," reported one officer, "did work in better order than heretofore, and seconded one another; which I am persuaded by God's providence was a terror to our enemies. God took away their hearts at this time; so that they fled from us this day and the next till noon at which we were within sight of Calais cliff and Dunkirk."

By then the Dutch fleet was in utter disarray. As Tromp wrote later in his report: "Through the carelessness or lack of experience in naval warfare of several captains and their officers, several of us ran one into another and were thrown into confusion."

In desperation, Tromp, with his smaller, shallower-draft vessels, sought escape among the shoals of the Continental coast, "to go where we cannot follow him, like the Highlanders to the mountains," as one English captain put it.

At this bitter juncture for the Dutch, Blake arrived to seal the battle. Driven from his sickbed by news of the fighting, he had boarded the 60-gun *Essex* and had run out of the Thames with reinforcements of 18 ships. Confronted with overwhelming odds, Tromp continued to make his retreat behind the sandbanks of the Dutch coast and remained there while the English cruised along the coast for a month or so. The Dutch admiral had been wounded in the face and remained sequestered, as much out of the agony of defeat as out of any physical pain, as rumors spread that he was dead.

Poor Tromp might well have wished himself dead, for never in the war had Dutch fortunes been lower. All told, the Dutch had lost 21 ships to the English, 11 of them captured—while the English had suffered not a single loss and only 12 ships disabled. The Dutch head of government, Johan de Witt, could only admit: "The condition of our common, dear fatherland, stands in my opinion at present in a great, troubled and almost desperate state, as if it were besieged and taken."

The English, now in full command of the Channel and the North Sea, pressed their advantage by blockading the Dutch coast so closely that virtually all Dutch maritime trade came to a standstill. Defeatism swept the seven provinces, particularly the coastal cities that had borne the brunt of naval warfare and stood the most to lose. Hunger riots erupted in the major cities as food prices shot up and once-prosperous citizens could not afford their accustomed fare.

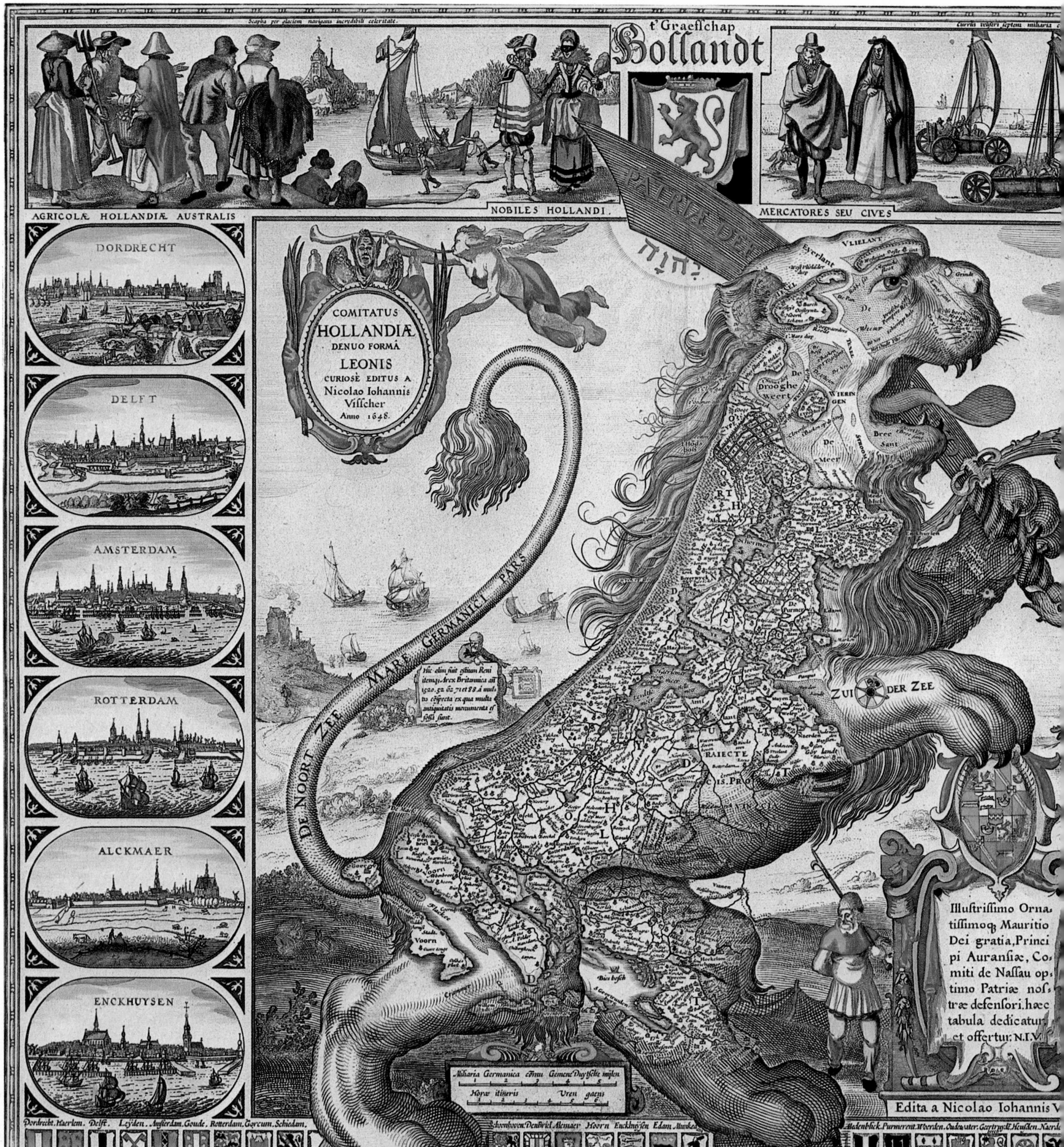
t'Graefschap
Hollandt
AGRICOLÆ HOLLANDIÆ AUSTRALIS
NOBILES HOLLANDI.
MERCATORES SEU CIVES
DORDRECHT
DELFT
AMSTERDAM
ROTTERDAM
ALCKMAER
ENCKHUYSEN
COMITATUS
HOLLANDIÆ
DENUO FORMÂ
LEONIS
CURIOSÈ EDITUS A
Nicolao Iohannis
Visscher
Anno 1648.
DE NOORT ZEE MARE GERMANICI PARS
ZUIDER ZEE
Illustrissimo Ornatissimoq; Mauritio Dei gratia, Principi Auransiæ, Comiti de Nassau optimo Patriæ nostræ defensori. hæc tabula dedicatur et offertur: N.I.V.
Edita a Nicolao Iohannis V

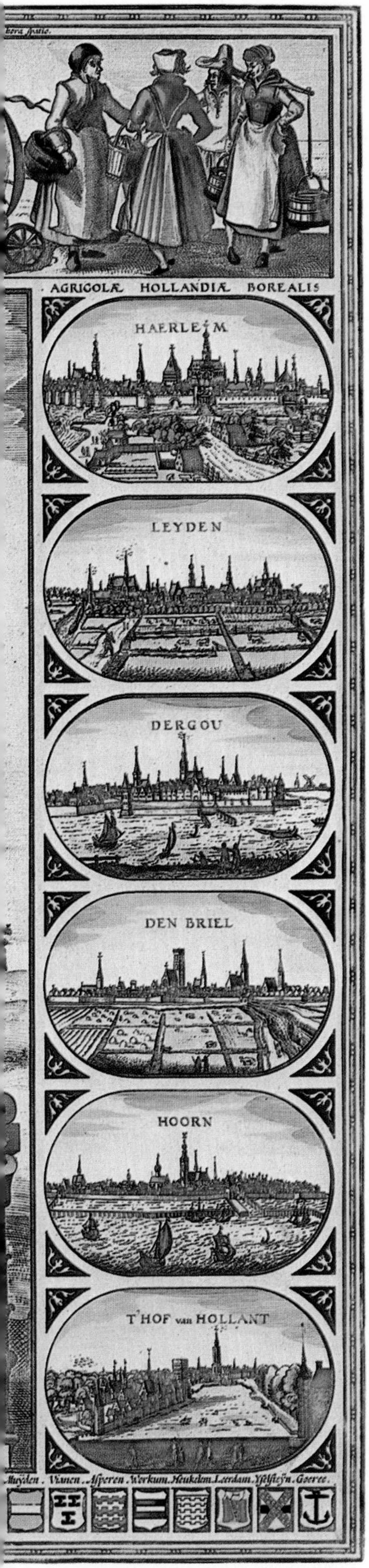
AGRICOLÆ HOLLANDIÆ BOREALIS
HAERLEM
LEYDEN
DERGOU
DEN BRIEL
HOORN
T'HOF van HOLLANT

The States-General ordered Tromp to sea as soon as possible to break the crushing English blockade. But Tromp faced severe tactical problems. The English fleet obviously was growing in power from the 118 vessels he had just fought. To have even a prayer of success, he would have to muster more than 100 combatants. About 100 men-of-war were refitting under his command in the Maas River estuary; another 27 were making ready to the north at Texel under his rival, Witte de With. But how to join them under the guns of the English?

On August 8 Tromp staged a masterful maneuver. Seizing on a strong northwest wind, he came out of the Maas and ran southeast, drawing the English after him and thus enabling de With to bring his vessels out from Texel. Tromp fought a short, sharp engagement with the English during the afternoon. Then in the night, while the intently pursuing English maintained a southeasterly heading, Tromp reversed course, tacked back to the north and joined up with de With.

By the time the English realized that they had been duped, the wind had veered around and was blowing a gale from the northeast. It took them an entire day to struggle back north to confront the combined forces of the Dutch fleet.

At last on August 10 both fleets stood out in parallel lines running westward from Scheveningen, near The Hague. For the first time, Dutchmen on shore could witness the outcome. The contending battle fleets were both in rough line-ahead formations. The English numbered about 120 ships, and so did the Dutch. The lines stretched across 16 miles of sea. Never had there been such an assemblage of men-of-war. As at the Gabbard Shoal, Blake was present in spirit only. His wound was still troubling him, and Monck was in command. Compared with some of the earlier battles, this one was brief but no less vicious. At 7 a.m. the English tacked toward the southwest and cleaved through the whole Dutch fleet, "leaving part on one side," said an English captain, "and part on the other of us," firing broadsides as they passed. The English then tacked a second time, to the northwest, as the Dutch tacked to the southeast. "We fought board and board with our enemies," said one Englishman—and "did very good execution," added another, describing how the fleets had sailed side by side, pouring fearsome broadsides into each other at point-blank range. In fact, said this captain, "this bout was most desperately fought by either almost at push of pike."

Tromp's ship, the *Brederode,* survivor of so many battles, was fiercely engaged, disappearing from time to time in clouds of smoke and sheets

Holland, most powerful of the seven provinces of the Netherlands, appears as a bellowing, sword-slinging lion rampant in this 1648 decorative map by cartographer Nicholas Vissher. Across the top are figures wearing the characteristic costumes of Dutch peasants, merchants and nobles, and two varieties of wind-powered vehicles: an iceboat and wind wagons. At the sides are perspectives of Holland's major cities.

of muzzle flame. Shortly after 11 a.m. there was a lull in the action. The *Brederode* flew a flag, calling for a parley of captains. Those who could were rowed in ships' boats to the flagship. And there, to their stunned dismay, they found their leader dead. There, said a captain, was "Admiral Tromp lying dead in his cabin, who having about 11 o'clock in the forenoon received a musket shot in the breast, died forthwith of it." His last words had been: "I am finished! Keep up your courage!"

Tromp's death was kept secret. His flag continued to fly on the *Brederode*. But the fight had gone out of every captain who knew of his death, and this infected the already hard-pressed Dutch fleet.

As the battle resumed, 25 Dutch captains abandoned their comrades and fled. De With, who was now in command, attempted to rally them, pursuing them angrily, yelling curses and firing bow chasers. "If they had been hanged on a previous occasion for similar offenses," he exclaimed, "they would not have done the same again now." But his efforts were hopeless. In the 13 hours of battle since 7 a.m., the Dutch had lost 13 warships sunk or burned, and a number captured; perhaps 4,000 Dutch sailors had been slain or wounded. The English lost only two ships sunk, and a little over 1,000 men killed or wounded. Two of the vessels they captured gave them particular satisfaction; they were the *Garland* and the *Bonaventure*, the two ships previously taken by the Dutch at the Battle of Dungeness.

De With had no alternative but to stagger home with those ships that still remained under his command. As might be expected, he leveled charges of gross cowardice against all those captains who had refused to fight. After a formal investigation, 13 captains were put on trial for dereliction of duty; of those, 11 were found guilty and a number were sentenced to severe punishments. One captain was sentenced "to stand with noose around the neck, his sword to be broken, with a kick under his rear end and to be hauled around the country as a rascal and to pay 600 florins" and costs. He was fortunate: another captain was sentenced to "be keelhauled three times with the noose around his neck"—which meant being heaved into the water and dragged under the belly of a ship. If the unfortunate malefactor survived drowning, the sentence continued, he was to be imprisoned for life.

But none of these punitive efforts did anything to mitigate the Dutch position. All told in the 15 months of fierce war, the Dutch had lost some 60 warships to various causes; thousands of men were dead or maimed. And the English controlled the seas. The Dutch were in a state of utter demoralization.

The war dragged through the winter of 1653, but without Tromp to lead the Dutch there was no more serious fighting. The English blockaded the Dutch, and the Dutch suffered miserably. Said an observer: "The sources of revenue that had always maintained the riches of the state, such as fisheries and commerce, were almost dry. Workshops were closed, work was suspended. The Zuyder Zee became a forest of masts; the country was full of beggars; grass grew in the streets, and in Amsterdam 1,500 houses were untenanted."

The English had undoubtedly won and could dictate the terms of the peace. The treaty was concluded at Westminster in April 1654, and the

The grim reaper holds the reins of a fiery chariot as Maarten Tromp, with a gesture of helplessness, is borne aloft to heaven in this allegorical engraving of the death of the valiant Dutch admiral at the Battle of Scheveningen in August 1653. Like Horatio Nelson in a later day, Tromp lost his life to a sharpshooter's musket ball, which hit him in the chest early in the melee.

Dutch were pleasantly surprised at the mildness of the English terms. Cromwell was not a vindictive victor. His major concern was less with the Dutch than with the English Royalists in exile on the Continent, and he made the Dutch forswear any assistance whatsoever to the young heir to the Stuart throne, Charles II. As for the Dutch themselves, Cromwell was willing to let bygones be bygones. He assured the Dutch that the world was in fact broad enough to accommodate the merchants of both nations. The Navigation Act remained; so did the ludicrous English insistence on being saluted in the Narrow Seas, which included the southern end of the North Sea, as well as the English Channel. The Dutch agreed to pay a large sum, £267,163, to English companies for loss of trade, and a small sum, £3,615, to the heirs of victims of the Massacre of Amboina *(pages 36-37)*—which came as a windfall to people who hardly recalled their unlucky kin. But that was about all.

Incredible battles had been fought at a terrible human cost, and little was changed except the nature of warfare at sea. But that was changed forever. And soon Robert Blake and William Penn would be called upon to orchestrate a whole new role beyond simple sea combat for the increasingly potent English Navy.

In celebration of the waters around them

"Through our thrifty and shrewd management," declared a group of Dutch merchants in 1629, "we have sailed all nations off the seas, drawn almost all trade from other lands hither and served the whole of Europe with our ships." This was no idle boast. The Dutch were the natural heirs to the sea. From primeval times the aptly named Netherlands was surrounded by the ocean, flooded by tides, defined by inland waterways. "Where else," commented a later Dutch historian, "could you have found a similar system of natural communications, a complete network of veins and arteries? You could cross the length and breadth of the country under sail, or with oars and towropes, safely, comfortably and with comparative speed."

From their myriad waterways, which separated each tiny community from the next, the Dutch gained a fierce independence and developed a vigorous rivalry between cities. By controlling the mouths of great rivers, they dominated the trade of Europe. With their countless fishing smacks, they made fortunes from the sea. And by extending their nautical genius to the ends of the earth, they built a mercantile empire that increasingly was the envy of the English. In 1644 a Dutch pamphleteer noted they had more than 1,000 vessels that could be used as warships to defend their maritime interests, another 1,000 merchantmen engaged in trade and 6,000 smaller ships used as fishing and inland transport. And these, he observed proudly, were manned by 80,000 of the finest seamen in the world.

With their coffers overflowing from the proceeds of fishing and trade and so many of them directly involved with the sea, the Dutch took pleasure in paintings that reminded them of their achievement. Today such works offer insights into their greatness—and into the nature of their water-dominated lives.

An Amsterdam landmark since 1480, when it was built as a medieval fort, the peak-roofed Schreierstoren in this work by Jacobus Storck is steeped in legend and history. For centuries it served as the harbor commissioners' office and was the scene of tearful farewells as Dutch wives said goodbye to sailors bound for the Indies—hence its name, which means "crying tower." The cantilevered bridgeworks on both sides of the tower raised drawbridges over canals that led into the heart of the old city.

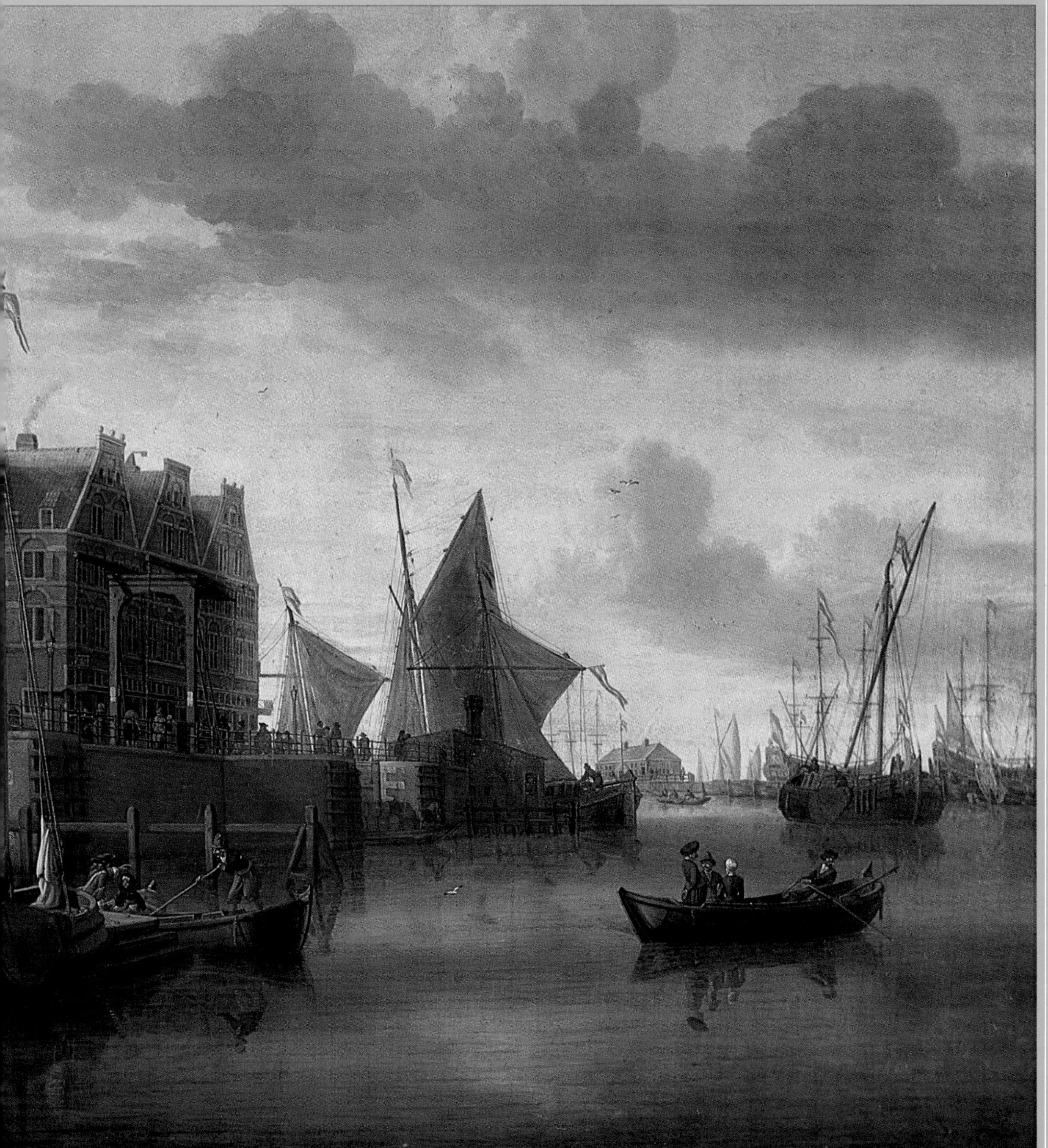

Avenues to a golden age

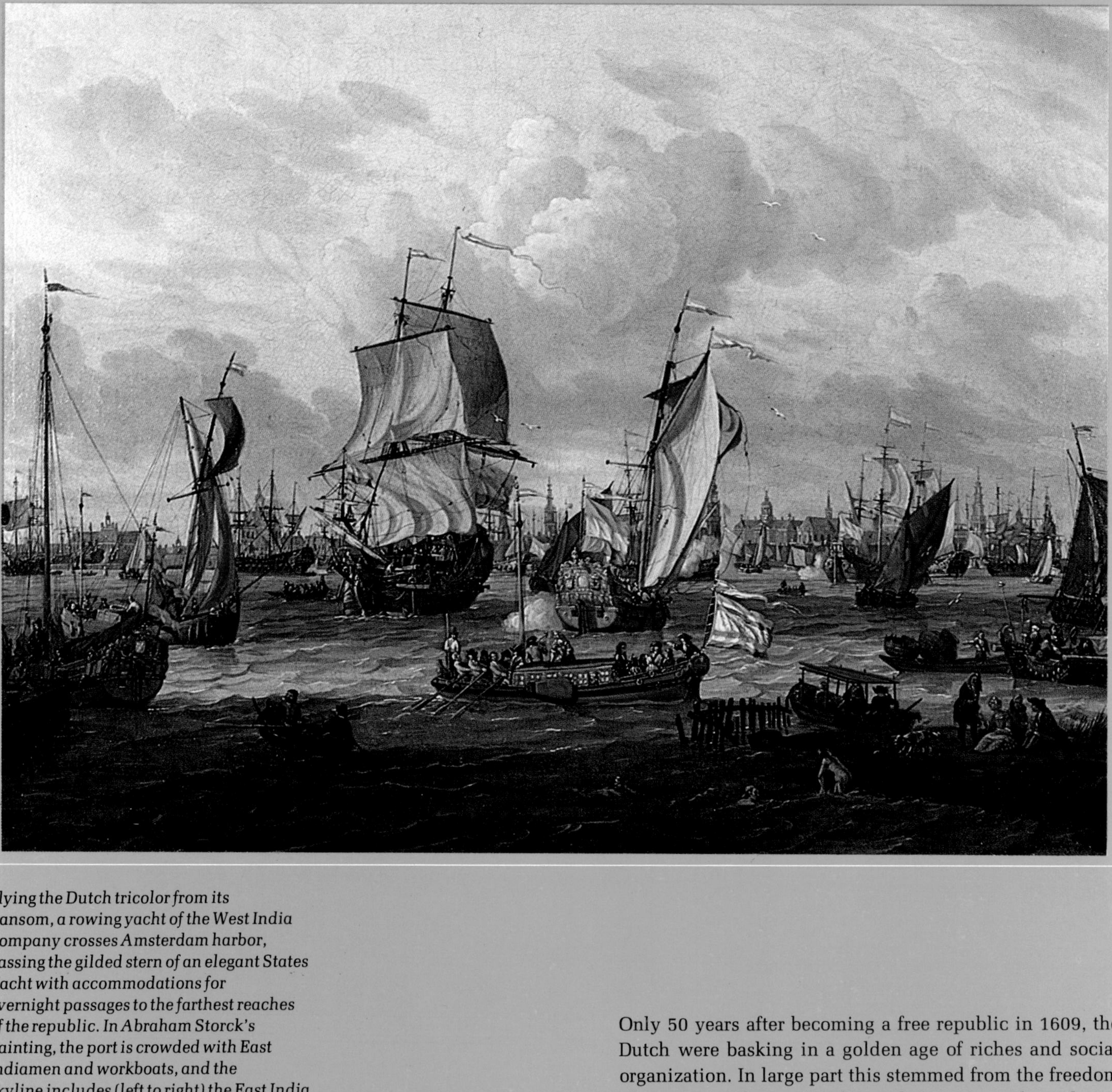

Flying the Dutch tricolor from its transom, a rowing yacht of the West India Company crosses Amsterdam harbor, passing the gilded stern of an elegant States Yacht with accommodations for overnight passages to the farthest reaches of the republic. In Abraham Storck's painting, the port is crowded with East Indiamen and workboats, and the skyline includes (left to right) the East India docks, Old Church and the Royal Palace.

Only 50 years after becoming a free republic in 1609, the Dutch were basking in a golden age of riches and social organization. In large part this stemmed from the freedom of movement they enjoyed over their rivers and canals at a time when the rest of Europe was still floundering in the mud of medieval roads and when travelers were at the mercy of highwaymen and contentious barons. By contrast, large numbers of people and great quantities of goods could be moved cheaply by rivercraft all across the Netherlands.

So comfortable were the Dutch with their water kingdom that they invented pleasure yachting—each man rich or poor finding summer satisfaction in boats ranging from ferryboats taking humble families on holiday excursions to the gaff-rigged luxury yachts of rich burghers.

Ghosting over the mirrored surface
near the port of Dordrecht, a passenger ferry
filled with ordinary folk glides past a
flock of ducks. In a nation where everything
happened on or near water, this
painting by Aelbert Cuyp in the mid-17th
Century captures the marriage of sea
and commerce fundamental to even the
poorest people commuting to work.
The wooden wings on the craft are leeboards
for stability when it is heeled over.

Fisheries to feed a continent

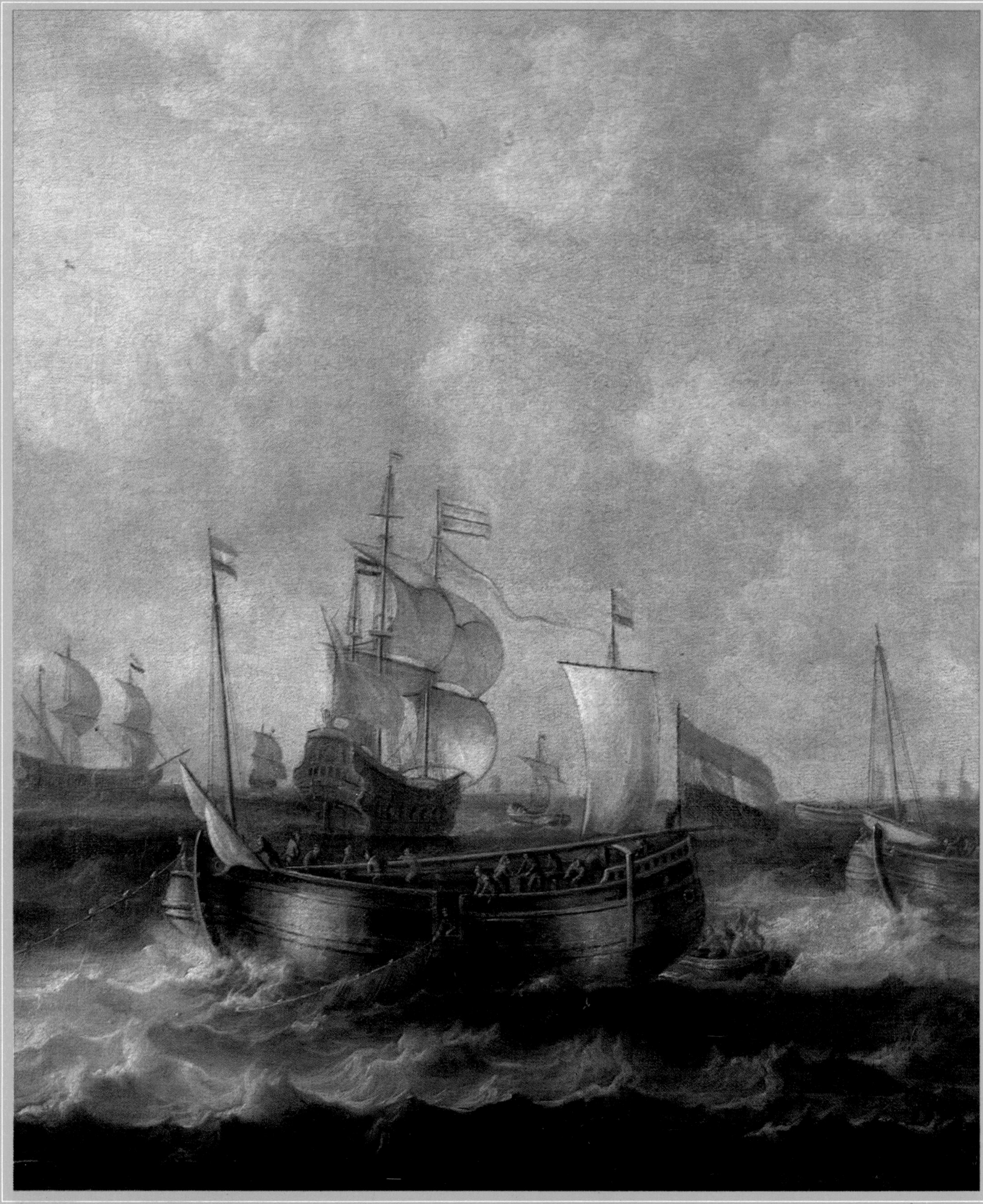

Selling their catch, the crewmen of a small Dutch fishing boat called a pink do a brisk trade on the beach with neighboring villagers in this painting by Simon de Vlieger. Fish—along with cheese—was a major export of the Netherlands.

Seining for herring on the choppy North Sea, the crew of a fat Dutch herring buss haul in their nets while a small square sail in her bow keeps the craft under way. Such ships as this one, in a painting attributed to Bonaventura Peeters, were constructed by the hundreds as the Dutch grew to dominate the European fishing industry. In the background a fleet of East Indiamen is homeward bound.

Vital to the welfare of millions in Europe was the Dutch discovery in the 14th Century that freshly caught herring could be salted and preserved indefinitely simply by pressing the fish in barrels between layers of salt. Famines following plagues in the Middle Ages had disrupted European agriculture, so the introduction of great quantities of Dutch salted herring soon led to its becoming a staple of diet and a primary source of protein throughout the Continent.

Their dominance of the great herring banks of the North Sea, and their virtual monopoly of the herring trade, made the Dutch fabulously wealthy in the 17th Century—but it also led to rivalry with England's fishing interests and contributed to animosities that eventually erupted into the Anglo-Dutch wars.

Sturdy traders for East and West

Packed with spices, silks and rare woods, a large fleet of Dutch East Indiamen sails back to Amsterdam in this painting by Andries van Eertvelt. Traveling in company and heavily armed with cannon, these merchantmen were almost immune to casual, piratical attack.

The great East India Company was only one pillar of Dutch commerce. Also contributing to the country's burgeoning wealth was the West India Company, which dispatched its sturdy vessels to the Caribbean islands, down the shoulder of South America to the bulge of Brazil, and all along the coast of West Africa.

Together the two companies poured immense fortunes into the coffers of burghers from Dordrecht to Amsterdam, and led to the creation of the largest merchant fleets the world had yet seen, a massive armada of some 568,000 tons in the 1670s. To the treasures of the East Indies, the West India Company added rich profits in commodities and slaves, both of which were transported by the thousands to the Caribbean and South America.

Pounded by a following sea, her mainmast gone by the boards, an armed merchantman races through a roaring squall with her canvas taken in except for the great square foresail, which has broken loose. In this painting by Willem van de Velde the Younger, a fishing pink at left fights to keep from broaching.

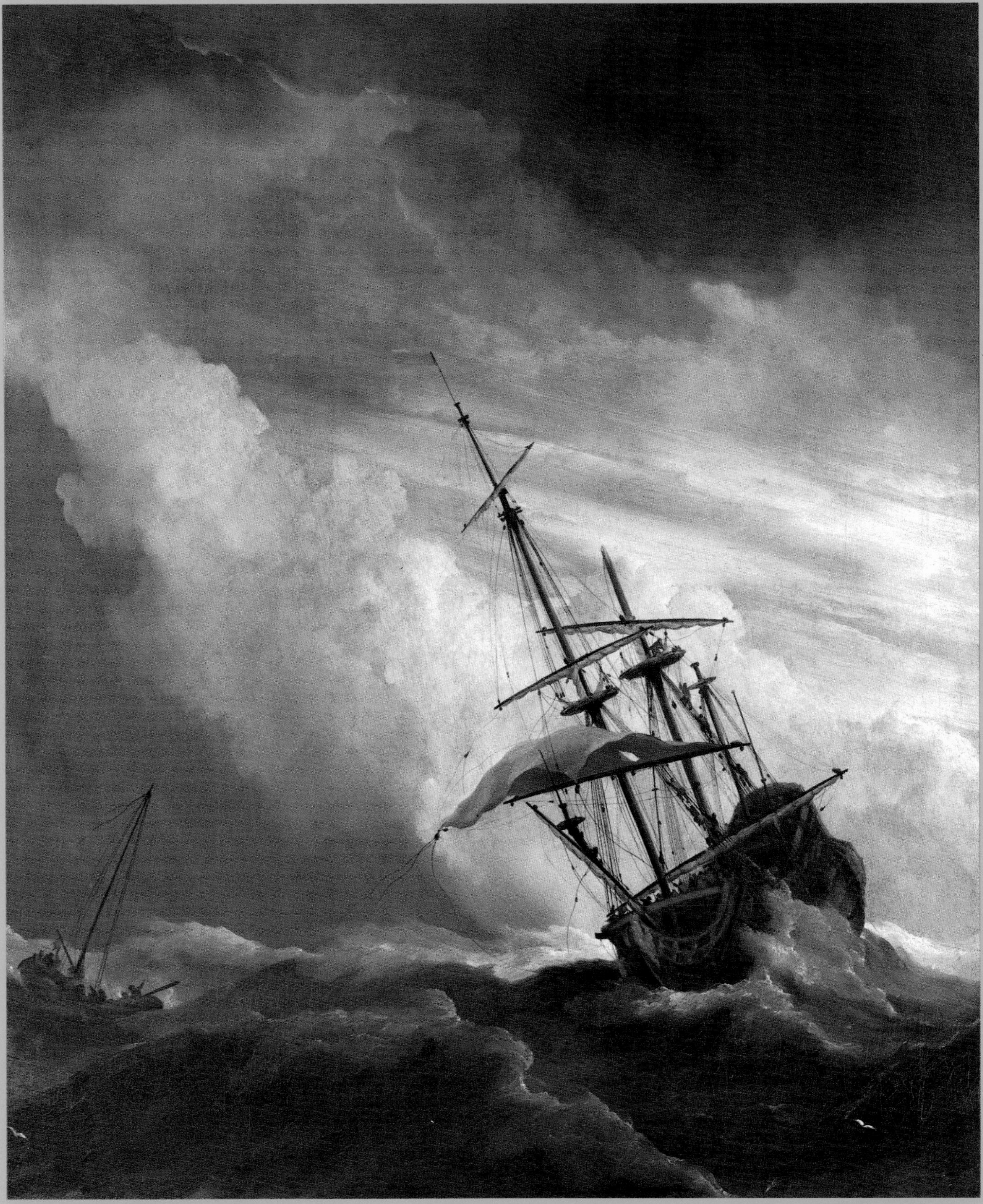

Chapter 3

A Spanish interlude between the wars

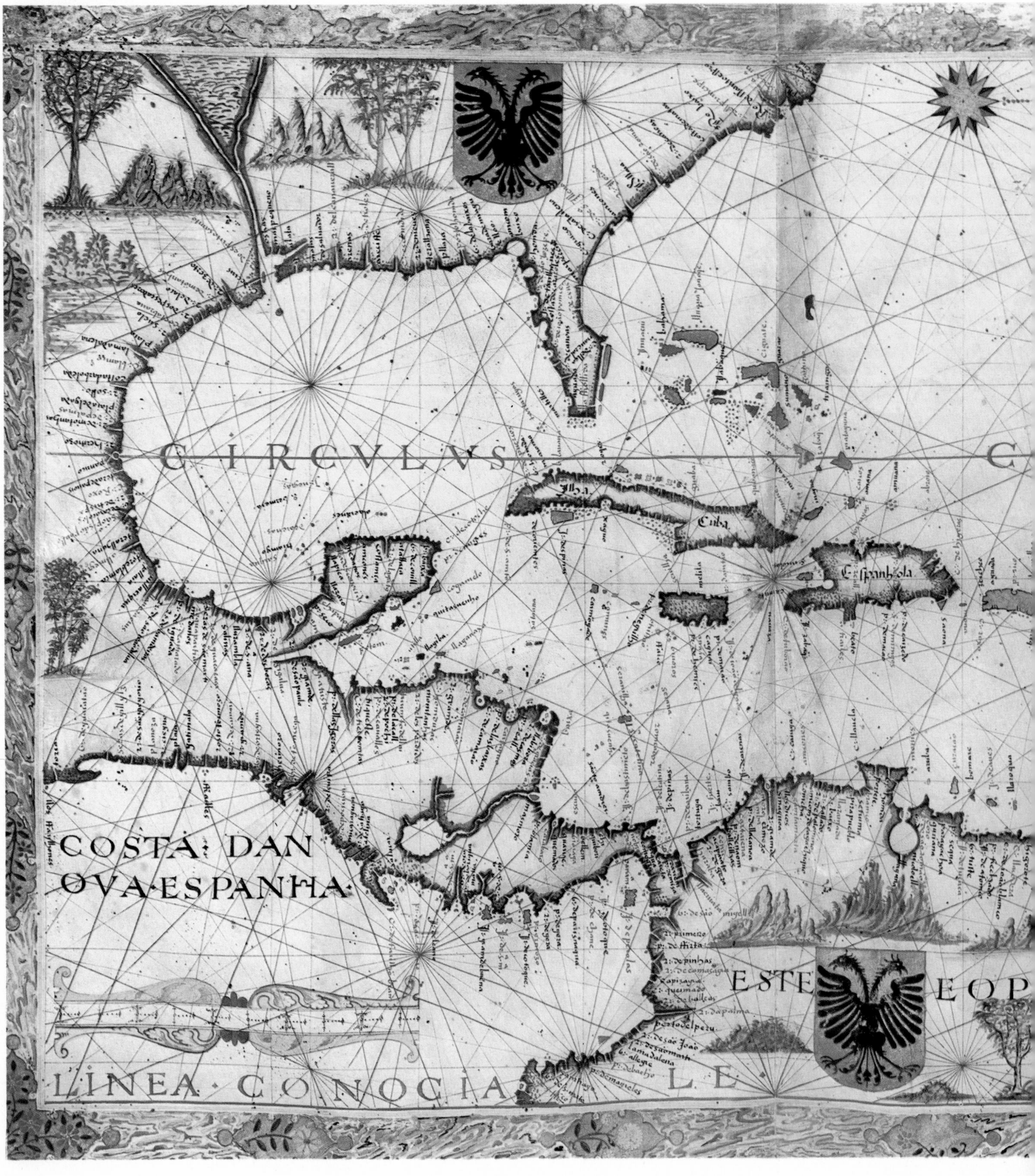
CIRCVLVS
Cuba
COSTA DAN
OVA ESPANHA
ESTE
EOP
LINEA CONOCIA
LE

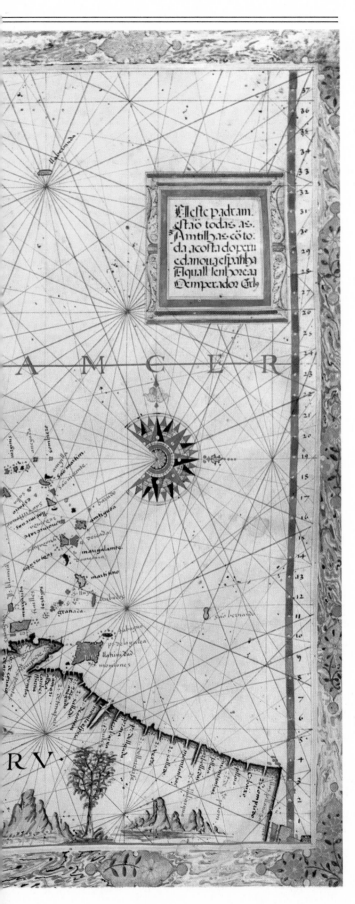

During the week before Christmas, 1654, an English fleet put out from Portsmouth into the gray, dark, winter seas of the Channel. There were 38 warships and four smaller supply craft with crews that totaled 4,690 seamen. They were loaded, in addition, with 2,910 soldiers. Bringing up the rear, on Christmas Day itself, the 60-gun man-of-war *Swiftsure* left Spithead wearing the flag of veteran General-at-Sea William Penn. The fleet's mission was so secret that it was given a code name: the Western Design, which suggested something of the secret it was intended to hide. Despite the unfavorable time of the year, the fleet was to cross the Atlantic to the West Indies. Once there, it was not to resume the recently concluded war against the Dutch by assaulting their West Indian and South American possessions, but to attack the dominant colonial power in the area—Spain—and to strip from the Spaniards as many of their island territories as possible. As Oliver Cromwell had succinctly put it in his order to the fleet: "The designe in General is to gain an interest in that part of the West Indies in the possession of the Spaniard. For the affecting whereof we shal not tye you up to a method by any particular Instructions, but only communicate to you what hath bin under our Consideration."

The operation was entirely Cromwell's brain child. As a stern Protestant, it is said, Cromwell had never been completely comfortable about war against the Dutch, because he believed the true enemies of all Protestant countries were Catholic France and Spain. It is also said that he needed a foreign war, like many another dictator, to distract his people's attention from troubles at home. In any event, he decided to make war on Spain by attacking with his new navy where Spanish lines of communication were stretched the thinnest—in Spain's American empire.

This was a different role for the budding English Navy and its newly developed men-of-war. The Anglo-Dutch war had been fought within two or three days of home ports, and fought entirely by the crews of the ships. But now, these same ships were set for a five weeks' outward voyage across a vast and hostile ocean. What is more, they were pestered with soldiers as passengers. Together, the Army and Navy—in what was looked upon as a great advance in tactics—would mount a combined operation. If successful, it would wrest for England vast new riches from an overseas empire in the West.

There was a second part to the plan—one that would also cast the Navy in a novel and powerful role. Cromwell intended to dupe, or at least

Spanish possessions in the New World were the target of Oliver Cromwell's imperial ambitions in 1654. The budding English Navy was given the task of supporting an Army invasion of Hispaniola, a prize just east of Cuba on this contemporary Portuguese map. But the landing was horribly bungled, and the English had to settle for Jamaica, the large, unidentified island to the west.

bemuse, the Spaniards in Europe while he was carrying out his Western Design across the Atlantic in the West Indies. Spanish spies would obviously get wind of the plan, but Spain could scarcely act in the absence of real evidence of English intentions and particularly not if the English were acting properly elsewhere. Cromwell therefore ordered a second fleet to be fitted for duty. This one, of 27 ships, was to be commanded by General-at-Sea Robert Blake, of Dutch War fame, and was also slated for long-range duty. It was to enter and patrol the Mediterranean, establish the prestige of the English fleet and thereby strengthen English influence in the area. Specifically, it was to attack the French, with whom the English were more or less permanently at odds; it was to strike at the notorious Barbary pirates of North Africa; and it was to maintain the friendliest of postures toward the Spanish—at least for the nonce. If all went well, Spain would be lulled in Europe while the Western Design was in progress in the Indies. When actual news of the English attack eventually reached Europe, English warships would be in position to thwart any Spanish reaction. It was a Machiavellian scheme.

Preparations for the Design had been going on since the summer. It had been even harder than usual to round up enough recruits. After the frightful casualties of the Dutch War and the Navy's continued inability to pay its men, it was no wonder volunteers were scarce. Even Blake himself, before he sailed, had to write to the Admiralty begging officials there to "make a bill for the payment of my salary unto the day of the date hereof, it being uncertain whether I may live to see you again." And the sailors, faced with the same doubt and the same long voyages, drew up a petition to Parliament and asked for their pay to be given every six months to attorneys, so that their families could have it. Blake's request was granted but the sailors' was not.

Nor was it only the pay that worried them. It was also sickness. The West Indies, as rumors spread of the fleet's destination, were a reputed hotbed of mysterious diseases. It was reported by a chronicler that "the seamen are so afraid of being sent to the West Indies that they say they would as soon be hanged." Everyone had heard of the later voyages of the Elizabethans, when whole expeditions had been ravaged by disease—in particular Drake's last voyage, in 1595, when the great captain himself had sickened and died out there.

The high command and even the government were also worried about the threat, and they did what they could about it. But because of the state of medicine at the time, they could not do much. Ashore, the health of the Navy was in the hands of a leading young physician, Dr. Daniel Whistler. But he confessed the limitations of his profession in a splendidly sonorous sentence: "It is the prerogative of the Great Physician in heaven to presage life or death according to His secret decree, a ray of whose all-seeing knowledge appears but dimly to us through narrow crannies of conjectural guess."

For the first time, a Physician to the Fleet was appointed to sail with the expedition. This might have been a big step forward. Ships' surgeons, although for the most part lacking in knowledge of general medicine, were trained in treating wounds, and especially in lopping off arms and legs. But the man selected, Paul de Laune, was a distinguished professor who had little practical experience and had never been to sea. Reports of the expedition offer no evidence that anyone ever consulted him; in fact the only evidence that he actually sailed is in the 1657 probate of his will, which records that he had died sometime before, in Jamaica—and that was not surprising since the hapless man was over 70.

Cromwell himself understood the fundamental cause of mortality in the Navy—overcrowding. He ordered Penn "to use the utmost care, in transporting the soldiers, to prevent sickness among them, to which purpose they are to be indifferently distributed for their numbers in the several ships, that no one ship may be overcharged with men, which may cause infection." But Penn apparently paid little attention. When the fleet departed Portsmouth, the bigger ships, including his flagship, the *Swiftsure,* carried only 30 soldiers each. Most of the troops were crammed into the smaller vessels. The *Katherine* and a ship unsuitably named the *Heartsease* normally had a crew of 70 each, including the gunners for each ship's 30 guns. The *Katherine* sailed with 200 soldiers on board, and the *Heartsease* with 160. Twenty even smaller ships were used as transports, carrying between them 1,800 troops, many of whom were so unwilling to go that they had to be rounded up and herded on board by saber-wielding cavalry.

Naval ships were always crowded, even with their normal crews: they needed far more men than merchant ships, so that they could man their guns in battle. The *Katherine* would normally have had about 25 men on watch, while another 25 off watch were eating or sleeping belowdecks. The other 20 or so would be specialists—gun captains, carpenters, boatswains and their mates—who did not keep watch but slept at night and worked by day. Normally, therefore, a ship of this size had space below for some 45 men to sleep. Now suddenly she needed space for 245 more—200 of whom were almost certain to be seasick.

Seasickness was seldom taken seriously by the sailors, who did not suffer from it. But for landlubbers like the soldiers of the Western Design, it was a torture beyond description. To begin with, they were forbidden to go out on the open upper decks, where they got in the way of the crew. Instead, they were shut away in the worst possible places for seasick men, down on the heaving, rolling gun decks, unventilated and lit only by a few candle lanterns swinging from the beams. The only sanitary arrangements were up on the head of the ship, either side of the bowsprit, under the open sky and over the open sea. Desperately seasick men had neither the strength nor the will to climb up there. They used buckets for everything, if they could find any that were not already overflowing. And if they could not, they used the corners of the decks where they lived. They had no way of cleansing themselves, and never took off their clothes. The only way to wash the deck was to sluice it down with buckets of sea water, which took the filth down through the hold, where their food was stored, and into the bilges. So they lived on top of a cesspit, lay in their own vomit and excrement, and of course infected one another with every intestinal disease they had brought on board.

Soldiers in those days may not have been very fastidious, but the farmers' sons among them would not have kept a pig in such conditions and expected it to thrive. Yet they themselves were expected to be fit and ready, the very moment their voyage ended, to rush ashore and fight.

The fleet made land in Barbados after five weeks at sea. The Navy reckoned it was an uneventful, successful crossing. Penn wrote to Cromwell: "The mercy of the Lord hath most eminently been seen amongst us hitherto, in the quick and fair passage He gave us"—though Penn did report the loss of one ship, the *Great Charity*, which simply disappeared in a squall shortly after the fleet's departure.

Barbados was already an English colony, and here Penn and his officers began plans for their mission to capture Spanish possessions in the West Indies. Of the three places proposed for launching the initial assault, Havana was considered too well fortified and too well manned; Cartagena—on the coast of modern Colombia—while rich, could not supply the victuals necessary for the invasion force and might too easily hide her wealth in the limitless countryside. Santo Domingo was selected. That city was virtually the only Spanish stronghold on Hispaniola, an island that was thought to be rich in gold and that would offer a retreat if further ventures failed. It would also be a good place for colonization.

The Dutchman who snared Spain's "Golden Bird"

Crews of the Spanish treasure fleet flee to shore in 1628 as Dutch boarding parties close in on the galleons in Cuba's Matanzas Bay.

On Barbados the Army officers saw assembled for the first time the soldiers they had to command: undisciplined, mostly untrained, half-starved and weakened by the voyage, ragged and mutinous. The men were not even properly armed. Four storeships had started late from England and had not arrived, and for want of anything better, the Army had to be equipped with homemade pikes as its main weapon.

The commander in chief was Robert Venables, a soldier of long experience but only recently promoted to general and hopelessly unequal to such a difficult situation. Despairing of the men he had, he set about recruiting more in Barbados and neighboring islands. He managed to round up more than 3,500 men—mostly small landowners and exiled Royalists—by promising them land in Hispaniola, and he let them bring women to nurse the sick and wounded. But as these new recruits had neither arms nor provisions, they only made matters worse.

Venables put all his men on half rations, and the whole dissatisfied crowd, some 11,000 in all, set sail for the last few hundred miles to Hispaniola. Scarcely had the fleet departed Barbados than Venables began to quarrel with everyone, especially with Penn, and the quarrels

The Dutch were just as swift as the English to perceive opportunities in the New World empire of the Spanish Crown. The Dutch West India Company, formed in 1621 by Amsterdam merchants, had as its aim "acts of hostility against the ships and property of the King of Spain." As its agent, it chose one Piet Hein, a famous Dutch captain who had already conducted a number of daring raids on Spanish colonies in the Caribbean and Brazil.

Hein's target was nothing less than the "Golden Bird," the great treasure fleet that came north annually from Peru, Mexico and other Spanish possessions. But for years Hein and his cohorts searched in vain. Finally, in 1628, the Dutch captain led an expedition of 31 ships into the waters off Cuba, and there he found his quarry.

On September 7 a lone Spanish bark blundered into the Dutch marauders and was captured. The next morning, Hein's squadron came on the main body of the Spanish fleet. The treasure ships were so deeply laden that some of them had their gunports blocked by chests of jewels and crates of bullion.

Slow and helpless, the galleons attempted to flee into Matanzas Bay, and the safety of a Spanish port. But the four galleons carrying all the gold and silver ran aground near the mouth of the bay. As Hein's boarding parties clambered up one side of the galleons the Spanish crews fled in panic over the other side.

The treasure—taken without a casualty—surpassed anyone's dreams: an incredible 180,000 pounds of silver, 134 pounds of the purest gold, plus thousands of chests of pearls and other gems. When the body was all sorted out, its total value was reckoned at 15 million guilders, or enough for the West India Company to declare a 50 per cent dividend.

Hein, of course, became the hero of all Netherlanders, but he took it in stride. "I've been in greater danger for them 20 times before," grumped the old captain, "and they would not have cared if my head had been taken off by a cannon ball." But he did not refuse the award of 7,000 guilders.

The Dutch also named Hein chief admiral of all their fleets. But alas, he did not live to enjoy his new role; on June 18, 1629, barely six months after his return, he was felled by a cannon shot in a fight with Dunkirk pirates.

CAPTAIN PIET HEIN

spread down through the ranks. The Navy despised the soldiery they were obliged to carry, and the soldiers distrusted the sailors who, they said, refused to share what food and weapons they had.

In mid-April, four months out from home, this hungry, halfhearted mob of men was put ashore on the beaches of Hispaniola in three widely separated groups. The nearest was six miles from Santo Domingo; the farthest was more than 30 miles away. The men were ordered to march on Santo Domingo and seize it forthwith.

They never got near the town. When they were ashore, they found what Venables described as a "land burnt up with drought, so that our horses and Men (the sun being in our Zenith) fell down for thirst; our very feet scorched through our Shoes with the Sand and Gravel." Water bottles had not been issued and the men made themselves sick by eating great quantities of oranges, lemons and limes in an attempt to slake their thirst. At night, lying out in the woodlands, the Englishmen were alarmed by the light of fireflies and the sinister clicking sounds of land crabs. Day and night, they were terrified of snakes.

No army ever needed leadership more badly, but Venables gave his men none. He was among the first to come down with dysentery, and he was obsessed by it. His letters and reports were full of his own "raving condition and great weakness," of "such cruel gripings that I could scarce stand," and a "grievous Flux" that made him unable to walk without a couple of men to support him.

It would be difficult for any general to command an army, let alone inspire it, while he had a severe stomach-ache, but men would have sympathized more with Venables if he had not complained so much. He had also annoyed his army by bringing his wife with him, and whenever things got too uncomfortable ashore, he retired at night by her side, on board his flagship, which was following along just offshore. There, he recovered so quickly that one suspects he suffered mainly from an acute attack of nerves. His men were a lot less fortunate. Their ills were real enough to kill 1,000 of them within a fortnight.

The attack was a farce. A small fort stood astride the route, a mile and a half from Santo Domingo. The Army advanced toward it, with Venables correctly enough in the lead. But the vanguard, on a road with a forest on either side, ran into a Spanish ambush, broke ranks and fled back down the road, throwing the rest of the Army into chaos. The only men who stood firm (so the Navy said) were a regiment of sailors—and one of them, named Henry Whistler (perhaps a relative of the doctor in England), wrote a bitterly sarcastic report that was typical of the Navy: "General Venables being one of the foremost, and seeing the enemy fall on so desperately with their lances, he very nobly run behind a tree and our sea regiment did fall on most gallantly, and put the enemy to flee for their lives, and coming where General Venables was got behind a tree he came forth to them. But was very much ashamed, but made many excuses: being so much possessed with terror that he could hardly speak."

Possessed with terror or not, Venables blamed everyone but himself for this disaster. He court-martialed his adjutant general for being the first to flee, and sentenced him to be "cashiered and his sword broken over his head, and to be made a Swabber to keep the Hospital ship

William Penn, commander of the English Naval forces, was so disgusted by the Army's inept invasion of Hispaniola that he threatened to "set sail and leave them."

Army commander Robert Venables blamed the Hispaniola calamity on troops "so cowardly as not to be made to fight." But he failed to rally his men after an ambush.

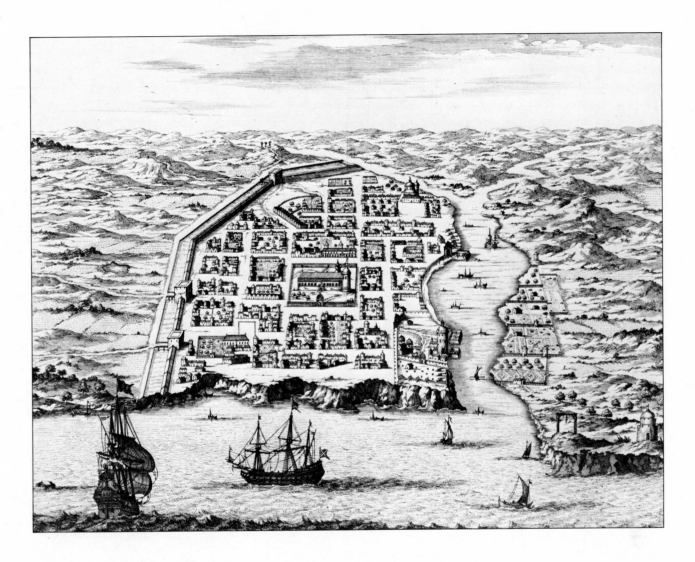

With a good natural harbor and a central location in the Indies, Santo Domingo, capital of Hispaniola, was in Cromwell's view a potential "magazine of men and provisions" for carrying on the conquest of the Caribbean. The English mistakenly thought the place undefended, and were stunned to find it well protected.

clean"—the first oblique reference to the use of a hospital ship in a navy. Presumably, she was a storeship on which the surgeons had been assembled, and to which the most seriously wounded and sick had been taken.

Though Penn must have known the truth about Venables' craven incompetence, the record gives no hint of disapproval. Rather, Penn's dispatches backed up the hapless general. Wrote the sailor: "We are ashamed of the cowardice of our men, which yet continueth, and were not the enemy as cowardly as themselves, they might with a few destroy our Army. But having conferred with the Officers this day they all agree that these People will never be brought to March up to that place again."

Penn resolved—"to our great grief and anguish of Spirit"—to leave Hispaniola and make an attempt on Jamaica instead. This was another nearby Spanish island, which was known from spies to have a smaller garrison—only a few hundred men.

Arriving off Jamaica on May 10, 1655, Penn said that he would not trust the Army again: this time, the Navy would be in charge of the attack. For ease of maneuvering in the shallow coastal waters, he went on board the smallest of all his ships, the *Martin*, a galley mounting only 12 guns. He took Venables with him, perhaps to show the general how a proper assault ought to be mounted. Penn then hoisted his battle flag and led the way to the island's principal strong point, Fort Caguaya on modern Kingston Harbor. Other small ships followed in his wake, and the big men-of-war anchored outside. There was a short sharp cannonade between the *Martin* and Fort Caguaya, which guarded the inner harbor. Ships' boats with a combined force of sailors and volunteer soldiers came in astern of the *Martin*. They cheered her as they passed.

Whistler was in the thick of it again—and reporting sourly on Venables. "All the time that the army was landing," he wrote, "Venables was walking aboard of the *Martin*, wrapped up in his cloak, with his hat over his eyes, looking as if he had been a-studying of Physic more than like a general of an army. But seeing the enemy all fled from their forts and none there to oppose our army, he did desire a boat, saying he would go ashore." And indeed the Spaniards had run. The island's only town, St. Jago de la Vega—later to be known as Spanish Town—surrendered next day, and the whole of Jamaica within a week.

Penn decided to consolidate the victory by garrisoning the island and turning it into a British colony. In any case, his army, if it could be called that, was too sickly and demoralized to move on. The men lived in a state of panic, without much discipline or organization, taking few orders from anyone. They condemned themselves to starvation by wantonly killing off the Spaniards' cattle, and continued to infect one another by unsanitary habits. Malaria, yellow fever, scurvy and beriberi swept through the ranks. "Greater disappointments I never met with," a soldier wrote sadly. "Never did my eyes see such a sickly time, nor so many funerals, and graves all the town over that it is a very Golgotha. Some of the soldiery are buried so shallow that the Spanish dogs, which lurk about the town, scrape them up and eat them. For my own part in 25 years have not I endured so much sickness as here with the bloody flux, rhume, ague, fever."

At the end of six months a muster was undertaken with great difficulty. Of the 7,000-odd soldiers who had embarked from England and Barbados, only 4,510 were still alive, along with 173 women and children (it was not recorded how many women and children had set out). Of these survivors, 2,316 men were sick. Only 2,194 men—less than one third of the original force—were deemed healthy and fit for duty.

As an English colony, Jamaica just survived. Strong men and a few strong women overcame the danger and filth; those who lived through the tropical diseases developed a tolerance for them and began to carve out the sugar plantations that would soon make Jamaica the most valued of English Caribbean possessions. But the Army, for any warlike intent, had ceased to exist, and no more of the grand scheme could be executed.

Once Penn recognized this, he did not tarry long in Jamaica. On June 25 he took half the fleet and sailed for home, leaving the other half to begin the settlement of the newly won territory, using it as a base to raid other Spanish possessions in the Caribbean. Venables contrived to get surgeons to say that he should go, too, for the sake of his health.

Back in England, Cromwell instantly clapped them both into the Tower of London. By any account, Venables deserved it. Penn's offense was more mysterious. Perhaps Cromwell was disappointed and angry at

NOTICIA
DE LAS INVASIONES
QVE LAS ARMAS DE INGLATERRA
HAN HECHO EN LAS
INDIAS.
FELIZ SVCESO,
QVE LAS REALES DE ESPAÑA
han tenido en ſu defenſa.

CON LICENCIA
En Madrid. Por la viuda del Lic. Iuan Martin del Barrio. Año 1655.

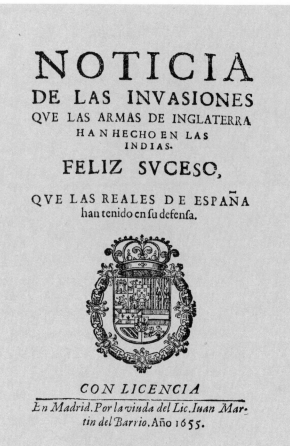

Demonstrating the fine art of the half-truth, Spanish and English pamphleteers both conclude that the English expedition to the West Indies was a rousing victory—each for its own side. The routing of the English in Hispaniola is the basis for the Spanish claim to a "happy success." Ignoring the Hispaniola ignominy, the English account trumpets the "great success" achieved in capturing Jamaica.

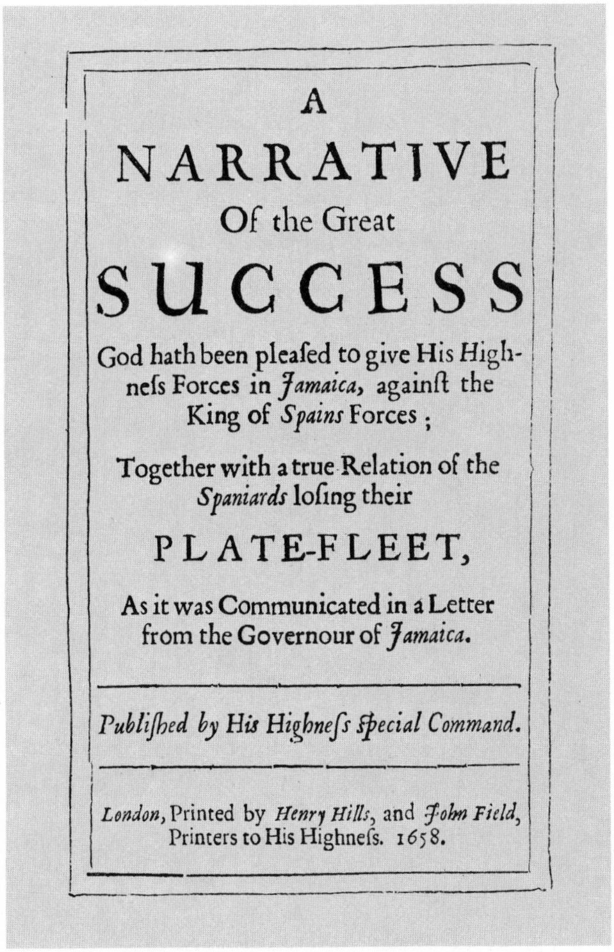

A

NARRATIVE

Of the Great

SUCCESS

God hath been pleaſed to give His Highneſs Forces in *Jamaica*, againſt the King of *Spains* Forces;

Together with a true Relation of the *Spaniards* loſing their

PLATE-FLEET,

As it was Communicated in a Letter from the Governour of *Jamaica*.

Publiſhed by His Highneſs Special Command.

London, Printed by *Henry Hills*, and *John Field*, Printers to His Highneſs. 1658.

Penn's failure to seize more of the Spanish islands. But it was said long afterward that Penn had attempted to betray Cromwell to the exiled King Charles II, that he had written to the King in Cologne and offered to bring his whole fleet over to the Royalist cause, and that the King had declined the offer because there was no port where he could have kept a fleet. It is not unlikely—Penn had done the same sort of thing before—and possibly Cromwell had got wind of it. Both Penn and Venables signed abject submissions to Cromwell, and were soon released.

In the Western Design, the English had suffered from an excess of ambition and a fatal overconfidence in the power of their new navy. The warships had weathered the long voyage and extended duty far from home ports in excellent style. And the sailors had fought courageously and well on Hispaniola and in the attack on Jamaica—presaging the establishment of a marine corps of seagoing infantrymen. But the Navy had not yet demonstrated an ability to transport large numbers of land-bound troops across an ocean with any real success. It would be centuries before the English—indeed, before anybody—learned to mount a large combined operation, with special transports for the troops and proper food, kit and equipment.

If the English were only marginally successful in the main goal of the Western Design—to secure territory from Spain—they were far more adept at carrying out the second part of Cromwell's plan: the thrust into the Mediterranean. For there they quickly learned to use the Navy as a powerful instrument of international politics.

General-at-Sea Robert Blake, with 4,000 men and some 900 cannon in his 27 ships, had arrived off the Spanish port of Cadiz on October 30, 1654, and had immediately put Cromwell's diversionary plan into effect. As might be expected, the Spaniards were apprehensive at the approach of a powerful English fleet. But Blake had moved swiftly to lull their fears. Anchoring peacefully, he had sent a letter to the Spanish King, Philip IV, expressing all good wishes toward the Spaniards and requesting hospitality in Spanish ports.

There followed a long charade in which Blake went charging off in pursuit of French and Barbary ships operating in the area. Observed an English officer named John Weale: "We see plain that we are not only a terror to the French, but also to the Turks." In no case did the English offer the least threat to the Spanish. By late fall, Blake had chased both the French and the Barbary corsairs into port, and had taken his fleet down the Mediterranean to Naples for supplies, rest and diplomacy.

The Italians warmly welcomed the English men-of-war. Here was a growing power in the Mediterranean, to be manipulated, if possible, as a counter to the French and Spanish, and most particularly to the heathen corsairs who had been terrorizing shipping for centuries. Blake enjoyed the cordiality of the Italians until the end of January, 1655. And then he swung into brilliant action against the Barbary corsairs.

Receiving intelligence of a concentration of ships along the North African coast, he crossed the Mediterranean and spent the better part of a month hunting down the Barbary armada. At last, on February 22, he found a fleet of nine galleys at Porto Farina, on the western shore of the

Gulf of Tunis. The enemy, as Blake reported, "was drawn up as near shore as they could, lightened and unrigged, their guns planted upon divers batteries upon the land, and a kind of formed camp, consisting of some thousands of horse and foot, as if they feared some invasion."

Blake withdrew to reprovision. On April 3 he returned—and scored a thunderous victory in which, for the first time, seaborne cannon annulled the natural advantages of shore batteries. Guns emplaced ashore were steadier and had greater arcs of fire. But Blake, with his well-drilled crews and an assist from the weather, overcame the handicap.

The frigates, followed by the larger ships, blew down on the Barbary ships and fortifications on an offshore breeze. In his usual laconic fashion, Blake described the fight: "We entered with the fleet into the harbour, and anchored before their castles, the Lord being pleased to favour us with a gentle gale off the sea, which cast all the smoke upon them, and made our work the more easy, for after some hours' dispute we set on fire all their ships, which were in number nine, and the same favourable gale still continuing, we retreated out again into the road."

Petty Wales
The Bulwark Gate
The Lieutenants Lodgings
RIVER
THAMES

The English lost no ships and only some 25 men, another 40 being wounded. The Moorish fleet had been destroyed and the shore fortresses had been abandoned in the face of the English fire. Blake humbly concluded his report: "It is also remarkable by us that shortly after our getting forth, the wind and weather changed and continued very stormy for many days, so that we could not have effected the business, had not the Lord appointed that nick of time in which it was done."

Blake's victory was all the more remarkable because he achieved it while seriously ill. He had never fully recovered from the wound he had suffered fighting Tromp in 1653, or the infection that had followed it, and now when he was nearly 60 his health had deteriorated alarmingly.

He often wrote letters to Cromwell complaining of the trials of his ships and men on the interminable cruises up and down the Mediterranean, and adding oblique complaints of his own weakness: "Our condition is dark and sad and like to be very miserable; our ships extreme foul, winter drawing on, our victuals expiring, all stores failing, our men falling sick through badness of drink, and eating their victuals boiled in salt water for two months space. And our mariners (which I most apprehend) apt to fall into discontents through their long keeping abroad. Our only comfort is that we have a God to lean upon although we walk in darkness and see no light. I shall not trouble your Highness with any complaints of myself, of the indisposition of my body, or troubles of my mind, my many infirmities will one day, I doubt not, sufficiently plead for me or against me, so that I may be free from so great a burden."

It was reported that Blake lived at sea on nothing but broths, jellies and cordials. Undoubtedly what kept him going was his austere religion, and his determination to do whatever duty was laid on him. He expected to die at his post. Anticipating it, he asked for another commander to be sent to assist him, and Cromwell on January 2, 1656, sent out Edward Mountagu, a fiercely loyal Army officer who had proved himself an outstanding regimental commander in the land battles against the Royalists a decade earlier. Cromwell had named him to the powerful Council of State and now was giving him added responsibility. Mountagu and

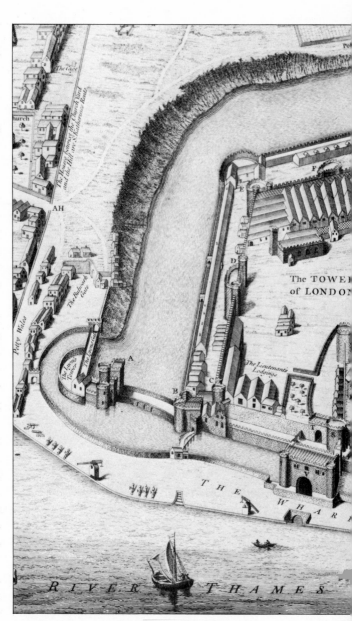

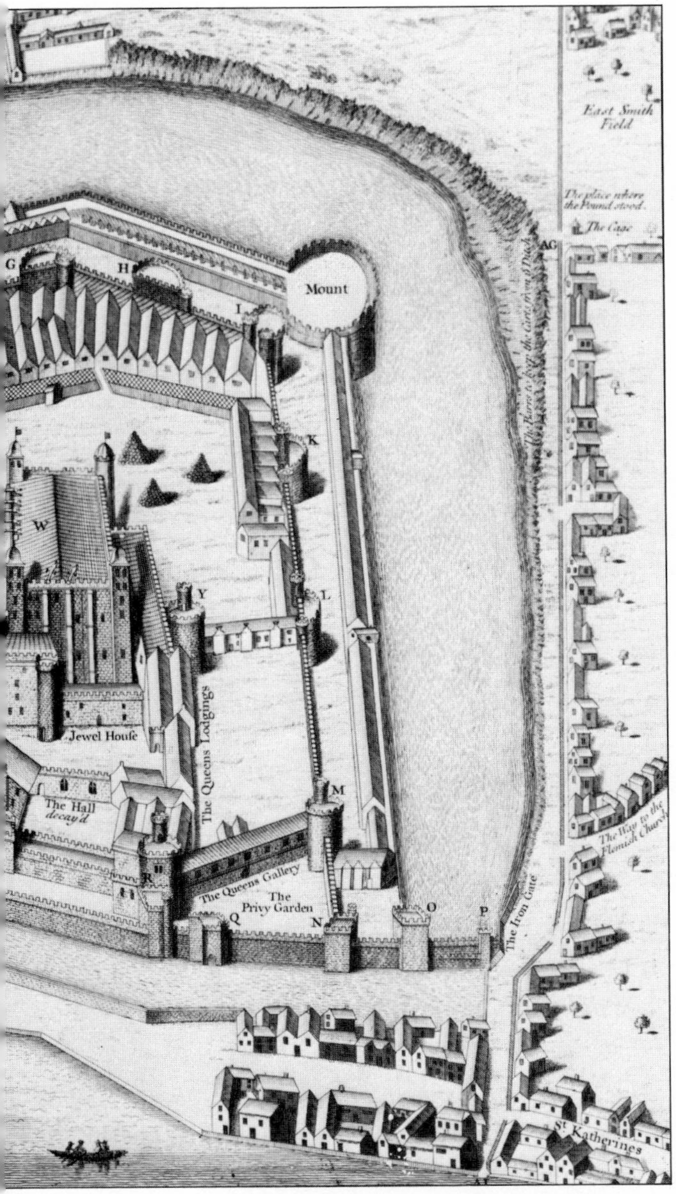
East Smith Field
Mount
Jewel House
The Queens Lodgings
The Hall decay'd
The Queens Gallery
The Privy Garden
The Iron Gate
St Katherines

Upon their return from their disappointing venture to the Indies, both William Penn and Robert Venables were clapped into the Tower of London, seen in this 16th Century view. So cowed was Venables by the noisome place that he wrote Cromwell piteous letters complaining that he was lodged "over a great draw-well which sent up unwholesome Vapours and damps." Penn bore up somewhat better, though to secure his release, he was forced to surrender his Naval commission.

Blake made an odd couple: Blake elderly, puritanical and cautious, and Mountagu young and reckless, and still so ignorant of the sea that he employed a sailor to make him a model ship so that he could study its rigging and see how it worked. But they cooperated, sharing the flagship *Naseby*. Under Blake's tutelage, Mountagu learned the tactics and strategies of attack. He quickly became a competent sailor, prepared for command, and cognizant of the practical needs of a fleet.

About this time, news reached Europe of Penn's attack on the Spanish island in the West Indies. Cromwell immediately dropped all pretenses. He ordered his two disparate commanders to clamp a blockade on the ports of Spain and prevent any reinforcements from being sent to Spain's New World possessions. He also instructed Blake and Mountagu to try to capture the next Spanish treasure fleet from the West Indies.

So began the English tactic of blockade and seizure that was to occupy successive fleets up to the time of Trafalgar a century and a half later. It was arduous duty in the extreme, waiting month after month offshore in the open Atlantic, in every kind of weather, so that the Spanish fleets did not dare come out of their harbors. The port Blake and Mountagu watched most closely was Cadiz, the usual landfall for treasure fleets crossing the Atlantic by southern routes. The English waited there for seven long months, the ships taking turns, three or four at a time, running down to the African coast or up to Lisbon for water, wood for galley fires and any fresh food they could get. It was a stroke of fate that when the action was finally joined, Blake and Mountagu were not on patrol.

In early September, 1656, the two commanders in their joint flagship, the *Naseby*, had left their station for water and provisions. The senior officer of the fleet on watch was Captain Richard Stayner in the 64-gun *Speaker*, with seven other ships in company ranging from 28 to 54 guns. A lookout in Stayner's crew sighted eight foreign sail against the setting sun, 15 miles off Cadiz, on September 8. The sails were those of the Spanish treasure fleet, 28 days out of Havana and now in sight of home.

The Spaniards took little notice of Stayner's ships but sailed on all that night, showing their lights and firing cannon salutes from time to time to announce their homecoming to the people of Cadiz. Stayner sailed with them, keeping a careful distance: though the Spaniards saw his ships, they apparently thought them friendly craft. At dawn on the 9th, Stayner bore down to engage the Spaniards.

There is no Spanish account of the fight or of their astonishment and dismay at the sudden attack. The only surviving English account is Stayner's report to Blake—a modest document, befitting a subordinate. "After some hours' dispute with them," he wrote, "there were two of their ships fired, after they were clapt on board, the one by the *Bridgewater*, and the other by the *Plymouth*, and the enemy seeing themselves unable to hold out, fired their ships themselves; whereby most of their lives were lost, as also some of our men which were on board; and the *Bridgewater* had some trouble getting herself clear of the ship which was fired, being board by board with her."

Stayner described how he had attacked "a Galleon conceiving her to have been their Admiral, which after proved to be so; after we had given her some broadsides, being very near a long time together, she at last struck to us. The ship which I took being very rich, and so much torn that it was very hard for us to have saved her; I have taken out as much plate as we could for the present, which is between 7 or 800 bars of silver.''

This was the sort of battle sailors dreamed of. Two Spanish ships were captured, three burned. Only the three smallest reached Cadiz safely, and one of those was not Spanish, but a Portuguese captive. The treasure taken was said to be worth £1 million, which would have been enough to build at least 50 first-class men-of-war.

By the Prize Laws, shares of this fortune belonged to the captors. But they did not wait for the tedious workings of the Prize Court. The more seaworthy of the two captured ships was escorted back to England. The silver and other treasures were landed at Portsmouth and carted in ammunition wagons under Army guard to London. But when the wagons arrived, they were found to contain only about one third of the original amount. Nobody ever discovered who had made off with the rest.

Quite possibly Mountagu, who had taken no part in the battle, but led the escort home, had managed to acquire a share of silver plate, fine textiles, cash and general cargo. Stayner protested later that he had more regard for his reputation than for money, and had "never got above £2,000''—but he was able to bequeath to his daughter a pearl and emerald necklace that had once belonged to an Inca empress in Peru. One captain supposedly made away with £60,000, and there were stories of more than one ordinary seaman who wound up with £10,000—a stupendous windfall for men whose pay was about £14 a year, when they could get it. But only two lesser offenders were caught and sentenced to minor penalties. On the whole, people sympathized with the embezzlers: given the chance, they would have done the same.

Robert Blake did not go home or take any part in the celebrations—much less in the illicit profits of the fight. He grimly stuck to his duty, and faced the ordeal of an entire winter on blockade. He and his ships barely survived a series of vicious gales. In February he wrote to Mountagu, who had remained in England: "The Lord hath been pleased in great mercy to provide for our safety and in particular for myself in supporting me against the many indispositions of my body. I cannot imagine the Admiralty Commissioners so insensible of my condition as to condemn me to the durance of another winter. Neither can I conceive it advisable to the public interest to keep out the squadron so long. But the goodness of the Lord toward us is never to be forgotten, is far greater than all the discouragements of men notwithstanding the great Tempests of Wind that we have encountered.''

It was a truly awesome bill of particulars that Blake then appended:
"*Fairfax* her head broke and torn away at the cutwater 8 foot down.
"*Plymouth* hath spoiled her powder and continues extreme leaky.
"*Worcester* complains in her quarter and hath spoiled all her bread.
"*Phoenix* lost her main mast sails rigging and all belonging to it and broke several seams.
"*Hampshire* lost foremast and boltsprit sails and all her rigging.
"*Newcastle* leaky continually pumping.
"*Foresight* leaky and very defective and bad about the stern.

An old rogue's views of duty in the Med

For English seamen a Mediterranean cruise was exotic duty compared with an assignment in the bleak and familiar North Sea. One tar who found it exciting was Edward Barlow, who made two voyages south in the 1660s and chronicled every adventure in a journal that he illustrated with drawings like those at right and on the following pages.

Barlow's first venture into the area occurred in June 1661 on board the 32-gun *Augustine*, one of a squadron sent to discipline the Algerians for plundering English merchantmen. But in one encounter the Algerians proved too well entrenched to defeat. In the only battle of this cruise, a ship-to-shore fight, Barlow noted, "the shot shattered our rigging very much." For the duration of the 10-month cruise, the fleet roamed the Mediterranean, escorting merchantmen, landing seamen to defend the Portuguese in Tangiers against the Moors, and generally making its presence felt.

Barlow, or "old rogue," as he termed himself, sampled the delights of sweet Malaga wine. "I was not used to drink such every day," he admitted, "and at last my head began to turn round." He attended a bullbaiting in the "Portingalle meteropelas" of Belem and announced that the women of the city "are very fair and handsome." After months on ship's biscuit, he savored the bread and oranges and lemons of Spain, and once raided a vineyard until "there came two or three Spaniards with guns and rapiers."

Barlow returned to the Mediterranean in 1668, now on the 52-gun *Yarmouth* as part of a 10-ship squadron. This time the Algerians were better behaved. Barlow recounted how a collection was taken in the fleet, each sailor contributing five shillings, in order to redeem 14 Englishmen from slavery in Algiers. Then the ships set off on a grand tour to "renew peace for the good of our merchants' trade." Barlow visited fabled Carthage, "but now it is all ruenated," and saw the lovely city of Messina "being built most of beautified alleblaster." He marveled at images of saints "in pure silver" in Genoa, and in Livorno wrote of "the bloodred coral which they get from the bottom of the sea."

In all the 12-month cruise, there was only one incident with the Algerians. At one point the squadron came upon an English merchantman that had been captured by the corsairs, who were "intending to make prizes of the goods. But seeing us coming, they let her go."

On a page in his journal, Edward Barlow sketched the occasion of his leaving home, shortly to enter upon a life at sea. His mother, as he recounts in the text above the picture, beckons him back, but Barlow could not be deterred, so fed up was he with a farmer's life of "ditching and thrashing and dunging among the cattle, and suchlike drudgery."

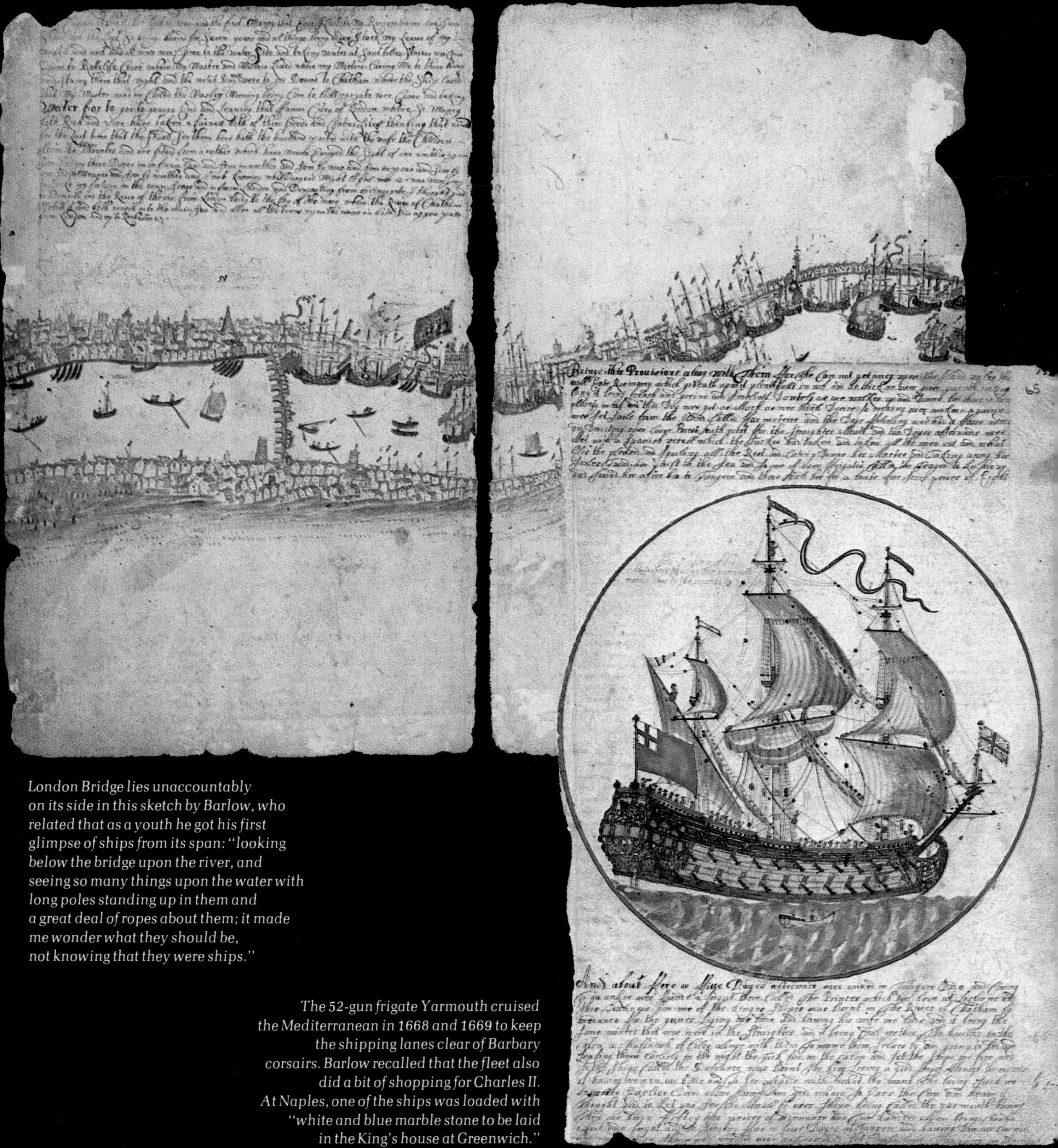

London Bridge lies unaccountably on its side in this sketch by Barlow, who related that as a youth he got his first glimpse of ships from its span: "looking below the bridge upon the river, and seeing so many things upon the water with long poles standing up in them and a great deal of ropes about them; it made me wonder what they should be, not knowing that they were ships."

The 52-gun frigate Yarmouth cruised the Mediterranean in 1668 and 1669 to keep the shipping lanes clear of Barbary corsairs. Barlow recalled that the fleet also did a bit of shopping for Charles II. At Naples, one of the ships was loaded with "white and blue marble stone to be laid in the King's house at Greenwich."

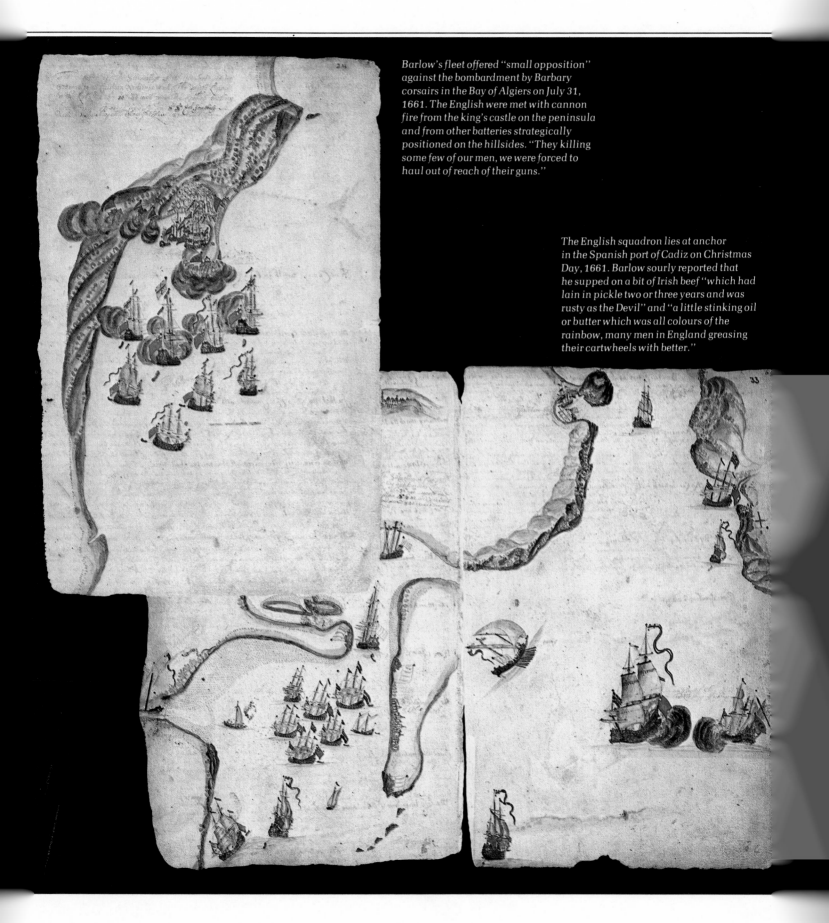

Barlow's fleet offered "small opposition" against the bombardment by Barbary corsairs in the Bay of Algiers on July 31, 1661. The English were met with cannon fire from the king's castle on the peninsula and from other batteries strategically positioned on the hillsides. "They killing some few of our men, we were forced to haul out of reach of their guns."

The English squadron lies at anchor in the Spanish port of Cadiz on Christmas Day, 1661. Barlow sourly reported that he supped on a bit of Irish beef "which had lain in pickle two or three years and was rusty as the Devil" and "a little stinking oil or butter which was all colours of the rainbow, many men in England greasing their cartwheels with better."

Clouds of black smoke roll over the water as Turkish and Italian galleys clash off the coast of Sicily near the volcanic islands that mariners called the "chimneys of Hell." Barlow's ship was on its way to Naples in 1668 when Barlow noted that the volcanoes made a "great thundering noise as ships pass by, and especially when it raineth hard, then it burneth fiercest and maketh most noise."

The Tuscan port of Livorno lies neatly tucked inside stout walls while the English fleet rides at anchor just off the mouth of the harbor early in 1669. Barlow described the cluster of houses outside the walls at right as a leper colony; the tower at right is a lighthouse and the three towers out from the shore are powder magazines. About the town itself, Barlow wrote: "Here are many kind-hearted courtesans and brothel houses where many a man empties his pockets of money."

"And most of the ships that have been out from the beginning complain exceedingly in their masts."

Nevertheless, February found the English fleet still on blockade station off Cadiz. And on the 19th of that month, an English merchant ship en route from Barbados to Genoa hailed the fleet to report that she had sighted 12 Spanish galleons eastward bound in the Atlantic on a course for the Canary Islands.

By then the audacious Stayner had rejoined the fleet and been promoted to rear admiral. He and a council of captains wanted Blake to choose six or eight of the ships and send them to intercept the Spaniards. But Blake refused. His ships were foul, storm-damaged and short of men and supplies; in addition, he had news that the Spanish were preparing a large fleet at Cadiz. Under such conditions he would not split the fleet. "The General," Stayner wrote, "was very angry with us, charging us to speak no more of it."

In the next few weeks, several such angry scenes were played out: Stayner and the captains always impatient for action and Blake insisting on delay. He may have been right, and the captains may have been too eager for another profitable fight. A month later, he was still stubbornly keeping his fleet off Cadiz.

Near the end of March, 1657, supply ships arrived from England with six months' food and what the fleet craved most, 20 tons of good English beer. It was off-loaded in record time. Wrote Blake: "No man living remembereth so much goods taken out in so short a time, without the least damage either to the provisions or the ships." Now the captains renewed their argument. More news had come in: the treasure fleet was at Santa Cruz on the island of Tenerife. At a council on the flagship on April 10, the captains again urged Blake to sail for Tenerife. "The General said little," Stayner noted, "and we stayed aboard all night."

A new source of doubt was in Blake's mind. Word had arrived that a Dutch fleet was in these waters, escorting a convoy. Nobody knew whose side the Dutch might take, that of the English or the Spanish. In fact, the Dutch were strictly neutral, but the rumors were wildly contradictory. One had it that they were planning to escort the Spanish treasure fleet home, another that they were planning to attack the treasure fleet in Tenerife. It was the latter story that finally brought Blake to a decision. To forestall the Dutch, he sailed on April 13 with all of his ships on a 700-mile voyage south to Tenerife.

The Spaniards in the islands sighted the English squadron on April 18, and were perfectly confident. There were a number of English prisoners from Hispaniola in the Spanish ships, and they subsequently reported that their captors had "derided us among themselves, and laughed our intentions to scorn, drank healths to our confusion and were for Spaniards very jolly." Well they might have been, for their fleet of 16 galleons lay at anchor close inshore in the bay of Santa Cruz, and the whole of the shore was fortified with castles and breastworks.

That evening, Blake held yet another council of war. Stayner, ever aggressive, proposed that 12 of the soundest frigates should make the attack on the morrow, while the rest of the fleet stayed outside the bay. Blake, according to Stayner's account, refused because the next day was the Sabbath, the day of rest. Stayner complained bitterly that the enemy was simply being given time to bolster defenses.

At 6 o'clock on Monday morning the council was called again. The captains stood in surly silence. "They said never a word," Stayner wrote, "till he earnestly desired them." Stayner himself announced that he had already told Blake his opinion "and would say no more until I knew better." At last, to force Blake to decide, the captains asked him to name 12 frigates to make the attack, and he chose four from each squadron. Then the captains requested that Stayner should command them. Blake asked Stayner if he agreed, and he replied, "With all my heart."

At 8 o'clock that morning, Stayner in the *Speaker* led 12 frigates in line-ahead formation into the bay beneath the forts, while Blake lay off with the larger men-of-war to fire on the defenses at longer range.

As ever in sailing navies, wind was the most important factor in Stayner's attack. Tenerife lay in the trade winds, and a steady northeasterly breeze almost always blew into the bay of Santa Cruz. Sailing in was easy. The problem was to sail out again when the battle was over.

Stayner devised a masterful solution. He ordered each frigate at the proper moment to drop an anchor offshore and let out three lengths— about 1,800 feet—of cable. Thus they would sail into the harbor on a tether, as it were. When they had done their job they would be able to haul themselves back along this tether with their windlasses until they reached their anchors, and would now have enough sea room to set their sails. However, to fight and maneuver while so tethered required a special technique. When they reached their desired position, a rope called a spring was attached to the anchor cable astern of the ship and was run around to the bow. This functioned as a pivot mechanism; by hauling on the spring, the men could swing the ship to bear on any target.

As Stayner's force neared the Spanish line, the column anchored parallel to the enemy's formation. Playing out their anchor cables and using their spring ropes, the British maneuvered into choice firing positions. Stayner worked himself in between two great galleons commanded by the Spanish admiral and the vice admiral. The Spanish ships were firing furiously, and so were the shore batteries. But two things were on Stayner's side in that perilous position: the high-built galleons screened his smaller and lower frigates from the guns of the forts, and the gun smoke blowing down on the onshore breeze helped to hide them. It was a virtual repeat of Blake's action against the Barbary corsairs in the Gulf of Tunis two years before.

Suddenly the powder magazines on the two Spanish flagships exploded. When the wreckage had fallen, all that could be seen of either was a single carved stern floating on the sea.

Through that gap in the Spanish line, Stayner came under heavy fire from the forts; he began to haul himself off by his anchor cable. Five of the other frigates had each overwhelmed a galleon, and each was trying to tow away her prize. One of these prizes was already burning, fired by her own crew. Blake, by now having entered the bay to neutralize the shore batteries, sent orders not to take prizes but to burn them. That made the captains angry: to them, and to the Navy in general, a prize was the main objective of a battle, a proof of victory and a source of profit.

An unassuming pine box houses what was one of Robert Blake's most valued and vital personal possessions, his compass. On a page torn from a logbook and affixed to the lid of the case are Blake's notes correlating compass points to degrees of latitude and longitude on his charts.

With its gilt-edged writing leaf and exquisitely inlaid drawers and cabinets, General Blake's portable desk was both a practical workplace and a symbol of his rank. The drawers were designed to hold papers, logbooks, writing implements and navigational instruments, the cabinets for drinks or medicines. The front flap folded up for stowage during battle.

No doubt Blake thought it would be difficult enough to get his own ships out of the bay, and impossible if prizes were in tow. But he had to repeat his order three times before the captains obeyed it. Then he sent in boats, still under cover of smoke, to take and burn the other nine ships that were far inshore. The boatswain from the frigate *Bristol* came upon three galleons moored together. With seven or eight men, he boarded the nearest of the three, whose crew had fled, and put a match to her. She blazed up and the flames set alight the other two. By mid-afternoon all of the 16 Spanish ships were wrecked, and nothing of them could be seen but the burning hulks and the masts of two that had sunk.

Stayner's ship, the *Speaker,* had been first into the bay, and she was last out. "We rode at anchor till the sun went down," Stayner wrote, "then the wind came off shore, and we set those pieces of sail we had, and cut away the anchor. Our ship was much torn. We had holes between wind and water four to five feet long and three to four feet broad, that we had no shift to keep her from sinking but by nailing hides over the holes and nail butt staves along the sides of the hides, for we had eight to nine feet of water in the ship that our pumps and bailing would hardly keep her free."

Even in calm water within the bay, the *Speaker's* masts were tottering, and as soon as she made the open sea all three of them fell. Another frigate stood inshore to take her in tow, and the next day they rigged temporary masts; she sailed all the way back to the nearest friendly base in Portugal with nothing but the hides to keep the sea out.

There was no prize money in this fight; the fleet had nothing material to show for its victory. But it had demonstrated beyond any doubt that it was master of the blockade-and-seizure tactic. Spain had not only failed utterly to dispatch reinforcements to aid its suddenly vulnerable New World possessions, it had even proved helpless to secure the transport of vitally needed treasure from those possessions. Here, as would become increasingly apparent to the English and the French, was dramatic proof that the sun was beginning to set on the age of Spanish Empire.

Now at last Cromwell decided that Blake had served long enough, and gave him permission to come home.

Blake was eager to go. He took the fleet back to Lisbon, where the British envoy reported, "The General is very weak: I beseech God to strengthen him." Following Cromwell's orders, Blake left 14 ships off Cadiz "for annoying the enemy," and sent five into the Mediterranean to seek out Turkish pirates. As he sailed with the remaining 11 ships, those left on blockade duty honored their homeward-bound commander with a 13-gun salute. But Blake, dour to the last, fired only one.

As his ships entered the English Channel, bound for the Thames, Blake sent a message to the Admiralty to remind them of the "sad condition" of those he had left behind. Then his own ship diverted to Plymouth, the nearest port. "Our coming in hither," his flag captain wrote, "was by order of the General, who desiring much to get once ashore before his death: but it pleased the Lord to order it as soon as we came to the entering of the Sound, Death seized on him." Another captain added: "His course was finished and his memorial should be blessed. As he lived, so he continued to the death, faithful."

Chapter 4

The nemesis of the dockyard thieves

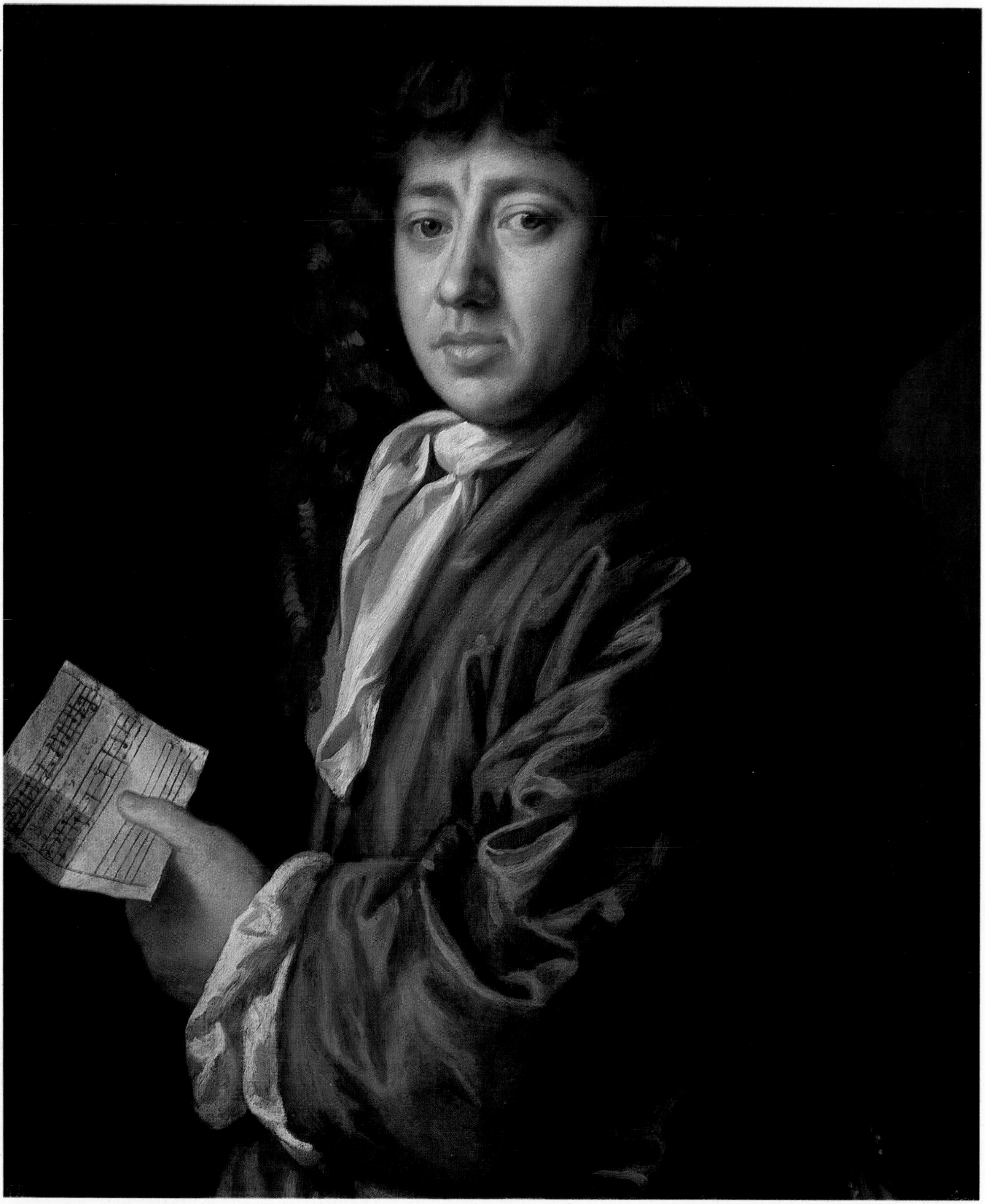

n May 1660 the great 80-gun *Naseby*, wearing the flag of General-at-Sea Edward Mountagu, commander of the English fleet, was at anchor off the coast of the Netherlands preparing for an occasion of supreme importance. Among her 500-man complement was a young seaman named Edward Barlow (*pages 89-92*), better educated than most, and this Barlow wrote in his diary: "Our ship flying three silk flags with sixteen silk penants or streamers and a silk jack, also a silk ancient with nine streamers of another sort: and having a cloth of scarlet going round about her, and all her round tops wound about with the same, the ship being as clean washed and scraped as a trencher."

This was a very different circumstance from the final battle of the war that had been fought against the Dutch off the same coast seven years before. Now Cromwell was dead; England was done with its only experiment in republican government, and the fleet, at Parliament's behest, had gone to the Netherlands with great rejoicing to bring King Charles II home from his exile. When the King came alongside the ship, Barlow wrote, "all the men in the ship gave a great and loud shout, many of them hurling their caps or hats into the sea as a token of their joy to see His Majesty." The flagship fired 70 guns three times in salute, the vice admiral fired all his, then the rear admiral, and then all the rest of the fleet, which made, said Barlow, "such a rattling in the sky as though it had been a great storm or tempest of thunder and rain."

In the same ship at the same ecstatic moment, another young man was also keeping a diary—a diary that was to become, long after his death, one of the most famous ever written. The diarist was Samuel Pepys. Unlike Barlow, Pepys had never been to sea before then and knew nothing whatever about the Navy. A poor relation of the illustrious Mountagu, he had come on board as the secretary to the general. Throughout the voyage he occupied himself with recording the pomp of the great occasion: "Infinite shooting off of guns," he wrote. And he had the heady experience of kissing the King's hand as His Majesty stepped on deck. "The King seems to be a very sober man," he remarked in his diary, "and a very splendid Court he hath in the number of persons of quality that are about him, English, very rich in habit."

Soon after arriving on board, the King set about changing the republican names of some of the ships. The flagship *Naseby*, built by Cromwell and named after the 1645 battle that ensured his victory, was immediately and pointedly renamed the *Royal Charles*; the *Richard*, named for Cromwell's son, became the *Royal James* for the King's younger brother James, Duke of York; the old *Prince Royal*, named the *Resolution* by Cromwell, was rechristened the *Prince Royal*; another man-of-war was named the *Happy Return*, to celebrate the occasion.

A number of Naval officers won new names as well. Among them were three who had served as Cromwell's generals-at-sea but who had changed their allegiance after Cromwell's death and his son's unsuccessful attempt to carry on in his place. Edward Mountagu, who had won fame while serving in the Mediterranean, became the Earl of Sandwich; George Monck, who had been one of Robert Blake's commanders during the First Dutch War, became the Duke of Albemarle, and William

Famed diarist Samuel Pepys was known in his own time as the hardheaded administrator who put to rights the English Navy's chaotic and graft-ridden dockyards and other shoreside establishments. "The right hand of the Navy" was how a top admiral, the Duke of Albemarle, termed him, yet the many-faceted Pepys also found time to enjoy the arts, and in this 1666 portrait displays his score for a song, "Beauty Retire."

Serjeants at Armes
Two Persons representing
the Duke of Normandy &
the Duke of Aquitaine
The Gentleman Usher
with the Black Rod
Garter principal
King of Arms
The Lord Mayor
of London
The Earl of Lindsey
Lord great Chamberlain
of England
The Earl of Northumberland
Lord high Constable of England
The Earl of Suffolk
Earl Marshal of
England
Footmen
Pages

Preceded by ranks of aristocrats, the Lord Mayor of London and other personages, and surrounded by pikemen, Charles II (bottom right-hand panel in this commemorative scroll) rides from the Tower of London to Whitehall on the eve of his coronation on April 23, 1661. "The King looked most noble," rhapsodized Pepys. "So glorious was the show with gold and silver," he added, "that we were not able to look at it, our eyes at last being so much overcome with it."

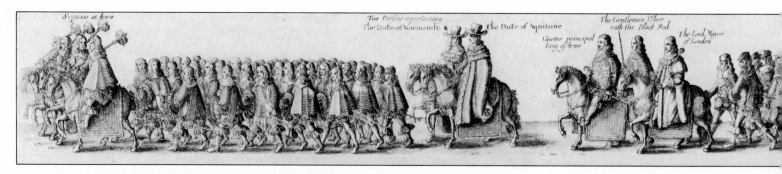

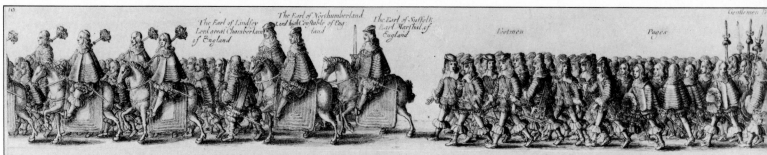

Penn, who had seized Jamaica, was knighted and became Sir William.

Both Monck and Mountagu had worked for the restoration of the King, and whatever feeling Charles might have harbored against these men, he found it the better part of wisdom to overlook their past association with Cromwell. He needed the budding English Navy, and these men were the professionals who had built it and knew how to run it. Over them the King placed his brother the Duke of York as Lord High Admiral. So the Navy put to sea with a new, royal air, under a duke, an earl and a prince.

"We weighed anchor," Pepys wrote, "and with a fresh gale and most happy weather we set sail for England." By the time they came ashore after a three-day voyage across the North Sea, the new King had lavishly dispensed largess all around, showering ducats, guilders and pounds sterling on everyone present, noble and lowly alike. Seaman Barlow got one gold coin, equal to half-a-month's wages. Pepys himself fell into a handsome £50, which doubled the value of his worldly assets. There soon followed a more formal tie with the Navy for Pepys. Mountagu named him to the post of clerk of the acts on the Navy Board. All told, the occasion was a real stroke of luck for a young man of Pepys's humble background. But it turned out that the appointment of Pepys was no less a stroke of great good fortune for the fledgling English Navy.

When King Charles II was welcomed by the fleet that day off the Dutch coast, the English Navy, for all its flaws and growing pains, was a proud inheritance, which he was happy to claim. Cromwell had built a superb fleet of warships. Despite all combat casualties in the First Dutch War and losses to other causes, the fleet totaled 157 men-of-war, three times the number of ships that Charles's father had commanded. But Cromwell had built and maintained the fleet largely on credit. For all his good intentions on wages, he had in the later years been forced to pay seamen

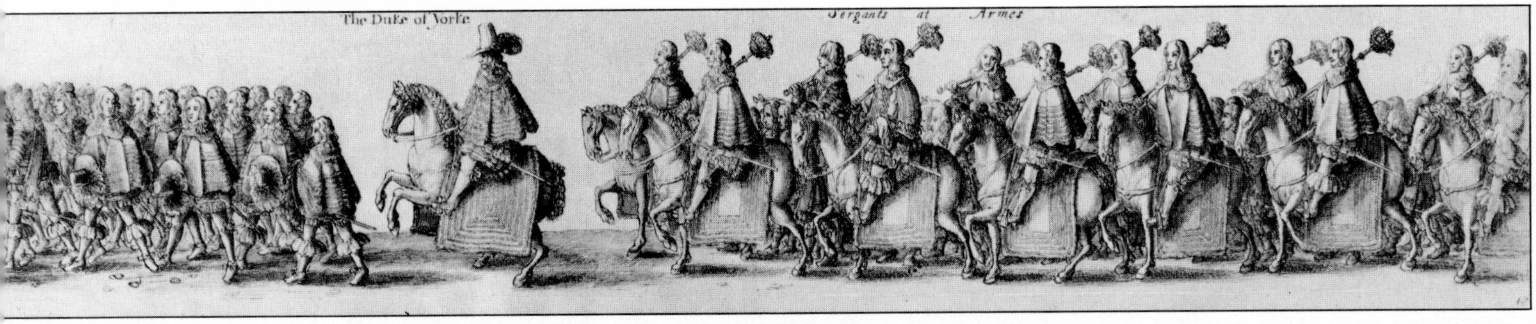
The Duke of Yorke
Sergants at Armes

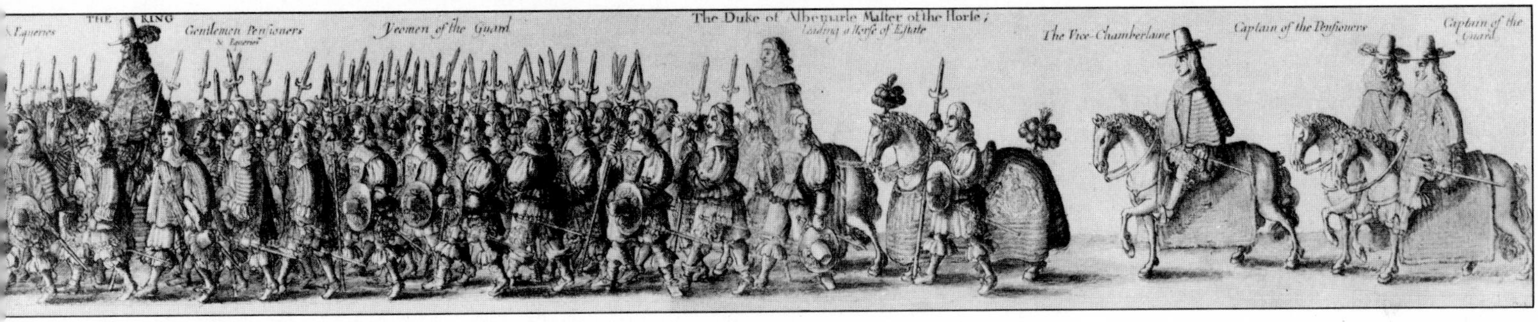
THE KING
Gentlemen Pensioners
Yeomen of the Guard
The Duke of Albemarle Master of the Horse;
The Vice-Chamberlaine
Captain of the Pensioners
Captain of the Guard

and dockyard workers in "tickets" instead of money. In theory, the tickets could be turned in for cash. But the Navy seldom had enough cash on hand for the men to redeem their tickets; some of these had gone unpaid for four years. And so with the Navy, Charles inherited the Navy's chronic debts, which had reached the astronomical figure of £1 million.

Moreover, there was not the slightest chance of reducing that debt so long as the Navy was being bled by graft and incompetence ashore. Robbing the Crown was a time-honored national custom. Under Charles's immediate forebears—his father, Charles I, and his grandfather, James I—Naval administration, such as it was in those early days, had been unbelievably corrupt. Nothing was done without bribery. Materials and stores were seldom bought unless a suitable bribe had been offered to the official who signed the order. Worse, in the dockyards, men stole and sold timber, rope and sailcloth, tar and nails and oakum; even guns were taken out of the King's ships and sold to foreign buyers.

Shipwrights charged the King for maintenance of ships that had been scrapped, and officers drew the pay of seamen who had died or never existed. (One captain even had his dog entered on his ship's books and drew a man's pay for it.) Pursers were notorious for giving short measure: it was said there was no such person as an honest purser. It was a vicious cycle; no matter how much money was scraped together, it soon ran out through the scuppers of corruption, raising the cost and perpetuating the debt.

Under Cromwell, Naval administration improved a bit and was, by the standards of the age, relatively efficient. His stern rule brought some men of rectitude into high positions—but not enough to wipe out swindling. The tradition of daylight robbery died hard. Officials continued to enrich themselves while work was neglected. Everyone knew about it, but nobody could do anything to stop it: a senior man would not accuse his juniors, for fear that his own misdeeds would be discovered.

These were the things that Charles II inherited when he was restored to the throne—and that the young Samuel Pepys acquired when he fell into the post of clerk of the acts.

Samuel Pepys was 27 when the King came home. Pepys's father was a London tailor, and his mother was also of the lower middle classes. His only good fortune of birth was that a great-aunt had surprisingly married the head of the rich and powerful family of Mountagu, one of whose scions was the general-at-sea (the new Lord Sandwich) who had taken Pepys on as a secretary. But that was good fortune enough. Pepys had grown into a young man of intense intellectual curiosity. He had already won a scholarship to Magdalene College, Cambridge. And when the general-at-sea favored Pepys with his influence, Pepys knew just how to make the most of it for himself—and for his country.

Pepys had never even heard of the clerk of the acts until he assumed the post. He was astonished to find that it made him one of the four members of the Navy Board, which ran the shore-based establishment of the Navy. The Board was responsible for building and maintaining all the King's ships and dockyards.

In his new role he brought order out of the chaos that was the Navy's shoreside establishment, and for the first time established real efficiency and honest dealing in English Naval administration. He was responsible for bringing about the first careful accounting of the Navy's records, introducing the first economical and business-like trading for the Navy's supplies, and paving the way for the first formal training schools for Naval personnel, teaching everything from gunnery and hand-to-hand cutlass combat to sail handling and rope splicing.

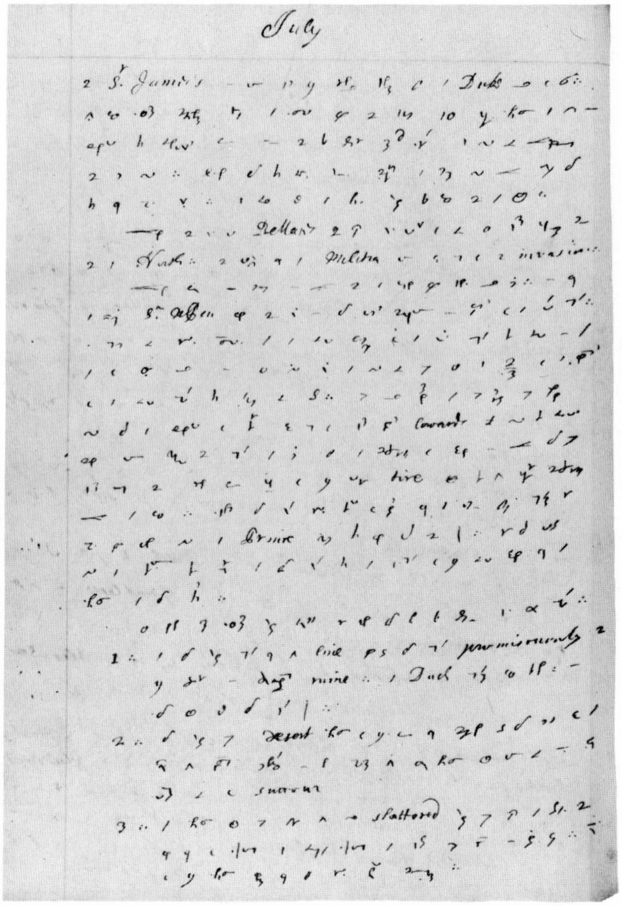

So extensive was Samuel Pepys's diary that he wrote it down in shorthand, as shown on this page dated July 4, 1666, recounting his conversations that day with Sir William Penn on the fighting tactics of the Royal Navy. Failing eyesight forced him to call it quits after eight and a half years and some 1,250,000 words. In a final entry, dated May 31, 1669, he wrote, "I . . . undo my eyes almost every time that I take a pen in my hand; and therefore, whatever comes of it, I must forbear."

Pepys accomplished his remarkable feat against a background of international tensions in which the Navy was becoming ever more valuable to England. Once again, animosity was rapidly mounting toward England's arch commercial rival, the Dutch Republic. Both nations managed to avoid outright war for another five years, partly out of the pragmatic (though not universally held) conviction that trade would benefit more from peace than from war. Johan de Witt, an officer of the Dutch States-General, observed that if the devil himself were sovereign of England, it would be necessary to live on friendly terms with him; Charles II's Lord Chancellor, the Earl of Clarendon, banking English fires, warned the King against the interruption to trade, "upon which the greater part of his revenue did arise." Meanwhile, both nations indulged in frequent name-calling and angry denunciations in press and Parliament. Both engaged in skirmishes in their far-off trade routes; in the year 1664 alone, English semi-official privateering attacks on Dutch shipping around the world yielded more than 100 prizes.

It is something of a mystery why Mountagu named Pepys as clerk of the acts. Perhaps he thought it would help his own career to have a servant of his own on the Navy Board.

Pepys himself later said that Mountagu did it by chance, not knowing what an important job it was. But Pepys was being modest; he should have said what an important job it was to become because he would make it so. In any case, one aspect of its importance was soon obvious. The very day after Pepys was installed, a lady gave him £5 in silver to use his influence in her husband's favor, and when he went home he "found a quantity of chocolate left for me, I know not from whom."

A week later somebody offered to buy the job from him for £500. It was understood that Naval jobs were bought and sold. The price depended not on the salary of the job (which in Pepys's case was £350 per year), but on the scope it brought for making money on the side and for selling other jobs or giving them to friends and relations. In another month or two, the price Pepys was offered had gone up to £1,000, which he wrote "made my mouth water." But he decided not to sell. "Chance without merit brought me in," he wrote in his diary, "and diligence only keeps me so, and will, living as I do among so many lazy people."

There was nothing truly contradictory in Pepys's attitude, not in that day. Considering the modesty of his salary, he was expected to accept gifts and indulge in a bit of influence peddling. It was woven into the social fabric of the times, and indeed he could not have survived had he eschewed it. Where Pepys differed from the vast majority of his contemporaries was in his approach to his job; he was as fiercely determined to see the Naval establishment function properly as he was greedy for personal gain. And because of that the Navy came out richer also.

The Navy Board contracted with London merchants for the timber, hemp, tar, sailcloth, candles and victuals it took to run the Navy, negotiated with Parliament to raise the money to pay for it, and answered for its actions directly to the Duke of York as Lord High Admiral. In the face of the alarming national debt that existed on Charles's accession, the main job of the Navy Board in 1660 was to reduce the size and expense of the fleet by laying up ships and discharging men. Reduction of expenses began modestly, first by dispensing with pilots in the Thames and then in early December by cutting down on the "unfitting expense of Powder" for "unusuall salutes"—meaning that now salutes would be fired only according to the Lord High Admiral's regulations. Harsher measures came in time; by 1664 several thousand men had been laid off from the dockyards.

As clerk of the acts, Pepys was the lowest ranking of the four officers on the Navy Board (the others being the treasurer, comptroller and surveyor). Initially he was expected to do no more than record the decisions of the Board, which met twice a week. For a man of his gregarious and inquisitive nature, the job left enough time to enjoy the life of London to the full, and every night to record the day's events in his diary.

But the same inquisitive disposition led him to explore the job itself. Soon he was making visits to the dockyards at Deptford and Woolwich, where he experienced an awakening. "Never till now," he wrote in his diary after a visit to Deptford, "did I see the great authority of my place, all the captains of the fleet coming cap in hand to us." Back in London he strolled through Thames Street, comparing prices of tar, oil, hemp, timber, cloth—and discovered that the flagmakers supplying the Navy were charging threepence a yard too much. He decided that he should not only record the Board's contracts but also sign the bills for the merchandise. Because the other members of the Board were content to col-

Samuel Pepys's London: a city ablaze with luminaries

The London that Samuel Pepys enjoyed when his work at the Navy Office was done was a cosmopolitan's delight. In contrast to Oliver Cromwell's stern Puritanism, King Charles II banished solemnity from his court, bestowing the title Master of Revels on playwright Thomas Killigrew, who had established the Theater Royal.

There, with his friend and fellow diarist John Evelyn, Pepys could enjoy a farcical comedy by John Dryden, a chivalrous melodrama featuring the captivating Margaret Hughes, or the licentious dialogue of frolicsome Nell Gwyn (she referred to the King as "my Charles the third" because he was the third of her lovers named Charles).

Pepys's own fondness for the fair sex was matched only by his love of music. "Music and women I cannot but give way to, what ever my business is," he told his diary.

This hedonism was tempered by an equally intense dedication to more serious interests. Pepys was an early president of the Royal Society, whose weekly discussions enlisted the greatest minds of England, including Sir Christopher Wren, architect of the new St. Paul's Cathedral, and chemist Robert Boyle, discoverer of Boyle's law governing the behavior of gases. Astronomer Edmond Halley, who predicted the arrival of Halley's comet, and mathematician Sir Isaac Newton, founder of modern physics, were also regular participants at the meetings of Pepys's "college of virtuosoes."

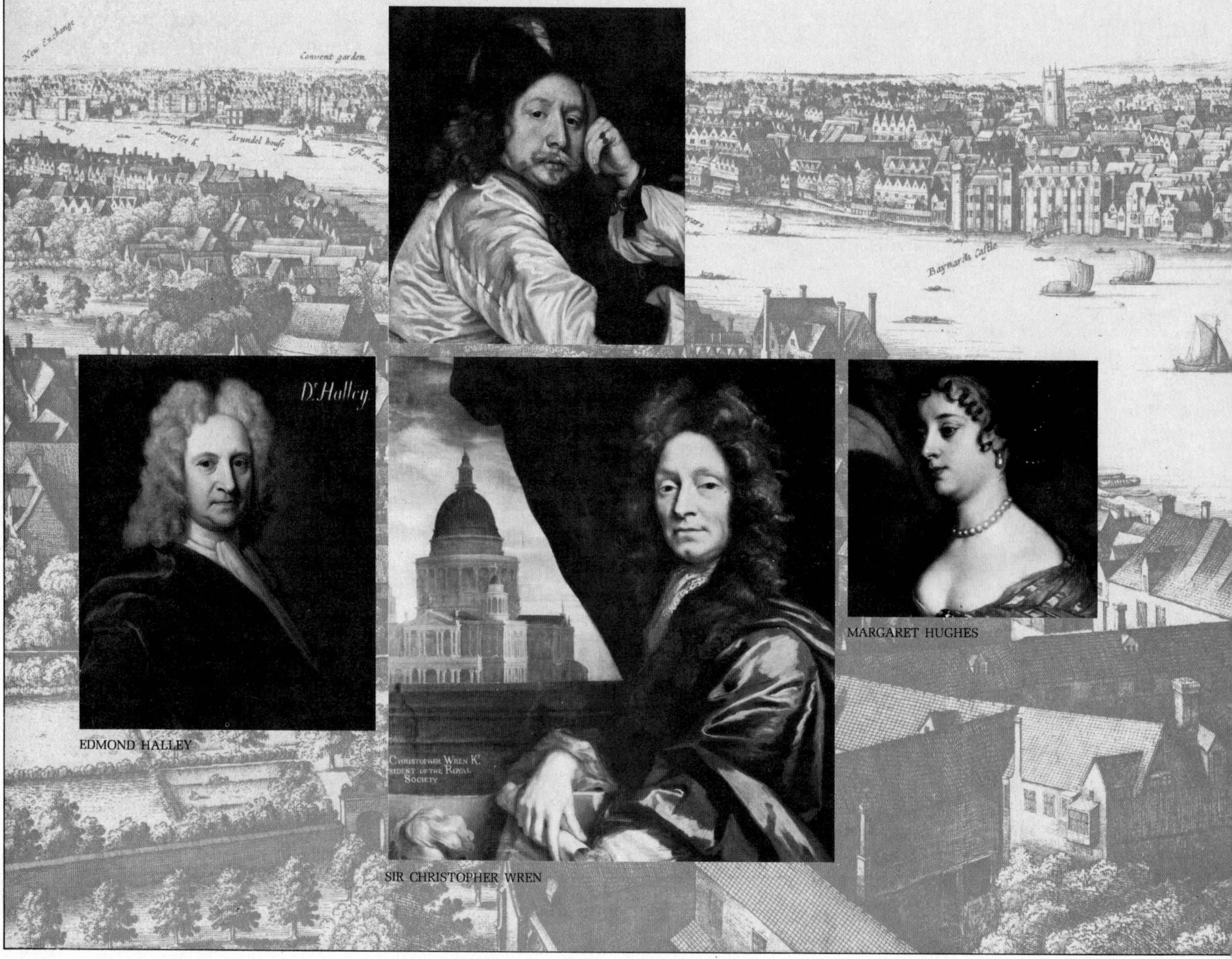
New Exchange
Convent garden.
Arundel house
D.r Halley
Christopher Wren K.t
sident of the Royal
Society

THOMAS KILLIGREW

EDMOND HALLEY

SIR CHRISTOPHER WREN

MARGARET HUGHES

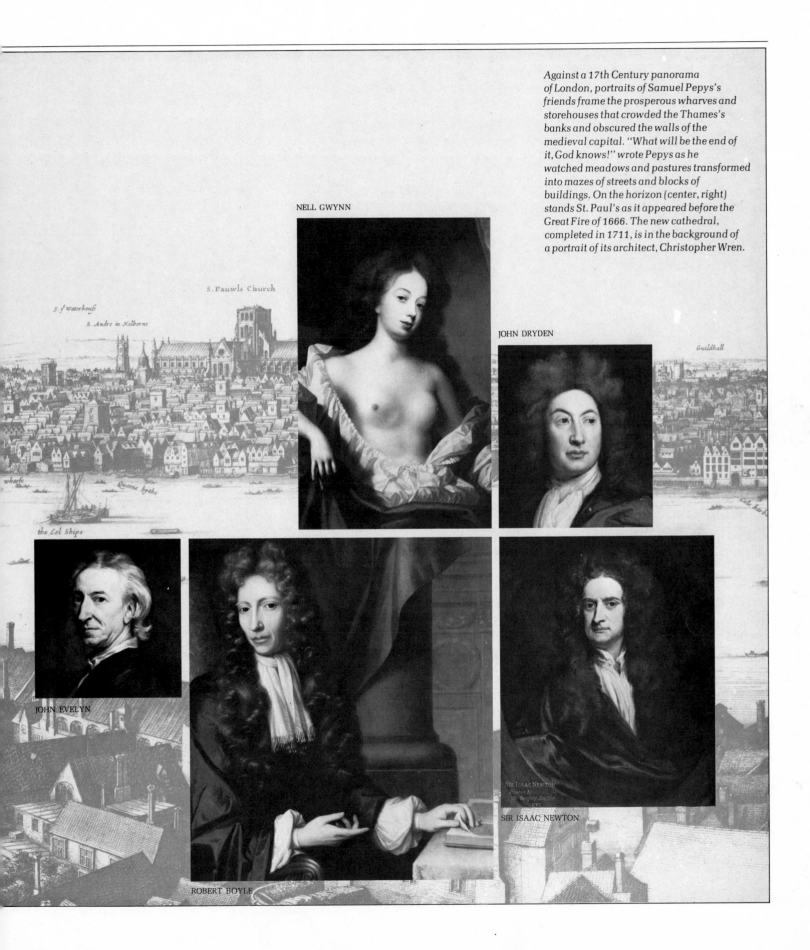

Against a 17th Century panorama of London, portraits of Samuel Pepys's friends frame the prosperous wharves and storehouses that crowded the Thames's banks and obscured the walls of the medieval capital. "What will be the end of it, God knows!" wrote Pepys as he watched meadows and pastures transformed into mazes of streets and blocks of buildings. On the horizon (center, right) stands St. Paul's as it appeared before the Great Fire of 1666. The new cathedral, completed in 1711, is in the background of a portrait of its architect, Christopher Wren.

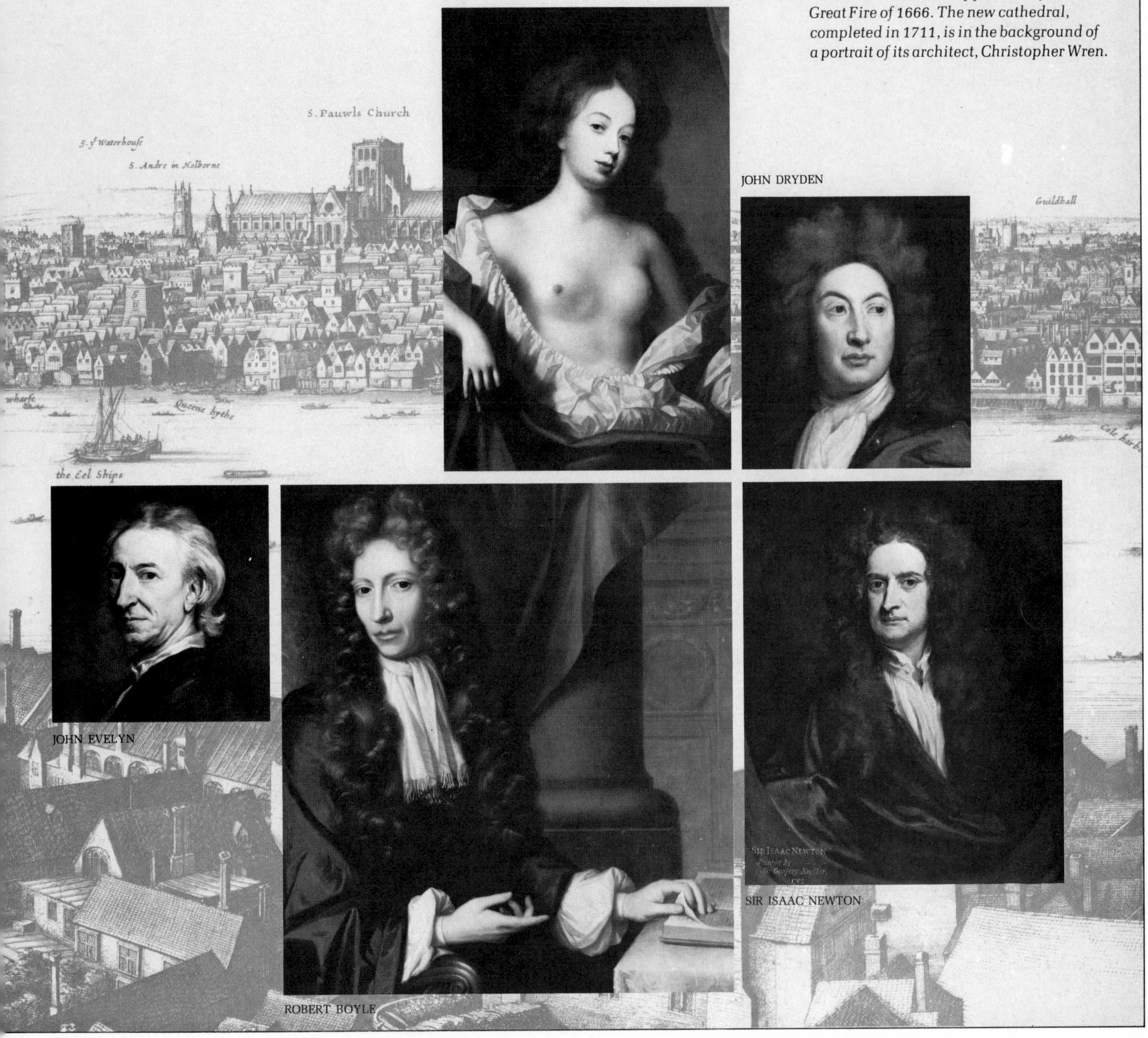
S. Pauwls Church
S. Andre in Holborne
Guildhall
wharfe
Queene hythe
the Eel Ships
SIR ISAAC NEWTON

NELL GWYNN

JOHN DRYDEN

JOHN EVELYN

ROBERT BOYLE

SIR ISAAC NEWTON

lect the emoluments of their jobs, Pepys had no interference from them.

Flags were only the merest of details that interested Pepys. Hearing that ill-fitted shrouds were breaking the masts of English ships, he took up the study of hemp (quizzing Dutch shipmasters he met in a tavern because he had heard that Dutch rope was superior). He learned the different merits of Baltic and North American timber, such as the proper ratio of their diameters to their length and the proper method of preserving the wood until ready for use. It soon became apparent that he knew more about glazing, canvas and lanterns than anyone else on the Board—and more about merchants and their prices as well. So he progressed from simply recording contracts to negotiating them on his own.

In September 1663 he made a contract with one of his legion of friends, Sir William Warren, for £3,000 worth of masts made of Baltic timber. At a price that was 5 to 7 per cent cheaper than that in past contracts, they were the best bargain made for the Navy in a quarter of a century.

As time went on and he gathered the business of the Navy Board increasingly into his own hands, it struck Pepys with some force what a fantastic fortune could be had from graft. "Good God," he wrote, "to see what a man might do were I a knave." Pepys was certainly no knave. Nor was he a saint, and he would have been foolish not to have seen to his own well-deserved profit. Whenever he made an appointment, signed a paper or drew up a contract, the person who benefited from it expected to give him a present. Often the package would contain some trifling gift for his wife. But it was sure to include a bonus for him as well. "When I came home, Lord! in what pain I was to get my wife out of the room without bidding her to go," he wrote of one incident, "and by and by, she being gone, it proves a pair of white gloves for her and forty pieces in good gold, which did so cheer my heart that I could eat no victuals almost for dinner for joy to think how God do bless us every day."

By May 1661 Pepys's net worth had risen from the modest £100 he had reckoned at the time of the Restoration to a welcome £500. But he took his cut in moderation and according to a certain code of ethics. When he supplied the discounted flags to the Navy, he pocketed £50, but he noted approvingly that he had saved the King twice that sum in the transaction. As a rule, Pepys figured that for every pound he pocketed, he could have fetched 10 had he chosen to be unscrupulous. To him, accepting these blessings was something quite different from such reprehensible practices as falsifying the books and stealing the stores.

Other qualities that in his mind came under the heading of reprehensible were laziness and sheer incompetence. He set himself to weed these evils out of Naval life. On a summer's day in 1662, for example, he met a captain in London who was extremely angry because his ship, the 24-gun *Rosebush*, was not ready in Woolwich dockyard. "So took boat," he later wrote, "and went down on board the *Rosebush*, and found all things out of order; but after frightening the officers there, left them to make more haste, and so on shore to the yard, and did the same to the officers of the yard, that the ship is not dispatched." He made a habit of frequently turning up without warning in the dockyards, sometimes so early in the morning that he routed the men in charge out of bed.

Very little escaped his notice. Viewing the Chatham dockyard on one occasion, Pepys wrote, "among other things, a team of four horses came close by, drawing a piece of timber that I am confident one man could easily have carried upon his back. I made the horses be taken away, and a man or two to take the timber away with their hands."

Even his seniors were subtly menaced with hints of exposure. When he discovered that Sir William Batten, the Surveyor of the Navy Board, was helping himself to money from the Chatham Chest—the wounded seamen's fund, to which every poor seaman contributed sixpence a month out of his lowly wages—Pepys used his considerable powers of persuasion to convince the Duke of York to set up a commission to oversee the management of the Chest. Action on this particular issue was slow in coming, but when it did, Pepys could take the credit. Eventually he was to give the Navy a core of uncomfortable conscience, and to free it of much of the crippling weight of thieves and rogues ashore.

That was not all this landsman did for the Navy. His vision ran centuries ahead. It annoyed him extremely that any young man of good birth could buy a commission and go to sea as an officer without adequate knowledge; he discerned that a navy in the long run must have a permanent corps of skilled professional officers at every level, men who would make a career of naval service. With Pepys's reforms, anyone aspiring to be a midshipman had to have two years at sea in some prior job; a lieutenant had to have three years' sea duty, one of them as a midshipman, and be able to pass an examination proving he knew the fundamentals of sailing a ship. Out of Pepys's regulations came the code of rigorous training that made of English Naval officers an elite and expert band.

There were two problems Pepys could do nothing about at first. One was getting the Navy into the black. Despite all the cutbacks in ships and personnel, the Navy's debt still stood at the enormous £1-million figure that Charles had inherited in 1660. In fact, the appropriations voted by Parliament for the Navy's day-to-day operations brought in only two-thirds the amount Pepys and his colleagues estimated as the need. As the Navy sank ever deeper into the financial mire, Parliament voted a series of universally detested excise duties on ale, beer and the newly popular tea and coffee. But though these alleviated the immediate concern of running the Navy, they could not solve its long-term money problems.

The other trouble Pepys could not eradicate was manning the fleet. A navy that had for so long left its men unpaid could not expect many volunteers, and there were scarcely enough to matter. In the desperate search for men, drastic use was made of the press gangs. Even in London, Pepys observed, any able-bodied man was likely to be seized like a criminal, held in prison, hauled by armed guards to the riverside in squads that were followed by lamenting wives and lovers, and sent down in boats to Chatham and Sheerness, where the fleet assembled. Pepys hated the practice, but there was little he could do about it. He confided to his diary: "More complaints arise, and justly, every day of the irregularities and violences committed in the pressing of men."

Across the North Sea the Dutch fleet at this time numbered around 135 specialized men-of-war crewed by some 20,000 officers and seamen. And one pamphleteer crowed that there were 1,000 more vessels among the merchant ships fit for war. But behind those healthy numbers, the Dutch were suffering from many of the same problems that afflicted the English—and a number of woes that were peculiar to themselves.

One of the greatest problems derived from the very independence of spirit that had put the little nation in the forefront of maritime powers in the first place. As a confederation of seven disparate provinces, the Dutch Republic had a navy whose shoreside administration was governed by not one admiralty but by five. Two of the provinces—Friesland and Zeeland—had admiralties of their own. And the dominant province—Holland—contrived to have three: one for the city of Amsterdam, one for the city of Rotterdam and one to represent the "North Quarter," which covered the area of West Frisia. Though all five of the admiralties in theory served the same republic, and all in theory were jointly responsible for the fleet, they were beset by local jealousies and handicapped by jockeying for political leverage.

In one instance, when Zeeland was lusting for an armed foray into Portuguese waters and Holland had a commercial problem to settle with Denmark, the Hollanders refused to oblige the Zeelanders with ships and money, while the Zeelanders stymied efforts of the Hollanders to work out a trade treaty with Denmark. Such bickering was seriously detrimental to the Navy both ashore and afloat. Sir George Downing, Charles II's envoy in the Netherlands, wrote home in 1664: "You have infinite advantages upon the account of the form of the government of this country which is a shattered and divided thing."

What the Dutch did share with the English was a universal distaste for the taxes levied to support the Navy. Because it had three admiralties Holland was expected to bear a heavy burden of the expense, and in fact contributed a mighty 50 per cent toward financing the Dutch Navy. In all provinces, Dutch citizens footed the bills through a burdensome series of taxes. The foundation of the system was an extraordinarily high sales tax, which hit the poor especially hard. The people of Leiden, for example, had to pay a sales tax of 25 per cent on their bread, 66 per cent on their beer and more than 100 per cent on their salt. On the rung above the lowly poor, middle-class manufacturers were pressed as well with taxes on imported raw materials.

There was still a third means of taxation, however, and this one reflected the Dutch pragmatic devotion to trade on any principle. When in the 1630s Prince Frederick Henry, then the nominal head of the Dutch Republic, had suggested an embargo on trade with the Spanish enemy, one Amsterdam merchant retorted that if he could make a profit by passing through hell, he would risk burning the sails of his ships to do so. Most of his fellow merchants shared his sentiment, and practicality ruled out disbarring Spain from Dutch trade. The dilemma was resolved by allowing the traffic to continue but requiring a license of those merchants who engaged in it.

The licenses for trade with the enemy provided a chief source of income to the five Dutch admiralties. They might have provided even more, had not so many of the large merchants evaded the license fees. One result of this evasion was that the provinces were almost constantly in arrears to the fleet. Even in Holland, the richest province, only the

The imposing office of the Amsterdam Admiralty, largest of the five Dutch Naval administrations, overshadows the municipal buildings in Prinsenhof Square in this mid-17th Century engraving. In addition to outfitting the most powerful fleet in the Dutch Navy, the Admiralty was responsible for regulating customs and marine traffic in Amsterdam's vast harbor, biggest and busiest in the land.

Amsterdam Admiralty was consistently paid up in its Naval dues.

Neither were the Dutch much less prone to corruption than their English neighbors, despite a common misapprehension to the contrary. In 1640 the Amsterdam Admiralty Board was rocked with scandal when its treasurer admitted that he had embezzled close to 200,000 guilders. Later, Ambassador Downing wrote home to England that "there is scarce any who come in the States-General but get in to make themselves a fortune by it and must be bought." And a Portuguese envoy recorded one delicate way in which the Dutch went about their corruption. A Dutch merchant desirous of the favors of another would pay a social call on his quarry at home. In the course of conversation he would drop, "as if by accident," the Portuguese wrote, "a jewel worth about a thousand crusados more or less into the hands of one of the children." No one would ask the tot to return the jewel—and so the bribe discreetly took place under the guise of innocent child's play.

The bookkeeping of the Amsterdam Admiralty Board, unlike that of Pepys's Navy Office, was at best confused and at worst downright dishonest. When the States-General repeatedly asked for a summary of income and expenditures, the Board answered evasively that "the necessary data are missing." Further evidence of corruption appeared in the appointment of the 15-year-old son of a prominent Amsterdam family to the rewarding position of first clerk. Since he was still in school, temporary replacements were found for seven years until he finally took up his sinecure at the age of 22. It was not recorded whether the youth drew a salary or shared in the rewards of his position while still a student.

For all its shortcomings, the Dutch Naval establishment had the edge on its English counterpart in one respect at least. The admiralties managed to pay their contractors on time—and also paid their dockyard workers and seamen. One excellent reason was that costs were lower for the Dutch. Shipbuilders and suppliers charged 30 to 50 per cent less than their English counterparts. While there was graft, there was none of the wholesale gouging that went on in England; perhaps the Dutch felt a greater sense of responsibility toward their newly independent republic.

The seamen's wages also were low—less than the 20 shillings a month theoretically accorded English crews—but the prompt and reliable payment went far toward making service in the Dutch Navy attractive. The result was that the Dutch had no need for the hated press gangs but actually had a surplus of volunteers. The sailors represented not only Dutchmen but also Germans and Scandinavians (whom the Dutch lumped together as "Easterlings") and even Englishmen. The marriage records for Amsterdam between 1651 and 1665—the years encompassing both Anglo-Dutch wars—show that 57½ per cent of the bridegrooms who listed their occupation as Dutch Navy men were foreigners. Of those, 4 per cent were English.

The polyglot fleet drew various reactions from Dutch commanders. One contemporary Dutchman asserted that a mixed crew was less apt to bring off a mutiny. Others saw the drawbacks. Though the records do not show it, there must have been serious problems of training. One captain wrote to Johan de Witt quoting his colleagues as complaining of having to "make do with inexperienced men, or with oafish Easter-

lings.'' Another pleaded with the authorities in Amsterdam for ''good trusty Netherlands' hearts.''

The Dutch Navy was a mixed bag in another vital respect: its top fleet commanders. The seven contentious provinces were adamant about each being represented afloat. When their fleet set sail it was composed therefore of seven squadrons, each subdivided into three detachments, totaling 21 in all—with 21 flag officers. The English three-squadron system enhanced tactical maneuver and command. But seven squadrons carried the division of responsibility well past the point of efficiency.

It was an unwieldy system at best, and could result in a chaos of conflicting orders. But in the first war with the English, the Dutch had in Maarten Tromp an admiral so brilliant, tactful and resourceful that he could unify all Dutchmen. Another such hero would appear in the person of Michiel Adriaenszoon de Ruyter when the next war erupted.

That eventuality was drawing closer every day as the decade of the 1660s approached its midpoint. ''I hope we shall be in good condition before it comes to break out,'' Samuel Pepys anxiously wrote in his diary toward the end of 1663. ''We all seem to desire it as thinking ourselves

Dutch Admiral Michiel de Ruyter (second from left) and his family gather in a pastoral setting for this 1662 portrait before the second war with the English. As successor to the late Maarten Tromp in command of the Dutch fleet, de Ruyter won fame as a dogged fighter and perhaps the most skilled naval tactician of his time. In contrast to aristocratic English officers, he was republican to the core, sweeping his own cabin and feeding the chickens he kept on deck.

to have advantages at present over them; for my part I dread it."

The great merchants and financial powers in England had always been split over whether it was more advantageous to trade in relative peace with the Dutch or to seek the advantages a victory in war would bring. And now, increasingly, the war party, as it was called, was making itself heard the loudest. The Navy, of course, had always been anxious to test its ships and evolve tactics against the Dutch. But the rising clamor for war placed King Charles II in a quandary. He was loath to provoke antagonism from France's Louis XIV, who was nominally an ally of the Dutch. However, he owed his return to the throne to Parliament. And merchants with representatives in Parliament were among those clamoring loudest for war. But Charles was a shrewd man with a number of tricks up his sleeve, and he found a way out of his dilemma.

As before—indeed as always—the Dutch and the English were abrasive competitors for overseas empire. The arena this time was not so much the Spice Islands of the East Indies as it was the New World and the coast of West Africa. Charles and his ministers cunningly devised a scheme that might serve two aims at once: it would deprive the Dutch of overseas wealth, and in so doing, perhaps goad them into war.

In March 1664 the King granted the Duke of York a several-hundred-square-mile tract in North America that extended from Delaware Bay to Connecticut. It included many English settlements, but also the territory called the New Netherlands, which had been claimed and settled by the Dutch. In his capacity as Lord High Admiral, the Duke sent a Naval expedition in May 1664 to take possession of the territory. Part of its mission was to humble the Dutch. The expedition was ready to fight to accomplish this, but it arrived off the North American coast to find the Dutch in disarray. The colonists were preoccupied with annoying Indian attacks. They were fed up also with the arbitrary rule of their governor, Pieter Stuyvesant. Without firing a shot, the settlers handed over the town of New Amsterdam, which was thereupon renamed New York.

The Dutch settlers may not have cared whom the place belonged to, provided their colonial lives were undisturbed. But the Dutch government at home cared very much, and this bloodless conquest pushed them a step nearer to a declaration of war.

Meanwhile, the English were busily striking a further series of sparks on another distant coast: the shores of tropical West Africa. The Dutch had been trading there profitably for ivory, slaves and gold since 1626. In the winter of 1662 a number of prominent Englishmen founded an organization called the Royal African Company. For appearance' sake, it was chartered as a private company, ostensibly to join peacefully in the trade. But the governor of the new company was the Lord High Admiral, the Duke of York; the King's cousin Prince Rupert, a former cavalry officer who was now a Navy admiral, was deeply involved in it, as were a number of Naval officials and leading merchants with Naval contracts. In return for granting the company a royal charter, King Charles II was to receive two thirds of all the gold brought home by the company.

As the Dutch were shortly to discover, the Royal African Company was a stratagem—aside from whatever profits it might return its high-powered backers. If things worked out right, the company might pro-

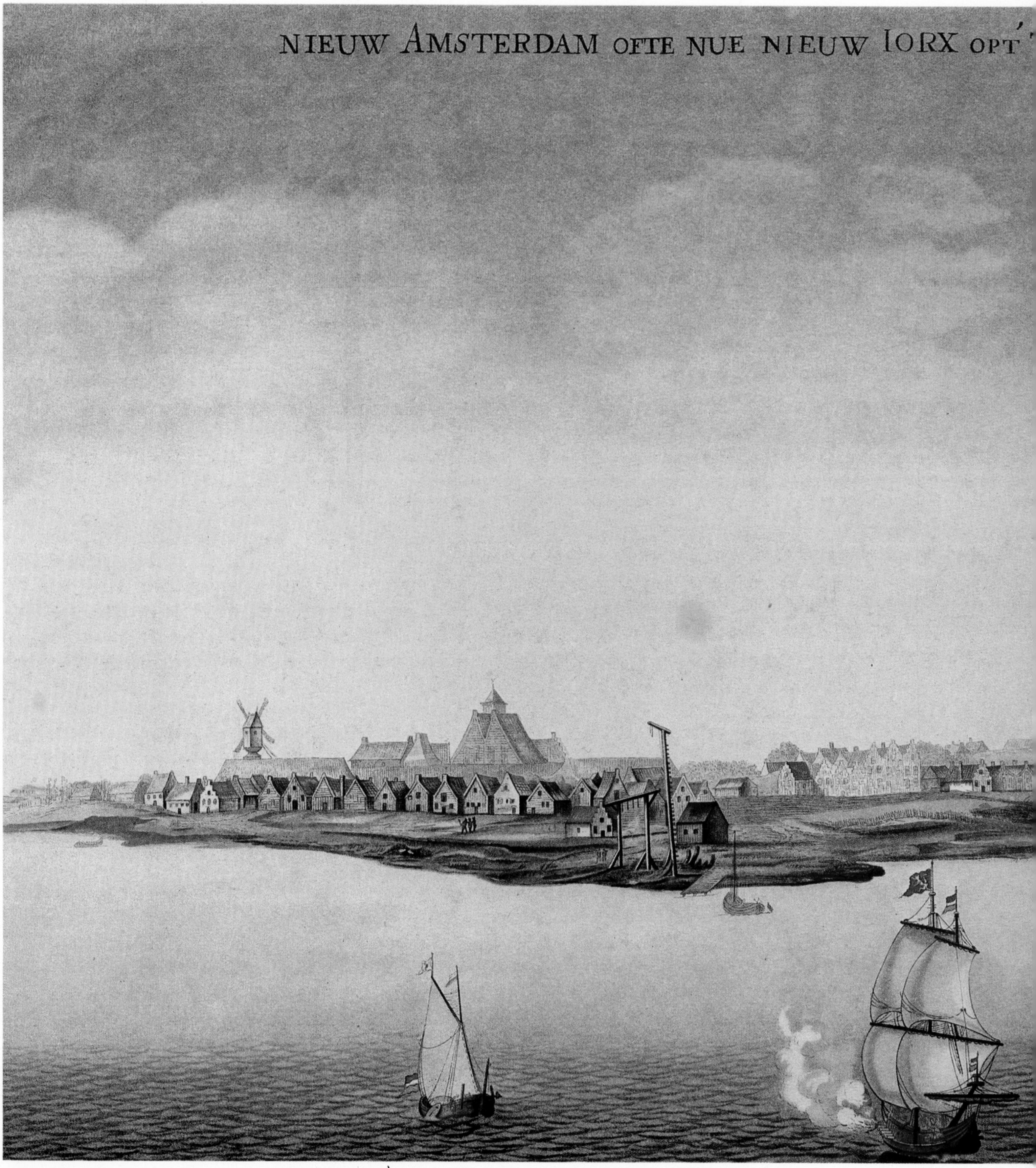
NIEUW AMSTERDAM OFTE NUE NIEUW IORX OPT'

:YLANT MAN

Trading vessels call at the old Dutch West India Company wharf in New York Harbor shortly after the town was taken by the English in 1664. The settlement —identified in this Dutch watercolor as "New Amsterdam now New York on the island of Man(hattan)"—was 38 years old when its governor, Pieter Stuyvesant, under pressure from the residents, surrendered to a fleet of English ships without even firing a shot.

voke and outrage the Dutch until they declared war; the King could then disown the responsibility.

In November 1663 the Royal African Company sent out an expedition to West Africa under Captain Robert Holmes, who set sail in the King's 40-gun ship the *Jersey*. Holmes was a wild, black-haired Anglo-Irishman who had risen from the ranks of the Royalist army under Prince Rupert's command in the Civil War and had remained the Prince's companion ever since. He was well-known as a bold and quarrelsome adventurer, one who could be trusted to do whatever was necessary to stir up a fight. And generally he won it. Sir William Coventry, one of the company's directors, called him "a man of an understanding fitt to make a warre, and a courage to make it good."

Now in the employ of the Royal African Company, he did what was expected of him—and more. His instructions were to assist in "protecting and promoting the Interests of the Royal Company, which is the sole end of your present voyage." In general he was to maintain the right of the company to trade where it pleased on the African coast, and he was specifically empowered "to kill, take, sink or destroy such as shall oppose you and to send home such shipps as you shall soe take." William Coventry, who wrote the orders, described them as "pretty bold." But they were not half so bold as the man who carried them.

Impatient to begin his campaign against the Dutch, Holmes could not wait until he reached the Gold Coast, where, as Coventry said, "It was intended by the Company the game should begin." Instead, on December 27, 1663, he seized a 300-ton West Indiaman outward-bound near the Cape Verde Islands, more than 600 miles north of the Gold Coast. Holmes next commenced shooting at a Dutch fort on Goree Island that served as headquarters for Dutch interests along the entire coast. To his undoubted surprise, after a token fight the Dutch governor sent out a boat with a white flag.

It was so absurdly easy that it was almost an embarrassment. "If I go beyond my instructions," Holmes wrote to Coventry, "I hope you and the rest of the Royall Company will mediate for mee." Whereupon he went on down the coast—committing outrage after outrage against the Dutch, and in a royal ship. The Dutch had built forts at the mouths of the major rivers to serve as refuges for the Dutch traders in case the local tribes turned angry. The forts were not designed to withstand bombardment from a ship. The men who manned them were mercenary soldiers or company agents, demoralized and lonely on that steaming, sickly coast, and unwilling to sacrifice their lives for their employers' property.

One by one the Dutch forts surrendered. Holmes sent some of his captives home to the Netherlands and released or pressed the rest. He helped himself to the products of their trade and left in each fort a few soldiers and Royal African Company agents.

Nor did Holmes face much resistance at sea. For some inexplicable reason, the Dutch had neglected to provide formidable escorts for their lightly armed merchantmen engaged in West African trade. Perhaps they felt that their dominant position was beyond challenge; perhaps they were simply being parsimonious. In any event, the *Jersey* was like a fox in a hen run. Holmes chased and boarded Dutch ships, divided his men among them, pressed captured seamen into service to fill out his crews and built up a fleet of his own in the finest of piratical styles. He justified his actions in reports home with spurious tongue-in-cheek tales of Dutch insolence and treachery. Starting with his single ship, the *Jersey*, by March 25, 1664, he had at least eight in company when in April he decided to attack two large Dutch forts.

From now on he was to find the going rougher. Cape Coast Castle was one of two forts that stood less than eight miles apart on the Gold Coast, both on the sites of 15th Century Portuguese settlements that had fallen to the Dutch. The second was Elmina Castle. Together they harbored 200 Dutchmen, more than 30 African warriors and several dozen 6-pounder guns. Scattered between and beyond the Dutch forts were English, Danish and Swedish trading settlements. The Dutch tolerated these rivals because they were relatively few in number, perhaps 100 all told, but there was no love lost between the men secure in the forts and those on the outside exposed to all the dangers of the wild continent.

Holmes brought his fleet to anchor a few miles up from Elmina and sent a letter in a canoe to the Dutch governor. In it he complained of injuries done by the Dutch to the English company. It was his usual device to provide some excuse for what he intended to do. He also recruited the help of everyone he could from the shore—the English and Scandinavian traders and a crowd of tribesmen led by a sympathetic chief whom the English called John Cabissa. The Dutch reply was vague and noncommittal and did not satisfy Holmes. He took five of his ships in line ahead and sailed as close as he could to nearby Cape Coast Castle. Each of the vessels fired broadsides at it as they tacked to and fro.

But the shots did no visible damage to the stout stone walls of the fort, and the shallows extended too far offshore for the fleet to move into much closer range. So Holmes began to put men and guns ashore. It was a tricky business to land the guns—6- and 12-pounders—from boats and canoes, and one was lost in the surf. The landing took several days, but in the end Holmes had a half-dozen guns trained on the landward side of the fort, backed by about 100 Europeans and 30 Africans.

Still it was no good. His impromptu army was a motley gang, many of whom, no doubt, were beachcombers and castaways who had turned up to see the excitement but not to take any risks. While the Africans waited, armed with nothing but their own knives and spears, the Europeans fired the guns at the safest possible range, and Holmes observed to his

The Dutch Boare Diſſected, or a Deſcription of HOGG-LAND.

A *Dutch man* is a Luſty, Fat, two Legged Cheeſe-Worm: A Creature, that is ſo addicted to Eating Butter, Drinking fat Drink, and Sliding, that all the World knows him for a ſlippery Fellow. An *Hollander* is not an *High-lander*, but a *Low-lander*; for he loves to be down in the Dirt, and *Boar*-like, to wallow therein.

THe *Dutch* at firſt,
When at the worſt,
The *Engliſh* did relieve them:
They now for thanks,
Have play'd baſe Pranks
With *Engliſhmen* to grieve them.
A Thoſe Spider-Imps,
As big as Shrimps,
Doe lively Repreſent,
How that the States
Spin out their Fates
Out of their Bowels vent.
B The *Indian* Ratt
That runs in at
The Mouth of Crocodile,
Eates his way through,
And ſhews well how
All Nations they beguile.
C The Monſtrous Pig,
With Vipers Big,
That Seven-headed Beaſt,
Shews how they ſtill,
Pay good with ill
To th' *Engliſh* and the Reſt.
The Vipers come
Forth of the Wombe,
With death of their ownMother:
Such are that Nation,
A Generation,
That riſe by fall of Other.
D One of the Rout
Was Whipt about
Our Streets for telling lyes:
More of that Nation
Serv'd in ſuch Faſhion
Might be for Forgeries.
E Their Compaſs is
An *Holland* Cheeſe,
To ſteer a Cup of Ale-by:
The Knife points forth
Unto the North
The Needle theſe Worms ſail-by.

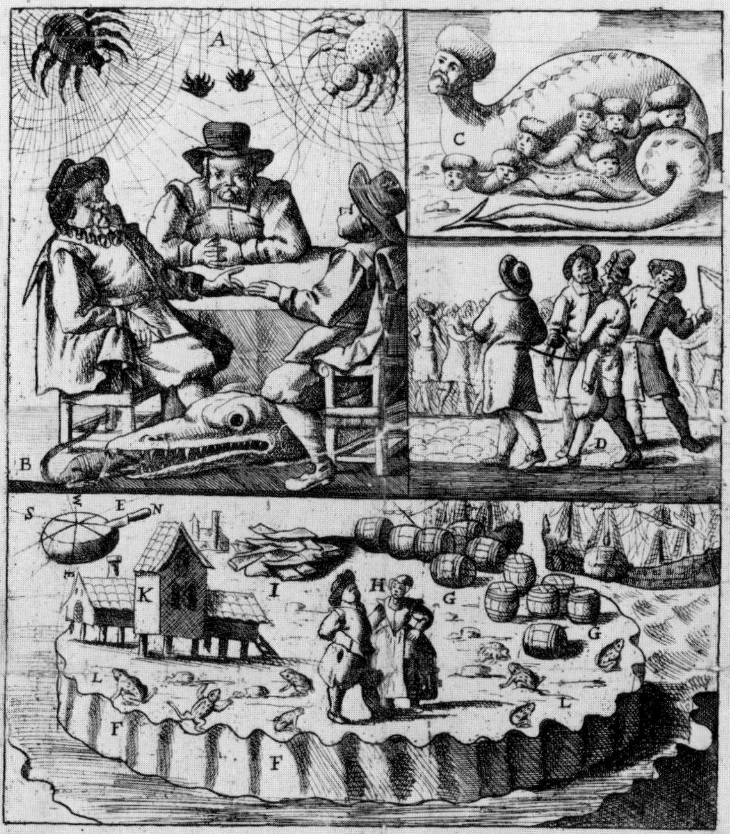
A
B
C
D
S E N
K
I
H
G
L
F

F Their Quagmire Iſle
('Twould make one ſmile)
In Form lyes like a Cuſtard:
A Land of Bogs
To breed up Hogs,
Good Pork with *Engliſh* Muſtard.
G If any asks,
What mean the Casks?
'Tis Brandy, that is here:
And Pickle-Herring,
(Without all Erring:)
'Tis neither Ale nor Beere.
H Thoſe Two you ſee,
That yonder bee
Upon the Bog-Land Walking;
Are Man and Wife,
At wofull Strife
About laſt Night's work talking.
He Drinks too long;
Shee gives him Tonguè,
In Sharp, hot-ſcolding Pickle,
With Oyle ſo glib
The ſame for Tib,
Her tipling man to Tickle.
I Spin all Day,
You Drink away
More then I get by Wheeling:
I doe by part,
Sayes he, Sweet Heart,
For I doe come home Reeling.
I The *Holland* Boare,
Hath Stock-Fiſh ſtore,
As good as can be eaten:
And ſuch they are,
As is their Fare,
Scarce good till ſoundly beaten.
K Their State-Houſe ſuch is,
It ſtands on Crutches,
Or Stilts, like ſome old Creeple:
L Frogs in great Number
Their Land doth Cumber,
And ſuch-like Croaking People.

An English broadsheet, in the form of a ditty that characterized the Dutch as a nation of fat hogs—complete with illustrations keyed by initials to each of the verses—typifies propaganda published amidst the rising clamor for renewed war in 1664. For their part, the Dutch responded by strengthening their already powerful navy. Seeing that war was inevitable, Pepys wrote, "We have put one another by each other's dalliance past a retreat."

fury that five out of six of their shots were missing the castle entirely. The Dutch fired back from time to time, with equal ineffectiveness.

The desultory duel went on for at least a fortnight. Holmes grew more and more impatient. All he needed was someone to open a breach. The African chief, John Cabissa, turned the scales at last. He enlisted a second chief who, according to Holmes, was "very earnest to storm the castle." Encouraged by the arrival of new black allies, the traders moved their guns forward to point-blank range. Holmes raised anchor and made sail to bring his ships in line for the final assault. But just as the attack was about to begin, a white flag was hoisted on the castle roof. The pragmatic Dutch saw the hopelessness of their position and surrendered.

A castle that could stand so long was really a prize worth having. Holmes left 50 men to garrison it. By then he was too shorthanded to try his luck at attacking Elmina too. But no matter. He sailed for home with his task

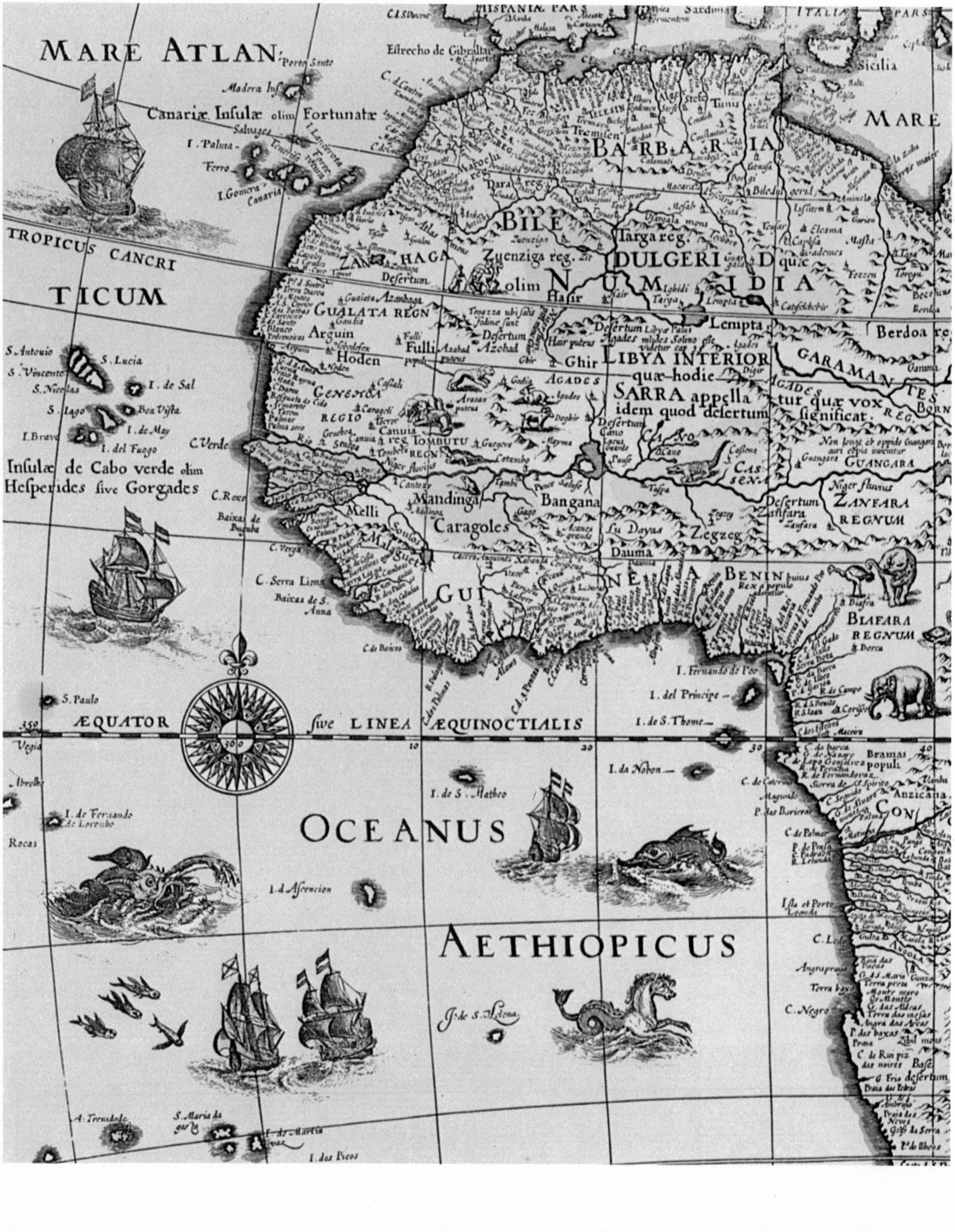
MARE ATLANTICUM
Canariæ Insulæ olim Fortunatæ
TROPICUS CANCRI
Insulæ de Cabo verde olim Hesperides sive Gorgades
Estrecho de Gibraltar
BARBARIA
BILEDULGERID
NUMIDIA
LIBYA INTERIOR quæ hodie SARRA appellatur quæ vox idem quod desertum significat.
GUALATA REGN
Zuenziga reg.
Targa reg.
Lempta
Berdoa
GARAMANTES
AGADES
TOMBUTU REGN
Mandinga
Caragoles
Melli
Bangana
Zegzeg
ZANFARA REGNUM
GUANGARA
GUINEA
BENIN
BIAFARA REGNUM
C. Verde
C. Serra Liona
ÆQUATOR sive LINEA ÆQUINOCTIALIS
I. de S. Thome
I. del Principe
I. Fernando de Poo
OCEANUS AETHIOPICUS
I. d Ascencion
I. de S. Matheo
CONGO
ANGOLA
Sicilia
MARE

*The capes and rivers of the fabled Gold
Coast of West Africa fill a highly detailed
1660 map by Amsterdam cartographer
Willem Blaeu, while tricolor-bearing Dutch
merchantmen ply the offshore waters
undisturbed. The fact was that in this year
West African trade was bitterly
contested by an English company that was
expressly chartered to seize and possess
gold mines, and to protect English traders
and their cargoes on the Guinea coast.*

*The agent of English aggression against
the Dutch in Africa was Robert Holmes, a
Navy captain of a wild and piratical
nature. A few months after arriving on the
Guinea coast, he wrote to his superiors
in London: "You have now all the trade in
your owne hands from Cape de Verd to
the Gould Coast . . . being the most
considerable trade in Christendome. I hope
you will take a resolution to keepe it."*

accomplished. One of Holmes's officers wrote that by his "bounty and
courage" he had "made soe perfect a conquest of this whole coast that
nothing but want of men hinders our intire possession."

Upon Holmes's arrival in England on January 9, 1665, the King and the
Royal African Company acted out an elaborate charade. Scarcely had
Holmes landed his treasure—a large quantity of gold plus exotic animal
hides and ivory "elephants' teeth"—than he was clapped into the Tower
of London on charges of having grossly exceeded his orders. In addition,
he was accused of having embezzled substantial amounts of loot. The
embezzlement charge was ludicrous; everyone would have been astonished had he not seen to his own nest. As for the charge of exceeding
orders, that was "a matter of jest," as Pepys put it.

Until their devious scheme of provoking the Dutch into war had succeeded, the King and the Royal African Company had to make it appear
that Holmes had acted on his own and was in disgrace. Thus if the Dutch
struck back, England could pose in the eyes of Europe as the injured
party. And the English made certain that the Dutch would strike back by
failing to return any of the ill-gotten goods Holmes had brought back.

The Dutch reacted to the fiasco in West Africa with profound anger. The
Dutch Navy was ordered to gird for war, and additional Naval taxes
levied on the provinces were paid without demur. The States-General
demanded a punitive expedition to avenge Holmes's blatant attacks on
the African posts—an operation that the Navy was pleased to mount.

In command was the country's premier admiral, 58-year-old Michiel de
Ruyter, who, like Tromp, was a lifelong seaman and a veteran in naval
combat. He had gone to sea at the age of 11 as a boatswain's boy, had been
made a captain in his late twenties and was named a rear admiral at 37.
He had participated in the actions against Spain and in the incessant
fight against pirates and privateers of all kinds. During the first war
against the English, his flagship *Lam* had been so damaged in the July
1653 battle off Scheveningen that she had to be towed home.

Like Tromp also, he was very much the common man, which endeared
him to his crews. An English diplomat, Sir William Temple, observed,
"Admiral de Ruyter I never saw in clothes better than the commonest sea
captain, nor with above one man following him, nor in a coach."

In August 1664 Johan de Witt ordered de Ruyter to sea with a fleet of
eight major men-of-war. His orders were to recapture the fallen forts and
set the Dutch African trade on its feet again. Said and done. One by one
the river-mouth forts that Holmes had taken were retaken—for the English agents and traders who occupied them were no more eager than the
Dutch had been to die in their defense. The only fort de Ruyter failed to
recapture was Cape Coast Castle; the English had reinforced the castle,
and the Dutch lacked the cooperation of the Africans in the area.

In the Netherlands, fury with the English continued to mount, until at
last on February 22, 1665, the States-General obliged Charles and the
Royal African Company by formally declaring war. The English scheme
had succeeded exactly as planned. Robert Holmes was immediately released from prison, pardoned for any and every offense he had committed, and was appointed to command the 52-gun *Revenge*.

"The war," Pepys wrote, "is begun: God give a good end to it."

The fire ship: a triumph of the incendiary's art

It was a characteristic of the 17th Century naval wars that wooden men-of-war, though they might be horribly battered, only rarely were sunk by gunnery. But they could be burned—and thus were developed the devilish little fire ships that accompanied the fleets in combat. A fire ship could not fight in the main battle. But in the hands of experts, and at the cost of its own destruction, it could administer the *coup de grâce* to an already damaged man-of-war.

Fire had been a weapon at sea from ancient times and it gained great favor in the late 16th Century when the English successfully employed crude unmanned fire ships against the Spanish Armada. By the mid-17th Century the technique had been so refined that specially equipped and manned fire ships were able to cling to their victims until both were consumed by the flames.

The Dutch fire ships in particular were a triumph of the incendiary's art, as can be seen opposite and on the following pages. The Dutch started with a small, expendable vessel, often a moderately fast ship called a *fluyt,* and substantially modified her for the mission. It took a skilled application of engineering and chemistry to make sure that the ship rapidly took fire and continued blazing with fierce intensity. Naturally, she had to be manned by a cool and dedicated crew, expert in ship handling and grappling, and it was no accident that they were paid double the wages of ordinary Dutch seamen.

On the attack, judgment and timing were everything. Even a damaged foe might still muster enough fight to disable the vulnerable fire ship before she reached her target. Once near the enemy, fire-ship crews had to put their vessel to the torch at precisely the right moment and then hurry to escape the flames. After that they were at the mercy of enemy sharpshooters as they rowed away in their longboat.

There is no record of how many English and Dutch men-of-war were destroyed by fire ships during the two wars. But in every major battle, warships succumbed to the incendiary assaults. So terrifying were the fire ships, according to a contemporary English account, that "men leaped overboard and drowned themselves for fear of burning."

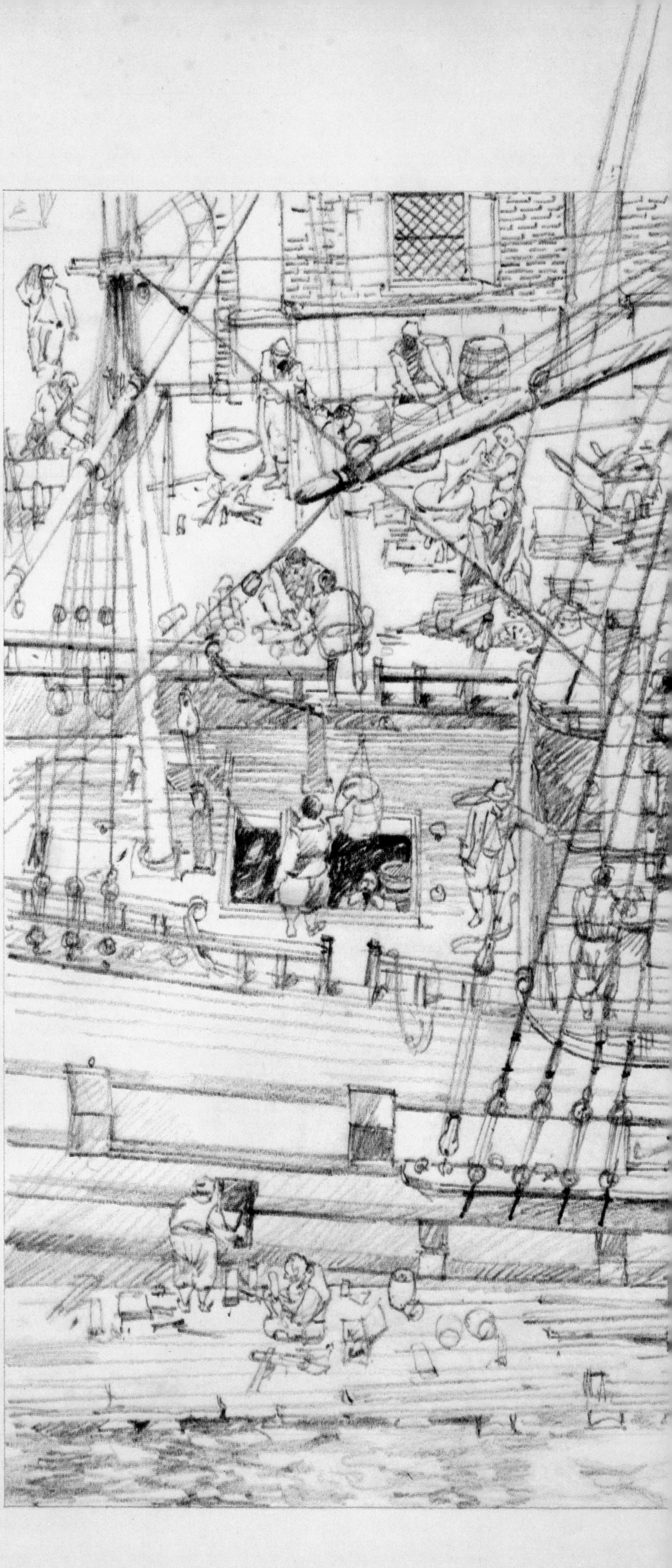

Dockside in the Netherlands, yard workers outfit an old supply ship as a fire ship. On floating platforms in the foreground, carpenters cut ventilation ports into the ship's sides, hinging their lids at the bottom so that they cannot shut once the ship is on fire. On the forecastle deck, wooden chimneys are fitted into holes cut in the deck: these served to shoot the flames from the fireroom belowdecks high into the rigging. At the main hatchway the troughs that will hold the combustibles—being prepared on the dock at upper left—are passed down to the main deck, while valuable cannon, no longer needed, are loaded onto an oxcart.

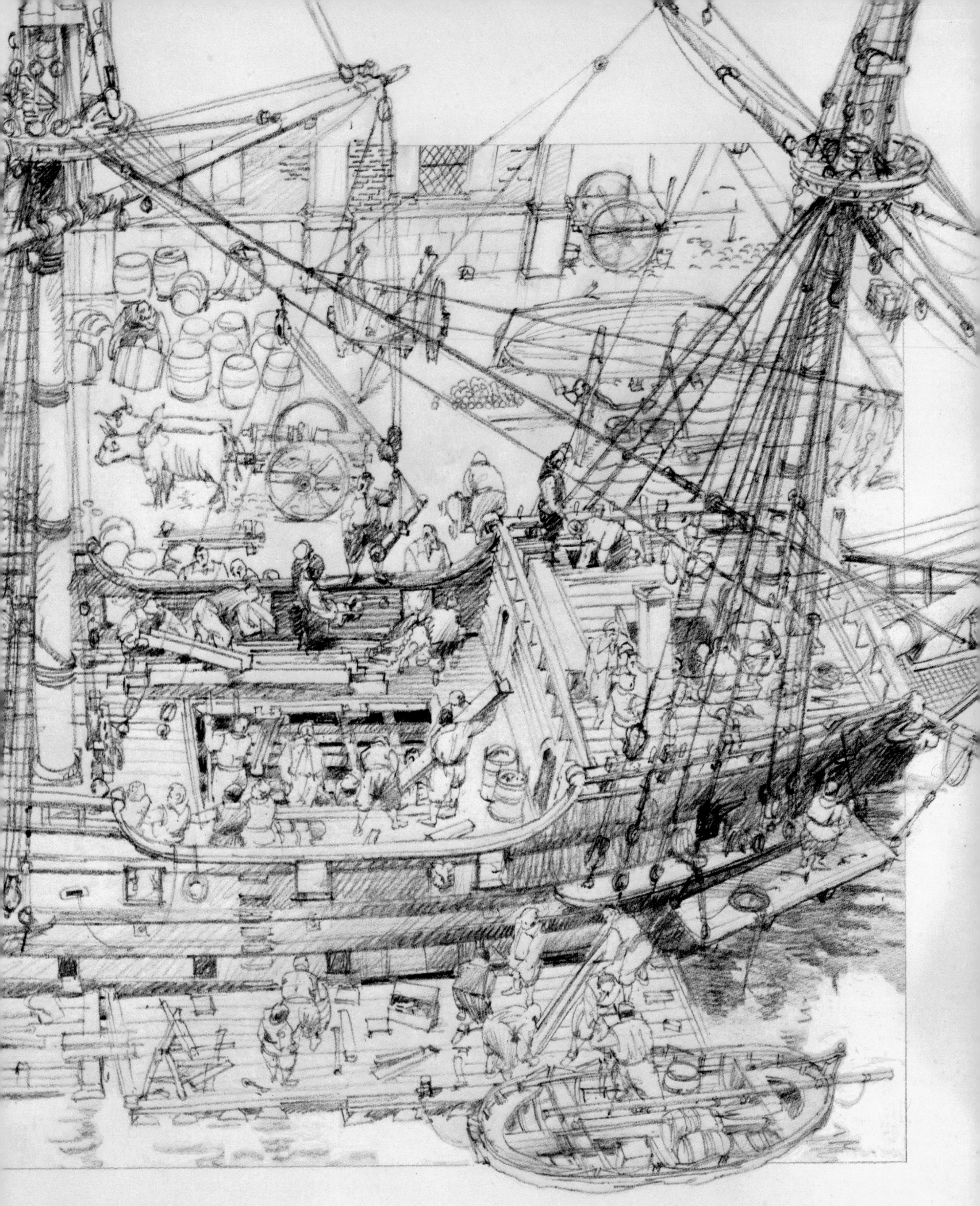

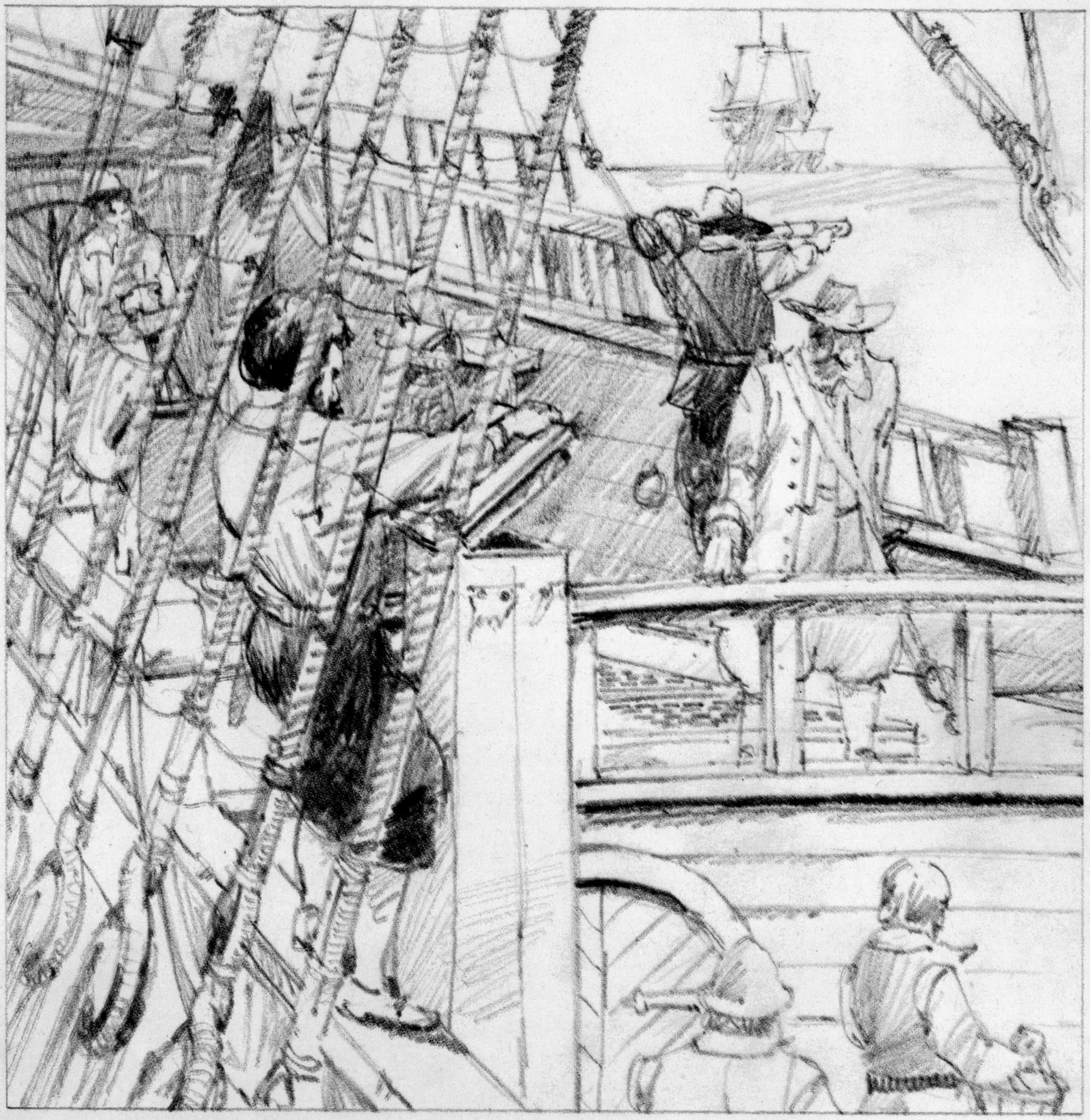

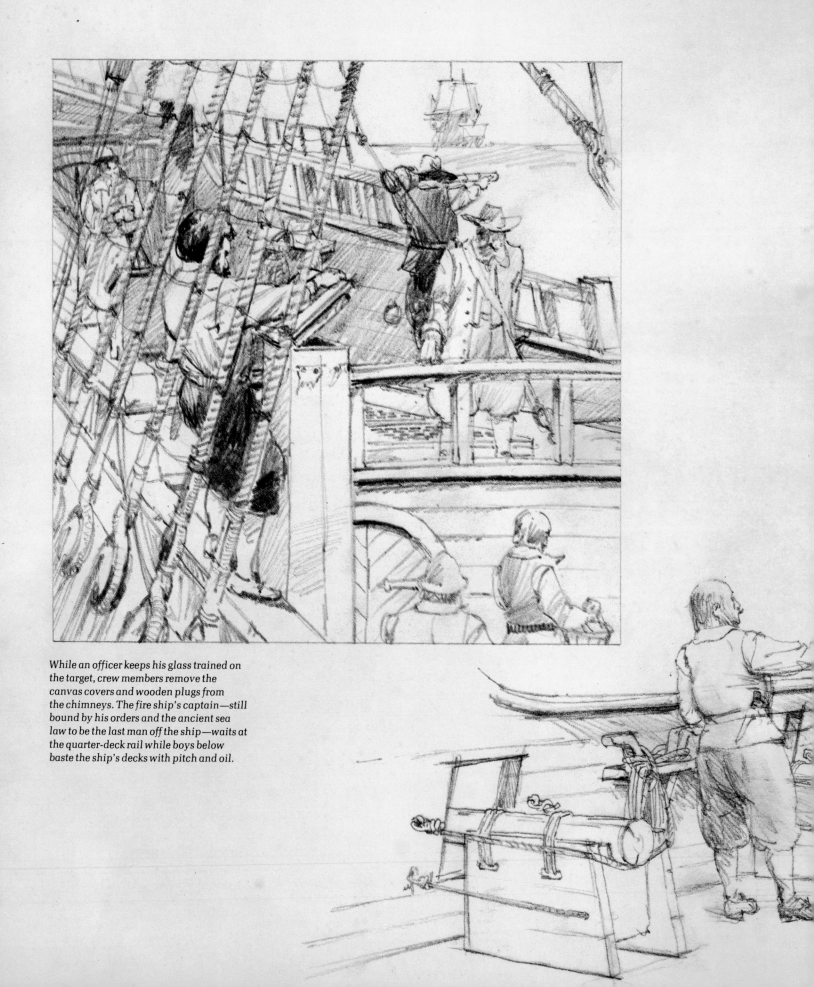

While an officer keeps his glass trained on the target, crew members remove the canvas covers and wooden plugs from the chimneys. The fire ship's captain—still bound by his orders and the ancient sea law to be the last man off the ship—waits at the quarter-deck rail while boys below baste the ship's decks with pitch and oil.

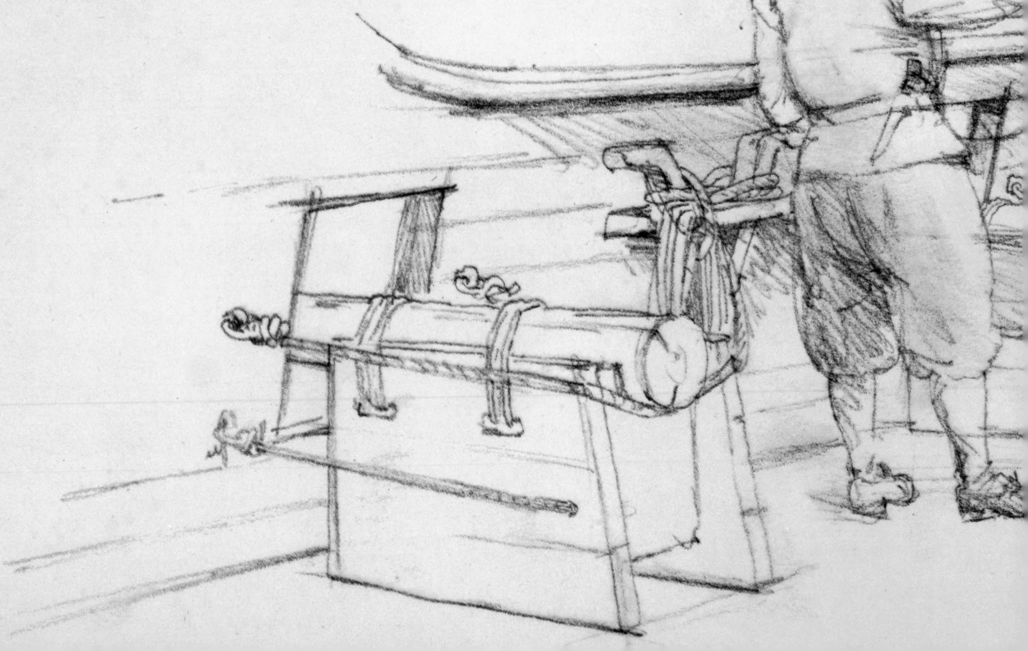

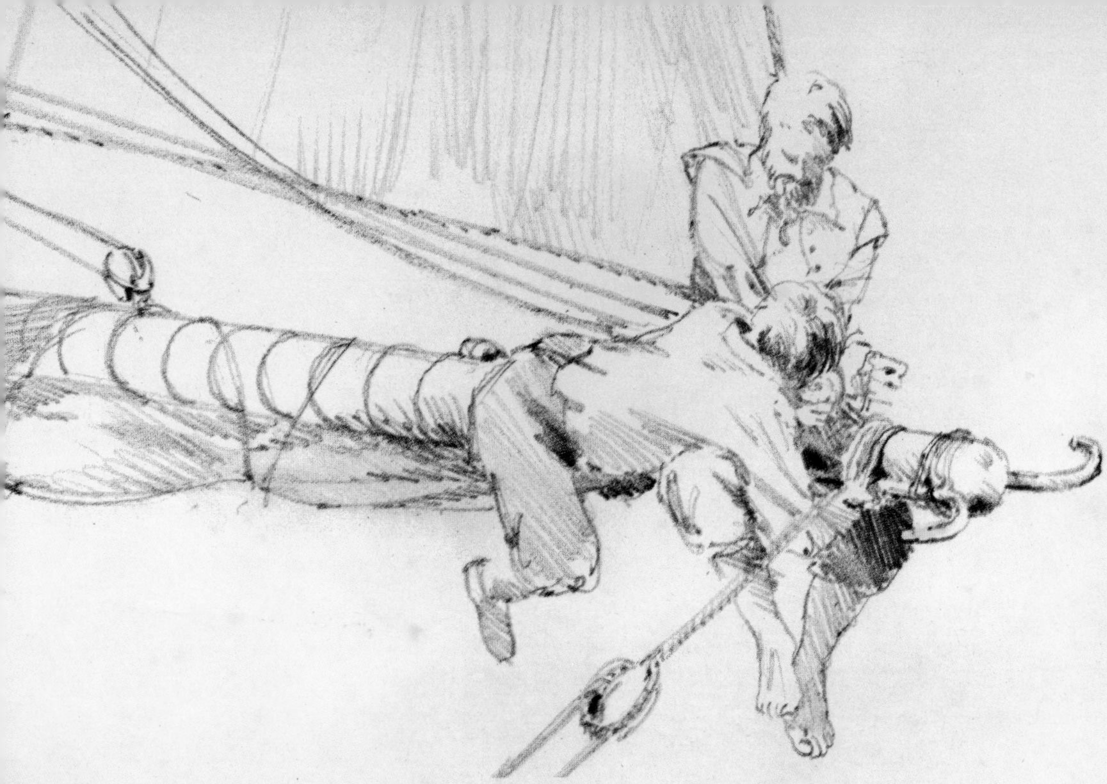

Straddling the end of the main yard, two crewmen make last-minute preparations by lashing on long sickle-like sheer hooks. The fire ship's foreyard and main yard were fitted with such hooks: when the fire ship crashed into her victim, the hooks would entangle the rigging and lock the two in an inescapable embrace.

Once the enemy warship to be attacked has been chosen, the boat in which the fire ship's crew will escape is swung overboard to be towed until needed. Two sailors unbatten the main hatch, exposing the fireroom, while three others prepare the grappling hooks that they will cast onto the enemy's deck to pull the ships together. Mounted at the gunports are wooden "cannon" to conceal the fire ship's purpose.

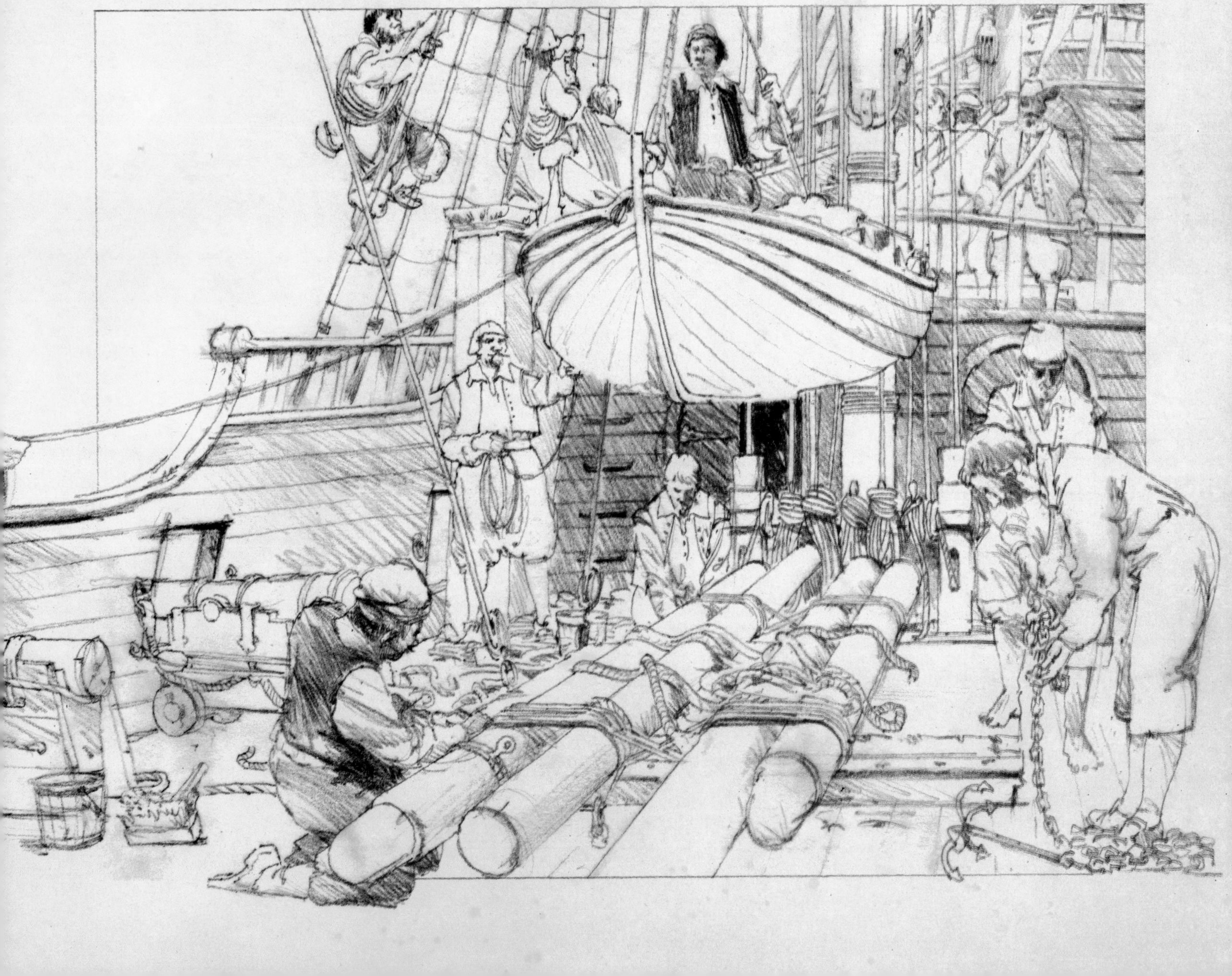

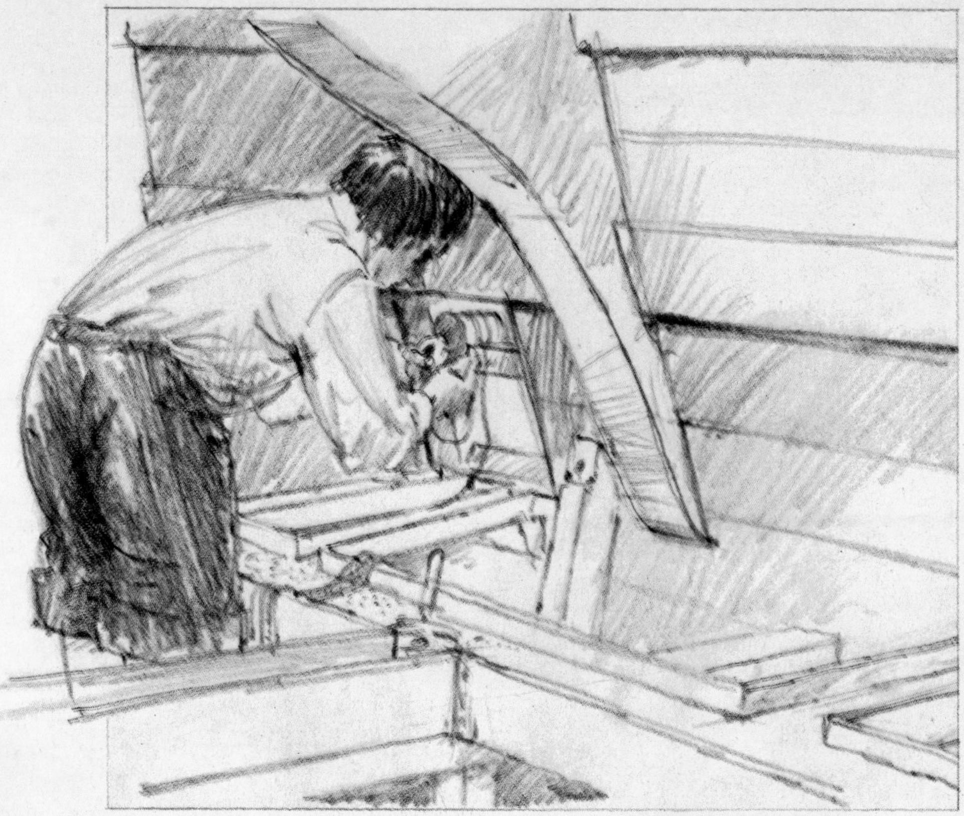

Belowdecks, the carefully strung network of pyrotechnic devices is readied. Small iron canisters filled with gunpowder have been set behind each fire port and wedged against a piece of wood fixed across the back of the port. A crewman lays a quick-burning fuse, meant to explode the canisters shortly before reaching the enemy ship, blasting open the port lids and letting in a rush of air to feed the flames.

Troughs filled with gunpowder, saltpeter, resin, sulfur and linseed oil, and packed with kindling, run the length and breadth of the fireroom. At right, a crewman strings a fuse between the troughs and a fire barrel also filled with combustible material. As the fire spreads from the troughs, it will ignite the fuse of the fire barrels, sending a spear of flame up the wooden chimneys into the sails of prey and predator alike.

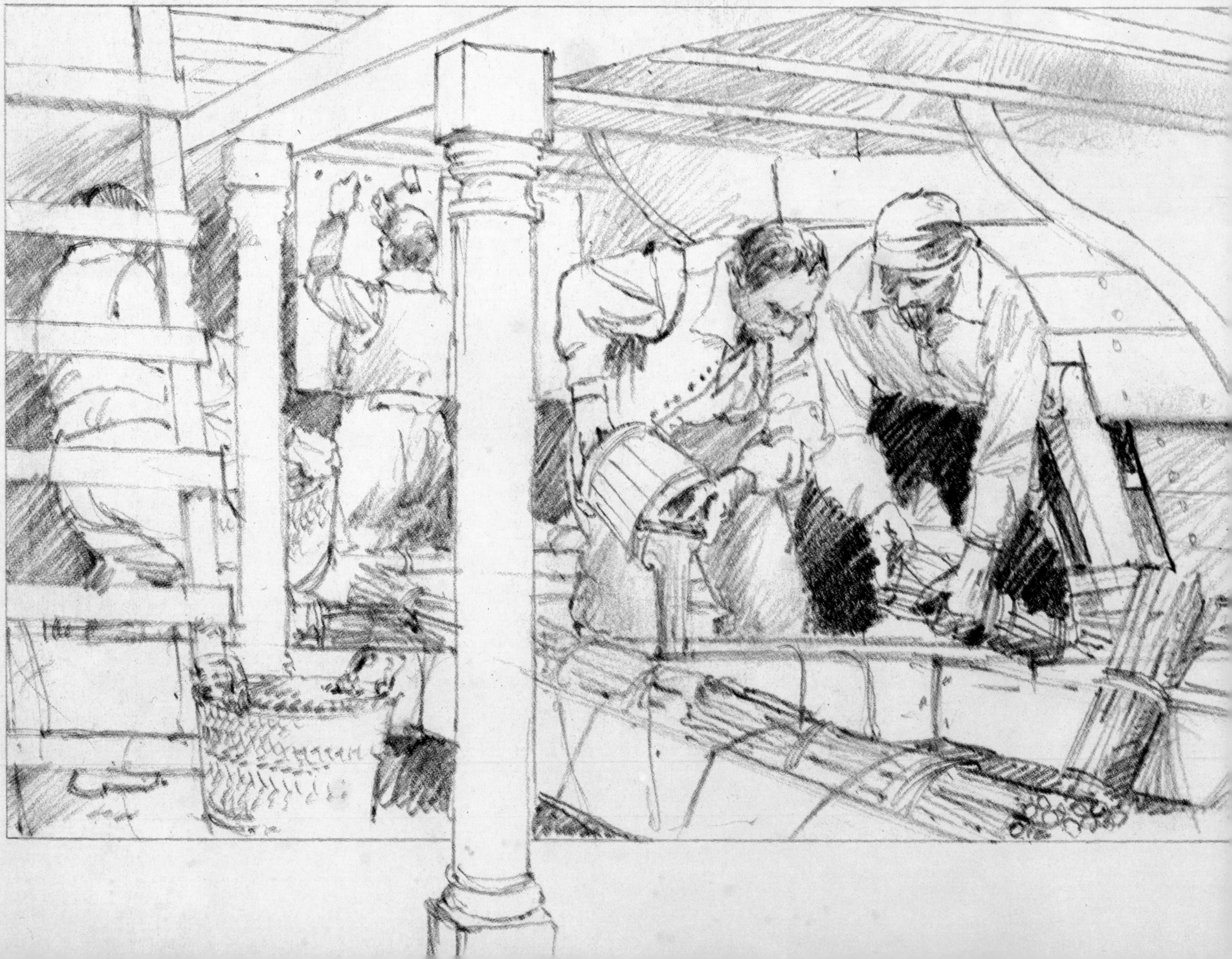

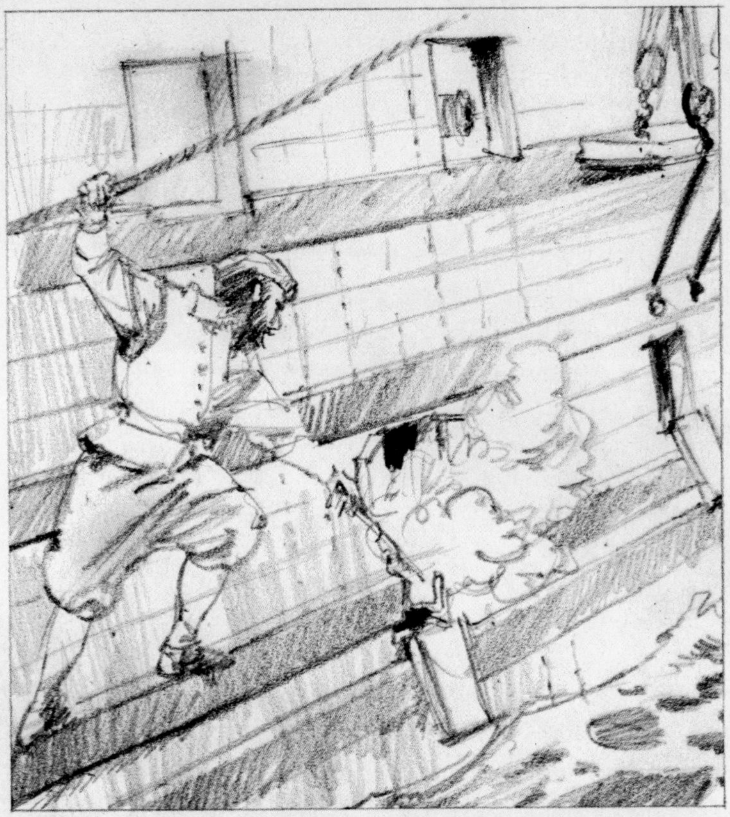

With less than 10 minutes separating the fire ship from her target vessel, a crewman balances on a wale and touches a burning fuse to the combustible mixture in the main fire trough, protruding through a specially enlarged three-door port. Once ignited, the fire will spread rapidly through the trenches of combustibles to the fire barrels and canisters positioned at the fire ports.

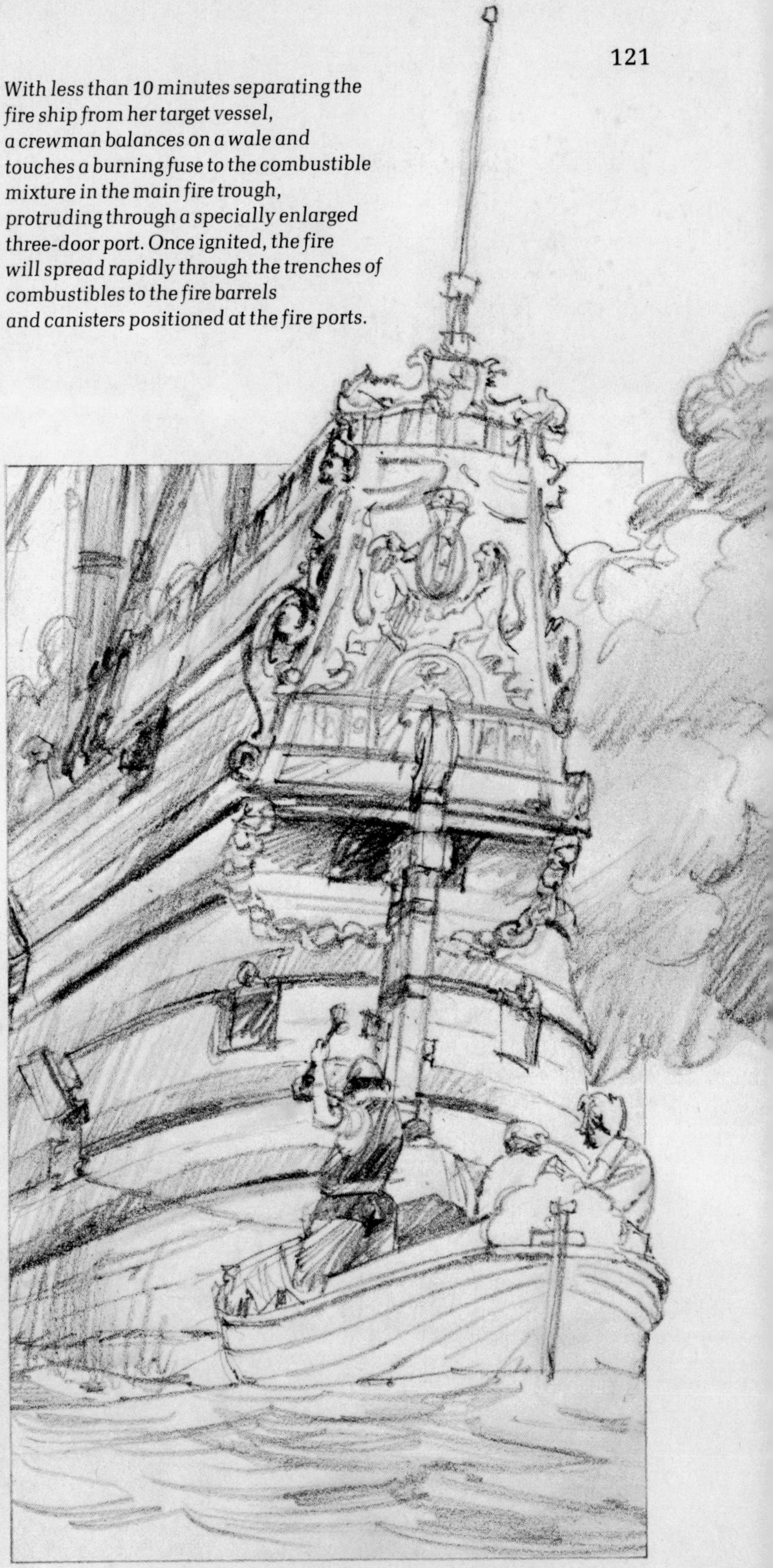

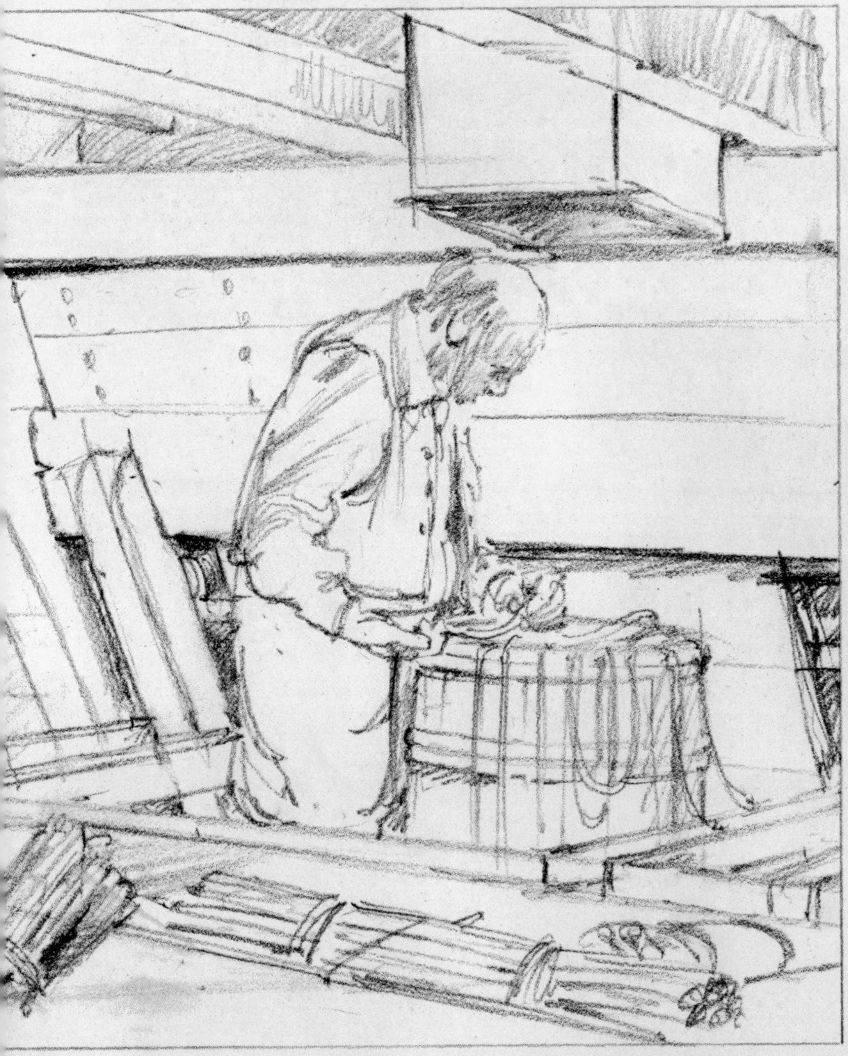

With flames already blossoming, members of the crew establish the course of the fire ship toward her victim by wedging the rudder. Wielding a heavy hammer, a sailor drives pieces of wood between the sternpost and the rudder, which will help to keep the floating fire bomb on course while foiling any attempt by the other ship's crew to board the fire ship and steer her away.

Amid the roar of blazing canvas and the grinding of spar and plank, the men of the unfortunate English man-of-war work frantically to break their vessel free of the fire ship. The crew vainly attempts to push away the burning hulk with a heavy timber, called a fire boom, that protrudes from a forward gunport. Because the captain of the fire ship has nimbly brought his ship against the enemy from the windward side, the flames sweep into the sails and rigging of the grappled English vessel. As in any successful sailing maneuver, the whim of the wind is critical to the success of the fire ship's venture.

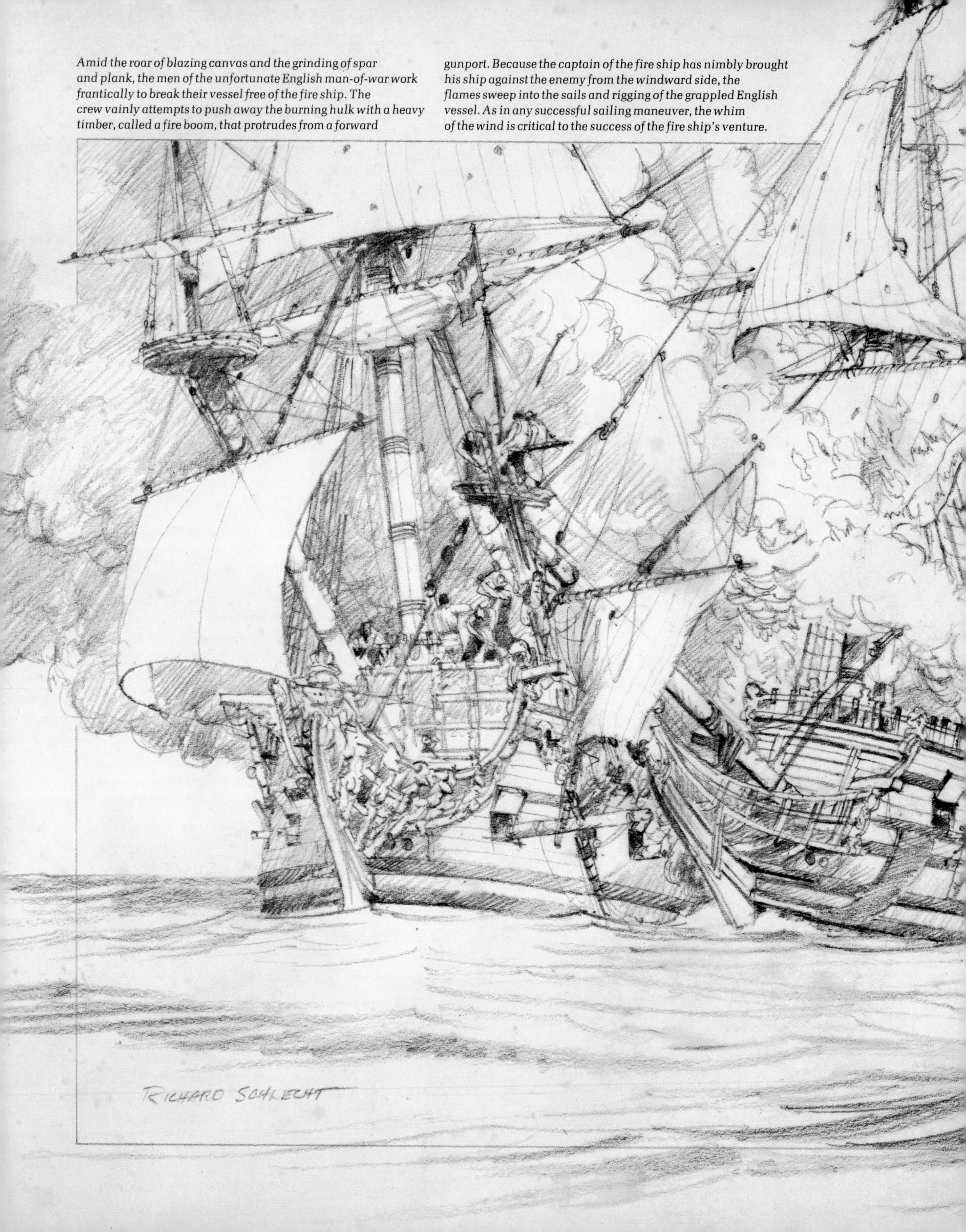
RICHARD SCHLECHT

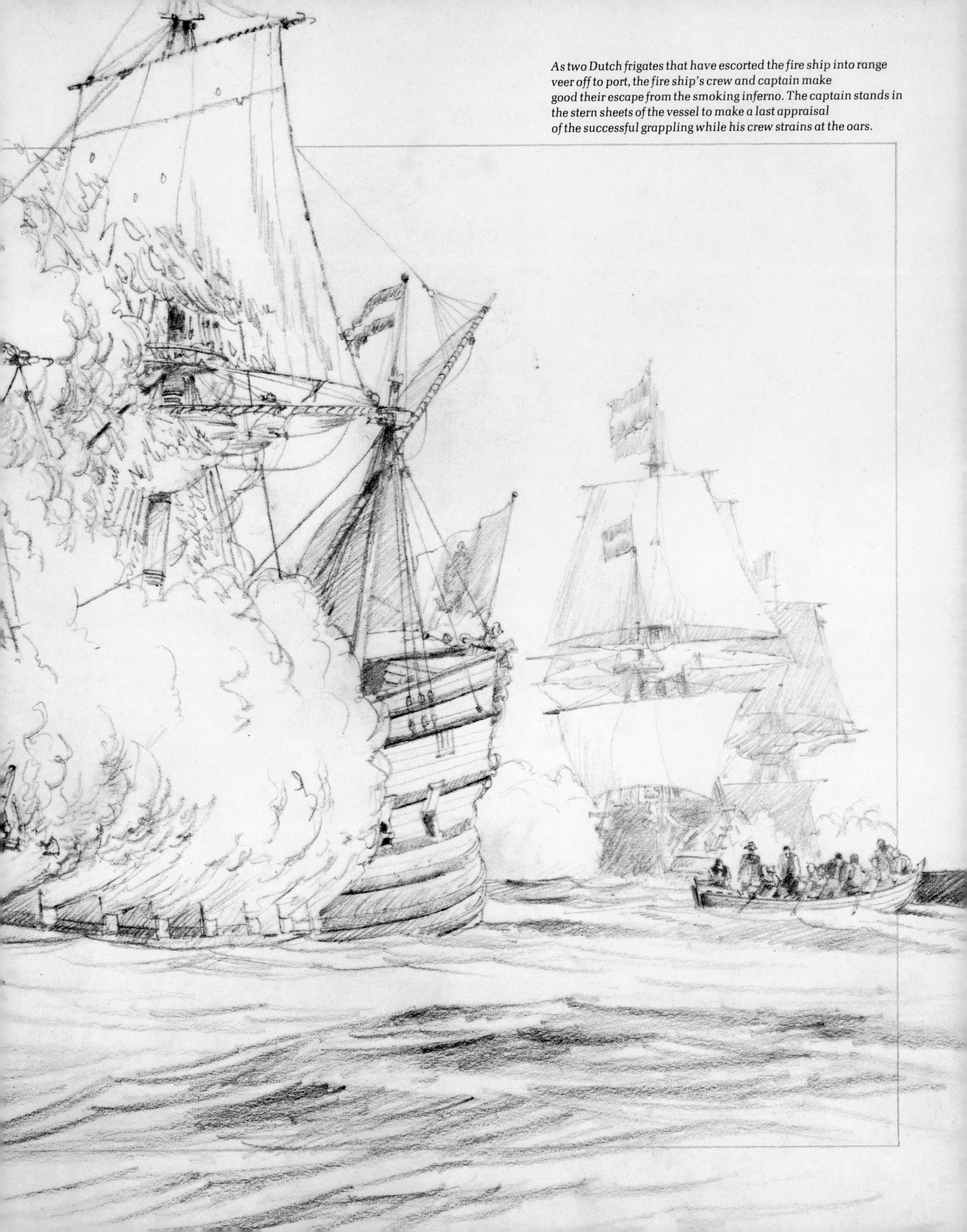

As two Dutch frigates that have escorted the fire ship into range veer off to port, the fire ship's crew and captain make good their escape from the smoking inferno. The captain stands in the stern sheets of the vessel to make a last appraisal of the successful grappling while his crew strains at the oars.

Chapter 5

"To fly is the fashion of cowards"

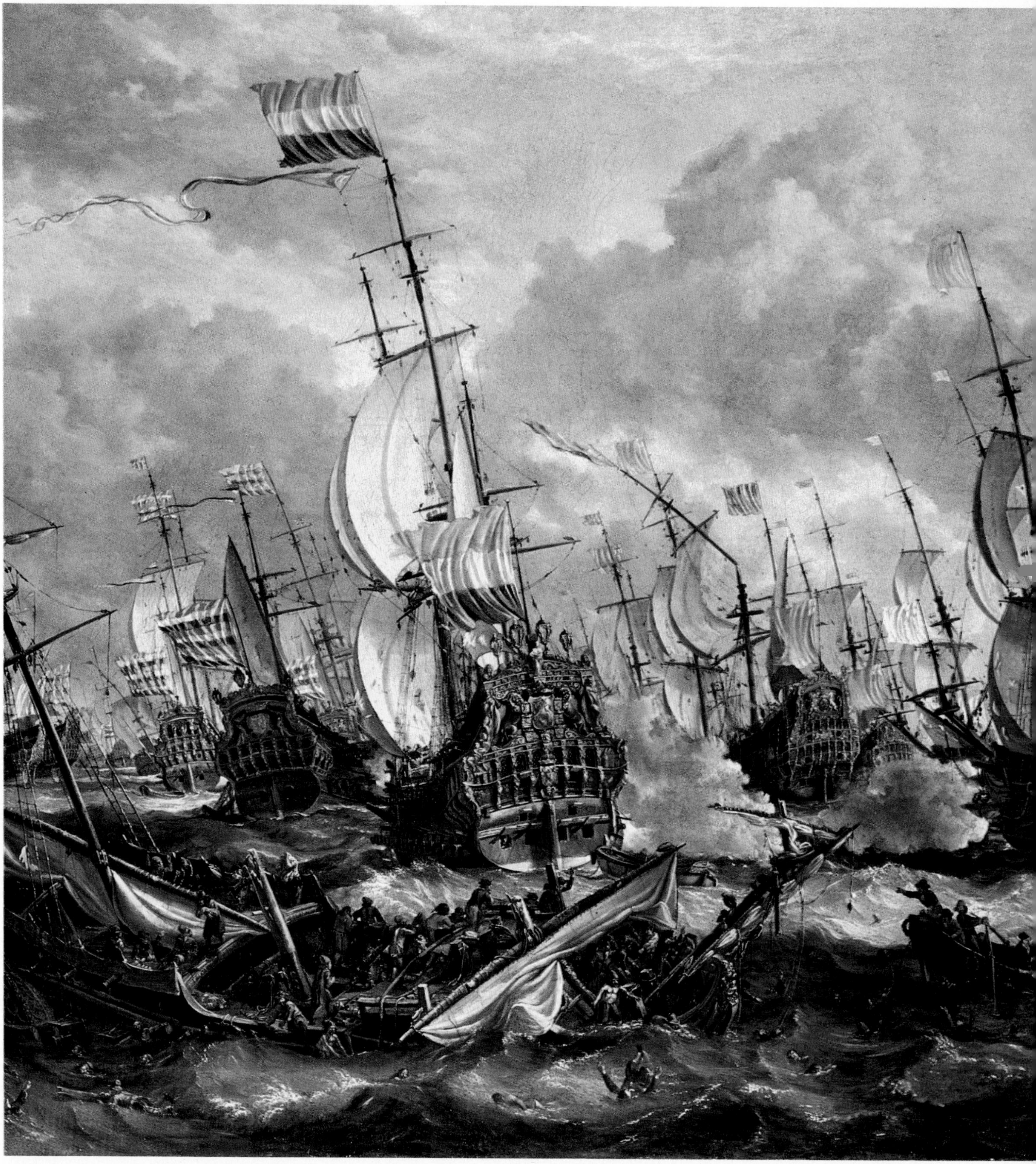

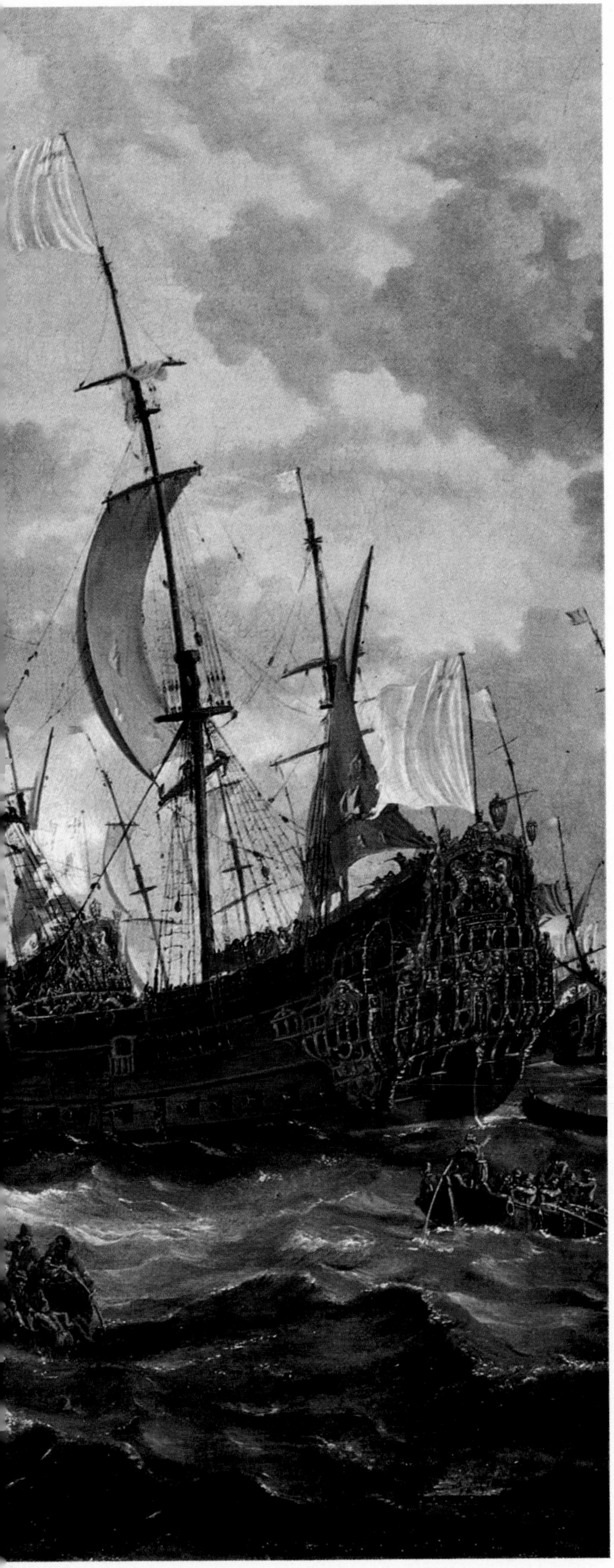

War had been declared in mid-winter, 1665. But it was early spring before the Duke of York sailed down the Thames from London in his yacht and hoisted his flag as Lord High Admiral in the *Royal Charles*, and it was May before the opposing fleets were finally at sea. The feisty Dutch were just as willing as the English to have another trial of strength, but neither side was in any great hurry to commence hostilities. They both had superb new fleets, much improved since the previous war a decade past, and they both had infinitely clearer ideas of battle tactics. But neither fleets nor tactics could be properly tested in changeable stormy weather; and in this war, unlike the first, no battles would be fought in winter, with its howling gales. There was a tacit agreement that winter battles were to be avoided.

The Dutch sent forth a formidable armada: 103 men-of-war with 30 fire ships and dispatch boats, manned by 21,631 men and mounting 4,869 guns. They would have preferred to wait for Michiel Adriaenszoon de Ruyter, who was the only officer all the disputatious admirals were willing to serve under, but this valiant was still in Africa, where he was attempting to retake the trading posts captured by Captain Robert Holmes. In his absence the Dutch appointed as commander in chief Jacob van Wassenaer, Lord of Obdam. He was a man of wide experience, second only in seniority to de Ruyter. He wore his flag on the *Eendracht*, a mighty man-of-war mounting 76 guns. Whatever it was that had caused the Dutch to build small in the previous war apparently no longer applied. For two other ships from the province of Holland had 76 and 78 guns—and most of the vessels in the fleet carried from 50 to 60 guns.

On June 11, 1665, off the east coast of England at Lowestoft, this vast array of sail was sighted hull down on the horizon by Captain James Lambert, who was out on patrol in the *Happy Return*. Lambert fired a cannon and let his topgallant sheets fly as a signal—for at anchor inshore of him was the entire might of the English fleet. "They all weighed," an eyewitness wrote, "and stood off to the Southeast, the wind East North East, fair weather."

Laconic words, but they evoke a scene of nautical splendor: for there, close to the low-lying shore on that summer's day, were 137 ships that simultaneously, in the hands of 21,006 men, weighed anchor and made sail on the signal of the Lord High Admiral. And it was no disorganized mass of shipping, as war fleets had been in the past. For the first time, an order of battle had been issued that gave every ship in the fleet its own

Spewing death and destruction, the English and Dutch lock broadside to broadside in the Four Days' Fight of 1666. Flying a tricolor (upper left) in this contemporary painting by the Dutch artist Abraham Storck is the flagship Zeven Provincien. Opposite her at right is England's Royal Prince, while in the foreground the battered Swiftsure surrenders to a Dutch boarding party.

position in the battle line, an idea that probably originated with the Earl of Sandwich—although the order was made in the name of the Duke of York. Sandwich by this time knew much more about ships than he had when he fought as plain Edward Mountagu alongside Blake in the Mediterranean. So the fleet stood out from shore, stemming the strong tide in an orderly line ahead five miles long, with fire ships and dispatch boats taking station like pilot fish abeam the great flagships.

Prince Rupert, Charles's cousin, led the van in the 78-gun *Royal James*. The commanding Duke of York led the center squadron in the *Royal Charles*, also of 78 guns, together with Sir William Penn, who was given the new title of captain of the fleet and the new responsibility of putting the Duke's intentions into the practical terms of signals. The Earl of Sandwich in the old but still formidable 86-gun *Royal Prince*, the biggest ship in either of the fleets, led the rear squadron. Among the great ships were another 20 of 58 to 76 guns, all prototypes of the ships of the line, which in the next two centuries fought for mastery of the seas until the coming of steam. All told, the English fleet mounted 4,192 cannon, 677 fewer than the Dutch. But more of the English guns were of large caliber and long range.

Two days passed before these fearsome armadas were within gunshot. With the onshore wind, the Dutch had the advantage of the weather gauge. Obdam could have chosen his moment to bear down and attack, but he did not do it. Everyone, Dutch and English alike, was astonished that he failed to give the signal, and nobody could ever explain exactly why he waited. An English seaman offered a lower-deck theory: "They loved not to fight near our shore, lest they should have too far to run home if they should be beaten." An angry Dutch captain had a somewhat less charitable opinion: "God Almighty either took away our admiral's brains, or else He never gave him any."

Whatever the case, it soon became academic. During the night of June 12 the wind veered into the southwest, and Obdam's chance had gone. The English were now to windward.

By that time, impatience had disorganized both formations. A number of Dutch captains had broken line and were beating upwind to the enemy. The English, too, after sailing close-hauled for two days and making several tacks, were not in a strict enough order to satisfy Sandwich. "Whereas our order of battle," he wrote, "was a line, so that every ship might have his part in fighting and be clear of his friends from doing them damage, yet many of our ships did not observe it, but luffed up to windward, that we were in ranks 3, 4 or 5 broad."

In the early dawn of June 13, when the first shots were fired, the fleets were on opposite tacks. Each ship had a shot at an enemy as it passed and then ceased fire until the next appeared. The rearmost ships had to wait an interminable time to engage; the van was entirely out of action once it had cleared the enemy line. After the first pass, both fleets reversed their courses and made a second pass. There was not much wind and both lines were immensely long, so that nearly five hours elapsed between the passes, and in between, there was a full hour when all the ships were out of range and firing ceased altogether.

This was no way to fight. It consumed vast quantities of ammunition

Victorious at the Battle of Lowestoft in June 1665, James, Duke of York—later to become King James II—poses in triumph with an anchor, crown and scepter (near right). To commemorate the victory, in which he successfully employed the new line-ahead battle formation, James commissioned artist Peter Lely to paint the portraits as well of all his commanders in the fight. Three of the most senior admirals (far right) were James's cousin Prince Rupert, Edward Mountagu, first Earl of Sandwich, and George Monck, first Duke of Albemarle.

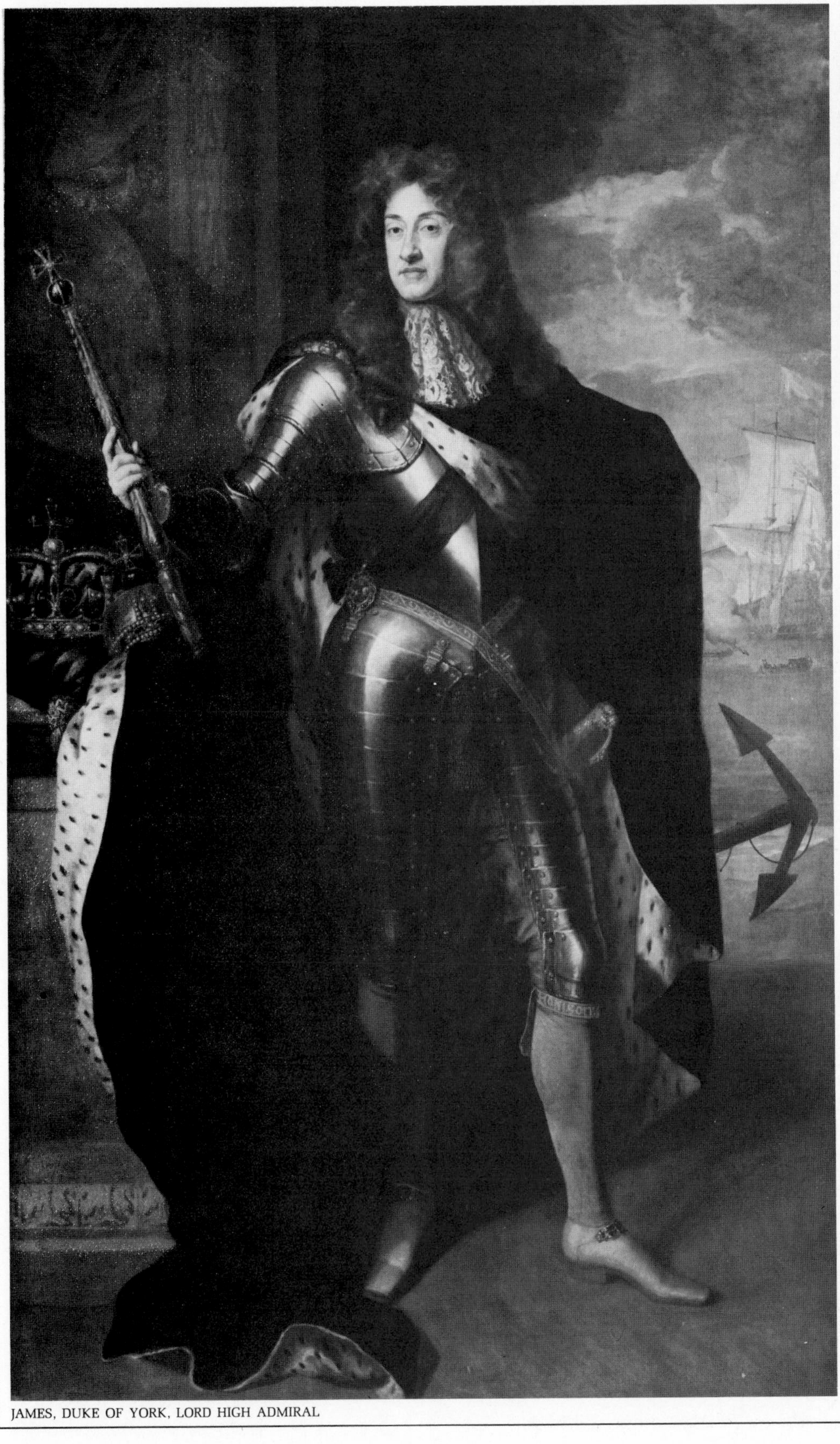

JAMES, DUKE OF YORK, LORD HIGH ADMIRAL

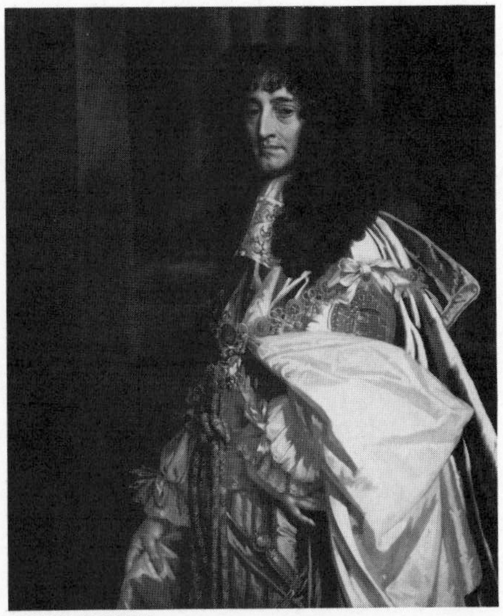

PRINCE RUPERT

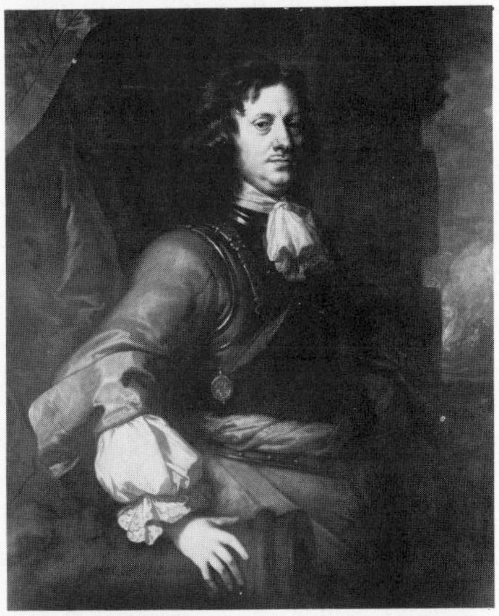

EARL OF SANDWICH

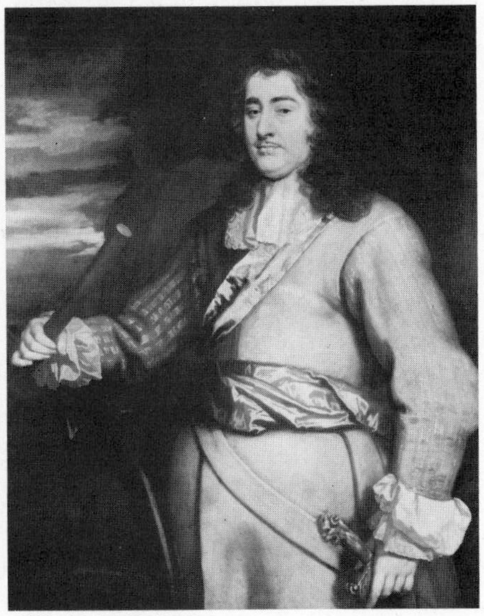

DUKE OF ALBEMARLE

and made a great deal of noise, but it might have gone on for days without reaching a conclusion. Both fleets realized what was needed, and after the second pass, the English made an attempt to get on the same tack as the Dutch were on. But in the midst of all the smoke and chaos, their maneuvers failed and another old-fashioned melee ensued. As the line tactic broke down, the admirals went hunting one another to engage in a personal duel and the squadrons dutifully following in their wake were bound to pile up in confusion.

Obdam and Sandwich themselves were the first to start an individual fight. "About two o'clock in the afternoon," Sandwich wrote, "Obdam and the *Oranje* and three or four more great ships plied me very hotly for two hours together, when His Royal Highness stretched it out ahead of me and most bravely himself entertained Obdam." On the *Royal Charles* a group of the Duke's followers stood beside him on the quarter-deck and were smashed to bits by a single flailing chain shot exactly as General-at-Sea Richard Deane had been killed in the earlier war. The Duke was drenched in their blood, and himself wounded in one hand by a flying splinter of skull.

The duel between the Duke of York and Obdam ended suddenly and terribly when the great *Eendracht* suffered a hit in her powder magazine and exploded. The blast could be heard in The Hague, some 60 miles away. Only five men were saved of her complement of 409.

Still undaunted, the Dutch fought on. The *Oranje*, a large converted East Indiaman, tried to board the Duke of York's *Royal Charles* and, as Sandwich explained, "was gallantly taken up by the *Mary* and then by the *Royal Catherine* and *Essex*." In this uneven fight the *Oranje* was captured after taking terrible losses. "An abundance of her men were killed and the ship scarce able to swim yielded, and after the men were taken out she was set on fire."

These stunning disasters started a chain reaction that could only have occurred in a Dutch fleet with its superabundance of admirals. Obdam had obviously been killed by the explosion of the *Eendracht*. Second in seniority to Obdam was a man of long experience named Jan Evertsen. But Evertsen was a Zeeland admiral, and the five admiralties had ordained for their own political reasons that if Obdam died, a junior Holland admiral named Egbert Meeusz Kortenaer should assume the command. However, Kortenaer had been mortally wounded early in the battle. He was still alive, and his ship was still flying his flag. But it was under the command of her first mate, Ate Intes Stinstra, who was in the process of pulling out of the battle. Seeing him go, Evertsen hoisted the flag of commander in chief. So did Cornelis Tromp, the great Maarten's son, who had no intention of deferring to a Zeeland commander.

Thus three ships were flying the senior flag, and nobody knew which one to follow. Most of the Dutch captains took Kortenaer's retreat as a signal to break off the battle, and the fleet fell into total confusion. They began "to turn their arses and run," as the victorious English put it.

In their haste, four Dutch ships collided in a mass and could not disentangle themselves before an English fire ship ran smartly in and put the lot to the torch. Three more Dutch ships also collided and were burned. And yet a third group of three heavily damaged ships surren-

With an evil yellow flash, the Dutch flagship Eendracht explodes in the June 1665 battle off Lowestoft, bringing an end to the fierce duel between the Eendracht and the Duke of York's Royal Charles. The blast, wrote Cornelis Tromp, a squadron commander in the fight, sent the Dutch fleet "into such a confusion that they all ran away from the enemy before the wind, and through that some ships fell foul of each other and were taken or burned by the English."

dered to Sandwich. He left them to be taken as prizes, but an overzealous fire ship, perhaps mistaking signals, ran in and burned them. "This cruel fact was much detested by us as not beseeming Christians," wrote Sandwich, who doubtless bemoaned the loss of prize money. The fire-ship captain was court-martialed for attacking ships that had already struck their flags. As darkness fell, the Dutch were in full retreat. The English formed line astern of the Duke of York in the *Royal Charles* to chase them toward their ports and fight them once more in the morning.

But the English failed to catch the Dutch again. When the day's fighting was done, the Duke went to bed, leaving Penn on deck to command the pursuit. The survivors of the Duke's personal staff were heard to remark that he had "got honour enough" and should not "venture a second time." His duchess, it appeared, had instructed the aides to see that her husband did not take too many risks. When the Duke was safely asleep, Lord William Brouncker went to Penn and announced that the Duke had ordered sail to be slackened.

Penn was surprised, but he did not waken the Duke to query the order. He carried it out, and the whole fleet astern of him had to do the same in order to keep station. The contemporary historian Bishop Gilbert Burnet wrote that "when the Duke had slept, he, upon his waking, went out upon the quarter-deck, and seemed amazed to see the sails slackened, and that thereby all hope of overtaking the Dutch was lost. He questioned Penn upon it. Penn put it upon Brouncker, who said nothing. The Duke denied he had given any such order; but he neither punished Brouncker for carrying it nor Penn for obeying it."

The consensus was that the Duke's entourage, who were far from being military men, had had enough of fighting and had lost their nerve. Without their timorous interference, the war might have ended there and then. It had already been a shattering defeat for the Dutch: they had lost at least 5,000 men, some 30 ships and three admirals. The English had lost only two ships and perhaps 800 men. The Dutch could not have survived another day of it.

In the Netherlands there were fierce vilifications. Three captains were shot; three were banished from the country; and three were publicly reduced in rank and were cashiered from the Navy. No formal charges were brought against Admiral Evertsen; but being a Zeeland admiral, he was subjected to gross indignities in Holland, culminating when he was set upon by a mob and pitched bodily into the water. Outraged, he refused to go to sea again. Cornelis Tromp expected to be named commander in chief but the position was intended for de Ruyter upon his return from Africa. Tromp was infuriated and his actions ever afterward betrayed a bitter resentment of de Ruyter.

The English commanders also fell to bickering. The Duke of York, having won the battle, retired to Hampton Court to rest on his laurels. The King appointed Sandwich and Prince Rupert as joint commanders in chief, but Rupert refused to share the command. Sandwich therefore became the sole commander.

By now it was July 27, and Sandwich sailed north in search of a Dutch East India convoy that had been reported off the coast of Norway on a circuitous route home to dodge the English. De Ruyter had entered the North Sea some six days ahead of the convoy and was sailing for the Netherlands. He arrived there on August 6 and by August 18 he was at sea again as commander in chief of the entire Dutch Navy with orders to escort the homecoming East India fleet and, if possible, to intercept the English. The two war fleets spent almost a month prowling all over the North Sea, as far north as Bergen and the Shetland Islands. Sandwich never did find de Ruyter. For "the sea is wide and fogs and nights advantageous for them to escape us by," as one of the English captains wrote regretfully. De Ruyter, however, had managed to encounter the merchant fleet and in convoy left Bergen for home, only to have his ships hopelessly scattered almost immediately by a violent northerly gale.

Following that storm, on September 13, the hard work of Sandwich and his fleet finally had some reward; in a fierce but brief battle they captured two Indiamen and four Dutch men-of-war that had been separated from the main Dutch fleet by the howling winds of the preceding days. Only the *Hector*, of 22 guns, was sunk. Having missed the bulk of the enemy convoy, Sandwich continued his search and in the following week the English fleet captured four more men-of-war, ranging from 40 to 70 guns each, and a number of merchantmen before finally deciding to return with the prizes to the Thames.

As it turned out, it was a most costly victory—both for Sandwich and for England. Sandwich should have delivered his captures to the Prize Court. Instead, he refused to wait for the tedious workings of the Prize Court, but broke open the cargoes and distributed much of the wealth among his friends and captains in the fleet. Sandwich himself boldly offloaded an immense amount of treasure onto small coasters, which took it straight to his own country estate. A week or so later, Samuel Pepys was taken aboard one of the looted Indiamen, where he saw "the greatest wealth lie in confusion that a man can see in the world. Pepper scattered through every chink, you trod upon it; and in cloves and nutmegs I walked above the knees: whole rooms full. And silk in bales, and boxes of copper-plate. As noble a sight as ever I saw in my life."

Pepys reported that seamen and officers were selling whole bags of diamonds and other gems, and himself invested in some of these ill-gotten bargains. But he got rid of them hastily enough when the affair grew into a monumental scandal.

Those who had succeeded in looting the Spanish galleon captured off Cadiz nine years before—possibly Sandwich among them—got away with it because the deed had been done quickly and quietly. The treasure simply evaporated. But this action, committed virtually in the open, was too gross even for an age inured to graft and thievery. Some people made excuses for Sandwich's behavior, including the easygoing King. In the end, however, there was such an outcry about the affair that he had to be dismissed as admiral and sent out of the country as ambassador to Spain. So England lost another high admiral. To fill this post, Prince Rupert had to be recalled. He set sail with a renewed and powerful enemy in front and an even more ominous enemy behind him: plague, the terrible Black Death that had started in April and was now ravaging London while sparing the Continent (*pages 132-133*).

At Christmastime a seaman in the fleet, Edward Barlow, wrote in his journal *(pages 89-92)*, "And the Sickness having been very fierce in London all the summer, so I thought good to send a letter to a friend at London to know of my friends' and acquaintances' health, and who were dead and who living; and in seven or eight days more I received an answer, wherein I received the bad news of my brother George being dead, and three of my uncle's children, and my mistress and master's son, and divers neighbours and acquaintances more, which was a great grief to me to hear; and I thought I should have died myself with grief."

The whole English fleet, especially the Londoners, sailed and fought that year with worry in their minds: their families were in more danger than they were themselves. London in the second half of 1665 was a city of the dead. Everybody who could afford it escaped to the countryside—or almost everybody. Samuel Pepys, unheroic by nature, was one of the few who deliberately braved the plague. He sent his wife away but remained at his post at the Navy Office—and wrote in a letter: "I have stayed in the city till above 7400 died in one week, and of them above 6000 of the plague, and little noise heard by day or night but tolling of bells; till I could walk Lombard Street and not meet twenty persons from one end to the other, and not fifty upon the Exchange; till whole families (ten and twelve together) have been swept away; till the nights (though much lengthened) are grown too short to conceal the burials of those that died the day before, people being thereby constrained to borrow daylight for that service; lastly, till I could find neither meat nor drink safe, the butcheries being everywhere visited, my brewer's house shut up, and my baker with his whole family dead of the plague."

The winter of 1665-1666 brought a respite, both from the war and from the plague, which spread with less horrifying speed in colder weather. The English used the time to rebuild, resupply and reman their fleet—the money came from a large loan from the English East India Company. The Dutch spent almost 11 million guilders to fit out a new fleet, one million guilders coming from the Dutch East India Company. The winter also brought them an ally. In January 1666 the French decided to honor a treaty with the Dutch by declaring war on England. The French turned out to be useless and halfhearted allies: though France had a fleet, her ships never fired a shot in the battles to come. But the fleet did cause one false alarm, which led to a mistake in strategy and a defeat of the English in the longest, hardest battle of all: the Four Days' Fight.

As winter softened into spring, Prince Rupert and the Duke of Albemarle boarded the *Royal Charles,* now mounting 82 guns, to take command of 80 men-of-war laying at the Downs, off the coast of Kent, for the start of the new fighting season. De Ruyter was also ready: under his command, the Dutch fleet of 85 warships was united as it had never been before. The English expected every day to see the enemy's masts beyond the Goodwin Sands. While they waited, a frigate arrived posthaste in the west of England to report that a French fleet of 36 sail was on its way from the Mediterranean and already approaching the mouth of the English Channel. King Charles decided to divide his fleet and ordered Rupert to go down the Channel in the 78-gun *Royal James* with a third of the

The Great Plague: London's dreadful visitation

The year 1665, in the midst of the Second Dutch War, saw the highest mortality rates among Englishmen in many a century. Combat casualties were the least of it. A hundred times as many Englishmen died at home in their beds or, if they were paupers, in the streets of London.

The killer was the mite-sized rat flea that brought the dread bubonic plague, or Black Death—so named because its victims' skin was blotched a horrid black. This agony of pus-filled sores, swollen groins and armpits, tremors, vomiting and delirium claimed about half of all those afflicted. The plague was no stranger to 17th Century Europe. In an average year in England, anywhere from a handful to a few thousand could be expected to die from the scourge. But the virulence of this particular year's outbreak was staggering.

The disease started in April in the teeming, rat-infested slums of London; it spread gradually at first, then faster and faster until suddenly it had the whole city in its awful grip. "The contagion chang'd its former slow and languid pace," wrote Dr. Nathaniel Hodges, one of the few doctors who remained in London to tend patients, "and having as it were got master of all, made a most terrible slaughter."

By midsummer the weekly Bills of Mortality issued by civil authorities were listing the dead in the thousands. "The plague above 6,000," wrote Samuel Pepys, "but it is feared the true number of the dead this week is near 10,000; partly from the poor that cannot be taken notice of, through the greatness of the number and partly from the Quakers and others that will not have any bell ring for them."

Pepys might have mentioned another reason for reticence. When authorities found a case of the disease, they

MEMENTO MORI

LONDON'S Dreadful Viſitation:
Or, A COLLECTION of All the
Bills of Mortality
For this Preſent Year:
Beginning the 27th. of December 1664. and ending the 19th. of December following:
As alſo, The GENERAL or whole years BILL:
According to the Report made to the KING's Moſt Excellent Majeſty,
By the Company of Pariſh-Clerks of London, &c
LONDON:
Printed and are to be ſold by E. Cotes living in Alderſgate-ſtreet, Printer to the ſaid Company 1665.

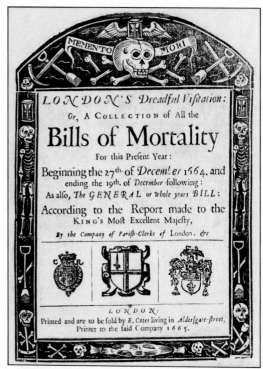

A skull and crossbones and other grim death symbols (above) bedeck the title page of "London's Dreadful Visitation; Or, A Collection of All the Bills of Mortality" for 1665, the year of the Great Plague. The bills listed the week's deaths by parishes and causes. Beyond the ghoulish fascination they held for benighted Londoners in this terrible year—at its peak the plague claimed more than 7,000 victims in one week (right)—the bills served the practical purpose of apprising authorities of the epidemic's course.

The Diſeaſes and Caſualties this Week.

		Impoſthume	11
		Infants	16
		Killed by a fall from the Bel-frey at Alhallows the Great	1
		Kingſevil	2
		Lethargy	1
		Palſie	1
		Plague	7165
Abortive	5	Rickets	17
Aged	43	Riſing of the Lights	11
Ague	2	Scowring	5
Apoplexie	1	Scurvy	2
Bleeding	2	Spleen	1
Burnt in his Bed by a Candle at St. Giles Cripplegate	1	Spotted Feaver	101
Canker	1	Stilborn	17
Childbed	42	Stone	2
Chriſomes	18	Stopping of the ſtomach	9
Conſumption	134	Strangury	1
Convulſion	64	Suddenly	1
Cough	2	Surfeit	49
Dropſie	33	Teeth	121
Feaver	309	Thruſh	5
Flox and Small-pox	5	Timpany	1
Frighted	3	Tiſſick	11
Gowt	1	Vomiting	3
Grief	3	Winde	3
Griping in the Guts	51	Wormes	15
Jaundies	5		

Chriſtned { Males 95, Females 81, In all 176 } Buried { Males 4095, Females 4202, In all 8297 } Plague 7165
Increaſed in the Burials this Week 607
Pariſhes clear of the Plague 4 Pariſhes Infected 126

The Aſſize of Bread ſet forth by Order of the Lord Maior and Court of Aldermen,
A penny Wheaten Loaf to contain Nine Ounces and a half, and three half-penny White Loaves the like weight.

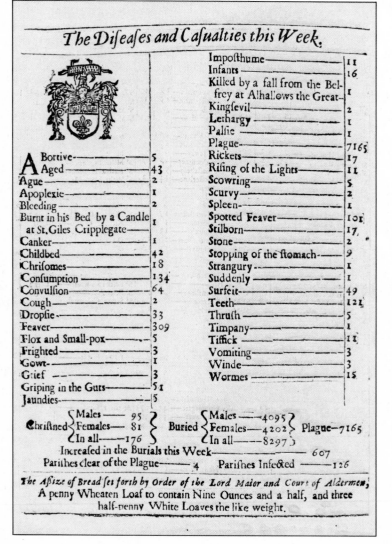

quarantined the house, confining all members; to see that the families obeyed, two watchmen were appointed to guard the door, where a foot-high red cross and a placard bearing the rueful legend "Lord Have Mercy upon Us" informed passersby of the contagion. "And such a solitude about those places," recalled the Reverend Thomas Vincent, "people passing by them so gingerly, and with such fearful looks, as if they had been lined with enemies in ambush, that waited to destroy them."

All through the summer the sickness raged, the weekly death totals mounting through the third week in September, when authorities counted 7,165. Then "the plague by leisurely degrees declined, as it had gradually made its first advances," wrote Dr. Hodges. The final toll was awesome. The official count was 68,596, but other estimates put it closer to 100,000—about a quarter of London's population.

As Londoners returned to their city, Pepys mused, half in jest, "it is a wonder what will be the fashion after the plague is done, as to periwiggs, for nobody will dare to buy any haire, for fear of the infection, that it had been cut off the heads of people dead of the plague." But the Londoners were a resilient citizenry. "The houses which before were full of the dead, were now again inhabited by the living," wrote Dr. Hodges, "and the shops which had been most part of the year shut up, were again opened, and the people again cheerfully went about their wonted affairs of trade and employ. They had the courage now to marry again. Even women before deemed barren, were said to prove prolifick. So that after a few months the loss was hardly discernable, and thus ended this fatal year."

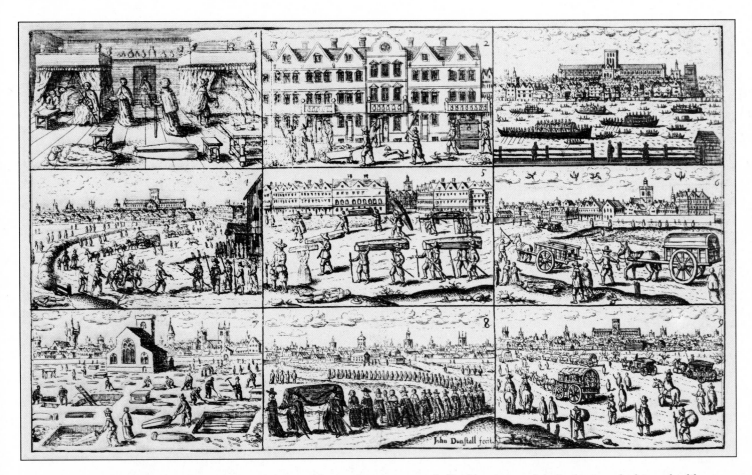

A 1666 broadsheet gave vignettes of plague-ridden London. In a stricken house (1) a family is confined indoors, one member dead by a coffin, others crowded two to a bed. Outside (2) the doors of afflicted houses are marked by crosses, while authorities patrol the streets, clubbing scavenging dogs and carting off the dead. By the Thames (3) thousands flee by boat, while in the countryside (4) halberd-bearing guards halt refugees and ask to see health certificates. Meanwhile the burial of the dead continues with lines of pallbearers (5) and hearses (6) converging on the graveyards (7); only the most prominent citizens could be accorded a proper funeral (8). But at last the plague was over (9), and Londoners "crowded back as thick as they had fled," recalled one survivor.

ships to meet the French, leaving Albemarle with the other two thirds to look after the Dutch.

It was a classic error of judgment. Instead of one powerful fleet, the English now had two that were weak. To compound the mistake, it was soon discovered that the frigate captain had been wrong. Word arrived that the strange fleet was not French but Spanish and that it was not closing in on the Channel but was minding its own business off the coast of Portugal. A frantic message was sent to Rupert to recall him. But in the most surprising gaffe of all, it was sent by coach in the ordinary mail, not by a special courier, and it took a week to reach him off the Isle of Wight. By then Albemarle, with 56 remaining ships, had spotted de Ruyter and his 85 vessels, and had decided to fight regardless of the odds.

Almost immediately Albemarle committed a grave tactical error. There was a strong southwesterly wind and a lumpy sea when he sighted the Dutch, who immediately set a course of southeast toward the coast of Flanders. Albemarle was obliged to turn into a parallel course upwind of them. In that position, all his ships had the wind on the starboard beam and were heeled to port, toward the enemy, and in the heavy seas most of them could not open their lower-deck gunports on the leeward side without the water rushing in. Taking and keeping the weather gauge always brought the advantage of freedom to maneuver, but it could have a disadvantage in a strong wind and sea. The fleet downwind could open its lower ports on the side that was facing the enemy, but the fleet upwind could not. The English had to fight the first encounters without their heaviest guns, the 48- and 32-pounders of the lower deck.

For three or four hours on that southeast course, Albemarle battled it out with the Dutch. Then the Flemish coast, and the shoal waters off it, loomed ahead. Either by luck or by tactical foresight, de Ruyter had put Albemarle in a corner. The Englishman had to alter course, and the only course he could make, with the land ahead and the enemy on his lee, was opposite to the one he was on. He signaled the fleet to tack together, and coming back, once again the lower gunports could not be opened. Running the fearsome gauntlet of Dutch fire, every English ship was damaged. Three or four were forced to fall out of line and were quickly put upon by Dutchmen.

One of those was the 65-gun *Henry,* the flagship of Rear Admiral Sir John Harman, a veteran captain who had recently been promoted. When she was surrounded she was battered on every side by shot from Dutch men-of-war, each striving for the kill. Soon she was completely disabled, sails and rigging in chaos. The Dutch now sent in a fire ship to grapple her. A lieutenant from the *Henry* jumped on board the blazing fire ship (whose crew, of course, had put off in their boats). He managed to loose the grappling irons, and then swung back on his own ship unhurt.

The Dutch sent in a second fire ship, which grappled the *Henry* on the other side and set her sails on fire. That caused a panic, and about 50 of the crew jumped overboard (first among them the parson, Pepys later noted slyly). Harman drew his sword and rushed round the deck, threatening to slaughter the next man who tried to leave the ship. The men rallied, but just as they were gaining control of the fire, a topsail yard came crashing down and broke the admiral's ankle.

Proof that time heals all wounds is this portrait, commissioned in 1674 by England's King Charles II, of Cornelis Tromp, son of the Dutch admiral Maarten Tromp and himself a commander against the English in the second Anglo-Dutch war. Charles had reason to favor Tromp, who supported the Prince of Orange, Charles's nephew, in a Dutch power struggle in the early 1670s.

A Dutch admiral in one of the attacking men-of-war bore up for the crippled ship and hailed Harman to surrender. "It has not come to that yet," Harman shouted back, and cut loose a murderous broadside, killing the Dutch admiral. That seemed to take the starch out of the Dutch. They ceased firing and moved on, content to leave the devastated hulk of the *Henry* drifting out of control. But with the amazing resource of early sailors, the *Henry*'s crew rigged some jury sail and took this ship 60 miles across the wind to the port of Harwich, where they landed their wounded and got to work to make her fit to fight again. Incredibly, by the next evening she was ready enough, and Harman sailed her out, broken ankle and all, to try to rejoin the battle.

At the end of the first day, Albemarle reckoned up his losses. In addition to his own flagship, the *Royal Charles*, he found that only 43 of his 56 ships were still fit for action, and in those 44, many men had been killed and many more were lying in agony on the lower decks. During the night he called a council of war of his captains and made a memorable speech: "If we had dreaded the number of the enemy, we should have fled: but though we are inferior to them in ships, we are in all things else superior. Let the enemy feel that though our fleet be divided, our spirit is entire. At the worst it will be more honorable to die bravely here on our own element than be made spectacles to the Dutch. To be overcome is the fortune of war, but to fly is the fashion of cowards."

So on the second day, they renewed the fight against a Dutch fleet that still had 80 combat-ready vessels—a margin of almost 2 to 1. It was a feat of discipline that at least brought a tribute from the Dutch. Their great statesman, Johan de Witt, said afterward, "Our own fleet could never have been brought on after the first day's fight, and I believe that none but theirs could; all that the Dutch discovered was that Englishmen might be killed and English ships be burned, but that English courage was invincible."

Brave though it was, the decision of the English to fight only brought disaster nearer. On the second day, against such overwhelming numbers, many more English ships were crippled, though none were sunk. By nightfall, Albemarle could count on 16 ships that still remained fit to fight, while the Dutch still had close to 80 combatants. In spite of their numbers, they too were severely battered. Cornelis Tromp, who was second-in-command, had had to shift his flag to another ship when his own was put out of action, and de Ruyter himself was lagging astern of the rest with his main yard and main-topmast down. Nevertheless, the Dutch had the advantage of numbers. For the English to battle head on any longer would amount to suicide, and Albemarle had commenced a fighting retreat toward the English coast, seeking to save his cripples.

He did it in style, despite the decreasing winds, which made the maneuver difficult. The worst-damaged ships were sent ahead, and the 16 fit ones formed a rear guard to protect them. The Dutch followed closely. As both fleets crept slowly and painfully north toward the mouth of the Thames, the Dutch tried time and again to break through the English screen. But they could not.

That afternoon of the third day, another fleet was sighted, far down to the southwest of the Strait of Dover. The sails, for all Albemarle knew, might be those of Prince Rupert hurrying to his rescue—or those of the French coming to help the Dutch polish him off.

It was an afternoon of breathless suspense. At last, just before dusk, the oncoming ships were made out to be Rupert's. But the joy and relief were short-lived. The seaman who kept a journal, Edward Barlow, described what happened: "We began to edge towards them; and being near to a sand which is called the Galloper through the unskilfulness of the pilots, thinking they had been farther off, we ran just upon it, the *Royal Charles* striking upon it, and some other great ships. And the *Royal Prince*, being the biggest ship and drawing the most water, stuck fast upon it, all the rest of the fleet sailing away and leaving her all alone: they durst not stay to help her for fear of running more of the Great Ships on the ground."

The *Royal Prince* was, of course, Phineas Pett's veteran *Prince Royal*, which had survived a dozen fierce engagements in her 56-year career. Refitted to mount 90 guns, 26 more than at first, the great vessel was now the flagship of Sir George Ayscue, who was second only to Albemarle in seniority. And her grounding was a terrible loss to the weakened fleet. The Dutch surrounded her and attacked her without mercy, and there was nothing anyone could do to help her. Hoping to save as many lives as he could, Ayscue struck his flag and surrendered to Cornelis Tromp. Tromp believed he could get the *Royal Prince* off the sand and take her home as a prize. But de Ruyter refused to spend the time when there was still an English fleet to deal with. He insisted that she be burned. And so she died, with a thunderous explosion when the flames reached her powder magazine.

Prince Rupert had now joined his 24 ships to the combat-fit survivors of Albemarle's battered squadron; during the retreat 17 damaged ships had been repaired enough to fight, giving Albemarle 33 combatants in all. Another three put out from the Thames, bringing the fleet to 60. Albemarle went on board Rupert's flagship, the *Royal James*, for a council. He was exhausted—as was every man in this fleet, after three days of battle and three nights of feverish labor to patch up the damage before the dawn. But Rupert and his squadron were fresh, and ashamed of wasting their time on the fool's errand down the Channel. The two admirals agreed to fight again despite the fact that they were still seriously outnumbered: there was still a last chance to salvage pride.

Seaman Barlow, at the other end of the scale of rank, understood the decision very well: "They concluded to set upon the Hollands fleet again the next day to see what fortune would befall them, being very loath that the groat-headed Flemings should go home victorious, though their fleet were still twice the number that we were."

The Dutch were exhausted too, and might well have withdrawn victorious. But, as Barlow wrote, "By sunrising the Hollands ships bore up to us, and the fighting began anew, very fiercely on both sides, Prince Rupert and his Vice-Admiral being engaged very hot, venturing into the midst of them and running into much danger, whereby in a small time they were very much disabled, losing a great many men."

As so often in the past, the fleets had commenced the action determinedly trying to fight in line of battle. But in the strong southwest winds, the exhausted crews in their battered ships could not keep forma-

Part of the shipboard silver of English Admiral George Ayscue, this biscuit box was a memento of war for Dutch Rear Admiral Isaac Sweers when Ayscue's flagship, the famed Royal Prince, was grounded and lost during the Four Days' Fight in 1666. To mark the change of ownership, Sweers emblazoned his coat of arms, and that of his wife, across the cover of the box, which bears Ayscue's palm-bordered shield on the front.

tion; the combat became a melee with broadsides thundering in every direction. Barlow himself was wounded in the leg by a spent cannon shot that came through the side of the ship. Hobbling lamely about, he was not much use that day to anyone. But he was extremely unwilling to see the fleet retire, admitting defeat, and when at last it inevitably happened, he made every possible excuse for it: "The fight continuing very hard till four of the clock in the afternoon, and few or none but were much disabled in one thing or another, and being engaged with so much odds that some of our ships began to retreat towards our own coast, and it being almost night and a mist arising, our General feared in the mist we might run aboard of one another. So our General made the sign to retreat, the mist increasing and it beginning to be dark; but the Hollands fleet made no great haste to follow us, being willing to leave off, having their bellies full as well as we."

That mist was a godsend. Both sides had fought to the limit of endurance. They needed an honorable excuse to stop, and the mist provided it.

Astonishingly, the first account to reach London made the battle a glorious victory. Again it was a frigate captain who breathlessly reported an utterly inaccurate story: the Dutch had fled, not half their fleet had escaped, and few if any of their flagships. "We were all so overtaken with this good news," Pepys wrote, "that the Duke of York ran with it to the King, who was gone to Chapel, and there all the Court was in a hubbub, being rejoiced over head and ears." He spent the evening watching the bonfires of joy in the streets with several ladies he knew.

The next day, as the truth began to come out, the gloom was all the deeper for the mistaken celebrations, and the battle began to seem a disgraceful defeat. The search for a scapegoat was almost hysterical. Most of the captains, and many other people, put the blame on Albemarle. Albemarle blamed the captains. Pepys quoted him as saying that he "never fought with worse officers in his life, not above 20 of them behaving themselves like men"—the most flagrantly unjust of all the accusations. Nobody dared to blame the King or the Duke of York, the Lord High Admiral, for the strategic error that lay at the root of it all. The only people nobody blamed were the seamen. As always, they had fought with the bulldog tenacity typical of English seamen.

Though the battle unquestionably was a victory for the Dutch, it had not really decided anything. Once again, the number of ships actually destroyed was remarkably small. Of the combined English fleet of 80 men-of-war, only four were total losses from combat damage. Another six were captured. The Dutch, for their part, lost but four from their original fleet of 85. The human casualties were worse by far. In the English fleet, two admirals and 12 captains were dead, along with some 2,500 seamen killed or wounded; another 2,000 were taken captive. The cost to the Dutch was three admirals and 2,500 men killed or wounded. But it was ships that counted more than men. Both sides knew that another battle would have to be fought, and very soon.

It is astonishing how quickly wooden ships could be repaired in those days. The English had scarcely a single undamaged ship in the fleet, and scores that needed complete new outfits of masts, rigging and sails. Yet

Perilous missions in the service of art

When the Dutch fleet sailed into combat during the wars with the English, it was often accompanied by a small, single-masted craft known as a galliot, dispatched by the commander in chief on a perilous mission of her own. She carried no armament, but she was not to lag back from battle. Quite the contrary, she was to go "before, behind," even "in the fleet," taking her passenger, artist Willem van de Velde, in any direction he deemed "expedient for the drawings he is going to make."

Van de Velde, joined by his son Willem in the second war, created a pen-and-ink documentary of the major sea battles between the Dutch and the English. During the fighting, the artists sketched furiously to capture the action. Back in their studio they transferred sketches to canvases, adding details of rigging. The artists then used a wash to turn the battle "notes" into spirited works known as grisailles.

Facing a troubled Dutch economy, the artists emigrated to England after the war, where in 1674 King Charles II granted each a £100 annual pension. There the artists also cleverly capitalized on a market for works that had not sold in the Netherlands—depictions of Dutch defeats during the two wars.

During the calm before the Four Days' Fight in 1666, the elder van de Velde sketched Dutch captains arriving for a council on board de Ruyter's flagship, the Zeven Provincien. The second sketch below is a scene from the battle itself by the younger artist van de Velde, who recorded ship position with a few deft pencil strokes and used a wash to depict lingering smoke from the destroyed English Prince Royal. Handwritten notes on the sketch indicate the colors of smoke and sky.

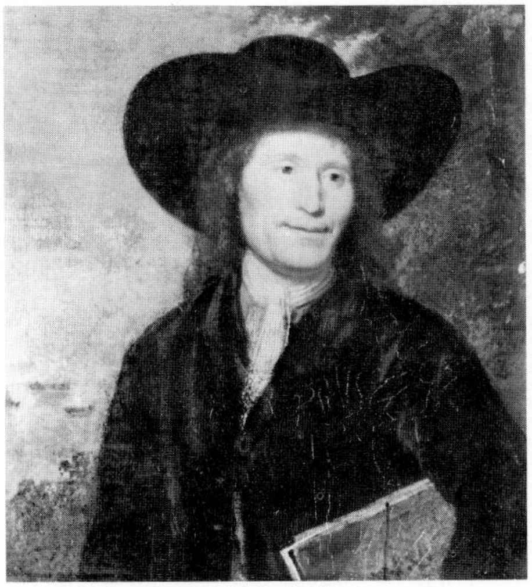

WILLEM VAN DE VELDE THE ELDER

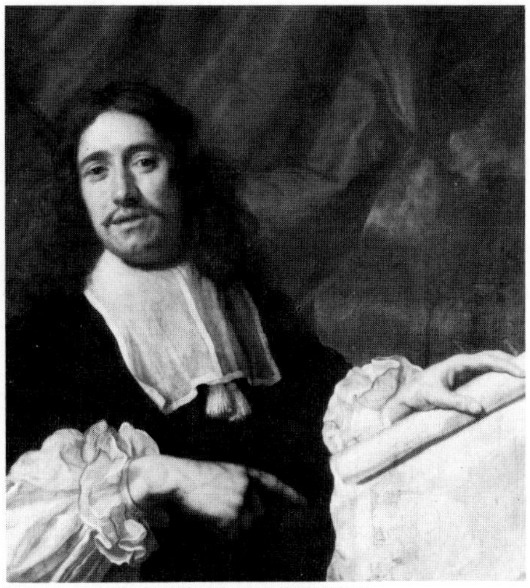

WILLEM VAN DE VELDE THE YOUNGER

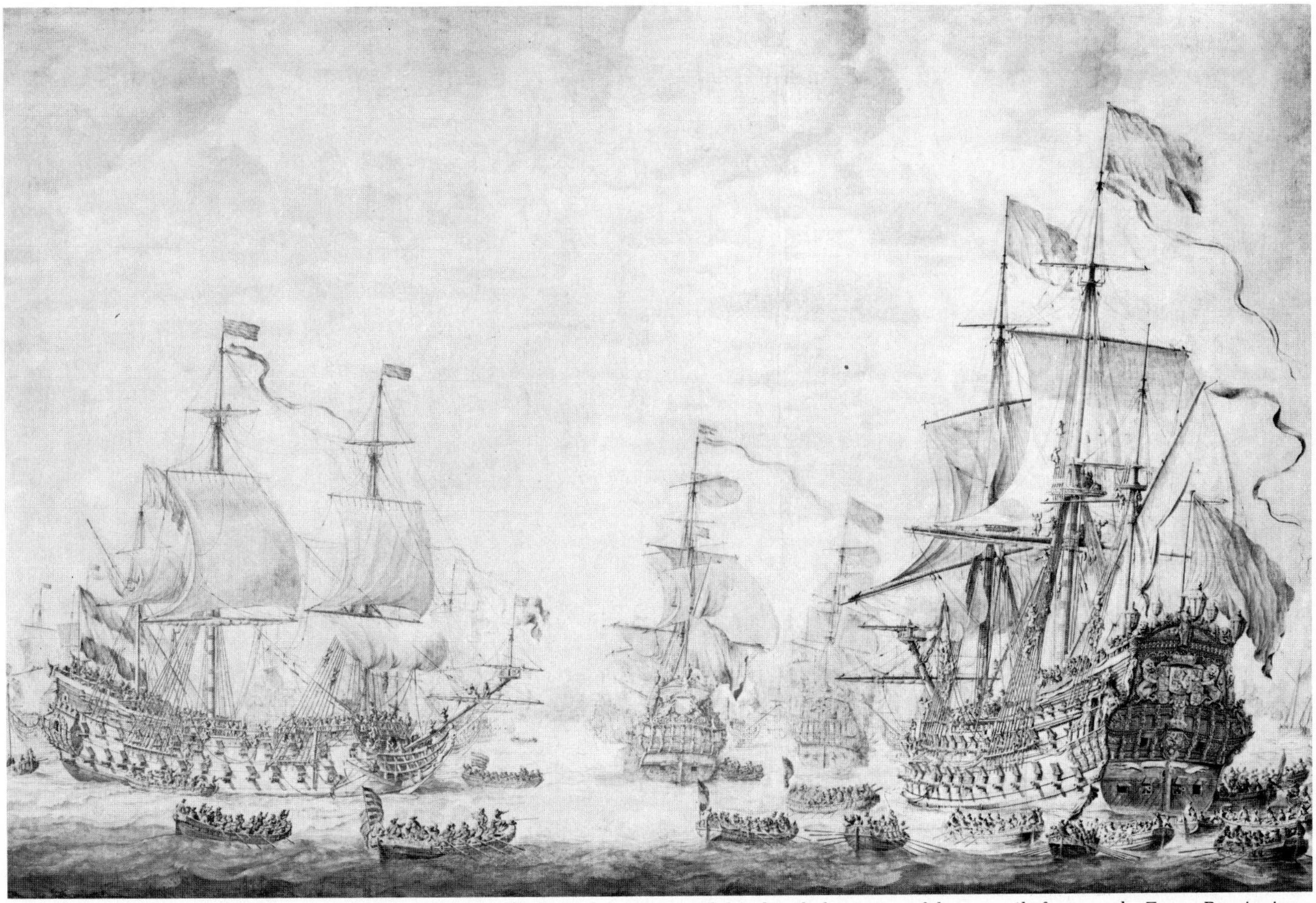

From his on-the-spot sketch (opposite, top), van de Velde the Elder later prepared this detailed painting of the council of war on the Zeven Provincien.

within six weeks, the fleet was ready to put to sea and have another go. The Dutch were even quicker.

Since the battle had ended off the mouth of the Thames, most of the work of refitting fell to Chatham dockyard on the Medway River, which runs into the south side of the Thames estuary. Here were the dry docks for building and repairs: there were stacks of planking seasoning in open sheds; ponds where the big logs for masts and spars were seasoned by floating in water; sawmills; smithies; sail lofts; and a ropewalk a quarter of a mile long, where men spun every size of rope and cable on machinery turned by hand. Here also was every kind of nautical craftsman, men who among them knew all there was to know about ships. In charge of it all, with the title of commissioner, was Peter Pett, the son of Phineas.

There were still many things wrong despite everything that Samuel Pepys had done to shape up the Navy's shore establishment. During that hectic year of 1666, Pett complained to the Navy Board that he was desperately short of materials and that his men were owed more than a year's pay. It is surprising they did any work at all. Yet when the fleet of battle-torn ships came limping up the river on the tide, the unpaid and dissatisfied shipwrights evidently pulled themselves together.

In such a crisis the building of new ships was halted, and an army of skillful men—perhaps 1,000 in all—went to work on repairs. The crews, of course, worked side by side: every man-of-war had her own carpenters, riggers and sailmakers, and every sailor knew how to knot and splice, and caulk a leaky seam. Everyone knew that across the North Sea the Dutch were efficiently doing the same work and would be back the moment they had finished.

The narrow river at Chatham was aswarm with boats going to and fro, carrying men and materials to the ships at anchor—the ships being taken in turn below the cranes that hauled out the stumps of masts and stepped new ones in their places. Hordes of men then clambered aloft to renew the rigging. Ashore in the ropewalk, the clanking machinery spun mile upon mile of rope, and in the sail lofts, patient men sat cross-legged and sewed the sails by hand with palm and needle. Over all sounded the hammers of carpenters, caulkers and blacksmiths. And at last, one by one, the ships shook out new sail, weighed anchor and dropped downriver to form up again as a fleet.

The English, 88 strong under Rupert and Albemarle sharing command in the *Royal Charles,* were waiting in the estuary of the Thames when de Ruyter came across with 89 men-of-war on July 22. For three days, both fleets maneuvered among the tides and shallows off the Essex coast, waiting for more favorable weather. Neither was particularly anxious to fight again in the strong winds that had beset the previous battle. There were thunderstorms, and each fleet had a ship dismasted by lightning. But on July 24 a light northerly wind came in and both fleets stood away toward the open sea. The next day they met. It was St. James's Day.

The St. James's Fight, as the English called it, was the first in which an eyewitness—James Pearse, the senior surgeon in the fleet—drew a series of battle plans on the spot (*pages 142-143*). They plainly show that both nations from the start had at last adopted the classic tactics of battle: both fleets are in line ahead on the same tack, and the lines converge until the leaders are in gunshot.

It was 10 o'clock in the morning when the first broadsides were fired, and soon the leading squadrons of both sides were pounding furiously away at each other, both standing off to the eastward and each ship engaged in a deadly duel with its opposite number. An hour later the center squadrons were locked in action, with de Ruyter in the 80-gun ship called the *Zeven Provincien*, and Rupert and Albemarle in the 82-gun *Royal Charles*. But the rear Dutch squadron was commanded by Cornelis Tromp, and as he came into range he abruptly altered course and to everyone's astonishment deliberately sailed right through the English line. The only reason for such a tactic that anyone could imagine at the time was that he detested de Ruyter and wanted to fight an independent battle of his own. He certainly succeeded in that: de Ruyter was puzzled and furious as the rearmost third of each fleet, the Dutch in pursuit of the English, sailed off in a fight on the opposite tack and was soon out of sight.

The main battle soon developed into an artillery duel in which the English had the upper hand. The stiff codes of Naval discipline enacted during the First Dutch War, the tighter selection system for junior officers instituted by Pepys, the emphasis on training, the homogeneity of English crews compared with the polyglot nature of Dutch crews all served to give the English the edge in gunnery. English gunners loaded faster and aimed better than their Dutch counterparts. And they had the added advantage of more 32- and 48-pound cannon that could wreak great destruction at long range. These advantages had been nullified to some extent in the swirling free-for-alls that characterized the early battles of this second war. But now as formal line-ahead tactics with massed firepower were being perfected, the English superiority in gunnery had a telling effect. The Dutch fought with superb courage, but the direct hits they suffered quickly wore them down. By midday, two hours after the battle was joined, three of the seven admirals of the leading Dutch squadron had been killed, and the ships of the squadron had been battered to a state where they could fight no more. They had no option but to flee as best they could to the eastward and home.

The two centers had a more equal fight, because the Dutch were personally led by de Ruyter, and the captains and crews were fighting under his inspiration. The *Royal Charles* was so severely damaged that Rupert and Albemarle had to shift their flags, being rowed across to the *Royal James*, a 78-gunner that was still in good order. The *Henry*, which had distinguished herself in the Four Days' Fight, did so again, now commanded by the fire-eating Robert Holmes, of Africa notoriety—now Sir Robert. She fought such a hot and savage battle with de Ruyter's flagship that the *Zeven Provincien* was entirely dismasted, and the Dutch ship had to fall back while jury masts were rigged.

By midafternoon both sides were too mauled and exhausted to continue an organized fight, and the whole mass of them, some 60 ships in all, drifted together southward out of control. On the splintered hulks the crews—those who were still alive—struggled desperately to get their ships under way again. Toward night the English managed to get into a

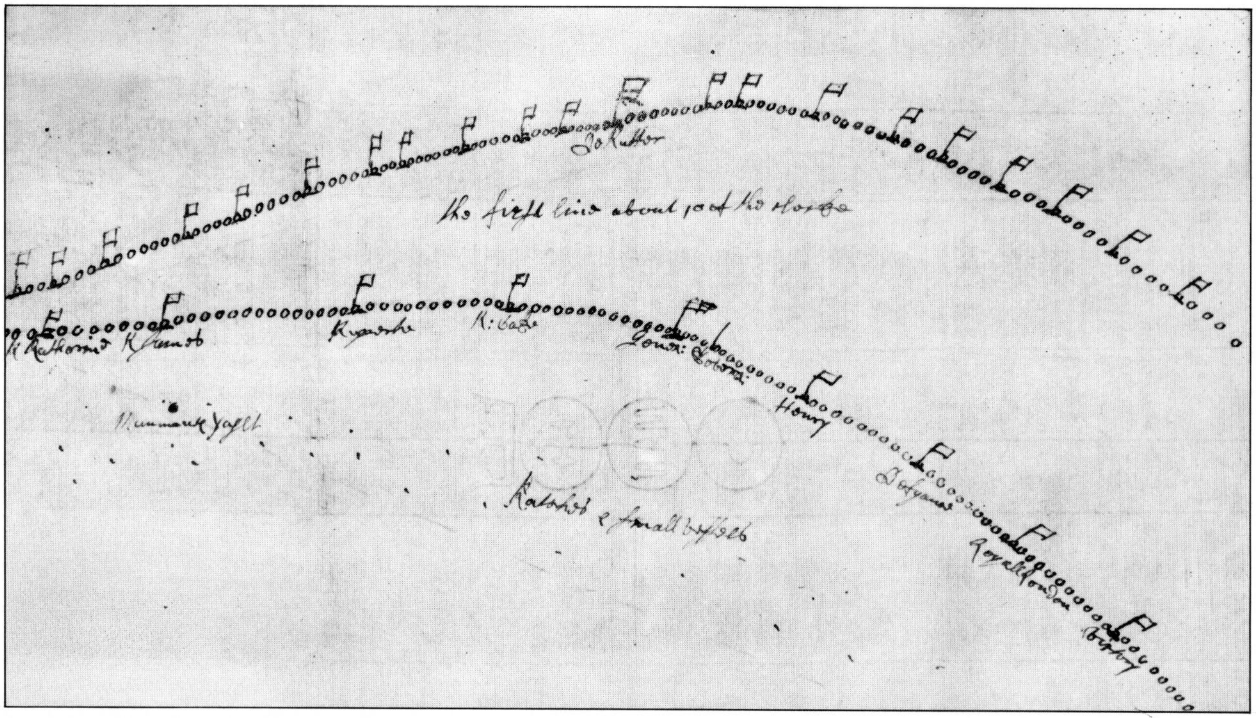

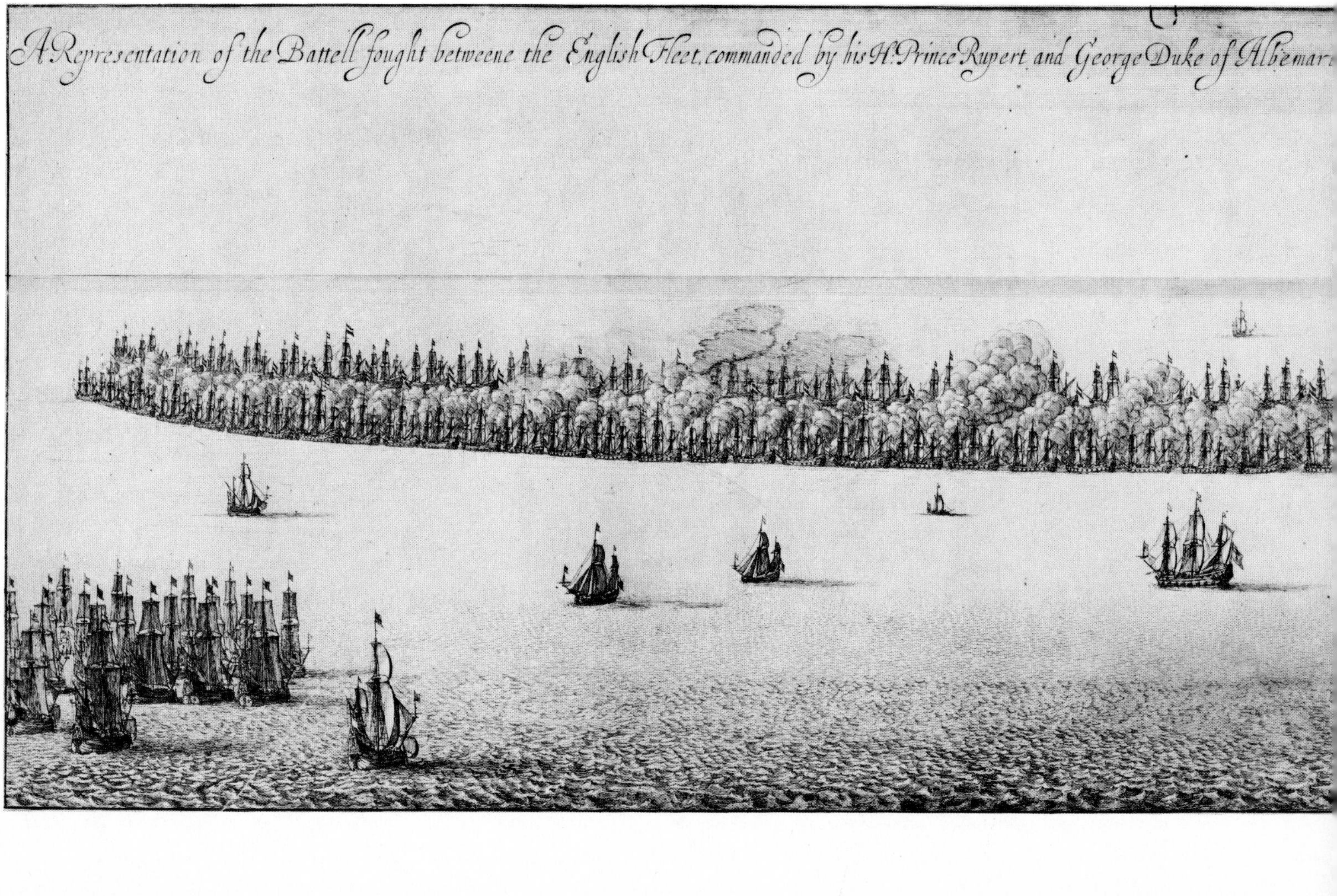
A Representation of the Battell fought betweene the English Fleet, commanded by his H: Prince Rupert and George Duke of Albemar

rough line and began to engage again. But de Ruyter had also re-formed his squadron and had organized a screen of the less damaged ships, such as Albemarle had used in the Four Days' Fight to shepherd the worst of the sufferers back to port. The battle went on in a desultory fashion all night. Two major Dutch ships were abandoned and left to burn. The English continued the pursuit until dawn found the combatants near the shallow channels off the Dutch coast. And at last, without competent pilots, the English broke off the action.

That day, on the far horizon, Rupert and Albemarle saw their rear squadron, and it was chasing Tromp. This was a surprise, to say the least: when they had last seen it, it was being chased. But somehow, during the night, it had won the weather gauge, and somehow—presumably from a dispatch boat—Tromp had learned that the rest of the fleet he had left had been defeated, so that he alone was at sea in the presence of the whole victorious English fleet. He also took refuge among the shallows.

It was the turn of the Dutch to fall into fierce recriminations. De Ruyter accused Cornelis Tromp of insubordination for breaking out of the main line of battle without permission. Tromp, in turn, accused de Ruyter of failing to protect the fleet's now-destroyed lead squadron. Each refused to serve again with the other. But Tromp was quite clearly in the wrong, and he lost his post.

The first real use of the line-ahead formation, which became the standard naval tactic, was diagramed (left) during the St. James's Fight in 1666 by English surgeon James Pearse. The Wenceslaus Hollar engraving (below), with equidistant ships firing tidy broadsides, exaggerates the skill of the English and Dutch forces but accurately reflects the enormous lengths of the battle lines.

Roy.l.l Charles; And the Dutch Fleet commanded by Adm.ll de Ruyter on the 25.th July 1666. Together with a List of the English Shipps & Capt.ns & their numbers of Men & Gunns.

As the battered Dutch fleet vanished into its home ports, Rupert and Albemarle came to anchor outside the ports with no enemy in sight. It was clear that they had won a tremendous victory. They had certainly repaid the Dutch for the humiliation of the Four Days' Fight. The English had lost only one man-of-war and two or three fire ships; scarcely 300 men had been killed or wounded, though five captains were dead. The Dutch lost some 20 ships, sunk or burned. Some 7,000 men were dead or wounded, along with four admirals and an undetermined number of captains killed. Albemarle and Rupert were in total control of the North Sea and they used this supremacy to their advantage. Triumphantly they sailed north along the Dutch coast capturing merchant ships and terrifying the coastal cities.

Hitherto, the wars between the English and the Dutch had been fought entirely at sea, and neither side had landed a single man on the enemy coast. But now the English decided to attack a small village on the island of Vlieland, which was said to have a vast amount of government stores in it, and to lead the adventure they chose Sir Robert Holmes.

Holmes's orders were to plunder and burn the town and bring off "the better sort of inhabitants"—which meant anyone who looked as if he had wealth or authority. No violence was to be done to "women or children, nor the inferior sort of people, unless in case of resistance." But when Holmes entered the difficult channel between the islands of Vlieland and Terschelling, he saw before him a much more worthy objective: an uncountable number of masts. The roadstead behind Tershelling was crammed with merchant ships.

Holmes sailed boldly into the harbor in daylight in a converted pleasure yacht called the *Fanfan*, which belonged to Prince Rupert, with two frigates (one of which ran aground), five fire ships and several hundred men in small ketches and longboats.

Two small Dutch warships came bravely out to meet him. One was grappled by the remaining frigate and set on fire. The other ran aground in the mud—for the little harbor was surrounded by tidal mudbanks. Her crew took to their boats. A fire ship bore down on the stranded Dutch

As a Dutch merchant fleet explodes in fiery clouds, terror-stricken crew members and citizens flee in boats in this Dutch print of the 1666 debacle in the harbor of Westerschelling. After the ships were reduced to what one eyewitness termed "so many consuming keels," freebooting English leader Robert Holmes sent men to pillage and torch the town. Crews lingered over the task with such relish, wrote Holmes, "that I was forced to set fire in some houses to windward of the towne to occasion the hastening of our men away."

ship. The English crew had already ignited the fire ship and put off in their own boat when the flaming fire ship also ran aground. Both crews rowed a race to board the Dutch warship. The fire ship's crew won, fought off the Dutch with their own guns and set her, too, on fire.

By now the crews of the merchantmen were making for their boats, and so were the people of the island. Hundreds of small craft hurried frantically away toward the Friesland coast. Holmes sent in all his boats, with orders not to plunder but to destroy. The men fired the first few ships and soon had to row away from the scorching heat. For the merchant ships, packed tightly together in the constricted space, set fire to one another until the entire mass of them was blazing and the column of smoke could be seen from the fleet offshore. There was never an exact count of the ships that were destroyed that afternoon. The official English figure was more than 150; the Dutch admitted to at least 114. For years afterward, this conflagration was known in England as "Sir Robert Holmes his Bonefire."

In financial terms, that one afternoon's work had done more damage than the English fleet had accomplished in the entire war. It would have been better if Holmes had left it at that. But he had not yet carried out the letter of his orders. He waited all night outside the smoking harbor. As dawn came up across the desolate mud flats, he gave the command: the boats cast off, and the men scrambled ashore and cautiously advanced toward what they took to be the little town of Vlieland. Most of the inhabitants had fled. The sailors now turned to plunder. They smashed their way into the houses and loaded themselves with so much booty that most of them could hardly stagger back with it. Among it, of course, was drink, and they spent so long in sacking the place that Holmes, bringing up the rear, set fire to the houses in order to drive his men out. Even so, after the last of the boats had put off, mournful and drunken cries were heard from the shore, and some boats had to go back to pick up the last of the stragglers.

When the news reached London, the burning of the ships was celebrated by lighting bonfires in the streets and firing the guns of the Tower. Burning ships was a justifiable part of a naval war. But some people were less easy in their conscience about the burning of the town. It was in fact a useless provocation. Holmes had not even burned the right town: the one with the government stores was on the island of Vlieland, and the one he torched was in Terschelling and had no government stores at all. Pepys was in doubt when he heard the first news of it: "I believe it is but a foolery either in the report or the attempt." There was an uneasy feeling that such a wanton act would bring retribution, from either the Almighty or the Dutch.

De Ruyter was at sea again, with a refitted fleet, scarcely three weeks after he had been forced back to port in the fight on St. James's Day. However, there was no more fighting before the winter came on. The two fleets met again, this time off the coast of France. But as the first shots were fired, a violent storm blew up, and both had to run for shelter. De Ruyter made for Dunkirk. The English put in to Portsmouth. And as they came to anchor in the roads, boats came out from shore bringing the news that had shaken the country: London was burning.

Chapter 6

Twin catastrophes: God's fire, Holland's revenge

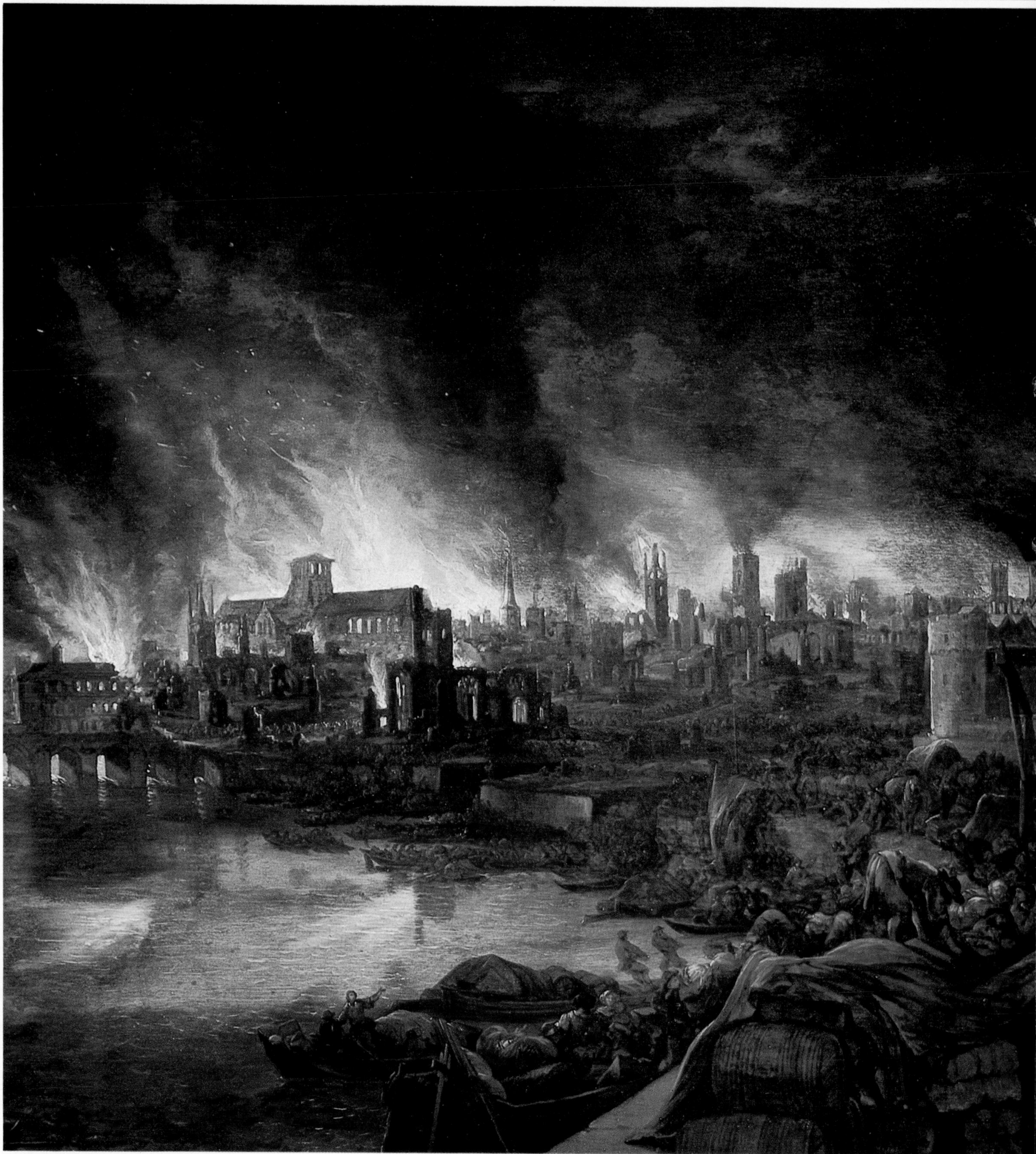

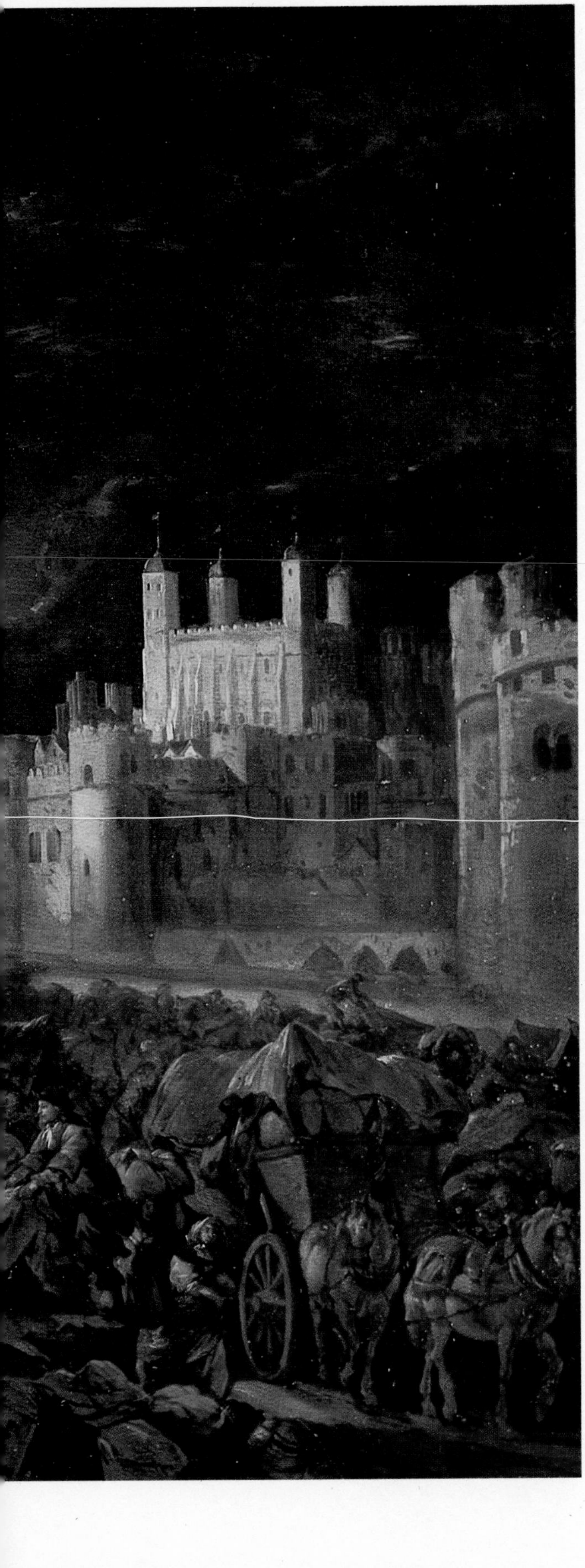

Moralists saw at once in the Great Fire of London in 1666 the vengeance of God for the burning of the harmless little island of Terschelling in the Netherlands. If they were right, the revenge was terrible. As it turned out, this cataclysmic fire would have a profound—for the English, a disastrous—effect on the naval war then raging up and down the Channel and in the North Sea. For it would help bring financial ruin on the English Navy, and render a vital portion of the fleet impotent at a critical juncture in the months to come.

Like so many such catastrophes, the fire seemed to begin out of nothing, with the merest of sparks. On Sunday, September 2, some soot started smouldering in the overheated chimney of a bakery on Pudding Lane in the center of London's commercial district, known as the City. The summer of 1666 had been long, dry and hot, and the cinders ignited the Star Inn on nearby Fish Street. A breeze fanned the flames, and fire fighters were slow to respond on this drowsy weekend afternoon. The fire crept along Fish Street and Pudding Lane down toward the river until it reached the ship chandlers' shops of Thames Street, with their stores of hemp, tallow, oil and spirits, and the heaps of coal and piles of timber along the wharves. Then, suddenly, the whole riverside area seemed to explode in a great searing gout of orange flame.

As in the time of the plague, a year before, the Navy's Samuel Pepys was in the thick of this new calamity. When it became apparent that the fire was out of control, he took a boat upriver to report to King Charles II, and to propose that firebreaks be made by razing entire rows of houses. He returned with the King's order to London's Lord Mayor "to spare no houses, but to pull down before the fire everyway." The unfortunate Mayor responded that he was making firebreaks as swiftly as he could, but that the fire was racing ahead of him—and in any case, the householders were bitterly resisting the leveling of their homes. Pepys told his diary of "poor people staying in their houses as long as till the very fire touched them, and then running into boats or clambering from one pair of stairs by the waterside to another."

At dusk, Pepys crossed the river to escape the heat "and saw the fire grow; and, as it grew darker, appeared more and more, and in corners and upon steeples and between churches and houses, as far as we could see up the hill of the City, in a most horrid, malicious, bloody flame. Only one entire arch of fire from this to the other side the bridge, and in a bow up the hill, for an arch of above a mile long. It made me weep to see it. The churches, houses, and all on fire and flaming at once, and a horrid noise the flames made, and the crackling of houses at their ruin."

Late that night, the fire reached the foot of the lane where Pepys lived, in a house attached to the Navy Office. Returning back across the river,

Refugees flee from the blazing heart of London during the Great Fire of September 1666. The three-day conflagration destroyed virtually the entire commercial district and profoundly crippled the English in the second Anglo-Dutch war.

he and his household joined the refugees. They loaded all their movable possessions and some of the Navy records into carts and boats for transportation out to the suburbs. To save the Navy Office, Pepys and Sir William Penn brought dockyard hands with explosives to blow up the buildings round it. That checked the flames. By now King Charles himself had arrived on the scene and, in a rare display of personal involvement, fought the fire shoulder to shoulder with the Londoners. The monarch moved from area to area, passing buckets, swinging a pickax, offering encouragement and handing out coins to workmen from a bag attached to the saddle of his horse. A contemporary letter tells of the King and the Duke of York "handling the water in bucketts when they stood up to the ancles in water, and playing the engines for many hours together," which encouraged the bystanders to fall to work "with effect, having soe good fellow labourers."

For four days the City burned. Sparks and "fire-drops," as Pepys called them, were borne westward on the wind over the newly cleared spaces and started fresh fires behind the backs of the exhausted working parties. Timber houses with plaster walls, pitch boarding and thatched roofs went up like torches, spreading their shower of sparks throughout the City. "Had you been at Kensington," wrote a resident in that borough, "you would have thought that it had been Doomsday, from the fire, and cries and howlings of the people. My gardens were covered with ashes of papers, linens and plaster-work blown there by the tempest."

Estimates of the dead ranged as high as 4,000. In material terms the cost was shattering. In those four days, the mercantile heart of the kingdom—a bit less than one square mile—had been destroyed: 13,000 houses, 87 parish churches, 44 company halls, the Guildhall, Royal Exchange and Custom House, the hospitals, libraries and prisons. The damage was between £8 million and £10 million, greater than the total cost of both the Dutch wars.

The ruins continued smouldering for months, and so did the effect on England. Nobody could quite believe that the calamity had been an accident. It was either an act of God or a treacherous plot. It was hysterically rumored that shadowy men had been observed lobbing fireballs into cellars. Who were these evil creatures? The Dutch, cried some people. But most of those who subscribed to the plot theory darkly laid the blame at the feet of their longtime political and religious foes: the French. Though the French had taken no active part in either of the Dutch wars, they were loosely allied with the Dutch, and it seemed perfectly believable to the bitterly anti-Catholic English that French "papists" under the young and ambitious King Louis XIV would seek to destroy by stealth and sabotage what they dared not assault in open combat. In fact, growing numbers of Englishmen concluded that they were fighting the wrong people and that the Navy's cannon might better be aimed at the detestable French.

Thus, with anti-French feelings running high, the war against the Dutch came under increasing scrutiny. And all the more so because it was turning into a financial debacle that, along with the fire, threatened to bankrupt England.

The first two years of the Second Dutch War had already cost England more than £3 million. The King, through Parliament, had raised nearly £2 million of this from land taxes, customs and excise duties, but that left a huge deficit of unpaid bills and increasingly restive creditors. Charles's embarrassment was the source of no little glee in Europe; as news of the Navy's plight circulated abroad, caricatures of the King were printed in Continental newspapers; one depicted him with his empty pockets turned inside out.

The question in England, as the fighting season of 1666 drew to a close, was how to finance the Navy for 1667. Since Parliament was obviously inadequate to the task, the King had hoped to borrow supplemental funds from London merchants and bankers. But all that went up in smoke in the Great Fire. Combing through the ashes of their businesses, the private guilds, shipping and livery companies were in no position to lend anyone anything. Whatever funds were found for the Navy would have to come from Parliament. And Parliament, like the creditors, was growing more and more uneasy about the Navy's solvency.

Before September was out, Pepys was sitting up night after night in his office preparing the Navy's accounts for a parliamentary inquiry. However carefully he reckoned, nothing could hide the fact that the Navy was nearly £1 million in arrears in its payments, and that thousands of pounds had disappeared in unaccountable swindles. In October, Pepys went before the Parliamentary Committee of Public Accounts and succeeded in bemusing the members—but not before deftly wriggling his way out of a comedy of errors. While waiting outside the courtroom for the inquiry to begin, he had handed his confidential book of papers to a page boy of Sir William Penn—only to discover that the boy had passed it on to the doorkeeper of the House of Commons. Pepys was beside himself, since "all the nakedness of the office lay open in papers within those covers." But even the halls of justice were not immune to temptation; Pepys got his papers back by greasing the palm of the doorkeeper.

Later, undergoing cross-examination by the Members of Parliament, Pepys, by his own account, "did make shift to answer them better than I expected." The outcome was that Parliament voted the King another £1,800,000. But where was it to come from? With commerce crippled by the fire, government revenues were scant and were needed for other purposes, including the rebuilding of London. Only one proposal won any favor in Parliament: it invited householders throughout the realm, who were taxed on the number of their chimneys, to pay a lump sum equivalent to the tax for an eight-year period and be free of paying the tax in the future.

But that would take time, and in the meanwhile the Navy had no ready cash to pay its creditors. One admiral had begged the Navy Office for money "to stop the bawlings and impatience of these people, especially of their wives, whose tongues are as foul as the daughters of Billingsgate." He begged in vain. Thousands of sailors were being discharged when their ships were laid up for lack of funds for maintenance and repairs. Many of the seamen had received no money for a year or more, and there was none to give them. They and their families, along with the sick and injured who had already been discharged, faced starvation. Those who remained in the Navy were grumbling louder than ever, and growing defiant. On January 2, Pepys wrote: "God have mercy on us! for we can send forth no ships without men, nor will men go without money, every day bringing us news of new mutinies among the seamen."

Mutiny was perhaps the wrong word; what happened was more like a strike. The seamen were not as a rule violent; they simply and firmly refused to go to sea again unless they were paid. The English Navy had come to the end of the road, which all habitual debtors must expect. Its creditors, the seamen, had foreclosed.

Curiously, King Charles greeted these developments with less alarm than might have been anticipated. Even before the fire, he had been sending out secret peace feelers to the Dutch. Actual negotiations had begun not long after Holmes's bonfire. Now the King took a calculated gamble that peace would be made before he had to pay to fit out the fleet again and reenlist men for the summer. He sent Lord St. Albans, a trusted confidant of the family (and possibly his mother's lover), to the Continent to open negotiations.

But the negotiations went extremely slowly. By January the envoys had not progressed beyond discussing where a peace conference might be held. In March they finally agreed on the Dutch town of Breda, about halfway between Amsterdam and Antwerp. It was late in May before ambassadors met, and then they spent time in a confusing protocol debate. Who should enter the conference chamber first? A room had to be found with several doors so that both delegations could enter simultaneously. And who should sit at the head of the table? The whole thing came to a halt while a search was mounted for a round table large enough to accommodate everybody.

The fact was that the Dutch were equally disenchanted with the war, and equally eager to bring it to an end. Moreover, the Dutch had little greater love for the French than did the English. They, too, were Protestant, with a natural antipathy toward Roman Catholicism. Despite the alliance, they distrusted Louis XIV and suspected him of territorial designs; in fact, they had uneasily witnessed a build-up of French forces in the regions to the south of their newly independent United Provinces. It was time to call a halt to the long, bloody and inconclusive battle with the English and to focus their attention on potential perils on land.

But the Dutch were in no great hurry for peace. They were still able to pay their crews and fit out a fleet, and they knew very well from their spies and from international gossip that the English could not. Their chief minister, Johan de Witt, was a brilliant and energetic man, and he was determined to negotiate from a position of strength. He had devised a stunning master stroke that would extract from the English sweet revenge for Holmes's infuriating bonfire, and at the same time would give the Dutch powerful leverage at the conference.

Writing from The Hague on May 31, Johan told his brother Cornelis that "the English envoys at Breda needed a sharp lesson to curb their arrogance." Cornelis was the mayor of the major city of Dordrecht and his brother's trusted confidant and adviser; he was also a man experienced in naval matters, having served in an admiralty for a number of years. On June 10, Johan informed Cornelis that little progress was being

Johan de Witt, Dutch chief of state from 1653 to 1672, personally masterminded the brilliant, river-borne attack on the English Navy yards in the Medway estuary near the Thames in 1667. Exhorting his officers not to return without achieving a "notable exploit," de Witt ordered them "to destroy or take all the English ships of war and to burn the King's magazines, the provisions and munitions of war that should be found in that place."

made at Breda and added cryptically that he "expected from Cornelis, from de Ruyter and from the other leading officers of the fleet deeds that would prove that they were the best plenipotentiaries for peace."

De Witt had a plan. What it was not even Admiral Michiel Adriaenszoon de Ruyter, again in command of the fleet, knew. But while the ambassadors were dancing their diplomatic minuet in Breda, Johan de Witt had his plan put in motion. The fleet was ordered to rendezvous off the island of Texel in the North Sea. When it had sailed clear of the land and there was no possible risk of a leakage of information, Johan de Witt personally went out to the flagship to give de Ruyter his orders. With him he brought his brother Cornelis, to represent him personally as a kind of supreme commander; Cornelis was to go to sea with de Ruyter and ensure that the plan was carried out, whatever the difficulties and whatever the cost.

It is understandable that Johan de Witt felt it necessary to put his brother on board with a figurative pistol to the tactical commander's head. For the plan appeared impossible. De Ruyter was ordered to sail audaciously into the estuary of the Thames, and then up the tortuous Medway River past every defense to Chatham, where the biggest vessels of the English Navy were laid up at moorings. There, he was supposed to destroy as many ships as he could, and burn or make off with those that he could not sink.

It was a plan that nobody but a landsman would have made: to a seaman it was mad. Even supposing that the whole of the English fleet would be laid up out of fighting condition and that the land defenses would be weak, there were still daunting hazards of navigation. The Thames estuary was notoriously full of sandbanks and other shallow areas where a large man-of-war would be stranded if she missed the tide. A square-rigged ship, unhandy to windward, could enter only with a wind between north and southeast—and having entered, she would have to wait for an opposite wind to take her out again.

The Medway was even worse than the Thames. Its estuary was a narrow winding channel with enormous mud flats, which were hidden during high water, and Chatham dockyard, where the English ships were lying, was seven miles up this tortuous waterway. A vessel needed a northeasterly wind to go in and a southwesterly wind to come out, and the tidal streams were so strong that a ship could enter the estuary only on the flood and go out only on the ebb. If the Dutch fought their way in, they would have to stay there and defend themselves until wind and tide allowed them to retreat.

De Ruyter disliked the idea, and made no bones about it. When the scheme was explained to his captains, they were aghast; a chronicler reported that one of them called it "manifestly ridiculous and impossible." But neither of the brothers de Witt was a man to be argued with; on board de Ruyter's flagship, Cornelis de Witt brought to bear all the power of the ruling States-General, of which Johan was head. The attack must proceed, and proceed at once, while the conference at Breda was getting under way. If the attack was successful, it would exact retribution for Terschelling and change the whole balance of the peace terms, which up to now favored the English.

The Dutch fleet—some 50 men-of-war, with the usual attendant fire ships and dispatch boats, together totaling about 80 vessels and more than 12,000 men—was sighted from the English shore on June 17. It was anchored in the King's Channel, one of the main entrances to the Thames. At first nobody either in or out of the Navy worried much about the enemy's appearance: because the Dutch fleet was lying at anchor, its presence was taken to be a mere demonstration of power. An attack while peace was being discussed seemed to be out of the question; it would flout all the rules (unwritten though they were) of this war at sea between the English and the Dutch.

But the English had entirely misread Dutch intentions. In fact the fleet had met bad weather on the crossing and some of its ships had lagged behind and were missing. De Ruyter was merely waiting for the right moment to attack. On the 18th he halted a Norwegian merchantman outward bound from the Thames, and her captain told de Ruyter that 20 English merchantmen were lying in the Hope, the reach of the Thames below the town of Gravesend. To Cornelis de Witt, who was growing impatient for action, that seemed to offer a chance for another bonfire in revenge. On the 19th, when the missing Dutch warships arrived, he persuaded de Ruyter to commence the operation by taking a squadron up the Thames after the 20 merchantmen.

The probe was a dismal failure—a reminder, if any were needed, that the attackers were at the mercy of wind and tide. The wind started out easterly, but before the Dutch ships reached the Hope it dropped, and when the tide turned, de Witt had to anchor to avoid being swept out of the river. In the meantime, the merchantmen had fled upstream while the wind was in the east and were now beyond reach. De Ruyter and de Witt called off the attempt and retreated back out of the Thames.

Nevertheless, this bold Dutch squadron had penetrated 20 miles up the Thames, farther than any enemy fleet since Viking times. The exploit set London in a panic. "The Distraction and Consternation was so great in Court and City as if the Dutch had been not only Masters of the River, but had really landed an Army of one hundred thousand Men," wrote Charles's minister, the Earl of Clarendon. "If the King's and Duke's personal Composure had not restrained Men from expressing their Fears, there wanted not some who would have advised them to have left the City." There was a frantic rush to commandeer all possible ships in the river and fit them out as fire ships. The English former general-at-sea, the Duke of Albemarle, hurried down to Gravesend—in company, according to Pepys, "with a great many idle lords and gentlemen with their pistols and fooleries"—and tried to organize defenses for the river. But almost all the population had fled, and in Gravesend not more than a dozen men could be found to protect the place.

By the next day, the panic had spread to the Medway. Peter Pett, still commissioner in charge of the dockyard, was a mild and indolent man; he showed none of the irascible independence of his father, who had so boldly built the *Prince Royal* at the opening of the century. Peter, hearing that 20 of the 80 Dutch ships were lying at the Buoy of the Nore, the naval anchorage just outside the Medway mouth where English fleets had been accustomed to lie in perfect security, suddenly took a terrible

Gravesend
the Hope
Gillingham
ROCHESTER

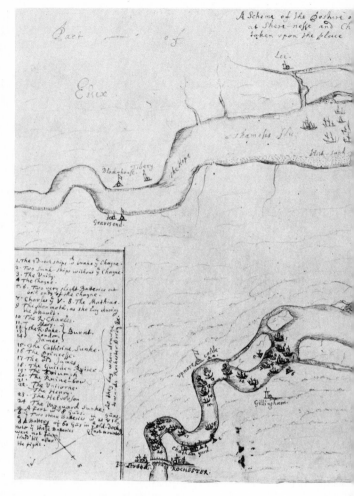

Dutch warships bottle up the mouths of the Medway and Thames Rivers in June 1667, in this sketch—keyed on the left to illustrate the position of the English fleet and defenses—drawn by Samuel Pepys's friend and fellow diarist John Evelyn. "A dishonour never to be wiped off!" wrote Evelyn, who blamed the Dutch success on the English Navy's "unaccountable negligence in not setting out our fleet in due time."

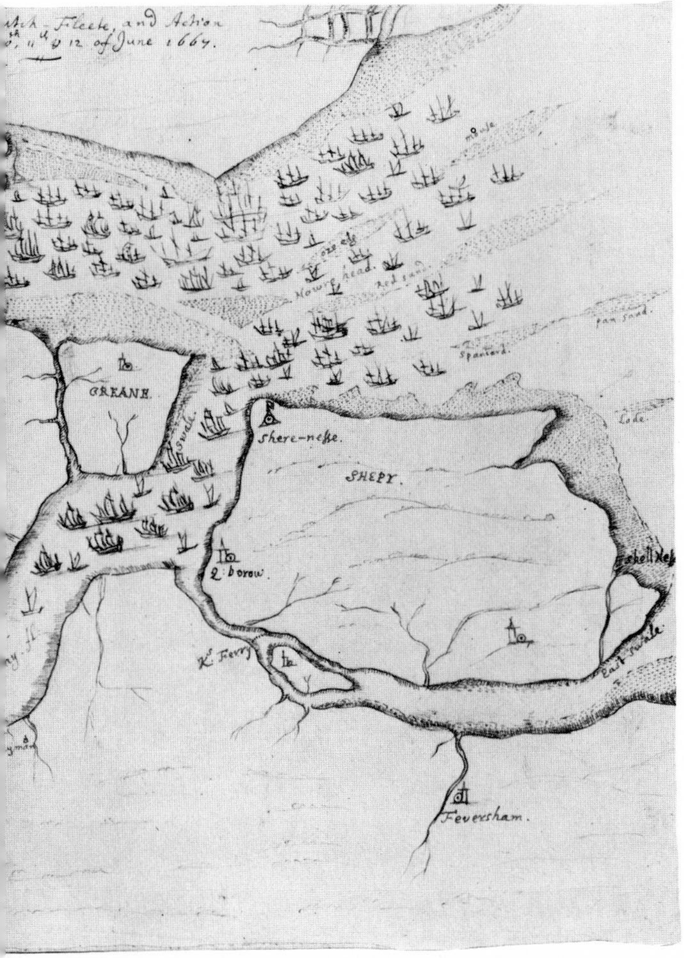
GREANE
Shere-nesse.
SHEPY.
Feversham.

fright. He thought that this squadron might attempt the Medway, and dispatched a note to the Navy Board asking advice. The commissioner, Pepys wrote, "was in a very fearful stink for fear of the Dutch."

In fact the huge dockyard had very little defense, except the natural difficulty any ships would encounter navigating the winding river. Nobody had ever conceived that an enemy fleet might come so far into the heart of England. Only 13 weeks before the Dutch came, the King had ordered shore defenses to be built round the naval ports to protect them during the winter lay-up. A new fort had been started on the point of land at Sheerness, commanding the entrance to the river, and in February the King himself had gone down to inspect it. But after the royal visit, most of the men at work on it disappeared—because, like the sailors and shipyard workers, they had not been paid. The work languished, and when the crisis came, the fortress was unfinished and only a few of its guns had been installed.

About seven miles up the Medway from Sheerness, an 800-yard iron chain, weighing 14½ tons, was stretched across the channel between the mud flats. The chain had been emplaced the previous May, and was suspended on floating wooden platforms. There was a system of pulleys to lower and raise it for the passage of friendly vessels. But as yet there were no guns on either bank to cover it with their fire.

Another four miles upriver, just below the dockyard, on the opposite side of the river, there was an Elizabethan fortress called Upnor Castle. About a dozen guns were mounted there and the dockyard itself had another half-dozen cannon. But neither the castle nor the dockyard had enough ammunition or enough gunners. Everything was weakened by the fatal lethargy that came from poverty, hunger and disillusionment.

As for the dockyard men, who were in charge of the laid-up warships in the river, the threat of attack was a final straw, and most of them disappeared with their families into the countryside. Behind them they left 18 major men-of-war, unmanned and more or less unrigged, among them the pride of the English Navy and the most powerful men-of-war in the world: the Duke of York's flagship *Royal Charles*, the *Royal Oak*, the *Royal James* and the *Loyal London*, all ranging between 1,021 and 1,230 tons and normally mounting from 70 to 90 heavy cannon.

Peter Pett's plea for advice was answered more thoroughly than he could have expected—or wished. Senior Navy and Army officers converged on the threatened river and began giving contrary orders. A Scottish regiment happened to be in Kent, and somebody ordered it to man the unfinished fort at Sheerness. It started to march there, but somebody else ordered it to turn round and go back again. Only one company—about 35 men—arrived at Sheerness. Another 100 sailors were sent downriver in two small ships to join the garrison of the fort. But both ships ran aground in the dark, and when they were floated off again more than half of the sailors had waded ashore through the mud and vanished. At that point, the Dutch commenced their attack.

In the late afternoon of June 20, on the rising tide, a Dutch squadron of 23 shallow-draft ships—six fire ships and 17 small-armed auxiliary yachts and trading craft—entered the river mouth on a northeasterly wind and began to bombard the fort at Sheerness. The few men inside manned what guns there were. But the guns were not properly mounted; at the first salvo most of them ran backward off their platforms into the mud and stuck there. The Dutch went on bombarding the fort until nightfall, and they landed 800 men to assault it from the shore. They need scarcely have bothered. At the final assault, they found only seven defenders at the guns. They found something else to please them, though: a vast store of timber, masts, spars, iron and brass, and barrels of gunpowder, resin and tar—a haul that the Dutch estimated as worth four or five tons of gold.

The news that Sheerness had fallen was brought up the river to Chatham—and the place fell into a state of confusion and panic. Albemarle raced to the dockyard from Gravesend; so did two of Pepys's colleagues of the Navy Board and at least three senior Army officers. All had their own ideas, but none had the means or the practical skill or the local knowledge to carry them out. They all started giving orders to Peter Pett, the only one who knew his way around. But he was not a fighting man at all, and had nobody to command except the remnants of the disgruntled dockyard workers. Soldiers and sailors, already disenchanted, saw that their highest commanders had not made any coherent plans and did not know what to do.

However, during the night of June 20, the commanders agreed on two things: to take the big ships, including the *Royal Charles*, upriver as far as they could go, and to take some small ones, mainly fire ships, downriver past the chain and sink them to block the channel. Albemarle ordered Pett to go ahead and do it, as if it were easy. But in the strong tides running through Chatham anchorage, it was far from easy.

The big ships could be moved only by towing them with boats on a rising tide; the small ships could go downriver only on the ebb. Pett asked for rowboats in order to move the *Royal Charles* and Albemarle said he could not have them: he needed them himself to take soldiers and shot to the shore batteries. Men were sent aboard the big ships, then taken off again to man the fire ships. The order to move the *Royal Charles* was canceled. Somebody insisted that she be used where she was, as a floating battery. Somebody else discovered that there was no powder or shot in her, and not many guns. The order to move her was reinvoked, but by this time the only pilot who could manage it had gone downriver with the fire ships.

During the next day, June 21, the English managed to sink five fire ships and two ketches in a narrow part of the channel below the chain. The operation was carefully observed by Dutch sloops and longboats making a reconnaissance. The Dutch then retreated to bide their time.

All through the night, the English forces labored with furious urgency—but to little effect. The harbor was full of boats being frantically rowed on errands of desperate importance, and being hailed out of the darkness and ordered to stop what they were doing and do something else. Large vessels were drifting out of control on the tide. The *Henry*, now mounting 64 guns, was let go from her moorings without any boats to tow her. She drifted up the river until she hit the bridge above Chatham at Rochester, hung there on the tide, drifted down again until she grounded on the ebb, floated up again on the flood and then, so Pepys

King Charles II and one of his many mistresses, Lady Castlemaine (right), scandalized London with their carefree attitude during the Medway debacle. According to the all-knowing Samuel Pepys, one night when the Dutch were less than 70 miles away from London "the King did sup with Lady Castlemaine at the Duchess of Monmouth's, and there were all mad in hunting of a poor moth."

was told, berthed herself "so well as no pilot could have done better."

Ashore, meanwhile, soldiers were struggling with guns in the Medway mud. There was no solid foundation to set the guns on; the troops were hunting for oak planking to build a platform and, as an alternative, looking for a piece of firm ground. Albemarle was issuing impossible orders "on pain of death" (and, one suspects, already rehearsing in his mind his own excuses for the disaster everyone could see was coming).

The only possible hope was a change of wind. But the wind stayed where it was, blowing gently but steadily from the river mouth. And early in the morning of June 22, across the mud flats, the masts of the Dutch were seen coming up the river on the tide. An advance squadron avoided the sunken English fire ships with scarcely a pause. This van consisted of three frigates, four armed yachts and two fire ships; astern of them was a line of more than 20 warships that stretched to the farthest distance in the morning light. At about 10 o'clock, the main force came round the last bend of the river and confronted the chain.

The Dutch did not know what chaos they had already created inside the harbor. It was an astonishing feat of daring to sail in as they did, and the English, who always admired daring, gave the credit to de Ruyter, but in fact he did not play the leading part in it. This was a small-ship action, and his place, at least in the early stages, was in command of the main fleet outside in the Thames.

The attack was organized by Cornelis de Witt, representative of the civilian leadership, in the face of objections from most of the senior admirals and captains. It was he who led the vanguard up the river, with an admiral named Willem Joseph Baron van Ghent and the junior captains of the frigates and fire ships. The crucial assault on the chain was made by Captain Jan van Brakel of the 40-gun frigate *Vrede*. He sailed right up to the site of the chain and boarded the only manned English ship outside the barrier, the frigate *Unity*. Her crew, in panic at their isolation, deserted her and swam ashore. Two Dutch fire ships came in astern of the *Vrede*. The first, the *Susanna*, hit the chain, stuck there and caught fire. The second, the *Pro Patria*, rode up full tilt on the chain, which was sagging a few feet underwater, and broke it with her weight.

Frigates and other small-armed ships came crowding past the now-futile chain with wind and tide behind them. Two guard ships above the chain were set on fire, and both blew up when the flames reached their magazines. So did the *Mary*, a 70-gun man-of-war that had been captured in an earlier battle from the Dutch and that had run aground in the chaos of the night before. Another major warship, the 66-gun *Monmouth*, was taken in tow upriver by boats at the last moment, ran aground off Upnor Castle, was floated again and reached comparative safety above the dockyard.

That left the *Royal Charles*, the proudest of them all, the flagship of the Duke of York and of Prince Rupert and Albemarle—now alone and deserted, half-rigged, most of her gunports empty, the victim of muddled orders. Astonishingly, the *Royal Charles* had still not been moved farther upriver to safety, and in the last resort two attempts by a handful of English crewmen had failed to put her to the torch. The men remaining on board now swam for their lives, and she was boarded and captured by a Dutch boat with a crew of nine. Impotently watching from upriver, one Englishman mused: "Our sick ships lay, like moulting fowl, a weak and easy prey." The English high commanders, Albemarle among them, saw the *Royal Charles*'s flag come down and the Dutch flag hoisted in its place. Cornelis de Witt went aboard her, a more powerful ship than the Dutch had ever possessed, and sat down in the Duke of York's cabin to write a justly triumphant report. Dating his dispatch, "In the *Royal Charles*, the 22 June, 1667, about two in the afternoon, lying in the River of Chatham," he went on to thank "God Almighty, who in His providence had deigned to humble the pride of the English nation by means of the glorious arms of their High Mightinesses the States-General."

And there, just above the chain, the Dutch advance paused—halted not by the English but by the turn of the tide.

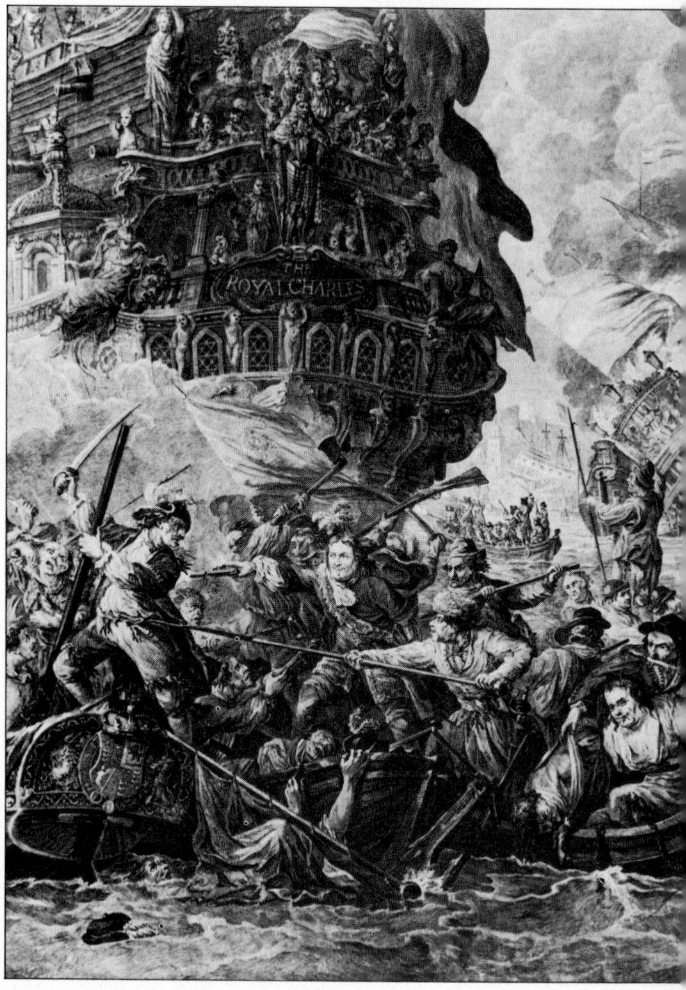
ROYAL CHARLES

Brandishing his cutlass, Admiral Michiel de Ruyter takes his longboat (at right) past the captured English flagship Royal Charles to finish off the remaining warships aground in the Medway. On the left in this fanciful commemorative engraving, Dutch sailors rout the remaining defenders, while at lower right the crumpled links of a protective chain, severed by the Dutch, droop into the water.

News of each step of this incredible disaster reached London with a time lag of a day. For the third time in three years, the city was reduced to panic—first the plague, then the fire, now this. Hour by hour, the Dutch were expected up the Thames. The King was advised to leave the capital: instead, he took a boat downriver to encourage the sinking of ships to block it, and the fitting out of fire ships. In their blind haste, his men made some costly mistakes: they passed up some empty vessels, while sinking seaworthy merchantmen in whose holds lay rich cargoes. Pepys, who still kept his fortune of £1,300 of gold in bags, sent it out of London once more, this time with his wife and father, who were given strict instructions to bury it in the garden of the family estate near Cambridge. They did, but made him angry by digging the hole in broad daylight while the neighbors were at church; anyone, he feared, might have seen them and dug it up again.

Rumors flew everywhere. Nobody knew what to believe. Everybody was looking for somebody to blame—the King, the papists, the Navy Board, the admirals. A man from Chatham told Pepys that English sailors on the Dutch ships—there were plenty of them—could be heard shouting that they had fought before for tickets (meaning Navy IOUs) and now were fighting for cash. Crowds of sailors' wives paraded the London streets, and they also were shouting: "This comes of you not paying our husbands." Drums beat through the city at night to call out the last reserves of militia. Stories of Dutch invasions came in from places all down the coast from Dover to Devon.

In Chatham, the night of June 22 was lit by flames of burning ships and flashes of desultory gunfire. The Dutch were not a mile away downstream, having advanced one and a half miles from the chain. The only remaining defenses between Chatham and them were ashore, in Upnor Castle on the north bank and in the lower part of the dockyard on the south, where a train of 10 heavy guns had arrived from the Tower of London. Above those defenses were a final two miles of water before the bridge at Rochester crossed the river. Further chaotic efforts were made that night to take the remaining ships into that last redoubt. Failing that, they would be abandoned. Albemarle gave another ill-considered order: sink all the ships at their moorings. Then it was canceled, in favor of

something a little less drastic: take them all upriver as far as possible, run them aground and hole them, thereby flooding them, to stop the Dutch from hauling them off.

That night the upper reaches again were full of the half-seen loom of moving ships, some more or less under control and others adrift and abandoned. The three biggest, the *Royal Oak*, the *Royal James* and the *Loyal London*, all ran aground close together in the mud just above the castle and were scuttled there, half full of water, embedded in the mud. The most splendid vessels that English art and science could create were left helpless and abandoned. Most of the rest, by morning, were huddled together in the last acute bend of the river just below the bridge. Albemarle spent the night with the men in the batteries. It was a curious scene: the unbending aristocrat, endowed with limitless authority, now at his wit's end to know how to use it, amid the sulky disenchanted soldiery. "Having no money to pay them," he wrote, "all I could do or say was little enough for their encouragement."

De Ruyter himself came up the river in the early part of the night: de Witt had sent him an imperious summons. The two of them conferred on board the captured *Unity*. They agreed to venture on the morning tide as far as Upnor Castle, and there to try to set the three big ships on fire. Five more fire ships were summoned from the fleet. Beyond that, nothing could be planned: everything, attack or escape, depended on the wind.

In the morning, battle was joined again, but now it was fought between the Dutch ships and the English batteries in the castle and the dockyard. Even the poorest of gunners ashore always had the advantage over ships: his platform was stable, and his targets were large and vulnerable. The range from the batteries to the center of the channel was only 300 yards, and proper batteries could hardly have avoided hitting the ships. But the batteries at Upnor Castle turned out, like the great chain, to be a phantom defense. Some of the gun carriages were rotten with age, many of the guns themselves were hopelessly rusted with disuse and—even worse—the cannon balls that had been hastily sent to the site of battle did not fit the bore of the old guns.

So, unburned and unsunk, the Dutch ships came on, urged forward by de Ruyter and de Witt, who were standing in an open longboat, shouting commands. The ships of war engaged the batteries. The fire ships passed them and grappled a victim each. First the *Loyal London* burst into flames, then the *Royal Oak,* and then the *Royal James.* A man observing from the dockyard wrote: "The destruction of these three stately and glorious ships of ours was the most dismal spectacle my eyes ever beheld, and it certainly made the heart of every true Englishman bleed."

The *Loyal London* and the *Royal James* were not burning fast enough to satisfy the Dutch, and they used their last two fire ships to reinforce the blaze. A huge smoke cloud rose over Chatham. Below in the lurid light of the fire, the guns of the ships and batteries thundered, and small Dutch boats darted among the falling embers directing the fire-ship crews and taking them off when their work was done.

The Dutch made no further attempt on the dockyard or the ships at the bridge. They had done enough. But the final humiliation for the English was still to come. The Dutch did not burn the flagship of the English fleet, the *Royal Charles*. They put a crew on board. People in the dock-yard, stunned by what had already happened, saw the great ship beginning to list and they guessed what the Dutch were up to—shifting her guns and everything movable across to one side, so that she would draw less water. They towed her to the center of the channel, and then, very calmly, out past the broken chain and down the river "at a time, both for tides and wind," Pepys recorded with grudging admiration, "when the best pilot in Chatham would not have undertaken it."

Pepys was overstating the case somewhat. As if on command from the Dutch, the wind had shifted from the northeast, which had favored their entrance, to the southwest, which aided their retreat from the Medway. And the tide now obligingly was at ebb. Still, towing this great vessel downriver past all obstacles was a feat of great magnitude, and Pepys was altogether correct in his admiration.

Here and there some English horsemen and foot soldiers gathered along the banks to fire on the enemy ships as they proceeded downriver. But the range was too great and their weapons too small for them to be more than a minor annoyance. The Dutch were far more worried about wind and water; the wind could shift back into the north at any moment, and the ebbing tide, for all the push it gave them, was lowering the river level and increasing the perils of the mudbanks.

At one point the frigate *Harderwijck*, carrying both de Witt and de Ruyter, went hard aground, and the two leaders hastily transferred to a smaller sloop for the remainder of their escape. The crew of the *Harderwijck* had to wait anxiously for the tide to flood before they could resume their passage. And even after all the Dutch had made good their departure from the Medway, the fleet then had to navigate the almost equally tricky Thames. There were hours of great concern when their prize, the *Royal Charles*, and three other ships grounded on sandbanks near the mouth of the Thames. But in time, they, too, were floated free. And at last, after 72 hours in the heart of the English Naval establishment, the Dutch sailed home in triumph without the slightest pursuit by the demoralized English.

As the *Royal Charles* was brought in victory to Holland, thousands upon thousands of cheering Dutchmen crowded the shores to see her come in. Soon afterward, Cornelis de Witt, Michiel de Ruyter and Willem van Ghent were each presented a handsome gold cup worth 25,000 guilders by their grateful government. Johan de Witt was showered with honors. "God be praised and thanked," he wrote, "for such a great mercy; and may he grant that the arrogance of the enemy may be curbed, and the present bloody war changed to an honorable and assured peace."

As for the *Royal Charles*, she never sailed again. The Dutch kept her on exhibit for a while, then laid her up until 1672 when they finally sold her for scrap timber at public auction—where she fetched 5,000 guilders. But they saved from her stern the carved royal coat of arms *(page 161)*, which they stored away among other treasured naval artifacts.

The English had suffered greatly at the battle on the Medway. Six of the fleet's major vessels had been lost. Two others had been captured, and several smaller ones scuttled. They estimated the amount of damage to

With their tricolors streaming in a blue enameled sky, Dutch ships sail around the outside of this gold goblet, which commemorated the Dutch triumphs during the 1667 Medway attack. Authorized by the government of Holland at a total cost of 72,000 guilders, three such goblets were cast and presented to Commander Cornelis de Witt and Admirals Michiel de Ruyter and Willem van Ghent "not as a reward" for their victories—they were suitably rewarded with cash—but simply as souvenirs to be kept in the men's families.

Around the edges of the conference room in Breda, disgruntled delegates continue to argue the merits of the treaty that ended the second Anglo-Dutch war, even while the plenipotentiaries vote for acceptance. Though the terms demanded by the Dutch were mild, the English were humiliated by the defeat. "Nobody is speaking of the peace with any content or pleasure; but are silent in it, as of a thing they are ashamed of," wrote Pepys.

be close to £200,000. There was also a commercial loss of considerable magnitude because the Dutch tore up coastal shipping and blockaded both the Medway and the Thames Rivers for some time *(pages 162-169).* When it was finally all over, the English were not bad losers—at least so far as the Dutch were concerned. It had been a shocking defeat, but the victims rather admired the victors for pulling it off—for their courage, their skill, and most of all perhaps for their chivalry. The Dutch had burned no houses. They took no plunder except for some random and unauthorized pillaging of sheep for provisions (and for that the Dutch Navy court-martialed their disobedient seamen). And only one civilian had been killed in the whole attack—an inquisitive man who watched the excitement from a neighboring hill and was struck by somebody's stray bullet.

The English even found a hero to redeem their pride. He was not a Navy man, but a Captain Archibald Douglas, who was in command of some Scots soldiers ordered on board the *Royal Oak.* The Scots had been detached from their unit at Margate and provided only a token force of resistance against the advance of the Dutch. When the vessel caught fire all of the men fled save Douglas, who remained on board till he died in the conflagration. Not long afterward an elegant eulogy, "The Loyal Scott," was written, describing his last moments:

Downe on the deck he layd himselfe and dyed,
With his deare sword reposeing by his side.
And on the flameing plancks he rests his head,
As one whoe huggs himselfe in a warme bed.
The Shipp burns downe and with his relicks sinks,
And the sadd streame beneath his ashes drinks.

The English were less generous in assigning blame for the fiasco. A great many Englishmen in high positions, commencing with the King, should have shared the blame, and everyone knew it. Indeed, the fundamental fault was the cynical immorality of the age, which allowed men of power to enrich themselves while sailors were left to starve. Some punishments were meted out to a few minor officers present at the Medway debacle. One was shot; another was sentenced "to have a halter put round his neck, and a wooden sword broke over his head," according to contemporary annals. And everyone in authority combined with one accord to whitewash himself and heap every scrap of blame on Peter Pett.

Poor Pett. Confused by the conflicting orders he had been given, and too weak a man to defend himself, he was a handy scapegoat, and as he had been in charge of the dockyard it was easy to blame all the cracks in its defenses on him. The ubiquitous Pepys observed that Pett's "faults to me seem only great omissions; in general I find him to be but a weak silly man, that is guilty of horrid neglect in this business all along." But the Duke of Albemarle lodged formal charges against Pett, and the House of Commons tried him and sentenced him to imprisonment in the Tower. He was let out four months later, when the recriminations had begun to die away.

By then, the peace had been signed at Breda. One might think that the Dutch, with such a victory, would have sought to impose crushing terms. But they did not. It may have been that the humiliation of the English at the Medway, the glorious revenge for Terschelling, was satisfaction enough. The Dutch were not a vicious people; it had not been a vicious series of wars. Of more practical import, the English still had a fleet, some dozen warships in squadrons from the east and south coasts, and were still a formidable foe for all their financial and other woes. Lastly, there were the French, looming ominously to the west. Far better to accept a stalemate, to agree to an honorable peace and be done with it. The treaty was remarkably restrained. The English made some minor concessions in their Navigation Act. The Dutch still admitted the English claim to be saluted in the Narrow Seas. The English conceded a Dutch claim to Surinam in South America, and the Dutch agreed to let the English keep a fort in West Africa. Two islands were exchanged: the Dutch kept Pulo Run, where the nutmeg trees were sprouting again, and the English kept Manhattan; both sides seemed satisfied.

In terms of power or territory, nobody won and nothing was lost or gained. But both nations had won something—experience. They had learned the science of naval warfare, and tested their skill. They had made the warship—while distinct from the merchant ship—a vessel vital to the security of trade. With the warship had evolved the important line-ahead tactics of sending ships into battle in orderly columns with plans aforethought—tactics that would serve well for two centuries, until Lord Nelson applied his genius to another kind of tactics at Trafalgar. Finally, they had done all this by developing a special strategy of warfare for use afloat. Merchants went on grumbling jealously, but the mutual respect and admiration between the fleets were shown in a small incident soon after the war.

De Ruyter's son Engel was 18 years old, and already a frigate captain. The Dutch chose to send him with his ship on a mission to London to pick up a Dutch plenipotentiary and bring the diplomat home. While in London young de Ruyter was received with the highest honor by the English admirals his father had defeated, and was knighted by King Charles II. It was a graceful salute.

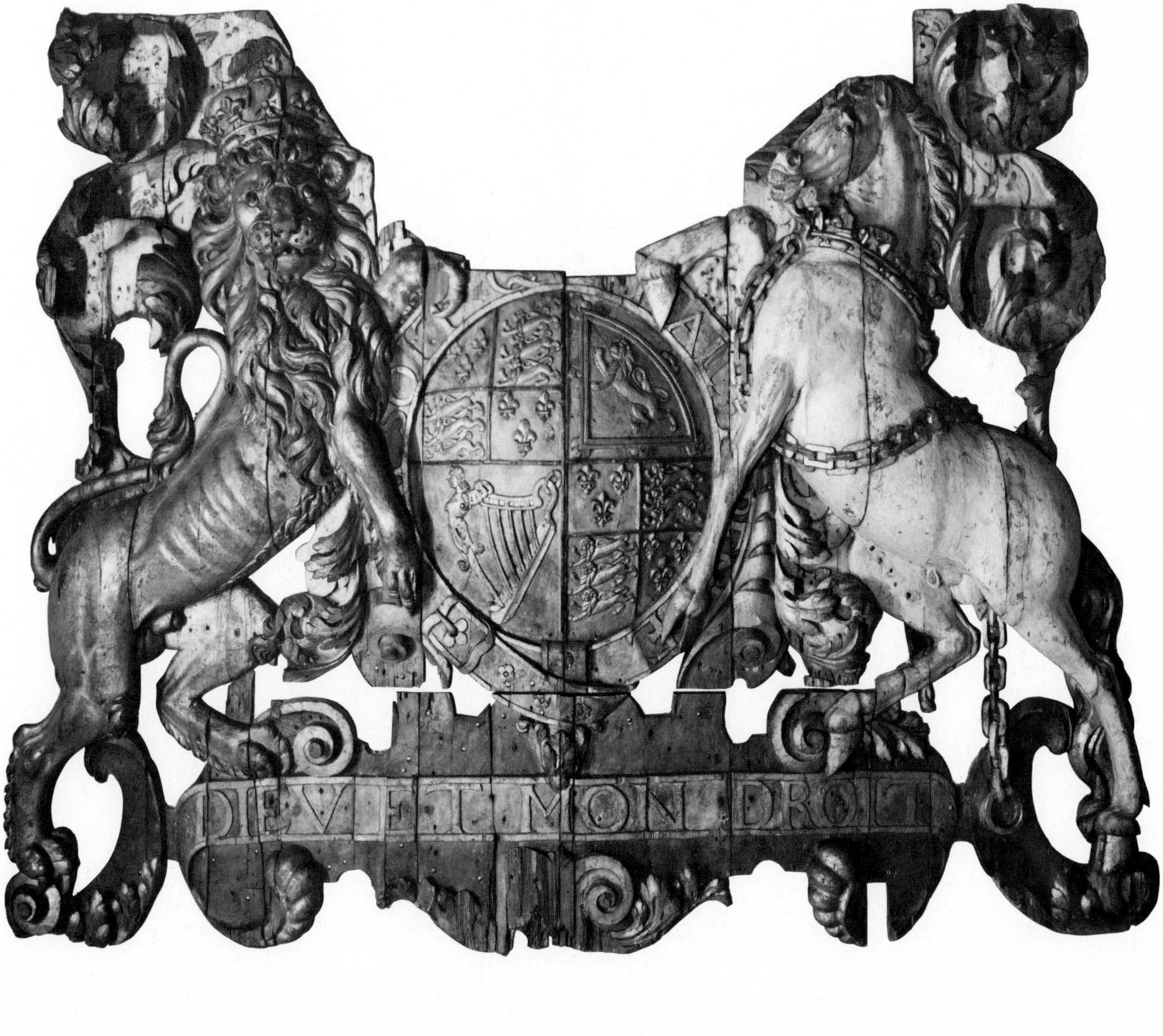
DIEV ET MON DROIT

The sternpiece with King Charles II's coat of arms was all that remained of the great flagship bearing his name, six years after her capture by the Dutch. The man-of-war that began life as the Naseby during Cromwell's short-lived Commonwealth was broken up for scrap lumber after being exhibited as a war prize.

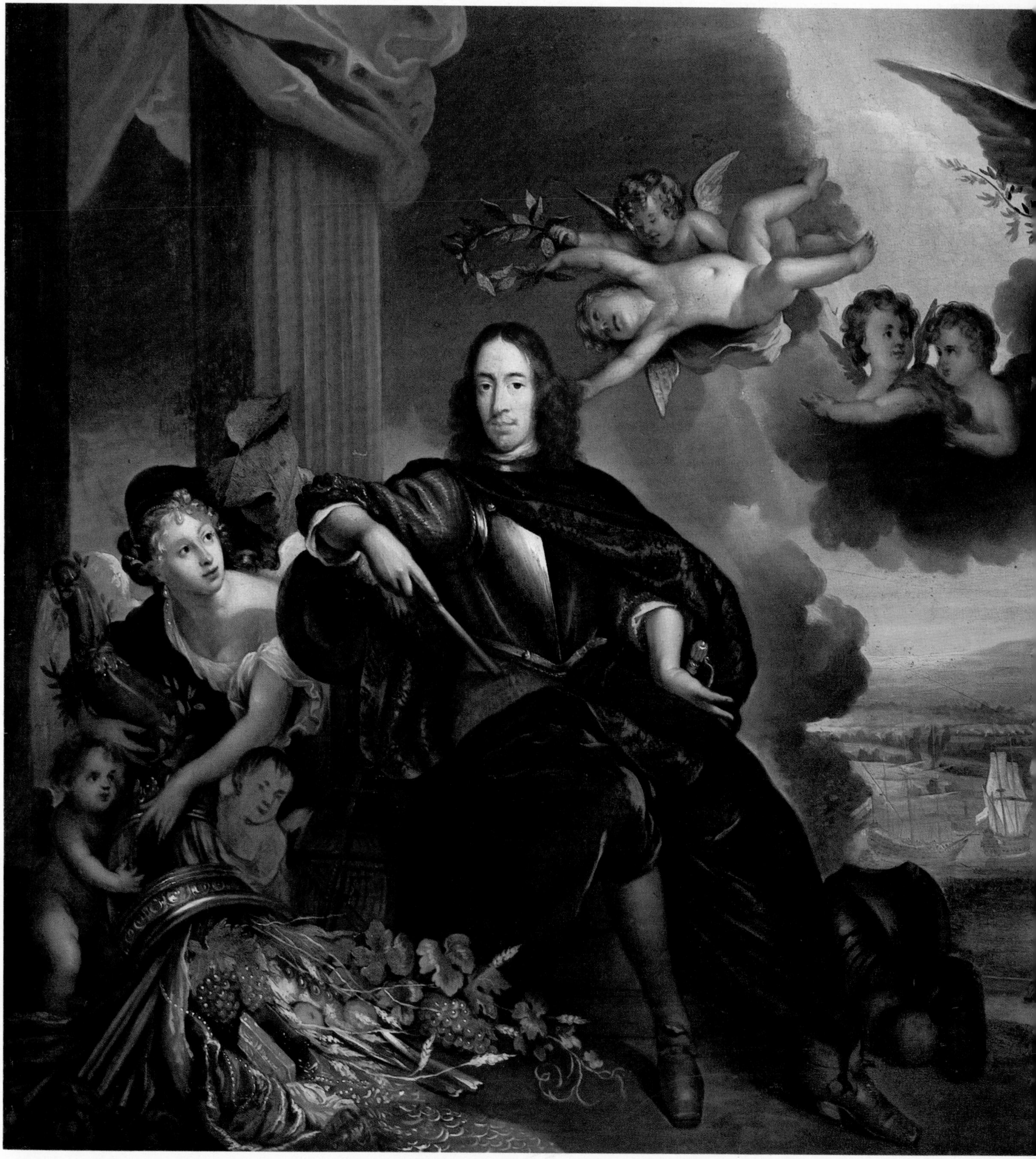

The greater victory that might have been

Loud was the rejoicing when the Dutch fleet returned in triumph from its historic foray up the Medway River into the heart of the English Naval establishment. Crowds paraded in the streets; poets sang of the Dutch "sea lions"; painters rushed to immortalize the heroes and record the death-defying tactics that led to the destruction of some of England's most formidable men-of-war and the capture of a flagship *(left and on following pages)*. But for one important Dutchman, the sweet draughts of victory had a sour aftertaste: the mission was not all that it could have been.

This man was Johan de Witt, Dutch chief of government, architect of the Medway raid and brother of Cornelis de Witt, the commander who carried it out. Once the initial attack had succeeded, Johan de Witt furiously urged brother Cornelis to press on to greater conquests. In letters to the fleet prowling English waters, he suggested a second venture into the Medway to destroy the remaining ships. He wrote of ravaging the dockyards on the adjacent Thames River, of attacking the port of Plymouth or Portsmouth, and possibly the Isle of Wight.

Cornelis responded by sending a 17-ship squadron north to destroy coastal shipping. A second squadron of 14 ships reconnoitered nearly 20 miles up the Thames to Gravesend before retreating upon receiving word of heavy shore batteries. Cornelis next mounted an assault with 1,400 soldiers and sailors on the fort at Harwich, 45 miles up the English east coast, and himself landed on English soil to direct the attack, standing within musket range of the defenders.

But the Dutch were beaten off, and thereafter Cornelis devoted himself primarily to blockading the Medway and the Thames, thus denying London its seaborne commerce. The Dutch blockade lasted for several months, until after a peace treaty was ratified, and caused Londoners no end of alarm and discomfort. But Johan de Witt remained unsatisfied that Cornelis' forces had done everything they could to humble the English. He expressed his sharp disappointment in a note to his brother, which ended with the Latin: *Vincere scit, victoriam ut nescit*—"He knows how to win a victory, but not how to exploit it."

Cornelis de Witt is attended by angels and cherubs in this allegorical painting commemorating the daring Dutch raid up England's Medway River. Dutch warships crowd the river to Upnor Castle (far right), where English men-of-war are ablaze. In the distance is the town of Chatham, last redoubt of the surprised and largely helpless English fleet.

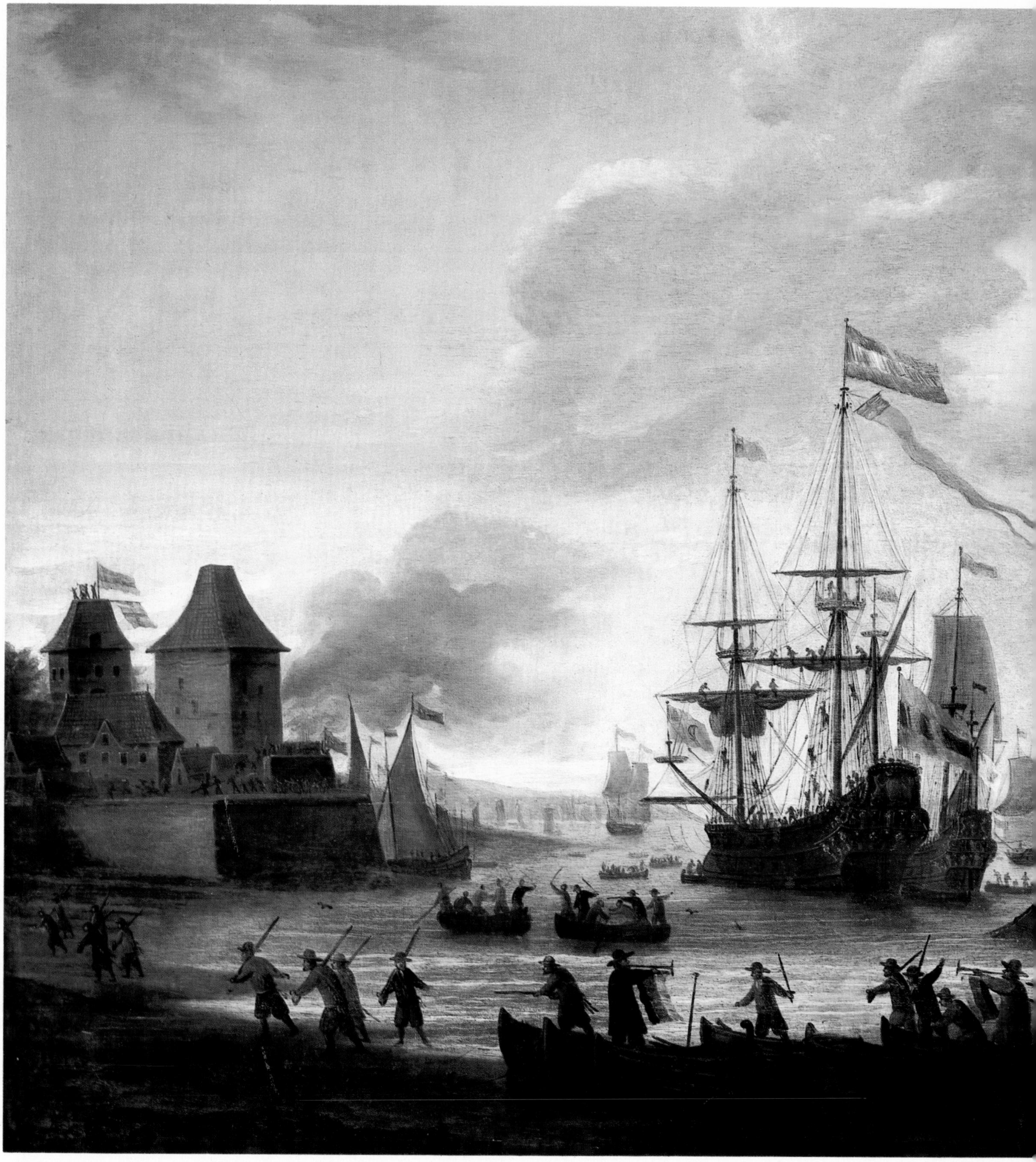

Dutch troops storm Fort Sheerness at the mouth of the Medway as two English men-of-war blow up offshore in this contemporary composite painting of battle scenes. "Our troops fought pluckily and had the upper hand," one of the attackers reported. "The colonel had two magazines and a small castle blown sky high."

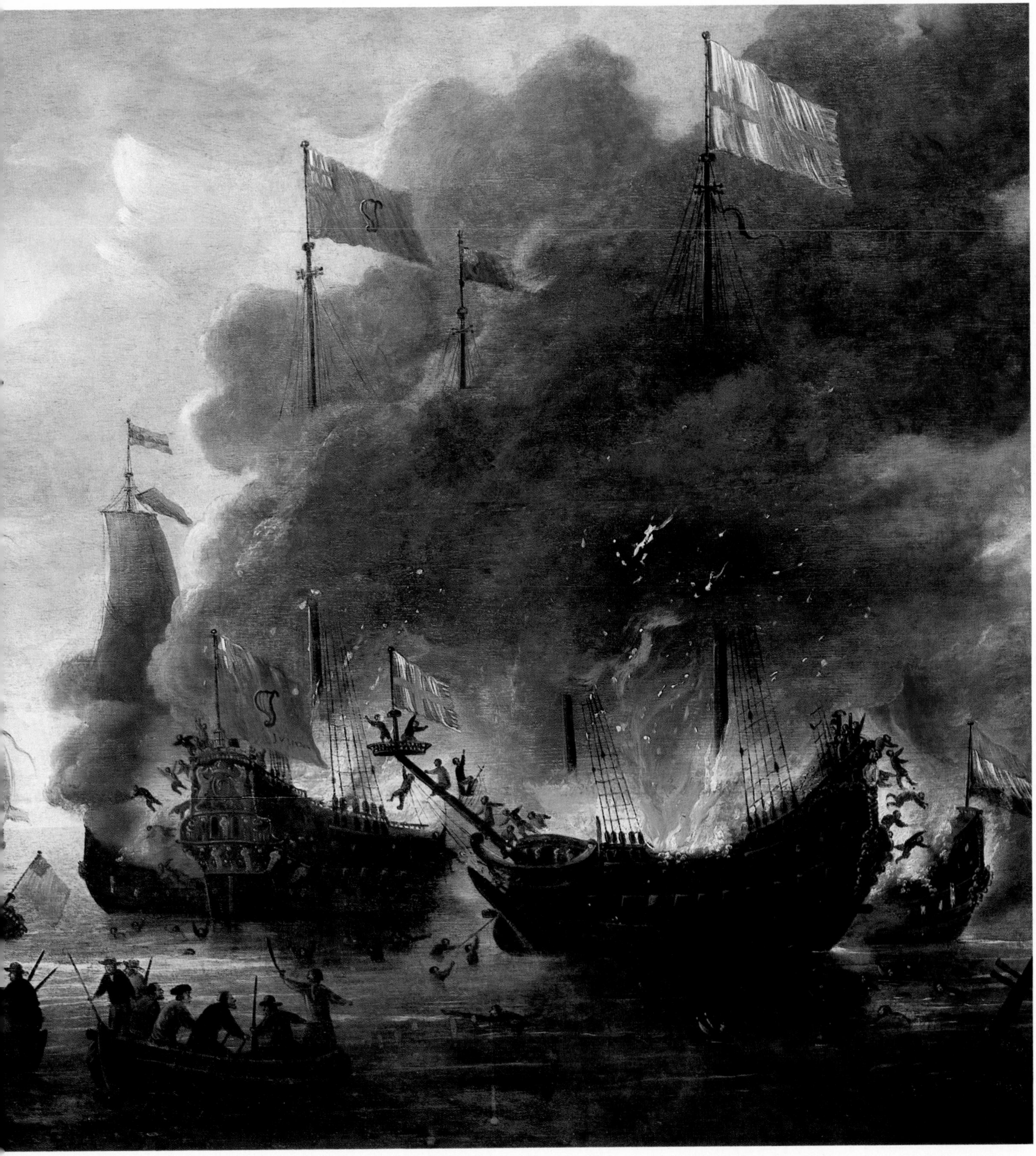

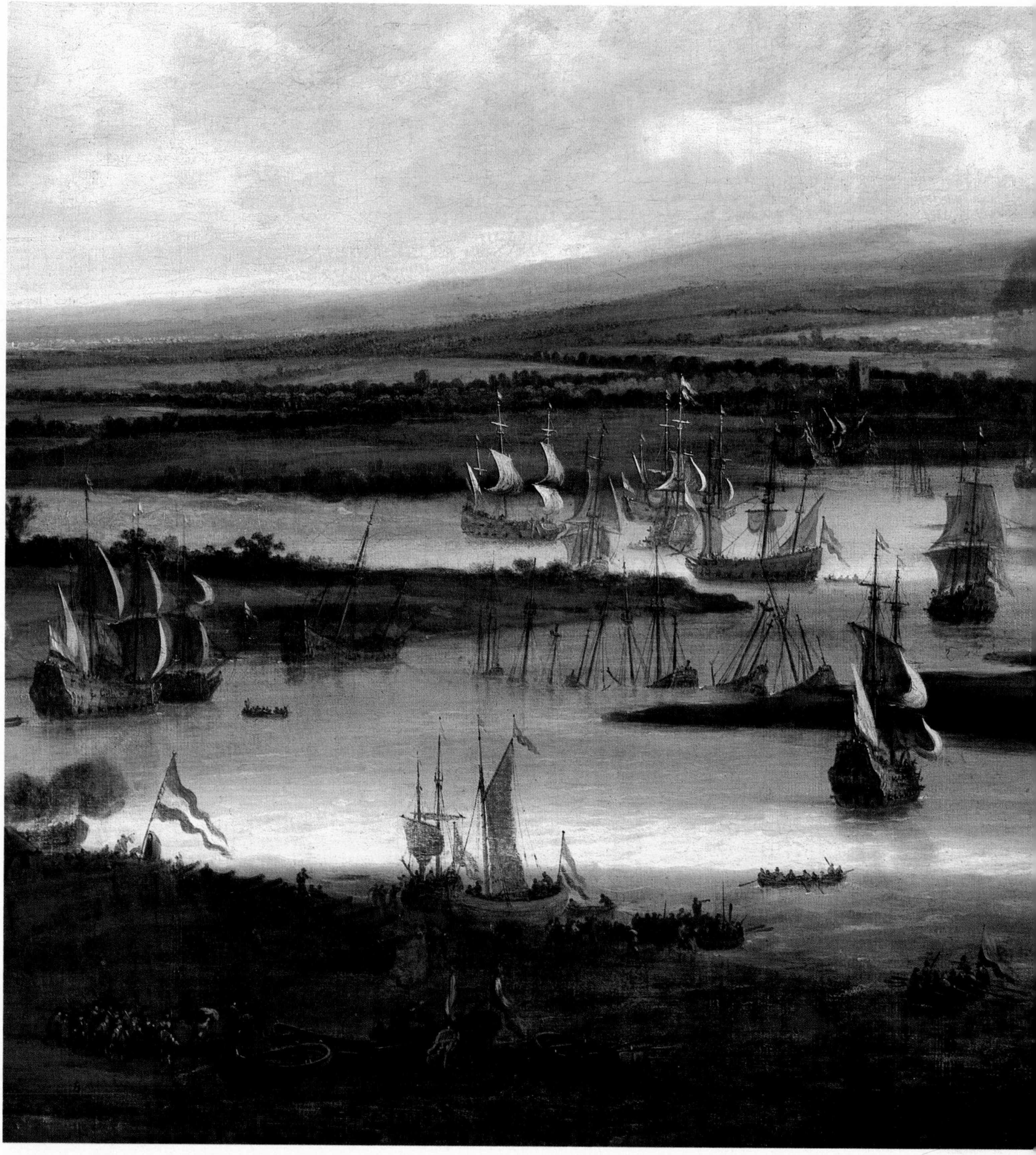

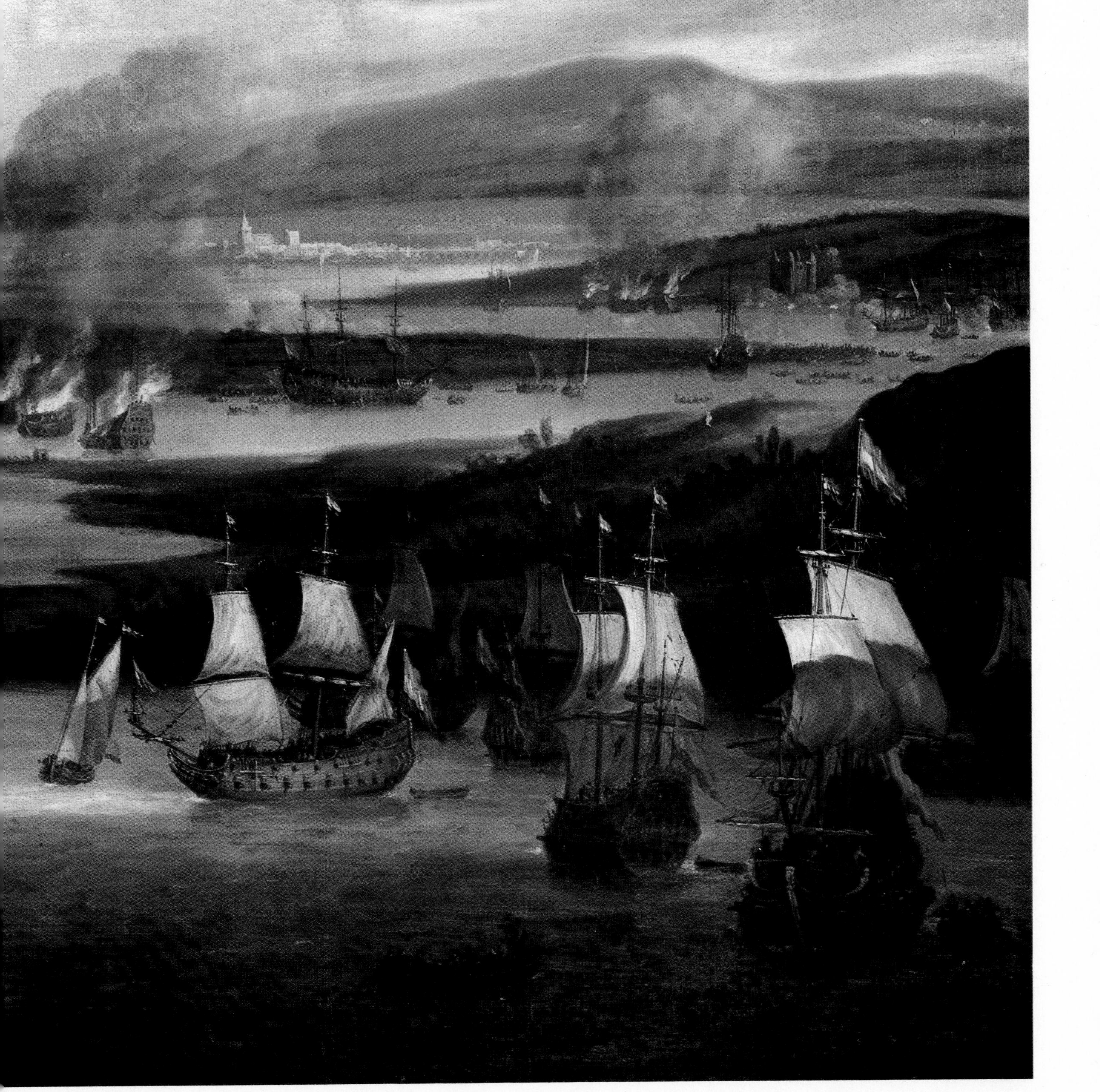

The panorama from Fort Sheerness (lower left) to Upnor Castle (far right) includes ships scuttled in vain to block the Dutch. It was to Pepys that an eyewitness described the taking of the Royal Charles "with a boat of nine men, who found not a man on board her, and presently a man went up and struck her flag and jacke."

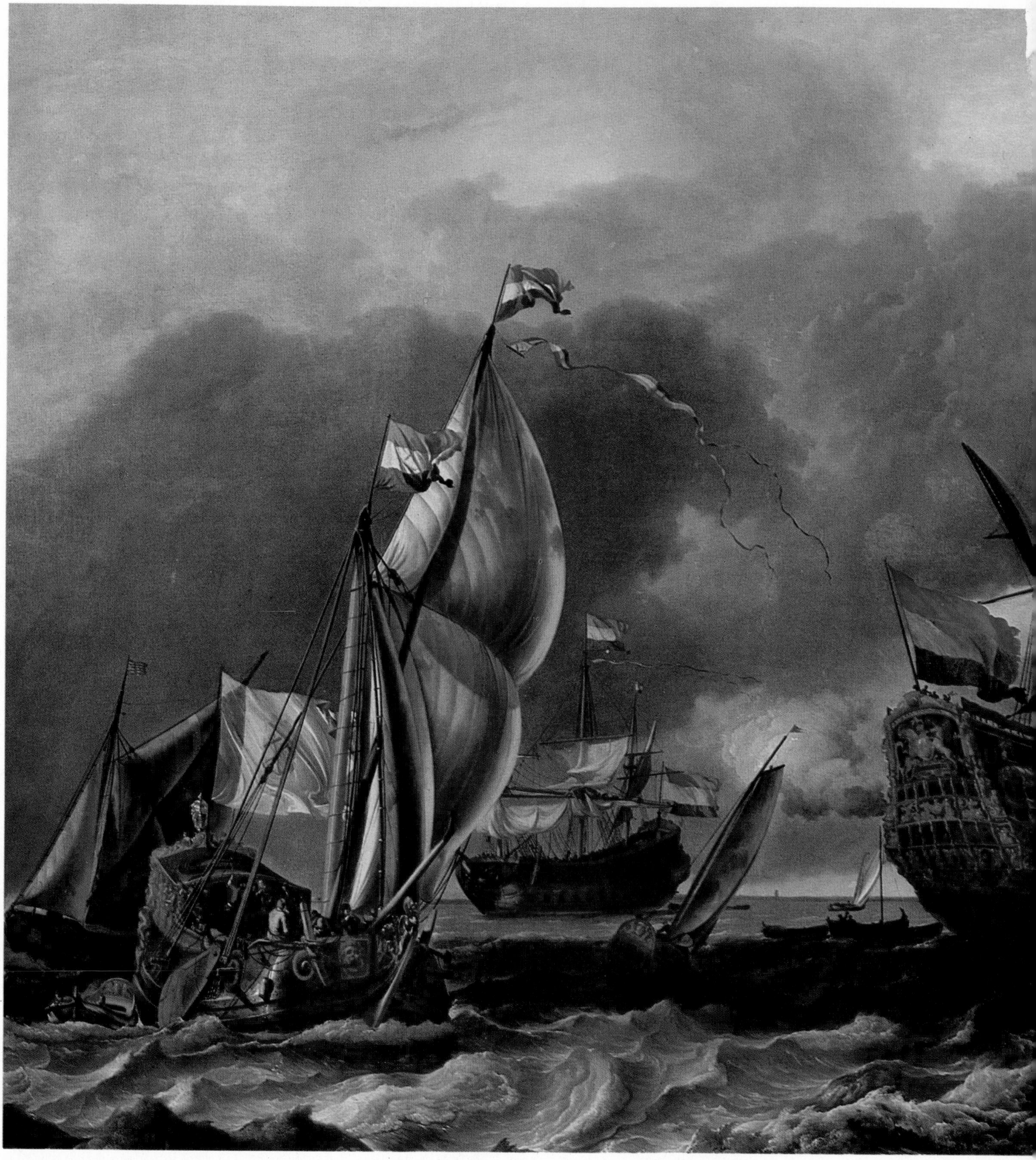

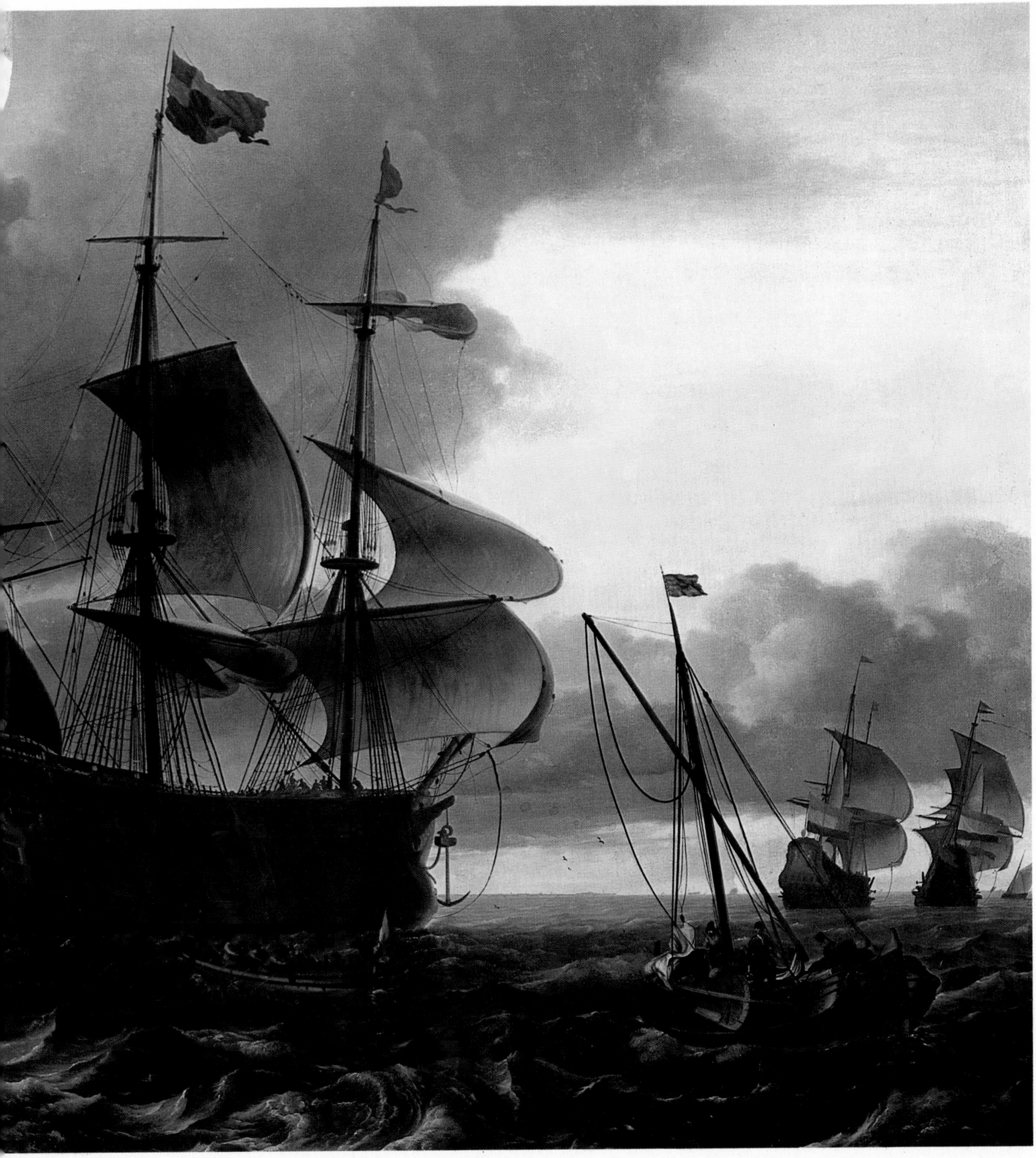

War prize of the Dutch, the Royal Charles (center) is escorted to Holland in this heroic painting. There was "such consternation among the enemy," wrote Cornelis de Witt, "that all the troops ran away from the ship the Royal Charles and part of them jumped into the water, and this was captured without any resistance."

Bibliography

Abbott, Wilbur Cortez, *The Writing and Speeches of Oliver Cromwell*. Russell and Russell, 1970.

Abel, Sir Wescott, *The Shipwright's Trade*. Cambridge University Press, 1948.

Abrahams, Peter, *Jamaica: An Island Mosaic*. Her Majesty's Stationery Office, 1957.

Anderson, R. C., ed.:
The Journal of Edward Mountagu, First Earl of Sandwich. Navy Records Society, 1929.
The Journals of Sir Thomas Allin, Vol. II. Navy Records Society, 1940.

Archibald, E. H. H., *The Wooden Fighting Ship in the Royal Navy*. Arco, 1968.

Ashley, Maurice, *Cromwell's Generals*. St. Martin's Press, 1955.

Atkinson, C. T., and Samuel Rawson Gardiner, eds., *Letters and Papers Relating to the First Dutch War, 1652-1654*, Vols. I-V. Navy Records Society, 1899-1912.

Bagrow, Leo, *History of Cartography*, revised and enlarged by R. A. Skelton. C. A. Watts, 1964.

Barbour, Violet, *Capitalism in Amsterdam in the Seventeenth Century*. Johns Hopkins Press, 1950.

Barlow, Edward, *Barlow's Journal*, transcribed by Basil Lubbock. Hurst and Blackett, 1934.

Bartel, Roland, ed., *London in Plague and Fire 1665-1666*. D. C. Heath, 1957.

Bathe, B. W., et al., *The Great Age of Sail*. Crescent Books, 1967.

Bell, Walter George, *The Great Fire of London in 1666*. Bodley Head, 1951.

Blewitt, Mary, *Surveys of the Seas*. Macgibbon & Kee, 1957.

Blok, Petrus Johannes, *The Life of Admiral de Ruyter*. Greenwood Press, 1975.

Boxer, C. R.:
The Anglo-Dutch Wars of the 17th Century. National Maritime Museum, 1974.
The Dutch Seaborne Empire, 1600-1800. Hutchinson, 1965.

Bricken, Charles, *Landmarks of Mapmaking*. Elsevier, 1968.

Bright, Mynors, and John Warrington, eds., *The Diary of Samuel Pepys*. J. M. Dent, 1953.

Bryant, Arthur, *Samuel Pepys: The Man in the Making*. Macmillan, 1933.
Samuel Pepys: The Savior of the Navy. Macmillan, 1939.

Casson, Lionel, *Illustrated History of Ships & Boats*. Doubleday, 1964.

Cipolla, Carlo M., *Guns, Sails and Empires*. Pantheon Books, 1965.

Clark, Sir George, *The Later Stuarts, 1660-1714*. Clarendon Press, 1956.

Clowes, G. S. Laird, *Sailing Ships*. His Majesty's Stationery Office, 1932.

Clowes, William Laird, *The Royal Navy*. Sampson Low, Marston, 1897.

Colledge, J. J., *Ships of the Royal Navy: An Historical Index*. David & Charles, 1969.

Corbett, Julian S., *The Successors of Drake*. Longmans, Green, 1900.

Cowburn, Philip, *The Warship in History*. Macmillan, 1965.

Culver, Henry, *Forty Famous Ships*. Garden City, 1936.

Curtis, C. D., *Blake, General-at-Sea*. Barnicott and Pearce, Wessex Press, 1934.

Danes, Godfrey, *The Early Stuarts 1603-1660*. Clarendon Press, 1959.

Davis, Ralph:
English Merchant Shipping and Anglo-Dutch Rivalry in the Seventeenth Century. National Maritime Museum, 1975.
The Rise of the English Shipping Industry. David & Charles, 1962.

Doyley, Edward, *A Narrative of the Great Success*. Henry Hills and John Field, 1658.

Elliott, J. H., *Imperial Spain, 1469-1716*. St. Martin's Press, 1964.

Falconer, William, *Falconer's Marine Dictionary*. David & Charles Reprints, 1970.

Falkus, Christopher, *The Life and Times of Charles II*. Doubleday, 1972.

Firth, C. H., ed., *The Narrative of General Venables*. Longmans, Green, 1900.

Franzen, Anders, *The Warship Vasa*. Norstedt and Bonnier, 1962.

Furber, Holden, *Rival Empires of Trade in the Orient, 1600-1800*. University of Minnesota Press, 1976.

Gaunt, William, *Marine Painting*. Secker & Warburg, 1975.

Geyl, Pieter:
History of the Low Countries. Macmillan, 1964.
The Revolt of the Netherlands. Ernest Benn, 1958.

Graham, Winston, *The Spanish Armada*. Doubleday, 1972.

Haley, K. H. D., *The Dutch in the Seventeenth Century*. Harcourt, Brace, Jovanovich, 1972.

Hannay, David, *The Great Chartered Companies*. Williams and Norgate, 1926.

Hart, Roger, *English Life in the Seventeenth Century*. Putnam's, 1970.

Howarth, R. G., ed., *The Letters and the Second Diary of Samuel Pepys*. J. M. Dent, 1932.

Huizinga, J. H., *Dutch Civilization in the 17th Century and Other Essays*. Collins, 1968.

Johnson, Paul, *Elizabeth I*. Holt, Rinehart and Winston, 1974.

Keevil, J. J., *Medicine and the Navy: 1200-1900*. E. & S. Livingstone, 1958.

Kemp, Peter, ed.:
History of the Royal Navy. Putnam's, 1969.
The Oxford Companion to Ships and the Sea. Oxford University Press, 1976.

Kennedy, Paul M., *The Rise and Fall of British Naval Mastery*. Baylis, 1976.

Koeman, C., *The History of Lucas Janszoon Waghenaer and his Spiegel der Zeevaerdt*. Sequoia, 1964.

Konijnenburg, E. Van, *Shipbuilding from Its Beginnings*. Congress of Navigation, 1930.

Kouwenhoven, John A., *The Columbia Historical Portrait of New York*. Doubleday, 1953.

Lacey, Robert, *Sir Walter Raleigh*. Atheneum, 1974.

Landström, Björn, *The Ship*. Doubleday, 1961.

Lewis, Michael, *The Navy Of Britain*. George Allen and Unwin, 1948.

Lielde, Jacob, *The Great Dutch Admirals*. Books for Libraries Press.

Lister, Raymond, *Antique Maps and Their Cartographers*. G. Bell & Sons, 1970.

Lloyd, Christopher:
Atlas of Maritime History. Arco, 1975.
The British Seaman. Fairleigh Dickinson University Press, 1968.

Long, A. G., *Some Things Nearly So: The Dutch Raid on the River Medway*. H. M. Dockyard, Chatham, 1967.

Lynam, Edward, *British Maps and Map-Makers*. Collins, 1947.

Macintyre, Donald, and Basil Bathe, *Man-of-War*. McGraw-Hill, 1971.

Mahan, A. T., *The Influence of Seapower upon History*. Little, Brown, 1918.

Maland, David, *Europe in the Seventeenth Century*. St. Martin's Press, 1966.

Marx, Robert F., *The Capture of the Treasure Fleet*. David McKay.

Mets, J. A., *Naval Heroes of Holland*. Abbey Press, 1902.

Newton, A. P., *The European Nations in the West Indies*. Barnes & Noble, 1933.

Ogg, David, *England in the Reign of Charles II*. Clarendon Press, 1934.

Ollard, Richard:
The Escape of Charles II: After the Battle of Worcester. Scribner, 1966.
Man of War: Sir Robert Holmes and the Restoration Navy. Hodder and Stoughton, 1969.
Pepys. Holt, Rinehart and Winston, 1974.
This War without an Enemy. Atheneum, 1976.

Oppenheim, M., *The Naval Tracts of Sir William Monson*, Vol. I. Navy Records Society, 1902.

Ortzen, Len, *Guns at Sea*. Galahad Books, 1976.

Osborne, Thomas, compiler, *The Collec-*

tion of Voyages and Travels from the Library of the Earl of Oxford, Vol. II. Thos. Osborne, 1745.

Penn, Granville, Memorials of the Professional Life and Times of Sir William Penn, KNT. James Duncan, 1833.

Perrin, W. G., ed., The Autobiography of Phineas Pett. Navy Records Society, 1918.

Powell, J. R., ed., The Letters of Robert Blake. Navy Records Society, 1937.
Robert Blake, General-at-Sea. Collins, 1972.

Powell, J. R., and E. K. Timings, eds., The Rupert & Monck Letter Book 1666. Navy Records Society, 1969.

Preston, Admiral Sir Lionel, Sea and River Painters of the Netherlands in the Seventeenth Century. Oxford University Press, 1937.

Quennell, Peter, and Alan Hodge, eds., The Past We Share. Prometheus Press, 1960.

Robinson, A. H. W., Marine Cartography in Britain. Leicester University Press, 1962.

Robison, Rear Admiral S. S. and Mary L., A History of Naval Tactics from 1530 to 1930, The Evolution of Tactical Maxims.

Banta, 1942.

Rogers, P. G., The Dutch in the Medway. Oxford University Press, 1970.

Rosenberg, Jakob, et al., Dutch Art and Architecture: 1600 to 1800. Penguin Books, 1977.

Sanderson, Michael, Sea Battles. David & Charles, 1975.

The Second Dutch War De Tweede Engelse Oorlog—1665-1667. National Maritime Museum, 1967.

Smith, Lacey Baldwin, This Realm of England, 1399-1688. Heath, 1971.

Stayner, Richard, The Naval Miscellany II, "A Narrative of the Battle of Santa Cruz." Navy Records Society, 1912.

Tannerbaum, Edward R., European Civilization since the Middle Ages. John Wiley, 1971.

Tavernier, Bruno, Great Maritime Routes. Viking, 1972.

Taylor, E. G. R., The Haven-Finding Art. Hollis & Carter, 1971.

Taylor, S. A. G., The Western Design. Solstice, 1969.

Tedder, Arthur W., The Navy of the Restoration. Cambridge University Press,

1915.

Van de Velde Drawings (A Catalogue of Drawings in the National Maritime Museum). Cambridge University Press, 1973.

Vere, Francis, Salt in Their Blood. Cassell, 1955.

Vreugdenhil, A., Lists of Men-of-War, 1650-1700: Ships of the United Netherlands, 1648-1702. Cambridge University Press, 1938.

Warner, Oliver:
Great Battle Fleets. Hamlyn, 1973.
Great Sea Battles. Spring Books, 1963.

Waters, David, The Art of Navigation in England in Elizabethan and Early Stuart Times. Hollis & Carter, 1958.

Williams, Jay, and editors of Horizon Magazine, The Spanish Armada. Harper and Row, 1966.

Wilson, Charles:
The Dutch Republic. McGraw-Hill, 1968.
Profit and Power: A Study of England and the Dutch Wars. Longmans, Green, 1957.

Willson, D. H., A History of England. Holt, Rinehart and Winston, 1967.

Acknowledgments

The index for this book was prepared by Gale Partoyan. The editors wish to thank the following: John Batchelor, artist, and David Lyon, consultant (pages 32-33), and Richard Schlecht, artist, and William A. Baker, consultant (pages 116-123).

The editors also wish to thank: In Italy: Professor Charles Wilson, Istituto Universitario Europeo, Fiesole, Florence; Laura Secchi, Director, Museo Navale, Genoa-Pegli. In London: R. Williams, Department of Prints and Drawings, British Museum; Wendy Evans, Communications Officer, Philippa Glanville and Rosemary Weinstein, Tudor and Stuart Period Department, The Museum of London; C. C. W. Terrell, Curator of Hydrography, R. J. B. Knight, Custodian of Manuscripts, Joan Moore, Department of Photography, A. W. H. Pearsall, Historian, E. H. H. Archibald, R. M. Quarm,

J. E. Tucker, Picture Department, National Maritime Museum; J. T. Roome, Department of Water Transport, The Science Museum; H. L. Blackmore, the Armouries, Tower of London; C. V. Wedgwood. Elsewhere in England: R. C. Latham, Librarian, Pepys Library, Magdalene College, Cambridge. In the Netherlands: Amsterdams Historisch Museum, Nederlands Scheepvaart Museum, Rijksmuseum, Amsterdam; Frans Halsmuseum, Haarlem; Atlas van Stolk, Prins Hendrik Maritiem Museum, Rotterdam; Rijksdienst voor Monumentenzorg, Zeist. In Sweden: Ulla Garell, Information Secretary, Björn Hedin, Photographer, Captain Bengt Ohrelius, Chief of Information, Hans Soop, Curator, Wasa Museum, Stockholm.

The editors also wish to thank: In Washington, D.C.: Stanley Kalkus, Director, Bar-

bara Lynch, Reference Librarian, John Vajda, Assistant Librarian, U.S. Navy Department Library; John C. Reilly Jr., Naval Historical Center. Elsewhere in the United States: Wendy Shadwell, Curator of Prints, The New-York Historical Society, New York City; Ken Dillon, Rosslyn, Virginia.

Particularly valuable sources of quotations for this book were: Letters and Papers Relating to the First Dutch War, 1652-1654, edited by C. T. Atkinson and Samuel Rawson Gardiner; Barlow's Journal, transcribed by Basil Lubbock; London in Plague and Fire 1665-1666, edited by Roland Bartel; The Diary of Samuel Pepys, edited by Mynors Bright and John Warrington; The Narrative of General Venables, edited by C. H. Firth; The Letters of Robert Blake, edited by J. R. Powell; The Dutch in the Medway by P. G. Rogers.

Picture Credits

The sources for the illustrations in this book are shown below. Credits from left to right are separated by semicolons, from top to bottom by dashes.

Cover: Rijksmuseum, Amsterdam.

Front and back end papers: Drawing by Peter McGinn.

Page 3: Martin de Vries, courtesy Rijksmuseum Nederlands Scheepvaart Museum, Amsterdam. 6, 7: Erich Lessing from Magnum, Paris, courtesy Fredinandeum Museum, Innsbruck. 8 through 11: Rijksmuseum, Amsterdam. 12, 13: Rijksmuseum Nederlands Scheepvaart Museum, Amsterdam. 14: National Portrait Gallery, London. 17: Frans Halsmuseum, Haarlem. 19: Photo Bibliothèque Nationale, Paris, courtesy Weidenfeld and Nicolson Archives, London. 20, 22: Edward Leigh by permission of the Master and Fellows of Magdalene College, Cambridge. 24: National Maritime Museum, London. 26: Photo Bibliothèque Nationale, Paris—Radio Times Hulton Picture Library, London. 27: Courtesy the British Museum. 28: National Portrait Gallery, London. 32, 33: Drawings by John Batchelor. 34, 35: By permission of the British Library. 36, 37: Rijksmuseum, Amsterdam—India Office Library and Records, London. 38: Amsterdams Historisch Museum. 40 through 45: Statens Sjöhistoriska Museum-Wasavaret, Stockholm. 46, 47: Derek Bayes, courtesy National Maritime Museum, London. 48: Rijksmuseum Nederlands Scheepvaart Museum, Amsterdam. 49: National Maritime Museum, London. 52, 53: Library of Congress. 55: Rijksmuseum, Amsterdam. 56: Rijksmuseum Nederlands Scheepvaart Museum, Amsterdam. 58: Library of Congress. 62: Atlas van Stolk, Rotterdam. 64, 65: Prins Hendrik Maritiem Museum, Rotterdam. 67: Rijksmuseum, Amsterdam. 68, 69: Amsterdams Historisch Museum. 70: Rijksmuseum Nederlands Scheepvaart Museum, Amsterdam. 71: © The Frick Collection, New York. 72, 73: Derek Bayes, courtesy National Maritime Museum, London. 74: National Maritime Museum, London. 75: Rijksmuseum, Amsterdam. 76, 77: Lee Batut, courtesy Palacio de Liria, Madrid. 80: National Maritime Museum, London. 81: Atlas van Stolk, Rotterdam. 82: Derek Bayes, courtesy Greenwich Hospital Collection, National Maritime Museum, London—Derek Bayes, courtesy Private Collection. 83, 84: Library of Congress. 85: The John Carter Brown Library, Brown University. 86, 87: By permission of the British Library. 89 through 92: Derek Bayes, courtesy National Maritime Museum, London. 95: Douglas Allen Photography, courtesy The Admiral Blake Museum, Bridgwater, England. 96: National Portrait Gallery, London. 98, 99: Courtesy the British Museum. 100: Edward Leigh by permission of the Master and Fellows of Magdalene College, Cambridge. 102, 103: Courtesy the British Museum (background). National Portrait Gallery, London; Peter Jackson Collection, London, courtesy Private Collection; National Portrait Gallery, London—National Portrait Gallery, London; by permission of the Council of The Royal Society, London; Peter Jackson Collection, London, courtesy The Earl of Jersey; by permission of the Trustees of the Will of J. H. C. Evelyn, Deceased; National Portrait Gallery, London (2). 106, 107: Rijksdienst voor de Monumentenzorg, Zeist, Netherlands. 108: Rijksmuseum, Amsterdam. 110, 111: J. Clarence Davies Collection, Museum of the City of New York. 113: Courtesy the British Museum. 114: Library of Congress. 115: National Maritime Museum, London. 116 through 123: Drawings by Richard Schlecht. 124, 125: National Maritime Museum, London. 127: National Portrait Gallery, London; Greenwich Hospital Collection, National Maritime Museum, London (3). 128, 129: Derek Bayes, courtesy Mrs. Peter Murdock. 132, 133: The Museum of London. 134: Derek Bayes, courtesy National Maritime Museum, London. 137: Rijksmuseum Nederlands Scheepvaart Museum, Amsterdam. 138: National Maritime Museum, London. 139: Rijksmuseum, Amsterdam, except top left, National Maritime Museum, London. 142, 143: By permission of the British Library—National Maritime Museum, London. 144: Atlas van Stolk, Rotterdam. 146, 147: The Museum of London. 150: Rijksmuseum, Amsterdam. 152, 153: Bodleian Library, Oxford. 154: The Walker Art Gallery, Liverpool. 155: Derek Bayes, by permission of the Rt. Hon. the Lord Barnard, TD. 156, 157: Museo Navale, Genoa-Pegli, Italy. 158: Rijksmuseum, Amsterdam. 159: Atlas van Stolk, Rotterdam. 161 through 167: Rijksmuseum, Amsterdam. 168, 169: Derek Bayes, courtesy National Maritime Museum, London.

Index

Numerals in italics indicate an
illustration of the subject mentioned.

A

Africa. *See* Pirates, Barbary; West Africa
Albemarle, Duke of (General George
Monck), 56, 61, 62-63, 65, 97-98; and
Dutch revenge, 152, 154, 155, 156-157,
160; quoted, 97, 135, 157; and second
Anglo-Dutch war, *127*, 130, 134, 135-
136, 137, 140, 141, 143-144
Amboina (East Indies), 31-35, *36-37*, 67
Amsterdam (Netherlands): Admiralty,
106-107, 108; bourse, *38*; harbor, *70*;
Schreierstoren, *68-69*
Anglo-Dutch wars, 6, 16-18, 27, 28, 30-39,
46-47, 77, 78; and East Indies, *36-37*;
fire ships in, *116-123*; first (1652-1654),
46-75, 98, 115; second (1665-1667), 109,
115, *124-145*, 147, *148-169*; treaty
ending, *159*, 160-161
Ark Royal (English), 15, *23*
Articles of War of 1653 (English), 59
Augustine (English), 89
Ayscue, Sir George, 136; silver of, *137*

B

Baker, James, 21
Baker, Matthew, painting by, *22*
Barbados (West Indies), 80-81, 84, 93
Barfleur, Battle of (1692), 29
Barlow, Edward, 98; journal of, *89-92*,
130, 136, 137; quoted, 97
Batten, Sir William, 105
Bergen (Norway), 130
Black Death (London), 130, *132-133*
Black Prince (England), 20
Blaeu, Willem, map by, *114*
Blake, Benjamin, 59
Blake, General-at-Sea Robert, *49*; and first
Anglo-Dutch war, 39, 48, 49, 51-63
passim, *62*, 67, 97; in Mediterranean,
126; possessions of, *95*; quoted, 48, 49,
51, 54, 56, 78, 86, 88-93; and West
Indies, 78, 85-88, 93-95
Bonaventure (English), 56, 66
Bourne, Major John, 50; quoted, 51
Bourne, Rear Admiral Nehemiah, 39
Boyle, Robert, 102, *103*
Breda (Netherlands), peace negotiations
at, 150, 151, *159*, 160
Brederode (Dutch), 35, 39, 49, 55, 60, *62*,
65-66
Bridgewater (English), 87
Bristol (English), 95
British Navy. *See* English Navy; English
ships
Brouncker, Lord William, 129
Burnet, Bishop Gilbert, quoted, 129

C

Cabissa, John, 112, 113
Cadiz (Spain), 85, 87-88, *91*, 93, 95,
130
Calais (France), 49, 63; Spanish Armada
at, *6-7*, 25
Cambridge University (England), 100
Canary Islands, 93
Cannon, introduction of, 21-23
Cape Coast Castle (Gold Coast), *112-113*,
115
Cape Gris-Nez (France), 60
Cape Verde Islands, 111
Cartagena, 80
Carthage (North Africa), 89
Castlemaine, Lady, 154, *155*
Charles I, King (England): and English
Navy, 98, 99; overthrow of, 27, 28, 30,
48, 49, 53; ship for, *24*, 25, 29, 35; and
ship money, 30
Charles II, King (England), 27, *28*, 30-31,
53, 67, 85, 90, 102, 106, 138; coat of
arms, *161*; coronation parade, *98-99*;
and Dutch revenge, 149, 150, 152, 153,
154, 156, 160, 161; and English Navy,
97-100, 101, 104, 105, 109; and Great
Fire, 147, 148; and second Anglo-Dutch
war, 126, 129, 130-134, 137; and West
Africa, 109-111, 115
Chatham Chest, 105
Chatham dockyard (England), 105, 140,
151-153, 154, 156, 157-158, *162-163*
Chaucer, Geoffrey, "Shipman," 21
Christopher of the Tower (English),
21
Church of England, 27
Clarendon, Earl of, quoted, 100, 152
Collins, Captain Greenvile, *Great Britain's*
Coasting Pilot, 53
Corsairs. *See* Pirates, Barbary
Coventry, Sir William, quoted, 111
Cromwell, Richard, 27, 97
Cromwell, Oliver, *26*, 27, 28, 30-31, 102;
and Anglo-Dutch wars, 48, 49, 51-53,
55, 56, 59, 67; and English Navy, 97, 98-
100; and Mediterranean, 85, 86-87, 95;
quoted, 77, 79, 83; ship for, *33*, 161; and
West Indies, 77-78, 79, 80, 84-85
Cuba, Matanzas Bay, *80*, 81
Cuyp, Aelbert, painting by, *71*

D

Danish: vs. Dutch, 106; traders, 112
De Laune, Paul, 79
De Ruyter, Engel, 161
De Ruyter, Admiral Michiel
Adriaenszoon: and Dutch revenge, 151-
152, 155, *156-157*, 158; family portrait,
108; goblet to, *158*; and second Anglo-
Dutch war, 108, 115, 125, 129, 130, 134,
135, 136, 140-143, 145; ship of,
138
De Vlieger, Simon, painting by, *73*
De With, Vice Admiral Witte, 55, *56*, 65;
quoted, 55, 66
De Witt, Cornelis: and Dutch revenge,
150-152, 155, 156, 157, 158, *162-163*;
goblet to, *158*; quoted, 156, 169
De Witt, Johan, 100, 107, 115, *150*, 151,
163; quoted, 63, 135, 150, 151,
158
Deane, General-at-Sea Richard, 56, 61, 62-
63, 128
Defoe, Daniel, quoted, 31
Deptford dockyard (England), 101
Devon (England), 36
Dordrecht (Netherlands), 71, 150
Dover (England), 39, 48, 49, 51, 56; Strait
of, 35, 39, 56, 136
Douglas, Captain Archibald, 159-160
Downing, Sir George, quoted, 36, 106,
107
Drake, Sir Francis, death of, 78
Dryden, John, 102, *103*
Dungeness, Battle of, 49, 56, 59, 66
Dunkirk, 63, 145; pirates, 81
Dutch East India Company, 31; and
second Anglo-Dutch war, 129-130; ship
of, *74*. *See also* Amboina
Dutch maps, *52-53*, *64-65*
Dutch Republic, 106-107. *See also* Dutch
ships
Dutch ships, 6, *68-75*, 105-108; vs.
English, *12-13*, *62*, 93, *162-169*; fire,
116-123, 134; herring fleet of, 54, 56,
72-73; vs. Portuguese, *34-35*; vs.
Spanish, *8-11*, 48, 55, *80-81*; and West
Africa, 109-115. *See also* Anglo-Dutch
wars
Dutch West India Company, 74, *80-81*;
wharf (New York), *110-111*; yacht of,
70

E

East Indies, 109. *See also* Amboina; Dutch
East India Company; English East India
Company
Easterlings, 107, 108
Edgar, King (England), 25
Edward III, King (England), 18
Eendracht (Dutch), 125, *128-129*
Effingham, Lord Howard of (Lord High
Admiral), 15; quoted, 53
Eikon Basilike, 27
Elizabeth I, Queen (England). *See*
Elizabethan ships
Elizabethan ships, 15, *22*, 23
Elmina Castle (Gold Coast), 112, 115
English Channel, *12-13*, 18, 25, 35, 36, 53-
54, 56, 59-60, *62*, 63, 67, 147; and Four
Days' Fight, 130-134, 136
English Civil War (1642-1651), *26-28*, 30,
31, 48, 49, 111
English East India Company, 35, 130
English Navy, 27, 28; Charles II and, 98-
100, 109; Cromwell and, 30-31, 98-99;
Fighting Instructions (1653), 61;
financial crisis of, 99, 105, 147, 149-
150, 153, 156; manual, *58*; Naval

Discipline Acts, 59; Pepys and, 97, 98, 100-105; *Sailing Instructions*, 61. *See also* English ships
English Pilot, The, Seller, 53
English pirates, 48
English ships, *14, 24, 32-33*; vs. Dutch, *12-13, 62*, 93; vs. French, *19, 21*, 23, 29, 78; vs. Spanish, *6-7*, 18, 77-95 *passim*, 130; and West Africa, 109-115. *See also* English Navy; Anglo-Dutch wars
Essex (English), 63, 128
Evelyn, John, 102, *103*; map by, *152-153*
Evertsen, Admiral Jan, 128, 129

F

Fair Isle channel, 55
Fairfax (English), 88
Fanfan (English), 144
Fighting Instructions (English, 1653), 61
Fire ships, *116-123*, 134; and Dutch revenge, 155, 157
Fishing boats, 54, 56, *72-73*
Flanders, 134
Flushing harbor (Netherlands), *17*
Foresight (English), 88
Fort Caguaya, 84
Four Days' Fight (1666), *124-125*, 130-137, *138*, 141, 143, 144
Frederick Henry, Prince (Dutch Republic), 106
French ships: vs. English, 21, 23, 29, 78, 85, 86; and second Anglo-Dutch war, 130-134, 136, 148, 150, 160
Friesland (Netherlands), 106, 145

G

Gabbard Shoal, Battle of (1653), *46-47, 62-63*, 65
Garland (English), 56, 66
Genoa, 89, 93
Gibraltar, 48; battle near (1867), *10-11*
Gold Coast (West Africa), 111-113, *map 114*
Goodwin Sands, 56, 130
Goree Island, 111
Gravesend (England), 152, 154, 163
Great Britain's Coasting Pilot, Collins, 53
Great Charity (English), 80
Great Harry (English), *20*, 21, 23, *32-33*
Greek fire, 19
Guinea. *See* West Africa
Gustavus II, King (Sweden), quoted, 40
Gwyn, Nell, *103*; quoted, 102

H

Halley, Edmond, *102*
Hampshire (English), 88
Happy Return (English), 97, 125
Hampton Court (England), 129

Harderwijck (Dutch), 158
Harman, Rear Admiral Sir John, 134-135; quoted, 135
Harwich (England), 135, 163
Havana (Cuba), 80
Hawkins, Sir John, 23
Heartsease (English), 79
Hector (English), 130
Hein, Piet, *81*; quoted, 81
Henri Grace à Dieu (English). *See Great Harry*
Henrietta Maria, Queen (England), 48
Henry (English), 134-135, 141, 154
Henry VII, King (England), 21, 23
Henry VIII, King (England), 21; ship for, *20, 32-33*
Henry, Prince (England), 15
Herring trade, 54, 56, *72-73*
Hispaniola, *map 77-78, 80-83*, 85, 93
Hodges, Dr. Nathaniel, quoted, 132, 133
Holland (Netherlands), *map 64-65*, 106-107. *See also* Dutch entries
Hollar, Wenceslaus, engraving by, *142-143*
Holmes, Sir Robert, 125, 141, 144-145, 150; quoted, 111, 113, 144; and West Africa, 111-*115*
Hope, the (Thames River), 152
Hospital ships, 82-83
Howard, Charles. *See* Effingham, Lord Howard of
Hughes, Margaret, *102*
Hundred Years' War, *19*

I

Impressment (of seamen), 52, 105, 112
Isle of Wight, 134, 163

J

Jamaica (West Indies), *map 76-77, 83-84*, 85, 98
James (English), 39, 49, 51
James I, King (England): and English Navy, 99; ship for, *14*, 15-16, 25
James II, King (England). *See* York, James, Duke of
Jamestown, 31
Jersey (English), 111-112
John, King (England), 35

K

Katherine (English), 79
Killigrew, Thomas, *102*
Kortenaer, Egbert Meeusz, 128

L

Lam (Dutch), 115
Lambert, Captain James, 125
Lane, Lady Jane, *28*
Leiden (Netherlands), 106
Lely, Peter, portraits by, *127*
Lisbon (Portugal), 87, 95
Livorno, 89, *92*

London (England): Black Death (1665), 130, *132-133*, 156; Bridge, *90*; Great Fire of (1666), 103, 145, *146-147*, 147-148, 149, 156; and Pepys, *102-103*. *See also* Tower of London
Louis XIV, King (France), 109, 148, 150
Lowestoft, Battle of (1665), 125, 126, *128-129*
Loyal London (English), 153, 157
"Loyal Scott, The," 160

M

Maas River, 65
Maen (Dutch), *8-9*
Manhattan Island, 160. *See also* New York
Mariner's Mirror, The (Waghenaer), *52-53*
Martin (English), 83-84
Mary (English), 128, 155
Mary Rose (English), 23
Mediterranean Sea: in Barlow's journal, *89-92*; English ships in, 78, 85-95, 97
Medway River, Dutch attack on, 151-160, *map 152-153, 156-157, 162-169*
Messina, 89
Monck, General George. *See* Albermarle, Duke of
Monmouth (English), 155
Moors, 86, 89
Mountagu, General-at-Sea Edward. *See* Sandwich, Earl of

N

Naples, 85, 90
Naseby (English), 31, *33*, 36, 87, 97, 161. *See also Royal Charles*
Navigation Act of 1651 (English), 27, 36, 67; changes in, 160
Nelson, Lord Horatio, 30, 61, 67, 161
Netherlands. *See* Dutch entries; Holland
New Amsterdam, 31, 109. *See also* New York
New Netherlands, 109
New World: English vs. Dutch, 109, *110-111*. *See also* West Indies
New York, 109; Harbor, *110-111*. *See also* Manhattan Island
Newcastle (English), 88
Newton, Sir Isaac, 102, *103*
North Africa. *See* Pirates, Barbary
"North Quarter" (Netherlands), 106
North Sea, 35, 36, 53, 67, 130, 144; and Dutch revenge, 147, 151; Gabbard Shoal in, *46-47, 62-63*, 65; herring banks in, *72, 73*
Norway, 54; and second Anglo-Dutch war, 129-130, 152

O

Obdam, Lord of (Jacob van Wassenaer), 125, 126, 128
Orange, Prince of, 134
Oranje (Dutch), 128
Oxford University (England), 49

P

Padilla (Spanish), *8-9*
Passenger ferry (Dutch), *71*
Pearse, James, drawings by, 140-141, *142*
Peeters, Bonaventura, painting by, *72*
Penn, General-at-Sea Sir William, 97-98, 100; and first Anglo-Dutch war, 52-53, 61, *62*, 67; and Great Fire, 148; quoted, 80, 83; and second Anglo-Dutch war, 126, 129, 149; and West Indies, 77, 79, 82, 83-85, 87
Pennsylvania, 52
Pepys, Samuel, 29, *96*, 134, 140, 141, 156, 167; diary of, *100*; and English Navy, 97, 98, 100-105, 107; and Great Fire, 147-148; London friends of, *102-103*; quoted, 97, 98, 101, 102, 103, 104, 105, 108-109, 113, 115, 130, 132, 133, 137, 145, 147, 149, 150, 152, 153, 154, 155, 158, 159, 160
Pett, Peter, 24, 25, 140; and Dutch revenge, 152-153, 154, 160
Pett, Phineas, *14*, 15-16, 25, *62*, 136, 140; quoted, 15, 16
Philip IV, King (Spain), 85
Phoenix (English), 88
Pirates: Barbary, 48, 78, 85-86, 90, *91*, 94; Dunkirk, 81; English, 48
Pleasure yachting (Dutch), *70*
Plymouth (England), 163
Plymouth (English), 87, 88
Portland (England), 59
Porto Farina (Gulf of Tunis), 85-86
Portsmouth (England), 145, 163
Portuguese ships, 89; vs. Dutch, *34-35*, 106; vs. Spanish, 6, 88
President (English), 36, 39
Press gangs. *See* Impressment (of seamen)
Prince Royal (English), *14*, 16, *17*, 25, 29, 31, 35, 36, 53, *62*, 97, 136, *138*, 152. *See also Resolution; Royal Prince*
Prins Willem (Dutch), 55
Privateering, 100
Prize Courts, 51, 130
Prize Laws, 88
Pro Patria (Dutch), 155
Pulo Run (East Indies), 160
Puritanism, 27, 30, 102

R

Race-built ships, 23-25, 35; *Wasa, 40-43*
Raleigh, Sir Walter, quoted, 6
Regent (English), 21
Resolution (English), 53, 62-63, 97. *See also Prince Royal; Royal Prince*
Revenge (English), 23, 25, 115
Richard (English), 97. *See also Royal James*
Rochester (England), 154, 156
Rosebush (English), 104
Rotterdam (Netherlands), 48, 51; Admiralty, 2, 106

Royal African Company, 109-115
Royal Catherine (English), 128
Royal Charles (English), 97, 125, 126, 128, 129, 130, 134, 136, 140, 141; Dutch capture of, 153, 154, 155-156, *156-157*, *166-169*; sternpiece, *161. See also Naseby*
Royal James (English), 97, 126, 134, 136, 141; and Dutch revenge, 153, 157
Royal Oak (English), 153, 157, 159-160
Royal Prince (English), 97, *124-125*, 126, 136; silver from, *137. See also* Prince Royal; Resolution
Royal Society (London), 102
Rupert, Prince (England): and second Anglo-Dutch war, 30, 126, *127*, 129, 130-134, 136, 140, 141, 143-144, 155; and West Africa, 109, 111

S

Sailing Instructions (English, 1653), 61
St. Albans, Lord, 150
St. Jago de la Vega (Jamaica), 84
St. James's Fight (1666), 140-141, *142-143*, 145
St. Laurens (Dutch), 50, 51
St. Maria (Dutch), 50
St. Paul's Cathedral (London), *102-103*
Sandwich, Earl of (Edward Mountagu), 86-87, 88, 97-98, 100, 126, *127*, 128-130; quoted, 126, 128, 129
Santa Cruz (Canary Islands), 93-94
Santo Domingo (Hispaniola), 80-83
Saracens, 19
Scheveningen, Battle of (1653), 65, *67*, 115
Schreierstoren (Amsterdam), *68-69*
Scotland: vs. England, 54; soldiers from, 159-160
Sea atlases, *52-53*
Seller, John, *The English Pilot*, 53
Sheerness, Fort (England), 153-154, *164-166*
Shetland Islands, 54, 130
Ship Money Fleet, 30
"Shipman," Chaucer, 21
Sluys, Battle of (1340), 19
Sovereign of the Seas (English), *24*, 25-29, 30, 31, 35
Spanish Armada, English defeat of, *6-7*, 15, 23-25, 35, 116
Spanish ships: vs. Dutch, *8-11*, 48, 55, *80-81*, 106, 115; vs. English, 18, 77-95 *passim*, 130; vs. Portuguese, 6; and second Anglo-Dutch war, 134. *See also* Spanish Armada
Spanish treasure fleet, *81*
Speaker (English), 87, 94, 95
Spice Islands, 109. *See also* Amboina
Stayner, Captain Richard, 87; quoted, 87-88, 93, 94, 95
Stinstra, Ate Intes, 128

Storck, Abraham, paintings by, *70, 124-125*
Storck, Jacobus, painting by, *68-69*
Strait of Dover, 35, 39, 56, 136
Stuyvesant, Pieter, 109, 111
Surat (India), *34-35*
Surinam (South America), 160
Susanna (Dutch), 155
Swedish ship, *Wasa, 40-43*
Swedish traders, 112
Sweers, Rear Admiral Isaac, silver of, *137*
Swiftsure (English), 77, 79, *124-125*

T

Tangiers, 89
Temple, Sir William, quoted, 115
Tenerife (Canary Islands), 93-94
Terschelling (Netherlands), *144-145*, 147, 151, 160
Texel (Netherlands), 65, 151
Thames River, *chart 52*, 163; and Dutch revenge, 151-152, *map 152-153*, 155, 156, 158, 159
Tower of London, 59, 84, *86-87*, 115, 156, 160
Trafalgar, Battle of, 30, 87, 161
Triboli, 21
Trinity House (England), Elder Brethren of, quoted, 29
Triumph (English), 56, 60
Tromp, Cornelis, 128, 129, *134*, 135, 136, 141, 143; quoted, 129
Tromp, Lieutenant Admiral Maarten Harpertszoon, 39, *48*, 49, 51, 53-56, 59-66 *passim*, *62*, 86, 108, 115; death of, 65, *67*; quoted, 48, 49, 51, 54, 55, 56, 60, 63, 66
Tunis, 48; Gulf of, 85-86, 94
Turks: vs. English, 85; vs. Italians, *92*
Tuynemans, Captain Bastiaen, 51

U

Unity (English), 155, 157
Upnor Castle (England), 153, 155, 156, 157, *162-163, 166-167*

V

Van Brakel, Captain Jan, 155
Van de Velde the Elder, Willem, *139*; paintings by, *138, 139*; quoted, 138
Van de Velde the Younger, Willem, 138, *139*; painting by, *cover, 138*
Van der Saanen, Captain Joris, 39
Van Eertvelt, Andries, painting by, *74*
Van Ghent, Admiral Willem Joseph, 155, 158; goblet to, *158*
Van Heemskerck, Admiral Jacob, 11
Van Wassenaer, Jacob. *See* Obdam, Lord of
Vanguard (English), *12-13*
Venables, General Robert, 81-85, *82*; quoted, 82-83, 87
Victory (English), 30

Vincent, Reverend Thomas, quoted, 133
Visscher, Nicholas, map by, *64-65*
Vlieland (Netherlands), 144-145
Vrede (Dutch), 155
Vroom, Hendrick Corneliszoon, paintings by, *6-13*

W

Waghenaer, Lucas, *The Mariner's Mirror*, *52-53*
Warren, Sir William, 104
Wasa (Swedish), *40-43*
Weale, John, quoted, 85
West Africa, 160; English vs. Dutch in,

109-115, *map* 114, 125
West Frisia (Netherlands), 106
West Indies, English vs. Spanish in, *map* 76-77, *77-85*, 87
Western Design (English fleet), *77-85*
Westerschelling harbor, *144*
Westminster, Treaty of (1654), 66-67
Whistler, Dr. Daniel, quoted, 78
Whistler, Henry, quoted, 82, 84
William II, King (Netherlands), 30
Woolwich dockyard (England), 101, 104
Worcester (English), 88
Wren, Sir Christopher, *102*

Y

Yarmouth (English), 89, *90*
York, James, Duke of, 97, 98, 101, 105, 109; and Dutch revenge, 153, 155; and Great Fire, 148; and second Anglo-Dutch war, 125, 126, *127*, 128, 129, 137
Young, Captain Anthony, 36, 39; quoted, 39

Z

Zeeland (Netherlands), 56, 106, 128
Zeven Provincien (Dutch), *124-125*, *138*, *139*, 141

Printed in U.S.A.